Preparing TEACHERS for the 21st Century

Framework for 21st Century Learning | Page Numbers

Framework for 21st Century Learning	Page Numbers
21ST CENTURY STUDENT OUTCOMES	
Core Subjects and 21st Century Themes	
Core Subjects	4–11, 87–95, 109–110, 338–340
Global Awareness	95-100, 141, 189, 219, 289, 324, 340, 386
Financial, Economic, Business and Entrepreneurial Literacy	142–143, 249–253
Civic Literacy	29–52, 114–115, 140–142, 268–281
Health Literacy	209–217
Learning and Innovation Skills	
Creativity and Innovation	70–74, 81–86, 118–133, 240–241, 375–380
Critical Thinking and Problem Solving	18–20, 81–86, 117–118, 193–195, 380–381
Communication and Collaboration	147–148, 208–209, 342–344, 376–377
Information, Media, and Technology Skills	
Information Literacy	1–12, 168–189
Media Literacy	388, 390
Information, Communications, and Technology (ICT) Literacy	17, 85–87, 128–129, 139, 225–226, 257, 289–290, 321–386, 353–357
Life and Career Skills	
Flexibility and Adaptability	80–87, 189–193, 357–360, 383–386
Initiative and Self-Direction	118–133, 285–289, 329–330, 377–378
Social and Cross-Cultural Skills	95–100, 144–148, 172–189, 201–204, 218–225
Productivity and Accountability	12–14, 161, 257–261, 346–348
Leadership and Responsibility	129–133, 193–195, 253–259, 309, 373–377, 390–392
21ST CENTURY SUPPORT SYSTEMS	
21st Century Standards	17–18, 159–160, 304–308, 341–342
Assessments of 21st Century Skills	64, 121–122, 310–321, 341–342
21st Century Curriculum and Instruction	107–118, 175–176, 227–228, 334–361, 380–381
21st Century Professional Development	18–20, 381–392
21st Century Learning Environments	126–128, 148–152, 371–384

FIFTEENTH EDITION

FOUNDATIONS
of American Education

Perspectives on Education in a Changing World

JAMES A. JOHNSON
Northern Illinois University

DIANN MUSIAL
Northern Illinois University

GENE E. HALL
University of Nevada, Las Vegas

DONNA M. GOLLNICK
National Council for the Accreditation of Teacher Education

Boston   Columbus   Indianapolis   New York   San Francisco   Upper Saddle River
Amsterdam   Cape Town   Dubai   London   Madrid   Milan   Munich   Paris   Montreal   Toronto
Delhi   Mexico City   Sao Paulo   Sydney   Hong Kong   Seoul   Singapore   Taipei   Tokyo

Vice President and Editor in Chief: Jeffery W. Johnston
Acquisitions Editor: Meredith D. Fossel
Development Editor: Amy J. Nelson
Editorial Assistant: Nancy Holstein
Vice President, Director of Marketing: Quinn Perkson
Senior Marketing Manager: Darcy Betts Prybella
Senior Managing Editor: Pamela D. Bennett
Senior Project Manager: Mary M. Irvin
Senior Operations Supervisor: Matt Ottenweller
Senior Art Director: Diane Lorenzo

Cover Designer: Candace Rowley
Cover Art: SuperStock
Photo Coordinator: Sandy Schaefer
Media Project Manager: Rebecca Norsic
Permissions Administrator: Becky Savage
Composition: S4Carlisle Publishing Services, Inc.
Printer/Binder: Worldcolor
Cover Printer: Lehigh/Phoenix
Text Font: Times

Credits and acknowledgments borrowed from other sources and reproduced, with permission, in this textbook appear on appropriate page within text. Photo credits can be found on page 415.

Every effort has been made to provide accurate and current Internet information in this book. However, the Internet and information posted on it are constantly changing, so it is inevitable that some of the Internet addresses listed in this textbook will change.

Library of Congress Cataloging-in-Publication Data
Foundations of American education : perspectives on education in a changing world / James
A. Johnson ... [et al.]. — 15th ed.
   p. cm.
 ISBN-13: 978-0-13-701252-7
 ISBN-10: 0-13-701252-7
 1. Education—Study and teaching—United States. 2. Education—United States. 3.
Teaching—Vocational guidance—United States. I. Johnson, James A.
 LB17.F67 2011
 370.973—dc22
                                                2009042474

10 9 8 7 6 5 4 3 2 1

www.pearsonhighered.com

ISBN 13: 978-0-13-701252-7
ISBN 10:   0-13-701252-7

We dedicate this 15th edition to the memory of three great educators who (along with James A. Johnson) brought this text to life more than 40 years ago. The reflective philosophical thinking of *Harold W. Collins*, the insights from leadership theory, law, politics, and finance from *John H. Johansen*, and the strong social commitment focused on meeting the needs of all students from *Victor L. Dupuis* continue to permeate this text.

We miss these three colleagues but will never forget that their ideas laid the foundation for this extraordinary textbook.

James A. Johnson, Diann Musial, Gene E. Hall, and Donna M. Gollnick

PREFACE

This best-selling text prepares future teachers to meet the challenges of tomorrow's classrooms through its thorough coverage of the foundations of American education, including the historical, legal, philosophical, social, and practical aspects of education. The fifteenth edition has been revised to engage future teachers in examining their changing role and the role of schools in today's diverse society.

The subtitle of this text, *Perspectives on Education in a Changing World,* emphasizes that today's educators must consider, reflect, and respond to divergent ideas drawn from different disciplines of study, different points of view, different experiences, different contexts, and different voices. This text helps students analyze these divergent perspectives through academic disciplines that include history, philosophy, politics, sociology, and the law. These disciplines are important to educators and so the historical and philosophical chapters have been moved up in the fifteenth edition. Students must recognize their impact on important issues such as diversity, reform, and their personal educational philosophy. Students need to understand these foundational concepts in the beginning of their learning so they can apply them to each step of their development as professional educators.

NEW TO THIS EDITION!

- **Chapter 6** *Place of Schools in Society* – Students are introduced to the different roles that schools play in our society. This chapter discusses the culture of schools, school choice, school levels—at rural, suburban, and urban schools—and concludes with a discussion of effective schools.
- **Chapter 13** *Becoming a High-Quality Teacher in a Changing World* – Students explore the changing nature of education and the importance of learning through professional development and educational research to gain a better understanding of what it takes to become a high-quality teacher.
- **Reflect on Diversity feature** – Located in every chapter, these features allow students to read about real classroom situations dealing with diversity. Students can further examine these issues and apply their knowledge by going to this text's online resource, MyEducationLab, to answer questions and receive hints and feedback.
- **Integrated Coverage of Technology** – Students can now view technology as an integrated piece of the instructional and learning process rather than as a separate entity.
- **Integrated Coverage of Educational Trends** – Chapters conclude with a new *Looking Ahead* section that introduces students to educational trends related to each chapter topic. This awareness will help students think critically about educational issues now so they will be better equipped to make decisions in their future classrooms.
- **Integrated Diversity Discussion** – Students are introduced to the challenges and rewards of teaching in today's diverse classrooms in each chapter. Marginal icons indicate where this discussion occurs in each chapter.
- **MyEducationLab** – The text's online resource offers ready-made assignments and activities set in the context of real classrooms. Fully integrated within the text, MyEducationLab provides opportunities for reflection and practice in an easy-to-assign format. For a full description of this text's MyEducationLab, see pp. vii–ix.

WELCOME TO THE FIFTEENTH EDITION!

The fifteenth edition of *Foundations of American Education* has been updated to acknowledge the fast-paced world of information that influences today's students and schools. A teacher's identity emerges and evolves in response to these changes. This edition offers multiple opportunities for students to make sense of the changes in the world, to determine a reflective response to the present, and to adjust responses as new changes emerge. The fifteenth edition continues to prepare teachers for tomorrow's classrooms, today's diverse student population, and the emerging trends in education today.

Prepare Teachers to Succeed in Tomorrow's Classrooms

The fifteenth edition focuses on the importance of becoming a high-quality teacher in a changing world. Education constantly changes and teachers need to keep learning through professional development and to keep up with educational research to teach in tomorrow's classrooms. With two new chapters—Chapter 6 and Chapter 13—this new edition challenges students to be open to change and acknowledge the diversity in American schools today. An integrated discussion of trends in educational technology invites students to embrace new methods of instruction. Explore this content that helps prepare teachers to succeed in tomorrow's classrooms:

- **Chapter 6** *Place of Schools in Society*
- **Chapter 13** *Becoming a High-Quality Teacher in a Changing World*
- **Teacher Perspectives** – Students read about the opposing sides of an educational issue by two educators and are directed to this text's online resource—MyEducationLab—to determine their stance on these important topics.
- **Journal for Reflection** – Found in every chapter, these activities give students the opportunity to pause and reflect on chapter content and how it relates to their own experiences in the classroom.
- **Preparing for Certification** – Located at the end of every chapter, these activities provide sample questions for state teacher certification exams such as the Praxis exam.
- **School-Based Observation activities** – This end-of-chapter activity invites students to apply chapter content through focused observations. Students have a chance to connect to the schools and classrooms in which they will teach.
- **Portfolio Development activities** – Students are encouraged to create artifacts for their teaching portfolio.
- **MyEducationLab**

Prepare Teachers for Diverse Classrooms

The fifteenth edition introduces readers to diversity in every chapter with a new text feature and an integrated discussion of today's diverse classrooms. Students are introduced to the social and educational issues faced by a diverse nation and are given opportunities to think critically and reflect on these issues. Explore the following content that will help prepare teachers for diverse classrooms:

- **Reflect on Diversity feature**
- **Integrated Diversity Discussion**
- **Global Perspectives** – These features provide students with a better understanding of educational practices in other countries and how they compare to practices in the United States. *Questions for Reflection* invite students to think about the topic and tie it to their future educational practices and classrooms.

Provide Teachers the Opportunity to Experience Real Classrooms

MyEducationLab is an online resource that offers ready-made assignments and activities set in the context of real classrooms. Fully integrated within the text, it provides opportunities for reflection and practice in an easy-to-assign format. MyEducationLab for this text includes:

- **Learning Outcomes** – Each topic of MyEducationLab connects intended learning outcomes to INTASC standards.

- **Building Teaching Skills and Dispositions** – Students can practice and strengthen skills that are essential to teaching. Students are first presented with a core skill, given an opportunity to practice the skill multiple times, and then critically analyze the skill.

- **Assignments and Activities** – These assignable exercises present content in an active format and provide questions that probe student understanding of a concept or strategy.

- **Book Specific Resources** – These resources are unique to this book and include:

  - **Study Plan Quiz with Review, Practice, and Enrichment**—Includes multiple-choice assessments tied to chapter objectives. Chapter-specific study plans offer multiple opportunities to master course content fully.

  - **Reflect on Diversity**—Located in every chapter, this feature allows students to read about real classroom situations dealing with diversity. Students can further examine these issues and apply their knowledge by going to MyEducationLab to answer questions and receive hints and feedback.

  - **Teacher Perspectives**—This popular text feature highlights two educators presenting opposing sides of an issue related to chapter content. Through MyEducationLab assignments, students are encouraged to develop personal stances on the issue.

Understand and Learn About Current Issues in Education Today

The fifteenth edition includes an integrated discussion of trends and current hot topics in education today.

- **Integrated Coverage of Technology**
- **Integrated Coverage of Educational Trends**
- **Education in the News**—Every chapter begins with a real current news article from publications such as *NEA Today*, *Education Week*, and newspapers from across the country. The articles focus on educational issues and invite students to reflect on topics such as virtual schools, standardized testing, diverse classrooms, students and families, financing schools, and more.

PEARSON
myeducationlab

The Power of Classroom Practice.

"Teacher educators who are developing pedagogies for the analysis of teaching and learning contend that analyzing teaching artifacts has three advantages: it enables new teachers time for reflection while still using the real materials of practice; it provides new teachers with experience thinking about and approaching the complexity of the classroom; and in some cases, it can help new teachers and teacher educators develop a shared understanding and common language about teaching. . . ."[1] As Linda Darling-Hammond and her colleagues point out, grounding teacher education in real classrooms—among real teachers and students and among actual examples of students' and teachers' work—is an important, and perhaps even essential, part of preparing teachers for the complexities of teaching in today's classrooms. For this reason, we have created a valuable, time-saving website – MyEducationLab – that provides you with the context of real classrooms and artifacts that research on teacher education tells us is so important for professional development. The authentic in-class video footage, interactive skill-building exercises and other resources available on MyEducationLab offer you a uniquely valuable teacher education tool.

---

[1] Darling-Hammond, l., & Bransford, J.,Eds.(2005). *Preparing Teachers for a Changing World.* San Francisco: John Wiley & Sons.

Instructors will find MyEducationLab easy to use and integrate into courses and assignments. Wherever you see the MyEducationLab logo in the margins or elsewhere in the text, follow the simple instructions to access videos, strategies, cases, and artifacts connected to assignments, activities, and learning units on MyEducationLab. MyEducationLab is organized topically to enhance the coverage of core concepts discussed in the chapters of your book. For each topic on the course you will find the following resources:

Connection to National Standards

Now it is easier than ever to see how your coursework is connected to national standards. In each topic of MyEducationLab you will find intended learning outcomes connected to the appropriate national standards for your course. All of the Assignments and Activities and all of the Building Teaching Skills and Dispositions in MyEducationLab are mapped to corresponding national standards and learning outcomes.

Assignments and Activities

Designed to save instructors preparation time, these assignable exercises show concepts in action through video, cases, and student and teacher artifacts and then provide thought-provoking questions that probe student understanding of these concepts or strategies. (Feedback for these assignments is available to instructors.)

Building Teaching Skills and Dispositions

These learning units help students practice and strengthen skills that are essential to quality teaching. Students are first presented with the core skill or concept and then given an opportunity to develop their understanding of this concept by watching video footage or interacting with other media and then critically analyzing the strategy or skill in classroom contexts.

IRIS Center Resources

The IRIS Center at Vanderbilt University (http://iris.peabody.vanderbilt.edu) – funded by the U.S. Department of Education's Office of Special Education Programs OSEP – develops training enhancement materials for pre-service and in-service teachers. The Center works with experts from across the country to create challenge-based interactive modules, case study units, and podcasts that provide research-validated information about working with students in inclusive settings. This text's MyEducationLab course integrates this content to enhance the content coverage in your book.

General Resources on Your MyEducationLab Course

The *Resources* section on your MyEducationLab course is designed to help your students pass their licensure exam, put together an effective portfolio, develop lesson plans, prepare for and navigate their first year of teaching, and understand key educational standards, policies, and laws. This section includes:

- *Licensure Exams*: Students can access guidelines for passing the Praxis exam, as well as state-specific tests. The *Practice Test Exam* includes practice questions, *Case Histories*, and *Video Case Studies*.
- *Portfolio Builder and Lesson Plan Builder*: Students can create, update, and share portfolios and lesson plans.
- *Preparing a Portfolio*: Students can access guidelines for creating a high-quality teaching portfolio that will allow them to document their growth as professional educators.
- *Licensure and Standards*: Links to state licensure standards and national standards provide a helpful reference resource .
- *Beginning Your Career*: Students can explore valuable information, advice and access tips on the following:
  - Resume Writing and Interviewing: Expert advice on how to write effective resumes and prepare for job interviews.
  - Your First Year of Teaching: Practical tips on how to set up a classroom, manage student behavior, and learn to organize for instruction and assessment.
  - Law and Public Policies: Specific directives and requirements students need to understand the No Child Left Behind Act and the Individuals with Disabilities Education Improvement Act of 2004.

Book-Specific Resources

REFLECT ON DIVERSITY

Located in every chapter, students read a practical classroom situation dealing with diversity. Students can then apply their knowledge by going to this text's online resource, MyEducationLab, to answer questions where they receive hints and feedback.

TEACHER PERSPECTIVES

This popular text feature highlights two educators presenting opposing sides of an issue related to chapter content. Through MyEducationLab assignments, students are encouraged to develop a personal stance on the issue.

STUDY PLAN

The MyEducationLab Study Plan provides multiple choice assessments tied to chapter objectives and are supported by study materials. A well-designed Study Plan offers multiple opportunities to fully master required course content targeted by objectives in each chapter:

- *Chapter Objectives* identify important learning outcomes for each chapter and provide focus for students as they read and study.
- *Multiple Choice Assessment*s, tied to each chapter's objectives, assess mastery of content through exercises that students can take as many times as needed. These quizzes provide overall scores for each objective and also explain why responses to particular items are correct or incorrect.
- *Study Material: Review, Practice and Enrichment* resources provide students with a deeper understanding of chapter content. After taking the Multiple Choice Assessment Quiz, students receive information regarding the chapter content on which they still need work. This review material includes text excerpts, activities with hints and feedback, and media assets (video, simulations, and additional cases).

Visit www.myeducationlab.com for a demonstration of this exciting new online teaching resource.

INSTRUCTOR SUPPLEMENTS

The text has the following ancillary materials to assist instructors in maximizing learning for all students. These instructor supplements are located on the Instructor Resource Center at **www.pearsonhighered.com**.

- **Instructor's Manual/Media Guide** provides concrete, chapter-by-chapter instructional and media resources with full integration of MyEducationLab.
- **PowerPoint Slides** are available to download for each chapter. Presentations include key concept summaries and other aids to help students understand, organize, and remember core concepts and ideas.
- **Test Bank** includes multiple-choice, true/false, short answer, and essay questions, as well as case studies and alternative assessment. The test bank contains page references and answer feedback.
- **Pearson MyTest** is a powerful assessment generation program that helps intructors easily create and print quizzes and exams. Questions and tests are authored online, allowing ultimate flexibility and the ability to efficiently create and print assessments anytime, anywhere! Instructors can access Pearson MyTest and their test bank files by going to *www.pearsonmytest.com* to log in, register, or request access.
- **Online Course Management.** Contact your local Pearson representative to learn how the online and instructor resources available with this book can be customized for delivery through today's popular learning management systems, including BlackBoard, WebCT, and more.

ACKNOWLEDGMENTS

We are sincerely grateful to the many colleagues, reviewers, and editors who have helped us over the years to make this text the most popular and widely used book in the field. We thank our publisher, Pearson, for its support and for enabling us to deliver the message that we as professional educators deem crucial for the preparation of teachers. In particular, we thank Amy Nelson, our outstanding development editor, as well as Meredith Fossel, for her work as our acquisitions editor. We also thank our colleagues and other members of the academic community for their assistance. We sincerely thank our current reviewers for their help and guidance: Samuel Cotton, Ball State University; Thuy Dao Jensen, University of Southern Indiana; Veronica L. Estrada, University of Texas-Pan American; Erwin V. Johanningmeier, University of South Florida; Thomas A. Kessinger, Xavier University; Lillian B. Poats, Texas Southern University; Carol Scateva, Lewis University; Heidi Schnackenberg, State University of New York, Plattsburgh and Vykuntapathi Thota, Virginia State University.

Finally, we thank our families and friends for supporting us throughout the revision process and appreciate the comments and recommendations from the faculty and students who have used previous editions of this book. Their suggestions have led to a number of changes in the current edition. We encourage all our readers to provide feedback for improving future editions.

ABOUT THE AUTHORS

JAMES A. JOHNSON, professor of education emeritus at Northern Illinois University, has been an educator for more than thirty-five years, serving as a public school teacher, teacher educator, and university administrator. He has been coauthor of fourteen editions of *Foundations of American Education,* as well as author or coauthor of a dozen other college textbooks.

DIANN MUSIAL, professor emerita of foundations of education and Northern Illinois University Distinguished Teaching Professor, has taught middle school science and mathematics in Chicago, served as principal of an Individually Guided Education elementary school, and worked in industry as director of training. She has directed more than twenty state and federally funded staff development grants, developed countless performance assessments and test item banks, and coauthored *Integrating Science with Mathematics and Literacy: New Visions for Learning and Assessment* (Corwin Press, 2008) and *Foundations for Meaningful Educational Assessment* (McGraw Hill, 2009).

GENE E. HALL, professor of educational leadership at the University of Nevada at Las Vegas (UNLV), has served for more than thirty years as a teacher educator, researcher, and university administrator. He is active in assisting teacher education institutions in their efforts to become nationally accredited. He is also internationally known for his research on the change process in schools and other types of organizations. He is the lead architect of the widely used concerns-based adoption model (CBAM), which organizational leaders and staff developers employ in studying and facilitating the change process. In addition to coauthoring the last five editions of this text, he is coauthor of *Implementing Change: Patterns, Principles, and Potholes,* Third Edition (Allyn & Bacon, 2011).

DONNA M. GOLLNICK is senior vice president of the National Council for the Accreditation of Teacher Education (NCATE), where she oversees accreditation activities. She is also past president of the National Association for Multicultural Education (NAME) and is a recognized authority in multicultural education. In addition to her work in teacher accreditation, she has taught in secondary schools and coauthored four editions of this text. She is also coauthor, with Philip C. Chinn, of *Multicultural Education in a Pluralistic Society,* Eighth Edition (Merrill, 2009).

BRIEF CONTENTS

Part I • The Teaching Profession

Chapter 1   Teaching in a Changing World   2

Part II • Historical Foundations of Education

Chapter 2   The Early History of Education in a Changing World   28

Chapter 3   Historical Perspectives of Education   56

Part III • Philosophical Foundations of Education

Chapter 4   Philosophy: Reflections on the Essence of Education   78

Chapter 5   Building an Educational Philosophy in a Changing
             World   104

Part IV • Sociological Foundations of Education

Chapter 6   Place of Schools in Society   138

Chapter 7   Diversity in Society and Schools   166

Chapter 8   Students and Their Families   200

Part V • Governance, Organization, and Legal Foundations
         of Education

Chapter 9   Organizing and Paying for Education   232

Chapter 10   Legal Perspectives on Education   266

Part VI • Curricular Foundations of Education

Chapter 11   Standards, Assessment, and Accountability   302

Chapter 12   Designing Programs for Learners: Curriculum and
             Instruction   334

Chapter 13   Becoming a High-Quality Teacher in a Changing
             World   366

CONTENTS

Part I **The Teaching Profession**

Chapter 1 Teaching in a Changing World 2
  EDUCATION IN THE NEWS: Heroes Every One 3
  Today's Teachers 4
    The Importance of Teachers to Society 4
    The Public View of Teachers and Schools 5
    Who Teaches? 7
    Teacher Supply and Demand 8
  GLOBAL PERSPECTIVES: TEACHING CHINESE TO AMERICAN STUDENTS 11
  Teaching as a Profession 12
    Professional Responsibilities 12
    Professional Knowledge 12
    Professional Skills 13
  REFLECT ON DIVERSITY: STUDENT BULLYING 13
  Quality Assurance 14
    Accreditation 14
    Licensure 15
    Advanced Certification 16
    Standards 17
    No Child Left Behind 18
  PROFESSIONAL DILEMMA: STANDARDIZED TESTS 18
  Reflecting on One's Practice 18
    Systematic Observation 18
    Informal Note-Taking 18
    Analysis of Practice and Reflection 19
    Reflective Journaling 19
    Folio/Portfolio Development 19
  Challenges Affecting Teachers 20
    Salaries in a Changing World 20
    Working Conditions 22
  TEACHER PERSPECTIVES: SHOULD DISTRICTS OFFER SIGNING BONUSES TO ATTRACT NEW TEACHERS? 22
  Beginning and Continuing a Teaching Career 23
    Becoming Licensed 23
    Searching for a Teaching Position 23
    Remaining a Teacher 23
  Looking Ahead: The Teaching Profession 24
  Summary 25 • Discussion Questions 26 • School-Based Observations 26 • Portfolio Development 26 • Preparing for Certification 26 • Websites 27 • Further Reading 27

Part II **Historical Foundations of Education**

Chapter 2 The Early History of Education in a Changing World 28
  EDUCATION IN THE NEWS: Teaching Patriotism—With Conviction 29
  The Beginnings of Education (to 476 CE) 30
    Non-Western Education 31
    Western Education 31
  Education in the Middle Ages (476–1300) 32
    The Dark Ages (400–1000) 32
    The Revival of Learning 33
  Education in Transition (1300–1700) 33
    The Renaissance 34
    The Reformation 34
  Educational Awakening (1700) 35
    The Age of Reason 35
  TEACHER PERSPECTIVES: IS "ABSTINENCE-ONLY" THE BEST SEX EDUCATION POLICY FOR SCHOOLS TO IMPLEMENT? 36
    The Emergency of Common Man 36
  Evolving Perspectives of Education in Our Developing Nation 37
    Colonial Education 37
  REFLECT ON DIVERSITY: RELIGIOUS BELIEFS IN THE CLASSROOM 39
    The Struggle for Universal Elementary Education 39
    The Need for Secondary Schools 40
  GLOBAL PERSPECTIVES: EDUCATIONAL IDEAS BORROWED FROM AROUND THE WORLD 41
    The Evolution of Teaching Materials 41
    Technology and History 45
  Meager Early Education for Diverse Populations 45
    Education of African Americans 45
    Education of Asian Americans 47
    Education of Hispanic Americans 48
    Education of Women 48
  GLOBAL PERSPECTIVES: MARIA MONTESSORI 49
  Private Education in America 50
    The Right of Private Schools to Exist 50
  PROFESSIONAL DILEMMA: HOW CAN THE BUSY TEACHER KEEP UP WITH HISTORICAL AND CONTEMPORARY RESEARCH? 50
    Parochial Schools 51

The Important Role of Private Education in America   51

Understanding and Using Educational Historical Research   51

Looking Ahead: Learning from Educational History   52

Summary 52 • Discussion Questions 53 • School-Based Observations 54 • Portfolio Development 54 • Preparing for Certification 54 • Websites 55 • Further Reading 55

Chapter 3   Historical Perspectives of Education   56

EDUCATION IN THE NEWS: History of the Federal Role in Education   57

More Students and Bigger Schools   58

Enrollment Growth   58

Need for More Schools   58

Need for More Teachers   58

School District Consolidation   59

Growth of Busing   59

Bigger School Budgets   59

Rapid Curricular Growth and Changes   59

TEACHER PERSPECTIVES: IS TEACHING MANNERS A GOOD USE OF CLASSROOM TIME?   60

Growth of Special Education Programs   60

Researching Educational Information Using Today's Technology   61

The Development of the Teaching Profession   61

Increasing Federal Involvement   61

The Professionalization of Teaching   62

REFLECT ON DIVERSITY: TESTING STUDENTS FOR NCLB   62

Continued Importance of Private Schools   63

Home Schooling   63

Continuing/Adult Education   63

Evolution of Educational Testing   64

Changing Aims of Education   65

Committee of Ten   65

Seven Cardinal Principles   65

The Eight-Year Study   65

"Purposes of Education in American Democracy"   65

"Education for All American Youth"   66

"Imperative Needs of Youth"   66

Preparation of Teachers   66

Colonial Teachers   66

GLOBAL PERSPECTIVES: EUROPEAN BEGINNINGS OF TEACHER TRAINING   67

Teachers as Indentured Servants   67

Teaching Apprenticeships   68

Teacher Training in Academies   68

Normal Schools   68

State Teachers' Colleges   69

Changes in Mid-Twentieth-Century Teacher Education   69

Recent Trends in Education   70

New Emphases in Education   70

GLOBAL PERSPECTIVES: JEAN PIAGET   72

Educational Critics   72

PROFESSIONAL DILEMMA: CAN A KNOWLEDGE OF HISTORY HELP TO IMPROVE MULTICULTURAL EDUCATION?   73

Changing Public Perspectives on Education   73

Major Educational Events of the Past Century   73

Looking Ahead: Looking Back to Help Us Look Ahead!   74

Summary 74 • Discussion Questions 75 • School-Based Observations 75 • Portfolio Development 75 • Preparing for Certification 75 • Websites 76 • Further Reading 77

Part III   Philosophical Foundations of Education

Chapter 4   Philosophy: Reflections on the Essence of Education   78

EDUCATION IN THE NEWS: Cheating Crisis in America's Schools: How It's Done and Why It's Happening   79

Structure and Methodology of Philosophy   80

The Branches of Philosophy   80

Thinking as a Philosopher   81

PROFESSIONAL DILEMMA: SHOULD MORALS AND VALUES BE TAUGHT IN PUBLIC SCHOOLS?   82

Technology and Philosophy   85

Schools of Philosophy and Their Influence on Education   87

Idealism   87

Realism   89

Pragmatism   91

Existentialism   93

Eastern and Native North American Ways of Knowing   95

Eastern Ways of Knowing   95

TEACHER PERSPECTIVES: SHOULD TEACHERS WEAR BUSINESS ATTIRE TO SCHOOL?   96

REFLECT ON DIVERSITY: CURRICULUM AND EASTERN WAYS OF KNOWING   97

GLOBAL PERSPECTIVES: THE FABRIC OF EASTERN WAYS OF KNOWING   98

Native North American Ways of Knowing   98

Looking Ahead: Increased Emphasis on the Development of Valued Dispositions   100

Summary 100 • Discussion Questions 101 • School-Based Observations 101 • Portfolio Development 102 • Preparing for Certification 102 • Websites 103 • Further Reading 103

Chapter 5   **Building an Educational Philosophy in a Changing World   104**

EDUCATION IN THE NEWS: Ethical Minds and Technology   105

The Dynamic Relationship between Philosophy and Education   106

What Does an Educational Philosophy Look Like?   107

Teacher-Centered Educational Philosophies   109

Essentialism   109

Behaviorism   110

Positivism   111

PROFESSIONAL DILEMMA: ADJUSTING THE ATTITUDE OF LEARNERS   112

Student-Centered Educational Philosophies   113

Progressivism   114

Humanism   115

Constructivism   117

Developing Your Own Philosophy of Education   118

Classroom Organization   120

Motivation   122

Classroom Management and Discipline   123

Classroom Climate   126

REFLECT ON DIVERSITY: CLASSROOM MANAGEMENT   126

Personal Learning Focus   128

Technology and Educational Philosophy   128

Your Philosophy of Education Beyond the Classroom   129

Teachers as Change Agents   129

Teachers as Leaders   130

TEACHER PERSPECTIVES: SHOULD TEACHERS EXPRESS THEIR VIEWS ON CONTROVERSIAL TOPICS IN CLASS?   131

GLOBAL PERSPECTIVES: THE WORLD AS A CLASSROOM   133

Looking Ahead: Increased Support for Charter and Magnet Schools   133

Summary 133 • Discussion Questions 135 • School-Based Observations 135 • Portfolio Development 135 • Preparing for Certification 135 • Websites 137 • Further Reading 137

Part IV   **Sociological Foundations of Education**

Chapter 6   **Place of Schools in Society   138**

EDUCATION IN THE NEWS: More Valley Students Signing Up for Virtual Schools   139

Roles of Schools   140

Citizenship   140

GLOBAL PERSPECTIVES: CITIZENSHIP EDUCATION IN AUSTRALIA   141

Workforce Readiness   142

Academic Achievement   143

Social Development   143

Cultural Transmission   143

Culture in Schools   144

Common Culture   144

Cultures of Families   145

Cultural Values   145

TEACHER PERSPECTIVES: SHOULD TEACHERS BE REQUIRED TO TAKE DIVERSITY TRAINING?   146

School Culture   147

Partnering with the Community   147

School Choices   148

Public Schools   148

Private Schools   150

Home Schooling   152

Virtual Schools: Crossing Boundaries with Technology   152

School Levels   152

Early Childhood Education   152

PROFESSIONAL DILEMMA: WHAT HAS HAPPENED TO PLAY?   153

Elementary Schools   154

Middle Level Education   154

High Schools   155

School Locations   155

Rural Communities   156

Suburban Communities   157

Urban Communities   158

REFLECT ON DIVERSITY: MAKE ME LEARN   159

Effective Schools   159

Criteria for Effective Schools   160

Looking Ahead: Greater Accountability for Student Learning   161

Summary 161 • Discussion Questions 162 • School-Based Observations 162 • Portfolio Development 163 • Preparing for Certification 163 • Websites 164 • Further Reading 164

Chapter 7   **Diversity in Society and Schools   166**

EDUCATION IN THE NEWS: For Students, Diversity Still Is Daily Lesson: Changing Ethnic Makeup Teaches Some to Beat Prejudice   167

Socioeconomic Status   168

Social Stratification   168

Class Structure   168

Poverty   169
Impact of Poverty and Low Income on Academic Achievement   171

Race and Ethnicity   172
Race   172
Ethnicity   172
Racial and Ethnic Disparities in Education   175
Teaching from a Cultural Context   175

REFLECT ON DIVERSITY: TEACHING THE TRUTH   176

Language   176
Language Diversity   176
Dialectal Diversity   177
Education for Language Diversity   177

Gender   179
Differences between Females and Males   179

TEACHER PERSPECTIVES: SHOULD ALL STUDENTS BE BILINGUAL?   180

Gender-Sensitive Education   182
Title IX   182

Sexual Orientation   183

Exceptionalities   184
Inclusion   185

PROFESSIONAL DILEMMA: INCLUSION OF STUDENTS WITH DISABILITIES   185

Disproportionate Placements   186
Response to Intervention   186

Religion   187

Multicultural Education   189
GLOBAL PERSPECTIVES: HISTORY CURRICULUM IN RWANDA   189

Incorporating Diversity   190
Providing Social Justice   191
Ensuring Equality   192

Looking Ahead: Teachers as Social Activists   193
Thinking Critically   193
Modeling Equity in the Classroom   193
Making Schools Democratic   194
Teaching for Social Justice   195

Summary   195 • Discussion Questions   197 • School-Based Observations   197 • Portfolio Development   197 • Preparing for Certification   198 • Websites   199 • Further Reading   199

Chapter 8   Students and Their Families   200
EDUCATION IN THE NEWS: Grant from Toyota Funds Program at Elementary Schools   201

Today's Families   202
PROFESSIONAL DILEMMA: FAMILY DIVERSITY   203

Parenting   203
Socioeconomic Status   203
Children Left Alone after School   207
Communicating with Families   208

Dangers Children Face   209
Child Abuse   209
Sexual Harassment   210
Other Violence   211

Challenges of Growing Up   214
Sexuality and Pregnancy   214
Substance Abuse   215
Economic Realities   216

Prejudice and Discrimination   217
Prejudice   218
Discrimination   219
Racism   219
GLOBAL PERSPECTIVES: COMING TO JUSTICE   219
Sexism and Other "Isms"   221

Engagement in School   221
Leaving School Early   221
TEACHER PERSPECTIVES: IS RETENTION BETTER THAN SOCIAL PROMOTION FOR STUDENTS?   222
Resiliency   224
REFLECT ON DIVERSITY: WHY BOTHER?   224

Equality of Access   225
Access to Technology   225

Looking Ahead: Greater Access to Quality Education   227

Summary   228 • Discussion Questions   229 • School-Based Observations   229 • Portfolio Development   230 • Preparing for Certification   230 • Websites   231 • Further Reading   231

Part V   Governance, Organization, and Legal Foundations of Education

Chapter 9   Organizing and Paying for Education   232
EDUCATION IN THE NEWS: Panel Approves School Finance Overhaul   233

School Districts: Organization and Finances   234
School District Organization   234
School District Expenditures   237

The Organization of Schools   237
The School Organization Chart   238
Innovations in School Organization   240

Organization of Education at the State Level   241
State Board of Education   241
Chief State School Officer   242
State Department of Education   242
State Legislature   243
Governors   244

Sources of Revenue for Schools   244
System of Taxation and Support for Schools   245

State Differences in the Funding of Education 246

State Sources of Revenue 246

Recent Challenges to School Finance within the States 248

Entrepreneurial Efforts to Fund Education 249

TEACHER PERSPECTIVES: SHOULD SCHOOLS ACCEPT CORPORATE ADVERTISING AND SPONSORSHIP? 250

State Aid 250

REFLECT ON DIVERSITY: ROBIN HOOD TAX LAWS 251

GLOBAL PERSPECTIVES: INTERNATIONAL COMPARISONS: EXPENDITURES PER STUDENT AS AN INDICATOR 252

The Federal Government's Role in Education 253

Leadership 253

The U.S. Department of Education 254

Educational Programs Operated by the Federal Government 254

No Child Left Behind 254

Federal Aid 256

Technology and School Administration 257

Politics and Accountability in Education 257

Politics: Neither Positive nor Negative 258

Politics across the Education System 258

School Politics 259

PROFESSIONAL DILEMMA: WHAT IS THE APPROPRIATE ROLE FOR TEACHERS WHEN THE POLITICS GET ROUGH? 259

Accountability 260

Looking Ahead: The Continuing Challenge of Funding Education 261

Summary 262 • Discussion Questions 263 • School-Based Observations 263 • Portfolio Development 263 • Preparing for Certification 264 • Websites 264 • Further Reading 265

Chapter 10   **Legal Perspectives on Education 266**

EDUCATION IN THE NEWS: Teacher Fired for Inappropriate Behavior on MySpace Page 267

Legal Aspects of Education 268

Legal Provisions for Education: The U.S. Constitution 269

Church and State 271

Segregation and Desegregation 276

Equal Opportunity 278

Opportunities for Students with Disabilities 279

Teachers' Rights and Responsibilities 281

Conditions of Employment 282

Right to Bargain Collectively 284

GLOBAL PERSPECTIVES: LEGAL ASPECTS OF EDUCATION IN OTHER COUNTRIES 285

Academic Freedom 285

Teacher Responsibilities and Liabilities 288

Teacher and Student Uses of Technology and the Law 289

E-Mail 289

Social Networking Risks 290

Cheating with Technology 290

Students' Rights and Responsibilities 290

Students' Rights as Citizens 290

REFLECT ON DIVERSITY: WHAT IF YOUR STUDENT'S MOTHER IS UNDOCUMENTED? 291

Students' Rights and Responsibilities in School 294

TEACHER PERSPECTIVES: SHOULD STUDENTS BE SUSPENDED FOR INAPPROPRIATE DRESS? 295

Looking Ahead: The Evolving Legal Aspects of Education 298

Summary 299 • Discussion Questions 299 • School-Based Observations 300 • Portfolio Development 300 • Preparing for Certification 300 • Websites 301 • Further Reading 301

Part VI   **Curricular Foundations of Education**

Chapter 11   **Standards, Assessment, and Accountability 302**

EDUCATION IN THE NEWS: High Marks for Schools May Become Hard to Get 303

Education Standards 304

Conceptions of Standards 305

Content Standards 306

21st Century Knowledge and Skills Framework 307

Federal Role in Standards 309

The Future of Standards-Based Education 309

Assessment 310

What Is Assessment? 310

Purposes of Assessment 310

Types of Assessments 312

REFLECT ON DIVERSITY: USING ASSESSMENTS FOR LEARNING 313

Performance Assessments 314

PROFESSIONAL DILEMMA: DEVELOPING PERFORMANCE ASSESSMENTS 314

Professional Aspects of Good Assessments 317

Accountability 320

Using Technology to Track Student Learning 321

International Comparisons 322

GLOBAL PERSPECTIVES: THE SUCCESS OF SOUTH KOREA 324

Testing Challenges 324

Equity within Accountability 326

TEACHER PERSPECTIVES: DOES PREPPING FOR HIGH-STAKES TESTS INTERFERE WITH TEACHING? 327

Looking Ahead: Learning to Assess for Student Learning 328

Performance Assessment for California Teachers (PACT) 329

Teacher Work Sample 330

Summary 331 • Discussion Questions 331 • School-Based Observations 332 • Portfolio Development 332 • Preparing for Certification 322 • Websites 333 • Further Reading 333

Chapter 12 **Designing Programs for Learners: Curriculum and Instruction 334**

EDUCATION IN THE NEWS: "Depth" Matters in High School Science Studies 335

What Is Curriculum? 336

Developing Curriculum 336

Curriculum Designs 338

GLOBAL PERSPECTIVES: GERMAN EDUCATION 340

Curriculum Resources 341

The Many Influences on Curriculum 342

Large-Scale Influences on Curriculum 343

Community Influences on Curriculum 344

School Site Influences on Curriculum 344

Selection and Management of Curriculum 344

The State's Role in Managing Curriculum 345

The District's Role in Managing Curriculum 345

Local Schools' Role in Managing the Curriculum 346

Evaluating Curricula 346

District and State Curriculum Evaluation Practices 347

National Curriculum Evaluation Studies 347

International Curriculum Evaluation Studies 347

Instruction: The Teaching Side of Curriculum 348

Instructional Objectives for Student Learning 348

Types of Instructional Objectives 348

Teaching Strategies 351

Direct Instruction 352

Indirect Instruction 352

Increased Emphasis on Science and Technology 353

Organizing Students to Maximize Learning 354

PROFESSIONAL DILEMMA: SHOULD I USE HOMOGENEOUS OR HETEROGENEOUS ABILITY GROUPING? 355

REFLECT ON DIVERSITY: THIS IS SCIENCE CLASS, NOT LANGUAGE ARTS 355

Research on the Use of Technology to Enhance Instruction 356

TEACHER PERSPECTIVES: SHOULD WE ABOLISH HOMEWORK? 356

Teaching Strategies for Diverse Students 357

Teaching Students with Language Diversity 357

Resources for Teaching ELL Students 357

Accommodating Students with Exceptionalities 358

Looking Ahead: Models for School Curriculum Reform 360

School Improvement 360

Accelerated Schools 361

Success for All 361

Institute for Learning 361

Summary 362 • Discussion Questions 363 • School-Based Observations 363 • Portfolio Development 364 • Preparing for Certification 364 • Websites 365 • Further Reading 365

Chapter 13 **Becoming a High-Quality Teacher in a Changing World 366**

EDUCATION IN THE NEWS: Newmarket Teacher Earns "ED"ie Award 367

Different Perspectives for Viewing Education and Teaching 368

Recent Trends in Attempts to Improve Education 368

Continuing Pressures to Reform Schools 368

Sixty Years of Increasing Federal Pressure to Change Schools 369

Reauthorization of ESEA as No Child Left Behind 371

A New President, A New Agenda for Education 372

Findings from Education Research and Development: Another Pressure for Changes in Teaching and Schools 372

Emerging Pressures and Indicators of Accountability Require Change in Schools 373

Expectations for Accountability Are Increasing 373

How to Recognize a High-Quality School 375

Data-Driven Decision Making 375

School Improvement Process 376

Professional Learning Communities 376

Parent and Community Involvement 376

High-Quality Schools Have Leaders That Make a Difference for Teachers and Students 377

REFLECT ON DIVERSITY: PARENT–TEACHER CONFERENCE 377

Checking a School for Indicators of High Quality 379

High-Quality Teachers Provide Evidence of Student Learning 379

What Evidence Will You Have to Show You Are a High-Quality Teacher? 380

High-Quality Teachers Use Student Learning–Centered Instruction 380

High-Quality Teachers Are Reflective and Have a Stated Educational Philosophy about Teaching and Learning 380

Ethics Is an Important Component of a High-Quality Teacher's Philosophy 381

High-Quality Teachers Have Three Types of Knowledge 381

Becoming a High-Quality Teacher Requires Change 384

Teachers Have Different Kinds of Concerns about Change 384

What Are Your Concerns about Becoming a Teacher? 384

GLOBAL PERSPECTIVES: TEACHER INDUCTION PROGRAMS HAVE A LONG HISTORY IN AUSTRALIA 386

Supportive Resources for Your First Year 386

Induction of New Teachers 387

The Future of Technology for Teaching and Student Learning 387

TEACHER PERSPECTIVES: SHOULD TECHNOLOGY BE USED IN EVERY CLASSROOM? 388

School-Based Administrators Can Be Important Supporters for New Teachers 389

Participating in the Profession 390

Teacher Unions 390

National Education Association 390

American Federation of Teachers 391

Professional Associations 391

Looking Ahead: Be the Best You Can Be 392

Summary 393 • Discussion Questions 394 • School-Based Observations 394 • Portfolio Development 394 • Preparing for Certification 394 • Websites 395 • Further Reading 395

References 397

Name Index 403

Subject Index 405

Photo Credits 415

SPECIAL FEATURES

EDUCATION IN THE NEWS

Heroes Every One   3
Teaching Patriotism—with Conviction   29
History of the Federal Role in Education   57
Cheating Crisis in American Schools: How It's Done and
    Why It's Happening   79
Ethical Minds and Technology   105
More Valley Students Signing Up for Virtual Schools   139
For Students, Diversity Still is a Daily Lesson: Changing
    Ethnic Makeup Teaches Some to Beat Prejudice   167
Grant from Toyota Funds Program at Elementary
    Schools   201
Panel Approves School Finance Overhaul   233
Teacher Fired for Inappropriate Behavior on MySpace
    Page   267
High Marks for Schools May Become Hard to Get   303
"Depth" Matters in High School Science Studies   335
Newmarket Teacher Earns "ED"ie Award   367

PROFESSIONAL DILEMMA

Standardized Tests   18
How Can the Busy Teacher Keep Up with Historical and
    Contemporary Research?   50
Can a Knowledge of History Help to Improve Multicultural
    Education?   73
Should Morals and Values Be Taught in Public
    Schools?   82
Adjusting and Attitude of Learners   112
What Has Happened to Play?   153
Inclusion of Students with Disabilities   185
Family Diversity   203
What Is the Appropriate Role for Teachers When the
    Politics Get Rough?   259
Developing Performance Assessments   314
Should I Use Homogeneous or Heterogeneous Ability
    Grouping?   355

TEACHER PERSPECTIVES

Should Districts Offer Signing Bonuses to Attract New
    Teachers?   22
Is "Abstinence-Only" the Best Sex Education Policy for
    Schools to Implement?   36
Is Teaching Manners a Good Use of Classroom Time?   60
Should Teachers Wear Business Attire to School?   96
Should Teachers Express Their Views on Controversial
    Topics in Class?   131

Should Teachers Be Required to Take Diversity
    Training?   146
Should All Students Be Bilingual?   180
Is Retention Better Than Social Promotion for
    Students?   222
Should Schools Accept Corporate Advertising and
    Sponsorship?   250
Should Students Be Suspended for Inappropriate
    Dress?   295
Does Prepping for High-Stakes Tests Interfere with
    Teaching?   327
Should We Abolish Homework?   356
Should Technology Be Used in Every Classroom?   388

GLOBAL PERSPECTIVES

Teaching Chinese to American Students   11
Educational Ideas Borrowed from Around the World   41
Maria Montessori   49
European Beginnings of Teacher Training   67
Jean Piaget   72
The Fabric of Eastern Ways of Knowing   98
The World as a Classroom   133
Citizenship Education in Australia   141
History Curriculum in Rwanda   189
Coming to Justice   219
International Comparisons: Expenditures per Student as
    an Indicator   252
Legal Aspects of Education in Other Countries   285
The Success of South Korea   324
German Education   340
Teacher Induction Programs Have a Long History in
    Australia   386

MYEDUCATIONLAB

Why Become a Teacher   7
Succeeding in Your First Year of Teaching   8
Licensure Standards   15
Using the INTASC Standards to Guide Teaching
    Practice   15
Licensure Exams   16
Reflection as an Essential Component of a Teaching
    Portfolio   19
Preparing a Portfolio   20
Beginning Your Career   23
Colonial Village   39
Educational History in the Making   52

Introduction to Teaching and Foundations of Education
    Interactive Timeline   74
Educational Philosophy and Teaching Practice   80
Writing a Subtraction Story   87
Educational Philosophy and Teaching Practice   107
Developing a Philosophy of Education   118
Classroom Management   125
City Scene   157
Characteristics of Effective Schools   160
Modifying Instruction for Student Diversity   175
Is this Child Mislabeled?   177
Episode 4: Leonard Baca on the Use of Native Languages
    in the Classroom   178
Parents as Child Advocates   185
RTI (Part 1): An Overview   187
Ethnic Identity   190
Incorporating the Home Experiences of Culturally Diverse
    Students   208
Tragedy at School   211
Keeping Students in School   224
Technology to Help Struggling Students   227
The Principal as Leader   238
Carol Bartlett, Principal   239
Grade Level Meeting   239
The Impact of NCLB on School Governance and
    Financing   254
Accommodations for Students with Exceptionalities   272
Brown vs. Board of Education   277
Legal Responsibilities of Teachers   288
Assessment Methods   310
Assessing Student Learning   312
Performance Assessment   314

Identifying Curriculum Types   338
Cognitive Development 3   349
Effective Teaching Methods   352
The Direct Instruction Model   352
Model Inquiry Unit   353
Cooperative Learning   354
Technology Improves Teaching Skills   357
Peer Observation and Feedback   376
Working with Parents and the Community   377
Teachers as Professionals: Two Principals' Views   378
Characteristics of Professionalism   380
The Multiple Roles of Teachers   386
Teaching at Different Grade Levels   386
Succeeding in Your First Year of Teaching   389
Professional Education Associations   391

REFLECT ON DIVERSITY

Student Bullying   13
Religious Beliefs in the Classroom   39
Testing Students for NCLB   62
Curriculum and Eastern Ways of Knowing   97
Classroom Management   126
Make Me Learn   159
Teaching the Truth   176
Why Bother?   224
Robin Hood Tax Laws   251
What if Your Student's Mother Is Undocumented?   291
Using Assessments for Learning   313
This is Science Class, Not Language Arts   355
Parent–Teacher Conference   377

FOUNDATIONS
of American Education

chapter one
TEACHING IN A
CHANGING WORLD

EDUCATION
IN THE **NEWS**

HEROES EVERY ONE

By **REG WEAVER**, NEA Past President
NEA Today, May 2005

We read about them every month in the pages of this magazine. We rub shoulders with them in our schools. We team up with them to make our communities better places.

Heroes.

The single mom who, after working hard all day as a high school custodian, trudges off to the local elementary school to meet with her child's teacher, instead of staying home and putting her feet up.

The retired music teacher who spends his mornings using music to teach language to preschool children with special needs. His students often learn to sing first and then to speak.

The middle school math teacher who stays late four days a week to tutor students in geometry and algebra so someday they will be able to attend college.

The cafeteria worker who, while dishing out the food she's cooked, keeps a vigilant eye on her diabetic students so they don't eat too much sugar and starch.

The elementary school teacher who goes to school at nights to learn Spanish so she can communicate with her students' parents.

The special education assistant who helps the special education teacher with children with the most severe disabilities—changing their diapers when they need changing.

The science teacher whose enthusiasm and preparation makes the subject come alive in her students' minds, lighting a fire that will glow for a lifetime.

The high school teacher who starts a chess club as an outlet for his most restless, high energy students—and then hauls them off to every chess tournament in the state.

The school bus driver who every year organizes a skiing weekend for inner city kids who otherwise would never get to ski or play in the snow.

The community college instructor who teaches English as a second language to immigrants at four different campuses and spends so much time in her car that her colleagues have dubbed her "the road scholar."

Heroes every one.

It is easy to take these folks for granted, though, because they don't toot their own horn. They're everyday people, not celebrities. I like to call them "unsung heroes." In fact, they don't think of themselves as heroes at all, and when someone like me sings their praises, it kind of embarrasses them. But that doesn't stop me.

Our unsung heroes are the exception to the rule that when all is said and done, more is said than done. Their actions speak louder than words. And in a society that rewards getting rather than giving, they give of themselves for the good of others, and then they give some more.

Yes, it is easy to take our unsung heroes for granted, but we must not. For they are the heart and soul of our Association. These are the folks who, when you come to them with a problem, always say: "What are we going to do about it?" They think in terms of possibilities rather than impossibilities, solutions rather than setbacks, and dos rather than don'ts.

Of course I am aware that a hero is often defined as somebody who does something dangerous to help somebody else. The firefighter who rushes into a burning building to save a child is definitely a hero. For me, however, the burn unit nurse who tenderly and skillfully cares for that firefighter's wounds through his long and agonizing recovery also qualifies as a hero. And so, too, do the many public school and college employees and retired and student educators I have had the privilege of meeting and knowing as president of NEA.

As educators and Association members, we are in the hope business, and these unsung heroes of ours, above all else, give us hope even during the times when hope seems ready to freeze over.

Unsung heroes of NEA, I am your number one fan!

QUESTIONS FOR REFLECTION

1. What is your perspective on the ideas about heroes suggested in this news item? Why?
2. What heroes would you add to those mentioned? Why?
3. What are some of the heroes that parents might have? Students? The general public?
4. What educational heroes would you expect to find mentioned in this chapter dealing with the education profession? Why?

Source: Reprinted by permission of the National Education Association.

LEARNING OUTCOMES

After reading and studying this chapter, you should be able to:

1. Articulate the role demographics play in determining teacher supply and demand and identify areas where teachers will be in high demand during the next decade.
2. Outline the professional responsibilities of a teacher as viewed by the public, parents, and professional colleagues. (INTASC 1: Subject Matter)
3. Identify the characteristics of professions and develop arguments for or against declaring teaching a profession.

4. Identify sources of evidence to show that you are developing the knowledge, skills, and dispositions outlined in the INTASC standards. (INTASC 1–10)
5. Identify some of the challenges that affect teachers, but not other professionals, and clearly articulate why you plan to pursue a teaching career.
6. Identify the basic requirements for the initial teaching license in the state where you plan to teach, including the types of tests and other assessments that are required.

We live in a world of rapid change, and many people have become so accustomed to change that they hardly take notice of it. People have many different perspectives on and opinions about schools, teachers, and education. Schools in general, and teachers in particular, are affected in many ways by this rapid change and by people's different perspectives on education. For instance, societal and parental expectations of schools constantly change; these expectations even change from parent to parent and from school to school.

These two realities—our rapidly changing world and the countless differing perspectives on education—greatly affect the work and lives of educators and are therefore developed in various ways and used as themes throughout this book. Each chapter approaches these topics by sharing pertinent information and posing thought-provoking questions regarding perspectives on education in a changing world. Our goal is to help you learn more about these important realities and to enable you to make informed progress toward developing your own professional perspectives on education and to better understand our changing world.

TODAY'S TEACHERS

About four million teachers provide the instructional leadership for public and private schools in the United States. Teaching is a profession that attracts the best and brightest college students into its ranks. Today's new teachers must meet rigorous national and state standards for entering the profession that did not exist a decade ago. Requirements for entering teacher education programs in colleges and universities are now more stringent than admission requirements for most other professions. Grade point averages of 3.0 and higher are becoming more common requirements for admission; tests and other assessments must be passed before admission, at the completion of a program, and for state licensure. Clearly, not everyone can teach.

Teacher candidates today are diverse in age and work experience. Some of you are eighteen to twenty-two years old, the traditional age of college students, but others of you are nontraditional students who are older and have worked for a number of years in other jobs or professions. Some of your classmates may have worked as teachers' aides in classrooms for years. Others may be switching careers from the armed forces, engineering, retail management, or public relations. Welcome to a profession in which new teachers represent such wonderfully diverse work experiences, as well as varying educational, cultural, and economic backgrounds.

The Importance of Teachers to Society

Society has great expectations for its teachers. "Nine out of ten Americans believe the best way to lift student achievement is to ensure a qualified teacher in every classroom," according to a national survey (Recruiting New Teachers, 1998). In addition to guiding students'

FIGURE 1.1

**Professions That Provide the Most Benefit to Society
According to Survey Respondents**

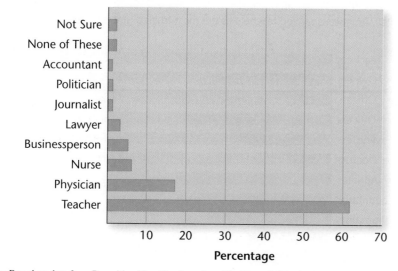

Source: Based on data from Recruiting New Teachers, Inc., *The Essential Profession: A National Survey of Public Attitudes toward Teaching, Educational Opportunity and School Reform,* Belmont, MA: Author, 1998.

academic achievement, teachers have some responsibility for students' social and physical development. They are expected to prepare an educated citizenry that is informed about the many issues critical to maintaining a democracy and to improving our world. They help students learn to work together and try to instill the values that are critical to a just and caring society. Teachers are also asked to prepare children and youth with the knowledge and skills necessary to work in an **information age**; information and its management are critical to education and society.

Given these challenging responsibilities, teaching is one of the most important careers in the world and especially in a democratic society. Although critics of our education system sometimes give the impression that there is a lack of public support for schools and teachers, the public now ranks teaching as the profession that provides the most important benefit to society. Public perceptions of the importance of teaching have improved over the years (Recruiting New Teachers, 1998). In fact, respondents to a survey about professions that benefit society ranked teachers first by more than a three-to-one margin over other important professionals such as physicians, nurses, businesspeople, lawyers, journalists, politicians, and accountants, as shown in Figure 1.1.

Teachers were also given a vote of confidence in a Gallup Poll that asked people to indicate the most trusted group of people in the country. The results, as shown in Figure 1.2, indicate that teachers were ranked first as the most trusted group in the country.

This public trust should be encouraging and perhaps a bit frightening to you as a future educator—encouraging because you will be entering a highly regarded and trusted professional group and frightening because you will be responsible for helping to uphold this public trust.

The Public View of Teachers and Schools

Teachers and the public agree that the quality of the teaching staff is of primary importance in selecting a school (Langdon & Vesper, 2000). Parents, guardians, and families know who the effective teachers are in a school and will do everything possible to ensure that their children are in those teachers' classes. At the same time, they know the teachers who are not as effective, and

information age The current age in which information and its management are critical to education and societal advancement.

FIGURE 1.2

Teachers Get America's Vote of Confidence

You may not make as much as a CEO or a pro baseball player, but your stock has a lot more currency than theirs in the eyes of the American public.

In a Gallup Poll, Americans ranked teachers as the most trusted group of people in the country.

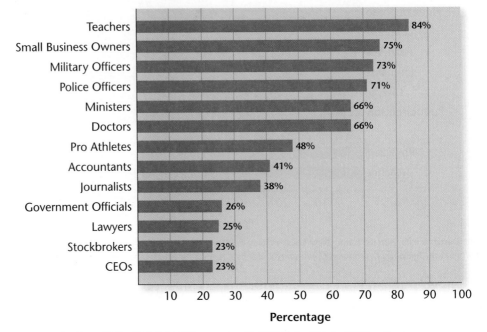

Source: Phi Delta Kappa/Gallup Poll, July 2002, as reported in *NEA Today*, October 2002, p. 9.

they steer their children into other classes if possible. They know the value of an effective teacher to the potential academic success of their children.

The annual Phi Delta Kappa/Gallup Poll survey on the public's attitudes toward public schools asks respondents to grade schools in both their local area and the nation as a whole. Figure 1.3 shows the results of the most recent survey, which indicates that parents generally give high grades to the school their oldest child attends.

This same annual PDK/Gallup Poll survey asks citizens to indicate the most serious problems facing our schools. The results are shown in Figure 1.4. Public school parents in their combined opinions view funding, overcrowding, and fighting as major school problems.

FIGURE 1.3

The Public's Opinion of Public Schools

	'08 %	'07 %	'06 %	'05 %	'04 %
A & B	**72**	**67**	**64**	**69**	**70**
A	30	19	26	31	24
B	42	48	38	38	46
C	14	24	24	21	16
D	5	5	5	6	8
Fail	4	3	4	4	4
Don't know	5	1	3	0	2

Source: William J. Bushaw and Alec M. Gallup, "The 40th Annual Phi Delta Kappa/Gallup Poll of the Public's Attitudes toward the Public Schools," *Phi Delta Kappan* (September 2008), p. 12. Reprinted by permission of *Phi Delta Kappan*.

FIGURE 1.4

The Public's View of Problems in Schools

	National Totals			Public School Parents		
	'08 %	'07 %	'06 %	'08 %	'07 %	'06 %
Funding	**17**	**22**	**24**	**19**	**26**	**21**
Discipline	10	10	11	3	5	7
Overcrowding	6	7	13	11	9	16
Fighting	6	6	5	8	8	4
Drugs	4	4	8	4	3	7
Good teachers	4	5	4	3	4	4
Standards	3	4	4	2	4	3

Source: William J. Bushaw and Alec M. Gallup, "The 40th Annual Phi Delta Kappa/Gallup Poll of the Public's Attitudes toward the Public Schools," *Phi Delta Kappan* (September 2008), p. 12. Reprinted by permission of *Phi Delta Kappan*.

Who Teaches?

Teachers should represent the diversity of the nation. However, white females are overrepresented in the teaching force, particularly in early childhood and elementary schools. Teachers come from varied backgrounds and hold a wide variety of perspectives. Some are Democrats, some Republicans, and some members of the Reform and other parties. Some belong to unions, but others don't. Teachers hold a variety of religious views. Because of these many differences, it is difficult to generalize about educators in the United States. However, taking a look at some of the similarities and differences among teachers may help you to understand the current teaching profession.

PROFILE OF U.S. TEACHERS. Although demographic data are elusive and constantly changing, the following snapshot of educators in the United States should help you get an idea of the profile of U.S. teachers.

In addition to being passionate about helping learners, teachers must be good managers and take time to collaborate with their colleagues.

According to the U.S. Department of Education, the United States has about 3.2 million public school teachers, about 400,000 private school teachers, and about 932,000 college and university faculty members. More than 60 percent of the teachers work at the elementary school level. In addition to teachers, our schools have about 411,000 administrative and education professionals. Approximately 1.25 million teachers' aides, clerks and secretaries, and service workers staff the nation's public schools. There are another roughly one million education-related jobs, including education specialists in industry, instructional technologists in the military, museum educators, and training consultants in the business world. So altogether, there are roughly six million educators in the United States, making education one of the largest professions in the country.

PEARSON myeducationlab

Go to the Assignments and Activities section of Topic 1 *The Teaching Profession* in the MyEducationLab for your course and complete the activity *Why Become a Teacher*.

REMAINING IN THE PROFESSION. Although many teachers make careers out of teaching, unfortunately, a relatively high percentage of classroom teachers eventually decide that teaching is not the profession they wish to pursue. It is estimated that approximately 20 percent of the new teachers hired annually are not teaching three years later. Teachers leave the classroom for a number of reasons. Some leave to raise children and some decide to return to school full time for an advanced

Most teachers enter and remain in their profession because of a desire to work with young people.

myeducationlab
Go to the *Assignments and Activities* section of Topic 14: *Professional Development* in the MyEducationLab for your course and complete the activity titled *Succeeding in Your First Year of Teaching.*

More information on rural and urban schools can be found in Chapters 7, 8, and 9.

induction Years one to three of full-time teaching.

mentoring An experienced professional helping a less experienced colleague.

degree. Others decide to pursue another career that might be more satisfying or pays a higher salary. Other reasons for leaving teaching are related to poor working conditions in schools, including lack of administrative support, perceived student problems, and little chance for upward mobility.

Like all other professionals, teachers become accomplished through experience. Most states do not grant a professional license to teachers until they have taught for at least three years. Teachers cannot seek national certification from the National Board for Professional Teaching Standards (NBPTS, which will be discussed in more detail later) until they have taught for three years. When teachers leave the profession in their first few years of practice, schools lose an important developing resource. Good professional development programs for teachers such as **induction** programs, which provide special help for new teachers during their first few years, also help to retain new teachers.

Many schools now have a system that provides **mentoring** among teachers. This peer mentoring system is designed to facilitate teachers helping one another. As part of a new teacher induction program, many of these schools assign an experienced master teacher to mentor beginning teachers.

When you search for your first teaching job, find out whether the school district provides induction programs, mentors, and professional development, especially for beginning teachers. These are services that help teachers improve their skills as well as their chances of being successful teachers for an entire career.

Teacher Supply and Demand

Many factors influence the number of teachers that a school district needs each year. The number of students in schools, the ratio of teachers to students in classrooms, immigration patterns, and migration from one school district to another influence the demand for teachers. The supply of teachers depends on the numbers of new teachers licensed, teachers who retired or left the previous year, and teachers returning to the workforce.

Sometimes the supply is greater than the demand, but various estimates for the next decade indicate a demand for new teachers beyond the number being prepared in colleges and universities. At this time, however, the United States does not seem to have a general teacher shortage. Instead, the problem is the distribution of teachers. School districts with good teaching conditions and high salaries do not face teacher shortages. However, inner-city and rural schools too often do not have adequate numbers of qualified and licensed teachers, in part because of lower salaries. There also are greater shortages of teachers in parts of the country with increasing populations, such as states in the Southwest.

TEACHER SUPPLY. The supply of new teachers in a given year consists primarily of two groups: new teacher graduates and former teacher graduates who were not employed as teachers during the previous year. Not all college graduates who prepared to teach actually begin teaching right after graduating. Generally, only about half the college graduates who have completed teacher education programs actually take teaching positions in the first few years after graduation.

It is estimated that nearly half the teachers hired by the typical school district are first-time teachers. A third is experienced teachers who have moved from other school districts or from other jobs within the district. Experienced teachers reentering the field make up the remainder of the new hires.

New Teachers. A number of new teachers are not recent college graduates. They are typically people who are changing careers or retirees from the military or business. These older new teachers with years of work experience often have completed alternative pathways into teaching through school-based graduate programs that build on their prior experiences. These teachers bring a valuable different perspective on education to their teaching positions.

Still other new teachers have no preparation to teach; some do not even have a college degree. More often they have a degree in an academic area such as chemistry or history, but have not studied teaching and learning or participated in clinical practices in schools. Some states and school districts allow these individuals to teach with only a few weeks of training in the summer. Participants in these programs are more likely to be dissatisfied with their preparation than are teachers who have completed either regular or nontraditional programs for teacher preparation. They often have difficulty planning the curriculum, managing the classroom, and diagnosing students' learning needs, especially in their first years of teaching. Individuals who enter the profession through this path leave teaching at a higher rate than other teachers.

Returning Teachers. A number of licensed teachers drop out of the profession for a time but return later in life. These teachers constitute about 20 percent of the new hires each year. Therefore, when you finish your teacher education program, you will be competing for teaching positions not only with other new graduates, but also with experienced teachers who are returning to the classroom or moving from one school district to another.

TEACHER DEMAND. The demand for teachers in the United States varies considerably from time to time, from place to place, from subject to subject, and from grade level to grade level. One of the major factors related to the demand for teachers is the number of school-age children, which can be projected into the future on the basis of birthrates. The projected demand for K–12 teachers is shown in Figure 1.5.

FIGURE 1.5

Relative Teacher Demand by Field

Fields with Considerable Shortage (5.00–4.21)			Fields with Some Shortage-con't. (4.20–3.41)	
Severe/Profound Disabilities	4.47		Middle School Principal	3.46
Mathematics Education	4.46		Library Science/Media Technology	3.46
Physics	4.39		Elementary Principal	3.42
Multicategorical	4.39		Fields with Balanced Supply and Demand (3.40–2.61)	
Mild/Moderate Disabilities	4.37		Speech Education	3.40
Chemistry	4.35		Gifted/Talented Education	3.34
Mental Retardation	4.34		School Social Worker	3.34
Emotional/Behavior Disorders	4.31		Family & Consumer Science	3.33
Bilingual Education	4.31		Counselor	3.29
Learning Disability	4.28		Languages—Classics	3.22
Visually Impaired	4.24		Elementary—Middle	3.20
Dual Certificate (Gen./Spec.)	4.23		Languages—French	3.13
Hearing Impaired	4.23		Music—Instrumental	3.13
Speech Pathologist	4.21		Languages—German	3.04
Fields with Some Shortage (4.20–3.41)			Music—Vocal	3.04
English as a Second Language/ELL	4.08		Journalism Education	3.03
Early Childhood Special Education	4.07		Music—General	3.01
Biology	4.06		Business Education	3.01
Earth/Physical Science	4.01		English/Language Arts	2.89
Audiologist	3.99		Elementary—Pre-Kindergarten	2.74
Physical Therapist	3.91		Art/Visual Education	2.74
Languages—Spanish	3.88		Elementary—Intermediate	2.73
General Science	3.87		Theatre/Drama	2.70
Occupational Therapist	3.82		Dance Education	2.69
School Nurse	3.80		Fields with Some Surplus (2.60–1.81)	
Technology Education	3.58		Health Education	2.57
Languages—Japanese	3.53		Elementary—Kindergarten	2.52
Agriculture	3.52		Elementary—Primary	2.41
Computer Science Education	3.52		Physical Education	2.33
Reading	3.52		Social Studies Education	2.20
Superintendent	3.50		Fields with Considerable Surplus (1.80–1.00)	
High School Principal	3.49		None	
School Psychologist	3.49			

From preliminary data supplied by survey respondents. In some instances, the averages are based upon limited input and total reliability is not assured.

Source: "Relative Demand by Field," in *2009 AAEE Job Search Handbook for Educators,* Columbus, OH: American Association for Employment in Education, Inc., 2009, p. 13. Reprinted with permission.

The number of school-age children in the United States is expected to increase during the next 10 years, requiring more teachers.

Many teachers will be retiring during the next decade, raising even further the number of new and reentering teachers needed to staff the nation's schools. As you plan your teaching career, you will want to consider a number of factors such as salary, benefits, cost of living, workload, and other forces that influence the demand for teachers. As you read the following, you will realize that many other factors may influence you as you decide what subjects you will teach and the area of the country where you will teach.

Student-to-Teacher Ratios. Obviously, one measure of a teacher's workload is class size. The number of students taught by a teacher varies considerably from school to school and from state to state. Elementary teachers generally have more students in a class than secondary teachers, but secondary teachers have five to seven classes each day. Figure 1.6 shows average student-to-teacher ratios in public schools in the United States.

The demand for teachers has increased, in part, because some states and school districts are limiting the student-to-teacher ratio, especially in the primary grades. In large school districts, lowering the student-to-teacher ratio by even one student creates a demand for many more teachers. Statewide initiatives to reduce the ratio have an even greater impact on the number of teachers needed.

Location of the School District. Within a given area because of say, new housing developments, population shifts may cause one school district to grow rapidly, build new schools, and hire new teachers, while a neighboring school district closes schools and reduces its number of teachers. Nevertheless, the greatest shortages are usually in urban schools with large proportions of low-income and culturally and linguistically diverse populations. Some teachers do not want to teach in large urban school districts because of poor working conditions in many schools and relatively low salaries compared to schools in the wealthier suburbs. Other teachers believe that teaching in a large city is both challenging and fulfilling. We recommend that you explore the advantages and disadvantages of teaching in districts of different sizes and locations.

FIGURE 1.6

Pupil/Teacher Ratio in Elementary and Secondary Schools, Selected Years

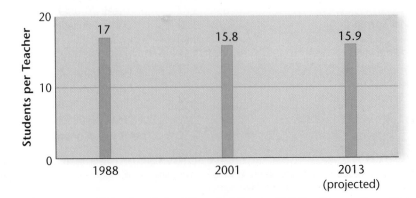

Source: U.S. Department of Education, National Center for Education Statistics, Common Core of Data surveys, various years.

Student enrollment also varies depending on the part of the country. In the next eight years, increases are expected in Arizona, Idaho, Nevada, and New Mexico; decreases are expected in most midwestern and northeastern states (Hussar & Bailey, 2008).

Teaching Field Shortages. Teacher shortages are more severe in some fields than others. For instance, the number of students diagnosed with various disabilities has increased considerably during the past decade and now totals more than 5 million throughout the country. As a percentage of total public school enrollment, the number of students requiring special education has risen considerably in recent years. Consequently, most school districts report the need for more special education teachers.

There is also a critical shortage of bilingual teachers. The need for bilingual teachers is no longer limited to large urban areas and the southwestern states. Immigrant families with children have now settled in cities and rural areas across the Midwest and Southeast. The projected demographics for the country indicate a growing number of students with limited English skills, requiring more bilingual and English as a second language (ESL) teachers than are available today. The Global Perspectives feature below provides an example of one school district's efforts to recognize and serve our increasingly diverse society.

Licensed mathematics and science teachers are prime candidates for job openings in many school districts. One of the problems in secondary schools especially is that teachers may have a state license but too often not in the academic area they are assigned to teach. The National Commission on Teaching and America's Future reported that nearly one-fourth of all secondary teachers do not have even a college minor in their main teaching field. This is especially true for mathematics teachers due to a shortage of candidates in this field.

Teachers often receive out-of-field assignments when teachers with the appropriate academic credentials are not available. Sometimes the assignments are made to retain teachers whose jobs have been eliminated as enrollments shift and schools are closed. The tragedy is that students suffer as a result—it is difficult to teach what you do not know. The federal legislation commonly referred to as the **No Child Left Behind Act (NCLB)** is designed to significantly reduce this out-of-field teacher assignment problem in the near future.

NCLB is explained more fully in various places later in this book—see the index for details.

Teachers from Diverse Backgrounds. Although the student population is rapidly changing and becoming more racially, ethnically, and linguistically diverse, the teaching pool is becoming less so. The number of Latino students is rapidly increasing, pulling almost even with the number of African American students in the 2000 census.

Having teachers from different ethnic and cultural backgrounds is extremely important to the majority of people in the United States (Recruiting New Teachers, 1998). Most school districts are seeking culturally diverse faculties, and districts with large culturally diverse populations are aggressively recruiting teachers from diverse backgrounds. The federal government and some states provide incentives to colleges and universities to support the recruitment of a more diverse teaching force. Another implication of the demographics of increasing student diversity is that all teachers need to become skilled at teaching in diverse schools and classrooms. Again, the Global Perspectives feature below provides an example of how some school districts are attempting to meet the demands of our rapidly changing global diversity needs.

No Child Left Behind Act (NCLB) A federal law passed in 2001 that sets goals for achievement for all students and requires that teachers meet certain qualifications.

GLOBAL PERSPECTIVES   Teaching Chinese to American Students

Our schools recognize that we live in a rapidly changing world in which more people now speak Chinese than any other language. China has become a major market, as well as a major supplier, for American industry. With these facts in mind, the Portland, Oregon, public school system instituted a K–12 Chinese-language instructional program for their approximately 50,000 students. Starting in kindergarten, students will study the Mandarin language and Chinese culture.

Questions for Reflection
1. What is your perspective on this idea?
2. What foreign language(s) are the most important for students to learn today?
3. At what grade level and intensity do you think foreign languages should be taught?

TEACHING AS A PROFESSION

Historically, fields such as law, medicine, architecture, and accountancy have been considered professions, but teaching has sometimes been classified as a semiprofession. This distinction is based in part on the prestige of the different jobs as reflected in the remuneration received by members of a particular profession. Although teaching salaries remain lower than those of most other professionals in most parts of the country, educators consider themselves professionals. The good news is that during the past decade the prestige of teaching has risen. Most teachers have master's degrees and continue to participate in professional development activities throughout their careers. They manage their professional work, designing and delivering a curriculum during a school year. They develop their own unique teaching styles and methods for helping students learn. In this section, we explore the factors that determine a profession and a professional and demonstrate that teaching itself is a full-fledged profession.

Professional Responsibilities

Being a professional carries many responsibilities. Professionals in most fields regulate licensure and practice through a professional standards board controlled by members of the profession rather than the government. Professional standards boards for teaching currently exist in about one-fourth of the states; other agencies have this responsibility in the remaining states. These boards have a variety of titles and typically include many practicing educators. Not only do these boards set standards for licensure, but they also have standards and processes for monitoring the practice of teachers. They usually have the authority to remove a teacher's license.

DEVELOPING PROFESSIONAL COMMITMENTS AND DISPOSITIONS. Successful teachers exhibit **dispositions** (beliefs, attitudes, and values) that facilitate their work with students and parents. Teachers' values, commitments, and professional ethics influence interactions with students, families, colleagues, and communities. They affect student learning, motivation, and development. They influence a teacher's own professional growth as well. Dispositions held by teachers who are able to help all students learn include the following:

1. Enthusiasm for the discipline(s) she or he teaches and the ability to see connections to everyday life
2. A commitment to continuous learning and engagement in professional discourse about subject matter knowledge and children's learning of the disciplines
3. The belief that all children can learn at high levels
4. Valuing the many ways in which people communicate and encouraging many modes of communication in the classroom
5. Development of respectful and productive relationships with parents and guardians from diverse home and community situations, seeking to develop cooperative partnerships in support of student learning and well-being.

LEARNING TO USE AND CONDUCT EDUCATIONAL RESEARCH. Another important professional responsibility of all educators is to be able to understand, evaluate, and use educational research results. Parents rightly expect teachers to utilize the best of educational research in their classrooms, just as we patients rightly expect our physicians to utilize the most recent medical research results when they provide us with medical treatment.

Teachers can begin to better understand and use good educational research by enrolling in courses dealing with educational research, attending meetings on the subject, reading educational research journals, and doing web searches on the topic. Teachers can also participate in research studies and, with proper background, even design and carry out their own action research to help solve problems they face in their classrooms.

↻ More helpful information on educational research can be found in every chapter.

Professional Knowledge

Professionals provide services to their clients, and their work is based on unique knowledge and skills grounded in research and practice in the field. Professions require their members to have completed higher education, usually at the advanced level. The competence of most professionals is determined in training by **authentic assessments** in real-life settings. Traditionally, professionals have had control of their work with little direct supervision.

dispositions The values, commitments, and professional ethics that influence beliefs, attitudes, and behaviors.

authentic assessment An assessment that measures one's ability to perform a task in a real-life situation.

One of the characteristics of a profession is that its members have some generally agreed-on knowledge bases for their work. This professional knowledge has evolved from research and practice in the field. Teachers who have prepared to teach are more successful in classrooms than those who have a degree only in an academic discipline. These competent and qualified teachers are key to student learning.

To be a professional, teachers must also know the subjects they will be teaching. For example, secondary teachers should major in the academic area that they later will teach so that they learn the structure, skills, core concepts, ideas, values, facts, and methods of inquiry that undergird the discipline. They must understand the discipline well enough to help young people learn it and apply it to the world in which they live. As students learn about a concept or skill, teachers must be able to relate the content to the experiences of students in order to provide meaning and purpose.

Professional Skills

One of the cornerstones of the field of teaching is knowledge about teaching and learning and the development of skills and dispositions that help students learn. Therefore, teacher candidates study theories and research on how students learn at different ages. They must understand the influence of culture, language, and socioeconomic conditions on learning. They also have to know how to manage classrooms, motivate students, work with parents and colleagues, assess learning, and develop lesson plans built on the prior experiences of fifteen to thirty or more students in the classroom. Teaching is a complex field. There are seldom right answers that fit every situation. Teachers must make multiple decisions throughout a day, responding to individual student needs and events in the school and community, all while keeping in mind the professional ethics required by the education profession. Incidentally, by taking this course, you are taking an important step toward developing the professional skills needed to be an effective educator.

Qualified teachers have also had the opportunity to develop their knowledge, skills, and dispositions with students in schools. These field experiences and clinical practices such as student teaching and internships should be accompanied by feedback and mentoring from experienced teachers who know the subject they teach and how to help students learn. Work in schools is becoming more extensive in many teacher education programs. Some teacher candidates participate in yearlong internships in schools, ending in a master's degree. Others work in professional development schools in which higher education faculty, teachers, and teacher candidates collaborate in teaching and inquiry. In both of these cases, most, if not all, of the program is offered in the school setting.

An example of the various kinds of problems that teachers face can be found in the Reflect on Diversity feature.

> More details about multicultural education are presented throughout this book, especially in Chapters 7 and 8.

REFLECTonDIVERSITY   Student Bullying

All year Jasmine has been teased by some of her eighth-grade classmates because she is very petite and at least six inches shorter than any of the other girls. One spring day when the class was supposed to be working on an assignment at their desks, Latoya started making fun of Jasmine again, first very quietly. Before long, the exchanges became louder.

"You're fat as a theater."

"Your mama's so ugly."

Then, Latoya hit too close to home when she responded "And your father's in jail."

Before the teacher could intervene, other students redirected the conversation around Jasmine's desk. As the room quieted down and students returned to their assignment, Mr. Brown decided to let it go.

After the girls crossed the street from school to begin the walk home through a wooded area, Jasmine confronted Latoya about her taunting in class. The exchanges between the two girls continued, again becoming very personal, when Latoya retorted with degrading remarks about Jasmine's size and boyfriend. Jasmine hit her. When Latoya returned the punches, Jasmine's cousin, Mitchyl, jumped in to help. Within a few minutes, Latoya was running back to school with numerous lacerations on her face, requiring stitches.

Questions for Reflection

1. Who was the bully and who was the victim in this altercation at school?
2. How could Mr. Brown have responded differently to the situation earlier in the day? What other steps could the teacher or other school officials have taken to try to prevent the after-school fight?
3. What action should the school take against either Jasmine or Latoya? What recourse does Latoya's family have?

myeducationlab To respond to these questions online, go to the *Book Specific Resources* section in the MyEducationLab for your course, select your text, and then select *Reflect on Diversity* for Chapter 1.

Most important to you as a future teacher, the No Child Left Behind Act requires that every classroom have a highly qualified, competent teacher who is fully certified and licensed in the areas being taught in every classroom. Like all sweeping pieces of legislation, the No Child Left Behind Act is controversial and has many critics. Because it will have a considerable impact on your future as an educator and citizen, we highly recommend that you review it more closely.

Some teachers feel that local, federal, and state requirements, such as NCLB and other various requirements and standards, place undue pressure on schools, teachers, and students to perform especially well on standardized tests. You will learn more about NCLB later in this book.

QUALITY ASSURANCE

One of the roles of professions and their standards is to provide quality control over who enters and remains in the profession. Most other professions, such as law, medicine, and dentistry, require candidates to graduate from an accredited professional school before they are eligible to take a licensing examination to test the knowledge and skills necessary to practice responsibly. Some professions also offer examinations for certification of advanced skills, such as the CPA exam for public accountants, or for practice in specialized fields such as pediatrics, obstetrics, or surgery. The same quality assurance continuum now exists for teaching. Figure 1.7 depicts a comprehensive quality assurance system for teaching that includes complementary sets of standards and assessments for initial teacher preparation, state licensure, national board certification, and continuing professional development.

Accreditation

Both public schools and teacher education programs are subject to **accreditation programs**, which are standards established by accreditation agencies, some of which are mandated and some of which are voluntary. Accreditation provides assurance to the public that graduates of programs are qualified and competent to practice. The proportion of accredited schools, colleges, and departments of education in a state has been found to be the best predictor of the proportion of well-qualified teachers in a state. Because well-qualified teachers are the strongest predictor of student achievement on national achievement tests, accreditation is an important first step of a quality assurance system for the education field.

accreditation programs Recognition given to educational institutions that have met accepted standards applied by an outside agency.

REGIONAL ACCREDITATION. The general concept of accreditation is related to an internal attempt on the part of a professional training system to examine and improve the quality of the profession that it serves. Six regional accreditation bodies offer accreditation to all K–12 schools and to colleges and universities. One of these six agencies, all of which are named by the general region

FIGURE 1.7

The Professional Continuum and Quality Assurance in Teaching

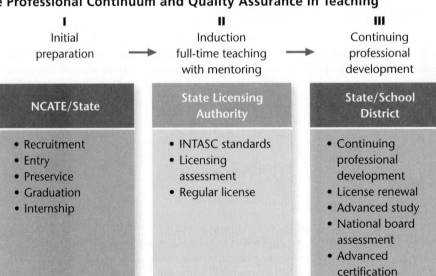

I	II	III
Initial preparation	Induction full-time teaching with mentoring	Continuing professional development
NCATE/State	**State Licensing Authority**	**State/School District**
• Recruitment • Entry • Preservice • Graduation • Internship	• INTASC standards • Licensing assessment • Regular license	• Continuing professional development • License renewal • Advanced study • National board assessment • Advanced certification

in which they function, is functioning in your state right now. For instance, the North Central Association of Colleges and Schools (NCA) covers a large number of states in the upper central part of the nation. You might want to inquire whether your own institution is accredited by one of these six regional accrediting agencies. There is a good chance that the schools in which you will eventually teach will also be involved in some type of regional accreditation.

NCATE. Do you know whether the teacher education program you are now in has NCATE accreditation? Your college or university is probably accredited by one of six regional accrediting bodies just discussed that apply standards to the university as a whole by reviewing its financial status, student services, and the general studies curriculum. However, professional accreditation in teacher education is granted to the school, college, or department of education that is responsible for preparing teachers and other educators. Fewer than half of the roughly 1,300 institutions that prepare teachers in the United States are accredited by the profession's major accrediting agency, the National Council for Accreditation of Teacher Education (NCATE). However, the NCATE accredited institutions graduate a majority of our new teachers. To learn more about the accreditation status of institutions, visit NCATE's website at www.ncate.org.

TEAC. Yet another somewhat smaller organization that offers accreditation to teacher education programs is the Teacher Education Accreditation Council (TEAC). This accrediting body, which was founded in 1997, is newer than NCATE and is dedicated to helping improve degree programs for professional educators.

Licensure

When you graduate, you will be required to obtain a teaching license for the state in which you wish to teach. The requirements for your license are determined by the state in which you teach.

STATE TEACHER CERTIFICATION. State licensure is a major component of a quality assurance system for professionals. To practice as a teacher, you must be granted a license from a state agency. A license to teach usually requires completion of a state-approved teacher education program and passing of a standardized test of knowledge. In addition, student teaching or an internship must be completed successfully.

States traditionally required candidates to take specific college courses, complete student teaching, and successfully pass a licensure examination for a license. Most states are now in the process of developing **performance-based licensing** systems. These systems will not specify courses to be completed; instead, they will indicate the knowledge, skills, and sometimes dispositions that candidates should possess. Future decisions about granting a license will depend on the results of state assessments based primarily on licensure test scores.

As mentioned, requirements for licensure differ from state to state. For this reason, if you plan to teach in a state different from the one in which you are going to school, you may want to contact that state directly for licensure information. The teacher certification officer at your institution should be able to provide you with licensure information and details about seeking a license in any particular state.

An initial teaching license allows a new teacher to practice for a specified period, usually three to five years, also known as the induction period. On completion of successful teaching during that period and sometimes a master's degree, a professional license can be granted. Most states require continuing professional development throughout a teacher's career and periodic renewal of the license, typically every five years.

INTASC. The ten principles of the **Interstate New Teacher Assessment and Support Consortium (INTASC)** have been adopted or adapted for licensure by many states. Figure 1.8 shows these ten INTASC principles, which describe what teachers should know and be able to do in their first few years of practice. You should be developing this knowledge and these skills in the college program in which you are currently enrolled.

Before granting a professional license, some states are requiring teachers to submit **portfolios**, which are scored by experienced teachers, as evidence of teaching effectiveness. The portfolios that you begin to compile during your teacher education program could evolve into the documentation you will later need to submit for your first professional license. Portfolios are discussed more fully elsewhere in this book (consult the index for locations) and at the end of each chapter.

To see a list of state certification and licensure offices throughout the U.S., go to the MyEducationLab for your course, select *Resources,* and then select *Licensure and Standards.*

myeducationlab

Go to the *Building Teaching Skills and Dispositions* section of Topic 1: *The Teaching Profession* in the MyEducationLab for your course and complete the activity titled Using the *INTASC Standards and Teaching Practice.*

performance-based licensing A system of professional licensing based on the use of multiple assessments that measure the candidate's knowledge, skills, and dispositions to determine whether he or she can perform effectively in that profession.

Interstate New Teacher Assessment and Support Consortium (INTASC) An organization that created a set of principles that describe what teachers should know and be able to do.

portfolio A compilation of works, records, and accomplishments that teacher candidates prepare for a specific purpose to demonstrate their learning, performances, and contributions.

FIGURE 1.8

INTASC Principles: What Teachers Should Know and Be Able to Do

1. The teacher understands the central concepts, tools of inquiry, and structures of the discipline(s) he or she teaches and can create learning experiences that make these aspects of subject matter meaningful for students.
2. The teacher understands how children learn and develop, and can provide learning opportunities that support their intellectual, social, and personal development.
3. The teacher understands how students differ in their approaches to learning and creates instructional opportunities that are adapted to diverse learners.
4. The teacher understands and uses a variety of instructional strategies to encourage students' development of critical thinking, problem solving, and performance skills.
5. The teacher uses an understanding of individual and group motivation and behavior to create a learning environment that encourages positive social interaction, active engagement in learning, and self-motivation.
6. The teacher uses knowledge of effective verbal, nonverbal, and media communication techniques to foster active inquiry, collaboration, and supportive interaction in the classroom.
7. The teacher plans instruction based on knowledge of subject matter, students, the community, and curriculum goals.
8. The teacher understands and uses formal and informal assessment strategies to evaluate and ensure the continuous intellectual, social, and physical development of the learner.
9. The teacher is a reflective practitioner who continually evaluates the effects of his or her choices and actions on others (students, parents, and other professionals in the learning community) and who actively seeks out opportunities to grow professionally.
10. The teacher fosters relationships with school colleagues, parents, and agencies in the larger community to support students' learning and well-being.

Each of these ten principles is accompanied in the full INTASC document with knowledge, dispositions, and performance expectations for candidates. INTASC content standards also have been developed for teachers of the arts, English language arts, mathematics, science, social studies, elementary education, and special education. INTASC standards can be accessed from the web at www.ccsso.org.

PEARSON
myeducationlab

To learn more about the Praxis exam, review test-taking strategies, and see sample questions, go to the MyEducationLab for your course, select *Resources,* and then select *Licensure Exams.*

National Board for Professional Teaching Standards (NBPTS) A national association that creates and publishes standards and offers certification to accomplished teachers.

PRAXIS. The Educational Testing Service (ETS) has developed a series of examinations, commonly called the *Praxis Series*™, that are designed to assess the knowledge and skills required to be an effective educator at various stages of a beginning teacher's career. Praxis I assesses academic skills, Praxis II assesses the subjects to be taught, and Praxis III assesses classroom performance. Some teacher education programs and most states make use of these tests as part of their admission, retention, graduation, and certification requirements. Perhaps you are familiar with these Praxis tests; you may even have taken some of them. In any case, you should become familiar with them. You can learn more about the *Praxis Series* by visiting its website at www.ets.org/praxis.

Advanced Certification

Advanced certification has long been an option in many professions but is relatively new for teaching. Like all issues related to education, requiring advanced certification is not supported by everyone.

Many states now have an advanced certification option for educators. Some states actually require teachers to progress through a series of certification levels, whereas other states have either optional levels of certification that are made available to teachers or only one certification level. You should inquire about the certification levels required or available in your state. You should also eventually understand the certification requirements and options in any school district in which you might consider working.

NBPTS. The **National Board for Professional Teaching Standards (NBPTS)** was established in 1987 to develop a system for certifying accomplished teachers. The first teachers were certified by NBPTS in 1995, and the number of teachers seeking national certification continues to increase. As of the printing of this book, nearly 74,000 teachers have achieved this national certification, and this number increases each year.

The NBPTS standards outline what teachers should know and be able to do as accomplished teachers. These standards state that nationally certified teachers:

1. Are committed to students and their learning.
2. Know the subjects they teach and how to teach those subjects to students.
3. Are responsible for managing and monitoring student learning.
4. Think systematically about their practice and learn from experience.
5. Are members of learning communities.

Why do teachers seek national certification? For one thing, recognition of accomplishment by one's peers is fulfilling. Nationally certified teachers are also aggressively being recruited by some school districts. Nationally certified teachers may also be paid an extra salary stipend of several thousand dollars. Your current teacher education program should be providing you with the basic foundation for future national certification.

To become eligible for national certification, you must teach for at least three years. The process for becoming nationally certified requires at least a year. You can learn the details about this opportunity by visiting the NBPTS website at www.nbpts.org or by going to this text's MyEducationLab.

The certification process requires the submission of portfolios with samples of student work and videotapes of the applicant teaching. In addition, teachers desiring NBPTS certification must complete a number of activities at an assessment center, where experienced teachers score the various assessment activities. Many teachers do not meet the national requirements on the first try but report that the process is the best professional development activity in which they have participated. Overwhelmingly, teachers report that they have become better teachers as a result. More and more parents in the future will likely desire nationally certified teachers in their children's classrooms.

Given the trend to include students with disabilities in general education classrooms, it is likely that some of your students will have special needs, no matter what grades or subjects you teach.

Standards

Standards and standards-based education are prevalent at all levels of education today. To finish your teacher education program, you will have to meet professional, state, and institutional standards that outline what you should know and be able to do as a novice teacher. When you begin teaching, you will be expected to prepare students to meet state or district standards. Assessments are designed to determine whether students meet the preschool–grade 12 standards at the levels expected. Most states require teacher candidates to pass standardized tests at a predetermined level before granting the first license to teach. Some states require beginning teachers to pass **performance assessments** based on standards in the first three years of practice in order to receive a professional license.

Standards developed by the profession (e.g., the INTASC and NBPTS standards just discussed) can be levers for raising the quality of practice. When used appropriately, they can protect students, including the least advantaged students, from incompetent practice (Darling-Hammond, 2000). Some educators view standards as a threat, especially when a government agency or other group holds individuals or schools to the standards, making summative judgments about licensure or approval. Others see standards as powerful tools for positive change in a profession or in school practices.

Standards and assessment are discussed in more detail in Chapter 11.

USING TECHNOLOGY TO BETTER UNDERSTAND STANDARDS. Just about all national and state educational standards can be rather easily found on the web. Standards created by professional organizations can also be accessed by checking the websites of those organizations. We highly recommend that you find and carefully examine any standards that apply to your major(s) and to

performance assessments A comprehensive assessment system through which candidates demonstrate their proficiencies in the area being measured.

the teaching areas that are of interest to you. You should also become familiar with the educational standards that apply to the state(s) in which you intend to teach. Such standards should be useful in guiding you through your remaining teacher education preparation.

No Child Left Behind

The No Child Left Behind Act (NCLB) was signed into law by President George W. Bush on January 8, 2002. This act, which is actually a reauthorized version of the earlier Elementary and Secondary Education Act (ESEA), is built around four national education reform goals: stronger accountability for student learning results, increased educational flexibility and local control, expanded educational options for parents, and an emphasis on using teaching methods that have been proven to work. The act received overwhelming support from the U.S. Congress and the administration and is likely to guide much of our public education for at least the next decade. This far-reaching law requires the tracking of all students' progress from grades 3 to 8 and also requires every student to pass the state proficiency test(s) by the end of the 2013–14 school year. The Professional Dilemma feature illustrates a rather common dilemma that teachers face concerning the current emphasis on tests.

⟳ More information on the use of technology in education can be found in each chapter.

REFLECTING ON ONE'S PRACTICE

It is interesting, and perhaps useful to educators, to note that physicians proudly claim to "practice" medicine throughout their careers. Many people have suggested that teachers should borrow this concept and also proudly undertake to "practice" teaching throughout their careers. This interpretation of the word *practice* implies that teachers, like physicians, should constantly strive to improve their performance—something that all good teachers do. This section provides you with a few practical suggestions as you prepare to "practice" your profession as a teacher.

Systematic Observation

As you proceed through your teacher education program, you should seize every opportunity to observe a wide variety of activities related to the world of education. For instance, in addition to the observation and participation assignments you will have as part of the formal teacher education program, you should volunteer to visit and observe a wide variety of classrooms. You should also attempt to find summer employment that allows you to work with young people. The more time you spend with children, the better you will understand them and be able to work with them.

Informal Note-Taking

As you observe teachers and classrooms, write down your observations. This type of note-taking can be done in a variety of ways. For instance, when you enter a classroom, write a brief descrip-

PROFESSIONAL DILEMMA   Standardized Tests

Testing is pervasive in our educational system today. Many school districts and states require students to pass tests to move from one grade to another grade. They must pass tests to graduate from high school and to enter most colleges and universities. Teacher candidates, like you, are required to pass standardized tests to be licensed to teach.

Not only are students and teacher candidates tested regularly and often, but also their schools and universities are held accountable for their performance on these tests. The aggregated results are published in newspapers and on websites. Schools and colleges are ranked within a state. Some are classified as low performing and lose part of their public funding. In some schools, teachers' and principals' jobs depend on how well their students perform on these standardized tests.

The standardized tests that are being used in elementary and secondary education are supposed to test for evidence that students are meeting state standards. For the most part, they are paper-and-pencil tests of knowledge in a subject area. Although the state standards are advertised as being developed by teachers and experts, many educators argue that many of the standards expect knowledge and skills that are developmentally inappropriate at some grade levels. In areas such as social studies, recall of specific facts that cover spans of hundreds of years is not an uncommon requirement.

It probably comes as no surprise that some teachers are teaching to the test, taking weeks out of the curriculum to coach students for the test. Some people believe that this constitutes a form of cheating. And due to pressure to do well on tests, some students find ways to cheat in an attempt to obtain higher scores.

Questions for Reflection
1. What are your perspectives on standardized tests at this point in your professional development?
2. What are some things that teachers can do to deal with the problems of standardized tests?
3. What are some of the factors that probably cause students to cheat?

tion of the setting, such as the physical appearance of the room, the number of students, the teaching devices available, and so on. Then systematically describe each thing you observe. The more detail you can record, the more you will learn from your observations.

Create a list of questions that interest you before you begin any given observation. If you are interested in how a teacher motivates students during a particular lesson, write down the question "What techniques does the teacher use to help motivate students?" Then record your observations under that question. The School-Based Observations feature, located at the end of each chapter, will help you get an idea of the types of observations you can make.

Analysis of Practice and Reflection

Once you have collected observations of teaching, children, classrooms, and schools, take time to think about what you have seen. Several techniques exist for systematically analyzing your observations, but equally important is taking time to reflect on these analyses. In our rush to get everything done, we frequently fail to take time to examine our experiences and impressions. However, being serious about finding time for thoughtful reflection is an important part of becoming an excellent teacher. The following processes can be helpful.

Reflective Journaling

Educators at all levels have come to realize that learners profit greatly from thinking reflectively about, and then writing down, what they learn in school. This process is called *reflective journaling*. If you are not now required to keep a journal in your teacher education program, we strongly recommend that you start doing so by completing the following Journal for Reflection feature. If you are required to keep a journal, we urge you to take this assignment seriously because you will learn much in the process.

━━━━━ JOURNAL FOR REFLECTION ━━━━━

Record your thoughts at this stage of your professional development about (1) the teaching profession, (2) its strengths and weaknesses, (3) your interest in teaching as a career, and (4) your excitement and doubts about working in the profession.

You can go about keeping a journal in many ways. All you need is something to write on and the will to write. A spiral notebook, a three-ring binder, or a computer works fine. Preferably at the end of each day (at the very least once each week), briefly summarize your thoughts about and reactions to the major events and concepts you have experienced and learned. Spend more time thinking and reflecting, and write down only a brief summary. We believe that your journal should be brief, reflective, candid, personal, and preferably private, something like a personal diary. Try to be perfectly honest in your journal and not worry about someone evaluating your opinions.

When you start to work in schools, you will discover (if you have not already done so) that teachers in elementary and secondary schools use journaling with their students. Something about thinking and then writing down our thoughts about what we have learned helps us internalize, better understand, and remember what we have learned.

Within each chapter in this book, we offer several suggestions for entries in your journal. We sincerely believe that reflective journaling throughout your teacher education program will enrich your learning and better prepare you for teaching.

Folio/Portfolio Development

As you move through your teacher education program and into your career as a teacher, you will find that you have been collecting stacks, boxes, and files of information and "stuff" related to you, your teaching, and the accomplishments of the students you have taught.

COLLECTING AND ORGANIZING MATERIAL. If you are like most teachers, you will not know for sure what to do with all of the teaching materials that you accumulate, yet you will be reluctant to throw any of it away. Be very careful about discarding material until you have organized a folio and anticipated the needs of various portfolios that you might have to prepare. A *folio* is an organized compilation of all the products, records, accomplishments, and testimonies of a teacher and his or her students. Imagine the folio as a large file drawer with different compartments and file folders. Some of the material included is related directly to you and your background. Other

PEARSON
myeducationlab

For more information on journaling and reflection, go to the MyEducationLab for your course and select *Resources, Preparing a Portfolio,* and then *Reflection as an Essential Component of a Teaching Portfolio.*

PEARSON
myeducationlab

For additional information about portfolios, go to the MyEducationLab for your course, select *Resources*, and then select *Preparing a Portfolio*.

items or artifacts reflect what others have said about you. Other materials may include examples of projects that your students have completed.

A *portfolio* is a special compilation assembled from the folio for a specific occasion or purpose, such as a job interview or an application for an outstanding teacher award. The portfolio might also be used by you and your professors throughout your teacher education program to document your performance in meeting state, professional, and institutional standards. Portfolios are required in some states as evidence that you should be granted a professional teaching license after the first few years of actual work in classrooms. Portfolios will also be required for NBPTS certification later in your career. A folio or portfolio can be organized in any way you think will be most useful.

The occasions on which other people recognize your contributions and achievements are called *attestations*. Awards, letters of commendation, newspaper articles, and information on elected positions and committee memberships are examples of attestation items to keep in your folio.

Through your efforts as a teacher candidate and teacher, students complete assignments, assemble projects, achieve on examinations, and receive awards. Compile the works and successes of the people you have worked with, along with photographs and video records of your classroom and student projects. You may want to include videotapes of your teaching with a description of your classroom context and a written analysis of your teaching. Also include copies of your best lesson plans, committee reports, grant proposals, and other products that have resulted from your efforts as a leader.

PORTFOLIO DEVELOPMENT TASKS. To help you start your folio, we have included at the end of each chapter several suggestions in the Portfolio Development section. We have selected topics and tasks that are important to you at this early point in your teacher education program; in fact, these suggestions anticipate some of the items you may need to include in future portfolio presentations.

CHALLENGES AFFECTING TEACHERS

The working conditions for teachers have improved measurably in recent years, and the following sections discuss some of the ways in which these improvements have been implemented. This information represents more good news for those who are preparing for careers in the education field.

Salaries in a Changing World

Teaching salaries vary considerably from state to state and from school district to school district. Table 1.1 shows average and beginning teacher salaries in each state. As you can see, salaries vary considerably from state to state. One reason for the higher salaries is a difference in the cost of living from one area to another. However, cost of living alone does not explain the differences. Some states and some school districts view teachers as professionals, have high expectations for them, support them through mentoring and professional development, use multiple assessments to determine teacher effectiveness, and pay salaries commensurate with those of other professionals.

SALARY DIFFERENCES. Each state's board of education is an agent of the state and is therefore empowered to set salary levels for employees of the school district it governs. Each school system typically has a **salary schedule** that outlines the minimum and maximum salary for several levels of study beyond the bachelor's degree and for each year of teaching experience. For example, a beginning teacher with a bachelor's degree might be paid $35,000, and one with a master's degree might be paid $42,000. Teachers with twenty years of experience might be paid $50,000 to $76,000, depending on the school district in which they are employed. Schools also pay extra for additional duties such as coaching or working with extracurricular activities.

The organization Recruiting New Teachers found that more than 75 percent of the public supported raising teachers' salaries. Over half of the respondents in this survey indicated that they would choose teaching as a career if they were guaranteed an annual income of $60,000. Further, they would recommend teaching as a career for members of their family if the salary was at this level (Who should teach, 2000). These findings suggest that the pool of available teachers would be much larger if teachers' salaries were higher.

ADDITIONAL BENEFITS. All full-time teachers receive additional benefits that, when added to their basic salary, constitute their total compensation package. When you pursue your first teaching position, you will want to inquire about these benefits as well as the salary. Although the salary is usually of first concern to a teacher, additional benefits are equally important over the long

salary schedule A printed negotiated schedule that lists salary levels based on years of experience and education.

Table 1.1 • Teachers' Beginning and Average Salaries by State

State	Beginning Salary 2004–2005	Average Salary 2004–2005	State	Beginning Salary 2004–2005	Average Salary 2004–2005
Alabama	$ 31,368	$ 38,186	Nebraska	29,303 a	39,441
Alaska	38,657	52,467	Nevada	27,957	43,212
Arizona	30,404	39,095	New Hampshire	28,279	43,941
Arkansas	28,784	41,489	New Jersey	38,408 a	56,635
California	35,760	57,604	New Mexico	33,730	39,391
Colorado	35,086	43,965	New York	37,321	55,665 b, c
Connecticut	39,259	57,760	North Carolina	27,944	43,343
Delaware	35,854	52,924	North Dakota	24,872	36,449
Florida	33,427	43,095 c	Ohio	33,671	49,438
Georgia	34,442	46,437 d, e	Oklahoma	29,174	37,879 d, e
Hawaii	35,816	47,833	Oregon	33,699	48,320 d
Idaho	27,500	40,864	Pennsylvania	34,976	53,281
Illinois	37,500	56,494	Rhode Island	33,815 a	56,432 a
Indiana	30,844	46,591 c	South Carolina	28,568	42,189
Iowa	27,284	39,284	South Dakota	26,111	34,039
Kansas	27,840	39,351	Tennessee	32,369	42,076 c
Kentucky	30,619	41,075	Texas	33,775	41,009
Louisiana	31,298	39,022 c	Utah	26,521	37,006
Maine	26,643	40,935	Vermont	26,461 a	44,346 c
Maryland	37,125	52,330	Virginia	33,200 a	45,377 c
Massachusetts	35,421 a	54,688 c	Washington	30,974	45,722
Michigan	35,557 a	53,959	West Virginia	26,704	38,404
Minnesota	31,632	47,411	Wisconsin	25,222	43,099
Mississippi	28,200	38,212 e	Wyoming	31,481	40,487
Missouri	29,281	39,064			
Montana	25,318	38,485	**50 states**	**$31,753**	**$47,602**

a=AFT estimate; b=median; c=includes extra-duty pay; d=includes employer pick-up of employee pension contributions where applicable; e=includes fringe benefits such as healthcare where applicable.

Source: American Federation of Teachers. 2007 Report. <www.aft.org>

Note: The salary information presented here was the latest available as this edition of the Job Search Handbook went to press. We encourage you to visit the website of the American Federation of Teachers at <www.aft.org> to locate updated information.

Source: "Teachers' Beginning and Average Salaries by State," in *2009 AAEE Job Search Handbook*, Columbus, OH: American Association for Employment in Education, 2009, p. 14. Reprinted with permission.

term. Additional benefits vary from school to school but frequently include some type of insurance benefits—hospitalization insurance, medical/surgical coverage, and major medical insurance. Somewhat less frequently, a teacher's medical insurance also includes dental care and prescription drugs; it may include coverage of eyeglasses and other types of less common medical services. Benefits often include a group life insurance policy as well.

Full-time public school teachers are usually eligible for retirement benefits as part of their total compensation package. These benefits also vary from state to state. In some states, teachers receive a combination of state teacher retirement and Social Security retirement. In other states, a teacher's retirement may depend totally on a state program and be divorced entirely from the federal Social Security retirement system. It is sometimes possible for teachers who move from state to state to transfer their retirement benefits to the state in which they ultimately retire. A teacher's retirement package is an extremely important part of the total compensation package and needs to be well understood by everyone entering the profession.

RECRUITMENT INCENTIVES. A shortage of teachers leads to a number of innovative strategies for recruiting teachers. Job fairs are held in areas where there is an apparent surplus of teachers so that school districts from areas of shortage can interview prospective applicants. Technology is being used in innovative ways too. For example, some districts have been willing to ship overnight a video telephone to an applicant so that he or she can be interviewed without having to travel. Others have provided moving expenses or help with housing.

Another way that some districts attract new teachers is by offering a contract signing bonus. This somewhat debatable practice is explored in the Teacher Perspectives feature.

Working Conditions

Almost everyone feels better about his or her work when the environment is supportive and conducive to high-quality output. The same is true for teachers and students. Like other factors in education, working conditions differ greatly from school to school. Within a single school district, the conditions can change dramatically across neighborhoods. Some schools are beautiful sprawling campuses with the latest technology. In others, toilets are backed up, paint is peeling off the walls, classes are held in storage rooms, or administrators are repressive. Most teachers who begin their careers in the second type of setting either aggressively seek assignments in other schools as soon as possible or leave the profession.

TEACHER PERSPECTIVES

Should Districts Offer Signing Bonuses to Attract New Teachers?

Difficulty recruiting a sufficient number of teachers has led some school districts to offer contract signing bonuses to new teachers. Needless to say, this is a controversial practice that is opposed by some experienced teachers.

YES

Virginia Hoover is a school social worker with eleven years in the Guilford, North Carolina, schools. She was the state's School Social Worker of the Year in 1997–98 and the Student Services Support of the Year in 1999.

Yes, I believe school systems should offer a sign-on bonus to staff. A bonus would definitely be an added attraction to new employees, whether they are graduating from college or just trying to get into education.

For new graduates, a bonus would help offset the expense of preparing their first classroom. Buying the materials and supplies needed to make classrooms inviting and exciting places for students can take a lot of money.

If a new teacher has to relocate to take the job, that's another expense. A bonus could relieve the stress of moving and help make the transition a more pleasant experience.

For the more seasoned staff person, a sign-on bonus would be a great help in meeting the expenses that come with taking a new job. . . .

As for me personally, I have no problem with systems offering such a sign-on bonus perk to attract capable people to education. I'm concerned about who will fill my role as social worker when I retire.

I won't be offended if my system begins offering a sign-on bonus to new staff. Those of us who are working hard pulling the load until vacant positions are filled would welcome the sight of quality applicants swarming to get those vacant jobs.

NO

Bob Kaplan teaches eighth-grade social studies at Jane Addams Junior High in Schaumburg, Illinois. He has taught for twenty-three years and served four times on bargaining teams, once as chairman, and most recently last spring.

Signing bonuses. What a great idea! What's next, no-cut contracts? Free agency? The traditional teacher pay scale may not be ideal, but it's fairer than having a rookie make more than a three-year veteran because the rookie teaches bilingual classes and the other teaches a multi-age elementary class.

If we were to have signing bonuses, who's going to determine what's more important for a bonus? Who's going to figure out how much of a bonus is deserved? Whatever happened to collective bargaining?

I can easily see a personnel director paying the extra dollars to fill a position. I can also foresee the same personnel director using these extra dollars as a backdoor to merit pay.

Our association needs to represent all members. These first-year teachers aren't even members yet. How, as a labor organization, can we explain to our members in their second or third year, "Gee, sorry you were too late for a bonus, but remember to keep paying your dues dollars!" . . .

Signing bonuses, on the surface, sound good. Administrators would love to fill tough positions by throwing money to a few.

But before we should even consider signing bonuses, we need standards and an effort to increase the supply for hard-to-fill positions. Let's use all this bonus money to reward teachers who have made and will continue to make a positive difference.

Source: Adapted from "Should Districts Offer Signing Bonuses to Attract New Teachers?" *NEA Today* (April 2000), p. 11. Reprinted by permission of the National Education Association.

What is your perspective on this issue?

myeducationlab To explore both sides of this issue and think about each perspective, go to the *Book Specific Resources*, section in the MyEducationLab for your course, select your text, and then select *Teacher Perspectives* for Chapter 1.

Teachers do work under very different conditions from those of most other professionals. Secondary and middle school teachers usually work with students in forty-five- to fifty-five-minute time periods with brief breaks between classes. Elementary and early childhood teachers are usually in self-contained classrooms in which they have few breaks, and they even have to supervise students during recesses and lunch periods. They have little time during the school day to work with colleagues or to plan for the next lesson or the next day. In many schools, teachers still have limited access to telephones or computers for support in their work.

BEGINNING AND CONTINUING A TEACHING CAREER

Becoming Licensed

Teachers must obtain a license before they can legally teach in public schools. Each state determines its own licensure requirements. Although requirements may be similar from state to state, unique requirements exist in many states.

LICENSURE TESTS. Most states require teacher candidates to pass one or more standardized tests at a specified level to be eligible for their first license to teach. Written assessments are required in many states, and many states require basic skills tests; in fact, many institutions require candidates to pass these tests before they are admitted into teacher education programs. More than half the states require candidates to pass tests in both professional pedagogical and content or subject area knowledge. The cutoff scores that determine passing are set by states and vary greatly. Teacher candidates who do not pass the test in one state may be able to pass in another state that has a lower cutoff score.

An increasing number of states are requiring future teachers to major in an academic area rather than in "education." Students complete courses in education, field experiences, and student teaching or an internship along with courses in a chosen academic major to become eligible for a license when the program is completed. You should clearly understand the requirements for a license in the state in which you are attending school and in any states in which you may wish to teach.

Searching for a Teaching Position

Teacher education candidates should begin thinking about employment early in their college careers. A helpful annual resource is the *Job Search Handbook for Educators* from the American Association for Employment in Education (www.aaee.org); it may be available in your college's job placement office. This handbook contains suggestions for preparing your résumé, cover letters, and letters of inquiry; it also provides excellent practical suggestions for improving your interviewing techniques. Information on teacher supply and demand in different fields is included in the handbook as well.

School districts typically would like applicants to present evidence that responds to the following questions, along with portfolios containing illustrations of performance, which are very helpful in this process:

1. Can the candidate do the job? Does the candidate have the necessary academic background? Can the candidate provide evidence that his or her students learned something? Does he or she know how to assess learning? Is he or she sensitive to the needs of diverse children? Can the candidate respond well to individual differences? How strong is he or she with regard to community activities?
2. Will the candidate do the job? What interview evidence does the candidate provide that communicates a professional commitment to getting the job done?
3. Will the candidate fit in? Is this candidate a good match for the needs of the district and the student needs as identified? How will the candidate work with other teachers and staff?
4. Will the candidate express well what he or she wants in a professional assignment? Does the candidate have personal and professional standards of his or her own?
5. Does the district's vision match the candidate's vision? Understanding the expectations of both the district and the candidate is critical if the candidate is to be successful.

Remaining a Teacher

Most educators feel that teaching improves dramatically during the first five years of practice. Often teachers hone their skills alone as they practice in their own classrooms and take advantage

PEARSON
myeducationlab

To see a list of teaching job websites, Go to the MyEducationLab for your Course, select *Resources, Beginning Your Career,* and then *Teaching Job Websites.*

of available professional development activities. A more promising practice is the assignment of mentors to new teachers to assist them in developing their skills during the early years of practice. Teachers who do not participate in an induction program (such as mentoring), who are dissatisfied with student discipline, or who are unhappy with the school environment are much more likely to leave teaching than are their peers (*Who should teach?*, 2000).

Experienced teachers see teaching as a public endeavor. They welcome parents and others to the classroom. As cooperating teachers and mentors, they become actively engaged with higher education faculty in preparing new teachers. They become researchers as they critically examine their own practice, testing various strategies to help students learn and sharing their findings with colleagues in faculty and professional meetings.

RENEWAL OF LICENSES. Most states require teaching licenses to be renewed periodically. A professional license is usually not granted until after several years of successful practice. Some states require a master's degree; a few require the successful completion of a portfolio with videotapes of teaching that are judged by experienced teachers. To retain a license throughout one's career, continuing professional development activities may be required.

LOOKING AHEAD: THE TEACHING PROFESSION

We all live in a rapidly changing world, including the professional world in which educators live. Many, if not most, of the topics discussed in this chapter will change over time; and you will need to keep up on current educational trends throughout your career as an educator.

Continuing professional development is one of the ongoing activities of career teachers. Often teachers return to college for a master's degree that may help to increase their knowledge and skills related to teaching and learning and the subjects they teach. They learn new skills such as the use of the Internet to help students learn. They learn more about the subjects they teach through formal courses, reading on their own and exploring the Internet, work in related businesses in the summers, or travel as time and resources permit. Teachers ask colleagues to observe their teaching and provide feedback for improving their work. They seek advice from other teachers and professionals with whom they work. They join and become active in professional organizations, attend and participate in professional meetings, read educational journals, explore and participate in educational research, keep up on world events, and so forth. Doing as many of these things as possible will improve your work as an educator and will even make your work more enjoyable.

Participants at the *2008 Phi Delta Kappa Summit on High-Performing Educators* developed a list of the qualities of a great teacher, which are shown in Figure 1.9. This list is a wonderful goal for you to keep in mind as you look ahead to your career as a "great educator."

FIGURE 1.9

A Great Teacher

- Has the ability to be flexible, optimistic, self-reflective, progressive, and innovative;
- Must possess the ability to build relationships with students and teachers and have a passion for teaching;
- Excites a passion for learning in his or her students through skilful facilitation, using 21st-century tools;
- Goes beyond the classroom as a collaborator with colleagues;
- Wants to improve himself or herself by learning good instructional skills;
- Is someone who knows the curriculum and works well as part of a team;
- Builds relationships and facilitates lifelong learning;
- Collaborates with families, peers, and the community;
- Shows appreciation and enthusiasm for cultural differences;
- Inspires others to achieve their potential;
- Understands the complexities of the teaching and learning environment;
- Has consistently high expectations for all students;
- Recognizes and adapts when he or she isn't getting through to students;
- Addresses the needs of the whole child;
- Uses assessment to inform instructional decision making; and
- Gives back through mentoring.

Source: Erin Young, "What Makes a Great Teacher?" *Phi Delta Kappan* (February 2009), p. 439. Reprinted by permission of *Phi Delta Kappan*.

SUMMARY

TODAY'S TEACHERS

- There are about four million public and private school teachers in the United States today.
- Teachers are generally highly regarded and respected today.
- Parents feel that overcrowding, discipline, and lack of adequate funding are some of the major problems in our public schools.
- Teacher supply and demand vary considerably from place to place.

TEACHING AS A PROFESSION

- Successful teachers are reflective about their work, as shown in their ability to gather, analyze, and use data to improve their teaching.
- These teachers have a natural curiosity about their work and are continually searching for better answers to the challenges they face.
- Teachers must continue to refine their professional skills throughout their entire careers to keep pace with our rapidly changing world.

QUALITY ASSURANCE

- A variety of agencies are attempting to improve the education profession through accreditation programs.
- Each state determines its own teaching requirements and issues its own teaching certificates.
- INTASC has created a list of ten principles that describe what teachers should know and be able to do.
- PRAXIS examinations are designed to assess the knowledge and skills required to be an effective teacher.
- The NBPTS is a system for granting certification for accomplished teachers.
- Standards and standards-based education are prevalent at all levels of education today.
- The NCLB act has been in existence since 2002 in an attempt to improve public education in the United States.

REFLECTING ON ONE'S PRACTICE

- You can learn a good deal about teaching through systematic observation and reflective journaling.
- Beginning in their teacher education programs, teachers should write in reflective journals, collect and organize information and data, and compile information from their folios into portfolios for specific purposes such as performance assessments and job applications.
- Collecting, organizing, and saving material you produce during your teacher preparation program can help you learn and be useful to you in the future.
- You should begin to develop a professional education folio now, if you have not already done so.

CHALLENGES AFFECTING TEACHERS

- Teacher salaries vary greatly from place to place.
- Typical additional benefits that teachers receive vary depending on the individual school district.
- Working conditions also vary greatly from school to school.
- Given all of this variability in salary and working conditions, you should explore and understand all of these conditions before you accept a teaching position.

BEGINNING AND CONTINUING A TEACHING CAREER

- People are typically required to take a variety of tests to become certified as teachers.
- You should begin your job application process early.
- Educators must constantly be attuned to the many different perspectives on education that are held by policy makers, parents, students, fellow educators, and society in general.
- Several big ideas about the teaching profession grow out of this chapter, including the fact that education is extremely important to the development of our society and that teachers play the key role in this important activity.

LOOKING AHEAD: THE TEACHING PROFESSION

- The field of education will continue to change rapidly in the future in the United States.
- There will also continue to be a great variety of perspectives on education in the future.
- You should strive to develop the skills and qualities needed to become a "great teacher," such as those listed in Figure 1.9.

DISCUSSION QUESTIONS

1. What are the characteristics of a profession? What are your arguments for or against recognizing teaching as a profession?
2. Why do shortages of teachers probably exist in some subjects and not in others?
3. What should national accreditation tell you about your teacher education program?
4. What is NBPTS certification and why is it important in a teacher's career?
5. Of what potential value are journals, folios, and portfolios in preparing to teach?
6. What support should school districts provide to teachers in the induction years to encourage retention in the profession beyond three years?

SCHOOL-BASED OBSERVATIONS

1. Begin a list of the teaching challenges that you observe in schools. Reflect on the challenges that you had not expected when you initially thought about teaching as a career and how those challenges may influence your decision to become a teacher. How much have the teaching challenges you have observed met your initial expectations?
2. Ask several teachers what their major challenges and satisfactions are as educators. Analyze their answers and think about the major challenges and satisfactions you may experience as an educator.

PORTFOLIO DEVELOPMENT

1. Your first folio development task is to find and organize the many materials, artifacts, and records that you currently have. Examples may include term papers, transcripts, awards, letters of recognition, and observation journals. Take some time now to find and begin organizing these materials. Organize them into logical categories. At various points in the future, you will be drawing items out of the folio to develop a portfolio for completion of student teaching or to apply for a teaching position or national certification.
2. The U.S. Department of Education now annually publishes a national teacher education report card, which includes information about all teacher education institutions in your state. Review the performance of candidates on state licensure tests in your field at your institution and other institutions in your state. Reflect on why there are differences in performance across institutions and whether state licensure tests are an appropriate measure of teaching competence. Place your written reflections in your portfolio.

myeducationlab To begin developing your own personal portfolio, go to the MyEducationLab for your course, select *Resources*, and then select *Portfolio Builder*.

PREPARING FOR CERTIFICATION

CERTIFICATION REQUIREMENTS

Because you are taking the course where this text is required, you are probably in the process of becoming certified to teach. The certification process for you includes completing a teacher education program such as the one you are in, and then being recommended by your institution to the state department of education for certification. The state may have additional requirements for certification beyond those of the institution. In many cases, those requirements include a standardized test or a series of tests, many times the PRAXIS Series™.

"The PRAXIS Series™ assessments are used for teacher licensure and certification by state departments of education and other certification agencies. The Praxis I® tests measure basic academic skills, and the Praxis II® tests measure general and subject-specific knowledge and teaching skills. The Praxis III® Teacher Performance Assessments assess the skills of beginning teachers in classroom settings. Praxis I® test is usually taken before admission to the teacher education program. The Praxis II® test is taken before student teaching, before graduation, or before certification/licensure. The Praxis III® is usually administered during the first year of teaching, where a trained observer is in the classroom to evaluate your teaching."

As you read further in this book, note how issues covered in the chapters relate to the topics covered in the Praxis II tests, particularly those on the Principles of Teaching and Learning (PLT) test. All teachers might take the PLT test if it is required by their respective states, no matter what the content area.

ANSWERING THE CHAPTER ESSAY QUESTIONS

In each of the subsequent chapters, you will find a question with this beginning prompt: Answer the following short-answer question, which is similar to items in Praxis and other state certification tests.

Following the prompt, you are given a question and then asked to examine your response using the Praxis general scoring guide. The general scoring guide provides this input:

A response that receives a score of 2:

• Demonstrates a thorough understanding of the aspects of the case that are relevant to the question

- Responds appropriately to all parts of the question
- If an explanation is required, provides a strong explanation that is well supported by relevant evidence
- Demonstrates a strong knowledge of pedagogical concepts, theories, facts, procedures, or methodologies relevant to the question

A response that receives a score of 1:

- Demonstrates a basic understanding of the aspects of the case that are relevant to the question
- Responds appropriately to one portion of the question
- If an explanation is required, provides a weak explanation that is supported by relevant evidence
- Demonstrates some knowledge of pedagogical concepts, theories, facts, procedures, or methodologies relevant to the question

A response that receives a score of 0:

- Demonstrates misunderstanding of the aspects of the case that are relevant to the question
- Fails to respond appropriately to the question
- Is not supported by relevant evidence
- Demonstrates little knowledge of pedagogical concepts, theories, facts, procedures, or methodologies relevant to the question

No credit is given for a blank or off-topic question.

(http://www.ets.org/Media/Tests/PRAXIS/pdf/0523.pdf, p. 8)

Keep this general scoring guide nearby as you answer the essay and short-answer questions for each chapter.

MYEDUCATIONLAB

myeducationlab Now go to Topic 1: *The Teaching Profession* in the MyEducationLab (www.myeducationlab.com) for your course, where you can:

- Find learning outcomes for *The Teaching Profession* along with the national standards that connect to these outcomes.
- Complete *Assignments and Activities* that can help you more deeply understand the chapter content.
- Apply and practice your understanding of the core teaching skills identified in the chapter with the *Building Teaching Skills and Dispositions* learning units.

- Check your comprehension on the content covered in the chapter by going to the *Study Plan* in the *Book Specific Resources* for your text. Here you will be able to take a chapter quiz, receive feedback on your answers, and then access *Review, Practice, and Enrichment* activities to enhance your understanding of chapter content.

WEBSITES

www.myeducationlab.com This text's MyEducationLab contains a wealth of enrichment material to help you learn more about the field of education.

www.teacher_teacher.com A website for recruiting teachers that also includes information about becoming a teacher and related topics.

www.ncate.org A list of institutions with teacher education programs accredited by NCATE and information about becoming a teacher are available on this website. It also includes links to state agencies and their licensure requirements.

www.nea.org A rich source of constantly updated information about the National Education Association, national educational issues, governmental activities related to education, and the teaching profession in general.

www.nbpts.org The website for the National Board for Professional Teaching Standards includes information on the process for seeking NBPTS certification as well as the board's standards, assessments, and publications.

www.theteacherspot.com A great resource for new teachers dealing with many topics (discipline, technology, teacher resources, etc.).

www.nasdtec.org Information on licensure requirements and state agencies that are responsible for teacher licensing are available on this website of the National Association of State Directors of Teacher Education and Certification.

www.zotero.org Helps students and teachers better find and organize learning material.

FURTHER READING

American Association for Employment in Education. (Published annually). *The job search handbook for educators.* Evanston, IL: Author. An excellent source of practical information for anyone searching for a teaching position.

Jacobson, L. (2005, June 22). Survey finds teachers' biggest challenge is parents. *Education Week,* p. 5. An informative report of the difficulties facing teachers.

Rathbone, C. H. (2005, February). A learner's bill of rights. *Phi Delta Kappan,* pp. 471–473. An excellent reminder to teachers and parents of the inherent learning rights of students.

Rose, L. C., & Gallup, A. M. The annual Phi Delta Kappan/Gallup Poll of the public's attitude toward the public schools. Published each September in *Phi Delta Kappan.* A wonderful annual source of information on the public's opinion on a wide variety of educational issues.

chapter two

THE EARLY HISTORY OF EDUCATION IN A CHANGING WORLD

TEACHING PATRIOTISM— WITH CONVICTION

By CHESTER E. FINN, JR.,
Phi Delta Kappan, April 2006

Americans will debate for many years to come the causes and implications of the September 11 attacks on New York City and Washington, D.C., as well as the foiled attack that led to the crash of United Airlines Flight 93 in a Pennsylvania field. Between the first and second "anniversaries" of 9/11, another development deepened our awareness of the dangerous world we inhabit and of America's role therein—the successful war to liberate Iraq from its dictator and his murderous regime. Of course, the consequences—and contentiousness—of that conflict continue to resonate daily in newspaper headlines and on the evening news. In these challenging times, educators rightly wonder about their proper role. What should they teach young Americans? How should they prepare tomorrow's citizenry? What is most important for students to learn?

These are weighty questions, and there is every reason to expect them to linger. But it is now clearer than ever that, if we wish to prepare our children for unforeseen future threats and conflicts, we must arm them with lessons from history and civics that help them learn from the victories and setbacks of their predecessors, lessons that, in Jefferson's words, "enable every man to judge for himself what will secure or endanger his freedom."

Jefferson was right when he laid upon education the grave assignment of equipping tomorrow's adults with the knowledge, values, judgment, and critical faculties to determine for themselves what "will secure or endanger" their freedom and their country's well-being. The U.S. Supreme Court was right, half a century ago, when, in the epoch-shaping *Brown* decision, it declared education to be "the very foundation of good citizenship."

Teachers know this better than anyone, and many need no help or advice in fulfilling their responsibility. They're knowledgeable, savvy, creative, caring, and—may I say it?—patriotic, as many fine teachers have always been. They love our country and the ideals for which it stands. Teachers must communicate to their students the crucial lessons from history and civics that our children most need to learn. The events of 9/11 and the war on terrorism that has followed create a powerful opportunity to teach our daughters and sons about heroes and villains, freedom and repression, hatred and compassion, democracy and theocracy, civic virtue and vice.

On 10 April 2003, David McCullough told a Senate committee, "We are raising a generation of people who are historically illiterate. . . . We can't function in a society," he continued, "if we don't know who we are and where we came from." The solemn duty of all educators is to make certain that all our children know who they are. Part of that can be accomplished by teaching them about America's founders, about their ideals, and about the character, courage, vision, and tenacity with which they acted. From that inspiring history, true patriotism cannot help but grow.

QUESTIONS FOR REFLECTION

1. What is your perspective on the need for schools to teach patriotism?
2. What are some of the ways teachers could do so if they wished?
3. What are some of the potential disadvantages to teaching patriotism in our schools?

Source: Reprinted with permission from *Phi Delta Kappan.*

LEARNING OUTCOMES

After reading and studying this chapter, you should be able to:

1. List some of the most important early educators in the world and explain their contributions to education. (INTASC 4: Teaching Methods)

2. Detail the major educational accomplishments of the ancient Greeks, the ancient Romans, and the Europeans of the Middle Ages, Renaissance, Reformation, and Age of Reason. (INTASC 3: Diversity)

3. Analyze what life was like for the colonial schoolteacher, student, and parent.

4. Articulate the roles local, state, and national governments played in colonial America soon after winning the War of Independence, in the 1800s, and in the early twentieth century.

5. Analyze how an understanding of early U.S. educational history might be used to improve teaching today. (INTASC 9: Reflection)

This part of the book briefly surveys the history of education. As you read this and the next history chapter, remember that historians see past events from various perspectives. *Celebrationist* historians, for instance, tend to see the brighter side of historical events and may tend, for example, to praise schools for past accomplishments. By contrast, *liberal* historians tend to study educational history through perspectives that focus on conflict, stress, and inconsistencies. *Revisionist* historians use yet another perspective, seeing celebrationist history as fundamentally flawed and concluding that we often learn more by studying what has been wrong with education than by rehearsing what has been right. *Postmodernist* historians believe that a person sees the history of education through the unique perspectives of her or his social class, race, ethnicity, gender, age, and so on. We challenge you to think critically as you read this and the next chapter and to formulate your own perspective through which to view educational history.

THE BEGINNINGS OF EDUCATION (TO 476 CE)

Informal education has been provided for children down through the ages by aboriginal people throughout the world. All people, regardless of their time and place in history, have cared for their young and attempted to prepare them for life's challenges. This was even true of the very earliest humans, who fed and protected their children and informally taught them—probably by

example and admonition—the skills they needed to survive as adults. For instance, Native Americans, who lived and flourished in North America for thousands of years before the first Europeans arrived and established formal schools, educated generations of their children. Many other early societies, including those in China, Africa, and South America, for example, also successfully provided education that their children needed to help build their flourishing cultures. Unfortunately, records do not exist that would help us better understand these earliest informal educational systems. If such records did exist, we would probably be quite impressed with the educational efforts of our aboriginal ancestors.

As written language came into use, humans felt the need for a more formal education. As societies became more complex and the body of knowledge increased, people recognized a need for schools. What they had

The aboriginal ancestors of today's Native Americans, like other aboriginal peoples, probably taught their children by admonition and example.

learned constituted the subject matter; the written language allowed them to record this knowledge and pass it from generation to generation.

Non-Western Education

It is impossible to determine when schools first came into existence. However, the discovery of cuneiform mathematics textbooks dated to 2000 BCE suggests that some form of school probably existed in Sumer (now part of Iraq) at that time. There is also evidence to suggest that formal schools existed in China during the Hsia and Shang dynasties, perhaps as early as 2000 BCE.

Western Education

It was not until about 500 BCE that a Western society advanced sufficiently to generate an organized concern for formal education. This happened in Greece during the **Age of Pericles**, 455–431 BCE. Greece consisted of many city-states, one of which was Sparta, a militaristic state whose educational system was geared to support military ambitions. The aims of Spartan education centered on developing such ideals as courage, patriotism, obedience, cunning, and physical strength. Plutarch (46–120 CE), a writer of later times, said that the education of the Spartans "was calculated to make them subject to command, to endure labor, to fight, and to conquer." There was relatively little intellectual content in Spartan education.

In sharp contrast to Sparta was Athens, another Greek city-state, which developed an educational program that heavily stressed intellectual and aesthetic objectives. Between the ages of eight and sixteen, some Athenian boys attended a series of public schools. These schools included a kind of grammar school, which taught reading, writing, and counting; a gymnastics school, which taught sports and games; and a music school, which taught history, drama, poetry, speaking, and science as well as music. Because all city-states had to defend themselves against aggressors, Athenian boys received citizenship and military training between the ages of sixteen and twenty. Athenian girls were educated in the home. Athenian education stressed individual development, aesthetics, and culture.

The Western world's first great philosophers came from Athens. Of the many philosophers that Greece produced, three stand out: Socrates (470–399 BCE), Plato (427–347 BCE), and Aristotle (384–322 BCE).

SOCRATES. Socrates left no writings, but we know much about him from the writings of Xenophon and Plato. He is famous for creating the **Socratic method** of teaching, in which a teacher asks a series of questions that leads the student to a certain conclusion. This method is still commonly used by teachers today.

Socrates traveled around Athens teaching the students who gathered about him. He was dedicated to the search for truth and at times was very critical of the existing government. In fact, Socrates was eventually brought to trial for inciting the people against the government by his ceaseless questioning. He was found guilty and given a choice between ending his teaching or being put to death. Socrates chose death, thereby becoming a martyr for the cause of education. Socrates' fundamental principle, "Knowledge is virtue," has been adopted by countless educators and philosophers throughout the ages. Incidentally, some historians speculate that Socrates might not really have existed, but rather might have been a mythical character created by other writers, which is something that many writers did at that time as evidenced by the rich Greek mythology we now treasure.

PLATO. Plato was a student and disciple of Socrates. In his *Republic,* Plato set forth his recommendations for the ideal society. He suggested that society should contain three classes of people: artisans, to do the manual work; soldiers, to defend the society; and philosophers, to advance knowledge and to rule the society. Plato's educational aim was to discover and develop each individual's abilities. He believed that each person's abilities should be used to serve society. Plato wrote, "I call education the virtue which is shown by children when the feelings of joy or of sorrow, of love or of hate, which arise in their souls, are made conformable to order."

ARISTOTLE. Like Plato, Aristotle believed that a person's most important purpose in life was to serve and improve humankind. Aristotle's educational method, however, was scientific, practical, and objective, in contrast to the philosophical methods of Socrates and Plato. Aristotle believed that the quality of a society was determined by the quality of education found in that society. His

More information on important educational philosophy pioneers can be found in Chapters 4 and 5.

Age of Pericles A period (455–431 BCE) of Greek history in which sufficiently great strides were made in human advancement to generate an organized concern for formal education.

Socratic method A way of teaching that centers on the use of questions by the teacher to lead students to a certain conclusion.

writings were destined to exert greater influence on humankind throughout the Middle Ages than the writings of any other person.

The early Greek philosophers, including Plato and Aristotle, articulated the idea that females and slaves did not possess the intelligence to be leaders and therefore should not be educated. Unfortunately, our world's current struggle with racism and sexism, deeply rooted in Western civilization, is traceable to the ancient world.

ROMAN SCHOOLS. In 146 BCE, the Romans conquered Greece, and Greek teachers and their educational system were quickly absorbed into the Roman Empire. Many of the educational and philosophical advances made by the Roman Empire after that time were actually inspired by enslaved Greeks.

Before 146 BCE, Roman children were educated primarily in the home, though some children attended schools known as *ludi*, where the rudiments of reading and writing were taught. The Greek influence on Roman education became pronounced between 50 BCE and 200 CE, when an entire system of schools developed. Some children, after learning to read and write, attended a *grammaticus* school to study Latin, literature, history, mathematics, music, and dialectics. These **Latin grammar schools** were somewhat like twentieth-century secondary schools in function. Students who were preparing for a career of political service received their training in schools of rhetoric, which offered courses in grammar, rhetoric, dialectics, music, arithmetic, geometry, and astronomy.

QUINTILIAN. One of the most influential Roman educators was Quintilian (35–95 CE). In a set of twelve books, *The Institutes of Oratory,* he described current educational practices, recommended the type of educational system needed in Rome, and listed the great books that were in existence at that time.

Regarding the motivation of students, Quintilian stated,

> Let study be made a child's diversion; let him be soothed and caressed into it, and let him sometimes test himself upon his proficiency. Sometimes enter a contest of wits with him, and let him imagine that he comes off the conqueror. Let him even be encouraged by giving him such rewards that are most appropriate to his age. (Quintilian, 1905, p. 12)

These comments apply as well today as they did when Quintilian wrote them nearly 2,000 years ago. Quintilian's writings were rediscovered in the 1400s and became influential in the humanistic movement in education.

The Romans had a genius for organization and for getting the job done. They made lasting contributions to architecture, and many of their roads, aqueducts, and buildings remain today. This genius for organization enabled Rome to unite much of the ancient world with a common language, a religion, and a political bond—a condition that favored the spread of education and knowledge throughout the ancient world.

EDUCATION IN THE MIDDLE AGES (476–1300)

By 476 CE (the fall of the Roman Empire), the Roman Catholic Church was well on the way to becoming the greatest power in government and education in the Western world. In fact, the rise of the church to power is often cited as a main cause of the Western world's plunge into the Dark Ages. As the church stressed the importance of gaining entrance to heaven, life on earth became less important. Many people viewed earthly life as nothing more than a way to a better life hereafter. You can see that a society in which this attitude prevailed would be less likely to make intellectual advances, except perhaps in areas tangential to religion.

The Dark Ages (400–1000)

As the name implies, the Dark Ages was a period when, in much of the Western world, human learning and knowledge didn't just stand still but actually regressed. This regression was due to a variety of conditions, including political and religious oppression of the common people. However, there were some examples of human progress during this time. In fact, some historians believe this historical period was not "dark" at all but rather an era of considerable human progress—another example of the differing perspectives with which historians view the past.

CHARLEMAGNE. During the Dark Ages, one of the bright periods for education was the reign of Charlemagne (742–814). Charlemagne realized the value of education, and as ruler of a large part

Latin grammar schools An early type of school that emphasized the study of Latin, literature, history, mathematics, music, and dialectics.

of Europe, he was in a position to establish schools and encourage scholarly activity. In 768, when Charlemagne came into power, educational activity was at an extremely low ebb. The church conducted the little educating that was carried on, mainly to induct people into the faith and to train religious leaders. The schools where this religious teaching took place included *catechumenal schools*, which taught church doctrine to new converts; *catechetical schools*, which at first taught the catechism but later became schools for training church leaders; and *cathedral* (or *monastic*) *schools*, which trained clergy.

ALCUIN. Charlemagne sought far and wide a talented educator who could improve education in the kingdom, finally selecting Alcuin (735–804), formerly a teacher in England. While Alcuin served as Charlemagne's chief educational adviser, he became the most famous educator of his day. It is reported that Charlemagne himself often sat in the Palace School with the children, trying to further his own meager education.

Roughly during Alcuin's time, the phrase **seven liberal arts** came into common usage to describe the curriculum that was then taught in some schools. The seven liberal arts consisted of the *trivium* (grammar, rhetoric, and logic) and the *quadrivium* (arithmetic, geometry, music, and astronomy). Each of these seven subjects was defined broadly; collectively they constituted a more comprehensive study than today's usage of the term suggests. The phrase *liberal arts* has survived and is commonly used now as a reference to general education as opposed to vocational education.

The Revival of Learning

Despite the efforts of men such as Charlemagne and Alcuin, little educational progress was made during the Dark Ages. However, between 1000 and 1300—a period frequently referred to as the "age of the revival of learning"—humankind slowly regained a thirst for education. This revival of interest in learning was supported by the rediscovery of the writings of some of the ancient philosophers (mainly Aristotle) and renewed interest in them and in the reconciliation of religion and philosophy.

THOMAS AQUINAS. Thomas Aquinas (1225–1274), more than any other person, helped to change the church's views on learning. This change led to the creation of new learning institutions, among them the medieval universities. The harmonization of the doctrines of the church with the doctrines of philosophy and education was rooted in the ideas of Aristotle. Himself a theologian, Aquinas formalized **scholasticism,** the logical and philosophical study of the beliefs of the church. His most important writing was *Summa Theologica,* which became the doctrinal authority of the Roman Catholic Church. The educational and philosophical views of Thomas Aquinas were formalized in Thomism—a philosophy that has remained important in Roman Catholic parochial education.

MEDIEVAL UNIVERSITIES. The revival of learning brought about a general increase in educational activity and the growth of educational institutions, including the establishment of universities. These medieval universities, the true forerunners of our modern universities, included the University of Bologna (1158), which specialized in law; the University of Paris (1180), which specialized in theology; Oxford University (1214); and the University of Salerno (1224). By the time Columbus sailed to North America in 1492, approximately eighty universities already existed in Europe.

Although the Middle Ages produced a few educational advances in the Western world, we must remember that much of the Eastern world did not experience the Dark Ages. Mohammed (569–632) led a group of Arabs who later captured northern Africa and southern Spain. The Eastern learning that the Arabs brought to Spain spread slowly throughout Europe over the next few centuries through the writings of such scholars as Avicenna (980–1037) and Averroës (1126–1198). These Eastern contributions to Western knowledge included significant advances in science and mathematics, including the Arabic numbering system.

EDUCATION IN TRANSITION (1300–1700)

Two very important movements took place during the educational transition period of 1300 to 1700: the Renaissance and the Reformation. The Renaissance represented the protest of individuals against the dogmatic authority the church exerted over their social and intellectual life. The Renaissance started in Italy (around 1300) when people reacquired the spirit of free inquiry that had prevailed in ancient Greece. The Renaissance slowly spread through Europe, resulting in a general revival of classical learning called *humanism.*

seven liberal arts A medieval curriculum that consisted of the trivium (grammar, rhetoric, logic) and the quadrivium (arithmetic, geometry, music, astronomy).

scholasticism The logical and philosophical study of the beliefs of the church.

The second movement, the Reformation, represented a reaction against certain beliefs of the Roman Catholic Church, particularly those that discouraged learning and that, in consequence, kept lay people in ignorance.

The Renaissance

The common people were generally oppressed by wealthy landowners and royalty during the eleventh and twelfth centuries. In fact, the common people were thought to be unworthy of education and to exist primarily to serve landed gentry and royalty. The Renaissance represented a rebellion on the part of the common people against the suppression they experienced from both the church and the wealthy who controlled their lives.

VITTORINO DA FELTRE. An important and influential educator during the Renaissance was Vittorino da Feltre (c. 1378–1446) (Smith & Smith, 1984, p. 84–88), a man from the eastern Alps region. Da Feltre studied at the University of Florence, where he developed an interest in teaching. He also developed a keen interest in classical literature and, along with other educators of that time, began to believe that people could be educated and also be Christians at the same time—a belief that the Roman Catholic Church generally did not share.

Da Feltre established several schools, taught in a variety of others, and generally helped to advance the development of education during his lifetime. He believed that education was an important end in itself and thereby helped to rekindle an interest in the value of human knowledge during the Renaissance.

ERASMUS. One of the most famous humanist educators was Erasmus (1466–1536), and two of his books, *The Right Method of Instruction* and *The Liberal Education of Boys,* formed a humanistic theory of education. Erasmus had considerable educational insight. Concerning the aims of education, he wrote:

> The duty of instructing the young includes several elements, the first and also the chief of which is that the tender mind of the child should be instructed in piety; the second, that he love and learn the liberal arts; the third, that he be taught tact in the conduct of social life; and the fourth, that from his earliest age he accustom himself to good behavior, based on moral principles. (Compayré, 1888, pp. 12–13, 88–89)

The Reformation

It is difficult for people today to imagine the extent to which the Roman Catholic Church dominated the lives of the common people through most of what is now Europe during the fifteenth and sixteenth centuries. The Roman Catholic Church and the pope had enormous influence over European royalty during this time. In fact, some historians suggest that the pope and other officials of the Roman Catholic Church were in some ways more powerful than many individual kings and queens. After all, the Roman Catholic Church could and frequently did claim that unless members of royalty abided by its rules, they were destined to spend eternity in hell—an extremely frightening prospect for any human being. Consequently, it is understandable that the church wielded great influence throughout most of Europe.

LUTHER. The Protestant Reformation had its formal beginning in 1517. In that year, Martin Luther (1483–1546) published his ninety-five theses, which stated his disagreements with the Roman Catholic Church. One of these disagreements held great implications for the importance of formal education. The church believed that it was not desirable for each person to read and interpret the Bible for himself or herself; rather, the church would pass on the "correct" interpretation to the laity. Luther felt not only that the church had itself misinterpreted the Bible, but also that people were intended to read and interpret the Bible for themselves. If one accepted the church's position on this matter, formal education remained relatively unimportant for the masses. If one accepted Luther's position, however, education became necessary for all people so that they might individually read and interpret the Bible for themselves. In a sense, education became important as a way of obtaining salvation.

IGNATIUS OF LOYOLA. To combat the Reformation movement, Ignatius of Loyola (1491–1556) organized the Society of Jesus (Jesuits) in 1540. The Jesuits worked to establish schools to further the cause of the Roman Catholic Church, and they tried to stem the flow of converts to the cause of Reformation. Although the Jesuits' main interest was religious, they soon grew into a great teaching order and were very successful in training their own teachers. The rules by which the Jesuits conducted their schools were stated in the *Ratio Studiorum;* a revised edition still guides Jesuit schools today. The improvement of teacher training was one of the Jesuits' main contributions to education.

COMENIUS. Among many other outstanding educators during this transition period was Johann Amos Comenius (1592–1670). Comenius is perhaps best remembered for his many textbooks, including *Orbis Pictus*. His books were among the first to contain illustrations. The invention and improvement of printing during the 1400s made it possible to produce books, such as those of Comenius, more rapidly and economically, a development that was essential to the growth of education. Much of the writing of Comenius reflected the increasing interest that was then developing in science.

LOCKE. John Locke (1632–1704) was an influential English educator during the late seventeenth century. He wrote many important educational works, including *Some Thoughts on Education* and *Essay Concerning Human Understanding*. He viewed a young child's mind as a blank slate *(tabula rasa)* on which an education could be imprinted. He believed that teachers needed to create a nonthreatening learning environment—a revolutionary idea at that time.

EDUCATIONAL AWAKENING (1700)

As we have suggested, educational progress in the world was slow and developed in only a few places through the seventeenth century. This section demonstrates why many of our current educational ideas can be traced to the early 1700s.

The Age of Reason

A revolt of the intellectuals against the superstition and ignorance that dominated people's lives at the time influenced education in this early modern period. This movement became the keynote of the period known as the **Age of Reason;** and François-Marie Arouet (1694–1778), a French writer who used the pen name Voltaire, was one of its leaders. Those who joined this movement became known as *rationalists* because of the faith they placed in human rational power. The implication for education in the rationalist movement is obvious: If one places greater emphasis on human ability to reason, then education takes on new importance as the way in which humans can develop this power.

Early educational efforts were closely tied to religious beliefs, so biblical teachings were emphasized. At the same time, premarital sexual relationships were strongly condemned. The accompanying Teacher Perspectives feature represents examples of contemporary educator views on the subject of premarital sex.

DESCARTES AND VOLTAIRE. The work of René Descartes (1596–1650) laid the foundations for rationalism. This philosophy evolved three axioms that gradually became well accepted by thinking people. These axioms were (1) that reason was supreme, (2) that the laws of nature were invariable, and (3) that truth could be verified empirically—verified by exact methods of testing. These ideas became the basis for disputing some of the traditional teaching of the church and for resisting the bonds that royalty had traditionally placed on the common people. These axioms also influenced the thinking of Voltaire. Voltaire was an articulate writer who was also brilliant, clever, witty, and vain—qualities that helped him become extremely influential. In fact, many authorities give him considerable credit for both the American and the French Revolutions, which took place during his lifetime.

FREDERICK THE GREAT. One of the influential leaders during the Age of Reason was Frederick the Great (1712–1786). Frederick was a friend of Voltaire's and supported the notion that education was of value. He was a liberal thinker for his time and one of the few leaders who did not attempt to force the common people into a particular form of religion. Frederick also permitted an unusual amount of free speech for his era and generally allowed the common people a degree of liberty that most rulers considered dangerous.

As a consequence, education had an opportunity to develop, if not flourish, during his reign as leader of Prussia. During Frederick's reign, Prussia passed laws regarding education and required teachers to obtain special training as well as licenses to teach.

Age of Reason The beginning of the modern period of education, a period in which European thinkers emphasized the importance of reason. The writing of Voltaire strongly influenced the rationalist movement.

TEACHER PERSPECTIVES

Is "Abstinence-Only" the Best Sex Education Policy for Schools to Implement?

Early school curricula were historically driven by a desire to help children read the Bible and develop strict moral standards. The debate about how to best help students develop socially acceptable sexual behavior carries on today, as shown in this debate.

YES

Elizabeth Bradley *teaches math at Lewiston High School in Lewiston, Maine, and won a Presidential Award in 2000 for her work. She has taught for fifteen years, interrupted by eight years as a business applications programmer.*

Consider this:

"Good morning, class. Today we're going to learn how to have safe sex (now referred to as 'safer sex' because safe sex doesn't really exist).

"We'll show you how to put a condom on a banana, and some other things you can do to minimize your risk of contracting an incurable disease, which may make you sterile (chlamydia), be a precursor to cervical cancer (HPV), or cause death (HIV).

"Oh, and you might end up pregnant. Then your choices are abortion ("one dead, one wounded," to quote a recent bumper sticker), adoption (a lifelong hole in your heart), or parenthood (a 24/7 commitment that will make school, college, work, independence, and emotional stability very difficult)."

Why can't we take the drinking and driving approach of "Just don't do it"? Statistics show that kids do care about what the adults in their lives have to say. . . .

Let's raise the standard and tell kids, unequivocally, what is in their best interest. Why is it that we want so much to protect their sexual activity, but not their very lives?

NO

Eileen Toledo *has taught English in middle schools for fourteen years, currently at the Pablo Avila Junior High School in Camuy, Puerto Rico. She runs the "Baby, Think It Over" program one period a week and wrote a master's thesis on it.*

The reality is that more students are becoming sexually active at earlier ages. As an educator, I had to get involved. I have been using "Baby, Think It Over" at my junior high school for five years. . . .

At school, we talk about child abuse, how to place babies to sleep correctly, and more. Students budget the weekly costs of caring for a baby. They inquire about jobs available to them at their age (13–16). Students realize how hard raising a baby can be for them. . . .

We also discuss STDs, and we talk about how making love is different from sex, which is what teens are having. Making love is a beautiful experience in a true relationship between adults ready and able to take on responsibilities, not teens who got pregnant by mistake. . . .

Yet I cannot be so naive as not to see that most teens become sexually active at an early age. So I must also talk about birth control. . . .

Students who have complete information about disease transmission and contraceptive use are the most likely to remain abstinent and will protect themselves if they choose to be sexually active. We have worked with over 400 students, and only three became pregnant in high school.

Source: Adapted from "Is 'Abstinence-Only' the Best Sex Education Policy for Schools to Implement?" *NEA Today* (February 2003), p. 23. Reprinted by permission of the National Education Association.

What is your perspective on this issue?

myeducationlab To explore both sides of this issue and think about each perspective, go to the *Book Specific Resources* section in the MyEducationLab for your course, select your text, and then select *Teacher Perspectives* for Chapter 2.

The Emergence of Common Man

The second pivotal trend of the early modern period that affected education was the concept sometimes called the **Emergence of Common Man**. Whereas the Age of Reason was sparked by a revolt of the learned for intellectual freedom, the thinkers who promoted the emergence of common man argued that common people deserved a better life—politically, economically, socially, and educationally.

ROUSSEAU. One of the leaders in this movement was Jean-Jacques Rousseau (1712–1778), whose *Social Contract* (1762) became an influential book during the French Revolution. Rousseau was a philosopher, not an educator, but he wrote a good deal on the subject of education. His most important educational work was *Émile* (1762), in which he states his views concerning the ideal education for youth. Rousseau felt that the aim of education should be to return human beings to their "natural state." His view on the subject is well summed up by the opening sentence of *Émile:* "Everything is good as it comes from the hand of the author of nature: but everything degenerates in the hands of man." Rousseau's educational views came to be known as *naturalism.*

Rousseau's most important contributions to education were his belief that education must be a natural process, not an artificial one, and his compassionate, positive view of the child. Rousseau

Emergence of Common Man A period during which the idea developed that common people should receive at least a basic education as a means to a better life.

believed that children were inherently good—a belief in opposition to the prevailing religiously inspired belief that children were born full of sin.

PESTALOZZI. Johann Heinrich Pestalozzi (1746–1827) was a Swiss educator who put Rousseau's theory into practice. Pestalozzi established two schools for boys, one at Burgdorf (1800–1804) and the other at Yverdun (1805–1825). Educators came from all over the world to view Pestalozzi's schools and to study his teaching methods. Pestalozzi enumerated his educational views in a book entitled *Leonard and Gertrude.* Unlike most educators of his time, Pestalozzi believed that a teacher should treat students with love and kindness.

Key concepts in the Pestalozzian method included the expression of love, understanding, and patience for children; compassion for the poor; and the use of objects and sense perception as the basis for acquiring knowledge.

Swiss educator Johann Heinrich Pestalozzi (1746–1827) put Rousseau's theory into practice.

HERBART. Johann Friedrich Herbart (1776–1841) was an educator who studied under Pestalozzi and was influenced by him. Whereas Pestalozzi had successfully put into practice and further developed Rousseau's educational ideas, it remained for Herbart to organize these educational views into a formal psychology of education. Herbart stressed apperception (learning by association). The **Herbartian teaching method** developed into five formal steps:

1. *Preparation:* Preparing the student to receive a new idea
2. *Presentation:* Presenting the student with the new idea
3. *Association:* Assimilating the new idea with old ideas
4. *Generalization:* Generalizing the new idea derived from combination of old and new ideas
5. *Application:* Applying the new knowledge.

Herbart's educational ideas are contained in his *Science of Education* (1806) and *Outlines of Educational Doctrine* (1835).

FROEBEL. Friedrich Froebel (1782–1852) was another European educator influenced by Rousseau and Pestalozzi who made a significant contribution to education. Froebel's contributions included the establishment of the first kindergarten (or *Kleinkinderbeschaftigungsanstalt*), an emphasis on social development, a concern for the cultivation of creativity, and the concept of learning by doing. He originated the idea that women are best suited to teach young children.

JOURNAL FOR REFLECTION

Select a person mentioned in this chapter (or another individual from the history of education who is of interest to you) and learn more about that person and her or his influence on today's schools. Make journal entry notes about what you learn.

EVOLVING PERSPECTIVES OF EDUCATION IN OUR DEVELOPING NATION

The earliest settlers to America from Europe brought with them a sincere interest in providing at least rudimentary education for their children. Naturally, they brought their European ideas about education with them and, soon after arrival, created educational programs throughout colonial America. This section will briefly examine these early colonial school programs.

Colonial Education

The early settlements on the East Coast were composed of groups of colonies: the Southern Colonies, centered in Virginia; the Middle Colonies, centered in New York; and the Northern

Herbartian teaching method An organized teaching method based on the principles of Pestalozzi that stresses learning by association and consists of five steps: preparation, presentation, association, generalization, and application.

Colonies, centered in New England. Each of these groups developed a somewhat unique educational system.

SOUTHERN COLONIES. The Southern Colonies soon were made up of large tobacco plantations. There was an immediate need for cheap labor to work on the plantations; in 1619, only twelve years after Jamestown was settled, the colony imported the first slaves from Africa. Other sources of labor for the Southern Colonies included Europeans from a variety of backgrounds who had purchased passage to the New World by agreeing to serve a lengthy period of indentured servitude on arrival in the colonies. There soon came to be two very distinct classes of people in the South— a few wealthy landowners and a large mass of laborers, most of whom were slaves.

The educational provisions that evolved from this set of conditions were precisely what one would expect. Few were interested in providing education for the slaves, with the exception of missionary groups such as the English Society for the Propagation of the Gospel in Foreign Parts. Such missionary groups tried to provide some education for slaves, primarily so that they could read the Bible. The wealthy landowners hired tutors to teach their children at home. Distances between homes and slow transportation precluded the establishment of centralized schools. When upper-class children grew old enough to attend college, they were usually sent to well-established universities in Europe.

MIDDLE COLONIES. The people who settled the Middle Colonies came from various national (Dutch, Swedish) and religious (Puritan, Mennonite, Catholic) backgrounds. This is why the Middle Colonies have often been called the melting pot of the nation. This diversity of backgrounds made it impossible for the inhabitants of the Middle Colonies to agree on a common public school system. Consequently, the respective groups established their own religious schools. Many children received their education through an apprenticeship while learning a trade from a master already in that line of work. Some people even learned the art of teaching school through apprenticeships with experienced teachers.

NORTHERN COLONIES. The Northern Colonies were settled mainly by the Puritans, a religious group from Europe. In 1630 approximately one thousand Puritans settled near Boston. Unlike people in the Southern Colonies, people in New England lived close to one another. Towns sprang up and soon became centers of political and social life. Shipping ports were established, and an industrial economy developed that demanded numerous skilled and semiskilled workers—a condition that eventually created a large middle class.

The curriculum of early colonial schools emphasized religious beliefs that were stressed in the schools at that time. Times have changed over the years, as illustrated in the accompanying Reflect on Diversity feature.

EARLY SCHOOL LAWS. These conditions of common religious views, town life, and a large middle class made it possible for the people to agree on common public schools and led to very early educational activity in the Northern Colonies. In 1642 the General Court of Massachusetts enacted a law that stated:

> This Co^t [Court], taking into consideration the great neglect of many parents & masters in training up their children in learning do hereupon order and decree, that in every towne y chosen men take account from time to time of all parents and masters, and of their children, concerning their ability to read & understand the principles of religion & the capitall lawes of this country.

This law did nothing more than encourage citizens to look after the education of children. Five years later (1647), however, another law was enacted in Massachusetts that required towns to provide education for their youth. This law, which was often referred to as the **Old Deluder Satan Act** because of its religious motive, stated:

> It being one chiefe proiect of y ould deluder, Satan, to keepe men from the knowledge of y Scriptures It is therefore orded [ordered], ye evy [every] towneship in this jurisdiction, aft y Lord hath increased y number to 50 household, shall then forthw appoint one w [with] in their towne to teach all such children as shall resort to him to write & reade & it is furth ordered y where any towne shall increase to y numb [number] of 100 families or househould, they shall set up a grammar schoole, y m [aim] thereof being able to instruct youth so farr as they shall be fited for y university [Harvard].

These Massachusetts school laws of 1642 and 1647 served as models for similar laws that were soon created in other colonies.

Old Deluder Satan Act An early colonial education law (1647) that required colonial towns of at least fifty households to provide education for youth.

REFLECTonDIVERSITY   **Religious Beliefs in the Classroom**

Kevin had been worrying for a week about the next unit in his biology class. It was supposed to introduce evolution, which he had learned from his family and at church was not the way the world developed. He liked science, but believed that science was wrong on this one. Ever since he was a baby he had been learning about creationism and how God created the world. His minister recently had told the congregation about the theory of intellectual design that countered the explanations of evolution. Kevin knew that Mr. Jenkins, his biology teacher, didn't attend Kevin's church. He didn't know his religious beliefs, but if Mr. Jenkins was going to teach evolution, he must not be very religious. He wondered what he should do when Mr. Jenkins began the discussion of evolution next week.

After Mr. Jenkins introduced the section on evolution on Monday, he called on Kevin, who had raised his hand. Kevin confidently stood and said, "Mr. Jenkins, are we also going to talk about intellectual design as part of this lesson?"

Somewhat surprised, Mr. Jenkins responded, "Son, intellectual design is not science. It is a nonsensical, stupid way to explain the development of species in our world. It has no place in my biology class."

Embarrassed, Kevin slid back into his seat. But he was going to talk with his parents and minister about Mr. Jenkins's brusque response to his question. He thought, "It isn't fair that other explanations of the world are totally dismissed. Other students in the class should know that research supports intellectual design as well."

Questions for Reflection

1. Why is Kevin so adamant that other perspectives on the development of the world should be explored in his biology class? Why does Mr. Jenkins think otherwise?
2. How would you have responded to Kevin's request to include intellectual design in this biology unit? Why?
3. What would have been taught about this topic in a science class during the Colonial period?

myeducationlab To respond to these questions online, go to the *Book Specific Resources* section in the MyEducationLab for your course, select your text, and then select *Reflect on Diversity* for Chapter 2.

TYPES OF COLONIAL SCHOOLS. Several different kinds of elementary schools sprang up in the colonies, such as the **dame school**, which was conducted by a housewife in her home; the writing school, which taught the child to write; a variety of church schools; and charity, or pauper, schools taught by missionary groups.

In 1635 the Latin Grammar School was established in Boston—the first permanent school of this type in what is now the United States. The grammar school was a secondary school. Its function was college preparatory, and the idea spread quickly to other towns. Charlestown opened its first grammar school one year later, in 1636, by contracting William Witherell "to keep a school for a twelve month." Within sixteen years after the Massachusetts Bay Colony had been founded, seven or eight towns had Latin grammar schools in operation. Transplanted from Europe, where similar schools had existed for a long time, these schools were aimed at preparing boys for college and "for the service of God, in church and commonwealth."

EARLY AMERICAN COLLEGES. Harvard, the first colonial college, was established in 1636 for preparing ministers. Other early American colleges included William and Mary (1693), Yale (1701), Princeton (1746), King's College (1754), College of Philadelphia (1755), Brown (1764), Dartmouth (1769), and Queen's College (1770). The curriculum in these early colleges was traditional, with heavy emphasis on theology and the classics. An example of the extent to which the religious motive dominated colonial colleges can be found in one of the 1642 rules governing Harvard College, which stated: "Let every Student be plainly instructed, and earnestly pressed to consider well, the maine end of his life and studies is, to know God and Jesus Christ."

The Struggle for Universal Elementary Education

When the colonists arrived in this country, they simply established schools like those they had known in Europe. The objectives of colonial elementary schools were primarily religious. These early colonial schools were meager by today's standards, but nevertheless, they were important forerunners of our contemporary schools.

MONITORIAL SCHOOLS. In 1805, New York City established the first *monitorial school* in the United States. The monitorial school, which originated in England, represented an attempt to provide economical mass elementary education for large numbers of children. Typically, the teacher would teach hundreds of pupils, using the better students as helpers. By 1840, however,

Go to the *Assignments and Activities* section of Topic 7: *History of Education* in the MyEducationLab for your course and complete the activity titled *Colonial Village*.

dame school A low-level primary school in the colonial and other early periods, usually conducted by an untrained woman (a dame) in her own home.

nearly all monitorial schools had been closed; the children had not learned enough to justify continuance of this type of school.

HORACE MANN. Between 1820 and 1860, an educational awakening took place in the United States. This movement was strongly influenced by Horace Mann (1796–1859). As secretary of the state board of education, Mann helped to establish **common elementary schools** in Massachusetts. These common schools were designed to provide a basic elementary education for all children. Among Mann's many impressive educational achievements was the publication of one of the very early professional journals in this country, *The Common School Journal*. Through this journal, Mann kept educational issues before the public.

In 1852, Massachusetts passed a compulsory elementary school attendance law, the first of its kind in the country, requiring all children to attend school. By 1900, thirty-two other states had passed similar **compulsory education** laws.

More detailed information on current school finances can be found in Chapter 9.

Financing public education has always been a challenge in America. As early as 1795, Connecticut legislators decided to sell public land and create a permanent school fund to help finance public schools. As more and more children attended school, other states soon took action to establish school funding plans as well.

HENRY BARNARD. The first U.S. commissioner of education was a prominent educator named Henry Barnard (1811–1900). He was a longtime supporter of providing common elementary schools for all children and wrote enthusiastically about the value of education in the *Connecticut Common School Journal* and in the *American Journal of Education,* which he founded. He had also served as the Rhode Island commissioner of public schools and as the chancellor of the University of Wisconsin before holding the prestigious position of commissioner of education for the entire United States. Barnard also strongly supported kindergarten programs for very young children as well as high school programs for older students.

REFLECTIONS ON EARLY U.S. ELEMENTARY EDUCATION. If we look back at the historical development of U.S. elementary education, we can make the following generalizations:

1. Until the late 1800s, the motive, curriculum, and administration of elementary education were primarily religious. The point at which elementary education began to be more secular than religious was the point at which states began to pass compulsory school attendance laws.
2. Discipline was traditionally harsh in elementary schools. The classical picture of a colonial schoolmaster equipped with a frown, dunce cap, stick, whip, and a variety of abusive phrases is more accurate than one might expect. It is no wonder that children historically viewed school as an unpleasant place. Pestalozzi had much to do with bringing about a gradual change in discipline when he advocated that love, not severe punishment, should be used to motivate students.
3. Elementary education was traditionally formal and impersonal. The ideas of Rousseau, Pestalozzi, Herbart, and Froebel helped change this condition gradually and make elementary education more student centered; this was becoming apparent by 1900.
4. Elementary schools were traditionally taught by poorly prepared teachers.
5. Although the aims and methodology varied considerably from time to time, the basic content of elementary education was historically reading, writing, and arithmetic.

The Need for Secondary Schools

Contemporary U.S. high schools have a long and proud tradition. They have evolved from a series of earlier forms of secondary schools that were created to serve the needs of society at various points in the nation's history.

common elementary schools Schools that originated in the mid-nineteenth century designed to provide a basic elementary education for all children.

compulsory education School attendance that is required by law on the theory that it is of benefit to the state or commonwealth to educate all people.

AMERICAN ACADEMY. By the middle of the eighteenth century, there was a need for more and better trained skilled workers. Benjamin Franklin (1706–1790), recognizing this need, proposed a new kind of secondary school in Pennsylvania. This proposal brought about the establishment, in Philadelphia in 1751, of the first truly American educational institution—the *American Academy*. Franklin established this school because he thought the existing Latin grammar schools were not providing the practical secondary education that youth needed. The philosophy, curriculum, and methodology of Franklin's academy were all geared to prepare young people for employment. Eventually, similar academies were established throughout America, and these institutions eventually replaced the Latin grammar school as the predominant secondary educational institution. They were usually private schools, and many of them admitted girls as well as boys. Later on, some academies even tried to train elementary school teachers.

Nearly all of the early educational ideas in America were borrowed from Europe, as explained in the accompanying Global Perspectives feature.

GLOBAL PERSPECTIVES   Educational Ideas Borrowed from Around the World

The educational ideas now implemented in the United States had their inception a long time ago. Our contemporary schools are a mixture of educational perspectives, ideas, concepts, and practices borrowed from around the changing world. Much of whatever credit and accolades our current American educational system receives must be shared with those who long ago conceived the idea of formal education and who then slowly developed and refined their educational concepts.

Questions for Reflection
1. As you read this chapter, look for some examples of our current educational practices that were inherited from other countries.
2. Attempt to learn about the evolution of education in a foreign country of your choice.

HIGH SCHOOL. In 1821 the *English Classical School* (which three years later changed its name to *English High School*) opened in Boston, and another distinctively American educational institution was launched. This first high school, under the direction of George B. Emerson, consisted of a three-year course in English, mathematics, science, and history. The school later added to its curriculum the philosophy of history, chemistry, intellectual philosophy, linear drawing, logic, trigonometry, French, and the U.S. Constitution. The school enrolled about one hundred boys during its first year.

The high school was established because of a belief that the existing grammar schools were inadequate for the day and because most people could not afford to send their children to the private academies. The high school soon replaced both the Latin grammar school and the private academy, and it has been with us ever since.

Information about current school organization is presented in Chapter 9.

JUNIOR HIGH/MIDDLE SCHOOL. About 1910 the first *junior high schools* were established in the United States. A survey in 1916 showed 54 junior high schools in thirty-six states. One year later a survey indicated that the number had increased to about 270. More recently, some school systems have abandoned the junior high school in favor of what is called the *middle school,* which usually consists of grades 6, 7, and 8.

The Evolution of Teaching Materials

The first schools in colonial America were poorly equipped. In fact, the first elementary schools were usually conducted by housewives right in their homes. The only teaching materials likely to be found then were a Bible and perhaps one or two other religious books, a small amount of scarce paper, a few quill pens, and perhaps hornbooks.

THE HORNBOOK. The **hornbook** was the most common teaching device in early colonial schools (see Figure 2.1). Hornbooks differed widely but typically consisted of a sheet of paper showing the alphabet, covered with a thin transparent sheet of cow's horn and tacked to a paddle-shaped piece of wood. A leather thong was often looped through a hole in the paddle so that students could hang the hornbooks around their necks. Hornbooks provided students with their first reading instructions. Records indicate that hornbooks were used in Europe in the Middle Ages and were common there until the mid-1700s.

As paper became more available, the hornbook evolved into a several-page "book" called a *battledore.* The battledore, printed on heavy paper, often resembled an envelope. Like the hornbook, it typically contained the alphabet and various religious prayers and/or admonitions.

hornbook A single page containing the alphabet, syllables, a prayer, or other simple words, tacked to a wooden paddle and covered with a thin transparent layer of cow's horn; used in colonial times as a beginner's first book or preprimer.

THE NEW ENGLAND PRIMER. Very few textbooks were available for use in colonial Latin grammar schools, academies, and colleges, although various religious books, including the Bible, were often used. A few books dealing with history, geography, arithmetic, Latin, Greek, and certain

FIGURE 2.1

Hornbook

The hornbook was the most common teaching device in colonial American schools.

classics were available for use in colonial secondary schools and colleges during the eighteenth century. The first real textbook to be used in colonial elementary schools was the *New England Primer.* Records show that the first copies of this book were printed in England in the 1600s. Copies of the *New England Primer* were also printed as early as 1690 in the American colonies. An advertisement for the book appeared in the *News from the Stars Almanac,* published in 1690 in Boston (see Figure 2.2). The oldest extant copy of the *New England Primer* is a 1727 edition, now in the Lenox Collection of the New York Public Library.

The *New England Primer* was a small book, usually about 2 by 4 inches, with thin sheets of wood covered with paper or leather. It contained fifty to one hundred pages, depending on how

FIGURE 2.2

1690 Advertisement

This 1690 advertisement promotes the *New England Primer,* the first true textbook to be used in colonial American elementary schools.

ADVERTISEMENT.

There is now in the Prefs, and will fuddenly be extant, a Second Impreffion of *The New-England Primer enlarged,* to which is added, more *Directions for Spelling:* the *Prayer of* K. *Edward* the 6th. and *Verfes made by Mr.* Rogers *the Martyr, left as a Legacy to his Children.*

Sold by *Benjamin Harris,* at the *London Coffee-Houfe* in *Bofton.*

FIGURE 2.3

Page from the *New England Primer*

How does this page from the *New England Primer* reveal the religious motive in colonial American education?

many extra sections were added to each edition. The first pages displayed the alphabet, vowels, and capital letters. Next came lists of words arranged from two to six syllables, followed by verses and tiny woodcut pictures for each letter in the alphabet. Figure 2.3 shows a sampling of these pictures and verses. The contents of the *New England Primer* reflect the heavily religious motive in colonial education.

BLUE-BACKED SPELLER. The primer was virtually the only reading book used in colonial schools until about 1800, when Noah Webster published *The American Spelling Book*. This book eventually became known as the *Blue-Backed Speller* because of its blue cover. It eventually replaced the *New England Primer* as the most common elementary textbook. Figure 2.4 shows a page from a *Blue-Backed Speller* printed about 1800.

The *Blue-Backed Speller* was approximately 4 by 6 inches; its cover was made of thin sheets of wood covered with light blue paper. The first part of the book contained rules and instructions for using the book; next came the alphabet, syllables, and consonants. The bulk of the book was taken up with lists of words arranged according to syllables and sounds. It also contained rules for reading and speaking, moral advice, and stories of various sorts.

TEACHING MATERIALS IN AN EARLY SCHOOL. By 1800, nearly two hundred years after the colonies had been established, school buildings and teaching materials were still very crude and meager. You can understand something of the physical features and equipment of an 1810 New England school by reading the following description written by a teacher of that school:

> The size of the building was 22×20 feet. From the floor to the ceiling it was 7 feet. The chimney and entry took up about four feet at one end, leaving the schoolroom itself 18×20 feet. Around three sides of the room were connected desks, arranged so that when the pupils were sitting at them their faces were toward the instructor and their backs toward the wall. Attached to the sides of the desks nearest to the instructor were benches for small pupils. The instructor's desk and chair occupied the center. On this desk were stationed a rod, or ferule; sometimes both. These, with books, writings, inkstands, rules, and plummets, with a fire shovel, and a pair of tongs (often broken), were the principal furniture.

FIGURE 2.4

Page from the *Blue-Backed Speller*

Noah Webster's *Blue-Backed Speller* came to replace primers around 1800. In addition to the alphabet, syllables, consonants, lists of words, and rules for reading and speaking, the *Speller* contained stories like the one shown here.

Instructors have usually boarded in the families of the pupils. Their compensation has varied from seven to eleven dollars a month for males; and from sixty-two and a half cents to one dollar a week for females. Within the past ten years, however, the price of instruction has rarely been less than nine dollars in the former case, and seventy-five cents in the latter. In the few instances in which instructors have furnished their own board the compensation has been about the same, it being assumed that they could work at some employment of their own enough to pay their board, especially the females. (Monroe, 1905, p. 282)

SLATES. About 1820 a new instructional device—the *slate*—was introduced in American schools. These school slates were thin, flat pieces of slate stone framed with wood. The pencils used were also made of slate and produced a light but legible line that was easily erased with a rag. The wooden frames of some of the slates were covered with cloth so that noise would be minimized as students placed the slates on the desk. Later on, large pieces of slate made up the blackboards that were added to classrooms.

By about 1900, pencils and paper had largely replaced the slate and slate pencil as the writing implements of students. The invention of relatively economical mass production of pencils in the late 1800s made them affordable for student use and led to their widespread use in schools.

MCGUFFEY'S *READERS.* In the same way that Noah Webster's *Blue-Backed Speller* replaced the *New England Primer,* William Holmes McGuffey's *Reader* eventually replaced the *Blue-Backed Speller*—selling about sixty million copies. These readers were carefully geared to each grade and were meant to instill in children a respect for hard work, thrift, self-help, and honesty. McGuffey's *Readers* dominated the elementary school book market until approximately 1900, when they were gradually replaced by various newer and improved readers written by David Tower, James Fassett, William Elson, and others.

One cannot help but be awed by the contrast and dramatic changes that have taken place in U.S. education today from its humble beginning centuries ago.

Technology and History

A wealth of wonderful technology is available to help you learn about history in general and history of education more specifically. For instance, doing a word search on just about any important history of education person will yield a wealth of information on that person. The same is true if you word search on just about any historical topic or object that may be of interest to you. For instance, searching on any of the teaching materials just mentioned, like "hornbooks" as an example, will provide you with not only written information, but also pictures of hornbooks. Searching for "education museums" will also provide you with a great deal of interesting educational history information from various sites.

We realize that you are already very familiar with word searching for information on the web, but we would like to remind you that searching for history of education information on the web is also a good resource, in case you have not yet done so.

JOURNAL FOR REFLECTION

1. Try to learn more about the historical development of education in the particular grade or subjects you are thinking of teaching.
2. Record in your journal any especially pertinent things you learn.

MEAGER EARLY EDUCATION FOR DIVERSE POPULATIONS

It is sad but true that students of color, girls, and students with disabilities have been historically badly underserved by our educational system and typically not even allowed to attend school until relatively recently.

Education of African Americans

Unfortunately, general efforts have been made only recently in this country to provide an education for African Americans. In the following subsections, we briefly explore why this was the case and discuss some of the early African American educators who struggled to correct this injustice (Davis, 1970).

EARLY CHURCH EFFORTS TO EDUCATE AFRICAN AMERICANS. Probably the first organized attempts to educate African Americans in colonial America were by French and Spanish missionaries. These early missionary efforts set an example that influenced the education of both African Americans and their children. Educating slaves posed an interesting moral problem for the church. The English colonists had to find a way to overcome the idea that converting enslaved people to Christianity might logically lead to their freedom. The problem they faced was how to eliminate an unwritten law that a Christian should not be a slave. The church's governing bodies and the bishop of London settled the matter by decreeing that conversion to Christianity did not lead to formal emancipation.

The organized church nevertheless provided the setting where a few African Americans were allowed to develop skills in reading, leadership, and educating their brethren. Often African Americans and whites attended church together. Eventually, some preachers who were former slaves demonstrated exceptional skill in "spreading the gospel." The Baptists in particular, by encouraging a form of self-government, allowed African Americans to become active in the church. This move fostered the growth of African American congregations; thus, Baptist congregations gave enslaved as well as free African Americans an opportunity for education and development that was not provided by many other denominations.

EARLY SCHOOLS FOR AFRICAN AMERICAN CHILDREN. One of the first northern schools established for African Americans appears to have been that of Elias Neau in New York City in 1704. Neau was an agent of the Society for the Propagation of the Gospel in Foreign Parts.

In 1807 several free African Americans, including George Bell, Nicholas Franklin, and Moses Liverpool, built the first schoolhouse for African Americans in the District of Columbia. Not until 1824, however, was there an African American teacher in that district—John Adams. In 1851, Washington citizens attempted to discourage Myrtilla Miner from establishing an academy for African American girls. However, after much turmoil and harassment, the white schoolmistress from New York did found her academy; it is still functioning today as the School of Education at the University of the District of Columbia.

> The more recent role of the federal government in educational affairs is discussed in Chapters 9 and 10.

Boston, the seat of northern liberalism, established a separate school for African American children in 1798. Elisha Sylvester, a white man, was in charge. The school was founded in the home of Primus Hall, a "Negro in good standing." Two years later, sixty-six free African Americans petitioned the school committee for a separate school and were refused. Undaunted, the patrons of Hall's house employed two instructors from Harvard; thirty-five years later, the school was allowed to move to a separate building. The city of Boston opened its first primary school for the education of African American children in 1820—one more small milestone in the history of African American education.

FREDERICK DOUGLASS. Born in slavery in Maryland in 1817, Frederick Douglass (ca. 1817–1895) ran away and began talking to abolitionist groups about his experiences in slavery. He attributed his fluent speech to listening to his master talk. Douglass firmly believed that if he devoted all his efforts to improving vocational education, he could greatly improve the plight of African Americans. He thought that previous attempts by educators to combine liberal and vocational education had failed, so he emphasized vocational education solely.

JOHN CHAVIS. African Americans' individual successes in acquiring education, as well as their group efforts to establish schools, were greatly enhanced by sympathetic and humanitarian white friends. One African American who was helped by whites was John Chavis (1763–1838), a free

Early efforts to provide formal education for African American children were few. The African American Children's School, shown here, was one example.

man born in Oxford, North Carolina. Chavis became a successful teacher of aristocratic whites, and his white neighbors sent him to Princeton "to see if a Negro would take a college education." His rapid advancement under Dr. Witherspoon soon indicated that the venture was a success. He returned to Virginia and later went to North Carolina, where he preached among his own people. The success of John Chavis, even under experimental conditions, represented another step forward in the education of African Americans.

PRUDENCE CRANDALL. A young Quaker, Prudence Crandall (1803–1890), established an early boarding school in Canterbury, Connecticut. The problems she ran into dramatize some of the Northern animosity to educating African Americans. Trouble arose when Sarah Harris, a "colored girl," asked to be admitted to the institution. After much deliberation, Miss Crandall finally consented, but white parents objected to the African American girl's attending the school and withdrew their children. To keep the school open, Miss Crandall recruited African American children. The pupils were threatened with violence; local stores would not trade with her; and the school building was vandalized. The citizens of Canterbury petitioned the state legislature to enact a law that would make it illegal to educate African Americans from out of state. Miss Crandall was jailed and tried before the state supreme court in July 1834. The court never gave a final decision because defects were found in the information prepared by the attorney for the state; the indictment was eventually dropped. Miss Crandall continued to work for the abolition of slavery, for women's rights, and for African American education. Prudence Crandall became well known, and she deserves considerable credit for the advances made by minorities and women in the United States.

BOOKER T. WASHINGTON. Booker T. Washington (1856–1915) was one of the early African American educators who contributed immensely to the development of education in the United States. He realized that African American children desperately needed an education to compete in society, and he founded Tuskegee Institute in 1880. This Alabama institution provided basic and industrial education in its early years and gradually expanded to provide a wider ranging college curriculum. It stands today as a proud monument to Booker T. Washington's vision and determination concerning the education of African American youth.

EARLY AFRICAN AMERICAN COLLEGES. Unfortunately, despite these efforts, African Americans received pathetically little formal education until the Emancipation Proclamation, issued by President Abraham Lincoln on January 1, 1863. At that time, the literacy rate among African Americans was estimated at 5 percent. Sunday school represented about the only opportunity most African Americans had to learn to read. In the late 1700s and early 1800s, some communities did set up separate schools for African Americans; however, only a very small percentage ever attended the schools. A few colleges such as Oberlin, Bowdoin, Franklin, Rutland, and Harvard admitted African American students, but, again, very few of them attended college then. There were even a few African American colleges such as Lincoln University in Pennsylvania (1854) and Wilberforce University in Ohio (1856); however, the efforts and opportunities for the education of African Americans were few relative to the size of the African American population.

Although there was no great rush to educate African Americans, the abolition of slavery in 1865 signaled the beginning of a slow but steady effort to improve their education. By 1890, African American literacy had risen to 40 percent; by 1910 it was estimated that 70 percent of African Americans had learned to read and write. These statistics showing the rapid increase in African American literacy are impressive; however, they are compromised by a report of the U.S. commissioner of education showing that by 1900, fewer than seventy of every one thousand public high schools in the South were providing for African Americans. Even worse, while educational opportunities for African Americans were meager, for other minority groups such as Native Americans and Hispanic Americans they were practically nonexistent.

Education of Asian Americans

The Second World War brought about what many consider unwarranted discrimination against Japanese Americans when the U.S. government placed more than 100,000 Japanese American citizens in internment camps and in some cases confiscated their property. Not until 1990 did the government officially apologize and pay restitution for having done so. In hindsight, many believe that this treatment of U.S. citizens of Japanese background constituted a form of discrimination.

In the decades following the Korean and Vietnam wars, the number of Asian immigrants to the United States has increased dramatically. Large numbers of Vietnamese, Cambodians, Laotians, and Thais have been included in this recent migration. Although many of these Asian immigrants have experienced considerable success, the majority have struggled to receive an education and find suitable jobs. Many feel that they have been discriminated against and have not received equal educational and employment opportunities. Yet many of the highest achieving high school students are Asian Americans, proof of the fact that their families typically place a high value on education.

Education of Hispanic Americans

The number of Hispanic American students in U.S. schools has increased dramatically over the past seventy years. But the historical background of this increase can actually be traced to the very first formal schools in North America. The earliest formal schools on this continent were started and conducted by Spanish missionaries in Mexico and the southwestern part of what is now the United States in the sixteenth century. Some historians even assert that the Spanish had established several "colleges" in North America before Harvard was founded in 1636. This assertion is probably true if one defines a mission school as a college, because some of them prepared boys for the ministry. As with the other early schools in the Americas, the missionaries established these early Spanish schools primarily for religious purposes—to help people read the Bible and thus gain salvation. Students at early mission schools in what is now Mexico and in Florida, California, Arizona, New Mexico, Cuba, and elsewhere were taught by Catholic priests in the Spanish language. After the United States won its independence and grew to include what we now think of as the Southwest, these early Spanish schools gradually became part of the larger English-speaking U.S. school system.

Multicultural education is presented in more detail in Chapters 6, 7, and 8.

Unfortunately, Hispanic American education did not develop as quickly or as well as that of the majority population. This discrepancy is due at least in part to the facts that many Hispanic Americans are in the lower income brackets, that many immigrated to the United States without well-developed English language skills, and that many suffered discrimination. Like other minority groups in the United States, Hispanic Americans have not historically been afforded equal educational opportunities. Schools in the southern and southwestern parts of the United States now have large numbers of Hispanic American students, and in many of these schools Hispanic American students are the majority or will become so in the relatively near future.

Education of Women

Historically, women have not been afforded equal educational opportunities in the United States. Furthermore, many authorities claim that U.S. schools have traditionally been sexist institutions. Although there is much evidence to support both of these assertions, it is also true that an impressive number of women have made significant contributions to educational progress.

Colonial schools did not provide education for girls in any significant way. In some instances girls were taught to read, but females could not attend Latin grammar schools, academies, or colleges. We will look briefly at a few of the many outstanding female educators who helped to develop our country's educational system, in spite of their own limited educational opportunities.

EMMA WILLARD. Whereas well-to-do parents hired private tutors or sent their daughters away to a girls' seminary, girls from poor families were taught only to read and write at home (provided someone in the family had these skills). Emma Willard (1787–1870) was a pioneer and champion of education for females during a time when there were relatively few educational opportunities for them. She opened one of the first female seminaries in 1821 in Troy, New York, and this school offered an educational program equal to that of a boys' school. In a speech designed to raise funds for her school, she proposed the following benefits of seminaries for girls:

1. Females, by having their understandings cultivated, their reasoning power developed and strengthened, may be expected to act more from the dictates of reason and less from those of fashion and caprice.
2. With minds thus strengthened, they would be taught systems of morality, enforced by the sanctions of religion; and they might be expected to acquire juster and more enlarged views of their duty, and stronger and higher motives to its performance.
3. This plan of education offers all that can be done to preserve female youth from contempt of useful labor. The pupils would become accustomed to it, in conjunction with the high objects of literature and the elegant pursuits of the fine arts; and it is to be hoped that both from habit and association they might in future life regard it as respectable.

4. The pupils might be expected to acquire a taste for moral and intellectual pleasures which would buoy them above a passion for show and parade, and which would make them seek to gratify the natural love of superiority by endeavoring to excel others in intrinsic merit rather than in the extrinsic frivolities of dress, furniture, and equipage.

5. By being enlightened in moral philosophy, and in that which teaches the operations of the mind, females would be enabled to perceive the nature and extent of that influence which they possess over their children, and the obligation which this lays them under to watch the formation of their characters with unceasing vigilance, to become their instructors, to devise plans for their improvement, to weed out the vices of their minds, and to implant and foster the virtues. And surely there is that in the maternal bosom which, when its pleadings shall be aided by education, will overcome the seductions of wealth and fashion, and will lead the mother to seek her happiness in communing with her children, and promoting their welfare. (Willard, 1893, pp. 12–14)

Many other female institutions were established and became prominent during the mid- and late 1800s, including Mary Lyon's Mount Holyoke Female Seminary; Jane Ingersoll's seminary in Cortland, New York; and Julia and Elias Mark's Southern Carolina Collegiate Institute at Barhamville, to name just a few. Unfortunately, not until well into the twentieth century were women generally afforded access to higher education.

Yet another important female educational pioneer, Maria Montessori, is discussed in the accompanying Global Perspectives feature.

GLOBAL PERSPECTIVES   Maria Montessori

Maria Montessori (1870–1952), born in Italy, first became a successful physician and later a prominent educational philosopher. She developed her own theory and methods of educating young children. Her methods utilized child-size school furniture and specially designed learning materials. She emphasized independent work by children under the guidance of a trained directress. Private Montessori schools thrive in the United States today.

Questions for Reflection
1. Do a key word web search on "Montessori" and record in your journal some of your reactions to what you find.
2. What is your perspective on the strong points and weak points of the Montessori method?

ELLA FLAGG YOUNG. Yet another example of an outstanding early female educator is Ella Flagg Young (ca. 1845–1918). Overcoming immense obstacles, she earned a doctorate at the age of fifty under John Dewey, was appointed head of the Cook County Normal School in Illinois, and became superintendent of the gigantic Chicago public school system in 1909—all achievements that were unheard of for a female at that time. She was also elected the first female president of the male-dominated National Education Association.

MARY MCLEOD BETHUNE. Mary McLeod Bethune (1875–1955) was one of seventeen children born to African American parents in Mayesville, South Carolina, and the first family member not born in slavery. She received her first formal schooling at age nine in a free school for African American children. It is reported that she would come home from school and teach her brothers and sisters what she had learned each day. She came to believe that education was the key to helping African American children move into the mainstream of American life, and she devoted her life to improving educational opportunities for young African American women. She eventually started the Daytona Normal and Industrial School for Negro Young Women and later Bethune-Cookman College, where she served as president until 1942. She also believed that education helps everyone to respect the dignity of all people, regardless of color or creed, and is needed equally by Caucasian Americans, African Americans, and all other Americans. Bethune went on to serve as founder and head of the National Council of Negro Women, director of the Division of Negro Affairs of the National Youth Administration, President Franklin D. Roosevelt's special adviser on minority affairs, and special consultant for drafting the charter of the United Nations. Bethune was an effective, energetic human rights activist throughout her life and also a dedicated and professional career educator.

THE NINETEENTH AMENDMENT. Various groups first took interest in advancing the cause of females in the United States in the mid-1800s. The women's rights convention held at that time passed twelve resolutions that attempted to spur interest in providing females more equal participation and rights in U.S. society. The Civil War also furthered interest in the rights of women throughout the country, very likely as a spin-off of the abolition of slavery. It is interesting to note that not all the people in favor of doing away with slavery supported improved rights for women. For instance, not until 1920, when the Nineteenth Amendment passed, did women have the right to vote.

Unfortunately, the right to vote did not necessarily do much to improve the status of women; females continued to be denied equal educational and employment opportunities. The civil rights movement after World War II served as another impetus to the women's movement and gave rise to an additional round of improvements for females in U.S. society. Some authorities would trace the emergence of the current feminist movement to the 1960s, when a variety of activist groups coalesced to work against discrimination of all kinds in U.S. society. Some groups and individuals feel that adequate educational provisions and opportunities for females, minorities, and those with disabilities are still lacking in our school systems today at all levels.

Although educators can learn a great deal from research, including educational history research, this requires time and determination, as explored in the accompanying Professional Dilemma feature.

PRIVATE EDUCATION IN AMERICA

Private education has been extremely important in the development of the United States. In fact, private schools carried on nearly all of the education in colonial times. The first colonial colleges such as Harvard, William and Mary, Yale, and Princeton were all private institutions. Many of the other early colonial schools, which can be thought of as **religion-affiliated schools,** were operated by churches, missionary societies, and private individuals.

religion-affiliated school A private school over which, in most cases, a parent church group exercises some control or to which the church provides subsidy.

The Right of Private Schools to Exist

In 1816 the state of New Hampshire attempted to take over Dartmouth College, which was a private institution. A lawsuit growing out of this effort ultimately resulted in the U.S. Supreme

---

PROFESSIONAL DILEMMA

How Can the Busy Teacher Keep Up with Historical and Contemporary Research?

Ask any teacher what her or his major problems are and "not having enough time" will likely be near the top of the list. So it is perhaps not surprising that many teachers find it difficult to keep up with current research that may help educators do a better job. And yet one of the important hallmarks of a professional is finding, evaluating, and implementing the results of valid and reliable research. For instance, when a person goes to a medical doctor, he or she expects that physician to be using knowledge based on the most recent medical research. By the same token, parents have a right to expect, when they send their children to school, that teachers will be using the most recent educational research in their educational practice. Thus, the professional dilemma is this: How do busy teachers locate, read, evaluate, and implement the best research results into their teaching? This task is made even more difficult by the fact that although a great volume of education research is constantly being conducted, a fair amount of it is not necessarily valid or reliable.

Teachers who are determined to put good research results into practice must first be able to read, understand, and evaluate educational research. To learn how to do this, you may need to take some basic research courses at a nearby college or university. You

may also need to read research reports found in a variety of professional journals in your specialty fields. This may mean subscribing to such journals or getting your school to make them available. You may also wish to attend a variety of professional meetings where research is presented and discussed. And after you locate good research findings, you will need to do careful planning when you implement these research results in your classroom.

Unfortunately, there is no simple solution to this professional dilemma. We know that because we, too, struggle with this problem. However, we are convinced that the first step to solving this dilemma is becoming determined to offer your clients (your students and their parents) the very best education possible. We also are convinced that to do so requires a knowledge of the best and most recent educational research.

Questions for Reflection
1. What are your feelings about this professional dilemma at this point in your career development?
2. What might you be able to do at this time to help you prepare to deal with this dilemma?
3. To what degree do you feel your current teachers are keeping up with, and using, research in their teaching?

Court's first decision involving the legal rights of a private school. The Supreme Court decided that a private school's charter must be viewed as a contract and cannot be broken arbitrarily by a state. In other words, the Court decided that a private school could not be forced against its will to become a public school.

Subsequent court decisions have reconfirmed the rights of private education in a variety of ways. Generally speaking, for instance, courts have reconfirmed that private schools have a right to exist and in some cases even to share public funds, as long as these funds are not used for religious purposes. Examples of such actions include the use of state funds to purchase secular textbooks and to provide transportation for students to and from private schools.

Not until after the Revolution, when there was a strong sense of nationalism, did certain educators advocate a strong public school system for the new nation. However, such recommendations were not acted on for many years. In the meantime, some Protestant churches continued to expand their schools during the colonial period. For instance, the Congregational, Quaker, Episcopal, Baptist, Methodist, Presbyterian, and Reformed churches all, at various times and in varying degrees, established and operated schools for their youth. It was the Roman Catholics and Lutherans, however, who eventually developed elaborate **parochial school** systems operated by their respective denominations.

Parochial Schools

As early as 1820 there were 240 Lutheran parochial schools in Pennsylvania. Although the number of Lutheran schools in that particular state eventually dwindled, Henry Muhlenberg and other Lutheran leaders continued to establish parochial schools until the public school system became well established. The Missouri Synod Lutheran Church has continued to maintain a well-developed parochial school system. Currently, there are approximately 1,700 Lutheran elementary and secondary schools, which enroll about 200,000 pupils, in the United States, and most of these schools are operated by the Missouri Synod Lutheran Church.

The Roman Catholic parochial school system grew rapidly after its beginnings in the 1800s. Enrollment in Catholic schools mushroomed between 1900 and 1960 from about 855,000 to more than five million students. The Roman Catholic parochial school system in the United States is now the largest private school system in the world.

A number of other religious groups have developed and operated their own parochial schools from time to time, and some of them still do today. Examples of such religious groups include the Mormons, Mennonites, and Quakers.

The Important Role of Private Education in America

The concept of public education—that is, education paid for by various governments (local, state, and federal)—is a relatively new idea in the history of U.S. education. For many years, if parents or religious groups wanted to provide education for their children, they had to do so with their own resources. In this part of the book, there have been many references to private schools and private education; at this juncture, we simply wish to reiterate the tremendous importance of private education. In fact, were it not for private education as the predecessor, it is difficult to imagine how we would have evolved a public education system. Private education still plays an enormously important role at all levels of education in the United States.

The major shift from private to public education occurred during the nineteenth century. For instance, in 1800 there was no state system of public education anywhere in the United States—no public elementary schools, secondary schools, or state colleges or universities. In fact, until the nineteenth century, all forms of education were private in nature—from elementary school through graduate school. By the year 1900, however, nearly all states had developed a public system of education running from elementary school through graduate school.

Understanding and Using Educational Historical Research

Unfortunately, some educators do not yet realize that having an understanding of historical educational research can help them be a more effective educator. Knowing about our educational past can help you take advantage of past educational successes and avoid repeating some past educational failures. When you face a problem or need to make a decision concerning your teaching, you should wonder what educational research, past and present, might help you make wise decisions that will improve your work with students.

Additional information on legal aspects of education can be found in Chapter 10.

parochial school An educational institution operated and controlled by a religious denomination.

An understanding of our educational past will also help you better realize how very, very important the work of educators has been in our society and throughout the world.

LOOKING AHEAD: LEARNING FROM EDUCATIONAL HISTORY

Go to the *Building Teaching Skills and Dispositions* section of Topic 7: *History in Education* in the MyEducationLab for your course and complete the activity titled *Educational History in the Making.*

This chapter illustrates that there have been many different perspectives on education throughout the ages, and that a number of big historical ideas have grown out of the more detailed history of education discussed in the chapter. These include the ideas that adults in early societies provided the informal education that they felt necessary for children to succeed in their society; that more formal schools likely came into existence only as people developed written languages; that all societies around the world have developed their own forms of education, down through the ages, designed to fulfill their unique needs; and that human progress has, in large part, depended on education.

Perspectives on education in a changing world is a part of the title of this book, and is a major theme throughout the book. Differing perspectives and change also apply to educational history. As pointed out earlier in this chapter, historians approach the understanding of history from differing perspectives and will undoubtedly continue to do so in the future. The world of education will also undoubtedly continue to change in the future, and this change will likely take place even more rapidly. So each of our individual attempts to understand educational history will undoubtedly vary from person to person and will undoubtedly evolve over time.

━━━ JOURNAL FOR REFLECTION ━━━

1. List some of the most important things you learned from this chapter.
2. Which, if any, of the items you listed will likely have practical value for you as a future educator?
3. In what ways?

SUMMARY

THE BEGINNINGS OF EDUCATION (TO 476 CE)

- Any study of the beginnings of formal education should start with the fact that parents have always attempted to provide, in one way or another, the informal education their children need to survive in their society.
- Formal schools very likely did not come into existence until four or five thousand years ago, as humans developed written languages.
- Current evidence suggests that one of the first well-organized educational systems was that evolved by the Greeks during what is today commonly called the Age of Pericles.
- Greek knowledge and schools eventually blended into Roman schools and libraries.
- Examples of important educators from this early period included Socrates, Plato, Aristotle, and Quintilian.

EDUCATION IN THE MIDDLE AGES (476–1300)

- The period from 400 until 1000 is often called the Dark Ages because of the lack of educational activity in much of the Western world.
- Alcuin was an example of one of the relatively few educators to make important contributions during the Dark Ages.
- During the later part of the Middle Ages, there was a revived interest in learning, as exemplified by the work of Thomas Aquinas and the establishment of medieval universities.

EDUCATION IN TRANSITION (1300–1700)

- This period of educational history is commonly marked by two historical movements: the Renaissance and the Reformation.
- The Renaissance represented a rebellion on the part of the common people against their economic, educational, and religious suppression under the royalty and landed gentry.
- These common people gradually demanded a better life and developed a spirit of inquiry, which created an interest in education and schooling.

- The fourteenth through eighteenth centuries saw sometimes erratic, but nevertheless fairly continuous, progression of educational development and advancement throughout much of the world.
- The Protestant Reformation led by Martin Luther, and the work of Ignatius of Loyola, did much to improve education during this time.

EDUCATIONAL AWAKENING (1700)

- In the Western world, this period is often divided into the Age of Reason, which emphasized people's rational and scientific abilities, and the Emergence of Common Man, which sought to create a better education and life for all people.
- Examples of people who contributed to educational advancement in various ways during this period were Descartes, Voltaire, Rousseau, Pestalozzi, Herbart, and Froebel.

EVOLVING PERSPECTIVES OF EDUCATION IN OUR DEVELOPING NATION

- Our earliest colonists brought their educational ideas and expectations with them from Europe and, soon after arriving in the New World, set about creating schools that fulfilled their needs.
- These efforts varied widely, from private tutorial education for plantation owners' children in the South, to religious schools in the Middle Colonies, to public schools in the North.
- Most education was driven by religious motives, and much of the formal education beyond that needed to read the Bible was provided only for boys from the more well-to-do families.
- Elementary and secondary education for all children developed slowly.
- Schools and teaching materials were humble and meager in Colonial America.

MEAGER EARLY EDUCATION FOR DIVERSE POPULATIONS

- Early efforts to provide education for the poor, people of color, and women were nonexistent or, at the very least, meager.
- Examples of early pioneers of African American education include Frederick Douglass, John Chavis, Prudence Crandall, and Booker T. Washington.
- Examples of female educational pioneers include Emma Willard, Maria Montessori, Ella Flagg Young, and Mary McLeod Bethune.

PRIVATE EDUCATION IN AMERICA

- The earliest education was provided by private schools, which have remained a very important part of our educational system.
- Parochial schools, conducted by religious groups, still prevail and make important contributions to education today.

LOOKING AHEAD: LEARNING FROM EDUCATIONAL HISTORY

- This chapter illustrates that perspectives on education have differed throughout the ages.
- A number of big historical ideas have grown out of the more detailed history of education discussed in the chapter.
- These include the ideas that adults in early societies provided the informal education that they felt necessary for children to succeed in their society; that more formal schools likely came into existence only as people developed written languages; that all societies around the world have developed their own forms of education, down through the ages, designed to fulfill their unique needs; and that human progress has, in large part, depended on education.

DISCUSSION QUESTIONS

1. What were the major contributions of several ancient societies to the development of education?
2. What factors contributed to the decline of education during the Dark Ages?
3. What were the strengths and weaknesses of Jean-Jacques Rousseau's ideas about children and education?
4. Discuss the evolution of elementary schools.
5. What historical conditions led to that uniquely U.S. institution, the comprehensive high school?
6. What are the highlights of the history of education of African Americans?
7. Discuss the roles that private schools have played in U.S. education.

SCHOOL-BASED OBSERVATIONS

1. More than two hundred years ago, Jean-Jacques Rousseau advocated that children be taught with love, patience, understanding, and kindness. As you work in the school, experiment with this basic approach to see whether it is effective. You might also wish to observe experienced teachers: To what extent do they teach children with love, patience, understanding, and kindness? We suggest that you experiment with other constructive ideas in this chapter as you observe and participate in the classroom.

2. As you work in schools, observe how they have changed relative to schools of the past. How are schools today similar to those of the past? How much and in what ways are students today similar to their historical counterparts? In what ways are they different?

3. While you are in the schools, visit with experienced teachers and administrators to discuss the ways that schools have changed over the years. Also ask how students, teaching methods, and parents have changed.

PORTFOLIO DEVELOPMENT

1. Make a list of historical educational ideas mentioned in this chapter that are still valid and useful for educators today.

2. Summarize the evolution of the goals of public schools in colonial America and the United States. Develop a chart that creatively portrays this evolution.

3. Write an essay on the importance of education in the historical development of the United States.

myeducationlab To begin developing your own personal portfolio, go to the MyEducationLab for your course, select *Resources,* and then select *Portfolio Builder.*

PREPARING FOR CERTIFICATION

1. One of the topics in the Praxis II Principles of Learning and Teaching (PLT) test is "Student Motivation and the Learning Environment." This section of the test includes reference to

   • Establishing daily procedures and routines
   • Establishing classroom rules
   • Using natural and logical consequences
   • Providing positive guidance
   • Modeling conflict resolution, problem solving, and anger management
   • Giving timely feedback
   • Maintaining accurate records
   • Communicating with parents and caregivers
   • Using objective behavior descriptions
   • Responding to student behavior
   • Arranging classroom space
   • Pacing and structuring the lesson

   In this chapter, you learned about the evolution of schools in the United States from colonial times to the present.

   Compare the climate for learning in early American schools with the climate in today's schools. How are schools' climates similar; how are they different?

2. Answer the following multiple-choice question, which is similar to items in Praxis and other state certification tests.

   The McGuffey readers were commonly used in U.S. schools in the 1800s. What was their major characteristic that contributed to modern curriculum development?
   a. The materials in each reader were sequenced by grade level and level of difficulty.
   b. They were the first materials to focus on phonics.
   c. They emphasized multicultural themes.
   d. They emphasized the concepts of learning by firsthand experience.

   After you've completed your written responses, use the Praxis general scoring guide provided in Chapter 1 to see if you can revise your response to improve your score.

MYEDUCATIONLAB

myeducationlab Now go to Topic 7: *History of Education* in the MyEducationLab (www.myeducationlab.com) for your course, where you can:

- Find learning outcomes for *History of Education* along with the national standards that connect to these outcomes.
- Complete *Assignments and Activities* that can help you more deeply understand the chapter content.
- Apply and practice your understanding of the core teaching skills identified in the chapter with the *Building Teaching Skills and Dispositions* learning units.

- Check your comprehension on the content covered in the chapter by going to the *Study Plan* in the *Book Specific Resources* for your text. Here you will be able to take a chapter quiz, receive feedback on your answers, and then access *Review, Practice, and Enrichment* activities to enhance your understanding of chapter content.

WEBSITES

www.myeducationlab.com To see an interactive timeline of the foundations of education, go to MyEducationLab, at www.myeducationlab.com, select *Resources*, and then *Introduction to Teaching and Foundations of Education Interactive Timeline*.

www.cedu.niu.edu/blackwell The Blackwell History of Education Museum and Research Collection is one of the largest collections of its kind in the world. Much of the collection is listed on this website. The Blackwell

Museum has developed a variety of instructional materials (also listed on its site) designed to help you learn more about the antecedents of early American and U.S. education.

www.historyofeducation.org.uk The *History of Education* journal of the History of Education Society, located in England, is a useful general source of educational history.

www.countryschoolassociation.org. A wonderful site for information on early one-room country schools.

FURTHER READING

Cremin, L. (1961). *The Transformation of the School: Progressivism in American Education, 1876–1957.* New York: Knopf. This and the next two entries are authored by one of the most respected educational historians of the twentieth century.

Cremin, L. A. (1970). *American Education: The Colonial Experience, 1607–1783.* New York: Harper & Row.

Cremin, L. (1990). *American Education: The National Experience, 1793–1976.* New York: Harper & Row.

Holmes, M., & Weiss, B. J. (1995). *Lives of Women Public Schoolteachers: Scenes from American Educational History.* New York: Garland. A well-done book about the important role of women educators.

Johnson, T. W., & Reed, R. F. (2002). *Historical Documents in American Education.* Boston: Allyn & Bacon. A compilation of many original resource documents pertaining to the history of education.

Morgan, H. (1995). *Historical Perspectives on the Education of Black Children.* Westport, CT: Praeger. A useful book containing a good deal of information about the history of African American children.

Szasz, M. C. (1988). *Indian Education in the American Colonies 1607–1783.* Albuquerque: University of New Mexico Press. An excellent source of information about the education of Native Americans during the colonial period.

chapter three

HISTORICAL
PERSPECTIVES
OF EDUCATION

EDUCATION
IN THE **NEWS**

HISTORY OF THE
FEDERAL ROLE
IN EDUCATION

The original U.S. Department of Education was created in 1867 to collect information on schools and teaching that would help the states establish effective school systems. While the agency's name and location within the Executive Branch have changed during the past 130 years, this early emphasis on getting information on what works in education to teachers and education policy makers continues to the present day.

The passage of the Second Morrill Act in 1890 gave the then-named Office of Education responsibility for administering support for the original system of land-grant colleges and universities. Vocational education became the next major area of federal aid to schools, with the 1917 Smith-Hughes Act and the 1946 George-Barden Act focusing on agricultural, industrial, and home economics training for high school students.

World War II led to a significant expansion of federal support for education. The Lanham Act in 1941 and the Impact Aid laws of 1950 eased the burden on communities affected by the presence of military and other federal installations by making payments to school districts. And in 1944, the "GI Bill" authorized postsecondary education assistance that would ultimately send nearly 8 million World War II veterans to college.

The Cold War stimulated the first example of comprehensive federal education legislation, when in 1958 Congress passed the National Defense Education Act (NDEA) in response to the Soviet launch of the *Sputnik* satellite. To help ensure that highly trained individuals would be available to help America compete with the Soviet Union in scientific and technical fields, the NDEA included support for loans to college students; the improvement of science, mathematics, and foreign language instruction in elementary and secondary schools; graduate fellowships; foreign language studies; and vocational-technical training.

The antipoverty and civil rights laws of the 1960s and 1970s brought about a dramatic emergence of the Department of Education's equal access mission. The passage of laws such as Title VI of the Civil Rights Act of 1964, Title IX of the Education Amendments of 1972, and Section 504 of the Rehabilitation Act of 1973, which prohibited discrimination based on race, sex, and disability, respectively, made civil rights enforcement a fundamental and long-lasting focus of the Department of Education. In 1965, the Elementary and Secondary Education Act launched a comprehensive set of programs, including the Title I program of federal aid to disadvantaged children, to address the problems of poor urban and rural areas. In that same year, the Higher Education Act authorized assistance for postsecondary education, including financial aid programs for needy college students.

In 1980, Congress established the Department of Education as a cabinet-level agency. Today, the Department of Education operates programs that touch on every area and level of education. The department's elementary and secondary programs annually serve more than 14,000 school districts and some 56 million students attending more than 97,000 public schools and 28,000 private schools. Department programs also provide grant, loan, and work-study assistance to nearly 11 million postsecondary students.

QUESTIONS FOR REFLECTION

1. What is your reaction to, and evaluation of, the evolution of the role of our federal government in education?
2. What do you believe were some of the reasons our federal government became involved in education matters?
3. How would you evaluate the current federal government's involvement in education?

Source: Adapted from *The Federal Role in Education,* Washington, DC: U.S. Department of Education. Retrieved January 30, 2009, from www.ed.gov?about/overview/fed/role.html.

LEARNING OUTCOMES

After reading and studying this chapter, you should be able to:

1. List and detail several of the most important changes that have been made in the U.S. educational system during the past half century. (INTASC 2: Development and Learning)
2. Explain the major changes in the evolution of the teaching profession.
3. Discuss the development of the major aims of American education. (INTASC 2: Development and Learning)
4. Explain the evolution of teacher training in colonial America and the United States.
5. Name some of the important major historical trends in American education.
6. Decide, explain, and defend the degree to which you believe it is possible to know, understand, and profit from the history of education. (INTASC 10: Collaboration)

MORE STUDENTS AND BIGGER SCHOOLS

Many dramatic changes have occurred in education in the United States during the past half century. Examples of these rapid and often controversial changes that represent various perspectives will be briefly discussed in this chapter. However, the big historical ideas presented in this chapter are (1) the phenomenal change and growth in both the size and complexity of U.S. educational establishments; (2) the tremendous new demands and expectations being placed on our schools and teachers by the current information age; (3) the major, as-yet unsolved challenge to our society and to our schools to provide excellent equal educational opportunities to all students; and, perhaps most important, (4) an understanding that the history of education is of very practical value in helping contemporary educators improve education.

Since World War II, U.S. education has been characterized by a great deal of growth and change: growth in terms of school enrollment, educational budgets, complexity, and federal influence, and change in terms of court decisions, proliferation of school laws, confusion about goals, school financial difficulties, struggles for control, and diversification of curricula.

Enrollment Growth

Perhaps the single most dramatic change that has occurred in education during the past sixty years is the sheer expansion in size of the educational enterprise. The total number of public school students in the United States has about doubled during the past seventy-five years. Although part of this rapid growth in school enrollment was attributable to overall population growth, a good part was due to the fact that greater percentages of people were going to school. Furthermore, people were staying in school much longer, as shown by the almost doubled enrollment in higher education.

Need for More Schools

As school enrollment dramatically increased, the need for new classrooms and buildings to house these students also increased. This need for new schools was generally concentrated in cities and suburbs. In fact, because of increased busing, school district consolidation, and shifting populations, some smaller rural schools were no longer needed, whereas more densely populated areas saw a drastic shortage of classrooms. Many schools had to resort to temporary mobile classrooms. Other strategies for coping with classroom shortages included larger classes, split scheduling that started some classes very early and others very late in the day, and classes held in a variety of makeshift areas such as gymnasiums, hallways, and storage closets. Many schools also rented additional space in nearby buildings. Fortunately, over time taxpayers were generally willing to approve the necessary bond referenda to provide the needed additional schools during this period of rapid growth in student enrollment.

Need for More Teachers

Naturally, this surge in student enrollment required many additional teachers, and at times colleges simply could not produce enough. To alleviate this situation, states lowered teacher certification requirements, sometimes to the point at which no professional education training was required at all. Over time, however, the nation managed to meet the demand for more teachers.

As one would expect, dealing with the increased numbers of students and teachers required a great deal more money. More buses had to be purchased, more books and other instructional materials had to be obtained, more school personnel had to be hired—more of everything was required to provide education to the burgeoning school population.

This is one of thousands of one-room country schools established to educate rural children during the westward movement in America.

School District Consolidation

The consolidation of school districts is another notable administrative trend during the past seventy-five years. The number of separate school districts was reduced from 117,000 in 1940 to about 14,000 today. There was a corresponding decline in the number of one-teacher schools over this same period.

Growth of Busing

Both the number and the percentage of students who are bused have increased considerably during the past seventy-five years, as have the total cost and per-pupil cost of busing. In addition to the general busing of students necessitated by school district consolidation, integration efforts have often involved busing students away from their neighborhood schools. Busing students to school is still a big operation for the U.S. educational enterprise. It is estimated that about 60 percent of all students are bused to school by about 450,000 school buses.

Bigger School Budgets

Educational growth has driven the nation's public education costs to record heights. This rapid increase is illustrated by noting that the approximate cost of public education was $2 billion in 1940, $5 billion in 1950, $15 billion in 1960, $40 billion in 1970, $97 billion in 1980, and $208 billion in 1990. Even if the figures are corrected for inflation, public education has become considerably more expensive: The percentage of the gross domestic product spent on education had risen from 3.5 percent in 1940 to 7 percent by 1980 (U.S. Department of Commerce, 1982, p. 23).

See Chapter 9 for more information on the current costs of education

Rapid Curricular Growth and Changes

As enrollments have increased and schools have grown larger, more diverse curricula and programs have been developed in U.S. schools. This rapid growth of programs places a great deal of work and pressure on teachers, school administrators, and school boards.

Curricular growth, like most change, was the result of an accumulation of many smaller events. One such event was the publication in 1942 of the report of the Progressive Education Association's Eight-Year Study (1932–1940) of thirty high schools. The study showed that students attending "progressive" schools achieved as well as students at traditional schools. This report helped to create a climate that was more hospitable to experimentation with school curricula and teaching methodologies. The publication of a series of statements on the goals of U.S. education (the "Purposes of Education in American Democracy," [Educational Policies Commission (EPC), 1944], the "Education for All American Youth" [EPC, 1944], and the "Imperative Needs of Youth" [EPC, 1952]) helped broaden our schools' curricular offerings.

As mentioned in the chapter-opening Education in the News feature, in 1958, shortly after the Soviet Union launched *Sputnik,* the world's first artificial satellite, Congress passed the National Defense Education Act (NDEA). This act provided a massive infusion of federal dollars to improve schools' science, mathematics, engineering, and foreign language programs. Eventually, innovative curricula such as SMSG mathematics, BSCS biology, and PSCS physics grew out of

Is Teaching Manners a Good Use of Classroom Time?

Historically, schools emphasized the teaching of manners, but schools today have tended to place less emphasis on this subject, a trend that some believe unfortunate.

YES

Kirk Hollinbeck teaches fourth grade at Procter Elementary in Independence, Missouri.

When children aren't taught manners at home, I believe the responsibility falls to the school. Teaching students how to respond when greeted, to say please and thank you, and to make eye contact are skills that last a lifetime. In recent years, mounting expectations, additional responsibilities, and dwindling resources have made teaching more stressful. How can we find time to teach manners and courtesy? I incorporate them into my student behavior expectations. I teach the importance of good manners and courtesy the first day and model positive behaviors all year. I teach "please" and "thank you" when I pass out pretzels or cereal for snack time. Students have two choices when I offer a snack: they can say "thank you" or "no thank you." Mouths drop when I take the snack back because a student forgot to say "thank you." I model courtesy through my interactions with students, colleagues, and parents. We practice how to make eye contact and discuss ways to respond when greeted.

I was surprised that many students have never been taught what to do when someone says "good morning." When I talk with a student or another adult, my students have learned that they must wait until our conversation has finished before I will talk to them. Is teaching manners and courtesy a good use of classroom time? Do you prefer adults who are polite or rude?

NO

Carolyn Cowgill is a retired teacher from the Central Bucks School District in Doylestown, Pennsylvania.

School is a social experience, and teachers will always spend some time each day dealing with manners. However, with so many academic subjects to thoroughly introduce, discuss, and lock in (especially with testing requirements), it should not be the teacher's responsibility to teach basic manners as part of the formal curriculum. Manners should be taught at home from the time a parent begins the dialogue while feeding and diapering the baby!

Before a child enters school, caretakers, parents, or relatives need to define traditional boundaries and reward courteous interactions with others. Before starting school, children must learn patience, to consider others' space and feelings, how to communicate their needs politely, and to treat each other with kindness. If parents have done their job, teachers only need to reinforce manners in the classroom and on the playground. Most children will accept the rules at school because they have already heard them at home, and having sets of rules makes children feel safe.

Further, because children pick up somewhat different cues for manners in each unique culture, families are the best teachers of manners. When children begin school, they then have a basis for observing their classmates and teachers and adapting to appropriate classroom manners.

Source: "Is Teaching Good Manners a Good Use of Classroom Time?" *NEA Today* (November 2006), p. 43. Reprinted by permission of the National Education Association.

What is your perspective on this issue?

PEARSON
myeducationlab To explore both sides of this issue and think about each perspective, go to the *Book Specific Resources* section in the MyEducationLab for your course, select your text, and then select *Teacher Perspectives* for Chapter 3.

---

these programs. Other school programs, such as guidance, were later funded through the NDEA. Note that in the case of the NDEA the federal government called on the schools to help solve what was perceived to be a national defense problem. Regardless of the motive, the NDEA represented another milestone that contributed significantly to the growth of the U.S. educational enterprise.

If one were to compare today's school curriculum with that of any school seventy-five years ago, one would find impressive changes. The 1940 curriculum was narrow and designed primarily for college-bound students, whereas today's curriculum is broader and designed for students of all abilities. This growth in the school curriculum has come about through the dedicated work of many people and represents one of the truly significant accomplishments in U.S. education.

For two diverse opinions on a potential curriculum topic, see the Teacher Perspectives feature.

Growth of Special Education Programs

See the index for more information about education for students with exceptionalities.

Perhaps curriculum growth is best illustrated in the area of special education. Public schools historically did not provide special education programs for children with disabilities; rather, they simply accommodated such children as best they could, usually by placing them in regular classrooms. Teachers had little or no training to help them understand and assist the special child. In fact, relatively little was known about common disabilities.

Not until the federal government passed a series of laws during the later twentieth century—including Public Law 94-142, the Education for All Handicapped Children Act—did schools begin to develop well-designed programs for students with disabilities. These new special education programs required teachers who had been trained to work with students with visual or hearing impairments, students with behavior disorders, and students with a range of other exceptionalities. States and colleges then developed a wide variety of teacher-training programs for special educators.

Researching Educational Information Using Today's Technology

As you already know, the Internet is a wonderful source of all kinds of information. This is especially true when you are looking for information about education, including both historical and current information. For instance, if you would like more information about educational research on just about any historical or contemporary topic, the web can help you rather quickly find such information. If you want to know more about historical research on any of the figures or topics mentioned in this chapter, try an Internet search. You must remember, though, that not everything on the web is accurate, so you need to be critical and selective about what you accept as authentic.

―――――――― JOURNAL FOR REFLECTION ――――――――

1. Interview a retired teacher about the educational changes she or he has observed over a lifetime.
2. Ask what advice this retired educator has for beginning teachers today and record the answers.

THE DEVELOPMENT OF THE TEACHING PROFESSION

The field of education has taken giant strides toward becoming a profession since World War II. In the following pages, we will briefly explore the increasing complexities of educational systems in the United States and look at some of the recent developments that have contributed to the professionalization of the field of education.

Increasing Federal Involvement

The federal government has played an important role in the development of national educational programs. This federal involvement in education has gradually increased over the years, and it reached a peak during the past seventy-five years.

The 1940s saw the nation at war, which provided the impetus for the federal government to pass a number of laws that affected education. The Vocational Education for National Defense Act was a crash program to prepare workers needed in industry to produce goods for national defense. The program operated through state educational agencies and trained more than seven million workers. In 1941 the Lanham Act provided funds for building, maintaining, and operating community facilities in areas where local communities had unusual burdens because of defense and war initiatives.

GI BILL. The GI Bill of 1944 provided for the education of veterans of World War II. Later, similar bills assisted veterans of the Korean conflict. The federal government recognized a need to help young people whose careers had been interrupted by military service. These federal acts afforded education to more than ten million veterans at a cost of almost $20 billion. Payments were made directly to veterans and to the colleges and schools the veterans attended. In 1966 another GI Bill was passed for veterans of the war in Vietnam. The initial cost of these acts amounted to a wonderful national investment because the government was repaid many times over by the increased taxes eventually paid by veterans who received this financial aid and later were employed.

NATIONAL SCIENCE FOUNDATION. The National Science Foundation, established in 1950, emphasized the need for continued support of basic scientific research. It was created to "promote the progress of science; to advance the national health, prosperity, and welfare; to secure the national defense; and for other purposes." The Cooperative Research Program of 1954 authorized the U.S. commissioner of education to enter into contracts with universities, colleges, and state education agencies to carry on educational research.

CATEGORICAL FEDERAL AID. Beginning in 1957, when the first Soviet space vehicle was launched, the federal government further increased its participation in education. The NDEA, the Vocational Education Act of 1963, the Manpower Development and Training Act of 1962, the Elementary and Secondary Education Act of 1965, and the International Education Act of 1966 are examples of increased federal participation in educational affairs. Federally supported educational programs such as Project Head Start, the National Teacher Corps, and Upward Bound are further indications of such participation.

Chapters 9 and 10 present more information on the administrative and financial aspects of federal involvement in education.

All of these acts and programs have involved categorical federal aid to education—that is, aid for specific uses. Some people believe that federal influence on education has recently been greater than either state or local influence. There can be no denying that through federal legislation, U.S. Supreme Court decisions, and federal administrative influence, the total federal effect on education is indeed great. Indications are that this effect will be even more pronounced in the future. It will remain for historians to determine whether this trend in U.S. education is a beneficial one.

THE STRUGGLE FOR EQUAL EDUCATIONAL OPPORTUNITY. The past half century has also been characterized by an increasing struggle for **equal educational opportunity** for all children, regardless of race, creed, religion, or gender. This struggle was initiated by the African American activism movement, given additional momentum by the women's rights movement, and eventually joined by many other groups such as Hispanic Americans, Native Americans, and Asian Americans. Other chapters of this book will discuss the details of this relatively recent quest for equal educational opportunity. We mention it briefly at this point simply to emphasize that the struggle for equal educational opportunity represents an important but underrecognized recent historical movement in education. Today, many observers are pointing out that with the accelerated growth of minority subcultures within this nation, our economic and political survival depends to a great degree on educational opportunities and achievements for all segments of U.S. society.

NO CHILD LEFT BEHIND. One of the federal government's recent major efforts to improve education and help children learn, especially disadvantaged children, is the sweeping legislation commonly referred to as No Child Left Behind (NCLB). While the goal of this law is admirable, it has been widely criticized, especially by the education profession. Examples of this criticism are that (1) sufficient funds have not been made available to effectively implement the law, (2) the mandated testing required by the law is not sufficiently valid or reliable and is too time-consuming, and (3) the law and testing do not take into account the extremely wide abilities of students. This law will be discussed in more detail throughout this book, but it is mentioned here as yet another example of increasing federal involvement in education. The accompanying Reflect on Diversity feature, pertaining to NCLB, presents a thought-provoking challenge for a hypothetical teacher.

> More information on NCLB can be found throughout the book. See the index for locations.

The Professionalization of Teaching

equal educational opportunity
Access to a similar education for all students, regardless of their cultural background or family circumstances.

Formal teacher training is a relatively recent phenomenon. Teacher-training programs were developed during the late nineteenth century and the first half of the twentieth century. By the midpoint of the twentieth century, each state had established teacher certification requirements. Since

---

REFLECTonDIVERSITY   Testing Students for NCLB

Because Dwayne has a learning disability, he is eligible for a special accommodation for the state tests that are conducted annually during the spring as part of No Child Left Behind (NCLB). Annette Beckett, a new teacher, has agreed to serve as the writer for the fourth grader during the next round of state assessments. She feels comfortable with this assignment because she had a dual elementary and special education major even though she is currently teaching in a second-grade classroom that does not have any students with disabilities. She also participated in an online training program for faculty who would be serving in this role for English-language learners and students with disabilities. She felt ready for the assignment.

During the test, Ms. Beckett sat next to Dwayne so that she could read to him from his test booklet. The process was working well. When they reached the section on comprehension, she read the passage, followed by the questions and possible answers from which Dwayne would have to choose. She paused to provide him time to respond. Dwayne, however, says, "Ms. Beckett, I didn't understand it. Please read it again."

Ms. Beckett thinks, "Does he really want me to read the whole passage again? He probably only needs to hear the middle section to respond to the question."

Questions for Reflection
1. If you were in Annette's position, what would you do? What are you required to do as the teacher providing the accommodation that Dwayne needs?
2. Could teachers or test prompters guide students to the correct answers? What could happen to a teacher who provided inappropriate assistance to a student?
3. What is the purpose of annual testing of student achievement that is one of the key elements of NCLB?
4. Why are many teachers concerned about the annual testing requirements of NCLB?

PEARSON **myeducationlab** To respond to these questions online, go to the *Book Specific Resources* section in the MyEducationLab for your course, select your text, and then select *Reflect on Diversity* for Chapter 3.

then, teacher training and certification have been characterized by a "refinement" or "profession-alization" movement.

In addition to teacher education, this professionalization movement has touched just about all facets of education: curriculum, teaching methodology, training of school service personnel (administrators, counselors, librarians, and media and other specialists), inservice teacher training, teacher organizations, and even school building construction. To understand clearly this professionalization movement, one need only compare pictures of an old one-room country school with a modern school building, read both a 1940 and a 2007 publication of the American Federation of Teachers or National Education Association, contrast a mid-twentieth-century high school curriculum with one from today, or compile a list of the teaching materials found in a 1940 school and a similar list for a typical contemporary school.

Continued Importance of Private Schools

As explained in Chapter 2, nearly all early schools in colonial America were private and religion was the main purpose of education. Children were taught to read primarily so that they could study the Bible, and most early colleges were private, established primarily to train ministers.

As the public school system developed, however, the religious nature of education gradually diminished to the point that relatively few U.S. children attended religious schools. There have always been certain religious groups, however, who have struggled to create and maintain their own private schools so that religious instruction could permeate all areas of the curriculum. The most notable of these religious groups has long been the Roman Catholic Church. During the past twenty-five years, though, enrollment in non-Catholic religious schools has grown dramatically, whereas Catholic school enrollment has declined.

Despite this recent trend, some Roman Catholic dioceses operate extremely large school systems, sometimes larger than the public school system in the same geographical area. The Chicago diocese operates the largest Roman Catholic school system, enrolling approximately 150,000 students.

With rare exceptions, private and parochial schools struggle to raise the funds they need to exist. They typically must charge a tuition fee, rely on private contributions, and conduct various fund-raising activities. In recent years, some school districts have made tuition vouchers available to parents who choose not to send their children to public schools.

Chapter 9 provides more information on private schooling in the United States.

Home Schooling

Many years ago, with few exceptions, the only parents who taught their children at home were those who lived so far from a school that it was impossible for their children to attend. In the past several decades, however, a growing number of parents have been choosing to educate their children at home—at least through the elementary grades and sometimes even through high school. The motivation for **home schooling** varies, but often it stems from a concern that children in the public schools may be exposed to problems such as drugs, alcohol, smoking, or gangs. Other parents have religious motives, wanting their children to be taught in a particular religious context. Still other parents, who may have had bad experiences with public schools, simply feel they can provide a better education for their children at home. Recent laws and court cases have generally upheld the right, within certain parameters, of parents to educate their children if they choose to do so. The number of parents providing home schooling has grown an estimated 15 percent each year in the last decade. A recent development among a minority of those who home school is a philosophy referred to as *unschooling*, in which parents provide no instruction but allow their children to learn through whatever they naturally do. As one would expect, the value of home schooling is widely debated in our society.

More information on home schooling can be found in Chapter 9.

Continuing/Adult Education

Many forms of education for adults have existed for at least two centuries in this country. Shortly after the United States became a nation, a need to help new immigrants learn English caused schools, churches, and various groups to offer English language instruction; factories found a need to offer job and safety training; churches taught adult religious instruction; and so forth. The New York public schools, as well as many other large schools, developed large English language programs as well as adult vocational programs for people who were unemployed. Adult education took a great variety of forms and quickly grew into a vast network of programs dealing with nearly all aspects of life in the United States.

home schooling Teaching children at home rather than in formal schools.

An example of a large early adult education development can be found in the Chautauqua movement at Lake Chautauqua, New York. Started in 1874 by the Methodist Sunday school, this adult education effort expanded to include correspondence courses, lecture classes, music education, and literary study on a wide variety of subjects throughout the eastern part of the nation.

Public schools increasingly offered adult education classes during the nineteenth century. Some of the larger public school systems, such as in Gary, Indiana, developed adult educational programs with an emphasis on vocational and technical training. Gradually, nearly all schools serving rural areas developed adult agricultural programs to improve farming methods.

In 1964 the Economic Opportunity Act provided adult basic education funding to help adults learn to read and write. Since that time there has been a proliferation of continuing/adult education programs of all types throughout the United States. These programs serve an increasingly important purpose in our rapidly changing society. They help new immigrants learn the English language, provide job training for people who are unemployed, update job skills, teach parenting skills, enable people to move to higher level employment, help people explore new hobbies, provide enrichment programs for retired folks, and generally make the world of education available to nearly all citizens regardless of age. The exploding popularity of the Elderhostel programs and other activities now offered for senior citizens and the crowded evening parking lots at high schools and colleges throughout the country attest to the popularity and success of continuing/adult education programs. In the future, as the world becomes increasingly complex and as more people remain active and healthy in old age, we predict that such adult/continuing education programs will continue to grow.

Evolution of Educational Testing

Educators have undoubtedly attempted to measure and assess student learning from the very beginning of formal education. However, it is only in the last sixty years that educational assessment has taken on vastly more importance, to the point in contemporary education that many feel assessment has become the tail that wags the educational dog. Let's briefly review this recent evolution of educational assessment.

Many historians suggest that the increased attention given to educational testing in the past sixty years was sparked by James Conant, who had become president of Harvard University in 1933. Conant and his colleagues were influenced by the developments in mental testing done by Alfred Binet in France and by Lewis Terman in the United States, which were used extensively by the U.S. Army to test recruits.

Conant seized on a relatively new test called the Scholastic Aptitude Test (SAT), developed by Carl Bright at Princeton University, as a way to assess a student's potential for success at Harvard. He also helped to create a new organization, called the Educational Testing Service (ETS), which became—and remains—the major power in the educational assessment area. By the 1960s, more than a million high school students were taking the SAT, which most colleges used as one criterion for admission.

Many so-called standardized tests have been developed during the past sixty years in an attempt to measure different kinds of aptitude, learning, motivation, and virtually every aspect of education. These standardized tests have come under much criticism from many educators, parents, and others, who question their fairness and accuracy. Even so they continue to be heavily used today.

Educators have faced increasing pressure in recent years to develop improved ways to assess student learning. Much of this pressure has come from taxpayers, government, and the industrial world, often in the form of a demand for greater accountability. Most states have implemented a required system of achievement testing. The results of these achievement tests are commonly used to evaluate and compare schools—a controversial and unfair practice, according to many educators.

In fact, while agreeing that accurate educational assessment is absolutely essential to the educational enterprise, a growing number of educators are questioning many aspects of the increasing emphasis on educational assessment. This important topic will be discussed in various places throughout the text. Suffice it to point out here that educational assessment has grown rapidly and taken on increasing importance, for better or worse, in the past sixty years.

See Chapter 11 for more information on educational assessment.

CHANGING AIMS OF EDUCATION

The aims of education in the United States have reflected changing perspectives on education over the years. During colonial times, the overriding aim of education at all levels was to enable students to read and understand the Bible, to gain salvation, and to spread the gospel.

After the colonies won independence from England, educational objectives—such as providing U.S. citizens with a common language, attempting to instill a sense of patriotism, developing a national feeling of unity and common purpose, and providing the technical and agricultural training the developing nation needed—became important tasks for the schools.

Committee of Ten

In 1892 a committee was established by the National Education Association (NEA) to study the function of the U.S. high school. This committee, known as the **Committee of Ten**, made an effort to set down the purposes of the high school at that time and made the following recommendations: (1) High school should consist of grades 7 through 12; (2) courses should be arranged sequentially; (3) students should be given very few electives in high school; and (4) one unit, called a Carnegie unit, should be awarded for each separate course that a student takes each year, provided that the course meets four or five times each week all year long.

The Committee of Ten also recommended trying to graduate high school students earlier to permit them to attend college sooner. At that time, the recommendation implied that high schools had a college preparatory function. These recommendations became powerful influences in shaping secondary education.

Seven Cardinal Principles

Before 1900, teachers had relatively little direction in their work because most educational goals were not precisely stated. This problem was partly overcome in 1918 when the Commission on Reorganization of Secondary Education published the report *Cardinal Principles of Secondary Education,* usually referred to as the Seven Cardinal Principles. In reality, the Seven Cardinal Principles constitute only one section of the basic principles discussed in the original text, but it is the part that has become famous. These principles stated that the student should receive an education in the following seven fields: health, command of fundamental processes, worthy home membership, vocation, civic education, worthy use of leisure, and ethical character.

The Eight-Year Study

The following goals of education, or "needs of youth," were listed by the Progressive Education Association in 1938 and grew out of the Eight-Year Study of thirty high schools conducted by the association from 1932 to 1940:

1. Physical and mental health
2. Self-assurance
3. Assurance of growth toward adult status
4. Philosophy of life
5. Wide range of personal interests
6. Aesthetic appreciations
7. Intelligent self-direction
8. Progress toward maturity in social relations with age-mates and adults
9. Wise use of goods and services
10. Vocational orientation
11. Vocational competence.

"Purposes of Education in American Democracy"

Also in 1938, the Educational Policies Commission of the National Education Association set forth the "Purposes of Education in American Democracy." These objectives stated that students should receive an education in the four broad areas of self-realization, human relations, economic efficiency, and civic responsibility.

Committee of Ten A historic National Education Association (NEA) committee that studied secondary education in 1892.

"Education for All American Youth"

In 1944 this same commission of the NEA published another statement of educational objectives, entitled "Education for All American Youth":

> Schools should be dedicated to the proposition that every youth in these United States—regardless of sex, economic status, geographic location, or race—should experience a broad and balanced education which will

> 1. equip him to enter an occupation suited to his abilities and offering reasonable opportunity for personal growth and social usefulness;
> 2. prepare him to assume full responsibilities of American citizenship;
> 3. give him a fair chance to exercise his right to the pursuit of happiness through the attainment and preservation of mental and physical health;
> 4. stimulate intellectual curiosity, engender satisfaction in intellectual achievement, and cultivate the ability to think rationally; and
> 5. help to develop an appreciation of the ethical values which should undergird all life in a democratic society.

"Imperative Needs of Youth"

In 1952 the Educational Policies Commission made yet another statement of educational objectives, entitled "Imperative Needs of Youth":

> 1. All youth need to develop salable skills and those understandings and attitudes that make the worker an intelligent productive participant in economic life. To this end most youth need supervised work experience as well as education in the skills and knowledge of their occupations.
> 2. All youth need to develop and maintain good health and physical fitness.
> 3. All youth need to understand the rights and duties of the citizen of a democratic society, and to be diligent and competent in the performance of their obligations as members of the community and citizens of the state and nation.
> 4. All youth need to understand the significance of the family for the individual and society and the conditions conducive to successful family life.
> 5. All youth need to know how to purchase and use goods and services intelligently, understanding both the values received by the consumer and the economic consequences of their acts.
> 6. All youth need to understand the methods of science, the influence of science on human life, and the main scientific facts concerning the nature of the world and of man.
> 7. All youth need opportunities to develop their capacities to appreciate beauty in literature, art, music, and nature.
> 8. All youth need to be able to use their leisure time well and budget it wisely, balancing activities that yield satisfactions to the individual with those that are socially useful.
> 9. All youth need to develop respect for other persons, to grow in their insight into ethical values and principles, and to be able to live and work cooperatively with others.
> 10. All youth need to grow in their ability to think rationally, to express their thoughts clearly, and to read and listen with understanding.

These various statements concerning educational objectives, made during the last century, sum up fairly well the historical aims of U.S. public education. These changing aims also show how perspectives on the purposes of education have evolved over time.

PREPARATION OF TEACHERS

Because present-day teachers have at least four—and often five to eight—years of college education, it is difficult to believe that teachers have historically had little or no training. One of the first forms of teacher training grew out of the medieval guild system, in which a young man who wished to enter a certain field of work served a lengthy period of apprenticeship with a master in the field. Some young men became teachers by serving as apprentices to master teachers, sometimes for as long as seven years.

Colonial Teachers

Elementary school teachers in colonial America were very poorly prepared; in fact, more often than not, they had received no special training at all. The single qualification of most teachers was that they themselves had been students. On the other hand, most colonial college teachers, private tutors, Latin grammar school teachers, and academy teachers had received some kind of college education, usually at one of the well-established colleges or universities in Europe. A few had received their education at an American colonial college.

The accompanying Global Perspectives feature presents information on an early teacher-training effort in Europe.

GLOBAL PERSPECTIVES — European Beginnings of Teacher Training

The first formal teacher-training school in the Western world of which we have any record was mentioned in a request to the king of England, written by William Byngham in 1438, requesting that "he may yeve withouten fyn or fee (the) mansion ycalled Goddeshous the which he hath made and edified in your towne of Cambridge for the free herbigage of poure scolers of Gramer" (Armytage, 1951).

Byngham was granted his request and established Goddeshous College as a teacher-training institution on June 13, 1439. Students at this college gave demonstration lectures to fellow students to gain practice teaching. Classes were even conducted during vacations so that country schoolmasters could also attend. Byngham's college still exists today as Christ's College of Cambridge University.

At that early date of 1439, Byngham made provision for two features that are still considered important in teacher education today: scheduling classes so that teachers in service can attend and providing some kind of student teaching experience. Many present-day educators would probably be surprised to learn that these ideas are nearly 600 years old.

Questions for Reflection
1. What are some of the probable reasons that any type of more formal teacher preparation was lacking in early history?
2. What is your perspective on Byngham's early efforts to provide teacher training?

Teachers in the various kinds of colonial elementary schools typically had only an elementary education themselves, but a few had attended a Latin grammar school or a private academy. It was commonly believed that to be a teacher required only that the instructor know something about the subject matter to be taught; therefore, no teacher, regardless of the level taught, received training in the methodology of teaching.

Because many colonial schools were conducted in connection with a church, the teacher was often considered an assistant to the minister. Besides teaching, other duties of some early colonial teachers were "to act as court messenger, to serve summonses, to conduct certain ceremonial services of the church, to lead the Sunday choir, to ring the bell for public worship, to dig the graves, and to perform other occasional duties."

Teachers as Indentured Servants

Sometimes the colonies used white indentured servants as teachers; many people who came to the United States bought passage by agreeing to work for some years as indentured servants. The ship's captain would then sell the indentured servant's services, more often than not by placing an ad in a newspaper. Such an ad, shown in Figure 3.1, appeared in a May 1786 edition of the *Maryland Gazette*. Records reveal that there were many indentured servants and convicted felons

---

Men and Women Servants
JUST ARRIVED

In the ship *Paca*, Robert Caulifield, Master in five Weeks from Belfast and Cork, a number of healthy Men and Women SERVANTS.

Among them are several valuable trademan, viz.

Carpenters, Shoemakers, Coopers, Blacksmiths, Staymakers, Bookbinders, Clothiers, Diers, Butchers, Schoolmasters, Millrights, and Labourers.

Their indentures are to be disposed of by the Subscribers,

Brown, and Maris
William Wilson

FIGURE 3.1

1786 Advertisement for Indentured Servants

among early immigrants who were advertised and sold as teachers. In fact, it has been estimated that at least one-half of all the teachers in colonial America may have come from these sources. This is not necessarily a derogatory description of these early teachers when we remember that many poor people bought their passage to the colonies by agreeing to serve as indentured servants for a period of years and that in England at that time, hungry and desperate people could be convicted as felons and deported for stealing a loaf of bread.

Teaching Apprenticeships

Some colonial teachers learned their trade by serving as apprentices to schoolmasters. Court records reveal numerous such indentures of apprenticeship; the following was recorded in New York City in 1772:

> This Indenture witnesseth that John Campbel Son of Robert Campbel of the City of New York with the Consent of his father and mother hath put himself and by these presents doth Voluntarily put and bind himself Apprentice to George Brownell of the Same City Schoolmaster to learn the Art Trade or Mastery— for and during the term of ten years And the said George Brownell Doth hereby Covenant and Promise to teach and instruct or Cause the said Apprentice to be taught and instructed in the Art Trade or Calling of a Schoolmaster by the best way or means he or his wife may or can.

Teacher Training in Academies

One of Benjamin Franklin's justifications for proposing an academy in Philadelphia was that some of the graduates would make good teachers. Speculating on the need for such graduates, Franklin wrote,

> A number of the poorer sort [of academy graduates] will be hereby qualified to act as Schoolmasters in the Country, to teach children Reading, Writing, Arithmetic, and the Grammar of their Mother Tongue, and being of good morals and known character, may be recommended from the Academy to Country Schools for that purpose; the Country suffering at present very much for want of good Schoolmasters, and obliged frequently to employ in their schools, vicious imported servants, or concealed Papists, who by their bad Examples and Instructions often deprave the Morals and corrupt the Principles of the children under their Care.

The fact that Franklin said some of the "poorer" graduates would make suitable teachers reflects the low regard for teachers typical of the time. The academy that Franklin proposed was established in 1751 in Philadelphia, and many graduates of academies after that time did indeed become teachers.

Normal Schools

normal school The first type of American institution devoted exclusively to teacher training.

Many early educators recognized this country's need for better-qualified teachers; however, it was not until 1823 that the first teacher-training institution was established in the United States. This private school, called a **normal school** after its European prototype, which had existed since the late seventeenth century, was established by the Reverend Mr. Samuel Hall in Concord, Vermont. Hall's school did not produce many teachers, but it did signal the beginning of formal teacher training in the United States.

The early normal school program usually consisted of a two-year course. Students typically entered the normal school right after finishing elementary school; most normal schools did not require high school graduation for entrance until about 1900. The nineteenth-century curriculum was much like the curriculum of the high schools of that time. Students reviewed subjects studied in elementary school, studied high school subjects, had a course in teaching (or "pedagogy" as it was then called), and did some student teaching in a model school, usually operated in conjunction with the normal school. The subjects offered by a normal school in Albany, New York, in 1845 included English grammar, English composition, history,

First State Normal School was adopted from European teacher training schools and is still standing in Lexington, Massachusetts.

geography, reading, writing, orthography, arithmetic, algebra, geometry, trigonometry, human physiology, surveying, natural philosophy, chemistry, intellectual philosophy, moral philosophy, government, rhetoric, theory and practice of teaching, drawing, music, astronomy, and practice teaching.

Horace Mann was instrumental in establishing the first state-supported normal school, which opened in 1839 in Lexington, Massachusetts. Other public normal schools, established shortly afterward, typically offered a two-year teacher-training program. Some of the students came directly from elementary school; others had completed secondary school. Some states did not establish state-supported normal schools until the early 1900s.

State Teachers' Colleges

During the early part of the twentieth century, several factors caused a significant change in normal schools. For one thing, as the population of the United States increased, so did the enrollment in elementary schools, thereby creating an ever increasing demand for elementary school teachers. Likewise, as more people attended high school, more high school teachers were needed. To meet this demand, normal schools eventually expanded their curriculum to include secondary teacher education. The growth of high schools also created a need for teachers who were highly specialized in particular academic subjects, so normal schools established subject matter departments and developed more diversified programs. The length of the teacher education program was expanded to two, three, and finally four years; this longer duration fostered development and diversification of the normal school curriculum. The demand for teachers increased from about 20,000 in 1900 to more than 200,000 in 1930.

The United States gradually advanced technologically to the point at which more college-educated citizens were needed. The normal schools assumed a responsibility to help meet this need by establishing many other academic programs in addition to teacher training. As normal schools extended their programs to four years and began granting baccalaureate degrees, they also began to call themselves *state teachers' colleges.* For most institutions, the change in name took place during the 1930s.

Changes in Mid-Twentieth-Century Teacher Education

Universities entered the teacher preparation business on a large scale around 1900. Before then, some graduates of universities had become high school teachers or college teachers, but not until about 1900 did universities begin to establish departments of education and add a full range of teacher education programs to the curriculum.

Just as the normal schools expanded in size, scope, and function until they became state teachers' colleges, so the state teachers' colleges expanded to become *state colleges.* This change in name and scope took place for most institutions around 1950. The elimination of the word *teacher* really explains the story behind this transition. The new state colleges gradually expanded their programs beyond teacher education and became multipurpose institutions. One of the main reasons for this transition was that a growing number of students coming to the colleges demanded a more varied education. The state teachers' colleges developed diversified programs to try to meet their demands.

Many of these state colleges later became state universities, offering doctoral degrees in a wide range of fields. Some of our largest and most highly regarded universities evolved from normal schools. Figure 3.2 diagrams the evolution of U.S. teacher preparation institutions.

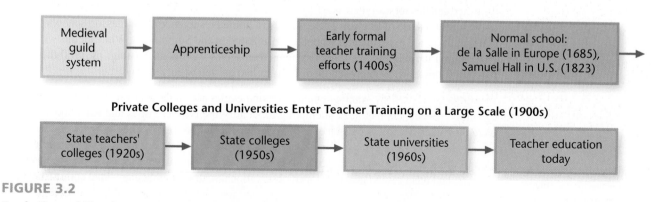

FIGURE 3.2

Evolution of Teacher Preparation Institutions

Obviously, establishing the teaching profession has been a long and difficult task. Preparation of teachers has greatly improved over the years from colonial times—when anyone could be a teacher—to the present, when people such as you must meet rigorous requirements for permanent teacher certification.

━━━━━━━━ ■ JOURNAL FOR REFLECTION ■ ━━━━━━━━

1. Describe and evaluate a learning experience you remember from your own school days.
2. What made the experience memorable, and what role did the teacher play in the learning process?

RECENT TRENDS IN EDUCATION

Education experienced major changes and a wide variety of perspectives following World War II when John Dewey, George Counts, William Bagley, W. W. Charters, Lewis Terman, and other intellectuals who had held sway during the first half of the twentieth century yielded to a somewhat less philosophically oriented breed of researchers represented by Abraham Maslow, Robert Havighurst, Benjamin Bloom, J. P. Guilford, Lee Cronbach, Jerome Bruner, Marshall McLuhan, Noam Chomsky, and Jean Piaget.[*] The Progressive Education Association closed its doors, and a series of White House conferences on children, youth, and education were inaugurated in an attempt to improve education.

No school system on earth has been scrutinized, analyzed, and dissected as profoundly and as mercilessly as that in the United States. From the late 1940s to the mid-1950s, educational institutions at all levels were not only flooded with unprecedented numbers of students but also censored and flailed unmercifully by self-ordained critics (Hyman Rickover, Arthur Bestor, and Rudolph Flesch). In retrospect this frantic rush to simultaneously patronize and criticize the institution seems a curious contradiction. The public schools were characterized as "godless, soft, undisciplined, uncultured, wasteful, and disorganized." Critics who remembered the high failure rates on tests given to World War II draftees were determined to raise the public's levels of physical fitness and literacy; others who detected a weakening of moral and spiritual values were eager to initiate citizenship and character education programs. The enrollments in nonpublic schools doubled, correspondence schools of all kinds sprang into existence, and the popular press carried articles and programs designed to help parents augment the basic skills taught within the school program. In 1955 there were an estimated 450 correspondence schools serving 700,000 students throughout the country.

New Emphases in Education

Fortunately, although some people were highly critical of the schools, not everybody panicked. There were physical fitness programs, character education projects, a general tightening of educational standards, and much more. J. P. Guilford, E. Paul Torrence, Jacob Getzels, and others explored the boundaries of creativity; Alfred Barr and D. G. Ryans carried out exhaustive studies of teacher characteristics; and just about everybody experimented with new patterns of organization. There were primary block programs, interage groupings, plans devised by and named for George Stoddard and J. Lloyd Trump, core programs, and a host of other patterns or combinations of plans structured around subject areas, broad groupings of subjects, or pupil characteristics. There were programs for the gifted and the not-so-gifted, and there was a new concern for foreign language instruction as well as the functional use of English. There was also a limited resurgence of Montessori schools and several one-of-a-kind experimental schools such as Amidon and Summerhill. While all this was taking place within the schools, the school systems themselves were consolidating; by 1960 there were only about one-third as many school districts as had existed twenty years earlier.

ANALYSIS OF TEACHING. Another emphasis found expression in the **analysis of teaching**. For half a century, researchers had been attempting to identify the characteristics and teaching styles that were most closely associated with effective instruction. Hundreds of studies had been initiated, and correlations had been done among them. During the 1950s, the focus began changing from identification of what ought to occur in teaching to scrutiny of what actually does occur. Ned Flanders and other researchers developed observational scales for assessing verbal communications

analysis of teaching Procedures used to enable teachers to critique their own performance in the classroom.

*We thank Dr. Donald Barnes for many of the ideas presented in this section.

between and among teachers and students. The scales permitted observers to categorize and summarize specific actions by teachers and students. These analyses were followed by studies of nonverbal classroom behaviors.

Another series of investigations involving the wider range of instructional protocols was patterned after the time-and-motion studies used earlier for industrial processes. Dwight Allen and several other educators attempted to analyze teacher behaviors, delineate the components of effective teaching, and introduce teacher candidates to the elements judged most important to good teaching. The change in focus from studies of teacher characteristics to analyses of what actually occurs in classrooms has offered educators highly fruitful insights into teaching and learning and has provided usable instruments for further investigations of classroom behavior. It is now possible to assess the logical, verbal, nonverbal, affective, and attitudinal dimensions of instruction, as well as the intricate aspects of cognition and concept development.

TEACHER EFFECTIVENESS. During the past 50 years, research has focused even more closely on the instructional patterns of effective teachers. The **effective teaching** movement based on this research offers today's teachers important skills. In common with the schoolteachers of sixty years ago, today's teachers learn to be strong leaders who direct classroom activities, maximize the use of instructional time, and teach in a clear, businesslike manner.

Effective teachers now employ structured, carefully delineated lessons. They break larger topics into smaller, more easily grasped components, and they focus on one thought, point, or direction at a time. They check prerequisite skills before introducing new skills or concepts. They accompany step-by-step presentations with many probing questions. Teachers offer detailed explanations of difficult points and test students on one point before moving on to the next. They provide corrective feedback where needed and stay with the topic under study until students comprehend the major points or issues. Effective teachers use prompts and cues to assist students through the initial stages of acquisition.

This recent emphasis on demonstration, prompting, and practice is a far cry from the relatively unstructured classroom activities of the recent past. We now emphasize carefully created learning goals and lesson sequences. It will be interesting to see whether the educational pendulum swings back to a new focus on student concerns and initiatives at some time in the future.

> More information on effective teaching can be found in Chapters 12 and 13.

THE EVOLUTION OF EDUCATIONAL TECHNOLOGY. In some sense, even very early educators made use of what might be considered forms of basic educational technology. For instance, if a caveman or cavewoman used a stick or a finger to draw a symbol of something in the dirt or sand in an effort to teach a child something, that might be considered a rudimentary form of educational technology. Printed words are a form of educational technology, and hornbooks used as early as the Middle Ages contained printed words. The use of pictures, such as those included in the form of woodcuts in early books, are also forms of early educational technology.

Needless to say, technology has evolved over time to the advanced forms that we are familiar with today—technological advancements that early educators undoubtedly never dreamed of. I wonder what forms of educational technology that we, during this age, cannot even imagine might be developed at some point in the future. What do you think?

STUDY OF THE LEARNING PROCESS. Several leading educational researchers in the United States and Europe have sought to analyze and describe how children learn. All of these investigators have stressed the importance of successful early learning patterns and the problems associated with serious learning deficits. They also believe that important elements within the environment may be changed or modified to promote learning. Lev Vygotsky, a Russian, developed a social development theory in the late 1800s that suggested social interaction among children plays a major role in cognitive development. His work contributed significantly to the founding of constructionist psychology.

Robert Havighurst, a University of Chicago professor, identified specific developmental tasks that he believes children must master if they are to develop normally. He even suggests there may be periods during which certain tasks must be mastered if they are to become an integral part of children's repertoire of responses. There may also be "teachable moments" (periods of peak efficiency for the acquisition of specific concepts/skills) during which receptivity is particularly high. Havighurst has caused educators to look carefully at the motivations and needs of children. Another important educational reseacher, Jean Piaget, also stressed evaluating the developmental stages of children, as discussed in the Global Perspectives feature.

effective teaching A movement to improve teaching performance based on the outcomes of educational research.

Jean Piaget

Jean Piaget (1896–1980) was a Swiss psychologist educated at the University of Paris. Through his work with Alfred Binet, who developed one of the first intelligence tests, Piaget became interested in how children learn. He spent long hours observing children of different ages and eventually created a theory of mental or **cognitive development**. Piaget believed that children learn facts, concepts, and principles in four major stages. Up until about age two, he suggested, a child is at the *sensorimotor stage* and learns mainly through the hands, mouth, and eyes. From about two to seven years of age, a child is at the *preoperational stage* and learns primarily through language and concepts. Between ages seven and eleven, a child's learning is characterized by *concrete operations*, which involve the use of more complex concepts such as numbers. The final learning stage identified by Piaget is called the *formal operations* phase. This stage typically begins between ages eleven and fifteen and continues throughout adulthood. During this final stage, the learner employs the most sophisticated and abstract learning processes. Although children do not all fit neatly into these categories, Piaget's work has contributed much to educators' understanding of the learning process and has helped teachers develop more appropriate teaching strategies for students at different developmental stages.

Questions for Reflection
1. What is your perspective on Piaget's theory of cognitive development? Why?
2. How might Piaget's ideas be useful today? Why?

Jean Piaget (1896–1980) was a Swiss developmental psychologist who researched children's stages of learning.

Many important educators were concerned about providing education for all children, including those of different ethnic and cultural backgrounds. The authors of this textbook believe that knowledge of educational history can help contemporary educators better serve students in general and, for example, can help them improve multicultural education, which is especially challenging to educators today. The accompanying Professional Dilemma explores this possibility.

A contemporary of Havighurst, Jerome Bruner of Harvard, has also postulated a series of developmental steps or stages that he believes children encounter as they mature. These involve action, imagery, and symbolism. Bruner's cognitive views have stressed student inquiry and the breaking down of larger tasks into components.

Benjamin Bloom, author of Bloom's Taxonomy of Educational Objectives and distinguished service professor at the University of Chicago, has attempted to identify and weigh the factors that control learning. He believes that one can predict learning outcomes by assessing three factors: (1) the cognitive entry behaviors of a student (the extent to which the pupil has mastered prerequisite skills), (2) the affective entry characteristics (the student's interest in learning the material), and (3) the quality of instruction (the degree to which the instruction offered is appropriate for the learner). Bloom's research is reflected in models of direct instruction, particularly mastery learning, in which teachers carefully explain, illustrate, and demonstrate skills and provide practice, reinforcement, corrective feedback, and remediation.

B. F. SKINNER. Burrhus Frederic (B. F.) Skinner (1904–1990) became one of the foremost early educational psychologists in U.S. education. He developed a **behavioral theory**, which was a theory focusing on outward behavior that suggested students could be successfully trained and conditioned to learn just about anything a teacher desired. This required the teacher to break down the learning into small sequential steps. Skinner even experimented with teaching machines that presented the learner with small sequential bits of information—an idea that has been revived today in the form of computer-assisted instruction. Skinner published many works, including *The Technology of Teaching, Beyond Freedom and Dignity*, and *Walden Two*. He contributed much to our present-day understanding of human learning and helped to advance the technology of teaching.

Educational Critics

Another change in education was shown by a phalanx of critics, all holding differing perspectives, including Edgar Friedenberg (*Coming of Age in America*), Charles Silberman (*Crisis in the Classroom*), Jonathan Kozol (*Death at an Early Age*), Ivan Illich (*Deschooling Society*), John Holt (*How Children Fail*), and even the federal government (*A Nation at Risk*, 1983), all focusing on low educational standards. Some critics, such as Silberman, urged schools to refurbish what they already have; others, including Illich, wanted to abandon the schools altogether. These critics have not gone unnoticed. Friedenberg's call for alternatives to traditional education, Silberman's endorsement of open education, and Kozol's plea for equal opportunity are all reflected to some degree in innovative programs currently being used from coast to coast.

cognitive development A learner's acquisition of facts, concepts, and principles through mental activity.

behavioral theory A theory that considers the outward behavior of students to be the main target for change.

PROFESSIONAL DILEMMA

Can a Knowledge of History Help to Improve Multicultural Education?

When you become a teacher, you will be expected to provide multicultural education for your students, regardless of the age level or subjects you teach. Most teachers today face the dilemma of wanting to provide their students with a high-quality multicultural program, but being frustrated by the lack of time and support for doing so.

As you will learn, racial and ethnic prejudice and injustice have been present throughout U.S. educational history. Unfortunately, there is still considerable racial and ethnic strife in the United States today, and much of this strife has filtered into the halls of education. Debates rage about how schools should meet the educational demands of a complex multicultural society. As a teacher, you will be expected to join in this debate and help search for answers.

James Banks, a leading researcher in multicultural education at the University of Washington, feels past efforts have been too superficial. He asserts that "additive approaches" treat multicultural material as "an appendage to the main story of the development of the nation and to the core curriculum." Instead, multicultural education should integrate multicultural perspectives throughout the curriculum, on an equal footing with white European perspectives.

Despite the lack of time and adequate school district encouragement and support, there are many things that a determined and creative teacher can do to integrate multicultural education throughout the curriculum. Teachers can also encourage the school district to develop and support comprehensive programs for multicultural education and then participate in developing these plans.

Questions for Reflection

1. What are the historical antecedents that have contributed to the lack of racial and ethnic understanding in U.S. society?
2. Should education programs seek to eliminate cultural differences among individuals or to preserve and perhaps celebrate them?
3. What can you do in your classroom to improve multicultural education? Why and how?
4. What additional information would you like about multicultural education, and where might you find such information?

Changing Public Perspectives on Education

A public opinion survey, first conducted in 1950 and repeated in 1999, revealed the following interesting shifts over this fifty-year span: In 1950, 24 percent of those surveyed thought that teachers should be asked their political beliefs, whereas in 1999 only 9 percent thought so; in 1950, 39 percent said that religion should be taught in the public schools, whereas in 1999 the number had increased to 50 percent; in 1950, 44 percent said that teachers were underpaid, whereas in 1999, 61 percent said so; and in 1950, 67 percent of those polled thought that students were being taught more worthwhile and useful things in school than children twenty years before, but in 1999 only 26 percent thought so. These shifts in public opinion about public schools provide food for thought for contemporary educators.

JOURNAL FOR REFLECTION

What are your perspectives on some of the relatively recent trends in education that you have observed or experienced? Record your responses in your journal.

Major Educational Events of the Past Century

As we moved into the twenty-first century, many people reflected on educational accomplishments in the United States during the past hundred years. As would be expected, opinions differ considerably on this subject. Ben Brodinsky, an education journalist, has suggested that the GI Bill of Rights should perhaps be considered the single most important educational event of the past century. He lists the desegregation of schools as the second most important and the federal Education for All Handicapped Children Act as the third most important educational event of the twentieth century.

Undoubtedly, many important educational events and accomplishments occurred during the twentieth century—the list could go on and on. One example of significant progress made by the U.S. educational system in the past seventy-five years is reflected in the increased percentage of students completing high school—from about 50 percent in 1940 to about 70 percent in 1990. What would you put on your list of the most important educational changes, events, and/or accomplishments of the last century?

It is difficult to draw meaningful inferences from recent events that have not yet stood the test of time. Implications of recent educational events will eventually be found in the answers to questions

myeducationlab

To see and use an interactive timeline of the history of education, go to the MyEducationLab for your course, select *Resources*, and then select *Introduction to Teaching and Foundations of Education Interactive Timeline.*

such as these: What should be the role of the federal government in education? How can equal educational opportunity be achieved in the United States? How professionalized should the school system be? To what degree should educational policy and practice be influenced by litigation? How will school reform movements change the practice of education? The answer to these questions, and other questions you may have in mind, will be colored by the perspectives through which people view the world, children, and schools. We believe that viewing all educational questions through well-informed historical perspectives yields more valid answers.

LOOKING AHEAD: LOOKING BACK TO HELP US LOOK AHEAD!

As we have pointed out a number of times, perspectives on education have changed historically, and are now changing ever more rapidly. This makes predicting the future of education very difficult—perhaps even nearly impossible and somewhat foolhardy. Rather than do so, perhaps our best advice to you is that you should expect many changes and ever diverse perspectives on education during your career as an educator. Of course, you will need to try to understand and adapt to these rapid changes, and the challenges they present to you as an educator. Knowing and understanding educational history will help you better do this.

SUMMARY

MORE STUDENTS AND BIGGER SCHOOLS

- During the past seventy-five years the U.S. education system has experienced unprecedented changes and growth in both size and complexity.
- The great increase in numbers of students over these years has created a challenging need for more school buildings and many more teachers.
- Population increases and shifts from rural settings to cities required bigger schools and large, elaborate school busing systems.
- There has also been an amazing expansion of educational curricula and program diversification for different types of students at all levels during the past sixty years.
- All of this growth in size and programs has resulted in a tremendous increase in school budgets.
- Programs for students with special needs have increased tremendously in recent history.
- There has also been notable growth in other educational programs designed to better serve the needs of the increasingly diverse student populations now found in our schools.

THE DEVELOPMENT OF THE TEACHING PROFESSION

- There have been many changes and improvements in the teaching profession during the past seventy-five years, as U.S. educational systems have grown in complexity, especially in funding and control.
- The federal government has increased its involvement in public education through legislation and agencies such as the GI Bill, the National Science Foundation, the National Defense Education Act, the Elementary and Secondary Education Act, Project Head Start, Upward Bound, and the National Teacher Corps, to name just a few.
- Each of these federal acts, while providing funds for specific school programs, has also placed new demands and regulations on our schools.

CHANGING AIMS OF EDUCATION

- An impressive series of important statements have been made over the years in an attempt to determine and articulate the essential aims of education in the United States.
- These statements clearly show how perspectives on education have changed over time.

PREPARATION OF TEACHERS

- The history of teacher preparation shows an evolution from very meager and humble beginnings centuries ago to a complex and professional state today.
- Educators should be proud of the history of advancement in the preparation of educators and be mindful and proud of the current rigorous professional training they receive.

RECENT TRENDS IN EDUCATION

- Many recent trends in education include professional advancements such as analysis of the teaching act, teacher effectiveness research, sociological studies, the development of new learning theories, and other research efforts designed to help us better understand and improve student learning.
- Widely read critics of our schools during the past sixty years include Friedenberg, Silberman, Kozol, Illich, and Holt.
- Various governmental agencies at the state and national levels have also been critical of our schools in recent years, resulting in many reports and calls for school reforms.

LOOKING AHEAD: LOOKING BACK TO HELP US LOOK AHEAD!

- We live in a rapidly changing world that challenges teachers to "keep up to date."
- Even our understanding of the history of education changes.
- Every current educational challenge can be informed by educational history.

DISCUSSION QUESTIONS

1. Other than those mentioned in this chapter, what additional recent educational developments seem particularly important to you? Why are they important?
2. Has the increased federal involvement in education been good or bad for schools? How so?
3. In your opinion, in what respect, if any, has education become professionalized?
4. In your opinion, how much progress has the United States really made in providing equal educational opportunity? Defend your answer.
5. What is happening in education at this very moment that is likely to be written about in future history of education books?

SCHOOL-BASED OBSERVATIONS

1. As you work in the schools, look to see how the continuing struggle for equal educational opportunity is progressing. Also, analyze what you observe in order to determine the degree to which teaching has been professionalized—a movement that has gained impetus during the last sixty years. Finally, as you participate in classrooms, look for evidence that the work of educational pioneers discussed in this chapter (such as Bloom, Skinner, and Piaget) has made an impact in U.S. classrooms.
2. Discuss with experienced educators the changes they have observed during their careers. Visit with veteran educational administrators to discuss changes they have seen in education over the years.

PORTFOLIO DEVELOPMENT

1. Prepare a creative educational history project (using a poster, videotape, audio recording, slide presentation, or some other creative medium) dealing with a topic, person, or idea that is of interest to you. Design your project so that it can be used as part of your job placement credentials.
2. Create a list of the most useful outcomes of U.S. education during the past sixty years. What can you as a beginning teacher learn, if anything, from your list?

myeducationlab To begin developing your own personal portfolio, go to the MyEducationLab for your course, select *Resources*, and then select *Portfolio Builder*.

PREPARING FOR CERTIFICATION

1. Two of the topics in the Praxis II Principles of Teaching and Learning (PLT) test are Students as Learners and Students as Diverse Learners. In Students as Learners one subcategory is Student Development and the Learning Process. This subcategory addresses "(1) theoretical foundations about how learning occurs; how students construct knowledge, acquire skills, and develop habits of mind." In Students as Diverse

Learners, the subcategory "(1) Differences in the ways students learn and perform" includes the following:

- Learning styles
- Multiple intelligences
- Performance modes
  - Concrete operational thinkers
  - Visual and aural learners
- Gender differences
- Cultural expectations and styles

In this chapter, you learned about the several researchers who developed theories about child development and learning processes. Make a list of the theorists and write two or three sentences about how they contributed to our understanding of how students think and learn.

2. Answer the following multiple-choice question, which is similar to items in Praxis and other state certification tests.

The effective teaching movement was based on research focusing on the instructional patterns of effective teachers. Which instructional pattern was *not* emphasized in the effective teaching movement?

a. Teachers emphasize demonstration, prompting, and practice in their teaching.
b. Teachers focus on student concerns and initiatives when constructing the lessons.
c. Teachers check prerequisite skills before introducing new skills or concepts.
d. Teachers emphasize carefully created learning goals and lesson sequences.

3. Answer the following short-answer question, which is similar to items in Praxis and other state certification tests.

Reread the 1952 list of "Imperative Needs of Youth." Think about the relevance of this list for students today. Select the two objectives that you believe are most important today and two of the objectives that you believe are least important today and explain your choices.

After you've completed your written responses above, use the Praxis general scoring guide provided in Chapter 1 to see if you can revise your response to improve your score.

MYEDUCATIONLAB

myeducationlab Now go to Topic 7: *History of Education* in the MyEducationLab (www.myeducationlab.com) for your course, where you can:

- Find learning outcomes for *History of Education* along with the national standards that connect to these outcomes.
- Complete *Assignments and Activities* that can help you more deeply understand the chapter content.
- Apply and practice your understanding of the core teaching skills identified in the chapter with the *Building Teaching Skills and Dispositions* learning units.

- Check your comprehension on the content covered in the chapter by going to the *Study Plan* in the *Book Specific Resources* for your text. Here you will be able to take a chapter quiz, receive feedback on your answers, and then access *Review, Practice, and Enrichment* activities to enhance your understanding of chapter content.

WEBSITES

www.scholastic.com/Instructor The Scholastic Instructor site contains a variety of educational materials such as articles, contests, free materials for teachers, and chats with other educators on many subjects, including the history of education.

www.si.edu This site provides links to each museum of the Smithsonian Institution in Washington, D.C., and includes much historical information.

www.cdickens.com/articles/dickjane.htm Information about the Dick and Jane readers that were used in many schools.

www.insight-media.com A wonderful source of information about history of education media.

FURTHER READING

Barton, K. C. (2005, June). Primary sources in history: Breaking through the myths. *Phi Delta Kappan,* pp. 745–757. A thought-provoking but controversial article concerning historical research.

Campbell, J. M. (1996). *The prairie schoolhouse.* Albuquerque: University of New Mexico Press. Contains information about rural schoolhouses common during the westward expansion of the United States.

Capella, G., Geismar, K., & Nicoleau, G. (Eds.). (1995). *Shifting histories: Transforming schools for social change.* Cambridge, MA: Harvard Educational Publishing Group. A detailed treatment of the history of education as it relates to social change in the United States.

Ravitch, D. (1983). *The troubled crusade: American education 1945–1980.* New York: Basic Books. An excellent account of the history of relatively recent (1945–1980) education in the United States, written by a well-respected educational historian.

Spring, J. (1994). *The American school 1642–1990.* White Plains, NY: Longman. A useful survey of the history of education in the United States.

Web, L. D. (2006). *The history of American education: A great American experiment.* Boston: Pearson Merrill Prentice Hall. A rather detailed treatment of the history of U.S. education.

chapter four

PHILOSOPHY: REFLECTIONS ON THE ESSENCE OF EDUCATION

CHEATING CRISIS IN AMERICA'S SCHOOLS

How's It's Done and Why It's Happening

Excerpt from **ABC PRIMETIME NEWS**

ABC News, April 29, 2009

Angelo Angelis, a professor at Hunter College in New York City, was recently grading some student papers on the story of Paul Revere when he noticed something strange. A certain passage kept appearing in his students' work, he said.

It went like this, Angelis told *Primetime*'s Charles Gibson: "Paul Revere would never have said, 'The British are coming, the British are coming'; he was in fact himself British, he would have said something like 'the Red Coats are coming.'"

Angelis typed the words into Google, and found the passage on one website by a fifth-grade class. Half a dozen of his college students had copied their work from a bunch of elementary school kids, he thought. The website was very well done, Angelis said. For fifth graders, he would give them an "A." But his college students deserved an "F."

Lifting papers off the Internet is one of the newer trends in plagiarism and technology is giving students even more ways to cheat nowadays.

Authoritative numbers are hard to come by, but according to a 2002 confidential survey of 12,000 high school students, 74 percent admitted cheating on an examination at least once in the past year.

In a six-month investigation, *Primetime* traveled to colleges and high schools across the country to see how students are cheating, and why. The bottom line is not just that many students have more temptation but they seem to have a whole new mind-set.

GET REAL

Joe is a student at a top college in the Northeast who admits to cheating regularly. Like all of the college students who spoke to *Primetime*, he wanted his identity obscured.

In Joe's view, he's just doing what the rest of the world does.

"The real world is terrible," he told Gibson. "People will take other people's materials and pass it on as theirs. I'm numb to it already. I'll cheat to get by."

Primetime heard the same refrain from many other students who cheat: that cheating in school is a dress rehearsal for life. They mentioned President Clinton's Monica Lewinsky scandal and financial scandals like the Enron case, as well as the inconsistencies of the court system.

Michael Josephson, founder of the Josephson Institute for Ethics, the Los Angeles–based organization that conducted the 2002 survey, said students take their lead from adults.

"They're basically decent kids whose values are being totally corrupted by a world which is sanctioning stuff that even they know is wrong. But they can't understand why everybody allows it."

AN ISSUE OF EXPEDIENCY

Even if the world were more ethical, students still have reasons for cheating. Some said they cheat because they're graded on a curve so that their score is directly affected by how other students do.

The pressure for good grades is high. "Grades can determine your future, and if you fail this then you're not going on to college, you're going to work at McDonald's and live out of a car," said high school student Spike.

A business student at a top state university said, "Everything is about the grade that you got in the class. Nobody looks at how you got it." He graduates in a few weeks and will go on to a job with a top investment firm.

Some students feel it is perfectly OK to cheat in some situations and in some courses. And some professors make it easy, students said. They overlook even the most obvious instances.

In fact, McCabe says, a survey of more than 4,000 U.S. and Canadian schools revealed half of all faculty members admitted ignoring cheating at least once.

WHERE IS THE TIPPING POINT?

"We are in a crisis," said Josephson. But he added, "I don't think it has to stay that way."

He said he was waiting for the tipping point, like Enron with business ethics, where there would be a sea change in attitudes towards cheating.

QUESTIONS FOR REFLECTION

1. Do you think that cheating in school is OK if teachers ignore it? Why? Why not?
2. Why would a student think it's OK to cheat when teachers grade on a curve?
3. What are examples of a tipping point that might change attitudes toward cheating?

LEARNING OUTCOMES

After reading and studying this chapter, you should be able to:

1. Define philosophy and describe methods of inquiry used by philosophers. (INTASC 1: Subject Matter)
2. List major philosophical questions associated with the three major branches of philosophy: metaphysics, epistemology, and axiology. (INTASC 1: Subject Matter)
3. Elaborate on the major tenets of idealism, realism, pragmatism, and existentialism. (INTASC 1: Subject Matter)
4. Relate philosophical concepts to teaching and learning. (INTASC 4: Teaching Methods; INTASC 5: Motivation and Management; INTASC 8: Assessment)
5. Compare writers from different schools of philosophy: Plato, Socrates, Kant, Martin, Aristotle, Locke, Whitehead, Peirce, Dewey, Rorty, Sartre, Nietzsche, and Greene. (INTASC 1: Subject Matter)
6. Describe the characteristics of Eastern and Native North American ways of knowing. (INTASC 3: Diversity; INTASC 9: Reflection)

STRUCTURE AND METHODOLOGY OF PHILOSOPHY

Philosophy provides a way to examine and interpret the world—to ask basic questions about human nature, beauty, principles of right and wrong, and how knowledge and reality are defined. Philosophical thinking helps to uncover the essentials—the basic principles that undergird teaching and learning.

The philosophical perspective is especially important because our personal philosophy of life is seldom explicit. Rather, philosophy resides in people's minds and hearts and is seldom expressed in words or specific ideas. Our personal philosophy becomes evident in the manner in which we respond to everyday problems and questions. The perspective of philosophy helps us to focus on the underlying issues and assumptions and beliefs that are not always evident to us in the hectic pace of contemporary life.

Because philosophy deals with underlying values and beliefs, it naturally pervades all aspects of education. The perspective of philosophy presents opposing views about human nature, knowledge, and the world in which we live. By examining these different, often opposing views, you will be able to identify your own philosophical position and state it in clearer language and concepts.

Although philosophy can be defined in many different ways, it is best thought of as a passion to uncover and reflect on the underlying meaning of things. Derived from the Greek *philos*, which means "love," and *sophos*, which means "wisdom," the word *philosophy* means "love of wisdom." Early philosophers did not claim to be wise; rather, they viewed themselves as reflective thinkers in search of wisdom. To many contemporary philosophers, conveying information or wisdom is not as important as helping others in their own search for wisdom.

Education presupposes ideas and questions about human nature, the nature of reality, and the nature of knowledge. These questions are ultimately of a philosophical character. Teachers must constantly confront the underlying assumptions that guide conduct, determine values, and influence the direction of all existence. Philosophy reminds teachers to continue the search for truth and not be satisfied with pat answers, even answers that are provided by so-called experts. To a philosopher, an expert is not one who professes truth; an expert is one who searches, questions, and reflects. Hence, the study of philosophy is at the heart of education.

The Branches of Philosophy

Philosophy includes branches that investigate large and difficult questions—questions about reality or being, about knowledge, about goodness and beauty and living a good life. Throughout the centuries, entire branches of philosophy have evolved that specialize in and center on major questions. For example, questions about the nature of reality or existence are examined in metaphysics, questions about knowledge and truth are considered in epistemology, and questions about values and goodness are central to axiology.

METAPHYSICS. **Metaphysics** is a branch of philosophy that is concerned with questions about the nature of reality. Literally, metaphysics means "beyond the physical." It deals with such questions as "What is reality?" "What is existence?" "Is the universe rationally designed or ultimately

myeducationlab

Go to the *Building Teaching Skills and Dispositions* section of Topic 8: *Philosophy of Education* in the MyEducationLab for your course and complete the activity titled *Educational Philosophy and Teaching Practice*.

metaphysics An area of philosophy that deals with questions about the nature of ultimate reality.

meaningless?" Metaphysics is a search for order and wholeness—a search applied not to particular items or experiences but to all reality and to all existence.

The questions in metaphysics, especially those about humanity and the universe, are extremely relevant to teachers and students of education. Theories about how the universe came to be and about what causes events in the universe are crucial if scholars are to interpret the physical sciences properly.

A teacher's classroom approach will be linked to the teacher's metaphysical beliefs. If, for example, the teacher believes that very specific basic knowledge is crucial to the child's intellectual development, it is likely that this teacher will focus on the subject matter. If, on the other hand, the teacher holds that the child is more important than any specific subject matter, it is likely that this teacher will focus on the child and allow the child to provide clues as to how he or she should be instructed.

EPISTEMOLOGY. **Epistemology** is a branch of philosophy that examines questions about how and what we know. What knowledge is true, and how does knowledge take place? The epistemologist attempts to discover what is involved in the process of knowing. Is knowing a special sort of mental act? Is there a difference between knowledge and belief? Can people know anything beyond the objects with which their senses acquaint them? Does knowing make any difference to the object that is known?

Because epistemological questions deal with the essence of knowledge, they are central to education. Teachers must be able to assess what is knowledge to determine whether a particular piece of information should be included in the curriculum. How people know is of paramount importance to teachers because their beliefs about learning influence their classroom methods. Should teachers train students in scientific methods, deductive reasoning, or both? Should students study logic and fallacies or follow intuition? Teachers' knowledge of how students learn influences how they will teach.

AXIOLOGY. **Axiology** is a branch of philosophy that deals with the nature of values. It includes such questions as "What is good?" and "What is beautiful?" Questions about what should be or what values we hold are highlighted in axiology. This study of values is divided into ethics (moral values and conduct) and aesthetics (values in the realm of beauty and art). Ethics deals with such questions as "What is the good life?" and "How should we behave?" One major question to be examined is "When does the end justify any means of achieving it?" Aesthetics deals with the theory of beauty and examines such questions as "Is art public and representative, or is it the product of private creative imagination?" Good citizenship, honesty, and correct human relations are all learned in schools. Sometimes these concepts are taught explicitly, but often students learn ethics from *who* the teacher is as well as from *what* the teacher says.

Both ethics and aesthetics are important issues in education. Should a system of ethics be taught in the public schools? If so, which system of ethics should be taught? Aesthetics questions in education involve deciding which artistic works should or should not be included in the curriculum and what kind of subject matter should be allowed or encouraged in a writing, drawing, or painting class. Should teachers compromise their own attitudes toward a piece of artwork if their opinion differs from that of a parent or a school board? Take a moment to consider the Professional Dilemma feature regarding the teaching of morals and values in public schools.

Thinking as a Philosopher

Philosophy provides the tools people need to think clearly. As with any discipline, philosophy has a style of thinking as well as a set of terms and methodologies that distinguish it from other disciplines. Philosophers spend much of their energy developing symbols or terms that are both abstract (apply to many individual cases) and precise (distinguish clearly). Developing ideas that embrace more and more instances (abstraction) while at the same time maintaining a clear and accurate meaning (precision) is difficult, but this tension is at the heart of the philosopher's task. The entire process is what is meant by *understanding*: uncovering the underlying, the foundational, and the essential principles of reality.

There is great variety in the ways philosophers think. Hence it is difficult to set forth a simple set of rules or thinking steps that can accurately be labeled philosophical thinking. To give you a sense of philosophical thinking, it is easier (and more accurate) to describe two different thinking styles that philosophers use interchangeably as they wrestle with large, unstructured

epistemology An area of philosophy that deals with questions about the nature of understanding and how we know things.

axiology An area of philosophy that deals with the nature of values. It includes questions such as "What is good?" and "What is value?"

PROFESSIONAL DILEMMA

Should Morals and Values Be Taught in Public Schools?

Should a teacher instruct students about values and matters of right and wrong? You may feel that this question demands an obvious affirmative answer. A problem arises, however, when you are asked to clarify the specific values that should be taught. How do you, as a teacher in a multicultural school setting, determine what moral values should be the focus of instruction?

One school of thought, influenced largely by the work of Lawrence Kohlberg, endorses direct instruction in moral development. The educational theorists who endorse this position contend that a body of morals exists that spans all cultures. This body of morals can be articulated at any point in time and should be taught directly to students in public schools. People—especially parents—may also feel that children are faced with an increasingly complex and dangerous society and cannot be expected simply to absorb the proper morals and values from the world around them. Because of this, the schools should step in.

In contrast to this point of view, those influenced by the educational theories proposed by Syd Simon in his text *Values Clarification*

reject the direct instruction of morals on the grounds that democracy demands that its citizens be free to clarify their own sets of values. This school of thought calls for public schools to refrain from the direct instruction of morals and asks teachers to help students define their own sets of individually selected values. The approach requires teachers to remain neutral in their presentations of opposing value systems. The teacher's role is simply to assist students in the clarification of the consequences of selecting any one set of morals or values.

This difficult problem of teaching morals and values is especially problematic for a democracy.

Questions for Reflection
1. Who do you think should select the values that are taught in a school district?
2. If the majority is given this right to choose the values, then what becomes of the individual rights of minorities?
3. Do your think it possible to teach a value-free curriculum?
4. Does the very act of instruction imply a certain value system expressed and upheld by the individual teacher?

questions. The first way of thinking can be labeled **analytic thinking**. Philosophers employ this style when they attempt to examine questions of the "what seems to be" type. A second philosophical style of thinking is called **prophetic thinking**. This style focuses on questions of the "what ought to be" type.

ANALYTIC WAYS OF THINKING IN PHILOSOPHY. When philosophers encounter a contemporary problem, they often spend time analyzing it in an attempt to clarify or find the "real" problem, not just the surface issues. To do so, philosophers use abstraction, imagination, generalization, and logic. These analytic thinking processes help focus the problem clearly and precisely.

Abstraction. The notion of **abstraction** covers a multitude of meanings. The word *abstract* is derived from the Latin verb *abstrahere*, meaning to "draw away." Abstraction, then, involves drawing away from a concrete level of experience to a conceptual plane of principles or ideas. The process of abstraction can be thought of as a three-step process that moves thinking from singular concrete instances to more general, universal ideas. The three steps involve (1) focusing attention on some feature within one's experience, (2) examining the precise characteristics of the feature, and (3) remembering the feature and its characteristics later so as to apply them to other instances or combine them with other ideas.

When teachers are asked to examine a new textbook series, for example, they will often be presented with promotional material about the important subject matter and learning tools that the series contains. The process of abstraction helps teachers pull away from the "bells and whistles" or the concrete examples in the text. Abstraction enables teachers to consider the underlying themes that are implicit and that provide a cohesive structure to the entire text series. Abstraction helps teachers uncover hidden messages.

Imagination and Generalization. According to Herbert G. Alexander (1987) the second step of analytic thinking is the use of imagination. Imagination can be thought of as the altering of abstractions. In philosophy the use of imagination assists the process of abstraction by filling in the details of an idea, selecting details, and relating ideas to one another.

Imaginative explorations occur in many different ways. Usually, they occur when a person first focuses on some abstraction or idea. Ideas come when one makes observations, reflects about past experiences, reads, views a dramatic work or piece of art, or converses with others. Once ideas are

analytic thinking A thinking strategy that focuses on questions of the "what seems to be" type; includes abstractions, imagination, generalization, and logic.

prophetic thinking A thinking strategy that focuses on questions of the "what ought to be" type; includes discernment, connection, tracking hypocrisy, and hope.

abstraction A thought process that involves drawing away from experiences to a conceptual plane.

selected, imaginative explorations can be made about them. Basic assumptions about things can be examined, arguments can be justified or clarified, and ideas can be distinguished from or related to other ideas. Experiential evidence, logical consistency, and a host of other criteria can be employed. The outcome of the whole imaginative process is the development of a system of ideas that has greater clarity and more interrelationships to other ideas or sets of propositions. This last step of the imaginative exploration process is sometimes referred to as generalization, because it ultimately results in the development of a comprehensive set of ideas.

Generalization sets ranges and limits to the abstractions that have been altered by imagination. As one's imagination relates more and more ideas to one another, the process of generalization determines which relationships should be emphasized or de-emphasized.

When teachers consider new ways to support student motivation, they can use these same processes. For example, teachers often imagine different types of mathematics contests or science Olympiads that might spur students' interests. As they imaginatively apply these contests to the classroom setting, teachers might abstract the competitiveness component as a necessary aspect of contests and Olympiads. Teachers might then wonder about the hidden messages of winning at the expense of others' losses. Teachers might generalize that the competitive approach could bring about knowledge wars; knowledge contests might make students less willing to share what they know with others. To complete this inquiry, teachers need to use logic.

Logic. Philosophy deals with the nature of reasoning and has designated a set of principles called logic. Logic examines the principles that allow us to move from one argument to the next. There are many types of logic, but the two most commonly studied are deductive and inductive logic. Deduction is a type of reasoning that moves from a general statement to a specific conclusion. Induction is a type of reasoning that moves in the opposite direction, from the particular instance to a general conclusion.

Philosophy provides tools that help people think clearly. It is important for educators to have a philosophy, both as a means of developing their ability to think clearly about what they do on a day-to-day basis and as a means of seeing how their workaday principles and values extend beyond the classroom to the whole of humanity and society. Figure 4.1, on page 84, describes how analytic ways of thinking help teachers solve a classroom problem. Studying philosophy enables you to recognize the underlying assumptions and principles of things so you can determine what is significant.

PROPHETIC WAYS OF THINKING IN PHILOSOPHY. In contrast to the search for underlying universal principles that is the focus of an analytic way of thinking, *prophetic thinking* seeks to uncover multiple, even divergent realities or principles. Prophetic thinking has emerged as a counterpoint to the highly successful but rigid analytic thinking style. According to Cornel West, a prophetic thinker is one who goes beyond abstraction. A prophetic thinker lives in multiple realities, feeling and touching these realities to such a degree that understanding is ultimately achieved. And a prophetic thinker understands multiple realities so well that bridges can be built between and among the multiple worlds. In his book *Prophetic Thought in Postmodern Times*, West (1993) identifies four basic components of prophetic thinking: discernment, connection, tracking hypocrisy, and hope.

Discernment. Discernment is the capacity to develop a vision of what should be out of a sophisticated understanding of what has been and is. This first component of prophetic thought is quite different from the abstract approach of the analytic thinker. The prophetic thinker is more concerned with the concrete, specific aspects of reality. To discern a situation is to take the entire situation into account to get beyond abstract principles. A discerning teacher is one who sees beyond mere test scores, beyond simple classroom rules. A discerning teacher examines the total content of a child's life and makes decisions based on this context. An outsider could criticize a discerning teacher for bending rules or being inconsistent. Yet a prophetic thinker would applaud the teacher for being wise. The prophetic thinker is a bit of a historian, building the future on the best of the past and present.

Connection. A prophetic thinker must relate to or connect with others. Rather than considering humankind in the abstract, prophetic thinkers value and have empathy for other human beings. They show empathy, the capacity to get in contact with the anxieties and frustrations of others.

FIGURE 4.1

Analytic Ways of Thinking: Focus and Solve Problems Clearly and Precisely

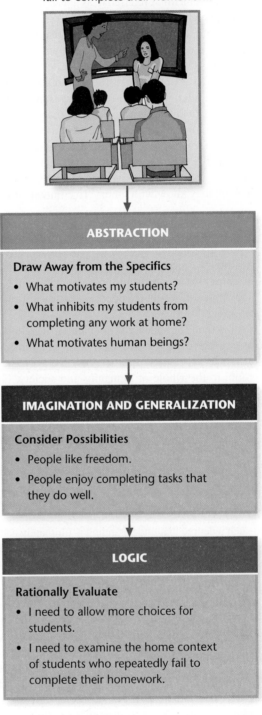

Specific Problem Confronts a Teacher
"Why do some students in my classroom
fail to complete their homework?"

ABSTRACTION

Draw Away from the Specifics

- What motivates my students?
- What inhibits my students from completing any work at home?
- What motivates human beings?

IMAGINATION AND GENERALIZATION

Consider Possibilities

- People like freedom.
- People enjoy completing tasks that they do well.

LOGIC

Rationally Evaluate

- I need to allow more choices for students.
- I need to examine the home context of students who repeatedly fail to complete their homework.

Many teachers really do care and work hard to help students. However, they are often unable to make the connection that would complete caring relations with their students. Teachers' willingness to empathize with students is often thwarted by society's desire to establish teaching on a firm scientific footing. But to students, the failure to connect means that teachers sometimes look as though they simply do not care. According to Nel Noddings (1993) both teachers and students have become victims in the search for the one best method of instruction.

Tracking Hypocrisy. Although the relationship between empathy and teaching is important, it is equally important for the prophetic teacher to identify and make known "the gap between principles and practice, between promise and performance, between rhetoric and reality" (West, 1993, p. 5). Tracking hypocrisy ought to be done in a self-critical rather than in a self-righteous manner. It takes boldness as well as courage to point out inconsistencies between school policies and practices, but when doing so a prophetic teacher remains open to others' points of view. New evidence might reveal that one's position is no longer valid, or it might enhance one's original thinking. Figure 4.2 on page 86, describes how prophetic ways of thinking help teachers solve a classroom problem.

Teachers not only teach content, but also find ways to help students seek connections to the world around them and apply ideas to their daily lives.

Hope. The fourth and perhaps most important component of prophetic thought is simply hope. West admits that given the numerous and horrific examples of people's inhumanity to one another, it is hard to take hope seriously. Still, without it, all thought is meaningless. West says:

> To talk about human hope is to engage in an audacious attempt to galvanize and energize, to inspire and to invigorate world-weary people. Because that is what we are. We are world-weary; we are tired. For some of us there are misanthropic skeletons hanging in our closet. And by misanthropic I mean the notion that we have given up on the capacity to do anything right; the capacity of human communities to solve any problem. (West, 1993, p. 6)

West challenges educators to see "skeletons" as challenges, not as conclusions. Even when confronted with educators' failures at creating a better community of scholars, the prophetic teacher must remember that the world is unfinished, that the future is open ended, and that what teachers think and do can make a difference.

Technology and Philosophy

Most of the time we think of technology as a tool that helps us work efficiently or improve the quality of a product. Philosophers of technology take a broader look at technology by asking questions about the consequences that technology has on the physical and human condition. For example, the philosopher Martin Heidegger (1993) believed technology provided the greatest danger, yet the greatest possibility for humankind. Heidegger was concerned about technology because it has the power to present information by emphasizing the worth of an object while de-emphasizing its dangers. He called this power of technology *enframing* and he was concerned that humans' ability to present things in a specific way could hide the actual essence of a thing.

With the release of new technologies increasing exponentially, other philosophers struggle to determine whether any one technology enhances or detracts from the essence of life and the natural order. Some philosophers contend that technology is developing so quickly that mankind no longer controls its direction. They contend that technology now has the power to develop autonomously because humans have become so dependent on it.

FIGURE 4.2

Prophetic Ways of Thinking: Uncover Multiple Realities or Principles

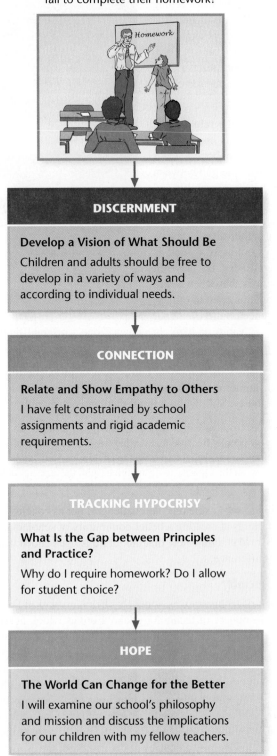

Specific Problem Confronts a Teacher
"Why do some students in my classroom
fail to complete their homework?"

DISCERNMENT

Develop a Vision of What Should Be
Children and adults should be free to
develop in a variety of ways and
according to individual needs.

CONNECTION

Relate and Show Empathy to Others
I have felt constrained by school
assignments and rigid academic
requirements.

TRACKING HYPOCRISY

**What Is the Gap between Principles
and Practice?**
Why do I require homework? Do I allow
for student choice?

HOPE

The World Can Change for the Better
I will examine our school's philosophy
and mission and discuss the implications
for our children with my fellow teachers.

John Dewey considered technology a natural component of the changing world. Because change is natural, then technology is natural. The key is to use our rational minds and inquiry to determine the effects of a technology and use it in ways that enhance but do not detract from the needs of all members in society.

No matter what you may think about technology, it is here to stay. Using the analytic and prophetic tools of philosophy can help direct the use of technology in ways that nourish society and schools. By constantly asking broader questions and encouraging students to do the same, schools can provide a forum for controlling and encouraging the development of technology.

═══ JOURNAL FOR REFLECTION ═══

Classroom activities that deal with what is good (right) or evil (wrong) are in the realm of axiology. Prepare lists of the goods and the evils of the U.S. educational system. Then, propose recommendations for change that might counteract as many of the evils as possible.

SCHOOLS OF PHILOSOPHY AND THEIR INFLUENCE ON EDUCATION

As philosophers attempt to answer questions, they develop answers that are clustered into different schools of thought. These schools of philosophical thought are somewhat contrived; they are merely labels developed by others who have attempted to show the similarities and differences among the many answers philosophers develop. As you examine the schools of thought described in this section, keep in mind that the individual philosophers who represent these schools are individual thinkers, like yourself, who do not limit their thinking to the characteristics of any one label or school of thought. Four well-known schools of thought that we discuss next are idealism, realism, pragmatism, and existentialism. In addition to these, we will touch on Eastern thought and Native North American thought. Technically, these two final clusters of thought are not termed schools because they encompass greater diversity and often extend beyond the limits of philosophy into beliefs, customs, and group values.

Idealism

Idealism's roots are found in the writings of Plato. **Idealism** is a school of philosophy that holds that ideas or concepts are the essence of all that is worth knowing. The physical world we know through our senses is only a manifestation or imperfect representation of the spiritual world. The spiritual world is everlasting and is not subject to change because it is perfect (metaphysics).

Idealists believe in the power of reasoning but de-emphasize the scientific method and sense perception, which they hold suspect. Rather, idealists contend that the rational mind has the ability to reason to the underlying ideas that support the physical world. All that is necessary is for the individual, through introspection, to search for these universal ideas that are lodged deep in our minds (epistemology).

Idealists search and value universal or absolute truths or ideas that will remain constant throughout the centuries. Idealists contend that truth, goodness, and beauty transcend and connect all other ideas and, hence, they are important to all cultures and peoples. Idealists contend that values are unchanging because they underlie all aspects of existence and are perfect (axiology).

EDUCATIONAL IMPLICATIONS OF IDEALISM. The educational philosophy of the idealist is idea centered rather than subject centered or child centered because the ideal, or the idea, is the foundation of all things. Knowledge is directed toward self-consciousness and self-direction and is centered in the growth of rational processes about big ideas. Some idealists note that the individual, who is created in God's image, has free will and that it is this free will that makes learning possible. The idealist believes that learning comes from within the individual rather than from without. Hence, real mental growth and spiritual growth do not occur until they are self-initiated.

What Should We Teach? Idealists' educational beliefs include an emphasis on the study of ideas or great works that persist throughout the ages. They also emphasize the importance of great leaders as examples for us to imitate. For idealists the teacher is the ideal model or example for

Go to the *Assignments and Activities* section of Topic 8: *Philosophy of Education* in the MyEducationLab for your course and complete the activity titled *Write a Subtraction Story*.

idealism A school of philosophy that considers ideas to be the only true reality.

Although the Socratic method dates back to 400 BCE, the art of asking probing questions and using dialogue to enhance learning is still widely used today.

the student. Teachers pass on the cultural heritage and the unchanging content of education, such as knowledge about great figures of the past, the humanities, and a rigorous curriculum.

How Should We Teach? Idealists emphasize the methods of lecture, discussion, and imitation. They believe that thinking clearly and accurately is critical to uncovering the big ideas that account for the universe. So, there is an emphasis on asking questions that spark thought. No one philosopher is an idealist. Rather, philosophers answer questions, and some of their answers are similar. These similarities are what make up the different schools of philosophy. To describe adequately any one school of philosophy, such as idealism, one needs to go beyond these general similarities to examine the subtle differences posed by individual thinkers. Plato and Socrates, Immanuel Kant, and Jane Roland Martin represent different aspects of the idealist tradition.

Matching Ideas from Philosophical Schools to Your Own. Studying the schools of philosophy can guide you in the development of your own philosophy of education. Throughout this chapter, simply jot down any ideas presented by a philosophical school (like idealism) that match your own. Then write down why these ideas make sense to you. You will probably find that ideas from different philosophical schools match your own thinking. So keep track of the school that relates to each idea you select. Because you have just reviewed the ideas of realism concerning what and how to teach, it would be wise to start recording your personal list based on these questions:

- What important knowledge and skills do I think should be taught?
- How should I teach these ideas and skills?

For more about Plato and Socrates, see Chapter 2.

PLATO AND SOCRATES. According to Plato (ca. 427–ca. 347 BCE), truth is the central reality. Truth is perfect; it cannot, therefore, be found in the world of matter because the material world is both imperfect and constantly changing. Plato did not think that people create knowledge; rather, they discover it. In one of his dialogues, he conjectures that humanity once had true knowledge but lost it by being placed in a material body that distorts and corrupts that knowledge. Thus, humans have the arduous task of trying to remember what they once knew.

The modern world knows the philosophy of Socrates only through Plato, who wrote about him in a series of texts called *dialogues*. Socrates (ca. 470–399 BCE) spoke of himself as a midwife who found humans pregnant with knowledge—knowledge that had not been born or realized. This Socratic "Doctrine of Reminiscence" speaks directly to the role of the educator. Teachers need to question students in such a way as to help them remember what they have forgotten. In the dialogue *Meno*, Plato describes Socrates' meeting a slave boy and through skillful questions leading the boy to realize that he knows the Pythagorean theorem, even though he does not know that he knows it. This emphasis on bringing forth knowledge from students through artful questioning is sometimes called the Socratic method.

IMMANUEL KANT. The German philosopher Immanuel Kant (1724–1804), in the *Metaphysics of Morals and the Critique of Practical Reason*, spelled out his idealistic philosophy. Kant believed in freedom, the immortality of the soul, and the existence of God. He wrote extensively on human reason and noted that the only way humankind can know things is through the process of reason. Hence, reality is not a thing unto itself but the interaction of reason and external sensations. Reason fits perceived objects into classes or categories according to similarities and differences. It is only through reason that we acquire knowledge of the world. Once again, it is the idea or the way that the mind works that precedes the understanding of reality.

JANE ROLAND MARTIN. Often labeled a feminist scholar, Jane Roland Martin (1929–) is a contemporary disciple of Plato's dialogues. In "Reclaiming a Conversation," Jane Roland Martin (1985) describes how women have historically been excluded from the "conversation" that constitutes Western educational thought. Martin advocates a return to Plato's approach. Dialogues such as the *Apology*, the *Crito*, and the *Phaedo* illustrate educated persons—well-meaning people of good faith, people who trust and like one another, people who might even be called friends— getting together and trying to talk ideas through to a reasonable conclusion. They engage in conversation, learning something from one another and from the conversation itself.

For Martin, to be educated is to engage in a conversation that stretches back in time. Education is not simply something that occurs in a specific building at a specific time. Nor is it simply training or preparation for the next stage in life. Education is the development of the intellectual and moral habits, through the give-and-take of the conversation, that ultimately give "place and character to every human activity and utterance." Education—the conversation—is the place where one comes to learn what it is to be a person.

RESEARCH ON THE USE OF SOCRATIC DIALOGUE TO ENHANCE REFLECTIVE LEARNING. The ancient philosophers Socrates and Plato believed that learning is best achieved through dialogue. When using Socratic dialogue, the teacher does not teach a subject by direct exposition. Instead, learners' beliefs are challenged by the teacher through a series of questions that lead learners to reflect on their beliefs, induce general principles, and discover gaps and contradictions in their beliefs. Using this type of questioning strategy is difficult when attempting to teach precise mathematical, scientific relationships so researchers set up a study in a science class to see if Socratic dialogue was effective in teaching science concepts (Kor, Self, & Tait, 2001).

In the Kor et al. (2001) study, students were asked to investigate a spring balance system on their own. The spring balance system models an experimental apparatus that verifies Archimedes' principle in a physics laboratory. One group of students investigated the spring balance system with the help of a teacher who assumed the role of a Socratic tutor and who prescribed immediate and intelligent feedback based on the Socratic questioning method. A second group of students investigated the spring balance system with the help of a Socratic tutor as well as the assistance of an articulation tool that provided direct instruction about problems similar to the spring balance system problem. After both groups of students investigated the spring balance system, students were post-tested. Results showed that all students improved their understanding of Archimedes' principle. However, students who received only the help of Socratic dialogue improved their understanding on a surface level and did not achieve a more abstract understanding of critical attributes. Students who were assisted by both Socratic dialogue and carefully structured problems significantly improved both surface level and abstract understanding concerning Archimedes' principle.

This research shows that Socratic dialogue is an effective teaching tool even in science. When teachers guide the development of students' understandings, learning occurs. However, when teachers wish to help students understand technical, abstract principles, Socratic dialogue needs to be enhanced by carefully structured, supporting problems that are designed to make explicit to the learner underlying critical entities that might be missed.

Realism

Realism's roots lie in the thinking of Aristotle. **Realism** is a school of philosophy that holds that reality, knowledge, and value exist independent of the human mind. In other words, realists reject the idealist notion that ideas are the ultimate reality. Figure 4.3 illustrates the dualistic positions of idealism and realism.

Every piece of the physical world is composed of matter. Matter takes on many forms or structures and this is what accounts for the different components that compose the world. The reason things look different from one another is due to the form that structures their matter (metaphysics).

Realists endorse the use of the senses and scientific investigation (reason) to find truth in the physical world. Knowing involves both sensation (taking in information through the senses) and abstraction (pulling out the underlying principles). By pulling out these underlying characteristics or principles, one can then classify things into different groups. Aristotle claims that the art of thinking well is to be able to distinguish things based on essential differences (epistemology).

realism A school of philosophy that holds that reality, knowledge, and value exist independent of the human mind. In contrast to the idealist, the realist contends that physical entities exist in their own right.

FIGURE 4.3

Dualistic Positions of Idealism and Realism

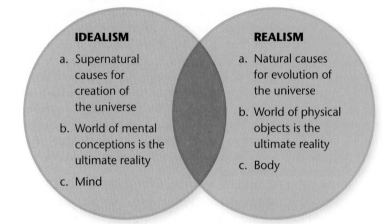

More information about realist-based curriculum and instruction can be found in Chapter 12.

Values and norms come from rights and responsibilities that derive from rational thinking. Because human beings have the ability to reason, then values and norms are those that are logical and consistent with the physical nature of the world. By studying the world logically, natural laws can be uncovered and values are derived from these natural laws (axiology).

EDUCATIONAL IMPLICATIONS OF REALISM. Contemporary realists emphasize the importance of scientific research and development. Curriculum has reflected the impact of these realist thinkers through the appearance of standardized tests, serialized textbooks, and a specialized curriculum in which the disciplines are seen as separate areas of investigation.

What Should We Teach? Realists contend that the ultimate goal of education is advancement of human rationality. Schools can promote rationality by requiring students to study organized bodies of knowledge, by teaching methods of arriving at this knowledge, and by assisting students to reason critically through observation and experimentation. Teachers must have specific knowledge about a subject so that they can order it in such a way as to teach it rationally. They must also have a broad background to show relationships that exist among all fields of knowledge. Thus, the realist curriculum would be a subject-centered curriculum and would include natural science, social science, humanities, and instrumental subjects such as logic and inductive reasoning.

How Should We Teach? Realists place considerable importance on the role of the teacher in the educational process. The teacher should be a person who presents content in a systematic and organized way and should promote the idea that there are clearly defined criteria one can use in making judgments (axiology). Realist teachers would emphasize the importance of teaching students to use experimental and observational techniques. In the school setting, they would teach logical, clear content and clarify how things differ from one another by classifying them. Realists would support careful testing of students' knowledge.

Matching Ideas from Realism to Your Own. As noted earlier in this chapter, studying the schools of philosophy can guide you in the development of your own philosophy of education. As you review the educational implications for realism, you will see that there are similarities between what realists say is important and what idealists also say is important. What differs is that realists recognize that ideas change, whereas idealists contend that ideas remain the same. Therefore, when it comes to teaching thinking skills, realists value experimental and observational thinking more than idealists would. Take time to reflect on realism and select what you think is worth teaching and how it should be taught.

Keep in mind that although we have described a number of general characteristics of realism, they can never fully capture the thinking of the individual philosophers who compose the school. It is important to examine the ideas of individual realist thinkers: Aristotle, Locke, and Whitehead.

ARISTOTLE. Aristotle (384–322 BCE) thought that ideas (forms) are found through the study of the world of matter. He believed that one could acquire knowledge of ideas or forms by investigating matter. To understand an object, one must understand its absolute form, which is unchanging. To the realist, the trees of the forest exist whether or not there is a human mind to perceive them. This is an example of an independent reality. Although the idea of a flower can exist without matter, matter cannot exist without form. Hence, each tulip shares universal properties with every other tulip and every other flower. However, the particular properties of a tulip differentiate it from all other flowers. Aristotle's writings are known for their analytic approach. In contrast to Plato, whose writings are in the form of a conversation, Aristotle took great care to write with precision.

JOHN LOCKE. John Locke (1632–1704) believed in the *tabula rasa* (blank tablet) view of the mind. Locke stated that the mind of a person is blank at birth and that the person's sensory experiences make impressions on this blank tablet. Locke distinguished between sense data and the objects they represent. The objects, or things people know, are independent of the mind or the knower insofar as thought refers to them and not merely to sense data. Ideas (round, square, tall) represent objects. Locke claimed that primary qualities (such as shapes) represent the world, whereas secondary qualities (such as colors) have a basis in the world but do not represent it.

> The little or almost insensible impressions on our tender infancies have very important and lasting consequences: and there it is, as in the fountains of some rivers, where a gentle application of the hand turns the flexible waters into channels, that make them at first, in the source, they receive different tendencies, and arrive at last at very remote and distant places.
>
> I imagine the minds of children as easily turned, this or that way, as water itself; and though this be the principal part and our main care should be about the inside yet the clay cottage is not to be neglected. (Locke, 1812)

ALFRED NORTH WHITEHEAD. Alfred North Whitehead (1861–1947), a philosopher and mathematician, attempted to reconcile some conflicting tenets of idealism and realism. He proposed "process" to be the central aspect of realism. Unlike Locke, Whitehead did not see objective reality and subjective mind as separate. He saw them as an organic unity that operates by its own principles. The universe is characterized by patterns, and these patterns can be verified and analyzed through mathematics.

> Culture is activity of thought and receptiveness to beauty and humane feelings. Scraps of information have nothing to do with it. . . . In training a child to activity of thought, above all things we must beware of what I will call "inert ideas"—that is to say, ideas that are merely received into the mind without being used, or tested, or thrown into fresh combinations.
>
> In the history of education, the most striking phenomenon is the schools of learning, which at one epoch are alive with a ferment of genius, in a succeeding generation exhibit merely pedantry and routine. The reason is that they are overladen with inert ideas. Education with inert ideas is not only useless: it is, above all things, harmful—Corruptio optimi, pessima. (Whitehead, 1929)

Pragmatism

Pragmatism's roots come from the thinking of a number of nineteenth-century American philosophers including Charles S. Peirce (1839–1914), William James (1842–1910), and John Dewey (1859–1952). **Pragmatism** is a process philosophy that stresses evolving and change rather than being. It differs from most forms of idealism and realism by a belief in an open universe that is dynamic, evolving, and in a state of becoming. There are no unchanging ideas (idealism) nor are there universal laws (realism). Because the underlying principle that explains the universe is change, many pragmatists claim that a metaphysical foundation for their thinking is unverifiable.

Because change is so important, pragmatists place a great deal of emphasis on the importance of understanding what it means to know. To the pragmatist, knowing is a transaction or a conversation between the learner and the environment. This transaction or conversation between learner and environment alters or changes both the learner and the world. Like the realist, the pragmatist believes that we learn best through experience, but pragmatists believe that the experience changes both the knower and the world. Whereas realists are concerned with passing organized bodies of knowledge from one generation to the next, pragmatists stress applying knowledge—using ideas as instruments for problem solving (epistemology).

pragmatism A late-nineteenth-century U.S. school of philosophy that stresses becoming rather than being.

More information about pragmatist-based curriculum and instruction can be found in Chapter 12.

Wedded as they are to change and adaptation, pragmatists do not believe in absolute and unchanging truth or values. Because we live in a constantly changing universe, values change too. What contributes to personal and social growth is the only underlying principle. We can clarify values by testing them and reconstructing them as needed. Values that work at one time or in one place or in one society might not work in another (axiology).

EDUCATIONAL IMPLICATIONS OF PRAGMATISM. Pragmatists stress the changing nature of reality. There are no absolutes and hence the teacher needs to help students learn to question what is and solve problems as they naturally occur. Realists and idealists call for a curriculum centered on academic disciplines, but pragmatists prefer a curriculum that draws the disciplines together to solve problems—an interdisciplinary approach. Pragmatists emphasize that truth is found in the real world, which is always changing. So, it is critical to present concepts as they relate to contemporary problems and questions. Figure 4.4 illustrates the relationships among realism, idealism, and pragmatism.

What Should We Teach? Because the world is always in flux, knowledge is subject to revision, so it is more important to know how to construct, use, and test knowledge claims. For pragmatists the most important thing to know is how to question what we know and how to reconstruct what we know to match the changing world. Therefore, pragmatists are less interested in transmitting large bodies of information; rather, they favor solving problems through interacting with the environment in an intelligent and reflective manner. Teaching students to use methods of scientific inquiry is a high priority.

How Should We Teach? Pragmatists view the school as a community of learners. Cultural diversity enriches society just as physical diversity enriches the universe. So, schools should use integrated and democratic teaching and learning approaches. Because the process of problem solving is more important than teaching specific subject matter, pragmatists prefer the use of learner-centered problems as a teaching focus. Facilitating student investigations and activities, providing technology and other resources, and encouraging students to collaborate as a learning community are the key characteristics of a worthy teaching approach.

Matching Ideas from Pragmatism to Your Own. Now take a moment to record the key ideas from pragmatism that match your own. You will find that pragmatism has components of both idealism and realism. For example, pragmatists value the development of theories or ideas (like idealism); they also note that ideas change and are subject to experimental and observational techniques (like realism). However, pragmatists contend that there are no underlying principles that account for the world other than the concept of change. This notion is not held by either realists or idealists.

FIGURE 4.4

Relationship of Realism, Idealism, and Pragmatism

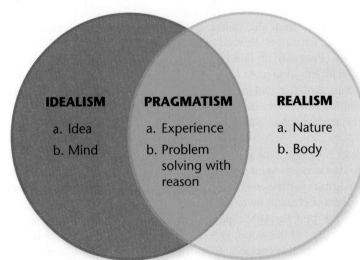

CHARLES SANDERS PEIRCE. Charles Sanders Peirce (1839–1914) is one of the earliest pragmatist thinkers. He introduced the principle that belief is a habit of action undertaken to overcome indecisiveness. He believed that the purpose of thought is to produce action and that the meaning of a thought is the collection of results of actions. For example, to say that steel is "hard" is to mean that when the operation of scratch testing is performed on steel, it will not be scratched by most substances. The aims of Peirce's pragmatic method are to supply a procedure for constructing and clarifying meanings and to facilitate communication.

JOHN DEWEY. Early in his philosophical development, John Dewey (1859–1952) related pragmatism to evolution by explaining that human beings are creatures who have to adapt to one another and to their environments. Dewey viewed life as a series of overlapping and interpenetrating experiences and situations, each of which has its own complete identity. The primary unit of life is the individual experience.

Dewey wrote the following passage early in his career. In it he shows his zeal for education as a social force in human affairs.

> I believe that all education proceeds by the participation of the individual in the social consciousness of the race. This process begins unconsciously almost at birth, and is continually shaping the individual's powers, saturating his consciousness, forming his habits, training his ideas, and arousing his feelings and emotions.
>
> In sum, I believe that the individual is a social individual and that society is an organic union of individuals. If we eliminate the social factor from the child we are left only with an abstraction; if we eliminate the individual factor from society, we are left only with an inert and lifeless mass. (Dewey, 1897)

RICHARD RORTY. Richard Rorty (1931–2007) was a contemporary pragmatist philosopher who spent much of his life reinventing the work of John Dewey in light of the chaotic, ever-changing view of the world. Rorty contended that reality is not fixed, and it is the task of thinkers to come up with a procedure for correctly describing the nature of reality. He argued that reality is the outcome of inquiry, and as human inquiry shifts so too will the nature of what we call *real*. Rorty contended that different disciplines have different avenues for studying the world and therefore these avenues of inquiry create different realities. The way an artist looks at the world and creates a work of art and the way a chemist looks at the world and develops a new way of looking at molecules both affect the very nature of what *is*. Essential to this point of view is the understanding that disciplines such as science, mathematics, art, and history are not rooted in a fixed reality but are constructed by groups of people who are trying to make sense of the world. Hence, disciplines are arbitrary contrivances and one discipline is as good as another. Also, because disciplines are created by persons, they are subject to all the foibles, limitations, and prejudices of any human convention.

Although Rorty did not speak directly to the field of education, his work provides a significant challenge to teachers. No longer can teachers represent expert knowledge as accurate or as true. Rather, expert knowledge is the current agreement of scholars at this point in time. Expert knowledge is simply a set of ideas and procedures that have been found to be useful. Rorty contended that a thinker should no longer be represented as a discoverer; rather, a thinker is more of a maker or cobbler who crafts meaning. People come together, agree on certain things, and then try to talk or reason their way to a sensible conclusion. Expertise is more a matter of "usefulness" than truth.

Existentialism

One way of understanding the heart of existentialism is to ponder a quote from Jean-Paul Sartre: "Existence precedes essence." **Existentialism** contends that reality is nothing more than lived existence, and the final reality resides within each individual. There is nothing absolute, not even change. There is no ultimate principle or meaning.

Existentialists believe that we live an alien, meaningless existence on a small planet in an unimportant galaxy in an indifferent universe. Each individual is the creator of her or his essence; each individual is the creator of her or his meaning. Whereas some people might be paralyzed by this view, existentialists are energized by their quest to clarify their identity and create meaning. You might say that the very meaninglessness of life compels us to instill life with meaning (metaphysics).

Knowing is a personal reflective process to existentialists. Existentialists accept the usefulness of scientific knowledge about the physical and psychological world, but they contend that this knowledge is limited. The most significant knowledge is personal and nonscientific. Knowledge is about the human condition and the personal choices that each human makes (epistemology).

existentialism A school of philosophy that focuses on the importance of the individual rather than on external standards.

More information about existentialism-based curriculum and instruction can be found in Chapter 12.

The key value for the existentialist is that human beings are free to make choices. However, this freedom is wrapped up in a search for meaning. We define ourselves; that is, we make meaning in our world by the choices we make. In effect, we are what we choose. We can choose to give up our freedom and allow others to define us or we can choose to be inner directed and authentic (axiology).

EDUCATIONAL IMPLICATIONS OF EXISTENTIALISM. The existentialist believes that most schools, like other corporate symbols, de-emphasize the individual and the relationship between the teacher and the student. Existentialists claim that when educators attempt to predict the behavior of students, they turn individuals into objects to be measured, quantified, and processed. Existentialists tend to feel that tracking, measurement, and standardization militate against the creation of opportunities for self-direction and personal choice.

What Should We Teach? According to the existentialist, education ought to be a process of developing a free, self-actualizing person—a process centered on the feelings of the student. Therefore, proper education does not start with the nature of the world and with humankind, but with the human individual or self. At school, students should be encouraged to discuss their lives and the choices they are making. Because we all live in the same meaningless predicament, we can learn by asking questions of one another, suggesting answers to concerns, and engaging in dialogue.

How Should We Teach? The existentialist educator would be a free personality engaged in projects that treat students as free personalities. The highest educational goal is to search for oneself. Teachers and students experience existential crises; each such crisis involves an examination of oneself and one's life purposes. Education helps to fill in the gaps with understanding that the student needs in order to fulfill those purposes; it is not a mold to which the student must be fitted. Students define themselves by their choices.

The existentialist student would have a questioning attitude and would be involved in a continuing search for self and for the reasons for existence. The existentialist teacher would help students become what they themselves want to become, not what outside forces such as society, other teachers, or parents want them to become.

Matching Ideas from Existentialism to Your Own. The ideas of existentialism are more difficult to apply to education in that they focus so much on the individual development of a person rather than on the transmittal of ideas and concepts about the world. However, existentialism does provide a perspective about the importance of responding to individual ways of thinking and understanding that is not evident in realism, idealism, or pragmatism. So, take a moment to consider the ideas of existentialism and those that match your own. Then write down why these ideas make sense to you. Remember to organize your personal list based on these questions:

- What important knowledge and skills do I think should be taught?
- How should I teach these ideas and skills?

Existentialist thinkers are as varied as the notions of individual thought and self-defined meaning would suggest. There are atheistic existentialists as represented by Jean-Paul Sartre, critical existentialists as exemplified by Friedrich Nietzsche, and humanistic existentialists such as Maxine Greene.

JEAN-PAUL SARTRE. Modern existentialism was born amidst the pain and disillusionment of World War II. Jean-Paul Sartre (1905–1980) broke with previous philosophers and asserted that existence (being) comes before essence (meaning).

Sartre saw no difference between being free and being human. This view opens great possibilities, yet it also creates feelings of dread and nausea as one recognizes the reality of nonbeing and death as well as the great responsibilities that accompany such radical freedom to shape oneself out of one's choices. The process of answering the question "Who are we?" begins at a crucial event in the lives of young people called the existential moment—that point somewhere toward the end of youth when individuals realize for the first time that they exist as independent agents.

FRIEDRICH NIETZSCHE. Friedrich Nietzsche (1844–1900) is an existential philosopher who stresses the importance of the individuality of persons. Throughout his writings, Nietzsche indicts the supremacy of herd values in modern democratic social systems. He criticizes the way social systems such as modern educational institutions foster a spirit of capitalistic greed. When

Nietzsche turns his attention primarily to social systems, human beings are portrayed much more as victims of social dynamics than as inferior or superior beings.

In Nietzsche's texts there is a strategy to liberate people from the oppression of feeling inferior within themselves, a teaching of how not to judge what one is in relation to what one should be. Although Nietzsche did not author a comprehensive teaching methodology, he teaches how to cultivate a healthy love of self-care, a taste for solitude, a perspective on perspective, literacy as a vital capacity, and an overall gratitude for one's existence. Nietzsche observed that most teachers and parents

> . . . hammer even into children that what matters is something quite different: the salvation of the soul, the service of the state, the advancement of science, or the accumulation of reputation and possessions, all as the means of doing service to mankind as a whole; while the requirements of the individual, his great and small needs within the twenty-four hours of the day, are to be regarded as something contemptible or a matter of indifference. (Nietzsche, 1986)

MAXINE GREENE. A theme that permeates most of Maxine Greene's work is her unyielding faith in human beings' willingness to build and transcend their lived worlds. To Greene (1917–) philosophy is a deeply personal and aesthetic experience. Her writing blurs the distinction between philosophy and literature. This is appropriate because Greene contends that living is philosophy. Greene (1988) asserts that schools must be places that offer "an authentic public space where diverse human beings can appear before one another as best they know to be."

The existentialist philosophy is one that supports the importance of humans developing their personal identities and determining what is and is not significant and worthy. In the above quote, Maxine Green states that schools are a place where diverse human beings can appear before others as they authentically see themselves. Many schools have policies about personal attire. The Teacher Perspective Feature explores the issue of requiring teachers to wear business attire in the classroom.

JOURNAL FOR REFLECTION

Now that you have developed a list of ideas from each of the classical philosophical schools that match your own, develop a paragraph that analyzes which philosophies tend to include the most similarities and the fewest to your own thinking.

EASTERN AND NATIVE NORTH AMERICAN WAYS OF KNOWING

Most studies of Western philosophy typically begin with the Greek philosophers. Yet there is evidence that Platonic philosophy owed much of its development to Eastern thinkers who emphasized the illusory quality of the physical world. In addition, native peoples from many lands have developed a way of thinking about life and education that extends and reorganizes the writing of Western thinkers. To ignore such ways of knowing would violate the very nature of philosophy that, as noted at the beginning of this chapter, is a search for truth.

Eastern Ways of Knowing

Although there are differences among the writings of the Far Eastern and Near Eastern philosophers, **Eastern ways of knowing**, as a group, stress inner peace, tranquility, attitudinal development, and mysticism. In general, Eastern ways of knowing emphasize order, regularity, and patience that are proportional to and in harmony with the laws of nature.

Western philosophy tends to emphasize logic and materialism; on the other hand, Eastern ways of knowing stress the inner rather than the outer world, intuition rather than sense, and mysticism rather than scientific discoveries. Western philosophers tend to begin with the outer, material world and abstract to concepts and underlying principles; Eastern ways of knowing begin with the inner world and then reach to the outer world of phenomena.

It is sometimes charged that Eastern ways of knowing are not philosophies but religions. Because the Eastern ways of knowing have such early beginnings and maintain a strong bent toward the spiritual side of nature, their stories maintain a language of gods and goddesses, much like Greek mythology. Unlike the Greeks, who tried to separate philosophy from religion, Eastern

Eastern ways of knowing A varied set of ideas, beliefs, and values from the Far and Near East that stress inner peace, tranquility, attitudinal development, and mysticism. When a man has pity on all living creatures, then only is he noble.

Should Teachers Wear Business Attire to School?

School districts differ in their policies regarding what type of attire teachers must wear. Because clothing is often considered a symbol of one's identity, the issue of wearing business attire is controversial.

YES

Ray Waters teaches English at Gulf Breeze High School in Gulf Breeze, Florida.

If educators want to be paid and treated as professionals, we should carry ourselves as professionals. An already tarnished image of public education is further sullied by teachers who choose to enter a classroom dressed for a day at the beach or for yard work.

Business attire in the classroom portrays an image of an educator who is proud of the work he or she does. What degree of respect can teachers expect to receive if they don't dress like adult role models intent on providing the very best education for their students? Would a doctor see patients in shorts and a T-shirt? Would an attorney enter a courtroom with flip-flops and Capri pants? Would a businessperson attend a corporate board meeting in a warm-up suit?

Our school, as with most high schools, has theme days—pep rally Fridays and homecoming week—when casual, or even bizarre, dress is encouraged. However, when the "fun" is over, school administrators should ensure that the faculty dress appropriately for the classroom. The job of an administrator is to create a culture at a school that accepts nothing short of the most professional behavior. Appropriate dress is not the only quality of professionalism, but it is the most conspicuous.

Evaluation instruments should include sections on professional dress. Warm-up suits, jeans, Birkenstocks, T-shirts, and Hawaiian print shirts are the daily attire of a few members of our faculty. High school students are mature enough to see hypocrisy. If students are required to meet an appropriate standard of dress, why aren't educators?

If educators are ever to enjoy the respect of the public and the compensation we deserve, let's start with something we can control. Let's outwardly show our pride in our profession by implementing dress codes for teachers.

NO

Eileen Elrod is a guidance counselor for Grayson County Schools in Virginia.

Form follows function and never is that more true than in defining "professional attire" in a school setting. Our duties are as varied as our job descriptions and attire must follow accordingly.

I will not forget the day I smugly walked down the hall after breakfast duty, proudly wearing my new dress pants and blouse, only to look down to see the label from a student's breakfast syrup container stuck to my pants. I've also learned that the red paint used in lower grades bonds permanently to better clothing.

My vest of bright green fabric depicting construction tractors might not portray the most professional air, but it stimulates children to talk. The merits of each tractor and brand have been described at length by even the quietest child. These were students who had been shy and uncertain of themselves. The vest got them talking.

Weaving dog and cat buttons into my shoelaces would not make a favorable impression in the corporate world, but it entertains young children who sit on the rug for a story.

My winter coat must lie either on a chair or on the floor because no closet or coat rack is available. Even those fortunate enough to have closets find them so full the doors won't close. Therefore, we wear washable work jackets.

I allow school spirit to override stereotyped professionalism when I wear the sweatshirts that are gifts from the wrestling team and coach. The gift of popular clothing is priceless and wearing these items tells team members, "You are important."

When choosing how we will dress our primary thought must be for our children and the tasks we do. We should not select clothing to make a fashion statement. Clothing is part of our curriculum.

Source: "Should Teachers Wear Business Attire to School?" *NEA Today* (February 2006), p. 45. Reprinted by permission of the National Education Association.

What is your perspective on this issue?

myeducationlab To explore both sides of this issue and think about each perspective, go to the *Book Specific Resources* section in the MyEducationLab for your course, select your text, and then select *Teacher Perspectives* for Chapter 4.

thinkers intertwined religious doctrines with philosophical views about the nature of the world and humans' interactions with it.

Eastern thinkers have always concerned themselves with education, which they view as a way of achieving wisdom, maintaining family structure, establishing law, and providing for social and economic concerns. Instruction includes the things that one must do to achieve the good life, and education is viewed as necessary not only for this life but also for achievement of the good life hereafter.

One good reason to study Eastern ways of knowing is that they offer vantage points from which to examine Western thought. Eastern ideas encourage one to question seriously the Western world's most basic commitments to science, materialism, and reason. Although we could analyze many more different types of Eastern thinking, we focus here on the ideas of the Far East

REFLECTonDIVERSITY   Curriculum and Eastern Ways of Knowing

Chi Mae Lin was thrilled to find out that she had been selected to participate in the curriculum committee at her rural high school in southern Nevada. She had been working as a Junior-Senior English teacher for only two years and she knew that this appointment was a sign that her teaching and professional conduct were making a difference in the minds of her colleagues. At the first meeting, committee members were asked to develop a required reading list for a specific course in an effort to keep the curriculum current and compatible with academic standards. Chi Mae was asked to prepare the reading list for Junior English.

After reviewing the current required reading list, Chi Mae noticed that all of the readings were written by American and European authors. So, she selected two new readings, one written by an author from Japan and another written by an author from Tibet. Her rationale for this change was based on the importance of expanding the students' perspectives about the nature of the world and humans' relationship to it.

On the day that Chi Mae made this proposal to the curriculum committee, she was surprised to find that the committee members were unimpressed with her selection. In fact, the committee's response

to her proposal seemed to generate hostility rather than debate. One committee member, with raised voice, shouted at her: "Why did you select two authors from the Middle East? Don't you know you are working with rural students living in the United States? The original documents are translations and were not even written in English."

Questions for Reflection
1. Why do you think Chi Mae thought that Japanese and Tibetan authors might expand students' perspectives about the nature of the world?
2. What did the committee member mean by reminding Chi Mae that she was working with rural students in the United States?
3. In what way would ideas from a piece of literature written in a different language offer students a new perspective?
4. Would it have been better if Chi Mae had suggested writings that were originally written in English by an American author with Japanese or Tibetan background? Why or why not?

myeducationlab To respond to these questions online, go to the *Book Specific Resources* section in the MyEducationLab for your course, select your text, and then select *Reflect on Diversity* for Chapter 4.

or Eastern Asia including India, China, and Japan because of their long, relatively stable traditions, enormous land area, and immense population. Consider the implications that Eastern ways of knowing have for curriculum in the Reflect on Diversity Feature.

INDIAN THOUGHT. Far Eastern Indian thought has a long, complex history and is permeated by opposites. To Western philosophers, opposites need to be reconciled, but to the Eastern mind, this need for consistency is unimportant. For example, great emphasis is placed on a search for wisdom, but this does not mean a rejection of worldly pleasures. Though speculation is emphasized, it has a practical character. Far Eastern Indian thinkers insist that knowledge be used to improve both social and communal life and that people should live according to their ideals. In Far Eastern Indian thought, there is a prevailing sense of universal moral justice, according to which individuals are responsible for what they are and what they become (Ozman & Craver, 2008).

CHINESE THOUGHT. The emphasis of Far Eastern Chinese philosophy is on harmony; correct thinking should help one achieve harmony with life. This harmony of government, business, and family should then lead toward a higher synthesis. Confucianism and Taoism provide two major contexts for Chinese thought.

For more than two thousand years, Confucian thought has influenced education, government, and culture in China. Confucius (551–479 BCE) believed that people need standards for all of life, so rules were developed for a wide range of activities. Confucian thought gives education a high place, but stresses building moral character more than merely teaching skills or imparting information. This moral approach has a practical component. Children should obey and defer to parents and respect the wisdom adults have gained in their journey through life. Following these principles enables children to become *chun-tzu*, persons distinguished by faithfulness, diligence, and modesty.

The central concept of Taoism is that of the "Tao," the Way or Path. The Tao is the way the universe moves, the way of perfection and harmony. It is conformity with nature. Perhaps the most significant aspect of the Tao is letting things alone, not forcing personal desires onto the natural course of events. It is a noncompetitive approach to life. Taoists believe that conflict and war represent basic failures in society, for they bring ruin to states and a disrespect for life.

JAPANESE THOUGHT. Japanese thought is rooted in Shinto, a way of thinking that recognizes the significance of the natural world. This respect for all nature permeates Japanese thought and life. Shinto accepts the phenomenal world (the world people apprehend through their senses) as absolute; this acceptance leads to a disposition to place greater emphasis on intuitive, sensible, concrete events rather than on universal ideas. On the social level, Japanese express this focus on the natural world through many artifacts, including the patterns of traditional kimonos. Within the house, flowers are arranged in vases and dwarf trees placed in alcoves, flowers and birds are engraved on lintels, and nature scenes are painted on sliding screens. Consider the fabric of Eastern ways of knowing in the Global Perspective Feature.

GLOBAL PERSPECTIVES — The Fabric of Eastern Ways of Knowing

Eastern thought is like a rich fabric of diverse ideas. It emphasizes sets of views that are quite different from the neat categorizations of Western thought. Eastern thought suggests that cohesive views can be achieved without the necessity of neat, hierarchically distinct categories. Although they are quite difficult to summarize, the philosophy and thought of the East suggest new ways of looking at long-accepted meanings and assumptions. As such, the study of Eastern thought is an important part of all future educators' preparation in an increasingly multicultural society.

Questions for Reflection
1. In what ways do Eastern ways of knowing affect character education programs?
2. What values would receive greater or lesser emphasis?

EDUCATIONAL IMPLICATIONS OF EASTERN WAYS OF KNOWING. Eastern educational thought places great emphasis on the teacher–student relationship. Change springs from this relationship; that is, the student is changed as a result of contact with the guru, master, or prophet. Eastern educational thought emphasizes transformation: The individual must be transformed to face life. Attitude shaping is important because the attitude a person holds toward life will determine the individual's levels of goodness and wisdom.

A recurring educational aim in Eastern ways of knowing is to put humanity in tune with nature. There is great emphasis on observing nature and learning through wanderings and pilgrimages. The importance of achieving wisdom, *satori,* enlightenment, or nirvana is supreme. All paths must lead to this, and from this wisdom spring virtue, right living, and correct behavior.

Native North American Ways of Knowing

Native North American ways of knowing A varied set of beliefs, philosophical positions, and customs that span different tribes in North America.

Just as the rich past and diverse cultures make it difficult to summarize Eastern thought, Native North American ways of knowing are equally difficult to synthesize. **Native North American ways of knowing** include a varied set of beliefs, positions, and customs that span different tribes in North America. These beliefs, positions, and customs center on the relationship of humans to all of nature, including the earth, the sun, the sky, and beyond. Because Native North American ways of knowing center on the relationship of humans to all of nature, it is sometimes difficult to separate knowing from a way of life. In fact, to understand is to live and to develop an ever closer, more profound human-to-nature relationship. The types of relationships and the symbols that inform these human-to-nature relationships differ widely among tribes.

Although Native North American ways of knowing differ across the four hundred–plus tribes in North America, these ways of knowing do have similar elements. They all include traditional stories and beliefs that dictate a way of

Native North American ways of knowing provide a perspective that connects knowledge to the earth that surrounds us and of which we are a part.

knowing and living. All include a reverence for nature and a sense of humans' responsibility to nature. And all groups make reference to a supreme being—although the names are different, the relationships vary, and the expectations of some supreme beings are interpreted through natural elements. Thus, the Black Hills are sacred to the Lakota, the turtle is revered as Mother Earth by the Ojibwa, and so on. Native North American ways of knowing are orally developed rather than written. Hence, they change slightly from age to age. Additionally, the ways of knowing are subject to interpretation by the shaman, or holy one.

For more about Native North American ways of knowing, see Chapter 6.

NAVAJO THOUGHT FOCUSES ON HARMONY AND INNER FORMS. The Navajo nation is the largest tribe in the United States. The Navajos' early history was nomadic, and their thoughts and customs are known for their unique ability to assimilate with and adapt to the thought and customs of other tribes. As with most Native North American cultures, the Navajo universe is an all-inclusive unity viewed as an orderly system of interrelated elements. At the basis of Navajo teachings and traditions is the value of a life lived in harmony with the natural world. Such a view enables one to "walk in beauty." To understand the Navajo worldview, one must note the teachings of the "inner forms" of things. These inner forms were set in place by First Man and First Woman. The concept of inner form is similar to the concept of a spirit or soul; without it, the Navajos say, the outer forms would be dead (Wilson, 1994a).

LAKOTA THOUGHT FOCUSES ON ONENESS WITH THE ENVIRONMENT. The Native American culture of the Great Plains, of which the Lakota form part, is based on mystical participation with the environment. All aspects of this ecosystem, including earth, sky, night, day, sun, and moon, are elements of the oneness within which life was undertaken. The Lakota celebrate the "sacred hoop of life" and observe seven sacred rites toward the goal of ultimate communion with Wakan-Tanka, the great Spirit (Wilson, 1994b).

HOPI THOUGHT FOCUSES ON A JOURNEY. The Hopi follow the path of peace, which they believe is a pure and perfect pattern of humankind's evolutionary journey. The Road of Life of the Hopi is represented as a journey through seven universes created at the beginning. At death the conduct of a person in accordance with the Creator's plan determines when and where the next step on the road will be taken. Each of the Hopi clans has a unique role to play, and each role is an essential part of the whole. Hopis must live in harmony with one another, with nature, and with the plan. Out of this complex interplay, then, the plan is both created and allowed to unfold.

> We feel that the world is good. We are grateful to be alive. We are conscious that all men are brothers. We sense that we are related to other creatures. Life is to be valued and preserved. If you see a grain of corn on the ground, pick it up and take care of it, because it has life inside. When you go out of your house in the morning and see the sun rising, pause a moment to think about it. When you take water from a spring, be aware that it is a gift of nature. (Albert Yava, Big Falling Snow, Hopi). (Wilson, 1994c)

EDUCATIONAL IMPLICATIONS OF NATIVE NORTH AMERICAN WAYS OF KNOWING. Native North American educational thought emphasizes the importance of nature. The pursuit of knowledge and happiness must be subordinate to a respect for the whole universe. To know is to understand one's place in the natural order of things. To be is to celebrate through ritual and stories the spirit that informs all reality. These principles encourage educators to study the physical and social world by examining the natural relationships that exist among things, animals, and humans. Studying ideas in the abstract or as independent entities is not as important as understanding the relationships among ideas and the physical reality. Native American thought supports the use of hands-on learning, making connections, holding discussions, and celebrating the moment. In fact, these very educational approaches are supported by many best practice educational research studies (Bransford, Brown, & Cocking, 2000; Donovan & Bransford, 2005).

Matching Ideas from Eastern and Native North American Ways of Knowing to Your Own. The ideas of Eastern and Native North American ways share a number of similarities. They both show a reverence for the world in which we live and value the importance of harmony with nature and each other. However, there are many different nuances to this theme based on the geographical location of writers (India, China, and Japan) as well as the tribe to which Native writers belong

(Cherokee, Lakota, and Hopi). So, take moment to consider the ideas of Eastern and Native American thinkers and determine which ones match your own. Then, write down why these ideas make sense to you. Remember to organize your personal list based on these questions:

- What important knowledge and skills do I think should be taught?
- How should I teach these ideas and skills?

━━━━━━━ **JOURNAL FOR REFLECTION** ━━━━━━━

Consider the four components of analytic and prophetic thinking as described in the first part of this chapter. Then, describe which aspects of these types of Western thinking fit Eastern and Native North American native ways of knowing.

LOOKING AHEAD: INCREASED EMPHASIS ON THE DEVELOPMENT OF VALUED DISPOSITIONS

As schools struggle to help students meet state and national standards, there is renewed interest and discussion among educators about the importance of developing more than academic understandings. National professional organizations (such as the National Council of Teachers of Mathematics and the American Association for the Advancement of Science) have called for an increased emphasis on developing characteristics such as curiosity, perseverance, open-mindedness, and inquisitiveness. These valued traits or dispositions are deemed to be important components of school curricula. Unfortunately, it is difficult to teach such dispositions and even more difficult to assess them with paper-and-pencil tests. Despite these difficulties, it is clear that a philosophy of education must include some consideration concerning such dispositions and how they can be developed.

SUMMARY

STRUCTURE AND METHODOLOGY OF PHILOSOPHY

- The study of philosophy permeates every aspect of the teacher's role and provides the underpinning for every decision.
- Philosophy revolves around three major types of questions: those that deal with the nature of reality (metaphysics), those that deal with knowledge and truth (epistemology), and those that deal with values (axiology).
- Decisions about the nature of the subject matter emphasized in a curriculum are metaphysical commitments to reality—what is real?
- Questions related to what is true and how we know are epistemological. Classroom methods are practices that aim to assist learners in acquiring knowledge and truth in the subject area.
- Classroom activities that deal with ethics (what is right or wrong), beauty, and character are in the realm of axiology (values).
- Analytic and prophetic thinking provide two approaches to the process of philosophy. Analytic thinking provides clarity and precision, whereas prophetic thinking fosters breadth and sensitivity.

SCHOOLS OF PHILOSOPHY AND THEIR INFLUENCE ON EDUCATION

- Four classical Western schools of philosophical thought (idealism, realism, pragmatism, and existentialism) were described. For each school of philosophy, representative philosophers and their ideas were provided to give prospective teachers a sense of how they might develop their own educational philosophy.
- Idealism is a school of philosophy that holds that ideas or concepts are the essence of all that is worth knowing. The physical world we know through our senses is only a manifestation or imperfect representation of the spiritual world.

- Realism is a school of philosophy that holds that reality, knowledge, and value exist independent of the human mind. In other words, realists reject the idealist notion that ideas are the ultimate reality.
- Pragmatism is a process philosophy that stresses evolving and change rather than being. It differs from most forms of idealism and realism by a belief in an open universe that is dynamic, evolving, and in a state of becoming.
- Existentialism contends that reality is nothing more than lived existence, and the final reality resides within each individual. There is nothing absolute, not even change. There is no ultimate principle or meaning.

EASTERN AND NATIVE AMERICAN WAYS OF KNOWING

- Eastern ways of knowing stress the inner rather than the outer world, intuition rather than sense, and mysticism rather than scientific discoveries. Order, regularity, and patience that are proportional to and in harmony with the laws of nature are key to a good life.
- Native North American ways of knowing include a varied set of beliefs, positions, and customs that span more than four hundred different tribes in North America. Beliefs, positions, and customs center on the relationship of humans to all of nature, including the earth, the sun, the sky, and beyond. To understand is to live and to develop an ever closer, more profound human-to-nature relationship.
- Both Eastern and Native North American knowing share an underlying sensitivity to nature and an emphasis on wisdom, virtue, spirituality, and harmony within the larger universe.
- The educational implications of these ways of knowing include the importance of teaching respect for the earth and awareness of the interrelationships among all things.

LOOKING AHEAD: INCREASED EMPHASIS ON THE DEVELOPMENT OF VALUED DISPOSITIONS

- As schools struggle to help students meet state and national standards, there is renewed interest and discussion among educators about the importance of developing more than academic understandings.
- National professional organizations (such as the National Council of Teachers of Mathematics and the American Association for the Advancement of Science) have called for an increased emphasis on developing characteristics such as curiosity, perseverance, open-mindedness, and inquisitiveness.

DISCUSSION QUESTIONS

1. How would you describe philosophy to a young child?
2. In your opinion, which is the most important aspect of a given philosophy (for the teacher): the metaphysical component, the epistemological component, or the axiological component? State the rationale for your choice.
3. Early Greek philosophers suggest that all knowledge is based on experience. Discuss the implications of this statement for teaching methodology.
4. Describe the ways that Eastern and Native North American ways of knowing might influence what and how you teach.

SCHOOL-BASED OBSERVATIONS

1. As you visit schools and classrooms, be alert for indications of philosophical concepts and different philosophical views. Examine the lesson plans that teachers have developed and consider whether their focus is on subject matter acquisition, the development of character, or the development of skills. These emphases can be a clue to the type of philosophy that a teacher endorses. You might wish to talk with teachers about their educational ideas.
2. Many schools have written statements describing their philosophy of education. Ask several schools to send you a copy of their philosophy of education. When you receive them, look for similarities and differences among the philosophical statements.
3. As you visit schools and classrooms, focus on the discipline approaches that teachers employ. What do these approaches imply about teachers' views of human nature?

PORTFOLIO DEVELOPMENT

1. According to idealistic philosophy, character education can be enhanced through study and imitation of exemplars/heroes in the historical record. Identify an exemplary educator from history and describe how you could teach character through that person's example. Place your essay in your folio as an example of your teaching methodology.

2. Assist a student as a mentor or tutor. Before beginning, gather samples of the student's thinking and schoolwork. Try to think like the student and by so doing uncover areas in which the student needs help. Develop a diagnosis that details what changes will be beneficial. Place these ideas in your folio as an example of your diagnostic and metacognitive skills.

myeducationlab To begin developing your own personal portfolio, go to the MyEducationLab for your course, select *Resources,* and then *Portfolio Builder.*

PREPARING FOR CERTIFICATION

1. One of the topics in the Praxis II Principles of Learning and Teaching (PLT) test is using "Ongoing personal reflection on teaching and learning practices as a basis for making professional decisions." In this chapter, you learned about two approaches to philosophical thinking—analytic and prophetic—that are useful tools to enhance instructional effectiveness. Think about a specific problem you might face in the subject or grade level you plan to teach. For example, you might not know much about the content in the textbook. Or you don't agree with the information in the textbook. You should select your own problem. Analyze that problem using the two approaches. How does each approach contribute to your understanding of the problem?

2. Answer the following multiple-choice question, which is similar to items in Praxis and other state certification tests.

   Two middle school teachers are discussing their philosophical beliefs about teaching and learning. Jan says, "I think it is very important that all students master an essential body of knowledge; I would like to teach a unit in my subject area that focuses on specific content and make sure that all students master it." Lee says, "I disagree. I think it is more important that students are able to apply knowledge to solve problems. I would teach an interdisciplinary unit that focuses on real issues so students can see how what they are learning applies to the real world." Lee's position more closely resembles

   a. realism
   b. idealism
   c. pragmatism
   d. existentialism

3. Answer the following short-answer question, which is similar to items in Praxis and other state certification tests.

   Some school districts have established mandatory service-learning programs to encourage students to develop an ethic of caring, involvement in the community, and citizenship. Do you believe service-learning projects should be a requirement for graduation? What are the benefits of such a requirement? What are the arguments against such a requirement?

DEFINITION OF SERVICE LEARNING

"Service-learning is the integration of community service activities with academic skills, content, and reflection on the service experience (Cairn & Kielsmeier, 1999). It combines meaningful service within a community with formal educational curriculum. Service-learning stands in sharp contrast to traditional community service in that it includes reflection and extends naturally from organized school curricula."

Karayan, S., & Gathercoal, P. (2005). Assessing service learning in teacher education. *Teacher Education Quarterly.* Retrieved July 19, 2009, from http://findarticles.com/p/articles/mi_qa3960/is_200507/ai_n14826938/

4. Answer the following short-answer question, which is similar to items in Praxis and other state certification tests.

   In the chapter, the authors define Western philosophies of education and Eastern ways of knowing. Find those sections in the chapter and reread them to make sure that you understand them. Compare and contrast a Western idea with an Eastern idea, providing examples from your own schooling where you can.

After you've completed your written responses above, use the Praxis general scoring guide provided in Chapter 1 to see if you can you revise your response to improve your score.

MYEDUCATIONLAB

myeducationlab Now go to Topic 8: *Philosophy of Education* in the MyEducationLab (www.myeducationlab.com) for your course, where you can:

- Find learning outcomes for *Philosophy of Education* along with the national standards that connect to these outcomes.
- Complete *Assignments and Activities* that can help you more deeply understand the chapter content.
- Apply and practice your understanding of the core teaching skills identified in the chapter with the *Building Teaching Skills and Dispositions* learning units.

- Check your comprehension on the content covered in the chapter by going to the *Study Plan* in the *Book Specific Resources* section for your text. Here you will be able to take a chapter quiz, receive feedback on your answers, and then access *Review, Practice, and Enrichment* activities to enhance your understanding of chapter content.

WEBSITES

www.philosophyofeducation.org The Philosophy of Education Society (PES) comprises educators who are committed to the critical normative and interpretive aspects of education. The mission of PES is to encourage scholarship in the field of philosophy of education; to discuss curricular, methodological, and institutional issues in the field; and to offer educators at large a forum for the philosophical analysis of educational issues. The site provides Internet resources, papers, and discussions that help teachers understand questions and concerns that flow from a philosophic perspective on education.

www.pdcnet.org The Philosophy Documentation Center (PDC) is a nonprofit organization dedicated to providing affordable access to the widest possible range of philosophical materials. Established in 1966, the PDC

provides access to scholarly journals, reference materials, conference proceedings, and instructional software. This site provides easy access to the ideas and writings of a wide variety of philosophers of education.

www.indigenous.ku.edu This is the website at the University of Kansas for the Global Indigenous Nations Studies Program. This program fosters and promotes scholarship focused on understanding the experiences and improving the lives of indigenous peoples around the world. It promotes and reports new knowledge concerning issues such as globalization, decolonization, empowerment, tribal sovereignty, ethnic and legal identity, social injustice, traditional beliefs, languages, public health, environmental resource management, and human rights.

FURTHER READING

Abel, D. C. (1992). *Theories of human nature*. New York: McGraw-Hill. Describes different views of human nature and discusses the implications for teaching, working, and living in society.

Bahm, A. J. (1995). *Comparative philosophy: Western, Indian, and Chinese philosophies compared* (rev. ed.). Albuquerque, NM: World Book. Compares different thinkers, ideologies, and philosophies from both the West and the East.

Cromer, A. H. (1997). *Connected knowledge: Science, philosophy, and education*. New York: Oxford University Press. Written by a physicist, this text argues that students' understanding needs to be connected; it provides practical suggestions that advance students' understanding in an orderly manner.

Littleton, S. C. (1996). *Eastern wisdom*. New York: Henry Holt. Describes Eastern thought drawn from India, China, and Japan and shows how such ideas enhance life.

Nerburn, K., & Mengelkoch, L. (1991). *Native American wisdom*. Novato, CA: The Classic Wisdom Collection. Describes the contributions of different Native American thinkers and suggests that their ideas need to be integrated into schools of learning.

Palmer, P. (1997). *To know as we are known: Education as spiritual journey*. San Francisco: Harper. Shows the close relationship between learning and becoming a person. Provides both spiritual and practical suggestions that challenge views of knowledge.

Sassone, L. (2002). *The process of becoming: A democratic Nietzschean philosophical pedagogy for individualization*. Chicago: Discovery Association. Explores in detail the many Nietzschean perspectives on education. It also offers a democratic Nietzschean pedagogy supplemented by contemporary radical democratic education reformers Paulo Freire, Ivan Illich, Jonathan Kozol, and Neil Postman.

Stevenson, L., & Haberman, D. J. (2008). *Ten theories of human nature*. New York: Oxford University Press. This book explores the ways that Confucianism, Hinduism, The Bible, Plato, Kant, Marx, Freud, Sartre, Skinner and Lorenze view the nature of human beings.

Waters, A. (Ed.). (2004). *American Indian thought*. Malden, MA: Blackwell Publishing. Presents essays written by Native American philosophers from various tribes in North America. The essays span issues related to epistemology, science, metaphysics, ethics, social and political philosophy.

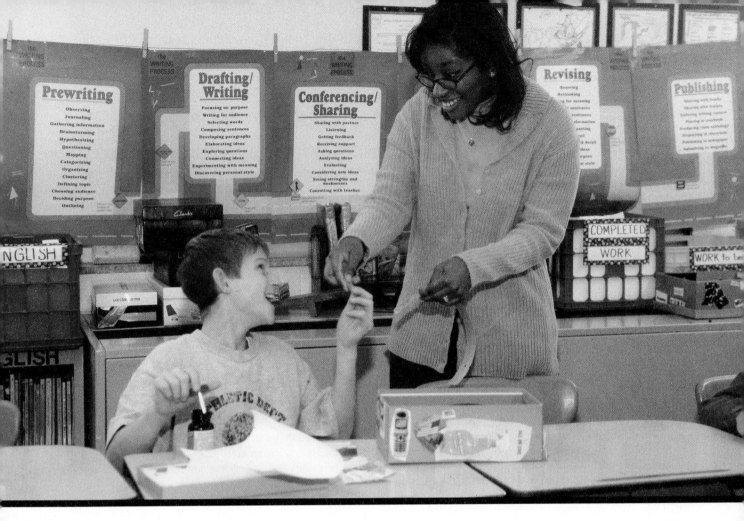

chapter five

BUILDING AN EDUCATIONAL PHILOSOPHY IN A CHANGING WORLD

EDUCATION
IN THE **NEWS**

ETHICAL MINDS
AND TECHNOLOGY

By **DEBRA VIADERO**,
Education Week, January 21, 2009

t's a familiar scenario: A teenager snaps a picture of underage classmates drinking alcohol at a party. The photos go up on a social-networking website and land on the desk of an athletic coach or a school administrator. The students pictured are suspended from school or booted off their teams

Researchers at the Harvard Graduate School of Education say stories like that one illustrate one of the ways new digital media are raising distinct ethical challenges and temptations for young people today.

"Even though many young people may not be ready to participate in the wider communities that digital media open up to them, there is no controlling information about yourself or others that gets posted," says Howard Gardner, the project's co-director. "It's a situation that's foisted upon young persons who are not ready for it."

Gardner, an eminent psychologist best known for his multiple-intelligences theory, is working with a team of researchers at Project Zero, the research center he helped create at the graduate school, to study how students' use of digital media affects the development of their "ethical minds."

Known as the GoodPlay Project, the study is being financed with a grant from the Chicago-based John D. and Catherine T. MacArthur Foundation. What researchers hope to do through the project is fill a gap in the burgeoning research literature on young people's use of digital media, including social-networking sites, blogs, online games, Wikipedia, and virtual worlds, such as Second Life.

While most studies are mapping out what young people are learning and doing in their digital lives, the GoodPlay Project is probing the ethical contours of those electronic worlds in an effort to better understand how digital technology shapes young people's character.

"What's interesting about the GoodPlay Project is that, while it is taking a broad look at the common, fundamental issues that involve youth and digital media, it is also taking a qualitative look at the idea that these young people are actually developing social norms that are quite different from adult values and behavior," says Mimi Ito, a cultural anthropologist at the University of Southern California in Los Angeles.

QUESTIONS FOR REFLECTION

1. In this article, Dr. Gardner and other researchers are studying how students' use of digital media such as social networking, blogs, online games, and virtual worlds helps shape young people's character. What are some ways that you think digital media shapes young people's character and what evidence do you have to support your thinking?

2. Mimi Ito, a cultural psychologist, notes that young people are developing social norms that are different from adult values and behavior. Using your own experience, identify ways that your own social norms have changed as a result of your use of digital media.

3. In what ways do you think that students' use of digital media could affect your approach to teaching?

Source: Copyright 2009 by *Education News.* Reprinted with permission.

LEARNING OUTCOMES

After reading and studying this chapter, you should be able to:

1. Identify the major tenets of the teacher-centered educational philosophies of essentialism, behaviorism, and positivism. (INTASC 1: Subject Matter)

2. Identify the major tenets of the student-centered educational philosophies of progressivism, humanism, and constructivism. (INTASC 1: Subject Matter)

3. Relate educational philosophies to learning and curriculum development. (INTASC 2: Development and Learning)

4. Relate educational philosophy to classroom organization, discipline practices, motivation, and classroom climate. (INTASC 5: Motivation and Management; INTASC 9: Reflection)

5. State the components of your personal philosophy of education. (INTASC 2: Development and Learning; INTASC 9: Reflection)

6. List the characteristics of teachers as change agents. (INTASC 9: Reflection; INTASC 10: Collaboration)

THE DYNAMIC RELATIONSHIP BETWEEN PHILOSOPHY AND EDUCATION

Educational philosophy can be analyzed as the application of philosophy to the classroom. The way curriculum is organized, the manner in which instruction is delivered, the character of school environments, and the processes used in testing and grading are informed by the philosophical views held by educators, parents, and legislators. Such views vary greatly among school districts and states. Table 5.1 describes the relationships between the four schools of philosophy that you studied in Chapter 4—idealism, realism, pragmatism, and existentialism—and education.

Educational philosophy is more than a set of words. It is embodied in the way teachers relate to students, other teachers, principals, and parents.

The four schools of philosophy described in Table 5.1 give rise to different, sometimes competing, learning foci, curricular goals, teaching methods, and approaches to character and aesthetic development. Educational philosophers attempt to develop cohesive ideas about teaching and learning by drawing on one or more compatible philosophies. They also attempt to clarify how these different approaches to curriculum, instruction, and assessment work or do not work together. For example, a behaviorist educational philosopher could focus on the mind, the physical world, or the social world. On the other hand, it would be inappropriate for the behaviorist to focus on personal choice because behaviorism essentially aims to control human behavior through teacher-directed reinforcement.

One strategy that can help you develop your own personal philosophy of education is to build on the educational philosophies of others. We describe six major educational philosophies in the first part of this chapter to show you how different philosophies give rise to divergent philosophies of education. We believe that this examination of different educational philosophies will prepare you, in the second part of the chapter, to develop your own philosophy of education.

The six educational philosophies presented in this chapter are organized according to the degree to which they focus on external (teacher-based) versus internal (student-based) authority. This same distinction (between a teacher-centered versus a student-centered authority) can also be used to group the philosophies studied in Chapter 4. As shown in Table 5.1, the ideas and principles that surround idealism and realism imply that external (teacher-centered) authority is important to the attainment of truth and goodness, whereas pragmatism and existentialism focus more on the innate worth of the individual (student-centered authority).

Table 5.1 • Educational Implications of Philosophy

Educational Aspect	Teacher-Centered Philosophies		Student-Centered Philosophies	
	Idealism	Realism	Pragmatism	Existentialism
Learning focus	Subject matter of the mind: literature, intellectual history, philosophy, religion	Subject matter of the physical world: mathematics, science	Subject matter of social experience	Subject matter of personal choice
Curriculum goal	The same education for all	Mastery of laws of the universe	Creation of a new social order	Personal freedom and development
Preferred teaching method	Teaching for the handling of ideas: lecture, discussion	Teaching for mastery of information and skills: demonstration, recitation	Problem solving: project method, product development	Individual exploration: discovery method, authentic pedagogy
Character development	Imitation of exemplars, heroes	Training in rules of conduct	Group decision making in light of consequences	Development of individual responsibility for decisions and preferences
Aesthetic development	Study of the masterworks; values of the past heritage	Study of design in nature	Participation in art projects based on cross-cultural and universal values	Development of a personal view of the world; self-initiated activities

Source: Adapted from Van Cleve Morris and Young Pai, *Philosophy and the American School*, 2nd edition. Boston: Houghton Mifflin, 1976. Copyright 1976 by Houghton Mifflin company. Reprinted with permission.

What Does an Educational Philosophy Look Like?

A philosophy of education is not just a set of written words; it is a reflective platform on which decisions about teaching and learning are made in an effort to develop learners. A teacher's practices in the classroom provide the clearest indicators of her or his personal philosophy. A worthy goal for beginning educators is to become comfortable with a variety of classroom practices that address the needs of learners. It is not a matter of selecting one methodology over another but rather of understanding different methodologies and using them responsibly. Figure 5.1 provides an example of a philosophy of education that developed and changed over time based on decisions that a teacher made and evaluated along the way. We will refer to this sample philosophy of education throughout this chapter in an effort to show how it relates to other educational philosophies and to a variety of instructional practices.

As you study the three teacher-centered educational philosophies of essentialism, behaviorism, positivism, you will find that many ideas are drawn from idealism and realism. You will also find that the three student-centered educational philosophies of progressivism, humanism, and constructivism draw primarily from pragmatism and existentialism. To varying degrees, each of these educational philosophies is used by classroom teachers and applied to the way teachers organize their classrooms, their instruction, and their assessments.

As you study these different educational philosophies, you will find that one or more of them clearly meshes with your own views. Make a note in your journal when you find a match between your own thinking and a specific aspect of an educational philosophy.

PEARSON myeducationlab

Go to the *Building Teaching Skills and Dispositions* section of Topic 8: *Philosophy of Education* in the MyEducationLab for your course and complete the activity titled *Educational Philosophy and Teaching Practice.*

FIGURE 5.1

Philosophy of Education Example: Teaching as Framing Ways of Knowing

Throughout my entire teaching and learning career I have been fascinated by the diverse ways each of us make sense of the world. Learning is inextricably intertwined with our identity; we know things as we know ourselves. Personal identity interacts with our knowledge of the world and this interaction is at the center of my teaching philosophy. For me, to be a teacher is to be a facilitator, a facilitator who mediates the educational environment in an effort to extend the personal understandings of students. This role of teacher as facilitator places front and center a tension: the tension between knowing a world as it is (objective knowledge) versus knowing a world in terms of self (subjective knowledge). This tension remains the central point around which my own philosophy of education revolves.

My early training in classical philosophy contributes greatly to the centrality of this tension. Readings by Aristotle, Descartes, and Kant influenced me greatly and made me think about the importance of uncovering truth. These and other classical writers struggled with subjective versus objective knowledge and through them I adopted the notion that objective truth is a worthy, absolute standard. I was influenced by this standard and early in my teaching career (perhaps, like many other beginning teachers) I sought to bring about "true" understandings in my students.

This implicit standard for objective truth was quickly shattered as I began my teaching career working with seventh- and eighth-grade students in an inner-city, poor neighborhood of Chicago. It was there among these children that I began to understand how the context of children's and adult's lives influence what they knew and how they know it. At first, I thought that my role as teacher was to display facts as facts and truth as truth. Little did I understand, then, that there is an integral relationship between who we are and what we know. Fortunately, as a teacher I remain a learner and through these early experiences in Chicago, I began to understand that although one might pose objective truth as a standard, there was no absolute argument in favor of such a standard. It was in Chicago that I began to view my teaching role no longer as a provider of truth, but as a prod or questioner who gently tries to extend and refine the personal understandings of my students. [See page 130.]

This turning point in my career has led me down a teaching and learning path that I continue to follow decades later. For me, I consider learning to be an artistic act; the learner fashions an understanding by linking and structuring past and present personal experiences into a whole. This whole idea is bounded or framed momentarily so that learners can internally view the whole and communicate or describe the way they know something.

On a clinical level, I have personally investigated this framing construct and found that employing this view of knowledge enables both me and my students to better understand what they seem to know as true and simultaneously be comfortable with subjecting their understanding to a dialectic process. Hence, I title my current educational philosophy Framing Ways of Knowing.

As a teacher I view myself as a facilitator who helps students both clarify what it is they seem to know and question the limits of that knowing. My instructional methods center on the development of learning situations that force a student to come to grips with her or his personal understanding. Hence, for me, teaching is the designing of educational experiences that bring out students' thinking. On the practical level, this means that I employ simulations, case studies, and problem-based learning events as well as readings, personal investigations, and presentations. [See page 120.]

An instructional event is incomplete, however, if it ends with a student simply clarifying a personal knowing. To me this knowing needs to always be challenged or at least submitted for review to other knowers. This final component of a learning event implies that to know is to frame a personal understanding, communicate it, and allow the community of scholars (other knowers) to respond and perhaps modify that understanding. That is, I do not simply conclude my courses of study with a final paper; rather I conclude it with a presentation based on a paper wherein students receive feedback and are challenged to develop new questions about their understanding. In fact, I explicitly state at the beginning of each new course that the epitome of a learner is the ability to frame a new question based on something he or she understands. [See page 128.]

One other anchor informs my educational philosophy: the development of big ideas. As a teacher I must constantly assess what type of understandings might develop learners' personal frames of thought. I have come to value the beauty and the usefulness of rich ideas that tend to cross disciplines but also bring structure and focus to individual frames of thought. Recently, the national standards movement has elucidated these ideas. Examples of rich ideas include equality, justice, power, authority, individuality, place, environment, voice, community (drawn from the social sciences) and interaction, cycle, time and space, matter and energy, organism, equilibrium, field, force (drawn from the physical sciences) and symmetry, scale, validation, replication, quantification, probability, population, and measurement (drawn from mathematical sciences) and form, function, line, color, hue, tone, mood (drawn from the arts). I find that by anchoring my teaching on the development of these larger ideas, students can better assess their own understandings and extend them through their exploration of these larger ideas. [See pages 121, 122.]

In the end I, as teacher, am really a learner. One who must constantly frame my own understandings, make sense of them, communicate them so that others may enter into a dialogue and a dialectic with me. Only within such a context can I maintain my right to teach in the midst of a community of learners.

TEACHER-CENTERED EDUCATIONAL PHILOSOPHIES

Essentialism, behaviorism, and positivism are educational philosophies that espouse a teacher-centered approach to teaching and learning. Each of these teacher-centered educational philosophies' approach to subject matter, classroom organization, teaching methods, and assessment places most of the responsibility on the teacher, whose job it is to enable students to learn what is important. Although each educational philosophy forms a distinct cohesive whole, all three are rooted in an authoritarian principle—that is, that truth and goodness are entities best understood by the person with expertise who is in authority. The students' role, then, is to attempt to master and follow the directions of those in power.

This chapter presents each educational philosophy's perspectives on curriculum, teaching, and learning. In addition, for each educational philosophy, we describe an illustrative classroom activity that is consistent with the educational philosophy. The classroom activity is further analyzed according to the nature of the learner (active or passive), the nature of the subject matter, the use of the subject matter, and the type of thinking that is emphasized (convergent—focused on right answers—or divergent—focused on developing multiple perspectives).

Essentialism

Essentialism holds that an educated person in a given culture must have a common core of information and skills. Schools should be organized to transmit this core of essential material as effectively as possible. The three basic principles of essentialism are (1) a core of information, (2) hard work and mental discipline, and (3) teacher-centered instruction. The back-to-the-basics movement is a truncated form of essentialism because it focuses primarily on the three Rs and discipline. Essentialism draws equally from both the philosophies of idealism and realism.

Essentialists are not so intent on transmitting underlying, basic truths; rather, they advocate the teaching of a basic core of information that will help a person live a productive life today. Hence, this core of information can and will change. This is an important difference in emphasis from the notions of everlasting truths that characterize the idealist. Essentialism stresses the disciplined development of basic skills rather than the idealist goals of uncovering essences or underlying principles.

ESSENTIALIST LEARNING FOCUS. Essentialism's goals are to transmit the cultural heritage and develop good citizens. The role of the student is that of a learner. School is a place where children come to learn what they need to know, and the teacher is the person who can best instruct students in essential matters. (See the Essentialist Class Activity.)

ESSENTIALIST CLASS ACTIVITY

Mr. Jackson's second graders had just learned to count money. He decided to let them play several games of "musical envelopes." Each student was given one envelope, with each envelope containing a different amount of paper "nickels," "dimes," "quarters," and "pennies." When the music stopped, students had to count the money in their envelopes. The one with the most money for each game got a special prize (Duck, 1981, p. 40).

In this essentialist class activity, the nature of the learner is *passive* because students are given very clear and direct instructions that do not permit individual approaches. The nature of the subject matter is *structured* in that students are required to approach the task in a singular, specific, organized way. The use of the subject matter is *cognitive*, and the thinking approach is *convergent* because there is little room for emotional involvement and there is only one correct answer for each envelope.

ESSENTIALIST CURRICULUM. The essentialist curriculum focuses on subject matter that includes literature, history, foreign languages, and religion. Teaching methods require formal discipline and feature required reading, lectures, memorization, repetition, and examinations. Essentialists generally agree about teaching the laws of nature and the accompanying universal truths of the physical world. Mathematics and the natural sciences are examples of subjects that contribute to the learners' knowledge of natural law. Activities that require mastering facts and information about the physical world are significant aspects of essentialist methodology. With truth defined as observable fact, instruction often includes field trips, laboratories, audiovisual materials, and nature study. Habits of intellectual discipline are considered ends in themselves.

essentialism An educational philosophy that holds that there is a common core of information and skills that an educated person must have; schools should be organized to transmit this core of essential material.

Essentialist teaching methods require formal discipline through emphasis on required reading, lectures, memorization, repetition, and examination.

Essentialism envisions subject matter as the core of education. Severe criticism has been leveled at U.S. education by essentialists who advocate an emphasis on basic education. Essentialism assigns to the schools the task of conserving the heritage and transmitting knowledge of the physical world. In a sense, the school is a curator of knowledge.

With the burgeoning of new knowledge in contemporary society, essentialism may be contributing to the slowness of educational change. In this context, essentialism has been criticized as obsolete in its authoritarian tendencies. Such criticism implies that essentialism does not satisfy the twenty-first-century needs of U.S. youth. Essentialist educators deny this criticism and claim to have incorporated modern influences in the system while maintaining academic standards.

For more information about reform movements, see Chapter 12.

ESSENTIAL SCHOOLS REFORM MOVEMENT. The Essential Schools movement is a contemporary school reform effort developed by Dr. Theodore Sizer that has many characteristics of essentialism. Sizer (2004) contends that students need to master a common core of information and skills, and he encourages schools to strip away the nonessentials and focus on having students "use their minds well." The Essential Schools movement does not specify what content is essential in a given culture at a given time. Rather, "essential schools" are required to analyze clearly what this core of information should be and to change the curriculum to emphasize this core.

The Coalition of Essential Schools (www.essentialschools.org) promotes a vision of schooling in which students engage in in-depth and rigorous learning. Essential schools select a small number of core skills and areas of knowledge that they expect all students to demonstrate and exercise broadly across content areas. Ten common principles have been developed by Dr. Sizer in collaboration with essential school participants to guide the efforts of the coalition. These principles include the following:

- Using the mind well with a focus on clear, essential learning goals
- An attempt to apply these goals to all students
- Personalized teaching and learning
- Emphasis on student-as-worker
- Student performance on real tasks with multiple forms of evidence
- Principal and teachers as generalists first and specialists second
- Budgets that do not exceed those of traditional schools by more than 10 percent
- Nondiscriminatory policies and practices.

Behaviorism

B. F. Skinner (1904–1990), the Harvard experimental psychologist and philosopher, is the recognized leader of the movement known as behaviorism. **Behaviorism** is a psychological theory and educational philosophy that holds that one's behavior is determined by environment, not heredity. Skinner verified Pavlov's stimulus–response theory with animals and, from his research, suggested that human behavior could also be explained as responses to external stimuli. Because of its focus on the careful examination of environment, behaviors, and responses, behaviorism is closely linked to realism. Other behaviorists' research expanded on Skinner's work in illustrating the effect of the environment, particularly the interpersonal environment, on shaping individual behavior.

behaviorism A psychological theory and educational philosophy that asserts that behaviors represent the essence of a person and that all behaviors can be explained as responses to stimuli.

BEHAVIORIST LEARNING FOCUS. Behaviorists holds that one's behavior is determined by environment, not heredity. This suggests that by carefully controlling the stimuli in the classroom, the teacher can significantly influence student behavior. Behaviorists believe that the school environment must be highly organized and the curriculum based on carefully developed behavioral objectives, and they hold that knowledge is best described as behaviors that are observable. They contend that empirical evidence is essential if students are to learn and that students must employ the scientific method to arrive at knowledge. The primary task of educators is to develop learning environments that lead to desired behaviors in students. (See Behaviorist Class Activity.)

BEHAVIORIST CLASS ACTIVITY

Students in Mr. Drucker's civics class were given merit tokens for coming into the room quietly, sitting at their desks, preparing notebooks and pencils for the day's lesson, and being ready to begin answering comprehension questions in their workbooks. On Fridays students were allowed to use their tokens at an auction to buy items that Mr. Drucker knew they wanted. Sometimes, however, students had to save tokens for more than two weeks to buy what they liked best (Duck, 1981, pp. 50–51).

In this behaviorist class activity, the nature of the learner is *passive*, in that students are carefully manipulated by providing responses to their behaviors that make students do what the teacher wants. The nature of the subject matter is *structured* in that the workbooks and comprehension questions are carefully focused and lead students step by step. The use of the subject matter is *affective* (having to do with feelings) because the teacher attempts to provide merit tokens that relate to what students desire. The thinking approach is *convergent* in that the comprehension questions require one correct answer.

BEHAVIORIST CURRICULUM: REINFORCEMENT. The concept of reinforcement is critical to teacher practices in behaviorism. The behaviorist teacher endeavors to foster desired behaviors by using both positive reinforcers (things students like, such as praise, privileges, and good grades) and negative reinforcers (things students wish to avoid, such as reprimands, extra homework, and lower grades). The theory is that behavior that is not reinforced (whether positively or negatively) will eventually be "extinguished"—will cease to occur. In general, behaviorists contend that learning takes place when approved behavior is observed and then positively reinforced.

A teacher may provide nonverbal positive reinforcement (smiling, nodding approval) or negative reinforcement (frowning, shaking the head in disapproval). Similarly, nondirective statements, questions, and directive statements may be positive or negative. Both children and adults respond to the models other people (peers, adults, heroes) represent to them by imitating the model behavior. Behaviorists contend that students tend to emulate behaviors that are rewarded.

Behaviorists have supplied a wealth of empirical research that bears on the problems of attaining self-control, resisting temptation, and showing concern for others. Behaviorists do not attempt to learn about the causes of students' earlier problems. Rather, the behaviorist teacher focuses on the here and now environment and must ascertain what is happening in the classroom to perpetuate or extinguish students' behavior. For example, if a student shouts out whenever she wishes and disturbs others in the class, the behaviorist teacher focuses on what response can be provided consistently to make this behavior cease. It does not matter what (in the past) may account for this unwanted behavior; the key is changing the current environment. Consider the Professional Dilemma feature about the challenges related to student boredom and a lack of interest in learning.

Positivism

The educational philosophy of positivism stems from what the social scientist Auguste Comte (1798–1857) described as "positive knowledge." Comte divided the thinking of humankind into three historical periods, each of which was characterized by a distinct way of thinking. The first was the theological era, in which people explained things by reference to spirits and gods. The second was the metaphysical era, in which people explained phenomena in terms of causes, essences, and inner principles. The third was the positive period, in which thinkers did not attempt to go beyond observable, measurable fact.

The positivist position rejects essences, intuition, and inner causes that cannot be measured. Empirical verification is central to all proper thinking. This educational philosophy rejects beliefs about mind, spirit, and consciousness and holds that all reality can be explained by laws of matter and motion. In sum, **positivism** limits knowledge to statements of observable

positivism A social theory and educational philosophy that limits truth and knowledge to what is observable and measurable.

PROFESSIONAL DILEMMA   Adjusting the Attitude of Learners

Teachers in today's schools meet face to face with an increasing number of attitude problems from some learners. These problems are manifested in a lack of respect for teachers, visual boredom in learning, and a lack of a career work ethic. The lack of respect may come from a societal image of teachers as "Those who can't, teach!" Additionally, whatever is wrong in society tends to be blamed on the teacher and the school program. Teacher authority is usurped by parents and the society, which challenge the teacher's right to discipline students, even the unruly ones. Some students call into question the worthiness of professional teachers, who are considered to have lower status when compared with other professions. The fact that teachers tend to be grossly underpaid for the type of workload they face may be questioned.

Some students exhibit boredom and are not motivated to learn because they do not see the relevance of what they are studying. To them, much of what they study seems to be important only for the tests they take and has no relevance to their lives. They yearn for assurance that teachers not only are competent but also care. The lack of a work ethic may be attributable to an environment that

provides everything material they need and want. This student problem may be related to the "good life" quality of a society that tends to have everything it needs. Many students have economically secure homes, are provided with an overabundance of goods and services, and are not held accountable for responsible activities in the family.

This dilemma does not paint a glowing picture of what is waiting for the teacher when she or he enters the classroom. If this picture is accurate and is to be altered, then the teacher needs to actively develop with the students a common ground for the establishment of respect for each other.

Questions for Reflection
1. How can the teacher show respect for the students and have the students show respect for the teacher?
2. How does the teacher prepare a learning environment that has meaning to the everyday life of the learner?
3. How does the teacher work with the home and community in providing a learning atmosphere in which students develop a work ethic and recognize its value?

fact based on sense perceptions and the investigation of objective reality. In the 1920s positivism became a rallying point for a group of scholars in Vienna. Because the group consisted largely of scientists, mathematicians, and symbolic logicians, positivism became known as logical positivism.

POSITIVIST LEARNING FOCUS. Direct instruction is a teaching and learning approach that requires teachers to clearly and precisely identify and state what a student needs to learn and master, as well as to restate this expectation through different media and assignments. It is a teaching and learning approach that places the responsibility for clear, precise expectations on the teacher. Once a teacher has identified precisely what students should know and be able to do, the teacher is expected to clearly describe to students exactly what they should know and be able to do. Teachers are encouraged to use repetition and have students practice and practice again, recite and recite again, what is to be learned. Teachers are further encouraged to have students repeat the main ideas of the instruction by using different media: oral recitation, writing, restating, drawing, and so forth. The key ingredient for this approach is the use of clear, uncluttered statements and restatements about the focus of learning.

This approach to teaching and learning fits the positivist educational theory because in such an educational approach knowledge is considered something that is clear and precise. If all knowledge is clear, precise, and the same for all, then teachers can be expected to require all students to learn the same knowledge. Direct instruction is possible because all knowledge that is worthy is also clear and precise. (See the Positivist Class Activity.)

Positivism focuses learning on acquisition of facts based on careful, empirical observation and measurement of the world.

POSITIVIST CLASS ACTIVITY

Humberto Diaz introduced the meaning of surface tension to his junior high science students. He then told students that they could observe surface tension by watching water drops come together as they were placed on the surface of a penny. During class he then distributed eyedroppers, water, and pennies to the students. He directed the students to determine how many drops of water could fit on the surface of the penny before spilling over. Students were to collect data and develop a data table and corresponding charts. At the end of the class, Mr. Diaz asked the students to discuss their findings and draw a conclusion about the surface tension of water.

In this positivist class activity, the nature of the learner is *active*, because students are asked to investigate and collect data on their own. The nature of the subject matter is *structured*, because students are provided carefully developed directions concerning what they are to do. The use of the subject matter is *cognitive* because students are provided questions that are focused on a single, important concept. The thinking approach is *divergent* because students are encouraged to think about how they will determine the number of drops that fit on a penny and why the numbers may differ across groups.

POSITIVIST CURRICULUM. Practiced as an educational philosophy, positivism focuses the curriculum on the acquisition of facts based on careful empirical observation and measurement of the world. Positivism requires schools to develop content standards that represent the best understandings of experts who have already uncovered important ideas based on their own observation and measurement. Students are encouraged both to master these expert understandings and to develop their own skills of observation, classification, and logical analysis.

Testing students' acquisition of content standards is a valued activity for the positivist educator. Creating objective tests that are free from bias is critical to education. Because empirical knowledge is proven by years of careful analysis, there is a set of truths that students should master and understand according to a clear set of criteria. The only way to ensure that such knowledge has been attained and understood is to test all students according to the same objective set of criteria.

Now that you have reviewed a description, learning foci, and curricular implications of essentialism, behaviorism, and positivism, you can better understand why they are grouped as teacher-centered philosophies. All of these educational philosophies are focused on developing on-task learners by using cognitive, highly structured learning tasks and strong teacher control. Although a variety of teaching methods can be used, all learning must be highly focused on learning concepts. Direct instruction is highly valued for its efficiency. In the next section, you will explore very different student-centered educational philosophies.

━━━━━ JOURNAL FOR REFLECTION ━━━━━

Consider the different teacher-centered educational philosophies and recall a teacher you know who seems to follow one of these educational philosophies. Describe the ways in which the teacher's actions represent the teacher-centered educational philosophy.

STUDENT-CENTERED EDUCATIONAL PHILOSOPHIES

Progressivism, humanism, and constructivism espouse a student-centered approach to subject matter, classroom organization, teaching methods, and assessment. Although each educational philosophy forms a distinct cohesive whole, all three are rooted in a student-centered principle, that is, the belief that truth and goodness belong to all persons no matter what their station. Teachers are learners and learners are teachers, and education is the process through which individuals help one another to clarify personal meaning.

As with the teacher-centered positions, we will present each student-centered educational philosophy's ideas on curriculum, teaching, and learning. In addition, for each philosophy we will describe a representative program along with an illustrative class activity. The class activity is further analyzed according to the nature of the learner (active or passive), the nature of the subject matter, the use of the subject matter, and the type of thinking that is emphasized (convergent—focused on right answers, or divergent—focused on developing multiple perspectives).

Progressivism

In the late 1800s, with the rise of democracy, the expansion of modern science and technology, and the need for people to be able to adjust to change, people in Western societies had to have a new and different approach to acquiring knowledge in order to solve problems. As noted in Chapter 4, a U.S. philosopher, Charles S. Peirce (1839–1914), founded the philosophical system called *pragmatism*. This philosophy held that the meaning and value of ideas could be found only in the practical results of these ideas. Later, William James (1842–1910) extended Peirce's theory of meaning and asserted that if an idea works well it can be considered true. The satisfactory working of an idea constitutes its whole truth. Pragmatism was carried much further by John Dewey, who insisted that ideas must always be tested by experiment. His emphasis on experiment carried over into his educational philosophy, which became the basis for what was usually described as progressive education (Dewey, 1916). **Progressivism** is an educational theory that emphasizes that ideas should be tested by experimentation and that learning is rooted in questions developed by learners.

From its establishment in the mid-1920s through the mid-1950s, progressivism was the most influential educational view in the United States. Progressivists basically favor human experience as a basis for knowledge rather than authority. Progressivism favors the scientific method of teaching and learning, allows for the beliefs of individuals, and stresses programs of student involvement that help students learn how to think. Progressivists believe that the school should actively prepare its students for change. Progressive schools emphasize learning *how* to think rather than *what* to think. Flexibility is important in the curriculum design, and the emphasis is on *experimentation*, with no single body of content stressed more than any other. This approach encourages *divergent thinking*—moving beyond conventional ideas to come up with novel interpretations or solutions. And because life experience determines curriculum content, all types of content must be permitted. Certain subjects regarded as traditional are recognized as desirable for study as well. Progressivist educators would organize scientific method–oriented learning activities around the traditional subjects. Such a curriculum is called experience centered or student centered; the essentialist and positivist curricula are considered subject centered. Experience-centered curricula stress the *process* of learning rather than the result.

Progressivism as a contemporary teaching style emphasizes the process of education in the classroom. It is more compatible with a core of problem areas across all academic disciplines than with a subject-centered approach to problem solving. It would be naive to suggest that memorization and rote practice should be ruled out. In progressive teaching, however, they are not stressed as primary learning techniques. The assertion is that interest in an intellectual activity will generate all of the practice needed for learning.

PROGRESSIVIST LEARNING FOCUS: DEMOCRACY. A tenet of progressivism is that the school, to become an important social institution, must take on the task of improving society. To this end, progressivism is deemed a working model of democracy. Freedom is explicit in a democracy, so it must be explicit in schools. But freedom, rather than being a haphazard expression of free will, must be organized to have meaning. Organized freedom permits each member of the school society to take part in decisions, and all must share their experiences to ensure that the decisions are meaningful.

Pupil–teacher planning is the key to democracy in classrooms and is the process that gives some freedom to students, as well as teachers, in decisions about what is studied. For example, the teacher might ask students to watch a film about an issue of interest and have them list questions about the issue that were not answered by the film but that they would like to investigate. Students and the teacher can then analyze the questions and refine them for research. Such questions can become the basis for an inquiry and problem-solving unit of study.

Progressivism views the learner as an experiencing, thinking, exploring individual. Its goal is to expose the learner to the subject matter of social experiences, social studies, projects, problems, and experiments that, when studied by the scientific method, will result in functional knowledge from all subjects. Progressivists regard books as tools to be used in learning rather than as sources of indisputable knowledge. (See the Progressivist Class Activity.)

progressivism An educational philosophy that emphasizes that ideas should be tested by experimentation and that learning is rooted in questions developed by the learner.

PROGRESSIVIST CLASS ACTIVITY

Mr. Brandese Powell asked his second graders to look at a cartoon that pictured a well-dressed man and woman in an automobile pulled by a team of two horses. The highway they were traveling along passed through rolling farmland with uncrowded meadows, trees, and clear skies in the background. He led a discussion based on the following questions:

1. What is happening in this picture?
2. Do you like what is happening in the picture? Why or why not?
3. What does it say about the way you may be living when you grow up?
4. Are you happy or unhappy about what you have described for your life as an adult?
5. How can we get people to use less gasoline now?
6. What if we could keep companies from making and selling cars that could not travel at least forty miles on one gallon of gasoline?

In this progressivist class activity, the nature of the learner is *active* because the teacher is asking open-ended questions that bring out the different ways that learners think about the picture. The nature of the subject matter is *ill structured*, because although there is an order to the questions, the direction that the discussion may take is open ended. The use of the subject matter is *cognitive* and *affective* because the concepts that underlie the picture are both rational and value laden. The thinking approach is *divergent* because there is no single, correct answer to the discussion questions.

PROGRESSIVIST CURRICULUM: CRITICAL PEDAGOGY. Many people believe that the socialization aspect of progressivism—the fact that it represents the leading edge of society and helps students learn how to manage change—is its most valuable aspect. However, progressivism is criticized for placing so much stress on the processes of education that the ends are neglected. Its severest critics contend that progressive educators have little personal commitment to anything, producing many graduates who are uncommitted and who are content to drift through life. Progressivists counter by stating that their educational view requires that students be taught to analyze world events, explore controversial issues, and develop a vision for a new and better world. Teachers would critically examine cultural heritages, explore controversial issues, provide a vision for a new and better world, and enlist students' efforts to promote programs of cultural renewal. Although teachers would attempt to convince students of the validity of such democratic goals, they would employ democratic procedures in doing so.

A contemporary version of progressivism is rooted in the work of Henry Giroux, who views schools as vehicles for social change. He calls teachers to be transformative intellectuals and wants them to participate in creating a new society. Schools should practice "critical pedagogy," which unites theory and practice as it provides students with the critical thinking tools to be change agents (Giroux, 1985).

Humanism

Humanism is an educational philosophy that is concerned with enhancing the innate goodness of the individual. It rejects a group-oriented educational system and seeks ways to enhance the individual development of the student. Humanism is rooted both in the writings of Jean-Jacques Rousseau and in the ideas of existentialism (as noted in Chapter 4). Rousseau (1712–1778), the father of romanticism, believed that the child entered the world not as a blank slate but with certain innate qualities and tendencies. In the opening sentence of *Émile*, Rousseau's famous treatise on education, he states that "God makes all things good; man meddles with them and they become evil" (Rousseau, 1979). Thus, Rousseau believed in humans' basic goodness at birth. He also believed that humans are born free but become enslaved by institutions. Humanistic education mingles some of these ideas from Rousseau with the basic ideas of existentialism.

Humanists believe that most schools de-emphasize the individual and the relationship between the teacher and the student. Humanists claim that as educators attempt to predict the behavior of students, they turn individuals into objects to be measured. According to the humanist, education should be a process of developing a free, self-actualizing person—a process that is centered on the student's feelings. Therefore, education should not start with great ideas, the world, or humankind, but with the individual self.

humanism An educational philosophy that contends that humans are innately good—that they are born free but become enslaved by institutions.

Humanists believe that education should be without coercion or prescription and that students should be active learners and make their own choices.

HUMANISTIC LEARNING FOCUS. Because the goal of humanism is a completely autonomous person, education should be without coercion or prescription. Students should be active and should be encouraged to make their own choices. The teacher who follows humanistic theory emphasizes instruction and assessment based on student interests, abilities, and needs. Students determine the rules that will govern classroom life, and they make choices about the books to read or exercises to complete.

Humanists honor divergent thinking so completely that they delay giving their own personal opinions and do not attempt to persuade students to particular points of view. Even though they emphasize the affective and thereby may make students feel a certain urgency about issues, it is always left to the individual student to decide when to take a stand, what kind of stand to take, whether a cause merits action, and, if so, in what kind of action to engage. (See Humanistic Class Activity.)

HUMANIST CLASS ACTIVITY

Ms. Fenway wanted her ninth graders to really recognize the effectiveness (and manipulation) of television, radio, and Internet advertising. She asked students to write down any five slogans or jingles they could remember and the products advertised. Ms. Fenway selected from their items at random and tested the class. For each slogan, class members had to identify the product advertised. The test was corrected in class by the students who were very surprised to find the grading scale reversed.

Those who had all correct answers received Fs, and those who had only one correct answer received As. When asked why she had reversed the grades, Ms. Fenway responded, "Because those of you who knew every product's slogan have been somewhat manipulated by advertising. On the other hand, those of you who knew very few products' slogans have avoided the influence of advertising." Ms. Fenway then told students the grades were not their actual grades, they were simply an indicator of how strongly we all are influenced by contemporary advertising.

She then asked whether students resented some companies' selling tactics. Then she and the class made a list of questions to ask themselves in order to avoid spending money in ways they might later regret. She also asked for specific examples of spending money for items they later wished they hadn't bought.

In this humanist class activity, the nature of the learner is *active* because the teacher asked students questions that were open ended and permitted the individual child to build on her or his own experiences. The thinking approach is *divergent* because there was no one correct answer or way of thinking about the answer. The nature of the subject matter is *structured* in that the teacher directed the questions and slowly unfolded each question to build on the prior one. The use of the subject matter is both *cognitive* and *affective*. It was cognitive because logic was required in the last question focused on avoiding spending money in ways that that students might regret. The activity was also affective because she built the activity around children's preferences for different products.

HUMANISTIC CURRICULUM. To humanistic educators, the curriculum of any school is found not so much in subject matter, but rather in the environment in which the subject matter is taught. Martin Buber's writings describe the heart of a humanistic school environment. In *I and Thou*, Buber portrays two different ways in which individuals relate to the outside world. In the I–It relationship, one views something outside oneself in a purely objective manner, as a thing to be used and manipulated for selfish ends. In contrast, I–Thou relationships are characterized by viewing other people as sacred entities who deserve profound respect. Such relationships focus on the importance of understanding and respecting diverse, subjective, personal meanings. Buber was deeply concerned that people were treated as objects (Its) rather than as Thou's, especially in business, science, government, and education (Buber, M., 1958).

Many students today believe that educators treat them as Social Security numbers stored in a computer. In college classes of 100 or more, it is difficult for teachers to remember students' names, let alone get to know them as individuals. Often teachers assign material, mark papers, and give grades without ever really conversing with students. When the semester ends, students leave class and are replaced by other, equally anonymous students. Buber did not believe that schools had to be this way. He contended that in a proper relationship between teacher and student, there is a mutual sensibility of feeling. There is empathy, not a subject–object relationship.

A humanistic school environment (in other words, its curriculum) is one in which people (both teacher and student) share their thoughts, feelings, beliefs, fears, and aspirations with one another. Nel Noddings (2005) labels this an *environment of caring*. According to humanists, this kind of caring relationship should pervade the educational process at all levels as well as society at large.

Inspired by humanism, many educators attempt to personalize education in less radical ways. Examples include individualizing instruction, open-access curriculum, nongraded instruction, and multiage grouping. Each of these approaches attends to the uniqueness of the learner. Block scheduling permits flexibility for students to arrange classes of their choice. Free schools, storefront schools, schools without walls, and area vocational centers provide humanistic alternatives to traditional school environments.

Educational programs that address the needs of the individual are usually more costly per pupil than traditional group-centered programs. Consequently, as taxpayer demands for accountability mount, humanistic individualized programs are often brought under unit-cost scrutiny. Nonetheless, growing numbers of educators are willing to defend increased expenditures to meet the needs of the individual learner within the instructional programs of the schools.

Constructivism

Constructivism is an educational philosophy that emphasizes developing personal meaning through hands-on, activity-based teaching and learning. Constructivism is closely associated with existentialism (as described in Chapter 4). The American Psychological Association (APA) has encouraged teachers to reconsider the manner in which they view teaching. The APA contends that students are active learners who should be given opportunities to construct their own frames of thought. Teaching techniques should include a variety of different learning activities during which students are free to infer and discover their own answers to important questions. Teachers need to spend time creating these learning situations rather than lecturing. Constructivist educators consider true learning to be the active framing of personal meaning (by the learner) rather than the framing of someone else's meaning (the teacher's).

Such a view of teaching and learning has profound ramifications for the school curriculum. If students are to be encouraged to answer their own questions and develop their own thinking frame, the curriculum needs to be reconceptualized. Constructivist theorists encourage the development of critical thinking and the understanding of big ideas rather than the mastery of factual information. They contend that students who have a sound understanding of important principles that were developed through their own critical thinking will be better prepared for the complex, technological world.

CONSTRUCTIVIST LEARNING FOCUS: PROBLEM-BASED LEARNING. Problem-based learning has recently emerged as a student-centered teaching and learning approach that is in keeping with constructivist tenets. Based on Dewey's concept of teaching through student-centered problems, this educational methodology centers student activities on tackling authentic contemporary problems. Problem-based learning is a radical approach in that it challenges educators to focus curriculum on student interests and current societal problems and concerns rather than on disciplinary content coverage.

In a problem-based experience, students are presented with a "hook." The hook might be a letter from a civic group, a request from an environmental agency, or any other motivating beginning. The hook describes a contemporary dilemma and requests students to take on some real-life role to solve the problem. Problem-based learning usually requires students to spend time finding the core problem, clarifying the problem, assessing what is and is not known about the problem, gathering needed data to complement what has been uncovered, and finally presenting a position statement and/or suggesting a solution. Throughout the process, teachers act as guides or coaches and give great latitude to student interest. Students learn content and skills within the problem context. Teachers spend time selecting problems that are compatible with student maturity levels and curricular needs. (See the Constructivist Class Activity.)

constructivism An educational philosophy that emphasizes hands-on, activity-based teaching and learning during which students develop their own frames of thought.

CONSTRUCTIVIST CLASS ACTIVITY

Reiko Nishioka's sophomore biology class had just completed reading Michael Crichton's novel *Jurassic Park* when a letter from movie producer Steven Spielberg arrived addressed to each student in the class. The letter requested each student's assistance in Spielberg's effort to determine what aspects of the novel were or were not scientifically accurate with regard to dinosaurs. The letter asked students to prepare a written summary and to send the summary, along with proper documentation, to Spielberg's production company. Because time was limited, Spielberg requested that the summaries be completed within three weeks. Reiko provided time for her students to think about the letter and then asked them to determine what they would do next.

In this constructivist class activity, the nature of the learner is *active* because students not only determine what it is they need to find out or learn but also how they will learn the material. The nature of the subject matter is *unstructured*, because students are free to tackle many different concepts based on their interest and they must figure out how they will learn the material. The use of the subject matter is *authentic* to real life because the content is embedded in a contemporary problem or concern. Finally, the thinking approach is *divergent* because there is no single correct answer to the problem.

CONSTRUCTIVIST CURRICULUM: PERSONALIZED LEARNING. Constructivist ideas about curriculum stand in sharp contrast to the authoritarian approaches we described earlier. Traditionally, learning has been thought of as a mimic activity, a process that involves students repeating newly presented information. Constructivism, on the other hand, focuses on the personalized way a learner internalizes, shapes, or transforms information. Learning occurs through the construction of new, personalized understanding that results from the emergence of new cognitive structures. Teachers and parents can invite such transformed understandings, but neither can mandate them.

Accepting this simple proposition—that students learn by shaping their own understandings about their world—makes the present structure of the school problematic. According to constructivist principles, educators should invite students to experience the world's richness and empower them to ask their own questions and seek their own answers. The constructivist teacher proposes situations that encourage students to think. Rather than leading students toward a particular answer, the constructivist teacher allows students to develop their own ideas and chart their own pathways. But schools infrequently operate in such a constructivist way. Typically, schools determine what students will learn and when they will learn it.

Now that you have reviewed a description, learning foci, and curricular implications of progressivism, humanism, and constructivism, you can better understand why they are grouped as student-centered philosophies. All of these educational philosophies are focused on students' interests, ideas, and contemporary societal problems. These philosophies use cognitive and affective subject matter and open-ended learning tasks and encourage students to take control of their own learning. Direct instruction by the teacher is limited and emphasis is on helping students develop their own perspectives and ways of thinking. In the next section of this chapter, you will explore your own thinking about teaching and learning in light of both teacher-centered and student-centered educational philosophies. Ultimately, you are asked to develop your own educational philosophy and also provide a rationale for your thinking.

JOURNAL FOR REFLECTION

Choose and write down a metaphor for each of the educational philosophies you have studied so far. For example, "constructivism is a shared voyage into new and uncharted territory." Then design a metaphor for your personal educational philosophy and clarify how it compares to the other metaphors.

DEVELOPING YOUR OWN PHILOSOPHY OF EDUCATION

PEARSON

Go to the *Assignments and Activities* section of Topic 8: *Philosophy of Education* in the MyEducationLab for your course and complete the activity titled *Developing a Philosophy of Education.*

This section helps you to clarify your role as a teacher in society and identify effective classroom practices. It offers a number of big ideas or key concepts that will challenge your image of what constitutes a good teacher. Ideas such as classroom environment or climate, voice and space, community of learners, and teacher as leader are presented to help you clarify your own approach to education. Which type of environment is best for today's students? How much teacher control is needed? Whose voices are predominant and whose voices are muted in today's classrooms? What teaching and learning methods will you use and how will you determine if these methods are working? These questions are examined and shown to be

FIGURE 5.2

Teacher-Centered versus Student-Centered Classroom Approaches

EDUCATIONAL PHILOSOPHIES

	Teacher Centered	Student Centered
	• Essentialism • Behaviorism • Positivism	• Progressivism • Humanism • Contructivism
Classroom Organization	Rigid/fixed; highly organized, from furniture to lessons	Open; flexible classroom furniture arrangement and teaching
Motivation	External controls	Internal incentives
Discipline	High teacher control	Equal teacher and learner control
Classroom Climate	Nurturing teacher voice; community of on-task learners	Teacher encourages student voices; community of inquirers
Learning Focus	Convergent thinking; focused subject matter	Divergent points of view; diverse subject matter
Teaching Styles	Extreme amounts of teacher talk; directed learning	Considerably less teacher talk, more learner talk; discovery-based learning
Leadership Styles	Teacher is primary authority source and evaluator	Teacher is model of participatory authority and evaluation

important to the development of a classroom climate that is either directed and didactic (like essentialism, behaviorism, positivism) or open and authentic (like progressivism, humanism, constructivism).

As you examine and refine your own philosophy of education, it is helpful to review how the six different educational philosophies relate to the contemporary classroom. Figure 5.2 summarizes how teacher-centered educational philosophies versus student-centered philosophies affect classroom organization, motivation, discipline, classroom climate, learning focus, teaching styles, and leadership styles. You may find that this chart quickly provides you a starting point for the clarification of your personal philosophy of education.

The physical setting of the classroom tends to reflect whether the teacher follows a directive or nondirective theory of education.

Classroom Organization

Because the way you organize your classroom encompasses and affects all other aspects of teaching and learning, it is useful to begin thinking about this topic first. All teachers must be able to organize their classrooms in such a way that they are conducive to teaching and learning. In fact, many school principals are quick to assert that the easiest way to predict the success of a beginning teacher is to evaluate his or her ability to organize the classroom.

A common misconception is that good classroom organization means maintaining a controlled atmosphere and refusing to allow any behavior that even looks ungoverned or unplanned. Actually, **classroom organization** is a multifaceted dimension of teaching that includes the content, methods, and values that infuse the classroom environment. It is a dimension of teaching that requires analysis and selection similar to that used in the identification of a preferred teaching philosophy.

Figure 5.2 shows how closely one's educational philosophy affects the different components of classroom organization.

THE PHYSICAL SETTING. The mere arrangement of classroom furniture and the use of classroom materials may be predicated on the teacher's perception of the learners as passive or active. Teacher-centered educational philosophies would support classrooms arranged in rows because this type of classroom arrangement has often been thought to be the best for classroom control and supervision. Also, this arrangement allows the teacher to capture the attention of students quickly and focus students on specific, important pieces of essential information.

Student-centered educational philosophies tend to support more open classrooms with small circles for special groupings in reading, mathematics, and other specific subjects. The teacher intends learning for the students to be divergent in nature, and the student is expected to be more active in the learning process. This is not to suggest that one type of classroom arrangement is better than another or that one theory is superior to another, but we do suggest that the teacher-in-training examine classroom theory as it relates to the physical environment for learning.

Let us return to the exemplar philosophy of education presented earlier in this chapter as Figure 5.1 and consider what type of physical setting this teacher might use. One key to determining this is as follows:

> As a teacher, I view myself as a facilitator who helps students both clarify what it is they seem to know and question the limits of that knowing. My instructional methods center on the development of learning situations that force a student to come to grips with her or his personal understanding. Hence, for me, teaching is designing educational experiences that bring out students' thinking. On the practical level, this means that I employ simulations, case studies, and problem-based learning events as well as readings, personal investigations, and presentations.

Based on this quote the teacher would most likely set up a classroom with a variety of learning centers (readings, hands-on activities, computer stations, video and audio resources with headphones, etc.). Student seats would be arranged in small groups to permit discussions. Students would be free to roam around the room much of time working on all sorts of learning activities and personal investigations.

JOURNAL FOR REFLECTION

classroom organization A multifaceted dimension of teaching that includes the content, method, and values that infuse the classroom environment, planning, and discipline practices.

Think about the different student seating arrangements in various classrooms. Sketch each seating arrangement and describe the types of student interaction and the types of learning that each seating arrangement supports. Draw the seating arrangement that you prefer, and describe the types of student interaction and learning that it encourages.

LESSON PLANNING. Careful lesson planning is mandatory if effective teaching and learning are to follow. If the learners are considered to be passive (teacher centered), the lesson plan might emphasize students' absorption of the factual content of the subject matter. Adherents of teaching styles that consider the learners to be active participants (student centered) would tend to emphasize thinking processes and skills and view the factual content of the subject matter as important but variable.

Regardless of the expectation for the learner, active or passive, all teachers need to plan sound lessons. Every lesson should be built from a basic set of general objectives that correspond to the overall goals of the school district. This is not to suggest that every third-grade classroom in a school district should have the same daily learning objectives for the students. Daily lesson objectives can vary from classroom to classroom depending on the particular needs of the students being served. However, if those daily teaching objectives are closely related to the overall objectives of the school district, then cross-district learning will reflect the school district's overall goals.

Lessons are often tied to some form of teaching units. These units should be planned in detail to include suggestions for teaching the lessons, types of materials to be used, and specific plans for evaluation. When it comes to designing teaching units, the differences between teacher-centered and student-centered styles become more pronounced. The reason is that the types of questions and learning content can differ greatly. For example, if a teacher is generally focused on teaching essential pieces of information and verifying that students understand this information in a very specific way, teaching units would tend to be shorter and focused on precise, specific learning outcomes. The unit would tend to have short, focused assignments based on some overall theme that students complete and submit for review by the teacher. On the other hand, if a teacher is focused on the development of big ideas that students learn and make sense of in their own unique way, learning units would tend to have a number of related investigations that students complete in an effort to make sense of the big ideas that underlie the teaching unit.

Initially, these are all decisions that must be made by the teacher based on the implications of her or his educational philosophy. Let us return to the educational philosophy example to determine what type of learning units this teacher would probably design:

> One other anchor informs my educational philosophy: the development of big ideas. As a teacher I must constantly assess what type of understandings might develop learners' personal frames of thought. I have come to value the beauty and the usefulness of rich ideas that tend to cross disciplines but also bring structure and focus to individual frames of thought. These ideas can be found in the work of great scientists, mathematicians, writers, poets, educators, artists, etc. Recently, the national standards movement has elucidated these ideas. Examples of rich ideas include equality, justice, power, authority, individuality, place, environment, voice, community (drawn from the social sciences) and interaction, cycle, time and space, matter and energy, organism, equilibrium, field, force (drawn from the physical sciences) and symmetry, scale, validation, replication, quantification, probability, population, and measurement (drawn from mathematical sciences) and form, function, line, color, hue, tone, mood (drawn from the arts).

Given that the teacher's educational philosophy is focused on large interdisciplinary ideas that students are to explore, the learning units would focus on one or more big ideas. The learning activities include a number of open-ended investigations during which students gather data and make sense of the information in their own words. Learning journals and a portfolio might be used to keep all of their information and insights organized. The teacher would coach each student along the way by asking probing questions in an effort to redirect each student and assist them by clarifying misconceptions.

For more information about student assessment and evaluation, see Chapter 11.

STUDENT ASSESSMENT AND EVALUATION. In assessing student progress and assigning grades, most teacher-centered and student-centered teachers use a variety of techniques including examinations, term papers, project reports, group discussions, and performance assessments. If the subject matter is treated as a bundle of information, teacher-made tests will tend to seek certain facts and concepts as "right" answers, suggesting emphasis on convergent thinking. However, if the subject matter is treated as big ideas that are applicable to problem solving, and if students are expected to engage in processes and develop skills to arrive at several "right" answers, teacher-made tests will tend to allow for divergent thinking.

How you develop your classroom philosophy will also dictate the emphasis you place on a student's academic performance. You must decide whether a student is to be compared with his or her peers or with a set of expectations based on individual needs and differences. Generally, teachers who support student-centered classrooms look for divergence in learning and tend to place less emphasis on group norms. Teachers who favor teacher-centered authority for the classroom with a stress on convergence in learning are more apt to favor student evaluation strategies that are based on group norms.

Returning to our exemplar educational philosophy, we can use the following segment to infer what types of assessment this teacher might use.

> I find that by anchoring my teaching on the development of these larger ideas, students can better assess their own understandings and extend them through their exploration of these larger ideas.

Based on this, the teacher would probably use a wide variety of assessments so that students could receive all sorts of feedback about their understanding. However, such a teacher would emphasize open-ended questions that allow students to construct their own answers rather than pick them in a multiple-choice test format. The reason for this is that the teacher wants students to think about big ideas and then describe their understanding of these ideas. Forced choice tests limit this exploration and hence essays, interviews, learning journals, and portfolios would be heavily employed.

Motivation

The concept of **motivation** is derived from the word *motive*, which means an emotion, desire, or impulse acting as an incitement to action. This definition of motive has two parts: First, the definition implies that motivation is internal because it relates to emotions, desires, or other internal drives; second, it implies that there is an accompanying external focus on action or behavior. Organizing a learning environment so that it relates to student needs and desires (internal) and also permits active participation in the learning process (external) is important to student motivation.

Teachers want students to be motivated to do many things: complete homework, be responsible, be lifelong learners, be on time, have fun, care about others, become independent. However, it is not always clear how one sets up a classroom environment that ultimately promotes these desired outcomes. For example, in a teacher-centered orientation, control is primarily in the hands of the teacher. In such a setting, motivation tends to come in the form of rules and regulations. Students are given clear directions concerning their responsibilities; and they are expected to follow these directions because the teacher is in charge. For some students, this clarity of expectations and rules is comfortable. Students achieve because they must; in such a setting, the second half of motivation (external action) is achieved, but not the first (internal desire). The reason students' internal motivation may suffer is that they recognize that both the task of teaching and the responsibility for their learning belong primarily to the teacher.

In a learner-centered setting, the responsibility for learning is primarily borne by the students. The teacher attempts to produce a climate of warmth and mutual respect. Students are encouraged to achieve specific outcomes, but ultimately, they are free to select those that most interest them. In this type of setting, the first aspect of motivation (internal desire) is achieved, in that students select the learning outcomes and processes that interest them; however, the second aspect of motivation (external action) is not as clearly achieved, in that students act according to their personal desires and these desires do not always match those of the teacher.

As a teacher, you should arrange the classroom environment so that it matches your personal philosophy. Your task is to consider carefully the "sources of power" that best reflect your philosophy of education. Figure 5.3 illustrates five different power sources that relate to five different

motivation Internal emotion, desire, or impulse acting as an incitement to action.

FIGURE 5.3

Sources of Power and Types of Motivation Responses

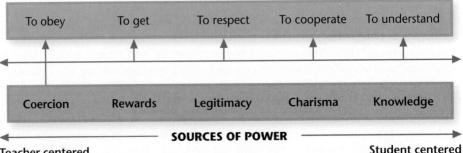
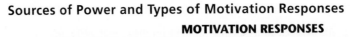

FIGURE 5.4

Teacher–Student Control Continuum

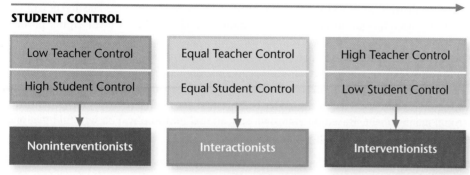

levels of motivation (Schmuck & Schmuck, 1983). Power can be coercive when the motivation is "to obey." Power can take the form of rewards when the motivation is "to get." Power can be seen as legitimate when the motivation is "to respect." Power can be in the form of charisma when the motivation is "to cooperate." Finally, power can be knowledge when the motivation is "to understand." Your philosophy of teaching could include all of these sources of power. All of them might be necessary at one time or another. On the other hand, it is important to assess how you set up your classroom rules and environment and make certain that they match your personal understanding of where power should lie in the teaching and learning process.

For more information about classroom management, see Chapter 12.

Classroom Management and Discipline

The attention given by the national media to disruptive behavior in the classroom has rekindled conflicting views regarding discipline. Polls of parents and teachers alike list discipline among the top issues confronting the schools. The main source of dissatisfaction for nearly two-thirds of today's teachers is their inability to manage students effectively. Teachers also are concerned about the effect disruptive behavior has on learning. The discipline dilemma—how to achieve *more* teacher control in the classroom while adhering to a more open philosophy that advocates *less* teacher control—precludes the development of a school discipline policy that would satisfy both views. Depending on the school district's expectations, the teacher might be caught between conflicting demands.

Carl Glickman and Charles Wolfgang (1978) have identified three schools of thought along a teacher–student control continuum (Figure 5.4). Noninterventionists hold the view that teachers should not impose their own rules; students are inherently capable of solving their own problems. Interactionists suggest that students must learn that the solution to misbehavior is a reciprocal relation between student and teacher. Interventionists believe that teachers must set classroom standards for conduct and give little attention to input from the students.

As you prepare to be a teacher, you need to identify your own beliefs regarding control in the classroom. The goal is to keep disruptive behavior at a minimum, thus enhancing the students' potential for learning as well as your own job satisfaction. Where maintenance of discipline is the primary concern, one might choose from among the entire range of possibilities along the Glickman–Wolfgang continuum regardless of one's own teaching style preference.

Figure 5.5 illustrates how classroom management relates to different types of teacher behaviors. In the following section, we examine three types of discipline along the teacher–student

FIGURE 5.5

Teacher Behaviors Related to Theories of Classroom Management

Choice Theory		Conflict Resolution			Assertive Discipline	
Visually looking on	Nondirective statements	Probing questions	Modeling	Reinforcement	Directive statements	Physical intervention
NONINTERVENTIONISTS		**INTERACTIONISTS**			**INTERVENTIONISTS**	

control continuum; that way you as a future classroom teacher can understand how different kinds of teacher behaviors can be used to support your preferred teaching philosophy.

TYPES OF DISCIPLINE. Whatever the personal philosophy of the teacher, he or she must address the wishes of the district when establishing classroom management schemes. The division of views on classroom discipline has inspired numerous books to assist teachers with discipline problems, and many special courses and workshops have been developed to deal with classroom discipline strategies. But because very few beginning teachers are given extensive exposure to discipline strategies in teacher preparation programs, the vast range of alternatives makes the choice of strategies difficult for teachers who have yet to develop their own styles. The following discipline approaches are described because they offer a variety of alternatives to classroom management. Based on your own educational philosophy, you will find that one or more of them is compatible with your own thinking.

Control or Choice Theory. The psychiatrist William Glasser has advanced **control theory** as a requisite for classroom discipline practices. He suggests that a person's total behavior is composed of feelings, physiology, actions, and thoughts. How a person manages these aspects of behavior makes up an operational definition of control theory. Glasser (1986, p. 46) asserts, "Control theory contends that we choose most of our total behaviors to try to gain control of people or ourselves."

Over time, Glasser (2000) realized that the term *control theory* was subject to misinterpretation, so he retitled his theory *choice theory*. He felt that the term *choice* reflected a better understanding of his ideas. Glasser states that people are driven by six basic needs. All of our choices and behaviors are based on the urgency for survival, power, love, belonging, freedom, and fun. If there is an imbalance in any of these six basic needs, people act out.

As a beginning teacher thinking about classroom discipline, you will find that choice theory encourages you to realize that it is somewhat natural and human for students not to take responsibility for disrupting class or deviating from classroom norms. As a matter of fact, even teachers often find it difficult to take responsibility for some of their own behaviors that deviate from the norm. Choice theory requires teachers to consider the many factors that can account for problem behaviors: physiology, feelings, urges, and so forth. Finally, teachers are encouraged to seek the assistance of counselors, social workers, and parents to fully understand what is causing the problem behavior and only then design an appropriate response.

Choice theory is one of the most difficult management approaches for a new teacher to implement. The majority of discipline problems in the classroom derive from the misguided efforts of students to achieve control. Unfortunately, many teachers think they must have complete control over the classroom. This type of classroom management allows no room for other individuals to have their need for control met. Consequently, student acting out behaviors increase. The first challenge to a new teacher is to evaluate the inappropriate behavior exhibited by the student, determine which need the student thinks is being met by that behavior, and think of appropriate replacement behaviors. The next step, according to choice theory, is to help the student identify the inappropriate behavior and the natural consequences of that behavior. This is done through a series of questions:

- What are you doing?
- What are you supposed to be doing?
- What is the rule?
- Are you making the best choices?

It is important for teachers not to impose artificial consequences. The final challenge is to get students to design a plan on their own. This can be accomplished by follow-up questions such as these:

- What is your plan?
- What choices do you need to make?
- What are you going to do to bring your plan into action?

Take another look at Figure 5.5 and you will see that choice theory falls within the noninterventionist type of classroom control. As a prospective teacher, you will need to evaluate whether control or choice theory is compatible with your view of human nature. If you believe that problem behavior is a natural consequence of our need to balance and fulfill natural urges for survival, power, love, belonging, freedom, and fun, then control theory will fit your philosophy of educa-

control theory A theory of discipline that contends that people choose most of their behaviors to gain control of other people or of themselves.

tion. If, however, you believe that humans are blank tablets who simply need to be directly taught the proper ways of acting, this approach probably won't be for you. You may find the next discipline approach (an interventionist) more compatible with your beliefs.

Assertive Discipline. Assertive discipline is a teacher-in-charge, structured classroom management approach designed to encourage students to choose responsible behavior. Developed by Lee Canter more than twenty years ago, this discipline approach is based on consistency, follow-through, and positive relationship building. The underlying tenet of this approach is that teachers have a right to teach and pupils have a right to learn.

Assertive discipline contends that the teacher has the right to determine what is best for students and to expect compliance. No pupil should prevent the teacher from teaching or keep another student from learning. Student compliance is imperative in creating and maintaining an effective and efficient learning environment. To accomplish this goal, teachers must react assertively, as opposed to aggressively or nonassertively.

Assertive discipline requires teachers to develop a clear classroom discipline plan. The classroom plan must clarify behaviors that are expected of students and clarify what students can expect from the teacher in return. The aim of the plan is to have a fair and consistent way to establish a safe, orderly, positive classroom in which teachers teach and pupils learn. The plan consists of three parts:

- *Rules* that students must follow at all times
- *Positive recognition* that students will receive for following the rules
- *Consequences* that result when students choose not to follow the rules.

According to assertive discipline, students cannot be expected to guess how a teacher wants them to behave in all situations. If students are to succeed in the classroom, they need to know, without doubt, what is expected of them. When students are not given the limits they need, they will act up in order to make the adults around them take notice. A student's disruptive behavior is often a plea for someone to care enough to make him or her stop.

Assertive discipline is not without critics. Some contend that assertive discipline is undemocratic. It conveys a message that only those with power have the right to make rules. Some teachers have responded to this criticism by allowing students to enter into the rule-making process. However, in the end, the assertive discipline teacher makes the final decision.

Other critics of assertive discipline claim that it is simplistic. Assertive discipline does not get at the root of some discipline problems. It assumes that by simply setting up clear rules and consequences along with providing positive feedback, all problem behaviors can be expunged.

In addition, some critics contend that children should obey rules because that is the right thing to do, not because there is some reward associated with obeying or some punishment for not obeying. The long-term implications of rewarding behavior as suggested by the assertive discipline model is that children obey because of positive feedback or because they are told to obey by an authority figure. Real discipline, according to the critics of assertive discipline, should be internal. Responsible behavior should be based on doing what is right.

Return to Figure 5.5 and revisit the behaviors that are associated with an interventionist theory of control. As a prospective teacher, you will need to assess to what degree assertive discipline and its related behaviors fit your philosophy of education. If your philosophy tends to be focused on the teacher's responsibility to control students, assertive discipline is compatible. If your philosophy is focused on students' authority, you would need to modify some of the assertive discipline tenets or not use this discipline.

Conflict Resolution. Another approach to discipline, conflict resolution focuses on the process of teaching students how to recognize problems and then solve them constructively. Students are taught to be conflict managers and are trained to deal with difficulties on the playground, in the hallways, and in the classroom. The student "managers" learn specific skills that enable them, for example, to guide a discussion about a problem between two people who are fighting. There are a variety of ways to train the students, but the underlying benefit is that the students solve their own problems with minimal assistance from adults. Advocates of conflict resolution contend that permitting students to share in the structure and even the enforcement of discipline policies helps them learn to contribute to the school and to society as a whole.

Peer mediation programs are closely associated with conflict resolution approaches. The focus of peer mediation is not so much the resolution of conflict but rather the proactive cultivation

PEARSON
myeducationlab

Go to the *Assignments and Activities* section of Topic 8: *Philosophy of Education* in the MyEducationLab for your course and complete the activity titled *Classroom Management*.

of a climate of peace. In these programs, students receive training in empathy development, social skills, and bias awareness. The overall goal of peer mediation training is to help students develop a social perspective wherein joint benefit is considered over personal gain.

Once again revisit Figure 5.5 and review the types of control behaviors that relate to an interactionist approach to classroom control. These behaviors are compatible with conflict resolution and peer mediation.

Discipline Guidelines. There is no cookbook formula for classroom discipline rules and procedures. Some general guidelines, however, can help the beginning teacher to establish some operating rules that will be accepted and practiced by students:

1. Students and teachers need to learn the importance of considerate behavior and communication.
2. Students need to be treated with respect. Students who are treated with respect develop strong self-esteem.
3. Teachers need to apply critical thinking skills when creating disciplinary rules or analyzing needed disciplinary action.
4. Teachers need to examine how their actions of a social or instructional nature may have helped trigger misbehavior.

The way the teacher introduces and uses these general principles for establishing rules for discipline will set the tone for classroom interactions, creating an environment that is conducive to learning and that minimizes classroom interruptions.

Classroom discipline strongly reflects the teacher's operating classroom philosophy. As you examine the educational philosophy that wins your interest and support, search for its applications to discipline in your classroom. The Reflect on Diversity feature discusses the choice of a classroom discipline approach.

Classroom Climate

classroom climate A holistic concept that involves a set of underlying relationships and a tone or sense of being and feeling in the classroom.

John Goodlad, in his observation of more than one thousand classrooms, found that differences in the quality of schools have little to do with teaching practices. Differences come from what Goodlad (1984, 2004) called an overall **classroom climate**. Classroom climate is not a simple set of rules or ways of acting; it is a holistic concept, one that involves a set of underlying relationships and an underlying tone or sense of being and feeling.

REFLECTonDIVERSITY   Classroom Management

Raja Manijue was concerned about his classroom management practices in his sixth-grade classroom. He had involved students in a discussion concerning his classroom discipline expectations at the beginning of the year and thought the students had agreed with his approach. Recently, however, Raja noticed that several of his students consistently challenged his authority when he called for silence and they often refused to stay seated during assignments.

After attending a professional development workshop on different classroom management approaches, Raja was impressed with an interactionist approach toward discipline that required students and teachers to negotiate classroom discipline rules and consequences. Raja notified students that he would hold a discussion on Monday to discuss new discipline rules and consequences; he asked all students to develop a list that they thought would be helpful and come prepared to share their ideas.

On Monday, Raja asked students to take out their list of ideas. He then went around the room and asked students to share one of their ideas. He was eager to hear what the students who were especially difficult to manage would suggest. Sadly, one after another refused to share her or his thinking. Raja explained that it was important to share

ideas so that everyone's thinking was included in the new discipline approach. However, the disruptive students refused to offer anything.

Disappointed by the disruptive students' refusal to share their thinking, Raja decided to call each of the students' parents and ask them for support. When he called the first parent and asked for help, he was shocked to hear "Why are you bothering me with this? As the teacher you need to demand that my son obey you. In my native country, teachers are in charge and students must listen. Students have no place in developing classroom rules."

Questions for Reflection
1. Why do you think the parent thought that Raja should not require students to participate in developing classroom rules?
2. What does the parent's response imply about her view of authority?
3. Should Raja modify his interactionist approach toward discipline in an effort to take into account this parent's view of authority? Why or why not?

myeducationlab To respond to these questions online, go to the *Book Specific Resources* section, select your text in the MyEducationLab for your course, and then select *Reflect on Diversity* for Chapter 5.

If your educational philosophy incorporates the importance of including the ideas of others and working collegially, you may incorporate some of the social networking components of the Internet or match students with experts from around the world. Ultimately, technology is a set of tools that provides access to many different resources. Your educational philosophy can guide you in determining the types of technology that best enhance students' ability to learn those concepts and skills that are of most worth.

Until now, we have concentrated on understanding how an educational philosophy connects to teaching and learning in the classroom. However, an educational philosophy extends beyond the classroom setting. The next section of this chapter describes ways in which your educational philosophy influences your relationship to the larger society.

━━━━━ JOURNAL FOR REFLECTION ━━━━

Describe the teaching method and classroom environment that you believe have been most effective for you as a learner. Identify the educational philosophy or philosophies that would encourage the teaching method and environment you have selected. Create a graphic that visually represents your own theory of teaching and learning.

YOUR PHILOSOPHY OF EDUCATION BEYOND THE CLASSROOM

The way you manage your classroom and the content, teaching methods, and values you stress will be based on your personal view of the proper role of the teacher in society. A classroom philosophy must incorporate this larger societal view into other views that relate to student learning and behavior in the classroom.

Schools play a role within the larger society. This role is determined by a number of factors: the expectations of society's leaders, economic conditions, the ideologies of powerful lobbying groups, and the philosophies of teachers. It is especially important for educators to examine the role of the school in terms of the larger society—because if such reflection does not occur, schools will merely reflect the status quo or the needs and desires of a single powerful group.

Teachers as Change Agents

An age-old question about the role of schools in a changing society concerns the proper role of the school and the teacher in relation to change. Should teachers be **change agents**, actively working for changes in the existing scheme of things? Or should they reemphasize eternal truths and cultural positions? This question of change versus transmission of ongoing values has been articulated in a variety of ways.

CHANGE AS ADAPTATION. Isaac L. Kandel (1881–1965) was a leader in the essentialist educational philosophy movement who advocated change as a process of **adaptation**. The adaptation approach emphasizes the importance of promoting stability in schools and enabling the individual to adapt to the larger environment (Kandel, 1938). The school should provide students with an unbiased picture of the changes that occur in society. But schools cannot educate for a new social order, nor should teachers use the classroom to promote doctrine. Change occurs first in society. Schools follow the lead.

If a teacher's educational philosophy is one in which the goal for teaching is the mastery of facts and skills so that students can enter society and get a job, that teacher would tend to look at change as the process of adaptation. Students would be taught to accept society as it is today and develop skills that make success in the world of work and daily life possible.

CHANGE AS RATIONAL PROCESS. John Dewey (1937) believed that schools have a part in social change. He contended that change continually occurs, often without a clearly defined direction. Schools need to assume a leadership role in this change because educators have the time to study newer scientific and cultural forces, estimate the direction and outcome, and determine which changes may or may not be beneficial. Schools need to provide an environment in which students can learn these analytic skills and participate in helping society determine the direction that is of most worth.

change agent A person who actively endeavors to mobilize change in a group, institution, or society.

adaptation In the context of social change, an educational approach that favors the promotion of a stable climate in schools to enable students to obtain an unbiased picture of changes that are occurring in society and thus to adapt to those changes.

If a teacher determined that students needed to participate in an ever-changing society, that teacher would tend to provide students with many opportunities to wrestle with problems that characterize society. Students would also be asked to constantly question their own thinking and share their ideas with others. Referring back to the sample educational philosophy presented at the beginning of this chapter, one could infer that change, as a rational process, is consistent with the following quote.

> This implicit standard for objective truth was quickly shattered as I began my teaching career working with seventh- and eighth-grade students in an inner-city, poor neighborhood of Chicago. It was there among these children that I began to understand how the context of children's and adult's lives influence what they knew and how they know it. At first, I thought that my role as teacher was to display facts as facts and truth as truth. Little did I understand, then, that there is an integral relationship between who we are and what we know.
>
> Fortunately, as a teacher I remain a learner and through these early experiences in Chicago, I began to understand that although one might pose objective truth as a standard, there was no absolute argument in favor of such a standard. It was in Chicago that I began to view my teaching role no longer as a provider of truth, but as a prod or questioner who gently tries to extend and refine the personal understandings of my students.

CHANGE AS DIALECTIC. Samuel Bowles and Herbert Gintis (1975, 2006) call for a dialectical humanism through which teachers can help students explore the tension between the individual and society. They identify a conflict, or **dialectic**, between the reproductive needs of society and the self-actualizing needs of the individual. Bowles and Gintis claim that entities such as schools, churches, peer groups, and town meetings attempt to mediate this tension between individual freedom and responsibility for the community. The problem schools face is that they are often unaware that they are mediating this underlying tension, and teachers are often caught in the middle of the dilemma. Teachers are asked to respond to the unique needs of the individual while simultaneously answering to the conflicting needs of society.

Bowles and Gintis call on teachers to develop a participatory democracy in which all interested parties learn both to pursue their interests and to resolve conflicts rationally. As a teacher, you will become part of the educational system. As part of this system, you will be asked to make decisions about student outcomes, discipline procedures, instructional methodologies, and assessment methods. Your decisions regarding these educational issues will be greatly influenced by how you perceive teachers as change agents. You will make different decisions depending on whether you determine that teachers need to help schools adapt, rationally change the social order, reconstruct, or participate in a dialectic. Your task is to consider carefully each of these change paradigms and select the one that matches your personal system of beliefs. Examine the Teacher Perspectives feature concerning the use of controversial topics in the classroom. It is a contemporary example of how communities' views about the proper role of schools can affect what is taught in the classroom.

dialectic A conflict between opposing forces or ideas; in change theory, this conflict is the one between individual needs and the needs of society.

Teaching can be looked at in a variety of ways, ranging from helping students create their own meaning to taking a deliberate stand and arguing for social change.

Teachers as Leaders

Teachers serve as leaders for their students. Evidence of this can be found in the testimonials that are offered by former students when they have become adults. Most students, whether they have achieved graduate degrees or have followed vocational pursuits immediately after high school, report remembering

TEACHER PERSPECTIVES

Should Teachers Express Their Views on Controversial Topics in Class?

Communities differ in their perspectives about the use of controversial topics in the classroom. Should schools advocate for social change by encouraging students to debate controversial topics? Should schools remain neutral about social change and refrain from encouraging students to deal with controversial issues?

YES

Rachael Rice is an artist and activist who teaches fifth- to eighth-grade art at Barre City Elementary and Middle School in Barre, Vermont.

If those views support civil and human rights, of course they should!

I believe one cannot advocate for children anywhere without advocating for children everywhere. This means advocating for children in Iraq, Afghanistan, and Palestine as well as in Western and European countries.

Advocating for peace is now considered controversial in my district, as are rainbows and pink triangles ("pro-gay"). Here at Barre City School, I have had a "Safe Space Ally" sign illegally stolen off my door by a former school board member. Our administration forbade me to replace it, citing "controversy."

At one time, the abolition of slavery, desegregation, and women voting were considered controversial topics. But today, we as teachers are freely encouraged to support equal rights around Dr. Martin Luther King's birthday, and to examine the effects of prejudice as we study the Holocaust or slavery. We are encouraged to educate students for participation in the democratic process, which depends so much upon the freedom to express dissent.

So the truth is that teachers are supported when they express controversial views, as long as their opinions are aligned with those of the majority.

Of course, it is extremely important for teachers who express strong opinions to respect the fact that some students may feel intimidated. That's why I tell all my students on the first day of school not to believe anything I say just because I say it.

I urge them to turn a critical eye toward their teachers as well as toward their studies.

They trust me to help create a safe environment in which unpopular sentiments may be expressed and responded to in appropriate, kind ways.

The best teachers teach students to think for themselves.

NO

Lacey Pitts is an NEA Student member in Americus, Georgia.

I do not believe teachers should share their opinions on controversial topics in the classroom. Too often teachers attempt to share their views to stimulate conversation, but only end up alienating students.

I am in college and still in a student's position, and I am not far removed from being a high school student. I was in a classroom where a teacher attacked my personal view and I remember how terrible it felt.

I was in tenth grade. The teacher opened a discussion of homosexuality in the classroom by stating that she felt homosexuality was wrong and a sin, implying that supporting such an alternative lifestyle was also wrong.

I was crushed, having family members and very close friends who were homosexual. I felt attacked for my love of these people and for accepting their lifestyle choices.

My teacher was supported by other students, but no one, not even I, advocated homosexuality. I was afraid of being told I was wrong and feared a personal attack by the teacher or other students. My voice was silenced in the classroom.

As educators, we must never allow this stifling to occur. Instead, we must strive to construct and foster environments that support differences in views and opinions by informing students of all arguments involved. We are in the classroom to guide, inform, and inspire our students.

When I become a teacher, I plan to play devil's advocate on controversial topics. I want my students to hear and consider all sides of an issue.

Impartiality is the key to allowing our students to think and decide their own stances on these topics individually.

Teachers must correct misstatements of facts, but a student's individual opinion should be allowed expression without fear of judgment.

Source: "Should Teachers Express Their Views on Controversial Topics in Class?" *NEA Today* (October 2005), p. 40. Reprinted by permission of the National Education Association.

What is your perspective on this issue?

PEARSON myeducationlab To explore both sides of this issue and think about each perspective, go to the *Book Specific Resources* in the MyEducationLab for your course, select your text, and then select *Teacher Perspectives* for Chapter 5.

---

teachers who had a personal impact on their lives. These students will usually discuss the leadership and modeling behaviors of the teachers they remember.

The idea of teachers as leaders suggests that the new teacher should be aware of the need to develop a beginning repertoire of leadership qualities to which students can look for guidance during their developmental years. These leadership qualities—and the practice of them—are highly dependent on the classroom philosophy that the new teacher puts into practice. Some beginning concepts for teacher leadership are vision, modeling behaviors, and use of power.

VISION. Classroom leadership behaviors begin when a teacher possesses both a vision and the intent to actualize that vision for the students. How a teacher actually puts his or her vision into practice depends wholly on the teacher's philosophical convictions. A **vision** is a mental construct that synthesizes and clarifies what you value or consider to be of highest worth. The clearer the vision or mental picture, the easier it is for a leader to make decisions or persuade or influence others. Formulating a vision requires reflection concerning what you believe about truth, beauty, justice, and equality. It is important to consider these issues and formulate a vision about how schools and classrooms should be organized and what ideas should be implemented.

Linda Sheive and Marian Schoenheit (1987) offer five steps to help leaders put their visions into action:

1. Value your vision.
2. Be reflective and plan a course of action.
3. Articulate the vision to colleagues.
4. Develop a planning stage and an action stage.
5. Have students become partners in the vision.

If teachers reflect on their vision, they can plan the course of action they need to use with their learners. Articulation provides teachers with an opportunity to share their vision with colleagues. Inservice or staff development sessions are excellent times to articulate a classroom vision. Visions require a planning stage and an action stage if they are to become reality. Planning and action stages should involve the students who are intended to be the receivers of this vision. For example, if a teacher wishes students to be reflective in their learning environment, then the teacher needs to help the students understand the benefits of reflectiveness and become partners in the planning. The teacher might engage the students in free and open discussions of the vision and its importance to the learning environment in the classroom.

MODELING. If teachers hold certain expectations of learner behaviors in the classroom, it is imperative that they model those behaviors with the students. If the classroom teacher is rigid and fixed in his or her classroom practices and creates an authoritarian atmosphere, then the students will probably respond accordingly. On the other hand, if the teacher provides a more democratic classroom, the students will respond similarly in their classroom encounters. We would caution that a laissez-faire environment will probably produce a classroom where learners have little or no direction. Teachers should consider the modeling effect on the classroom environment and exhibit behaviors consistent with their philosophy of education.

EMPOWERMENT. The concept of power in the classroom should not be considered good or bad; power in itself has no value structure. The use of power, however, gives it a good, poor, or bad image. All leaders have power that is associated with their position, but the successful leader is judicious in its use. The nature of the teaching position entrusts a teacher with power both within and outside the classroom. How a teacher uses power in the classroom or in the school building is wholly determined by the classroom philosophy the teacher wants to project.

Teachers' use of power can be classified into two different styles: teacher centered and learner centered. A teacher-centered power style is based on an authoritarian construct for the classroom. Learners are not expected to be active verbally in the learning process but are generally expected to be receivers and practicing users of teacher-given information. Learning is very convergent. It is selected and given to the learner in the particular way in which the teacher wishes the student to acquire it.

A learner-centered power style views the learner as someone who is verbally active and who seeks divergence in learning. Learner-centered power styles encourage the active participation of the learner in exploring learning and helping to determine the extent to which he or she will engage in alternative approaches. Learning is very divergent. These power styles tend to recognize differences in learning, individual interests, and higher order learning.

Past and present practices in schools tend to lean heavily on the teacher-dominant style. Therefore, although many teachers in training study both categories of teaching styles, they tend to see only one major type in practice when they visit schools. We suggest that you continually study both major styles so that you can apply either one as needed on the basis of your classroom objectives for students and your classroom philosophy.

Teachers' use of power extends beyond the classroom. Teachers, by their very occupation, are empowered with both rights and responsibilities. They have a unique obligation to advocate for the needs of children, to remind society of its obligations to coming generations, to look

vision A mental construction that synthesizes and clarifies what a person values or considers to be of highest worth.

GLOBAL PERSPECTIVES   The World as a Classroom

This chapter encourages you to examine your beliefs and assumptions in an effort to develop a personal philosophy of education. It is also important to consider the limitations that such a philosophy can impose. For example, to what degree does your philosophy of education incorporate the larger world of thinkers? Does your philosophy affirm or disaffirm varied thinking schemes, varied beliefs, and varied ways of arriving at answers? Relating to global neighbors is no longer just a matter of respecting differences. If educators are truly to relate and work collaboratively, their thinking schemes need to intermingle with those of other educators, educators who may have vastly different ways of thinking. Yet a personal philosophy implies the development of a cohesive set of views about knowledge and the nature of the world. Teachers must balance this need to intermix against the importance of clarifying an individual point of view; this is the challenge the world classroom presents to every teacher.

Questions for Reflection
1. How might you present to another teacher your own views about what knowledge is of most worth?
2. What can you do if you are asked to team teach with another educator who views knowledge differently than you do?

beyond material wealth, and to consider the spiritual wealth of knowledge. Teachers, by virtue of their occupation, are given certain rights to speak and be heard. The greater society looks to teachers for guidance concerning the future health of the world. The Global Perspectives feature encourages you to consider the world as a classroom.

JOURNAL FOR REFLECTION

Develop a statement that depicts how you intend to function as a teacher/leader within the larger society. Describe one position you support related to a political action.

LOOKING AHEAD: INCREASED SUPPORT FOR CHARTER AND MAGNET SCHOOLS

Throughout this chapter we have emphasized the importance of carefully developing your personal educational philosophy. The need to be clear about your personal approach to teaching and learning becomes especially important as calls for alternative approaches to teaching and learning increase. These calls have fueled increased interest and support for the development of magnet and charter schools. Magnet and charter schools are those that provide alternative approaches to education. Some magnet and charter schools emphasize an interdisciplinary theme such as the environment or the development of the arts. Other magnet and charter schools emphasize a unique teaching and learning approach such as a Montessori approach or a constructivist approach. Still other magnet and charter schools emphasize a social activist or democratic approach to school climate.

This increased emphasis on public support for alternative teaching and learning magnet and charter schools requires teachers to show that they have reflected and developed personal educational philosophies that are consistent with these alternatives to the standard curriculum. By explicitly developing your own personal views about the nature of knowledge and the nature of teaching you will be in a better position to determine if a charter or magnet school is appropriate for you.

SUMMARY

THE DYNAMIC RELATIONSHIP BETWEEN PHILOSOPHY AND EDUCATION

- Educational philosophy can be analyzed as the application of philosophy to the classroom.
- The way the curriculum is organized, the manner in which instruction is delivered, the character of school environments, and the processes used in testing and grading are informed by the philosophical views held by educators, parents, and legislators.
- Idealism and realism reflect a teacher-centered approach to education because they place greater responsibility on teachers to teach specific content and thinking skills.
- Humanism and existentialism reflect a student-centered approach to education because they place more emphasis on developing students' individual meaning.

- A philosophy of education is not a set of written words. It is a platform on which decisions are made and life is led.
- One strategy that can help teachers develop their personal philosophy of education is to build on the educational philosophies of others.

TEACHER-CENTERED EDUCATIONAL PHILOSOPHIES

- Teacher-centered educational philosophies (essentialism, behaviorism, and positivism) emphasize the importance of controlling the subject matter content, thinking processes, and discipline procedures within the classroom setting.
- Essentialism holds that there is a common core of information and skills that an educated person in a given culture must have.
- Behaviorism is a psychological theory and educational philosophy that holds that one's behavior is determined by environment, not heredity.
- Positivism is an educational philosophy that rejects beliefs about mind, spirit, and consciousness and holds that all reality can be explained by laws of matter and motion.

STUDENT-CENTERED EDUCATIONAL PHILOSOPHIES

- Student-centered educational philosophies (progressivism, humanism, and constructivism) place less emphasis on the external control of the teacher and more emphasis on developing students' personal meaning.
- Progressivism promotes individual student inquiry, humanism stresses student freedom, and constructivism emphasizes the importance of supporting personal meaning.
- The humanistic educational philosophy is concerned with enhancing the innate goodness of the individual. It rejects a group-oriented educational system and seeks ways to enhance the individual development of the student.
- Constructivism is an educational philosophy that emphasizes developing personal meaning through hands-on, activity-based teaching and learning.

DEVELOPING YOUR OWN PHILOSOPHY OF EDUCATION

- One way of clarifying your philosophy of education is to examine the different aspects of teaching and determine your own preferences for classroom organization, student motivation, discipline approach, and classroom climate.
- Classroom organization includes the way you set up your classroom, the way you develop lesson plans and implement those plans, and the way you assess students.
- Motivation approaches include noninterventionist, interactionist, and interventionist.
- Classroom climate involves the type of voice you choose to encourage and how much space your provide for collaboration and discussion.
- Most teachers use various aspects of different educational philosophies as they determine the specific type of classroom organization, discipline, motivation, and classroom climates that they prefer. For this reason, we encourage an eclectic approach—an approach that draws on many different sets of ideas.

YOUR PHILOSOPHY OF EDUCATION BEYOND THE CLASSROOM

- In life, one must consider the implications of a philosophy of education for acting responsibly in society. What types of societal change match your philosophy of education, and what type of responsible leadership does your philosophy compel you to assume?
- Teachers can choose to be a change agent in society by helping students prepare to enter society (adaptation), by helping students deal with change in a rational way (rational process), or by directly working on specific change initiatives (change as dialectic).
- Teachers can lead by modeling and empowerment.

LOOKING AHEAD: INCREASED SUPPORT FOR CHARTER AND MAGNET SCHOOLS

- The need to be clear about your personal approach to teaching and learning becomes especially important as calls for alternative approaches to teaching and learning increase.
- These calls have fueled increased interest and support for the development of magnet and charter schools.

DISCUSSION QUESTIONS

1. What were the characteristics and behaviors of one of your favorite teachers who had a teacher-centered educational philosophy? Of a favorite teacher who had a student-centered educational philosophy?
2. When might a teacher focus on personalized situations involving such things as death or injustice to stimulate student learning? How would such a strategy relate to the back-to-the-basics expectations of many U.S. schools?
3. Experienced teachers often advise a beginning teacher: "Be firm with the students and let them know at the beginning how you intend to teach your classes." Is this advice good or bad? Discuss the pros and cons of such a tactic.

4. Constructivism rules out some of the conventional notions about educating youth. It emphasizes students' construction of personalized understandings of the world rather than an established curriculum. What implications does constructivism have for grouping students?
5. Teachers must be able to manage the classroom in such a way that the environment created is conducive to teaching and learning. How do you plan to organize your classroom to set up such an environment?
6. What is your vision of democracy in the classroom? To what degree should students be permitted to decide what they will study, when they will study, and how they will study? Why?

SCHOOL-BASED OBSERVATIONS

1. This chapter contains examples of classroom activities associated with various educational theories. As you work in the schools, take the class activity features placed throughout this chapter with you and see whether you can determine which educational philosophies you observe in use. Then decide which educational philosophy you subscribe to and determine whether your own classroom activities are consistent with your personal educational philosophy.

2. Interview several teachers who organize their classrooms and teaching materials differently. Using probing questions, try to uncover the educational philosophy or philosophies that account for the differing teaching approaches.
3. Prepare a synopsis of your overall philosophy of education. Then interview a teacher who seems to teach and organize the classroom the way you would. Ask the teacher to review your synopsis.

PORTFOLIO DEVELOPMENT

1. Select one major concept from one of the national standards documents (available in your college library). Describe ways that you might help students learn a particular concept. You might consider methods that helped you learned a concept. Then, determine and explain which educational philosophy or philosophies match your description best. Include this description and explanation in your portfolio as an example of your ability to analyze lessons in terms of theories.
2. Prepare a synopsis of your overall philosophy of education perspective. Include your views about

classroom organization, motivation, discipline, and climate. Try to develop a graphic that clearly shows how all of these components connect and are consistent with your overall perspective.
3. Develop a statement that depicts how you intend to function as a teacher/leader within the larger society. Describe one position you support related to political action.

PREPARING FOR CERTIFICATION

1. One of the topics in the Praxis II Principles of Learning and Teaching (PLT) test is "Types of communications and interactions that can stimulate discussion in different ways for particular purposes" through the use of a variety of strategies (for example, "providing for learner understanding, helping students articulate their ideas and thinking processes, promoting risk taking and problem solving, facilitating factual recall, encouraging convergent and divergent thinking,

stimulating curiosity, helping students to question, promoting a caring community").

In this chapter, you learned about six major educational theories and the various teaching and learning approaches, classroom practices, and educational programs of study related to each theory. Review each of the theories, paying particular attention to the relationship between how students learn and the teaching and learning strategies consistent with each theory. Which theory seems most compatible with your own beliefs and philosophy? Which theory seems least compatible?

2. Answer the following multiple-choice question, which is similar to items in Praxis and other state certification tests.

   Ms. Jones, a second-grade teacher, began a language arts lesson by reading the beginning and middle of a story to the children. Instead of reading the end of the story, however, she asked the students to create an ending of their own. The children wrote their own endings and then read them aloud. Ms. Jones then read the story's ending, and she and the class talked about the many ways a story can end. Which educational theory appears to guide Ms. Jones's lesson? Describe your reasons for selecting the educational theory.
   a. Behaviorism
   b. Constructivism
   c. Positivism

3. Answer the following multiple-choice question, which is similar to items in Praxis and other state certification tests. If you are unsure of the answer, review the opening section of this chapter.

   Which of the following activities would most clearly be an inappropriate activity to encourage divergent thinking in a mathematics lesson on patterns and shapes?
   a. Children will identify and match pictures of three-dimensional shapes while playing a board game with peers.
   b. Children will create patterns using different shapes of pasta noodles and write how many pieces are in their designs.
   c. Children will use an online program in which they correctly identify shapes.
   d. Children will search for shapes in the classroom and make a chart listing the types and numbers of shapes found.

4. Answer the following short-answer question, which is similar to items in Praxis and other state certification tests.

   What is meant by the terms *teacher-centered locus of control* and *student-centered locus of control*? Give three examples of teaching practices or learning activities that you might observe in two classrooms—one dominated

by teacher-centered locus of control and the other dominated by student-centered locus of control.

5. Several topics in the Praxis II Principles of Learning and Teaching (PLT) test relate to the content of this chapter, including "effective classroom management," "strategies to promote positive relationships," "cooperation," and "purposeful learning." Items included in this category include the following:
   • Establishing daily procedures and routines
   • Establishing classroom rules
   • Using natural and logical consequences
   • Providing positive guidance
   • Modeling conflict resolution, problem solving, and anger management
   • Giving timely feedback
   • Maintaining accurate records
   • Communicating with parents and caregivers
   • Using objective behavior descriptions
   • Responding to student behavior
   • Arranging classroom space
   • Pacing and structuring a lesson

   Review the Classroom Climate section of this chapter. How will you build on John Goodlad's findings about positive classroom climate, Henry Giroux's conception of voice, and Maxine Greene's conception of space in your own classroom?

6. Answer the following short-answer question, which is similar to items in the Praxis and other state certification tests.

   The Jefferson Elementary School staff is debating the merits of the assertive discipline program developed by Lee Canter. One of the teachers, Leslie Brown, is strongly in favor of the program. Another teacher, Robin James, strongly opposes the program. What arguments might Leslie make in favor of the assertive discipline program? What arguments might Robin make against the program?

After you've completed your written responses to the questions above, use the Praxis general scoring guide provided in Chapter 1 to see if you can you revise your responses to improve your score.

MYEDUCATIONLAB

myeducationlab Now go to Topic 8: *Philosophy of Education* in the MyEducationLab (www.myeducationlab.com) for your course, where you can:

• Find learning outcomes for *Philosophy of Education* along with the national standards that connect to these outcomes.
• Complete *Assignments and Activities* that can help you more deeply understand the chapter content.
• Apply and practice your understanding of the core teaching skills identified in the chapter with the *Building Teaching Skills and Dispositions* learning units.

• Check your comprehension on the content covered in the chapter by going to the *Study Plan* in the *Book Specific Resources* section for your text. Here you will be able to take a chapter quiz, receive feedback on your answers, and then access *Review, Practice, and Enrichment* activities to enhance your understanding of chapter content.

WEBSITES

www.ed.uiuc.edu/EPS/Educational-Theory *Educational Theory* is a quarterly publication that fosters the continuing development of educational theory and encourages wide and effective discussion of theoretical problems within the education profession. You will find this journal filled with contemporary concerns that relate to teaching and learning.

www.funderstanding.com/content/constructivism Funderstanding contains a variety of theories on learning, instruction, assessment, influences, history of education, learning patterns, educational reforms, as well as additional links.

http://pbln.imsa.edu The Illinois Mathematics and Science Academy (www.imsa.edu) has developed a network of problem-based learning programs, ideas, examples of problem-based learning in classrooms, access to a problem-based learning teachers' network, and other resources that relate to the use of problem-based learning in contemporary schools.

www.criticalthinking.org The Foundation for Critical Thinking is dedicated to providing educators, students, and the general public with access to information about critical thinking, theory and practice, concepts, techniques for learning and teaching, and classroom exercises.

www.theteachersguide.com The Teachers Guide is a web-based company that provides information, professional articles, resources, books, virtual field trips, and educational software related to classroom management, educational psychology, special education, and so on. Click on Class Management for more information.

www.nwrel.org/scpd/sirs/5/cu9.html The School Improvement Research Series website provides introductions, definitions, and research on discipline practices. Discussions include research findings, teacher training in classroom management, discipline of multicultural students, specific discipline programs, and ineffective discipline practices. The site also includes a summary of research perspectives on improving school and classroom discipline.

FURTHER READING

Campbell, D. M., Cignetti, P. B., Melenyzer, B. J., Nettles, D. H., & Wyman, R. M., Jr. (1997). *How to develop a professional portfolio: A manual for teachers*. Boston: Allyn & Bacon. This booklet provides a comprehensive look at what is needed to develop a professional portfolio for education professionals.

Carlson, R. (2003). *The don't sweat guide for teachers: Cutting through the clutter so that every day counts*. New York: Hyperion. How to deal with the demands of teaching and still enjoy the job. Gives strategies for creating surprise, modeling respect, and being a talent scout.

Joyce, B. R., Weil, M., & Calhoun, E. (2000). *Models of teaching* (6th ed.). Boston: Allyn & Bacon. This book describes the relationship between different approaches to teaching and various educational theories. It shows that most teaching methods tend to draw from several related educational theories rather than a single educational theory.

Kohn, A. (1993). *Punished by rewards: The trouble with gold stars, incentive plans, A's, praise, and other bribes*. Boston: Houghton Mifflin. Dr. Kohn describes the unexpected consequences of using reinforcement practices and cautions against the dangers of providing rewards to enhance good behavior.

Ladson-Billings, G. (1994). *The dreamkeepers: Successful teachers of African American children*. San Francisco: Jossey-Bass. A reflective look at different teaching strategies in terms of their effectiveness with African American students.

MacKenzie, R. J. (2003). *Setting limits in the classroom*. Roseville, CA: Prima. Offers up-to-date alternatives to punishment and permissiveness beyond the usual methods. Also offers special tools for handling the "strong-willed" student.

Martin, J. R. (1995, January). A philosophy of education for the year 2000. *Phi Delta Kappan, 77*(1), 21–27. This article describes the work of an existentialist and how to develop a philosophy of education that is consistent with existential principles.

Noddings, N. (2005). *The challenge to care in schools: An alternative approach to education* (Advances in contemporary educational thought series) (2nd ed.). New York: Teachers College Press. This book offers a comprehensive discussion of the importance of caring as well as specific examples of a caring classroom environment.

Strike, K. A., & Soltis, J. F. (1985). *The ethics of teaching*. New York: Teachers College Press. A careful analysis of the ethics surrounding the life of a teacher. Drs. Strike and Soltis provide thoughtful questions and ideas that help teachers reassess their own ethical positions.

Torp, L., & Sage, S. (2002). *Problems and possibilities: Problem-based learning for K–16 education* (2nd ed.). Alexandria, VA: Association for Supervision and Curriculum Development. Provides a specific approach to the implementation of problem-based learning. The approach is supported by educational theories, and a clear set of steps for developing a problem-based learning unit is presented.

chapter six

PLACE OF SCHOOLS
IN SOCIETY

EDUCATION
IN THE **NEWS**

MORE VALLEY STUDENTS SIGNING UP FOR VIRTUAL SCHOOLS

By RAY PARKER

The Arizona Republic, May 24, 2009

An increasing number of Arizona's 62,000 high-school graduates have chosen a route suited to the MP3 generation: online classes.

At Primavera Online High School, one of Arizona's largest public high schools, about 9,000 students take classes in English literature, Spanish and calculus. They join clubs, enter science fairs, and talk one-on-one with their teachers.

No one complains about the mystery meat at the school cafeteria, and no one ever gets asked to, or snubbed at, a school dance.

More than a decade after being created by state lawmakers, the 14 Internet-based schools in Arizona have become a quiet force in the state's education system. These full-time, tuition-free, virtual schools allow students to learn at any time and from any computer.

More than 26,000 students took online courses in 2008, and enrollment numbers are growing. An estimated 1,475 students in Arizona are graduating from virtual schools this year.

"We've experienced the growth because I believe kids want more flexibility in their high-school careers, and many because of the economic times, want to work . . . and our classes are available 24 hours a day," said Primavera Online Principal Dane Van Deinse.

Kayla Gibson, 18, who will graduate this week from Primavera Online, said it was easy for her to complete schoolwork online "even though it does take a lot of self-motivation to complete the work."

Some virtual-school students are enrolled in traditional middle and high schools but use the online courses as supplements. Others are home-school students who use virtual classes as a small or large part of their curriculum since online classes encompass grades K–12.

The Legislature in 1998 passed the Technology Assisted Project-Based Instruction (TAPBI) program to "improve pupil achievement and extend academic options beyond the four walls of the traditional classroom."

Two school districts, Deer Valley Unified and Mesa Public Schools, and two charter schools, Sequoia Choice and Arizona Virtual Academy, have participated since the beginning, while 10 new providers have been added for a total of 14 virtual schools.

Online schools received a total of $57.4 million from the state in 2008; their funding is based on student enrollment.

TAPBI student enrollment increases each year: there were 10,800 students in 2005, 15,200 in 2006, and 24,100 in 2007.

Virtual schools set up shop in office buildings where administrators, technical workers and customer-service staff work. When signing up for a class, the student gets an introductory phone call from the teacher. Students follow detailed lesson plans and communicate with the teacher by phone or by e-mail at least once a week.

Geoffrey Wall, 17, of Tempe, will graduate this week from Arizona Connections Academy. He will enter Arizona State University in the fall as an art major.

"What I liked was the freedom because I had the ability to use my time the way I wanted to use it," he said.

As a former ice skater, Wall spent a lot of time practicing in the rink. He said the virtual school helped him fulfill his Arizona education requirements and taught him a lot about working independently.

"If I was picking up on something really quickly, I could just keep going," Wall said.

Taking classes outside of classrooms requires some adjustments. Art students send drawings to teachers by mail or create them on computers. Some students enter "discussions" in virtual classes that are similar to chat rooms. Science students conduct experiments in their kitchens.

The schools have tried to create extracurricular activities by forming online clubs and other programs, such as science fairs with projects posted on school Web sites.

The system works for Shawntae Swartz, 15, of Tempe. Swartz takes online classes through Primavera while enrolled in the 3-D animation program at East Valley Institute of Technology in Mesa.

"In anything there's going to be ups and downs, but I can get credits faster and at my own pace," she said.

QUESTIONS FOR REFLECTION

1. Have you ever taken online courses? How did you like them? What were the advantages and disadvantages of this mode of delivery of instruction?
2. What are some of the limitations of virtual schools like Primavera Online High School?
3. Do you have any interest in teaching in a virtual school or online courses? Why or why not?

LEARNING OUTCOMES

After reading and studying this chapter, you should be able to:

1. Understand generally accepted roles of schools and how they contribute to the socialization of children and youth.
2. Describe culture, its characteristics, and its impact in schools. (INTASC 3: Diversity)
3. Discuss characteristics of school culture that contribute to effective schools that support student learning.
4. Describe the school choices available to parents in a growing number of larger school districts.
5. Understand why schools have evolved into different groupings of students by age and grades. (INTASC 2: Learning and Development)
6. Identify some of the differences between rural, suburban, and urban schools and their impact on students.
7. Identify some of the characteristics of effective schools in which students learn at high levels.

ROLES OF SCHOOLS

Schools play many roles in society. They not only teach literacy and computation, they also reflect society's high ideals such as universal education for all children. At the same time, they reflect society's bad practices by sometimes contributing to racial and socioeconomic divides by, for example, tracking disproportionate numbers of students of color, low-income students, and English-language learners into special education. Schools do not always ensure that students in gifted programs and advanced placement courses match the racial and socioeconomic makeup of the students in schools. Schools in high-poverty areas are much more likely to be staffed by teachers who are inexperienced and not fully qualified.

━━━━━━━━━ JOURNAL FOR REFLECTION ━━━━━━━━━

Which of the following ideals do you think schools should mirror? Why?

- Be a model of our best hopes for society and a mechanism for remaking society in the image of those hopes.
- Adapt students to the needs of society by preparing them for specific roles and jobs.
- Serve the individual hopes and ambitions of their students and parents.

Our own philosophical and political perspectives help determine how we view the roles of schools. Should schools primarily support democratic equality, social efficiency, social mobility, or some other goal? Advocates of democratic equality view education as a public good through which all students should be exposed to a liberal arts education and learn to be productive citizens in a democracy. Proponents of social efficiency believe that schools should serve the private sector by preparing students for future jobs. People who support **social mobility** view education as an asset that can be accumulated and used for social competition. Credentials become very important for gaining a competitive advantage over others to secure a desirable position in society (Labaree, 1997).

School boards, educators, parents, and communities have their own beliefs and perspectives about the basic roles of schools. Their beliefs may draw on national reports calling for the reform of education. Through such reports and discussions and debates among educators, policy makers, and others, U.S. society continually refines and redefines its ideas about schools. The five roles described in the following sections are a sampling of those most often mentioned by educators and the public. Most schools address each of these roles, but in any given school or community, one goal may receive more prominence than others. Think about them as you develop your own views regarding the roles of schools in society.

social mobility The movement of an individual or family up or down in social class such as moving from the lower class to middle class as one finishes college and earns a larger income.

Citizenship

Most people agree that schools should help students become good citizens. There is less agreement about the meaning of the term *good citizens* and how schools should go about preparing them. In some schools, especially elementary schools, students sometimes receive a grade or rating on their citizenship within the classroom. Students often take a civics or government course or have studied citizenship issues in social studies courses.

America's Civic Health Index has identified the following categories as signs of desirable civic behavior:

- Connecting to civic and religious groups,
- Trusting other people,
- Connecting to others through family and friends,
- Giving and volunteering,
- Staying informed,
- Understanding civics and politics,
- Participating in politics,
- Trusting and feeling connected to major institutions, and
- Expressing political views (*American Civic Health Index: Broken Engagement.* Washington, DC: National Conference on Citizenship, 2006).

The involvement of large numbers of youth in the 2008 national elections, even though they were not old enough to vote in many cases, is a positive sign of engagement in the civic affairs of the nation. Teachers also model civic behavior and are more or less engaged in community and political activities locally, nationally, or internationally. Australian educators approach citizenship education in a similar way to U.S. educators. Their own involvement in related activities is described in the Global Perspectives feature.

GLOBAL PERSPECTIVES — Citizenship Education in Australia

How do teachers themselves practice citizenship and reflect their lived experiences in the classroom? Citizenship education in Australia has traditionally been teaching a set of knowledge. But with a rapidly changing world that is impacted by the forces of globalization, the notions of citizenship are changing, with greater emphasis being placed on diversity, globalization, social justice, human rights, and equality. Based on the assumption that the teaching of citizenship is influenced and mediated by teachers' own lived experiences as cultural beings, researcher Joan G. Dejaeghere examined the privilege and power that active engagement in a local, national, or international community could provide participants.

The sense of belonging was important in determining the relationships educators had with others and the communities in which they interacted. Their sense of belonging was strengthened by feeling included in the community and having "a shared identity around common values, ideals, or issues." The educators who had privilege and power in the rights that they could enact at each level had a strong sense of belonging.

Two other factors affected the Australian educators being active citizens at some level. One depended on their access to resources and knowledge, and the second was their own personal involvement in the issues. Their access to resources was determined by their own socioeconomic status, where they lived in comparison to the sources of power in Australia, and their connections to sources of economic and political power outside of the country. Participants who lived on the east coast of Australia felt that they had greater influence because they were close to the national center of political power. Those who participated in international organizations and worked internationally felt that they had power

and privilege in some global communities. All of the participants thought that they had little, if any, influence on the major issues affecting the global community such as the injustices and great gaps among people in economic stability.

The educators who participated in this study regarded citizenship as engaging with social and civic changes that include addressing "social injustices and global issues, such as the environment." They indicated that these issues should be addressed in schools as part of citizenship education. Although students in Australia report that their classrooms are generally open to such discussions, they rarely occur. Issues around the privilege and power of citizenship were seldom addressed in the classroom, which limited students' ability (1) to begin to think critically about the issues outlined as important in citizenship education and (2) to become active participants in a democracy.

Questions for Reflection
1. How did the educators participating in this study define citizenship education?
2. What advantages do you think you would experience if you became an active citizen who is involved in making the changes necessary to serve all people well?
3. How could students be taught to be active citizens? What are some projects in your community in which students might be interested? How could you help them become involved with those projects and develop their citizenship skills?

Source: From "Citizenship as Privilege and Power: Australian Educators' Lived Experiences as Citizens," by J. G. Dejaeghere, August 2008, *Comparative Education Review, 52*(3), pp. 357–380.

Citizenship education in public schools implicitly values patriotism and loyalty to one's country.

The National Council for Social Studies (NCSS) includes a standard on civic ideals and practices. The focus in citizenship education or in civics and government courses is usually on the structure of the U.S. political system and on treasured documents such as the Constitution and Bill of Rights. Patriotism and nationalism are the foundations of these courses and the school's **hidden curriculum**, which is the implicit set of values taught by teachers. One of the limitations of citizenship education that has this focus is that students might not have the opportunity to grapple with the problems and issues that are inherent in a democratic society such as racism, sexism, and the reasons for the great gaps in income among groups. Students might learn the civic values but never be challenged to discuss inequities among groups in society.

Preparation for citizenship cannot be taught in a single course. Schools work to develop democratic citizens who respect others, believe in human dignity, are concerned about and care for others, and fight for justice, fairness, and tolerance. Students learn through practice in the classroom how to be active, involved citizens. Schools not only teach about participation in society, they also model democratic practice through the equitable participation of students in our schools.

Democratic schools are discussed in more detail in Chapter 7.

Workforce Readiness

Since the release of the report *A Nation at Risk* in 1983, national reports on education have expressed concern about the quality of the workforce. The emphasis on the education of workers today focuses on preparing them for jobs in a global economy. For example, a 2009 report of the National Governors Association began its report *Building a High-Quality Education Workforce* with "The long-term health of each state's economy rests on the state's ability to educate and eventually employ citizens who contribute to its economy by filling jobs in a variety of sectors."

Some employers complain that schools do not provide students with the basic skills and behaviors necessary to participate effectively in today's global economy. Business owners want graduates to have the vocational skills appropriate to the job, but they also want them to have dispositions or values and attitudes such as punctuality and a good work ethic. A lack of agreement exists about the nature of the necessary skills, especially in an economy in which the greatest job growth is now in the service sector where people of color and women have disproportionately high representation (U.S. Census Bureau, 2008, Table 596). At the same time, the country's leaders worry that not enough engineers, computer scientists, and other workers in the STEM (science, technology, engineering, and mathematics) professions are being produced to meet the needs of the country. The production of U.S. students in these areas has fallen behind that of other nations.

The "real" goal of schools continues to be debated. Is it to ensure students have the knowledge and skills to keep the economy competitive in a changing world where new jobs continually emerge? Is it to help students learn a trade, learn how to learn, or learn how to take orders and follow the rules? This question is particularly important when conditions change as rapidly as they do in today's society. The vocation for which one is prepared initially may become obsolete within a few years. The *Framework for 21st Century Learning* (Partnership for 21st Century Skills, 2007), which is supported by many business leaders, calls for today's students to master the core subjects of English, reading or language arts, world languages, arts, mathematics, economics, science, geography, history, government, and civics. It expects them to develop global awareness, civic literacy, health literacy, and financial, economic, business, and entrepreneurial literacy. Students also need to be creative, be able to think critically and problem solve, and be able to communicate and collaborate with others. They must have information, media, and tech-

hidden curriculum The implicit values and expectations that teachers and schools convey about what is important for students to learn.

nology skills to work effectively in today's workforce. They must be able to adjust to change and adapt to new occupations and life situations as they arise. Meeting all of these expectations will be a major challenge for schools.

Academic Achievement

Media reports of student scores on achievement tests highlight a school's ability to offer students a strong academic background. Some school districts base their reputations on how well their students perform and how many are admitted to colleges. In some communities, parents camp out overnight to be first in line to enroll their children in a preschool that will provide the jump start needed for success on future tests to ensure later admission to prestigious colleges and universities.

Countries and their education systems are compared through student scores on international tests. When the scores of U.S. students fall below those of students in other countries, parents and policy makers demand changes. Concern about performance in reading, writing, and mathematics periodically leads to a back-to-basics movement in which the traditional academic subjects are emphasized. During these periods, frills such as the development of self-esteem, leisure activities, and anything that takes time away from academic study are condemned as a misuse of public funds. In response, many states and school districts have increased the length of the school day to provide more time to learn academic subjects.

Attention to academic achievement focuses on meeting standards in academic areas, the arts, health, and physical education. As a result, many schools have revised their curricula to be standards based. Standardized tests used by states and school districts reflect these standards. The emphasis is on testing students annually to determine if they are at grade level. Low-income students, students of color, and females are expected to learn at the higher levels historically expected of middle-class white students. School systems' reputations and their state funding are dependent on how well students perform on these tests when a school does not make **adequate yearly progress (AYP)** as required under the federal No Child Left Behind Act.

Social Development

Schooling also provides opportunities for students to develop their social skills by interacting with others. In this process, students should learn to respect others; they also learn a set of rules for working appropriately with peers and adults. Although schools usually do not provide a course that teaches skills in social development, appropriate behavior is constantly reinforced by teachers and other school professionals in the classroom and on the playground.

Teachers can give students opportunities to work with other students from diverse racial, gender, language, religious, and ability groups; one of the by-products of these interactions is that students learn more about their similarities and differences. Teachers can encourage interactions across groups through **cooperative learning** activities in which students from different groups are placed together. Other team projects allow students who might not seek one another out otherwise to work together. A part of teaching is helping students learn to work together positively.

Cultural Transmission

Schools around the world are expected to transmit the **culture** of their nation to young people so they can both maintain it and pass it on to the next generation. Schools have often approached this task by teaching history with an emphasis on important events and heroes. This emphasis helps children learn the importance of patriotism and loyalty. Formal and hidden curricula reflect and reinforce the values of the national culture—the principles, standards, and qualities the culture endorses.

These national values and rules are so embedded in most aspects of schooling that most teachers and students do not realize they exist. The only exceptions may be students who do not feel a part of the **common culture** or whose families have recently immigrated. In these cases, students and families quickly learn that schools might not reflect or support aspects of their culture that differ from the common culture. This dissonance between schools and families is most noticeable when students are from backgrounds other than Northern and Western European or whose native language is not English. Students from religious backgrounds that have not evolved from Judeo-Christian roots may also question the culture that is being transmitted at school. The challenge for educators is to transmit the common culture while including the richness and contributions of many who are not yet accepted as an integral part of that culture. In this way, schools begin to change and expand the common culture.

The *21st Century Learning Knowledge and Skills* framework is discussed in more detail in Chapter 11.

The consequences of not meeting AYP are discussed in Chapters 8 and 11.

adequate yearly progress (AYP) The annual progress report of how students in a school performed on the state's achievement tests as required by No Child Left Behind. Schools whose students are not performing at grade level are labeled by the state as "low performing."

cooperative learning An instructional strategy for grouping students from different groups and learning abilities to work collaboratively on projects and assignments.

culture Socially transmitted ways of thinking, believing, feeling, and acting within a group of people that are passed from one generation to the next.

common culture The shared values, traditions, history, experiences, and behaviors that are common across groups in society.

CULTURE IN SCHOOLS

Culture provides a blueprint for how we think, feel, and behave in a society. It imposes rules and order to help us understand the subtleties of our shared language, nonverbal communications, and ways of thinking and knowing. No matter where we live in the world, we have the same biological and psychological needs, but the ways we meet those needs are culturally determined. The location of the group, available resources, and traditions have a great influence on how and what we eat, how we groom and dress, how we teach and learn, and how we interact with each other. The meaning and celebration of birth, marriage, old age, and death also depend on our culture. It influences all aspects of our lives.

Culture is learned, shared, adapted, and dynamic. We learn our culture through **enculturation,** which occurs when parents, grandparents, religious leaders, teachers, television shows, and our neighbors teach us the culture and its acceptable norms of behavior. We internalize cultural patterns so well and so early in life that we often have difficulty accepting different, but just as appropriate, ways of behaving and thinking by others, sometimes leading to miscommunications and misunderstandings in society and the classroom. When schools use a different language or linguistic pattern from that used at the home of students or when students' behaviors have different meanings at home than at school, dissonance between schools and the home can occur (Heath, 1983). Understanding cultural differences and learning to recognize when students do not share our own cultural patterns are critical steps in the provision of an equitable learning environment.

Culture is not stagnant. It is dynamic, continually adapting to serve the needs of the group. We adapt our culture as we move from one section of the country to another or around the globe as do some of our students who are new immigrants or whose families are in the armed services. Cultures differ, in part, because of the geographic region in which we live. For example, Eskimos who live with extreme cold, snow, and ice have developed different cultural patterns than groups in the South Pacific islands with limited land and an unlimited body of water. Technological changes in the world and society also transform cultures. For example, new technologies allow robots to perform routine jobs and provide the opportunities for more people to work from home. Although technological changes and globalization are welcomed by many groups, others, especially indigenous groups such as American Indian tribes, Alaska Natives, and the Igorots of the Philippines find they are destroying their cultures and ways of life (Mander & Tauli-Corpuz, 2006).

Common Culture

The legal system, democratic elections, and middle-class values of American society, which serve as the foundation for many of our institutions and traditions, came from Western and Northern Europe. As new immigrants assimilated into society over a few generations, a common culture evolved. It is reflected in the ways most middle-class families live. These commonalities make it fairly easy for people to identify us as "American" when we are visiting other countries.

Historically, the common culture has been defined by those in power, who were primarily white, middle-class Protestants whose ancestors began immigrating from Western and Northern Europe five centuries ago. Until recently, European American men dominated the country's political system, holding the highest government and corporate positions. In this role, they had great influence over the institutional policies and practices that maintained their power and discriminated against other groups. The Civil Rights struggles of the 1960s and 1970s opened the political and corporate worlds to a growing number of women and persons of color. During this period, legislation was passed to protect the rights of all people and promote greater equality across groups in education, housing, and other areas. Our history as a nation of many diverse groups and our experiences in struggling for equality across groups has further refined our common culture.

What are some of the characteristics of the common culture? Universal education and literacy for all citizens are valued. A job or career must be pursued for a person to be recognized as successful. Fun is usually a relief from work. Technology in all of its forms, from cell phones to the computer, has a great impact on our lives, especially those of young people. Achievement and success are highly valued and demonstrated by the accumulation of material goods such as houses, cars, boats, clothes, and vacations. Individualism and freedom are core values that undergird the common culture of the United States. Members believe that individuals should be in charge of their own destiny and success. Freedom is defined as having control of one's own life with little or no interference by others, especially by government (Bellah, Madsen, Sullivan, Swidler, & Tipton, 2008).

enculturation The process of learning the characteristics and behaviors of the culture of the group to which one belongs.

Mass communications, which have been enhanced by technology and the Internet, influence our view of ourselves and others. They contribute to the development of a universal culture that mirrors in many ways the common culture of the United States. Some critics of this globalization worry that the positive aspects of ethnic cultures are losing ground as television and movies teach a common culture around the world.

Cultures of Families

Although we share the common culture as we interact in schools and at work, a family's unique culture may take precedence in the homes of your students, especially if they do not feel they are full-fledged members of the common culture. Students arrive at school with the traditions, language, and behaviors of their families' cultures. To some families, their **ethnicity** (for example, African American, Navajo, German American, or Korean American) most correctly defines who they are. They may speak a language other than English at home. Families also range along a continuum from poor to wealthy, which may affect students' health and well-being and their ability to engage effectively in school. Some families continue to be greatly influenced by the discrimination they face because of their race, ethnicity, immigration status, language, or religion.

Groups in the United States are discussed in greater detail in Chapter 7.

Knowing more about your students' cultural identity can help you make schooling and the curriculum more real or authentic for them. It also shows that you respect their families and communities. How can you know more about the cultures of the various communities and your students? You could participate in community activities and celebrations that will provide an understanding of students' cultural traditions. You could volunteer with community groups to coach, tutor, or serve food at a homeless shelter. You could actively participate in school activities in the evenings and on the weekends that provide the opportunity to interact more with other students in the school and their parents. Another approach to learning more about the cultures of your students is to take classes in ethnic studies, women's studies, religious studies, sociology, or anthropology to build your knowledge base. Two views about diversity training are presented in the Teacher Perspectives feature.

When we meet our students for the first time, we usually identify them immediately by their gender and race and maybe their ethnicity. We may not know their religion and its importance to their families unless they are wearing a garment or jewelry associated with a specific religion. We may not know the importance of their ethnicity or language. Therefore, we need to be very careful about stereotyping them based on factors that can be easily identified. Culture is far more complex and important in students' own identity than we can know without much more information.

Cultural Values

Although schools are expected to transmit the culture of the United States to the younger generation, educators do not always agree on *whose* culture should be transmitted. Is it always the common culture even though diverse racial, ethnic, language, and religious groups have their own cultures with different traditions, experiences, and histories? How can schools begin to accommodate all of these differences?

Some conservative politicians and popular talk show hosts argue that schools should ignore diversity. They believe that all students should learn the common heritage and adopt the common culture as their own. Multicultural theorists and educators present another perspective. They argue that student diversity enriches the school community. They believe in a pluralistic approach in which cultural differences are valued and integrated throughout the curriculum and all activities of the school. In this approach, teachers draw on the cultural backgrounds and experiences of students to teach academic knowledge and skills.

Incorporating the cultures of students in the curriculum is discussed in Chapter 7.

Parents' choices of religious schools, home schooling, or ethnocentric schools have been based in part on the **values** that parents believe schooling can impart. Although schools usually do not offer a course in which values are explicitly presented and discussed, values implicitly influence the formal and hidden curriculum. Curricula usually support the common culture and the current ideological, political, and economic order of society. For example, in the common culture, individualism is much more highly regarded than the rights of groups (Bellah et al., 2008). Some believe that public schools do not value their religion. Some parents do not want their children exposed to the secular values of a public school or what they perceive to be "foul" language and disrespectful behavior by students. Although these values may not seem controversial to some readers, they can be the cause of extensive debate and emotional pleas at school board meetings and community forums.

ethnicity A shared national origin or the national origin of one's ancestors when they immigrated to the United States.

values Principles, standards, and qualities that are considered worthwhile or desirable.

Should Teachers Be Required to Take Diversity Training?

How can you learn about cultures different than your own, especially those that are represented in the school in which you are teaching? Many teachers, as pointed out below, have taken a course on multicultural education when they were in college, but a number of experienced teachers have not had formal training related to diversity. These two teachers present their perspectives on whether such training is needed.

YES

Mary Cartier is a Student member at Michigan State University. She is a junior studying Secondary Spanish Education with a minor in Teaching Speakers of Other Languages.

Looking around my education classes at Michigan State University, I often see only White, female students. In fact, it's the highest demographic of teachers anywhere. Students need to know that their teachers respect and accept them, not only on an individual level, but also as members of society. If they don't see themselves in their teachers, students want to know that at least they're understood.

All educators will, no matter where they work, teach students from different backgrounds than their own, whether they are from a different social class, race, ethnicity, sexual orientation, or level of physical ability. Diversity training can help educators relate more effectively to students who are different from themselves.

In one of my very first classes at MSU, I was able to mentor a young kindergartner, whom I will call Jack. A young African-American student, Jack was unaware of the connotations of race, but he immediately noticed the difference between his own skin color and mine. I didn't ignore his comments, but rather chose to use the occasion as an opportunity to help him understand that there are many different types of people in the world. I feel this was important for me to do because as an African-American male, Jack will soon grow up to realize that race has many real consequences in life. Ignoring that fact would have been a disservice to both of us.

Children don't come into this world knowing how to discriminate—it's a learned behavior that can be stopped or prevented. Kids spend many hours in schools, and if they can be in an environment that breaks stereotypes and creates unity through diversity, it can continue the progress of social justice for our next generation of children.

NO

Suzanne Emery is a Retired member who taught English and journalism in San Diego City Schools.

Of course, every September a faculty does need a "heads-up" session on the year's groups of kids, of their home life, their homeland, and needs. The same holds true when there is an influx of students in the middle of the year, as happened after Hurricane Katrina. These sessions are necessary tools, but quite different from required diversity trainings.

Too much in-service for employed teachers can be so demeaning, dumbed down, and even insulting, that required diversity training for all teachers would merely push the scale farther and infuriate the ones most needing some enlightenment. And it is a fallacy to assume that only the traditional "majority" members could use some enlightenment. Prejudice and downright ignorance is colorblind. We reflect our backgrounds, our families, our religions, and our communities.

Additionally, at least half of the people now teaching have entered the profession in the past five years, all earning credentials which have specified, in most states, at least one course or strand in meeting the needs of a culturally diverse student population. The experienced faculty have, for the most part, been "in-serviced" almost annually in various sensitivities of their community. For San Diego, that included everything from language variations for native African-American kids, to practices of Hmong families, to ways to involve differently-abled kids in field trips, to how it is that our Muslim girls can become track stars while wearing head coverings and workout sweats.

As futile as it is to teach ethics to politicians who already know right from wrong, it is folly to believe a few mandated diversity meetings can fundamentally change classroom behavior. Teachers already recognize that their students are very diverse, but must eventually achieve similar success.

Source: "Should Teachers Be Required to Take Diversity Training?" *NEA Today* (May 2006), p. 41. Reprinted by permission of the National Education Association.

myeducationlab To explore both sides of this issue and think about each perspective, go to the *Book Specific Resources* in the MyEducationLab for your course, select your text, and then select *Teacher Perspectives* for Chapter 6.

Additionally, the emphasis on individualism and competition prevalent in many schools is not compatible with the cooperative patterns practiced by American Indian tribes and in many Latino and African American communities. These differences can lead to conflict between parents and schools and among groups within a community. Parents turn to the courts when they believe that schools have acted inappropriately. They may not believe that the schools use a democratic process in which they can be heard or that the community will support their petitions. School prayer, creationism, the banning of books, sex education, and segregation are among the areas that have been tested in the courts.

Because parents and other groups in a community may vehemently disagree about the values to be reinforced in schools, teachers should be aware of their own cultural values. Knowing their own values as well as those of the families represented in the school should help teachers prepare for potential conflicts. Expectations can vary greatly from one community or school to another. When a controversial topic, program, or book is being initiated, good communications with families will be critical in making the transition smoothly.

JOURNAL FOR REFLECTION

How does your family describe your cultural background? What characteristics about your culture, if any, were not valued in school? What characteristics of students from different ethnic, language, or religious backgrounds than you were not valued in school?

School Culture

A school also has a culture, which generally reflects the nation's common culture and the community in which it is located. A school's culture provides meaning for the students and educators who participate in that environment. Schools have their own unwritten rules and norms for behavior including how students interact with the teacher and each other. They develop their own traditions and rituals related to athletics, extracurricular clubs, graduation exercises, school social events, and the ways teachers interact with each other and parents. They have mascots, cheerleaders, school colors, and school songs that distinguish them from another school. Over time, they have developed reputations for the academic achievement of students or the prowess of their football, basketball, or other sports team. They also develop reputations for the establishment of a safe or dangerous environment. Some schools are influenced greatly by the religions and cultures of the children's families, others by the presence of a university or large military base. The cultural patterns that develop in a school can have a powerful impact on the academic performance of students and the ways that teachers feel about their work and students (Deal & Peterson, 1999).

Schools develop histories and memories that are transferred from generation to generation. Some students become the school leaders, fitting easily into the school culture. Some thrive in a cultural environment where they are popular and have many friends. School helps them meet their academic and social needs. Other students never seem to fit into the school culture; some because the school culture is very different than their own family's culture and adapting to the school culture causes dissonance at home. Other students feel marginalized and alienated, which may lead to their leaving school before graduation. As a result, some graduates have very positive memories of their schools and retain lifelong feelings of pride about them. Others remember never fitting in and never being understood by their peers and teachers.

Partnering with the Community

Partnerships between schools and communities can help bridge the disconnect that sometimes exists between school and community cultures. They can also support academic achievement and the development of positive relationships with young people. Community partners could include local businesses, the Chamber of Commerce, charitable organizations, churches, civic groups, foundations, local government, local media, museums, military groups, nonprofit associations, senior citizens, and youth groups. They may be able to contribute time, money, people, or expertise to enrich the work of schools on behalf of students. Some partners are able to assign employees or volunteers to work with students, teachers, or administrators. Others are able to contribute equipment such as computers and other resources needed by the school.

Educators can also bring the community into the school. Parents and grandparents of your students may be willing to teach about their own traditions and histories. Immigrant parents may be willing to discuss their country of origin and the reasons they immigrated to the

Competition in athletics and other extracurricular activities reflects the traditions of a school's culture.

United States. Some community members may be willing to assist you in working with students whose native language is not English; some may be willing to tutor students in reading and mathematics. You could ask people from the community to describe their jobs or a community project. The community includes many resources on which you could draw for assistance, including grandparents, employees at local businesses, museum staff, staff at community agencies, and public officials such as firemen and policemen. Bringing the community to the classroom could be helpful in garnering broader support for the school and its students.

Field trips provide an opportunity for students to develop a better understanding of the local community and other communities. School projects also provide opportunities for students to become involved in the community. A growing number of schools expect students to participate in service learning or community projects such as planting trees, cleaning up a park, or assisting elderly people and young children. Students could conduct research on a community need that could lead to changes. President Barack H. Obama has called for all citizens to take more responsibility in their neighborhoods. School projects that move students into the community help them understand the role of citizenship and their responsibility to the larger community.

SCHOOL CHOICES

In the past, parents had no say in which public school their children would attend. Children were assigned to a school based on their home address. Now increasing numbers and types of options to the traditional neighborhood public school are available. The parents of nearly one in four students have chosen a private school or a nontraditional school within the public system. The problem for many parents now is not whether they have a choice, but which school is best for their children. Many of these options are available within public school districts as well as private schools.

Public Schools

The schools that were established after Europeans began to settle the United States were private and attended by the children of the elite owners of property. By the 1830s, "common schools," which were designed, in part, to reduce the tensions across socioeconomic groups, were being attended by students from families of different social classes. During this period, most African American, Hispanic, and American Indian students attended segregated schools if they were in school at all. In many parts of the country these students and low-income students did not attend school regularly and, when they did, it was often for only a few grades.

When immigrant Roman Catholic families expressed concerns about the Protestant bible being taught in the common schools in 1842, riots erupted in Philadelphia and New York City. When the two sides could not reach agreement on the curricula, the Roman Catholic Church established its own private schools (Spring, 2001). Over time, the curriculum of the public schools, which continued to be supported by taxes, became more secular. Many policy makers and educational leaders continue to see education as a way to reduce the social and economic inequities that exist in society.

Any student today has the right to attend the public school in his or her neighborhood; in fact, children are required to attend school until they are sixteen to eighteen years old, depending on the laws of the state in which they live. Nearly 50 million students were enrolled in public P–12 schools in 2008, and that number is projected to increase to more than 54 million by 2017 (Planty et al., 2008).

Discussions about providing parents a choice of schools that their children can attend were initiated in the 1980s when the federal government funded **magnet schools**. In 1990 the state of Wisconsin passed legislation to provide low-income families in Milwaukee the opportunity to use a **voucher** to send their children to a private school. With the passage of NCLB, parents were allowed more options for choosing a school. The Obama administration's education policies also encourage the establishment of additional **charter schools** to offer more educational options to students.

Most public school options allow for increased parent and student involvement in school decision making. All represent, in some way, a break with the traditional public school. The creation of choices also causes competition between schools, which some people believe will lead to more efficiency and effectiveness. However, the research to date, though limited, does not provide clear evidence of a trend toward higher student achievement (Buckley & Schneider, 2007; U.S. Department of Education, Institute of Education Sciences, 2005).

The historical development of public schools is discussed in greater detail in Chapter 2.

magnet schools Public schools with a focused curriculum such as the arts or mathematics and science. These schools are designed to attract a diverse student population from across a school district or state.

voucher A check or credit granted by a school district or state to parents to pay part or all of the tuition for their children to attend a private school.

charter schools Public schools established by teachers, parents, nonprofit organizations, and others under a contract with the state or local school district. They are exempt from many state and district regulations as they design and deliver programs for improving the academic performance of students.

MAGNET SCHOOLS. Many school districts have been pressured by citizens and ordered by the courts to equalize the proportions of students from different racial groups in each school. One response, especially by large urban school districts such as those in Houston and Kansas City, has been to develop special academic programs and custom-designed facilities that will attract all students—hence the name *magnet* schools. Elementary, middle, and high school magnets exist. The school might emphasize the performing and visual arts, math and science, or the liberal arts. Whatever the theme, the faculty, curriculum, and all students in the magnet school are there because of their interest in the school's theme.

CHARTER SCHOOLS. Charter schools, which are supported by public funds, are one approach to providing families choice within the public school system. They have been started by academic institutions, nonprofit foundations, teachers, and parents for a variety of reasons. Although all charter schools are supposed to provide students with a strong academic background that meets the requirements of NCLB, some focus more directly on academics with a goal of most of their students attending and completing college. These types of schools include Montessori schools, Edison Schools, experiential learning schools, KIPP (Knowledge Is Power Program) academies, and online virtual schools. Founders of other charter schools have designed a curriculum and climate that are centered in the ethnic heritages of the students and community. Others have created schools around a particular philosophy that teachers and parents support.

Charter schools are established through a contract with either a state agency (for example, the State Department of Education) or a local school board for a specific time period, usually three to five years. The contract, or charter, lays out how the school will operate in exchange for receiving public funding. Charter schools have greater autonomy than traditional public schools and can be released from district and state regulations such as hiring licensed teachers or using the district's textbooks. However, charter schools are still held accountable for student learning and, in most settings, having a diverse student body.

Exponential growth in the number of charter schools has occurred since the first one was established in Minnesota in 1991. As of 2007, forty states and the District of Columbia had passed legislation to permit the establishment of charter schools. States with strong charter laws have the largest number of charter schools with Arizona, California, Delaware, District of Columbia, Florida, and Texas having the most (Center for Education Reform, 2006). More than 4,500 charter schools, serving 1.3 million students, existed in 2008, making up 5 percent of the public schools in the country (Center for Education Reform, 2007). As you might expect with the majority of charter schools located in central cities, the percentage of African American, Hispanic, and American Indian students is higher than in other public schools. They are generally smaller than other public schools as shown in Figure 6.1, and more likely to be located in the central city

FIGURE 6.1

Enrollment in Charter and Traditional Public Schools

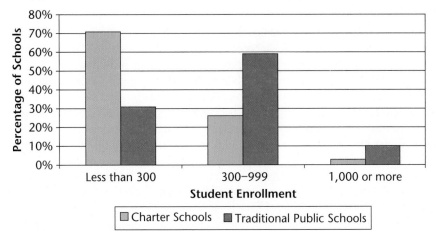

Source: U.S. Department of Education, National Center for Education Statistics. (2007). *The condition of education 2007* (NCES 2007-064, Indicator 32-1). Washington, DC: U.S. Government Printing Office.

(U.S. Department of Education, National Center for Education Statistics, 2007). Three in four charter schools provide elementary education or are combined elementary and secondary education (Center for Education Reform, n.d.).

Many public schools, especially charter schools, are contracting with for-profit and nonprofit companies to manage all or part of the operations of schools (Buckley & Schneider, 2007). These **educational management organizations (EMOs)** sometimes manage the school curriculum, instruction, assessments, and education of teachers. More often they manage specific operational activities such as payroll, budgeting, and personnel management. They may contract to provide supplemental services such as tutoring students when the school does not meet adequate yearly progress as expected by NCLB. They include Edison Schools, Mosaica Advantage, Chancellor Beacon, and Sylvan Learning Centers.

VOUCHERS. Without a doubt, the most controversial school choice option is school vouchers. At its simplest, a voucher program issues a check or a credit to parents that can be used to send their child to a private school. Generally, the argument for vouchers is based on equalizing educational opportunity for students of color and students from low-income families. Advertisements on television and the radio by groups such as the Black Alliance for Educational Opportunity and conservative groups point out to listeners that vouchers will allow them to remove their children from a failing public school to attend a private school that will provide them opportunities for future success—a very attractive proposal.

Wisconsin adopted the first law that allowed low-income families in Milwaukee to use a voucher to move their children from a public to a private school with a voucher of public funds. Ohio adopted a similar voucher plan for Cleveland families in 1996. The most expansive use of vouchers is in the District of Columbia as a result of Congress enacting a voucher program for 1,600 students in 2004 (Howell & Peterson, 2002), but the use of vouchers in the District of Columbia may be eliminated by the Obama administration. Nevertheless, vouchers have not been as popular as charter schools for providing school choice.

Most voucher programs are funded with state tax dollars. However, some voucher programs are funded by private foundations and occasionally individuals. For example, in the Edgewood Independent School District in San Antonio, Texas, a group of business executives offered $50 million over ten years for vouchers for students from low-income families to attend any private school or public schools in other school districts. The publicly financed programs have restrictions on who is eligible, as in Florida, where the state plan allows vouchers to be used only after the state has designated the public school as a failing school. Typically, the amount of a voucher is equivalent to the amount the public school received for each student. The debates about vouchers center on the use of public dollars to support private schools. The most serious point of contention is when the voucher funded with state education money is used to pay for a child to attend a religious school. This raises constitutional questions about the separation of church and state. Some national organizations have been active in opposition to voucher programs because they see this choice as undermining public education.

Legal issues related to the separation of church and state are presented in Chapter 10.

Private Schools

School choices also exist outside the public school system. These range from elite secondary schools (mainly in the Northeast), to alternative schools for high school dropouts, to faith-supported schools, to schools that are operated for profit. Although enrollment in private schools had grown to 5.3 million by 2001, it had declined to 5.1 million by 2005 (Broughman, Swaim, & Keaton, 2008).

Private schools vary greatly in purpose, organization, and size, and they serve students from all racial, religious, economic, and language backgrounds. Some are progressive and innovative; some are conservative and traditional. They are both large and small, day and boarding, single-sex and coeducational. On the average, fewer students are enrolled in private schools than in noncharter public schools. Ninety percent of private schools are at the elementary or combined elementary and secondary levels. In addition to regular elementary and secondary schools, private schools include Montessori, special education, vocational, technical, alternative, and early childhood schools (Broughman et al., 2008). Such schools have been an integral part of our nation's educational resources since colonial times. Because each private school is free to determine and practice its own philosophy of education, the spirit and environment vary from school to school, even though schools may display similar organizational structures and educational programs.

educational management organizations (EMOs) Market-oriented, for-profit businesses with whom school districts contract to manage a school and deliver instruction or to manage some of the administrative functions of a school such as payroll or personnel management.

FIGURE 6.2

Religious Orientation of Private Schools

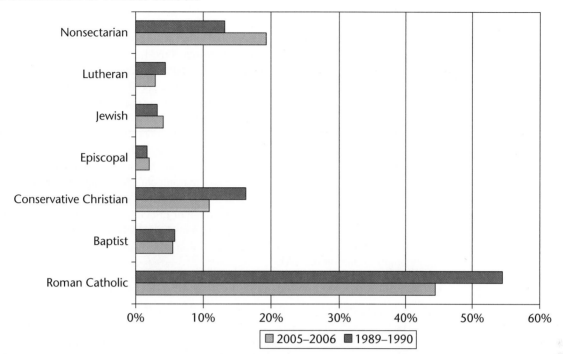

Source: Council for American Private Education. (n.d.). *Facts and studies.* Germantown, MD: Author. Retrieved January 20, 2009, from http://www.capenet.org/facts.html; Broughman, S. P., Swaim, N. L., & Keaton, P. W. (2008). *Characteristics of private schools in the United States: Results from the 2005–2006 private school universe survey* (NCES 2008-315). Washington, DC: National Center for Education Statistics, U.S. Department of Education.

PAROCHIAL SCHOOLS. Four of five private schools are parochial—that is, schools that are supported by religious organizations. The culture of a parochial school may have a positive impact on student achievement. Some researchers have found that students, especially African American and Hispanic students, who attend religious schools perform better on standardized tests than their public school peers (Broughman et al., 2008). Many religious groups sponsor schools, including the Amish, Muslims, Jews, Quakers, Catholics, and many Protestants. However, enrollment in different religious schools has shifted during the past fifteen years. Although enrollment in Roman Catholic schools is higher than in any other private school, it is less than in the past, as shown in Figure 6.2.

SINGLE-SEX EDUCATION. Most single-sex schools and colleges today are private with a goal of helping their students develop confidence, academic achievement, and leadership skills by building on their unique learning styles and cultural experiences. Schools or academies in some urban areas have been established for young African American men with the goal of developing their self-esteem, academic achievement, and leadership to improve their opportunities for enrolling in and being successful in college and life. Federal regulations in 2002 allowed

Parochial schools are parents' most popular choice if they choose to send their children to a private school.

public schools to experiment with single-sex education to improve the achievement of both girls and boys. As a result, some public schools have established segregated courses within a coed school.

Home Schooling

This rapidly growing form of schooling requires no public support; instead, children learn at home with one of their parents serving as the teacher. By spring 2007, 1.5 million students were being schooled at home. They represent 2.9 percent of the K–12 population—up from 1.7 percent in 1999 (U.S. Department of Education, Institute of Education Statistics, 2008). Teaching a home-schooled student requires parents to relearn subjects, organize each day's instruction, and then teach it. One of the advantages, as well as potential weaknesses, is that in most states the subjects taught are self-determined. This can work in favor of students' interests but may also contribute to gaps in their education.

Why do parents choose to home school their children? In a national survey of parents, three reasons were prominent. Two in three parents indicated that they taught their children at home because they were concerned about the school environment, they wanted to provide religious or moral instruction that was not available at a school, or they were dissatisfied with the academic instruction provided at a school (U.S. Department of Education, Institute of Education Statistics, 2008). The evidence is clear that for many students home schooling is a success. For example, home-schooled fourth graders watch less television and in high school they score an average of eighty points higher on the SAT.

Virtual Schools: Crossing Boundaries with Technology

The opportunities for students to meet in a classroom online is quickly becoming commonplace. **Virtual schools** and courses exist across the span of schooling from preschool through college and into professional development for teachers and other workers. The number of students enrolling in online courses has increased from 45,000 in 2000 to more than a million in 2008 (Christensen, Horu, & Johnson, 2008).

The most common reason for a student to participate in an online school is that the course is not available in the traditional school building (Trotter, 2008). For example, students in rural areas have taken courses in foreign language and other subjects because teachers for those subjects are not available in their schools. Advanced placement (AP) courses via technology are also popular. A growing number of high school students are using online courses for credit recovery when they have not completed core courses required for graduation (Davis, 2009). As the article that opened this chapter indicated, some students prefer the online environment. Online technologies also provide a valuable resource for students who are being home schooled.

──────── **JOURNAL FOR REFLECTION** ────────

How do you feel about allowing parents to choose a school for their children? Of the choices discussed in this section, in which would you prefer to teach? Why?

SCHOOL LEVELS

By the mid-nineteenth century, many elementary-aged children attended common schools, but it was not until the end of that century that high schools began to be established. Schooling was not further divided into early childhood and middle level education until the twentieth century. In this section, we explore why education was split into different levels based on the age of students.

Early Childhood Education

virtual school Education program offered without the teacher and student being in the same room or location for instruction. Most programs are offered online via web-based technologies.

The fields of child development and psychology were influenced by G. Stanley Hall, a professor at Johns Hopkins University, at the end of the nineteenth century. He defined childhood as the years between ages four and eight, which remains the age range for primary education in today's schools. Between 1930 and the 1950s, early childhood education programs had a behaviorist orientation, in which good habits were developed through exercise and drill. With a renewed interest in Piaget and the developmental stages of childhood, the field later took on a developmental approach. By the beginning of the twenty-first century, the field had been forced to emphasize academics, including the assessment of young children. One of the resulting changes is discussed in the Professional Dilemma feature.

PROFESSIONAL DILEMMA

What Has Happened to Play?

A new research study shows that "play is disappearing from kindergarten classrooms," reports Edward Miller of the Alliance for Childhood. Early childhood educators, researchers, and advocates decry the fact that the country's emphasis on academics and accountability has pushed play out of kindergarten classrooms. Perhaps the pendulum has swung too far to the side of cognitive development to the demise of other skills that are identified in the *21st Century Learning Knowledge and Skills* framework: collaboration, critical thinking, creativity, and physical activity. Some advocates worry that the removal of play is contributing to mental health problems and obesity in young children. The amount of time now available for free play—games, make-believe, and artwork of their choice—has moved to the background, if it exists at all. Because recesses have been eliminated or limited in time in a number of schools, some states are considering legislation requiring recesses in pre- and elementary schools. Is it time for the pendulum to swing the other way or can educators and policy makers reach a balance that includes both ends of the continuum to develop a whole, healthy child with the appropriate cognitive knowledge and skills?

Source: Jacobson, L. (2008, December 3). Children's lack of playtime seen as troubling health, school issue. *Education Week, 28*(14), 1, 14–15.

Questions for Reflection
1. Why does the elimination of play in early childhood programs concern some researchers and advocates of children? Do you agree with them? Why or why not?
2. What has led to the reduction of play time in so many schools? How have teachers lost control of their classrooms to outside forces?
3. Who should be involved in the development of a more balanced approach to teaching preschoolers and kindergartners?

By 1985 the National Association for the Education of Young Children (NAEYC) had developed a voluntary accreditation system with standards for preschools, kindergartens, and child care centers; more than 10,000 programs are now accredited. Over time, the qualifications for preschool teachers have increased. States now require preschool teachers to hold a bachelor's degree and be fully certified to work in public preschools and kindergartens. Many day care centers for prekindergarten children require day care workers to have completed at least an associate degree.

Some parents choose to send their children to a Montessori school in which the teacher is the facilitator of learning. The Montessori model, which was developed by medical doctor Maria Montessori, includes little or no large-group instruction, especially for three- to six-year-olds. The teacher works with one child at a time or with a small group of children. Built into every day at a Montessori school is one uninterrupted three-hour work period during which children are allowed to explore their environment without being required to attend any individual or small-group activities. The Montessori classroom must be well organized into subject-based work centers where children interact with the classroom materials. A typical classroom may have thirty to thirty-five students ranging in age from two and a half to six years old with one teacher and one nonteaching assistant. The same teacher remains with the same students while they grow through this developmental stage. Older children help teach the skills they have already learned to the younger children, allowing the teacher to observe and record the skills mastered for the child's portfolio, which is the only form of assessment used. No grades are given, and no forms of punishment or rewards are used.

Another popular approach to early childhood education is the High Scope model that is based on the belief that children are active learners and on the child development theories of Jean Piaget. Students explore materials within structured subject-based centers where items and shelves are clearly labeled with pictures and words so children can experience environmental print and categorize materials. High Scope classrooms have a fixed daily schedule and regular classroom routines with the goal of helping children who are economically disadvantaged achieve greater school success and develop social responsibility. It is designed to provide students with language and literacy, logic and mathematics, music and movement, and creative learning activities to contribute to their cognitive, physical, and affective development. The teacher creates a portfolio with examples of each child's work and completes developmental checklists to show growth throughout the year. High Scope teachers make regular home visits to help parents learn how to work with their children and to learn more about a student's home culture and language to ensure that they are reflected and respected in the classroom.

The Reggio Amelia approach to early childhood education originated after the end of World War II at the Diana School in the city of Reggio Amelia in Northern Italy. It was designed to meet the social, emotional, and educational needs of all children ranging in age from birth to six years old. Children are subdivided into an infancy group for children up to three years old and into a school group for three- to six-year-olds. A group of up to twenty-four children grows together with the same two teachers, an assistant, and the support of parent volunteers for a three-year cycle. Teachers collaborate with each other, parents, children, and community members in meeting the individual needs of each student. The curriculum is project based, allowing teachers to build on known areas of interest, such as dinosaurs, shadows, and community- or family-inspired events and interests. While working on their projects, children are encouraged to collaborate with other children to explore information and materials. A sense of community is developed in the school by having some common areas where children from all of the classes can mingle and interact. These common areas include a small-group room, a kitchen for children to have snacks, a multiage-appropriate physical development/tumble room, and other small play areas. The Reggio approach ensures that children, their families, their teachers, and the entire community take an active role in the education of each child.

Typical early childhood classrooms in the United States incorporate one or more of these approaches to instruction. A school district may have both the federally funded Head Start and prekindergarten classrooms in schools that use the same packaged curriculum, but also include elements of the Montessori, High Scope, and Reggio Amelia approaches. Some school districts offer specialized early childhood programs such as Montessori and language immersion programs in addition to the regular Head Start or prekindergarten classes.

Elementary Schools

One-room schools with a teacher who taught all subjects to students of all ages were built in many rural communities in the nineteenth century as the population moved west. The first school based on grades was established in 1848 in Boston—the city that was on the leading edge of establishing the roots of our educational system. In the Quincy School, teachers worked in a classroom with fifty-six students who sat at desks. This model was adopted across the country and changed little throughout the twentieth century. Over time, class sizes became smaller, averaging 15.8 students by 2005 (Planty et al., 2008) with student/teacher ratios lower in smaller rural schools and higher in large urban schools. By the beginning of the twenty-first century, desks were no longer bolted to the floor and in many classrooms, students sat at tables or movable desks that could be easily moved together for group activities.

For more information on the history of elementary schools, see Chapter 2.

Most elementary teachers work in self-contained classrooms with twenty to thirty students who move to the next grade with a different teacher at the end of a school year. In some schools, teachers team teach with specialists in mathematics, science, reading, language arts, and social studies. Some schools have resource teachers who work with classroom teachers to accommodate students with special needs. Some schools practice looping in which teachers remain with the same students for two to three grades.

Middle Level Education

Like early childhood education, middle schools owe their beginnings to psychologist G. Stanley Hall who found that early adolescents were neither children nor adults. He lobbied for an education that would better serve students between elementary and high school (Beane, 2001). The first step in this evaluation was the establishment of junior high schools, but for reasons different than that students are young adolescents. Because of the large influx of immigrant children and the increasing number of students not passing to the next grade, elementary schools were overcrowded. School districts established junior high schools, which were often attached to high schools, to relieve the overcrowded elementary schools (Beane, 2001). The number of junior high schools peaked at 6,000 in the 1960s, but then had declined to 632 by 2001 (McEwin, Dickinson, & Jenkins, 2003). They had become miniature high schools that many believed were not effectively serving young adolescents.

Although middle level educators believe that early adolescents deserve an education different from that provided in elementary and secondary schools, the early middle schools evolved when the baby boom generation of the 1950s overcrowded elementary schools. Rather than building more elementary schools, an option was to add a wing to the high school for students in the fifth or sixth to ninth grades. A research report from England also assisted in the establishment of middle schools when it reported that the average age for puberty had declined from ages twelve to fifteen to ages ten to fourteen, which encompassed students in grades 5 or 6 through 8 (Beane, 2001). Middle schools were designed to focus on the developmental and academic needs of young adolescents. The ideal was to have clusters of teachers and students. Middle level educators were expected to be more affectionate and sensitive to young people.

The middle school is generally defined as "a school having at least three grades and not more than five grades, and including at least grades six and seven." As the number of junior high schools declined, the number of middle schools grew to more than 13,000. Middle schools today usually focus on academic achievement that is provided in a positive and nurturing climate. Collaborative and cooperative learning strategies are popular. Most schools are working to eliminate the tracking of students by creating heterogeneous groups in which cultural diversity is celebrated and diverse learning styles are recognized. Many middle schools have adopted team teaching and block scheduling.

High Schools

After the first high school was established in Boston in 1821, the numbers grew slowly until the end of that century. They grew even more during the Great Depression of the 1930s when children were pushed out of the workforce and into high schools. Many states raised their compulsory school attendance to ages fourteen or sixteen during that period (Olson, 2000), contributing to high schools becoming an important institution in society.

Because many high schools, especially in urban areas, are not serving students well, a number of reforms have been proposed for them by groups as diverse as the Bill and Melinda Gates Foundation and the National Governors Association.

High schools today are being attacked as wastelands for young people. In a number of urban schools, less than half of the African American and Hispanic students are finishing high school within four years (Swanson, 2009). Governors, businesses, and organizations have established committees to reform high schools with the goal of changing the school culture to improve student achievement and increase graduation rates. High school "reforms, [Bill] Gates and others have argued, need to focus on raising academic standards, connecting students' studies to their lives outside of school, and addressing the anonymity of the nation's many large, comprehensive high schools" (Toch, Jerald, & Dillon, 2007).

The Bill and Melinda Gates Foundation has supported the development of small learning communities in high schools in numerous communities across the country. These small communities could be the high school itself with 150 to 400 students (Conchas & Rodríguez, 2008). They could be "schools within schools," which may be organized around a theme such as medical or technical careers. Teachers in these small schools develop common visions and goals and work together to realize them. More high school reforms can be expected during the next decade.

JOURNAL FOR REFLECTION

Based on your own high school experience and observations in other high schools, what reforms do you think would improve high schools?

SCHOOL LOCATIONS

The people who share the space and place in which we live have a great influence on our culture and lives. We become comfortable with the place where we live, understanding what is expected of us and others. When we move from one area of the country to another, we may suffer some cultural shock, having to learn the culture of the new area. The same is true for students and families as they move from one district to another, especially if they have moved to a new region of the country.

Since the 1970s, many individuals and families have migrated from the Northeast and Midwest to the South and West. The aging of the population in the Northeast and Midwest has led to a decrease in school enrollments, resulting in a loss of revenues for schools and the closing or consolidation of many of them. Half of the U.S. population now lives in the South and West, compared to 48 percent in 1970. One-fourth of the population lives in California, Florida, and Texas alone. Nearly one in five Florida residents is over sixty-five years old, and 15 percent of the population in Iowa, Maine, North Dakota, Pennsylvania, and West Virginia is retired (U.S. Census Bureau, 2008, Table 16).

FIGURE 6.3

Size of Schools in the United States

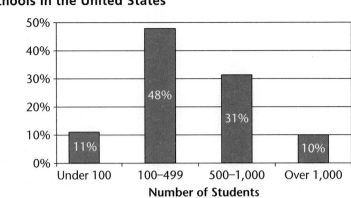

Source: U.S. Census Bureau. (2009). *Statistical abstract of the United States: 2009* (Table 231). Washington, DC: Author.

Nearly four in five people in the United States live in towns, cities, and metropolitan areas with a population of 2,500 or more (U.S. Census Bureau, 2008, Table 28). Teaching in an isolated rural area hundreds of miles from a large shopping mall is very different from teaching in a wealthy suburban area with access to a wide range of cultural and sporting events.

In 2006, there were 97,382 schools in 15,728 school districts (U.S. Census Bureau, 2008, Tables 231 and 232). The average enrollment in the nation's schools was 521 with over half of the students attending schools with enrollments of less than 500, as shown in Figure 6.3. One in four students attends the largest 100 school districts; 43 percent of the nation's students attend the largest 500 school districts (Dalton, Sable, & Hoffman, 2006). Students in the largest 100 school districts are ethnically, racially, and linguistically diverse with 29 percent of their students being African American, 7 percent Asian American, and 34 percent Latino. Nearly half of them are eligible for free lunch; 12 percent have one or more disabilities; and 12 percent are enrolled in English-language programs (Dalton et al., 2006). In this section we examine the characteristics of rural, urban, and suburban areas that may help you determine where you would like to teach.

Children in farming communities experience aspects of life that are foreign to most city and suburban students.

Rural Communities

Twenty-one percent of the population lives in rural areas or in towns with fewer than 2,500 residents (Dalton et al., 2006). By urban and suburban standards, families live long distances from one another, and children may travel long distances to school. To the rural family, however, the distances are not great, and a feeling of neighborliness exists. The social structure is less stratified than in more populous geographical areas, and everyone may appear to know everyone else. Values tend to be somewhat conservative as compared to other areas.

Workers in rural areas generally are poorly paid for their work, earning about three-fourths of the wages paid in urban areas. Although housing costs may be lower, other expenses are not much different. As a result, 14 percent of the rural population lives in poverty, which is slightly higher than the total population (U.S. Census Bureau, n.d.). Poverty is disproportionately high on American Indian reservations, but also exists on the Midwestern plains, western ranches, and farms across the country. Some rural areas depend heavily on low-skilled immigrant labor, allowing large farm owners to prosper while workers earn such low wages they can hardly sustain themselves. Employment in manufacturing is limited in rural areas.

An increasing number of urban and suburban dwellers choose to live in these areas, commuting to their employment in more populous metropolitan areas. These transplants are generally young and well educated. They are fleeing the complexities of city life to acquire self-reliance and self-confidence, to return to a physically healthier environment, or simply to be able to own an affordable home. In some instances, this exodus to a rural area has caused problems for schools because the newcomers' values sometimes clash with those of the more traditional rural community. Family living habits and expectations for school programs differ, and some newcomers demand increased social services. In many rural communities, it takes a considerable length of time for newcomers to be accepted into the social structure.

One in five students attends rural schools (U.S. Department of Education, National Center for Education Statistics, 2006). These schools have a larger percentage of white and American Indian students than other areas of the country, but the Hispanic population in a number of rural areas is growing. The schools are generally smaller than ones in cities, and the student-to-teacher ratio is lower. Rural students perform better on national achievement tests than their central city peers but less well than students in most suburban schools (U.S. Department of Education, National Center for Education Statistics, 2006).

Despite the pivotal role of schools in rural life, these schools face real difficulties. In some school districts, teacher shortages may result in the staffing of schools by teachers with limited academic background in the subjects they teach. Not all courses (for example, art and foreign languages) can be offered because of the limited number of teachers. Principals may be assigned to several schools, and support services may be limited because of the lack of funds. Teachers in rural areas sometimes feel isolated, especially if they are not from the area. In some rural communities, one-room schools still exist where a single teacher teaches all subjects to students in grades K–8. As ethnic diversity increases in these areas, teachers will be confronted with cultures and languages to which they may have had little or no exposure.

Rural communities cherish their small schools where all students know each other, all of the teachers, and most community members. They usually fight proposals for consolidating schools because of the long historical traditions associated with a school. In addition, they worry about consolidated schools being so far away that they cannot actively participate in their children's and grandchildren's education. Some students end up riding a bus for one or more hours daily to reach a new school.

Suburban Communities

Nearly half of the U.S. population now lives in the suburbs. The suburban population has become diverse as middle-class families of color have moved into them from cities. The suburbs are becoming even more economically, racially, ethnically, linguistically, and religiously diverse as new immigrants settle in them. Some communities actively solicit and celebrate diversity. In others, it is discouraged. Breaking past patterns of immigrants settling in their own enclaves in cities, today's immigrants from Central America, South America, Asia, and the Middle East often bypass cities and move directly into the suburbs or rural areas.

High-tech companies have found the suburbs ideal for their development and research on software, electronics, and biotechnologies. Entrepreneurs and professionals are attracted to suburban research parks, often moving into elite housing developments near their jobs. The production of the products (for example, silicon chips) of these companies usually occurs in other places (O'Mara, 2006), guaranteeing economically segregated communities. However, the suburbs are populated not only by the upper middle class; poverty now exists there as well as in cities and rural areas. The National Center for Children in Poverty reports that 31 percent of suburban children under age eighteen live in families with incomes below the poverty level (National Center for Children in Poverty, 2008).

Families often move from cities to the suburbs to ensure that their children receive a better education. Funding for schools has traditionally been better in the suburbs than other areas. Wealthy suburbs boast beautiful school buildings, sometimes on sprawling campuses, with the latest in

Go to the *Assignments and Activities* section of Topic 6: *School Organization* in the MyEducationLab for your course and complete the activity titled *City Scene*.

technology, qualified teachers, advanced placement courses, gifted and talented programs, and numerous extracurricular activities. However, not all suburban schools are of this high quality. Students who are English-language learners, who are from low-income families, or who are from backgrounds other than European are more likely to attend the older schools in the region.

Enrollments in suburban schools are, on the average, smaller than those of urban schools, but nearly 40 percent of the high schools have nine hundred or more students (U.S. Department of Education, National Center for Education Statistics, 2003). The proportion of students eligible for free or reduced-price lunch is less than in other areas (Planty et al., 2008). Students outperform their rural and urban counterparts on achievement tests (U.S. Department of Education, National Center for Educational Statistics, 2005), and more suburban students than students from other areas attend college. Safety is less of a concern for students, parents, and teachers. With changing demographics in the suburbs, however, these conditions are beginning to change—particularly in suburban areas next to major cities.

Urban Communities

Urban areas are usually rich in educational and entertainment resources such as libraries, museums, theaters, professional sports, colleges, and universities. People from different economic and cultural backgrounds intermingle in many parts of a city. An expensive restaurant can be on one block with a soup kitchen on the next block. Homeless people and families are more visible in urban areas as affordable housing becomes scarcer and the number of public housing units does not meet the needs of the population.

Mega-cities around the world are home to one-half of the world's population. The largest city in the United States is New York City with a population of around 8.3 million (U.S. Census Bureau, 2008, Table 26), which grows to 18.8 million when extended into the metropolitan area that includes its suburbs (U.S. Census Bureau, 2008, Table 16). The United States has 51 metropolitan areas with over one million residents (U.S. Census Bureau, 2008, Table 16). The population's diversity is usually greater in these metropolitan areas than in other areas of the country, often including many new immigrants from around the world. The majority of the foreign-born population in the United States lives in cities. Those in which more than one in five of its residents are foreign-born include Los Angeles (40 percent), San Jose (39 percent), New York City (37 percent), San Francisco (36 percent), Houston (28 percent), Boston (27 percent), El Paso (27 percent), Dallas (27 percent), San Diego (27 percent), Phoenix (23 percent), Las Vegas (23 percent), Chicago (22 percent), and Austin (20 percent) (U.S. Census Bureau, 2008, Table 40). Almost one in five elementary and high school students has at least one foreign-born parent (U.S. Census Bureau, 2008, Table 220).

The urban population is diverse. Hispanics are the majority population in San Antonio and represent more than 25 percent of the population in Texas's other large cities. They are a large portion of the population in many California metropolitan areas, including Los Angeles (44 percent), Riverside (45 percent), San Diego (30 percent), and San Jose (26 percent). San Jose, San Francisco, and Los Angeles are home to the largest proportion of Asian Americans in the United States. African Americans make up more than 25 percent of the population in the metropolitan areas of Memphis, New Orleans, Atlanta, Richmond, Virginia Beach, and Washington, DC (U.S. Census Bureau, 2008, Table 21). Even with this diversity, many residential areas remain segregated by race, ethnicity, and socioeconomic status.

Cities provide creative energy for many of their inhabitants, but they are oppressive and dangerous for others. Many families live in safe environments with good schools, parks, and recreational facilities. Others live in toxic environments that contribute to high incidences of asthma and other diseases. Some sections of the city are scarred by gunshots and graffiti. Ambulances, police raids, and funerals for young people in these parts of the city are common occurrences.

Schools across a city look different and serve their students differently. Upper middle class parents are more able to donate funds to assist their schools when teachers of art and music have been cut from the district's budget. When their children are not learning at the expected level, they can hire tutors. Although many low-income parents are engaged actively in their children's education, the proportion of upper middle class parents involved is higher. They talk with teachers; they ensure that their children have the best teachers; they encourage their children to study and participate in extracurricular activities; and they monitor their children's performance. Low-income parents lack the same **cultural capital**. Their income does not permit them to support school activities in the same way.

cultural capital The knowledge and ideas required to maintain or gain status and power in society.

REFLECTonDIVERSITY   Make Me Learn

Mr. Huang starts his Algebra I class even though only half of the students have arrived. When Jamal walks in ten minutes late, he sits at the back of the room and begins talking about last night's basketball game.

"Jamal, where's your homework?" says Mr. Huang.

"Ain't got it," he says as he turns back to his friends.

"How do you think you can pass this class without turning in your homework?" Mr. Huang returns to the problem on the blackboard. "Who can solve this equation?" he asks the few students who are listening.

Around the room, students are tuned into their iPods or talking to their neighbors. In the back of the room, they are arguing about whether LeBron James or Kobe Bryant is the best NBA player. Only two students hand in their homework, and most will be lucky to get a "D" at the end of the grading period.

Jamal walks over to the wall to check his average. It is under 30. On his way back to his desk, he tells a friend, "No way he's gone to fail me. He knows I'll come after him. He's not keeping me from graduating."

Mr. Huang walks over to Jamal's desk to remind him that his mother asked Mr. Huang to tutor him after school. "Why haven't you met me after school? There's no way you can pass this class without some extra help. Let's start by putting away that iPod."

"No way, man. You can't tell me what to do. When I feel like it, I will meet you for tutoring. I don't have the feeling yet."

Another student in the back of the room jumps up, saying, "I'm tired of this. Anybody going with me," and starts out of the classroom.

"I'm with you," Jamal retorts as he leaves his seat and departs the room.

Questions for Reflection

1. No learning appears to be happening in this classroom. Why is Mr. Huang having such a difficult time handling the students in his classroom?
2. What strategies would you use to engage these eleventh graders in Algebra I?
3. The National Governors Association, the Gates Foundation, and others are calling for a major reform of high schools. What changes need to occur in urban schools like this one to develop an academic environment that promotes learning?

Source: Adapted from "Will Jonathan Graduate?" by L. O. Parker, November 11, 2007, *The Washington Post 130*(341), pp. A1, A16–A18.

myeducationlab) To respond to these questions online, go to the *Book Specific Resources* section in the MyEducationLab for your course, select your text, and then select *Reflect on Diversity* for Chapter 6.

A school may serve as a refuge for some urban students. However, some students have less than desirable classrooms and schools that do not provide maximum conditions for learning. They sometimes meet in basement corridors or storerooms without windows as chronicled in books by Jonathan Kozol. Kozol (2000) calls on society not to provide "a narrow gate for children of the fortunate and favored. There should be one gate. It should be known to everyone. It should be wide enough so even Pineapple [a low-income student] can get in without squeezing" (p. 296). Urban schools can be difficult for both students and teachers as described in the Reflect on Diversity feature.

Urban schools can be highly centralized, authoritative, and bureaucratic. However, a growing number of urban school districts are allowing the communities to elect their own school boards. Those with reform-minded leaders are reducing the bureaucracy, becoming more decentralized, and allowing parents more choice in their schools. In a few cities such as New York City and Washington, DC, mayors have taken over the management of their schools with the goal of reforming schools and improving student learning.

Magnet schools are popular in urban areas. Six percent of the schools in the one hundred largest school districts are magnet schools, enrolling 9 percent of the students (Dalton et al., 2006). High schools are more likely to be large (that is, more than nine hundred students) in cities than in other areas of the country (U.S. Department of Education, 2003). The average student-to-teacher ratio in urban schools is only slightly higher than in suburban schools (Anderson & Summerfield, 2007). Research suggests that small class size is critical to improving learning in areas with students who are socially and economically disadvantaged (Leithwood & Jantzi, 2009).

EFFECTIVE SCHOOLS

Educational reformers are calling for a break with the past. They believe that too many teachers do not believe that all children can learn, and, as a result, do little to help students in our lowest income communities to learn to read, compute, and develop the knowledge and skills necessary to be self-sufficient in the future. They believe that state and local district regulations can be obstacles to teaching all students to learn. They believe that teacher unions are part of the problem. The unions are perceived by this group as defenders of incompetent teachers who are not helping students learn. Critics charge that teacher candidates are not being prepared by colleges and universities to work with

myeducationlab

PEARSON

Go to the *Building Teaching Skills and Dispositions* section of Topic 6: *School Organization* in the MyEducationLab for your course and complete the activity titled *Characteristics of Effective Schools*.

students from diverse populations in schools with the greatest need and the lowest academic performance. With new school leaders in cities across the country focused on reform, teachers identified as "ineffective" are being replaced with energetic, enthusiastic, and smart teachers who have generally majored in an academic area, but have no preparation in how to teach.

Effective schools first began to be studied in the 1980s to try to determine the characteristics of schools in which students had high academic performance. One of the early leaders in this movement, Ron Edmonds, focused his research on effective schools for students of color. These researchers found that the educators in these schools had a shared vision and goals for their work. They were concerned about teaching and learning, which was reflected in purposeful teaching and high expectations for their students. These schools also had strong and positive home-to-school partnerships.

It is true that effective teachers make a difference in student learning. Research shows that students who have effective teachers for at least three years in a row will perform at academically higher levels than students who were not lucky enough to have one of those teachers (Bransford, Darling-Hammond, & LePage, 2005; Sanders & Rivers, 1996). The value added to academic achievement by effective teachers has led to movements for greater accountability of educators for student learning. The No Child Left Behind Act was the federal approach to holding teachers and principals accountable by assessing student learning through state achievement tests. States are developing data systems that can track student achievement to a specific teacher. Some states and school districts are also developing plans for financially rewarding teachers who are able to improve the learning of their students as measured on state tests.

School culture also appears to have a great influence on student learning. The early research on effective schools found that they "had a climate and ethos that was purposeful and conducive to learning" (Deal & Peterson, 1999). The culture of a school can

- Foster school effectiveness and productivity;
- Improve collegial and collaborative activities that foster better communication and problem-solving practices;
- Foster successful change and improvement efforts;
- Build commitment and identification of staff, students, and administrators;
- Amplify the energy, motivation, and vitality of a school staff, students, and community; and
- Increase the focus of daily behavior and attention on what is important and valued (Deal & Peterson, 1999).

Of course, school culture can also do just the opposite of the list above. Some schools do not have a culture that supports academic learning and positive development for all students. Reformers think that these toxic schools can be turned around under their leadership with capable teachers, the removal of barriers such as teacher tenure, and more effective and efficient personnel and financial operations.

In most discussions today, effective schools are ones whose students are performing above grade level. Their curriculum is generally **standards based** and assessments are **performance based**. Teachers in these schools do not limit their teaching to preparing students to take a state standardized test. They encourage students to be problem-solvers and critical thinkers as well as ensuring that they know the subject matter. The nonprofit group Education Trust has found that the schools that teach all children to high standards have "clear goals; high expectations; rigorous coursework; extra instructional help when needed; and strong teachers who know their subject matter and how to teach it" (Education Trust, 2006). Two other important factors are explicit standards and assessments that provide teachers feedback on what students are learning. Under those conditions, African American and Hispanic students are performing at the same levels as white students (Education Trust, 2006).

Criteria for Effective Schools

The U.S. Department of Education annually recognizes Blue Ribbon schools that are either high-performing schools or dramatically improved public and private schools. Students in the high-performing schools must be achieving in the top 10 percent of their state on state tests. To be designated as a dramatically improved school, at least 40 percent of their students must be from disadvantaged backgrounds and have dramatically improved their performance to high levels. Since its inception in 1982, more than six thousand schools have received this recognition (U.S. Department of Education, 2009).

For more in-depth discussion of standards and assessments, see Chapter 11.

standards-based curriculum Course work that is based on explicit outcomes of what students should know and be able to do in a subject at a specific grade level as identified in standards.

performance-based assessment A comprehensive assessment system through which candidates demonstrate their proficiencies in the area being measured.

A number of organizations have also identified effective schools. For example, Education Trust has identified schools with large African American and Hispanic student populations in which those students are performing at high levels. The list of these schools is available at www2.edtrust.org.

LOOKING AHEAD: GREATER ACCOUNTABILITY FOR STUDENT LEARNING

No matter which curriculum approach or school reform effort a school adopts, the bottom-line goal should be to ensure that all of its students are learning at high levels regardless of their race, ethnicity, native language, socioeconomic status, physical ability, or gender. Academic achievement will continue to be one of the primary purposes of schools. Teachers are being held accountable for their ability to improve academic achievement. School leaders will continue to examine the school cultures that support effective schools and try to duplicate that culture in a larger number of schools. The number of parents who choose charter or magnet schools may increase as they seek schools that will help their children learn at the high levels expected by states.

Accountability is discussed in greater detail in Chapter 11.

Because No Child Left Behind requires schools and school districts to disaggregate test data by race, language, and disability, the differences in academic performance among groups has become very public. In some schools all students are performing at high levels, but in too many schools, students of color, English-language learners, and students with disabilities are falling behind their white, able-bodied peers whose native language is English. In the next chapter, we will explore the nation's diversity and the challenges that schools face as they build on that diversity to ensure that all students learn at high levels.

SUMMARY

ROLES OF SCHOOLS

- Schools serve many purposes, including the development of citizenship, preparation for work, the development of academic and social competence, and the transmission of the culture to another generation.

CULTURE IN SCHOOLS

- Culture determines the way we behave and think within society and its subgroups.
- A group of people who live in the same country generally share a common culture that is incorporated into the policies and institutions of society, including schools.
- Families have their own unique cultural backgrounds based on their ethnicity, native language, and religion that may be accepted positively by schools or be at dissonance with the school culture.
- Not all parents, communities, and educators agree on the values and content to be taught in schools, which can lead to the courts being called on to resolve the differences.
- Schools have their own cultures with histories and traditions that affect the way students and teachers behave.
- A school's culture is important in supporting student learning.
- Involving the community in schools not only helps community members become better advocates for the schools, but provides needed assistance for educators and students.

SCHOOL CHOICES

- Parents have always had the option to place their children in private religious, single-sex, and independent schools.
- Parents in larger school districts have a growing number of options within the public schools as the number of magnet and charter schools increases.
- In a few school districts, parents can receive a voucher to move their children from a public to a private school at public expense.

SCHOOL LEVELS

- Schools have been divided into grades to serve students who are at the same age level.
- Governors and philanthropists are calling for the reform of high schools to prepare students for a changing world and improve graduation rates.

SCHOOL LOCATIONS

- The place in which we live affects our cultural identity and lived experiences.
- Life and schools are different depending on whether we live in rural, suburban, or urban areas.
- Poverty is greater in central city and urban areas, but is growing in suburban areas.
- Schools in suburban areas, except those closest to urban areas, have greater financial support, and students perform at higher levels on achievement tests.

EFFECTIVE SCHOOLS

- Academic achievement is at the heart of effective schools, in which all students learn at high levels regardless of their race, native language, or disability.

LOOKING AHEAD: GREATER ACCOUNTABILITY FOR STUDENT LEARNING

- Teachers and schools are now being held accountable for learning by all students as measured by students' performance on state achievement tests.

DISCUSSION QUESTIONS

1. Students and families bring their cultures into the classroom. Teachers also bring to school their cultures, which may be different than that of their students. What problems can arise if teachers establish their own culture as the norm to be followed in the classroom? What cultural norms should guide a classroom in which students are culturally diverse?

2. Since the release of *A Nation at Risk* in 1983, the school curricula for early childhood education through high school have become standards based and the performance of students assessed regularly. What school purpose guided preschool to grade 12 education during this period?

3. You may be assigned to a school in which community members monitor the curriculum to ensure that their values are reflected. What curriculum content could spark debates in the community? How important will it be to keep parents and other community members informed?

4. Charter school advocates often indicate that state and district regulations are obstacles to good schools that help students learn. What regulations are they talking about? How might those regulations prevent a school from being as effective as it could be?

5. Most states match the licenses that teachers receive to a specific subject or age level of students, which in turn matches the school levels discussed in this chapter. Why are teachers not generally granted a single license to teach students across the P–12 grades? What teachers can receive a license that crosses all of the grade levels?

6. The numbers of students in central cities and rural areas are somewhat equal as is the income status of their populations. What are the obstacles to a good education that students face in these two different settings? What are the positive elements of their school locations that could contribute to a more effective education for students in those two areas?

SCHOOL-BASED OBSERVATIONS

1. Select a charter school in your area to visit. During your observations, identify characteristics of the school culture, students, teachers, and instruction that are similar to and different from the neighborhood schools that you have attended or observed. Record your observations in your journal or portfolio.

2. Visit a rural, suburban, or urban school and systematically record characteristics such as the ethnic and racial composition of the students, the income level of families, the size of the student population and teaching force, the student-to-teacher ratios, the general school climate, and other observable characteristics. What appears to be working well at the school? What appears to be problematic at the school?

PORTFOLIO DEVELOPMENT

1. To develop an understanding of school culture and its role in the establishment of effective schools, record the characteristics of schools by one of the following two approaches:
   a. When you visit a school, record the condition of the school, the characteristics of documents on the walls of the building, the type of instruction observed in classrooms, the reflection of students' cultures in the school, the mission of the school, and generally how students and teachers feel about the school. Also record the diversity of the school population, which is usually available on the website, and how students are performing on state-required standardized tests. As you look at your observations and data, write a paper or newspaper article about how the school culture supports (or does not support) student learning.
   b. Review a selected number of the U.S. Department of Education's Blue Ribbon schools (http://www.ed.gov/news/pressreleases/2008/09/09092008.html) or the effective schools identified by Education Trust (http://www2.edtrust.org/EdTrust/Product+Catalog/main.htm#sp). Write a report or newspaper article about the school cultures of some of the schools that appear to be serving their students well, at least in terms of improving their academic achievement.

2. Some critics of charter schools worry that the establishment of charter schools will harm public schools. Write a paper on the strengths and disadvantages of charter schools. Include in your paper an analysis of the contributions charter schools could make to public schools and whether you think their establishment is harming public schools.

PREPARING FOR CERTIFICATION

1. The PRAXIS II Principles of Learning and Teaching (PLT) has a section titled "Students as Learners." This section of the test includes reference to "understanding the influence of individual experiences, talents, and prior learning, as well as language, culture, family, and community values on students' learning":
   • multicultural backgrounds
   • age-appropriate knowledge and behavior
   • the student culture at school
   • family backgrounds
   • linguistic patterns and differences
   • cognitive patterns and differences
   • social and emotional issues

   Reread the elements that make up Culture in Schools. Using the descriptors above from the PRAXIS II and the elements from the text related to a school's culture, define the culture that existed in your high school.

2. Answer the following multiple-choice question, which is similar to items in Praxis and other state certification tests.

   In many districts, school choices are made available to parents for a variety of reasons. Reread the opening segment of the chapter about virtual schools. Virtual schools exist in most states, and at most levels (elementary, middle school, high school). In addition, single courses can be taken at those levels, and in the colleges and universities. Several reasons are given for students taking online courses. Which of the following does NOT often justify attendance in a virtual school:
   a. Credit recovery
   b. Comfort in the virtual environment
   c. Cost
   d. Unavailability of course on home campus.

3. Answer the following short-answer question, which is similar to items in Praxis and other state certification tests.

   Although schools are expected to transmit the culture of the United States to the younger generation, educators do not always agree on *whose* culture should be transmitted. Describe what you feel would be an ideal culture for the school where you might teach. How are they similar and different?

4. Answer the following short-answer question, which is similar to items in Praxis and other state certification tests.

   Some school reformers believe vouchers are an effective means of improving education. Describe the purpose of vouchers and how they work. List two arguments for vouchers and two arguments against the use of vouchers in public education.

After you've completed your written reponses for the above questions, use the Praxis general scoring guide provided in Chapter 1 to see if you can revise your response to improve your score.

MYEDUCATIONLAB

myeducationlab) Now go to Topic 3: *Schools and Society* in the MyEducationLab (www.myeducationlab.com) for your course, where you can:

- Find learning outcomes for *Schools and Society* along with the national standards that connect to these outcomes.
- Complete *Assignments and Activities* that can help you more deeply understand the chapter content.
- Apply and practice your understanding of the core teaching skills identified in the chapter with the *Building Teaching Skills and Dispositions* learning units.

- Check your comprehension on the content covered in the chapter by going to the *Study Plan* in the *Book Specific Resources* section for your text. Here you will be able to take a chapter quiz, receive feedback on your answers, and then access *Review, Practice, and Enrichment* activities to enhance your understanding of chapter content.

WEBSITES

www.capenet.org The Council for American Private Education (CAPE) includes facts and information about private schools, a list of blue ribbon private schools, and links to job banks.

www.edreform.com The Center for Education Reform is supportive of school choice. Its website discusses issues around choice and provides information on supportive state legislation and becoming active in school reform efforts.

www.govhs.org The Virtual High School Global Consortium is a nonprofit organization that offers online courses and professional development.

www.naesp.org The National Association for Elementary School Principals provides access to resources for elementary school teachers.

www.naeyc.org The website of the National Association for the Education of Young Children provides a number of resources on teaching preschoolers and primary students from diverse racial and language groups as well as students with disabilities.

www.nassp.org The website of the National Association for Secondary School Principals is a resource for studies on middle and high schools, a list of "breakthrough schools" serving students from families in poverty, and policies affecting high schools and their students.

www.nmsa.org The National Middle School Association's website includes professional development kits, publications on middle level education, and avenues for becoming involved in advocacy activities.

FURTHER READING

Conchas, G. Q., & Rodríguez, L. F. (2008). *Small schools and urban youth: Using the power of school culture to engage students*. Thousand Oaks, CA: Corwin Press. Examining the structural and cultural features of small learning communities in four schools in Oakland and Boston, the authors provide a clear, practical description of small schools that work.

Deal, T. E., & Peterson, K. D. (1999). *Shaping school culture: The heart of leadership*. San Francisco: Jossey-Bass. Although this book is written for school leaders, it provides valuable information about school cultures that contribute to effective schools and those that have led to toxic cultures. The descriptions of school cultures that have been effective in diverse communities are helpful.

Kincheloe, J. L., & hayes, k. (Eds.). (2007). *Teaching city kids: Understanding and appreciating them*. New York: Peter Lang. The authors of the chapters in this book explore how marginalized students in our urban schools have the resiliency to make it through, and how teachers can assist them in overcoming the racist and classist agendas that exist in many urban schools.

Price, H. B. (2008). *Mobilizing the community to help students succeed*. Alexandria, VA: Association for Supervision and Curriculum Development. This former president of the National Urban League describes strategies that teachers might use to inspire and reward academic achievement in the most challenged school districts. He promotes the use of the community to motivate students to be successful.

chapter seven

DIVERSITY IN SOCIETY AND SCHOOLS

FOR STUDENTS, DIVERSITY STILL IS DAILY LESSON

EDUCATION
IN THE NEWS

Changing Ethnic Makeup Teaches Some to Beat Prejudice

By **CARRIE COPPERNOLL**,
The Oklahoman, August 21, 2008

Growing up in Edmond, most of Gabrielle Anderson's friends were white. Now that she's in college, most of her friends are black. She's not sure, though, if that means she's changed or society has.

"If a person's going to be kind to me, I'm going to be their friend," said Anderson, a black 20-year-old junior at Oklahoma City University. "I don't think everybody has that mentality. I think you have to be taught that."

Anderson said she hopes people her age are learning the same lessons she did growing up. Their generation lives in a much different society than their parents or grandparents experienced.

OKLAHOMA NOW MORE DIVERSE

Oklahoma has become a more diverse state since the civil rights movement and even in recent years, according to figures from the U.S. Census Bureau. When Clara Luper's 13 youths sat down at the Katz lunch counter in 1958, about 1 in 10 Oklahomans were nonwhite, according to the census. When high school students were born in the early 1990s, about 1 in 5 Oklahomans were nonwhite. In 2006, about 1 in 4 Oklahomans were nonwhite.

Acceptance of such statistics becomes more important as Oklahoma becomes more diverse, said Seth McNayr, 17, of Oklahoma City. McNayr, who is white, has many friends of other races but says sometimes he feels like others look at him with suspicion.

ETHNIC BACKGROUNDS DRAW CURIOSITY

"They'll assume that we're afraid of them or that we don't like them," he said. "But I don't see why something our grandparents might have thought or even our parents may have thought would affect us."

Yet stereotypes are common among all age groups, said Sydney Cole, 17, of Oklahoma City.

"There still is racism here today," she said. "You don't see it as often as you did in the past, but it's definitely still here. . . . You can't take it personally."

Cole's mother is American Indian. Her father is black.

"People are always wondering exactly what race I am," she said. "I look like I could be anything. . . . It's actually a good opportunity for me to talk about my family and our history."

One of Cole's friends, Ayeh Aguilar, has been told several times she looks "exotic." She's half Venezuelan and half Iranian—a heritage that she's often asked about. She learned about the civil rights movement in school and said that kind of education is vital.

"What happened (to minorities) was wrong," said Aguilar, 17, of Oklahoma City. "But since that happened, we know now to grow from it and to make things better for the future and for future generations as well."

CAMP OPENS COMMUNICATION ABOUT DIVERSITY

Aguilar spent a week this summer at a diversity camp called "Anytown, Oklahoma." The camp was hosted by the Oklahoma Center for Community and Justice. More than 50 teens from throughout the state met near Tulsa to discuss cultural differences and issues facing young people.

The students talked about race, ethnicity, religion, culture and other issues, said Hannibal Johnson, Anytown founder and director.

The students are open for discussion, Johnson said, because diversity is something they deal with every day.

"I hope they end up curious about other people and their backgrounds," Johnson said. "I hope they step outside their comfort zone—beyond their neighborhood, beyond their congregation. I hope they become a catalyst for change."

QUESTIONS FOR REFLECTION

1. How would you describe the diversity of students in Oklahoma? How has it changed since 1990?
2. How different is the diversity in Oklahoma from where you grew up? Why do you think those differences exist?
3. Why do you think these students see race differently than their parents did?

LEARNING OUTCOMES

After reading and studying this chapter, you should be able to:

1. Understand that academic achievement is influenced by societal factors related to race, ethnicity, language, gender, and exceptionalities. (INTASC 3: Diverse Learners)

2. Identify different instructional strategies for assisting English language learners in learning English and the academic content that will help them achieve at levels necessary to improve their participation in higher education. (INTASC 3: Diverse Learners)

3. Understand the need for providing appropriate accommodations in the classroom for students with disabilities. (INTASC 3: Diverse Learners)

4. Understand the importance of building on the experiences and cultures of students and their families for instruction. (INTASC 1: Content and 3: Diverse Learners)

5. Discuss the importance of diversity, equality, and social justice in delivering high-quality education for all students. (INTASC 3: Diverse Learners)

SOCIOECONOMIC STATUS

Most people want the "good life," which in the United States includes a decent job, affordable housing, good health, a good education for their family members, and periodic vacations. One measure used to estimate the good life is **socioeconomic status (SES)**, which is the primary indicator of the standard of living families are able to maintain. It also has a great impact on one's chances of attending college and attaining a job that ensures material comfort throughout life.

Socioeconomic status serves as a criterion to measure the economic condition of individuals. It is determined by one's occupation, income, and educational attainment. Wealth and power are other important factors that affect the way one is able to live, but these data are difficult to measure. We may be able to guess a family's socioeconomic status if we know such things as where they live, their jobs, the type of car they drive, the schools their children attend, and the types of vacations they take.

Social Stratification

Most societies are characterized by **social stratification**, in which individuals occupy different levels of the social structure. Wealth, income, occupation, and education help define these social positions. However, high or low rankings are not based solely on SES criteria. Race, age, gender, religion, and disability can contribute to higher or lower rankings as well. Although members of most **ethnic groups** can be found at all levels of the socioeconomic status scale in the United States, those from northern and western European backgrounds historically have been represented at the highest levels.

Social mobility remains one of the core values of the U.S. culture. We are told that hard work will lead to better jobs, higher income, and a better chance to participate in the good life. We read stories of individuals who were born in poverty but through hard work became wealthy as corporate presidents, prestigious publishers, successful writers, athletes, or entertainers. Although upward mobility continues to occur, the chances of moving from poverty to riches, no matter how hard one works, are low without interventions such as a college education and lots of good luck. Individuals who are born into wealthy families are likely to attend good schools, finish college, and find high-paying jobs (Family income, 2008). They are raised with high expectations, have the economic resources to assist them in meeting these expectations, and usually end up meeting them.

Class Structure

We often divide students and their families into distinct classes based on the economic level of their families. Individuals who do manual work for a living are sometimes described as "working class" or "blue-collar" workers. When farm laborers and service workers are included in the working class, this group represents 46 percent of the employed population (U.S. Census Bureau, 2008, Table 600). Most members of this class have little control over their work. Some of the jobs are routine, mechanical, and not challenging. Work sometimes is sporadic and affected by an economy in which employees face layoffs, replacement by computerized equipment and other advances in technology,

socioeconomic status (SES) The economic condition of individuals based on their own or their family's income, occupation, and educational attainment.

social stratification Levels of social class ranking based on income, education, occupation, wealth, and power in society.

ethnic groups Groups based on the national origin (that is, a country or area of the world) of one's family or ancestors in which members share a culture and sense of common destiny.

part-time work, and unemployment as jobs move to locations with cheaper labor. Benefits such as vacation time and health plans are often limited. The education required for working-class jobs is usually less than that required for many middle-class positions, except for skilled and crafts workers who have had specialized training and may have served apprenticeships.

Most people who don't perceive themselves as poor or rich identify themselves as middle class. Annual middle-class incomes for a family of four range from $45,000 to $88,000, encompassing more than 30 percent of the population (Rose, 2000). It includes both blue-collar and professional or managerial workers. For most of the middle class, $88,000 would be the top of their earning potential, and this is often possible only because both spouses work. Families in this class have very different lifestyles at opposite ends of the income continuum. Clerical workers, technicians, and salespeople in the group have less control over their jobs than the professionals, managers, and administrators who often supervise them. These workers tend to have somewhat better benefits than do members of the working class. The professionals in this group expect to move beyond $88,000 in their careers with the goal of becoming one of the 10 percent of U.S. families earning more than $150,000 annually (U.S. Census Bureau, 2008, Table 674).

Many professionals, managers, and administrators receive incomes that are above $100,000, which places them in the more affluent upper middle class, but they often believe that their condition is universal rather than unique. Many think that most of the U.S. population shares the same affluence, advantages, and comforts. A $100,000 salary in a neighborhood where most families earn more than $250,000 seems low; in another neighborhood, a family making $100,000 would be considered well off. Professionals are men and women who have usually obtained professional or advanced degrees. They include teachers, lawyers, physicians, college professors, scientists, and psychologists. Excluding teachers, most of these families earn far above the median income of $58,407 (U.S. Census Bureau, 2008, Table 674). Successful executives and businesspeople are the managers and administrators in this group. These workers usually have more autonomy over their jobs and working conditions than working- and lower-middle-class workers.

The upper class consists of wealthy and socially prominent families. The income and wealth of members of this class are far higher than those of the other classes, and the gap is growing. As the recession unfolded in 2008, you may have heard a great deal about the high salaries earned by corporate chief executive officers and Wall Street executives. For example, in 1980 corporate chief executive officers earned forty-two times as much as their employees; by 1990 they earned eighty-five times as much; and by 2007 the multiple had grown to 344 (Anderson, Cavanagh, Collins, Pizzigati, & Laphan, 2008). These great differences contribute to limited interactions with members of other classes. Children in this class rarely attend public schools, isolating them from peers of other social classes. The greatest assimilation of lifestyles and values probably occurs among members of ethnically and culturally diverse groups in the upper class.

Poverty

The U.S. government established a poverty index in the 1960s that indicated the income that would be used to determine poverty regardless of where the family lived with the exception of Hawaii and Alaska. The 2009 federal guidelines set the threshold at an annual income of $22,050 for a family of four (Foss, 2009). These poverty thresholds are set at about half the income needed to meet basic needs, including housing, food, child care, and transportation (Foss & Couthen, 2008). As a result, many families are above the poverty level, but still do not have an adequate income to purchase their basic needs. Many members of these low-income families work in full- or part-time jobs that pay such low wages they cannot pull their families out of poverty.

Using the federal guidelines for 2006, 36.5 million persons (12.3 percent of the population) and 7.7 million families (9.8 percent of all families) earned incomes below the poverty level. Although 67 percent of the population living below the poverty level is white, only 10.3 percent of all whites in the country live in poverty (U.S. Census Bureau, 2008, Tables 691 and 693). The percentage of other racial and ethnic groups in poverty is higher because of disparate jobs and incomes. The median income of Asian American families was $74,612 in 2006, compared to whites' median income of $61,280. African American families and Hispanic families earned $38,269 and $40,000, respectively, or 62 and 65 percent as much as whites (U.S. Census Bureau, 2008, Table 673). Although this income disparity among groups decreases when one compares two-income families with the same level of education, it does not disappear. Women who work full time year-round also encounter discriminatory practices that keep their incomes at 72 percent of those of men (U.S. Census Bureau, 2008, Table 681).

FIGURE 7.1

Persons in Poverty in the United States in 2006

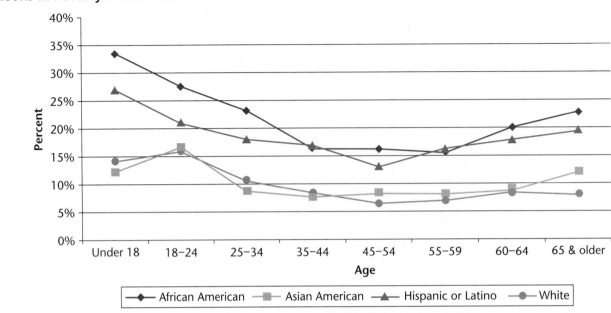

Source: U.S. Census Bureau. (2008). *Statistical abstract of the United States: 2009* (128th ed., Table 691). Washington, DC: U.S. Government Printing Office.

Children, the elderly, and most persons of color suffer disproportionately from poverty, as shown in Figure 7.1. Seventeen percent of U.S. children live in poverty (U.S. Census Bureau, 2008, Table 690). Another 22 percent of the nation's children live in low-income families above the federal poverty level. Thus, 39 percent of our children live in low-income families, often making them eligible for free or reduced-price lunches in schools and special academic programs (Foss & Couthen, 2008). The percent of U.S. children in poverty is more than double that of most other major industrialized nations. A number of industrialized nations have reduced child poverty levels to below 5 percent. Of 37 industrialized nations, the United States has a higher poverty rate for children than all nations except Poland, Mexico, and Turkey (Organisation for Economic Co-operation and Development, 2008). As with adults, Hispanic and African American children are more likely to live in low-income families, as shown in Figure 7.2.

Children under the age of six are more likely to live in low-income families than older children (Foss & Couthen, 2008). These young children need nurturing families and other adults. High-quality educational experiences can contribute to their cognitive and social development in

FIGURE 7.2

Children (Birth to Age Eighteen) in Low-Income Families by Racial and Ethnic Group in 2007

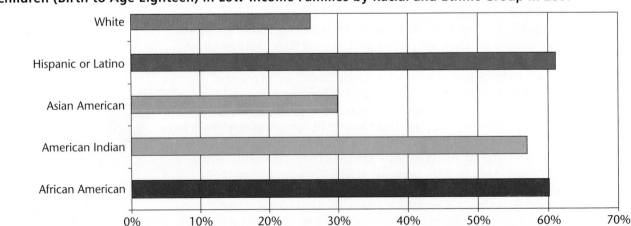

Source: National Center for Children in Poverty. (2008, October). *Basic facts about low-income children: Birth to age 18*. Retrieved on May 9, 2009, from http://nccp.org/publications/pub_845.html

very positive ways. Programs that help parents develop their parenting skills have also been found to improve the academic achievement of students who are suffering from the harsh economic conditions in which their families live. Education programs include Early Head Start and preschools for three- and four-year-olds, which are being offered by a growing number of schools with low-income students.

More information about parenting and early childhood education programs can be found in Chapter 8.

Impact of Poverty and Low Income on Academic Achievement

Although students in the eighth and twelfth grades whose parents have not finished high school have improved their scores on national mathematics tests since 1978, their performance is still not equal to that of students whose parents have finished high school and college—factors that generally correlate with higher incomes (National Center for Education Statistics, 2009). Low-income students also do not perform as well on the National Assessment of Education Progress (NAEP) tests that are given annually to fourth, eighth, and twelfth graders, as shown in Figure 7.3.

Factors outside of school contribute to the performance of students in school. Students of color and students from low-income families are more likely to be exposed to environmental hazards such as lead and mercury. The chances of these students being hungry and eating nonnutritious foods are greater than for their more affluent peers. School factors that contribute to their lower academic performance include less access to certified and experienced teachers. They are more likely to have substitute teachers because teachers are absent more than in schools where the students are white or from higher income families. The turnover of teachers from year to year is also greater. They also have less access to technology in their schools. During the summer, low-income students and students of color do not participate in education enrichment programs at the same rate as their classmates, limiting their chances to grow academically at the same rate (Barton & Coley, 2009).

Receiving a quality education is critical for low-income students to improve their chances of entering college and earning a middle-class income or above as adults. As a teacher, you should hold high expectations for the academic performance of these students and ensure that they are learning the subjects that you are teaching. In your teacher education program, you should learn how to assess student learning and make adjustments to your instruction when students are not getting it. Understanding what students know when they enter your classroom and being able to draw on real-world experiences that are meaningful to your students will contribute to your being successful with low-income students.

FIGURE 7.3

Performance on NAEP Reading Tests by Family Income*

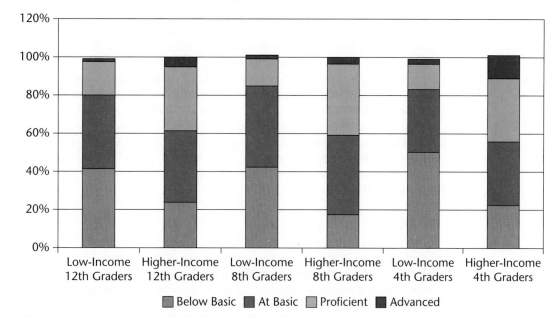

*Low income is defined as students eligible for free or reduced-price lunches at schools.

Source: U.S. Department of Education, National Center for Education Statistics. (2005, 2007). *NAEP data explorer.* Washington, DC: Author.

RACE AND ETHNICITY

American Indian tribes and Alaska Natives are the only indigenous ethnic groups in the United States. Therefore, more than 99 percent of the U.S. population, or their ancestors, came from somewhere else at some time during the past five hundred years. The families of your students often identify with a country of origin, although the geographical boundaries may have changed since their ancestors emigrated. A growing number of people have mixed heritage, with ancestors from different parts of the world.

Although many people now identify themselves by their **panethnic membership** (for example, as African American or Asian American), race remains a political reality in U.S. society. It has become integrally interwoven into the nation's policies, practices, and institutions, including the educational, economic, and judicial systems. As a result, whites have advantages that are reflected in higher achievement on tests and higher incomes in adulthood. The issue of race encompasses personal and national discussions of affirmative action, immigration, desegregation, and a color-blind society. Race and ethnicity may be linked, but they are not the same. Both influence one's cultural identity and status in society.

Race

Race and gender are among the first physical characteristics we notice when we meet another person. Many people inappropriately use race to explain differences among people's behaviors, languages, socioeconomic standing, and academic achievements. Although race is no longer accepted as a scientific concept for classifying people, it has become a social construction for identifying differences. We are sometimes asked to indicate our race or our panethnic identity on forms that we complete.

Our ideas about race are created from experiences in our own racial group and with other groups. They are also informed by reflections of racial differences in the media. Race has become politicized and institutionalized in the policies and actions of judges, teachers, legislators, police, employers, and others who are in charge of institutions that affect people's lives. Our stereotyped views of race usually bestow positive attributes and high status on our own race and negative attributes or low status on others.

Skin color is a signifier of race but does not capture its meaning. Many people have mixed racial backgrounds that place them along a continuum of skin color; they might not be obviously white, black, brown, or otherwise easily identifiable as one race or another as was true for several of the students in the article that opened this chapter. At one time, state laws declared a person's official race as nonwhite if a small percentage of his or her racial heritage was other than white. The official message was, and continues to be, that white is the ideal and that anything else, even small percentages of a race other than white, is less than ideal. This example is one of many ways in which race affects our everyday lives and becomes an integral part of our identity. Whether we like it or not, race continues to be used to sort people in society.

Persons of color usually identify themselves by their race or ethnic group and are usually identified as such by others. They are confronted with their race almost daily in encounters with employers, salespeople, and colleagues or as they watch the evening news. Whites, on the other hand, are seldom confronted with their race; in fact, many see themselves as raceless. White has become the norm against which persons of color are classified as *other*. As a result, many whites are unable to see how their race has privileged them in society. When you are unable to recognize racist policies and practices in the school or do not confront them, you may lose the trust and confidence of students of color. Being fearful to address race and racial disparities in your classroom and school will not serve your students well.

Ethnicity

The national origin of our family is the primary determinant of our ethnicity. We share a common history, language, traditions, and experiences with other members of our ethnic group that help sustain and enhance the culture of the group within the United States. Identity with our ethnic group is strongest when we maintain a high degree of interpersonal associations with other members of our group and share common residential areas.

Ethnic cohesiveness and solidarity are strengthened as members organize to support and advance the group, fight discrimination, and influence political and economic decisions that affect

panethnic membership Ethnic membership based on national origin from a continent such as Africa, Asia, or North America.

FIGURE 7.4

Panethnic and Racial Composition of the U.S. Population

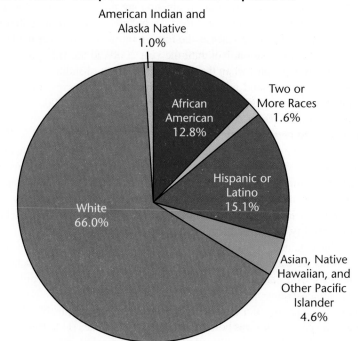

Source: U.S. Census Bureau. (2008). *Statistical abstract of the United States: 2009* (128th ed., Table 8). Washington, DC: U.S. Government Printing Office.

the group as a whole. In the 1960s, civil rights struggles led to calls for changes in schools, colleges, government programs, and employment to support equality across ethnic groups. During this period, African, Hispanic, Asian, and American Indians called for recognition of their ethnic roots in the school curriculum. By the 1970s, European ethnic groups, especially those of southern and eastern European origins, had also joined this movement. Ethnic studies programs were established in colleges and universities and some high schools to study the history, contributions, and experiences of groups that had traditionally been excluded.

The U.S. Census Bureau reports population data on the racial and ethnic groups shown in Figure 7.4, but these broad classifications do not accurately describe the ethnic diversity of the country. For example, there are more than five hundred American Indian tribes. Most panethnic classifications include numerous ethnic groups with identities and loyalties linked to specific countries. Asian Americans include recent immigrants and people whose ancestors emigrated from countries as diverse as India, Korea, Japan, and the Philippines. Hispanics include people from Mexico, Central America, Puerto Rico, Cuba, Spain, and South America. Although Africans continue to emigrate to the United States, most African Americans have long historical roots in this country; many have ancestors not only from Africa but also from Europe and American Indian tribes. European Americans range from western Europeans who may have lived in the United States for several hundred years, to those from eastern Europe who immigrated in large numbers at the beginning of the twentieth century, to recent immigrants from Russia and other former Soviet countries. The largest number of people identify their ancestry as German (17 percent), Irish (12 percent), English (9 percent), Italian (6 percent), and Polish (3 percent) (U.S. Census Bureau, American FactFinder, 2008c). By 2050, almost half of the population will be non-European (Day, n.d.).

━━━━━━━ JOURNAL FOR REFLECTION ━━━━━━━

How do you characterize your ethnic and racial heritage? What has been the nature of your interactions with other groups? Have your experiences been positive or negative? How could you better get to know individuals from ethnic and racial groups different than your own?

The United States is often referred to as land of immigrants who left their original homelands because of economic hardship or political repression. However, this picture is only partially true. The groups that have suffered most from discrimination are those who are indigenous or whose ancestors entered the country involuntarily. American Indians were here long before Europeans and others appeared. They suffered greatly as the foreign intruders took over the land and almost annihilated the indigenous population. Not until the year 2000 did the U.S. government admit to the near genocide of native peoples when the head of the Bureau of Indian Affairs apologized for "the agency's legacy of racism and inhumanity that included massacres, forced relocations of tribes and attempts to wipe out Indian languages and cultures" (Kelley, 2000).

The ancestors of most African Americans were brought involuntarily to America by slave traders as a commodity to be sold. They were not treated as full humans until well into the nineteenth century. Not until late in the twentieth century did Africans begin to voluntarily immigrate to the United States in any significant numbers. Mexican Americans in the Southwest were inhabitants of lands that were annexed as part of the spoils for winning the Mexican-American War; they did not immigrate. Today, many Mexicans would like to immigrate to this country, but, prevented by immigration laws, they instead cross the border illegally to obtain jobs and have better opportunities for economic stability. However, illegal immigrants constantly face possible deportation, loss of everything they have gained in this country, and separation from their families. You may know students whose parents were arrested and deported while their children were in school. Children of illegal immigrants may worry about this scenario happening to them, which could lead to inattention and stress that affects their concentration and academic performance.

Schools are early recipients of a growing number of new immigrants. Nearly one in four students have at least one parent who was born outside the United States (U.S. Census Bureau, 2008, Table 220). Immigrants today are settling beyond the traditional urban areas of California, Florida, Illinois, New Jersey, New York, and Texas. States that have had limited ethnic diversity in the past are becoming home to students from other countries as immigrant families are sponsored by persons in these communities or settle in rural areas and small to medium-sized towns because of jobs and values that are similar to their own.

The school population is becoming more diverse at a faster rate than the population as a whole, in part because women of childbearing age are more diverse than the older population. The student population is also more diverse than its teachers as shown in Figure 7.5. The degree and nature of diversity in schools vary by the region of the country. The percent of students who are Hispanic or Asian American is greater in the West. Schools in the South have the largest

FIGURE 7.5

Race, Ethnicity, and Gender of Students and Teachers

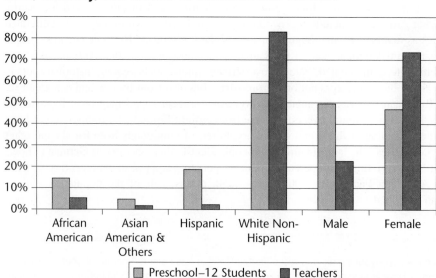

Source: U.S. Census Bureau. (2008). *Statistical abstract of the United States: 2009* (128th ed., Tables 241 and 254). Washington, DC: U.S. Government Printing Office.

percentage of African American students. Midwest schools have the least diversity, although the number of Hispanic students is growing in that area (Planty et al., 2008, Indicator 5). Having greater knowledge of the history and experiences of the diverse groups attending your school will improve your understanding of your students and their families. It also sends a message to families and communities that you care about them and their experiences.

Racial and Ethnic Disparities in Education

Students of color who have a long history of inequitable treatment in society and the education system have closed the achievement gap with Asian American and white students since the 1970s, but have not eliminated it. Although today's schools place a greater emphasis on academics for all students regardless of their race, ethnicity, gender, or socioeconomic status, students of color except for Asian Americans are not yet participating equally in higher level courses and programs, nor scoring at the same level on achievement tests. For example, African American participation in advanced placement (AP) courses and performance on AP exams is far below that of other groups. Hispanic students are more likely to be in mathematics classes taught by teachers who have not majored in mathematics. The classes in which students of color sit generally have more students than other schools. They change schools more frequently than white students and have greater fear for their safety in schools. All of these factors have an effect on cognitive development and academic achievement (Barton & Coley, 2009). They are factors that could be changed for the purpose of improving academic achievement.

The pattern of academic achievement for most students of color is similar to that of low-income students. The percent of white fourth-grade students scoring at the proficient level or above on NAEP tests of reading is more than twice that of Hispanic and African American students. The gap grows wider by the eighth grade and even wider by the twelfth grade. Although today all students are performing at higher levels on NAEP's mathematics test, the gap between whites and students of color is increasing (Barton & Coley, 2008).

Teaching from a Cultural Context

Teaching is complex. You cannot determine the learning styles, prior knowledge, or cultural experiences of students by simply knowing that they are from a specific ethnic group or SES level. You will need to observe and listen to students and their parents as well as assess student performance to develop the most effective teaching strategies. Being able to validate the cultures of students and communities may be helpful in improving student learning. As a result, students begin to feel that teachers care about them, which is a first step in building a foundation for trust between teachers and students who are from different racial and ethnic groups. A part of building trust is to teach the history of a group truthfully, which sometimes requires presenting it from the different perspectives of the participants in history. Members of different ethnic and racial groups experienced history differently based on their power in society. The Reflect on Diversity feature on the next page explores one teacher's dilemma about teaching a common American story about Thanksgiving.

To demonstrate respect for students' backgrounds and experiences, you should be able to help students see the relationship between subject matter and the world in which they live. Students should see themselves in the representations (that is, books, examples, word problems, and films) that are used in a classroom. An effective teacher teaches the same concept by explaining it in different ways, relating it to something meaningful in students' lives, and demonstrating it in multiple ways. For most beginning teachers, these various explanations may be limited; with experience, you will be able to draw on many different strategies to take advantage of each student's learning style and cultural patterns.

An inclusive curriculum begins to reflect the reality of our multicultural world rather than only the piece of it that belongs to the culture of the teacher. For example, learning science and mathematics would be enhanced for American Indian and other students if the knowledge and traditions of various tribes and nations were incorporated into the curriculum. Researchers Sharon Nelson-Barber and Elise Estrin report that

> Many American Indian students have extensive knowledge of mathematics and science knowledge that is rooted in naturalist traditions common to Native communities and arrived at through observation and direct experience. Because many Indian communities follow traditional subsistence

Go to the *Building Teaching Skills and Dispositions* section of Topic 2: *Student Diversity* in the MyEducationLab for your course and complete the activity titled *Modifying Instruction for Student Diversity.*

REFLECTonDIVERSITY   Teaching the Truth

It's November—the time of the school year that many elementary teachers teach about American Indians and Thanksgiving, even though the traditional story is not true. Mrs. Starkes was no different. She was setting up her PowerPoint presentation to introduce the unit to her fourth graders in rural Texas.

"Are we going to talk about Indians today?" Joe asked excitedly.

"Yes," Mrs. Starkes replied.

"I am so excited," the petite blond girl in the first row squealed. "My great, great grandmother was Cherokee."

Mrs. Starkes was always surprised at how many of her students claimed to have American Indian ancestors, especially in November. She was determined to break the stereotypes that her students had of American Indians. She knew that some of the other teachers were teaching the Thanksgiving story with toothpick tipis, feathered headdresses, and paper-bag Indian vests. She wanted to break the Disney World view of American Indian princesses who saved early European settlers.

How could she break the myth that the Pilgrims provided a great feast for their American Indian neighbors to celebrate the harvest? It's the same story that the parents of most of her students learned when they were in school. The truth was difficult and depressing. Do her students have any idea that the Cherokees were driven from their homes in the Southeast and forced to walk the "Trail of Tears," which killed one in four of them, to their new government homes in Oklahoma?

"Do you know where Indians live today?" she began the lesson.

"In tipis," a number of students shouted. "In a longhouse," another student offered.

Questions for Reflection

1. How would you respond to the stereotypes the students have about American Indians and help them develop a better understanding of the real history and current experiences of American Indians?
2. What is appropriate to teach fourth graders about the history of Thanksgiving?
3. Why do many myths and untruths about ethnic groups persist in our classrooms?

myeducationlab To respond to these questions online, go to the *Book Specific Resources* section in the MyEducationLab for your course, select your text, and then select *Reflect on Diversity* for Chapter 7.

Source: Adapted from Starnes, B. A. (2009, February). Thoughts on teaching: Teaching the truth is not easy. *Phi Delta Kappan, 90*(6): 448–449. Copyright Phi Delta Kappa International, www.pdkintl.org, 2009. All rights reserved.

lifestyles, parents routinely expose their offspring to survival routines, often immersing the children in decision-making situations in which they must interpret new experiences in light of previous ones. Unfortunately, a majority of teachers recognize neither Indian students' knowledge nor their considerable learning strategies. Thus, not only is potentially important content knowledge ignored but well-developed ways of knowing, learning, and problem solving also go unrecognized. (Nelson-Barber & Estrin, 1995)

Some parents and communities have become so upset at schools' unwillingness to respect and validate their cultures that they have established charter or private schools grounded in their own rather than the common culture. Afrocentric schools exist in a number of urban areas. Some Hispanic and American Indian groups have established schools in which their cultures are at the center of the curriculum. Jewish, Islamic, Black Muslim, Lutheran, Catholic, Amish, and other schools reinforce the values, beliefs, and behaviors of their religions in private schools across the country.

LANGUAGE

Language interacts with our ethnic and socioeconomic background to socialize us into linguistic and cultural communities. Children learn their native or heritage language by imitating adults and their peers. By age five, they have learned the syntax of their language and know the meanings of thousands of words. When cultural similarities exist between the speaker and listener, spoken messages are decoded accurately. But when the speaker and listener differ in ethnicity or class, miscommunication can occur. Even within English, a word, phrase, or nonverbal gesture takes on different meanings in different cultural groups and settings. You will need to recognize that miscommunications between you and your students may be due to inaccurate decoding rather than the lack of linguistic ability.

Language Diversity

More than 54 million U.S. residents speak a language other than English at home (U.S. Census Bureau, American FactFinder, 2008b). One in five school-aged children live in homes where a language other than English is spoken (Planty et al., 2008, Indicator 7). While the majority of the population whose native language is not English speak English very well, you may have in your classroom new immigrant students who know little or no English and have very limited school experiences in their home countries. Around 6 percent of the nation's children have difficulty speaking English (Planty et al., 2008, Indicator 7).

As immigrants assimilate into the common culture of the United States, their native language is often replaced by English within a few generations. The native language is more likely to be retained when schools and the community value bilingualism. As commerce and trade have become more global, professionals and administrators have realized the advantages of knowing a competitor's culture and language. They are encouraging their children to learn a second language at the same time that many of our educational policies are discouraging native speakers from maintaining their native language while learning English. The movement in some states for English-only usage in schools, in daily commerce, on street signs, and on official government documents highlights the dominance of English desired by some citizens. Seven states (Arizona, Arkansas, California, Connecticut, Massachusetts, New Hampshire, and Wisconsin) ban or restrict the use of student's native languages for instruction.

In addition to English-language learners (ELLs), your classroom may include a student with a hearing disability. Hearing disabilities affect 0.2 percent of the population (Planty et al., 2008, Indicator 8). The language used by many of these students is American Sign Language (ASL) with its own complex grammar and well-regulated syntax. As with oral languages, children learn ASL very early by imitating others who use the language. To communicate with people without hearing disabilities, many individuals with hearing disabilities also use signed English, in which the oral or written word is translated into a sign. ASL is a critical element in the identity of people with hearing disabilities. The language can be more important to their identity than their membership in a particular ethnic, socioeconomic, or religious group.

Dialectal Diversity

The majority of the population uses Standard English for official and formal communications. However, numerous regional, local, ethnic, and class (or SES) dialects are identifiable across the country. Each has its own set of grammatical rules that are known to its users. Although each dialect serves its users well, Standard English is usually viewed as more credible in schools and the work world. For example, most individuals involved in the media use Standard English. Although teachers may be bidialectal, they are expected to use Standard English as the example that should be emulated by students.

Many Americans are bidialectal or multidialectal in that they speak Standard English at work but speak their native or local dialect at home or when they are socializing with friends. Social factors have an influence on which dialect is appropriate in a specific situation. At one time, students were not allowed to use a dialect other than Standard English in the classroom. Some schools have proposed using the dialect of the community as a teaching tool, but such proposals usually have limited public support. Today, students are generally allowed to speak their dialects in schools but are encouraged to learn Standard English to provide them an advantage when they later seek employment.

One instructional approach is to systematically teach the communication patterns necessary to work effectively within the common culture. In this strategy, students' communication patterns are still valued, but they learn when it is to their advantage to use Standard English. In other words, they become bicultural—they are able to function in the different cultures of the school and their home. Teachers who also learn to function effectively in more than one culture will gain respect from students and begin to genuinely model a multicultural pedagogy.

Education for Language Diversity

A growing number of English-language learners are populating schools in large cities. However, the majority of them live in six states: Arizona, California, Texas, New York, Florida, and Illinois. California itself educates one in three of the ELLs in the country. Even small cities and rural areas are now home to immigrant families and their children. Since 1995, the number of ELLs has grown by more than 300 percent in Alabama, Indiana, Kentucky, Nebraska, North Carolina, South Carolina, and Tennessee (Educational Testing Service, 2008). ELLs in our schools are diverse with

FIGURE 7.6

Who Are the English-Language Learners in Schools?

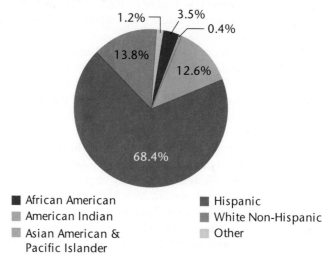

Source: EPE Research Center. (2009, January 8). Spanish is spoken by the vast majority of English-language learners, quality counts. *Education Week, 28*(17): 12.

most of them being Hispanic as shown in Figure 7.6. More than 450 languages are spoken in the nation's schools. The most common native or heritage languages are Spanish, Korean, Vietnamese, Chinese, Tagalog, Hmong, German, and Russian.

The growing number of ELLs in U.S. schools calls for educators to understand language learning and how to help students learn English while they are learning mathematics, science, and other subjects. Differences between the languages used at home and at school can lead to dissonance between students, their families, and school officials. Many students who enter school with limited English skills are not only trying to learn a second language but also adjusting to a new culture.

Members of Congress, state legislators, and school board members regularly debate strategies for teaching English-language learners. The debate centers on whether to use students' native languages in instruction. One instructional strategy is **bilingual education**, which uses both English and the native language. Another strategy immerses English-language learners in English-only classrooms. Other strategies bridge the two. Many school districts and some states require bilingual education if a specific number of students who speak the same native language are enrolled in a school. This approach requires teachers who are fluent in both English and the native language.

No Child Left Behind calls for ELLs to become English proficient and meet standards as measured by standardized tests. Voters in some states have passed state initiatives that limit language assistance to ELLs to one year. The problem with this approach is that research shows that one year of English instruction is generally not enough time to develop proficiency for academic success in classes taught only in English. The amount of time required for English proficiency "depends on multiple factors, including the child's age, level and quality of prior schooling of the child, parents' education level, type and quality of instruction provided, the child's exposure to English in his or her community, and quality of the teachers" (Civil Rights Project, 2002). For most ELLs, at least five years is required to develop language skills and academic achievement equal to that of native English speakers (Civil Rights Project, 2002). The result is that these students may fall further behind their classmates in conceptual understanding of the subjects being taught. For example, the number of English-language learners who are at the proficient or above level on NAEP's reading and mathematics tests is 25 percent less than their English-speaking classmates (Two lenses, 2009).

At least six different approaches are used to teach academic content to English-language learners (Genesee, 1999). Sheltered instruction, newcomer programs, and transitional bilingual education approaches are designed to integrate students into the common culture. Although the native language may be used for instruction early in the program, the goal is to move to English-only instruction as soon as possible, usually between one and four years. In sheltered instruction, teachers teach the academic subjects at the same time that they are teaching English to students. The newcomer programs are designed for new immigrants who have limited or no experience with English

Go to the *IRIS Center Resources* section of Topic 2: *Student Diversity* in the MyEducationLab for your course and watch and listen to the podcast titled *Episode 4: Leonard Baca on the Use of Native Languages in the Classroom.*

Other aspects of No Child Left Behind are discussed in Chapters 1, 9, and 11.

bilingual education An educational strategy that uses English and the native language of students in classroom instruction.

and often have limited literacy skills in their native language. These programs are sometimes found within a school; some large school districts have one or more schools specifically for new immigrants. The most successful programs are those which students attend for as many as four years (Genesee, 1999). Teachers using these two approaches—sheltered and newcomer—should have knowledge and skills in teaching **English as a second language (ESL)**.

In transitional bilingual education, academic subjects are taught in the native language as students learn English. Gradually, more and more of the instruction is conducted in English. After a few years, students in transitional bilingual education move into classes with instruction in English only. Developmental bilingual education, by contrast, supports bilingualism and literacy in both English and the native language. Both languages have equal status, and both are used for instructional purposes.

Bilingual education uses both the native languages of students and English in classrooms to ensure that students learn the academic concepts being taught.

Two immersion language programs use a second language for instruction and help students understand and appreciate a second culture while maintaining their own native culture and language. World languages immersion is designed for English speakers who want to learn a second language in a classroom that uses Spanish, French, Japanese, Farsi, or another language for instruction. Issues around students becoming competent in two languages are debated in the Teacher Perspectives feature on the next page. Two-way immersion is used to develop bilingualism in all students as language training is integrated with academic instruction. Classes usually have an equal number of English speakers and speakers of another language.

As a school decides the appropriate approach for teaching English-language learners, parents must be involved in the discussions and decisions. Together, educators and parents will have to decide whether they want to promote bilingualism among all students or only among the English-language learners. Is the goal for English-language learners to become competent in both English and their native language or to move into English-only instruction as soon as possible? Each approach has learning implications for students and cost implications for school systems.

For a curricular perspective on teaching English-language learners, see Chapter 12.

Legal issues related to English-language learners are discussed in Chapter 10.

GENDER

We are culturally different because of our gender even when we are members of the same socioeconomic, ethnic, and religious group. We often segregate ourselves by gender at social gatherings, seek different types of jobs, and are expected to take on different family roles. The ways we think and act are defined by both biology and the expectations of our culture and society. Our gender may also influence the way we treat boys and girls and young women and young men in our classrooms.

Differences between Females and Males

Learning the gender of a baby is one of the important rites of parenthood. However, the major difference between infant boys and girls is the way adults respond to them. There are few actual physical differences, particularly before puberty. The socialization process in child-rearing and schools is a primary determinant of gender identity and related distinctive behaviors.

By age two, children realize that they are a girl or a boy; by five or six, they have learned their gender and stereotypical behavior. In most cultures, boys are generally socialized toward achievement and self-reliance, girls toward nurturance and responsibility. Differences in the expectations and behaviors of the two genders may be rooted in their groups' ethnicity, religion, and socioeconomic status.

In schools many girls and boys perform differently in academic subjects and behave differently in the classroom. For years boys outperformed girls in mathematics, but the latest data show

English as a second language (ESL) An educational strategy for teaching English to speakers of other languages without the use of the native language for instruction.

TEACHER PERSPECTIVES

Should All Students Be Bilingual?

Many immigrant students enter school using a language other than English. The role of schools in teaching them English and encouraging the maintenance of their own native language has long been debated. Another side of the coin is the importance of native English speakers learning a second language so that they are fluent in at least two languages. This debate illustrates two teachers' perspectives on these issues.

YES

Douglas Ward is a bilingual learning disabilities resource teacher at William Nashold Elementary school in Rockford, Illinois. He is in his third year of teaching and is certified in bilingual special education and several other fields.

Yes, all students should be bilingual. Unfortunately, in the United States very few students become truly proficient in a foreign language. That is one reason for the shortage of foreign language and bilingual teachers.

Before the world wars, many immigrants in the United States used their native languages daily while they learned English. But the world wars and isolationist policies created a climate in which it was unpopular to speak anything but English. In some cities, fines were imposed on anyone caught speaking a foreign language in public business.

Many descendants of immigrants never learned their parents' or grandparents' native languages—in my case, Polish and German—because of these attitudes. My grandparents and parents, pressured by society, did not understand the importance of passing on their languages to me.

Learning a foreign language involves more than learning how to read, write, and speak. More important, it teaches students about a culture. Lack of understanding of cultural differences causes intolerance and war.

The people of the United States and the world need to be, not just tolerant, but accepting of other cultures. We need to embrace and celebrate our many cultures. Studying a foreign language and becoming bilingual opens one's mind to new thinking and creates new opportunities to communicate with other people.

Language can be the key to a lasting peace between enemies. Learning another language is the best way to make friends.

Students in many other countries learn at least one foreign language in their public schools. In the United States, few schools even offer a foreign language in elementary school.

As global businesses and trade expand, the need to know a second language is growing tremendously. Many businesses in other countries want to do business with us. Their salespeople speak English and know our customs. We need people who know other languages and cultures so that our exports will increase and our economy will become stronger.

Learning another language may also spill over into other areas. Research shows that bilingualism leads to cognitive advantages that may raise scores on some intelligence tests.

Studies also show a correlation between knowing two languages and linguistic abilities that may facilitate early reading acquisition. That, in turn, could boost academic achievement.

NO

Suzanne Emery retired last year after thirty-five years of teaching English and journalism, the last twenty-five at San Diego's Mira Mesa High School. She reviews questions for California's high school exit exam and edits the San Diego Education Association newsletter.

American education cannot be all things for all people.

We've agreed generally on the need to improve achievement in the basic curriculum. Bilingualism should not be added to the mix. Nor should it join all the other mandates that politically correct states and school districts impose: cultural holidays, parenting classes, good health activities, well-rounded social growth, adequate physical activities, proper nutrition, and suicide prevention.

A second language is always a luxury. It is needed only for the college bound and then only in certain majors.

We're told that European countries require two languages. But many European countries are very small, so bilingualism is a survival skill. And few other countries try to educate 100 percent of their children, as we do. In Europe, education is at the top of parents' priorities. Need we talk about the distractions here?

And what is the second language of bilingual children around the world? It is English. We need to educate our own kids for success in that universal language. Our schools can barely gather materials and teachers for the standard curriculum, let alone for another language.

If schools required a second language, what would it be? Spanish, Japanese, or French? How should we decide? What about all our students who speak Hmong, Farsi, or Tagalog? Would we mandate a third language for them?

Comfort in two languages is valuable in many venues and often desired for reasons of tradition. But families that want another language can do what they've always done: Saturday school, magnet schools, and temple classes.

If a district is so insular that it lacks the diverse quilt of contemporary America, its sterility and guilt should not be visited on the rest of the country.

So many American schools are like mine in San Diego where students regularly exchange videos with relatives in Vietnam, make the annual family pilgrimage to Mexico, edit the Islamic Center's youth newsletter, and produce pamphlets in graphic arts class for the Buddhist temple.

Here in California, with the nation's largest enrollment of newcomers, the challenge is to prepare all students for world-class competition, culminating with a high school exit exam in English, because English communication is key to success in academics and in adult life. That also applies to the rest of the country.

We cannot afford another diversion added to the overflowing plate of public education.

Source: "Should All Students Be Bilingual?" *NEA Today* (May 2002), p. 11. Reprinted by permission of the National Education Association.

What is your perspective on this issue?

myeducationlab To explore both sides of this issue and think about each perspective, go to the *Book Specific Resources* in the MyEducationLab for your course, select your text, and then select *Teacher Perspectives* for Chapter 7.

that girls and boys are now performing at the same levels on state achievement tests. Girls are now majoring in mathematics in college, earning nearly half of the math degrees (Quaid, 2008). Differences in performance on achievement tests include the following:

- Girls outperform boys on reading and writing achievement tests.
- Males outperform females on both the verbal and mathematics sections of the SAT although the gap on the verbal portion is small.
- On the ACT girls outscore males on the English and reading sections, but males perform better on the mathematics and science sections.
- Differences on achievement tests between white females and males are greater than among other racial and ethnic groups (Corbett, Hill, & St. Rose, 2008).

Some researchers attribute these gender differences to the development of specific hemispheres at the top of the brain. Females tend to have a well-developed left side of the brain, which is associated with verbal skills such as reading, speaking, and writing. The right side, which boys use more often, is associated with spatial skills of measuring and working with blocks or other objects (Corbett et al., 2008). Other researchers dispute this claim as they find female and male performance more alike than different, suggesting that previously observed gender differences are not solely determined by biology. They find that the variations in performance and behavior are greater within male and female groups than between them (Thorne, 2002).

A major difference between males and females is how they are treated in society. For example, women earn less than men throughout their life span, as shown in Figure 7.7. In addition, society generally places men in positions of superiority, as evidenced by their disproportionate employment in the highest status and highest paying jobs. Sometimes this relationship extends into the home, where the father and husband may both protect the family and rule over it. At times this relationship leads to physical and mental abuse of women and children.

Gender-specific behavior is sometimes stereotypically reinforced in classrooms. Girls are more likely to be quiet, follow the rules, and help the teacher. Boys and young men tend to be rowdier and less attentive. Some working-class males develop patterns of resistance to school and its authority figures because schooling is perceived as feminine, emphasizing mental rather than manual work (Arnot, 2004).

Males are also not well served by socialization patterns. Some do not fit neatly with the stereotypical vision of masculinity. Some males are more comfortable working as preschool teachers, nurses, or librarians—traditionally female careers—but may have learned that those jobs are inappropriate for "real men."

Single-sex schools focus on developing the confidence, academic achievement, and leadership skills of young women or men by using the learning styles and cultural experiences central

FIGURE 7.7

Income of Males and Females Working Full Time Year-Round

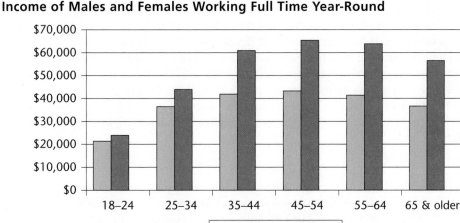

Source: U.S. Census Bureau. (2008). *Statistical abstract of the United States: 2009* (128th ed., Table 681). Washington, DC: U.S. Government Printing Office.

to their gender. Schools in some urban areas have been designed for African American young men to validate their culture and develop their self-esteem, academic achievement, and leadership capacities in order to confront the hostile environments they sometimes face in society.

Gender-Sensitive Education

Schools have played an important role in helping many young women realize their potential. Still, not all educators are sensitive to how they treat boys and girls in ways that influence learning. If gender **equity** existed, females and males would be expected to participate at nearly the same rates in academic courses. Let's look at some of today's realities:

- Girls and boys enroll in mathematics courses, including higher level courses, at about the same rate (Lacampagne, Campbell, Damarin, Herzig, & Vogt, 2007).
- Nearly half of students taking physics courses in high school are female, but they are only one in four of the college graduates in physics (Burger et al., 2007).
- Only one in five engineering college students is female—an increase of only 5 percent over the past 20 years (Burger et al., 2007).
- Girls participate differently in computer science courses; they are more likely to be in courses for word processing than programming courses (Burger et al., 2007).
- Girls (36 percent) are more likely to complete three or more years of foreign language than boys (24 percent) (Brantmeier, Schueller, & Wilde, 2007).
- High school girls take biology courses at a slightly higher rate than boys. The number of females and males earning doctorates in biological sciences is almost equal. The majority of students preparing to be veterinarians are female (Burger et al., 2007).
- Girls are more likely to participate in AP courses and take AP tests (Handwerk, Tognatta, Coley, & Gitomer, 2008).

To promote gender equity, females should be encouraged to get involved in mathematics, science, and computer science. Males should be encouraged to participate in areas in which they are underrepresented: the fine arts, foreign languages, advanced English, and the humanities.

A gender-sensitive education provides equity to boys and girls and young women and young men. It does not mean that all students are always treated the same. Different instructional strategies may be needed for the two groups to ensure participation and learning. Understanding cultural differences among females and males is important in developing appropriate teaching strategies. Not all girls and young women respond to instruction in the same way. Their other group memberships intersect with their gender in determining their interactions with teachers and effective instructional strategies. Multicultural teaching affirms students' gender and experiences in ways that promote learning for both males and females.

Teachers in gender-sensitive classrooms monitor interactions among girls and boys as well as their own interactions with the two genders. They intervene when necessary to equalize opportunities between them. If boys are not performing as well as girls in language arts or girls are not performing as well in mathematics, the challenge is to develop approaches that will improve all students' performance.

Different educational strategies that draw on students' cultural strengths may be needed to equalize performance in knowledge and skill development for girls and boys. Although competitive strategies are effective for many white boys, most girls and boys from other racial groups are more successful in collaborative settings. Instruction should include hands-on laboratory experiences, collaborative learning, practical applications, group work, and authentic learning to build on the learning styles of different students. The goal is to help both females and males learn the subject matter. Teachers will need to draw on multiple teaching strategies to reach this goal.

Title IX

Title IX of the 1972 Higher Education Amendments is the major legislation that addresses the civil rights of girls and women in the education system. It requires federally funded colleges and schools to provide equal educational opportunity to girls and women. Title IX has been credited for increasing the number of girls and young women participating in college preparatory courses, completing professional degrees in college, and participating in sports. In the year that Title IX passed, only 7 percent of law degrees were earned by females as compared to 48 per-

equity The state of fairness and justice across individuals and groups; it does not mean the same educational strategies across groups but does expect equal results.

cent in 2006. Eight percent of the medical degrees and 13 percent of the doctorates were awarded to females in 1970, but by 2006, women received 49 percent of all medical degrees and 48 percent of all doctorates (U.S. Census Bureau, 2008, Tables 286 and 289).

Participation in sports is associated with higher levels of family satisfaction. However, many families report that their daughters do not have the same opportunities to participate in organized sports at school as their sons (Sabo & Veliz, 2008). Although Title IX has led to a dramatic increase in the number of females involved in sports, providing them equal opportunities has been the most controversial part of Title IX. It requires the percentage of male and female athletes to be substantially proportionate to the percentage of females and males in the student population. In addition, the school must have a history and continuing practice of expanding opportunities for the underrepresented gender to participate in sports. Even if a school is not meeting the proportionate expectation, the school must be fully and effectively meeting the interest and abilities of the underrepresented gender (Staurowsky et al., 2007).

The number of girls and women participating in sports has increased dramatically since 1972. When Title IX was passed, fewer than 300,000 girls participated in high school sports. That number has increased by 1,000 percent, with more than 3 million high school girls now participating in high school sports (National Federation of State High School Associations, n.d.). The number of women participating in college sports has increased from 32,000 to more than 175,000 (DeHas, 2009). Some groups argue that Title IX has led to the elimination of some men's sports as women's sports have expanded. However, boys participate in high school sports at a higher rate than girls (Staurowsky et al., 2007). Although access to school sports is similar for girls and boys in many communities, a gap exists in low-income and urban schools where fewer girls participate in athletics and physical education (Staurowsky et al., 2007).

Title IX prevents discrimination in education programs based on gender. Schools must make provisions for girls and young women to participate in intramural, club, and interscholastic sports.

SEXUAL ORIENTATION

The majority of gay adults report feeling different from other children before they entered kindergarten (Mondimore, 1996). The common understanding among the research community is that sexual orientation is not chosen; one is born with it (Ost & Gates, 2004). Some cultural and religious groups believe that homosexuality is a choice of lifestyles. These groups place high value on heterosexuality and denigrate or outlaw homosexuality as part of their religious doctrine or community mores. Nevertheless, it is estimated that 5 to 10 percent of the population is lesbian, gay, bisexual, or transgender (LGBT). Gay men and lesbians are concentrated in some areas such as Vermont and San Francisco, but they live all over the country. The 2000 census found same-sex couples living in 99.3 percent of all counties in the country (Ost & Gates, 2004).

Gays and lesbians often face discrimination in housing, employment, and social institutions, as evidenced when schools and universities prohibit the establishment of gay student clubs. Homophobia, as expressed in harassment and violence against gays and lesbians, is tolerated in many areas of the country. Society's prejudices and discriminatory practices result in many gays and lesbians hiding their sexual orientation and establishing their own social clubs, networks, and communication systems to support one another.

Isolation and loneliness are the experiences of many gay and lesbian youth. If gays and lesbians openly acknowledge their sexual orientation or appear to be LGBT, they are likely to be harassed and face reprisals from peers and, sometimes, school officials. Structures within the schools do not provide the same kind of support to LGBT students that is available to other students. Sixty-four percent of LGBT students fear for their safety in schools. They feel more

See Chapter 8 for more discussion about sexual harassment.

comfortable and safer in schools when faculty and staff are supportive, LGBT people are portrayed in the curriculum, gay–straight alliance or similar clubs exist, and a comprehensive policy on harassment is enforced (Ost & Gates, 2004). Most educators often know little about this group and have had few or no contacts with LGBT people who are "out," or open, about their sexual orientation. They may not have taught students whose parents are gay or lesbian. Without a better understanding of homosexuality, teachers may find it difficult to work effectively with LGBT students or the children of gay and lesbian parents.

EXCEPTIONALITIES

More than forty-nine million people, or 15 percent of the population over five years old, have a **disability** (U.S. Census Bureau, American FactFinder, 2008a). About one-fourth of the persons with a disability indicate that their disability existed at birth or developed before they were age twenty. The number of people with disabilities increases with age; more than 39 percent of the population over age 65 has a disability (U.S. Census Bureau, 2008, Table 34). Those with physical disabilities can be readily recognized by their use of supports such as a cane, braces, or wheelchairs. Some individuals are labeled very early in their school careers as *mentally retarded, emotionally disabled,* or with some other disability. Figure 7.8 shows the number of students with different disabilities in today's schools. Critics of labeling declare this system to be demeaning and stigmatizing.

Some educators make a determination as early as kindergarten about the potential of students with disabilities, which can lead to low academic expectations for students who could perform at high levels if appropriate accommodations were made for their disability. Fifty-seven percent of students with disabilities are earning a high school diploma; 15 percent of them receive a certification of attendance (Planty et al., 2008, Indicator 22). Students with disabilities are 11 percent of the undergraduate population (U.S. Census Bureau, 2008, Table 277). Dropout rates for this population are relatively high. Persons with disabilities are disproportionately underrepresented in the labor force, sometimes because they are unable to go to work, but more often because the workplace has not made the accommodations that would make it possible for them to work productively.

Persons without a disability may react with disdain toward individuals with disabilities, viewing them as inferior. But like all other individuals, people with disabilities want to be recog-

Dropouts are discussed in greater detail in Chapter 8.

disability A long-standing physical, mental, or emotional condition that can make it difficult for a person to perform activities such as walking, climbing stairs, dressing, bathing, learning, or remembering.

FIGURE 7.8

Children and Youth Receiving Services under the Individuals with Disabilities Education Act (IDEA)

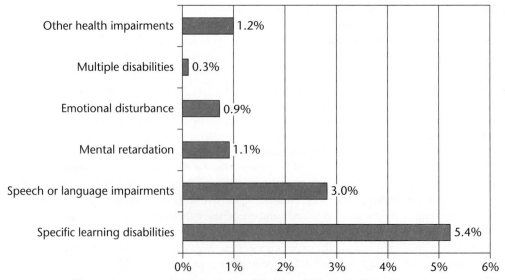

Source: Planty, M., Hussar, W., Snyder, T., Provasnik, S., Kena, G., Dinkes, R., KewalRamani, A., and Kemp, J. (2008). *The condition of education 2008* (NCES 2008-031). Washington, DC: National Center for Education Statistics, Institute of Education Sciences, U.S. Department of Education.

nized as persons in their own right. They have the same needs for love and the same desire to be as successful as persons without disabilities. Instead, society has historically not accepted them as equals. Some individuals with severe disabilities are placed in institutions out of the sight of the public. Others are segregated in separate schools or classes. Too often they are rejected and made to feel inept and limited in their abilities.

Inclusion

Inclusion is the practice of fully integrating all students into the educational process, regardless of their race, ethnicity, gender, socioeconomic status, religion, physical or mental ability, or language. Students see themselves represented in the curriculum as well as in classes for the gifted. (Historically, inclusion referred primarily to the integration of students with disabilities in general education classrooms.) Inclusion of all students requires collaboration among adults, including parents, who work with students with disabilities. You should not be expected to serve as both the teacher and specialist. Ideally, teachers of general education collaborate with a special educator, accompanied by a teacher's aide when needed and appropriate specialists, such as a speech/language pathologist, occupational therapist, physical therapist, vision specialist, adaptive physical education teacher, school psychologist, or school nurse. As a member of the team, you are expected to individualize instruction by following each student's **individualized educational plan (IEP)**. At times, students with disabilities may be pulled out of the classroom for special services, but these special sessions should be limited and should be used only to meet complex individual needs. The challenges you may face in an inclusive classroom are described in the Professional Dilemma feature. It is quite likely that you will have a number of students with disabilities in your classroom during your career. Will you know how to best serve these students or where to seek assistance?

myeducationlab

Go to the *Assignments and Activities* section of Topic 2: *Student Diversity* in the MyEducationLab for your course and complete the activity titled *Parents as Child Advocates*.

inclusion The integration of all students, regardless of their background or abilities, in all aspects of the educational process.

individualized education plan (IEP) A program designed to meet the needs of a child eligible for special education services. The plan helps educators understand the child's disability and provides directions for the services to be provided by teachers and other school professionals.

PROFESSIONAL DILEMMA   Inclusion of Students with Disabilities

Over time, classroom teachers have been given increased responsibility for making sure the needs of a child with an IEP are met in their classroom. Although a child may enter the classroom with an IEP requiring support from special educators, ultimately and legally it is the teacher's responsibility to make sure the IEP is implemented in the classroom. It is also the teacher's responsibility to handle any behavior or social difficulties that may occur in the classroom. Furthermore, the teacher must work with special educators to adapt lessons and assignments to the ability level of all students. Teachers must promote success for all learners rather than expecting failure.

Picture yourself as a teacher in an inner-city second-grade classroom. You have twenty-five students from low-income homes and several children for whom English is their second language. Among these students are three children with IEPs and four learners who are making limited academic progress but do not qualify for special education services.

The three children with IEPs have varied needs. One child is a girl in a wheelchair with physical needs requiring a nurse to accompany her in the classroom. Another child is an eight-year-old boy who was born with Down syndrome. He too has multiple needs, including speech/language therapy, occupational therapy to work on his fine-motor skills, and a behavior plan monitored by the school psychologist. The third child has attention deficit/hyperactivity disorder (ADHD). His academic skills lag behind by a full year below grade level, and his attention span is minimal during periods of instruction.

In addition to these three children with IEPs, four children are reading at the first-grade level. Although these children are obvi-

ously having difficulties with reading, writing, and spelling, they do not currently qualify for special education services because their performance level is not two standard deviations below their intelligence quotient–derived ability level.

Unfortunately, there is no reading specialist in your school to help teach the learners performing below grade level. Furthermore, the special education teacher is only required to provide direct services to the students with IEPs for two hours a week. A special education assistant has been assigned to assist with the children with IEPs in your classroom, but her time is split between all twelve first- and second-grade classes, so you are lucky to have her assistance on a daily basis. If the special educator or assistant is out for any reason, a substitute is rarely provided.

Questions for Reflection
1. What would you do to include the student in the wheelchair in as many classroom activities as possible and to encourage social interactions with her peers?
2. What would you do to make sure the child with Down syndrome is accepted and included by his peers?
3. Where would you designate that the child with ADHD take his breaks in the classroom, and what would you provide to make him feel as though he were having a break?
4. What would you do to differentiate instruction to meet the needs of the children who aren't reading at grade level but do not receive special education services?
5. How will you meet the needs of all the other students in your classroom and teach them at each of their ability levels?

Many students with disabilities are included in classrooms and other school activities alongside students who do not have disabilities. All students benefit from this arrangement, with improved outcomes for students with disabilities and an enhanced appreciation for diversity among all students.

A curriculum perspective on teaching students with disabilities can be found in Chapter 12.

One of the goals of inclusion is to provide students with disabilities the same opportunities for learning academic content to which others are exposed. Most students with disabilities can achieve at the same levels as their peers without disabilities, but they may require accommodations that allow them to access the content, the instruction, and the tools for learning. These accommodations may require physical changes in the classroom, such as increasing the height of a desk so that students in wheelchairs have a work space. It may require the provision of computers for students who cannot hold or control a pencil. It may require books in Braille or the use of sign language and taped books.

Researchers are finding improved student outcomes for students with disabilities who are in inclusive classrooms. Students without disabilities also receive positive benefits. Inclusion helps them become more tolerant of others, appreciate diversity, and be more responsive to the needs of others (Lipsky & Gartner, 1996).

Disproportionate Placements

Thirteen percent of all public school students are provided special education services under the Individuals with Disabilities Education Act (IDEA), which requires that students with disabilities be provided a free and appropriate public school education (Planty et al., 2008, Indicator 8). African American students, English-language learners, and students from low-income families are more likely to be in special education classes. Some of these disparities are shown in Figure 7.9. Students labeled *mentally retarded* or *emotionally disabled* disproportionately are from low-income families. Low-income children are also overrepresented in classes for students who are seriously emotionally disturbed. Middle-class students are more likely to be classified as having a *learning disability*. This pattern is also found in the placement of males and students of color in special education and gifted classes. African American and American Indian students are overrepresented in the disability categories of learning disability, mental retardation, and emotionally disturbed, as are males in general (National Center for Education Statistics, 2005). On the other hand, Hispanic, African American, and American Indian students are underrepresented in gifted and talented programs. You will need to monitor the reasons for your referrals of students to be tested for placement in these classes to ensure that you are providing equity in the delivery of education services.

Disproportionate placements of students in special education and gifted education programs may be due to a number of factors. Tests used for placement may be biased against low-income students, English-language learners, and students who have not assimilated into the common culture. Some educators who recommend students for special programs are intolerant of cultural differences and do not want students in their classes who they believe will disrupt the classroom. Schools should monitor recommendations and placements to find out if students from some groups are being disproportionately placed in these programs and take corrective action if needed.

Response to Intervention

The regulations for the Individuals with Disabilities Education Act, which was reauthorized by Congress in 2004, promoted the instructional model Response to Intervention (RTI) for identifying special education students. A growing number of early childhood and elementary teachers link lessons with frequent monitoring to identify students who may need special education services. RTI is a three-tiered screening system that allows teachers to determine whether stu-

FIGURE 7.9

Students with Disabilities by Race

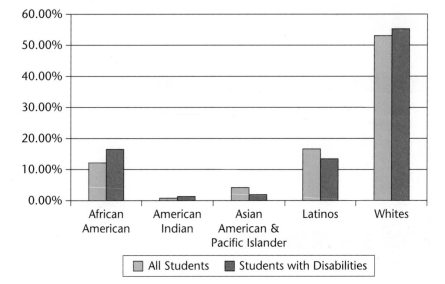

Source: Wirt, J., Choy, S., Rooney, P., Hussar, W., Provasnik, S., and Hampden-Thompson, G. (2005). *The condition of education, 2005* (NCES 2005-094), Indicator 6. Washington, DC: National Center for Education Statistics, U.S. Department of Education.

dents are learning, using interventions as necessary. The first tier is instruction for all students. The second tier is generally small-group instruction for students who are having difficulty. The third tier is individualized instruction for students who need a more intensive level of instruction. Students in the third tier may be eligible for special education services. The RTI screening process is replacing other procedures that have been used in the past to identify special education students.

PEARSON
myeducationlab

Go to the *IRIS Center Resources* section of Topic 2: *Student Diversity* in the MyEducationLab for your course to explore the module titled *RTI (Part I): An Overview.*

RELIGION

Religion can have a great influence on the values and lifestyles of families and can play an important role in the socialization of children and young people. Religious doctrines and practices often guide beliefs about the roles of males and females. They also provide guidance regarding birth control, marriage, child-rearing, friendships, and political attitudes.

By age five, children are generally able to identify their family's religious affiliation. Although 64 percent of the population report that religion is an important part of their daily life, less than half attend a religious service on a weekly basis (Newport, 2009). However, strong religious perspectives are reflected in the daily lives of many families.

Religious pluralism flourishes in this country. Members of religions other than those with Judeo-Christian roots are increasing. Other families declare themselves atheists or simply do not participate in an organized religion. Some individuals and families live in religious cults that are established to promote and maintain a religious calling. Some religious groups believe that their religion is the only correct and legitimate view of the world. Other groups recognize that religious diversity has grown out of different historical experiences and accept the validity of diverse groups. At the same time, every major religion endorses justice, love, and compassion as virtues that most individuals and nations should try to achieve.

Although they are not as dominant as earlier in U.S. history, Protestants are still clearly in the majority as shown in Figure 7.10. Within each of the major religious groups, distinct denominations and sects have the same general history but may differ greatly in their beliefs and perspectives on the correct way to live. Most Western religions are compatible with the values of the common culture; they usually promote patriotism and emphasize individual control of life.

FIGURE 7.10

Religious Diversity of the U.S. Population

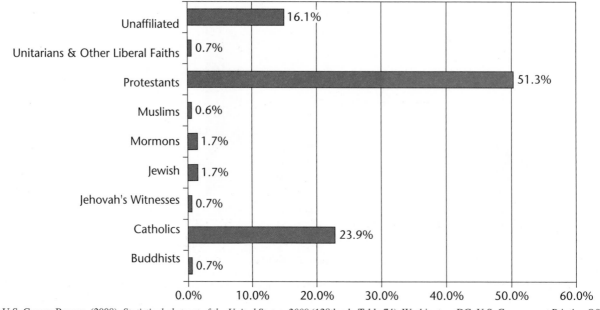

Source: U.S. Census Bureau. (2008). *Statistical abstract of the United States: 2009* (128th ed., Table 74). Washington, DC: U.S. Government Printing Office.

Public schools cannot advance a religion, but neither can religion be ignored in the curriculum. Diverse religious beliefs should be acknowledged and respected in classrooms and schools.

Legal issues about religion in schools are discussed in Chapter 10.

With the influx of immigrants from Asia, Africa, and the Middle East during the past few decades, religious diversity among the population has increased further with greater numbers of families practicing non-Western religions such as Islam, Hinduism, and Buddhism. The interaction of these faiths with Western religions and their impact on society has yet to be determined. In the meantime, students from diverse religious backgrounds appear in classrooms. You will need to respect these differences if you are going to serve the students and community well.

For many people, religion is essential in determining their cultural identity. Some religious groups, such as the Amish and Hutterites, establish their own communities and schools to maintain their religion, foster mutual support, and develop group cohesiveness. Members of groups such as the Mormons promote primary relationships and interactions with other members of the same faith. Most social activities are linked to religion, and institutions have been developed to reflect and support their religious beliefs. In many rural areas, the church is the center of social and community activities.

Families appear satisfied with schools when the schools reflect the values that are important in their religion. But they may attack schools when the curriculum, assigned readings, holidays, school convocations, and graduation exercises are perceived to be in conflict with their religious values. Many court cases during the past century have helped to sort out these issues.

JOURNAL FOR REFLECTION

How has your religious background had an influence on your perceptions of persons with other religious beliefs? How will you respond if the school district in which you teach asks you to teach something that is against your religious beliefs?

MULTICULTURAL EDUCATION

Diversity, social justice, and equality provide the foundations for **multicultural education**. Multicultural education holds educators morally and ethically responsible to help all students learn, regardless of their socioeconomic status, ethnicity, race, language, gender, religion, or ability. Teachers and administrators are expected to view all aspects of education—including the curriculum, teacher and student interactions, staffing patterns, discipline, and extracurricular activities—through a multicultural lens to ensure that the needs of students from diverse groups are an integral part of the education process.

Many educators think they are offering multicultural education simply by including information about groups other than their own in a lesson. This additive approach is evident in black history and women's history months or in highlighted sections of textbooks that discuss, for example, Japanese Americans. In some schools, attention to multiculturalism begins and ends with tasting ethnic foods and participating in ethnic festivals. Although these activities contribute to a superficial understanding of differences, they do not help students understand the history and experiences of diverse groups. The politics around incorporating diverse perspectives in the curriculum are not unique to the United States as can be seen in the Global Perspectives feature about developing a history curriculum in Rwanda.

multicultural education An educational strategy that values diversity, promotes social justice, and provides equality to all students regardless of their race, ethnicity, gender, language, sexual orientation, religion, or ability.

GLOBAL PERSPECTIVES   History Curriculum in Rwanda

What is taught in classrooms is often controlled by those in control of the country. After the genocide and wars in 1994 in the African country of Rwanda, the new government, which was controlled by the Tutsi, suspended the teaching of history. Officials needed time to determine the version of history that would be taught, which is not unusual in a country at the end of a traumatic political conflict.

The goal of the Rwandan government was to develop a curriculum to (1) promote a unified identity while understanding the historical context and (2) incorporate the realities of continuing ethnic identities in the country. Because the government's educational policy required that only the official history narrative be taught in schools, tensions were high among the teachers and curriculum developers from different ethnic groups. If they disagreed with the official narrative, they could be placing themselves in danger. Almost half of the population reported a different historical account of events than the one being incorporated into the curriculum.

Researchers from the University of California–Berkeley worked with Rwandan educators to develop the official curriculum. In addition to determining the historical account of ethnicity and the colonial role of Belgium in setting the stage for ethnic conflicts, the researchers wanted to help the teachers set a climate for critical thinking about what had happened.

Because the government wanted the curriculum to promote a national identity, it chose not to recognize the country's ethnic groups—Tutsi, Hutu, and Twa—that had migrated to the area over time. The official curriculum blamed the Belgian colonizers for perpetuating the migration story, which indicated which group arrived first, leading the Hutus to believe that the land was theirs and the Tutsis were later invaders of the land. This version of history showed the Rwandans as a peaceful people before the colonizers arrived. As with all history, some of the official accounts appear to be correct and others less likely so. The goal of the government was to eliminate the ethnic identities that led to earlier conflicts.

Because the government accused people who disagreed with their narrative of having a "genocidal ideology" that could lead to persecution, teachers decided that it was safer not to teach about ethnic groups in their history classes. They also decided that allowing debate among students about the truth or real facts would not help clarify the issue and, in fact, could be dangerous. Besides, teachers in Rwandan schools traditionally were transmitters of information, not facilitators of discussion and learning. Thus, a new history curriculum was implemented in Rwanda, but it was not one that allowed questioning of the official perspective of history.

Questions for Reflection
1. How did Rwandan politics influence what was included in the country's history curriculum?
2. How does this history curriculum support policy for assimilating ethnic groups into a common culture?
3. What are parallel examples in the curricula of U.S. schools?

Source: Freedman, S. W., Weinstein, H. M., Murphy, K., and Longman, T. (2008, November). Teaching history after identity-based conflicts: The Rwanda experience. *Comparative Education Review, 52*(4): 663–690.

A major dimension of multicultural education is the integration of principles of diversity, social justice, and equality throughout the curriculum. The curriculum for all academic areas should reflect these principles. Adding a course on ethnic studies or women's studies to the curriculum is an easy way to introduce students to the culture, history, and experiences of others, but it is not enough. Many students will be more willing to learn if their cultures are valued and integrated throughout the curriculum. As they learn within their own cultural context, they see themselves and their cultures valued by the teacher and school authorities.

In some schools, of course, teachers still face fairly homogeneous student populations who have little exposure to racial, language, and religious diversity or the multicultural reality of the country as a whole. But even with limited ethnic and racial diversity, most schools have males and females from different religious and socioeconomic backgrounds. The ethic of social justice is just as important in these settings as in those with greater ethnic and language diversity. To provide a well-rounded and balanced curriculum for these students, you will need to work harder at bringing different perspectives to presentations and discussions. You probably will need to develop innovative strategies for providing direct exposure to diversity and issues of equality.

In multicultural education, classrooms and schools are models of democracy and equity. This effort requires educators to:

1. Place the student at the center of the teaching and learning process.
2. Promote human rights and respect for cultural differences.
3. Believe that all students can learn.
4. Acknowledge and build on the life histories and experiences of students' group memberships.
5. Critically analyze oppression and power relationships to help students understand racism, sexism, classism, and discrimination against persons with disabilities, gays, lesbians, the young, and the aged.
6. Critique society in the interest of social justice and equality.
7. Participate in collective social action to ensure a democratic society.

Although you should begin to struggle with these issues now, the process of learning about others and reflecting on one's attitudes and actions in these areas is a lifelong activity.

Incorporating Diversity

Go to the *Assignments and Activities* section of Topic 2: *Student Diversity* in the MyEducationLab for your course and complete the activity titled *Ethnic Identity.*

For centuries, women, people with low incomes, and members of oppressed ethnic and religious groups have fought for an education equal to that available to persons with power in the country. Courageous educators established schools to educate students of color when they were not allowed to attend school. Early in the twentieth century, Carter G. Woodson established the Association for the Study of Negro Life and History to study and write about the history and culture of African Americans. Along with Woodson, W. E. B. DuBois, Charles C. Wesley, and other scholars provided the foundation for the study of racial, ethnic, and other groups. By the 1920s, the Intercultural Service Bureau in New York City was promoting the incorporation of intercultural education into the curriculum to increase knowledge about new immigrants, improve tolerance among groups, and reduce prejudice against them. In 1954 the Supreme Court declared illegal separate-but-equal education for black and white students in *Brown v. Board of Education*. The civil rights struggles of the 1960s laid the groundwork for new curriculum content about African Americans, Hispanics, American Indians, and Asian Americans. Attention to equity for women, individuals with disabilities, and English-language learners soon followed. These events led to the development of multicultural education.

Multiculturalism has been the subject of public and academic discussion during the past forty years. Editorials, national news programs, radio talk shows, and debates among college students and faculty periodically focus on the importance of diversity in society and the school curriculum. Simply put, the perspective of one side is that the recognition and promotion of diversity will strengthen the nation. The other perspective views the promotion of diversity as dividing the nation and leading to greater conflict among groups. This second perspective also argues that the Western tradition is denigrated when diversity and multiple perspectives are highlighted.

Campaigns for political office include debates about immigration, provision of services to undocumented workers and their children, English-only policies, as well as gay rights. Multiculturalists argue that multicultural education will help unify a nation comprised of numerous ethnic groups who have long faced discrimination. They believe that individuals should have the opportunity to learn more about one another and to interact on an equal basis in schools and society. They also believe that members of diverse groups can maintain their diverse history, traditions, and cultures while developing together a common civic culture. An outgrowth of these debates has been the establishment of general education requirements for ethnic, women's, and global studies in colleges and universities. Most states also expect teacher education candidates to study diversity and to be able to incorporate it into their teaching. Most of the developing state and national standards for preschool through college curricula include references to diversity.

VALIDATING STUDENT VOICES. In multicultural education, all participants have **voice**. Teachers do not dominate the dialogue. Students, especially low-income students and students of color, often do not think that teachers are interested in them, their cultures, or their perspectives. They do not see their voices valued in the educational system.

Including student voices in the classroom dialogue is not always easy. Many students have limited experience with active participation in their own learning. When the classroom climate begins to include student voices, students may express anger and be confrontational; they may test the limits of the language that can be used and the subjects that can be broached. Allowing student voices to be an integral part of classroom discourse may test your patience as you and your students figure out how to listen and contribute to the learning process. At the same time, tolerance, patience with one another, and the willingness to listen will develop as student voices contribute to the exploration of the subject matter.

Respect for differences is key in affirming student voices. For many educators, this affirmation requires relinquishing the power they have traditionally had as the voice of authority with the right answers. Class time no longer is monopolized by teacher talk. The meaningful incorporation of student voices requires the development of listening skills and the validation of multiple perspectives, languages, and dialects. It should allow students to participate in the dialogue through speaking, writing, and artistic expression. It should allow them to use the modes of communicating with which they feel most comfortable while teaching them other modes.

The affirmation of student voices requires that educators listen to the voices of *all* students. It is particularly important to hear the voices of students of color, low-income students, girls and young women, English-language learners, and students with disabilities. One of the goals of multicultural education is to validate the voices and stories of all students. The stories or narratives of others will increase student knowledge and tolerance of differences. Many students will learn to value both their own culture and those of others. In the process, teachers and students will also learn that they have much in common.

USING TECHNOLOGY TO LEARN ABOUT OTHERS. The Internet has opened many possibilities for interactions with students and adults in cultures beyond school boundaries. It allows students in inner-city Chicago to talk directly with students in rural New Mexico or Tokyo, Japan. Students in some classrooms are pen pals with students in another part of the country or another part of the world. You can find lesson plans on the Internet to help you with planning lessons about different groups in the school community or groups from other countries. Websites allow you and your students to visit new areas and people. Students in other countries are working with U.S. students on school projects, sharing information, and even making their reports together using Web 2.0 technologies. Using technology, teachers and students together can explore the world and interact with other students and adults from diverse groups. One resource for this work is a website created by two San Diego teachers to connect students and teachers from around the world. You may want to check it out at www.globalschoolnet.org.

Providing Social Justice

Social justice focuses on how we help others who are less well off than we are. Most religions measure the quality of a society by the justice and care it gives to those in the greatest need—the homeless, the sick, the powerless, and the uneducated. The ethic of social justice, especially as it relates to teacher–student relationships, is essential in the teaching profession, along with other moral commitments. Social justice in education requires schools to provide all students equal access to a high-quality education. Practices that perpetuate current inequities are confronted and strategies for eliminating them employed.

voice The right and opportunity to speak and be heard as an equal.

social justice Concept of society in which justice for all people is valued and society's benefits are shared equally.

Schools reflect the inequities of the broader society. As you reflect on the inequitable conditions in schools, ask yourself the following questions:

- How fair is it for some students to attend school in dilapidated, foul-smelling, crowded buildings while others attend classes in beautiful buildings with future-oriented technology and well-groomed grounds?
- How fair is it for wealthier students to have the most experienced and best-qualified teachers, who also earn the highest teaching salaries?
- How fair is it that wealthier students are exposed to an intellectually challenging curriculum and experiences while many low-income students have limited numbers of advanced placement classes offered in their school?
- How fair is it that students of color, especially males, students with disabilities, and English-language learners are pulled out of regular classes and isolated in segregated classes during much of the school day?
- How accurate are curricula and pedagogy that do not reflect the rich plurality of the people, histories, experiences, and perspectives of the groups that make up the United States and the world?

Educators ask themselves numerous questions about school practices if they are serious about providing social justice in schools. A theory of social justice suggests that school systems give those students with the fewest advantages the most advantages in their education and schooling to begin to ensure an equal and fair playing field. The goal might be to use the best-funded and most successful schools as the norm for all schools, with the least advantaged receiving the greatest resources for education. Practices today are usually the reverse with the most economically advantaged students attending attractive and safe schools with the greatest resources and most qualified teachers. Resources for education are not shared equally across groups.

Ensuring Equality

The application of civil rights laws and a drastic reduction in discriminatory practices could contribute greatly to the provision of fairness and justice in the distribution of societal benefits, including education. Schools should question whether their policies and practices are equitable. One step in this investigation might be an examination of how accessible gifted, talented, and honors programs are to students from diverse groups. A truly egalitarian society ensures not only that their schools are safe, adequately staffed, and supportive of learning but also that the schools of other people's children have the same amenities. Such a society works toward the elimination of racism, sexism, and other forms of discrimination in education.

JOURNAL FOR REFLECTION

How has your own education reflected diversity, social justice, and equality? What experiences will help you work effectively with students from groups different than your own?

EQUAL EDUCATIONAL OPPORTUNITY. One way to address equality in the educational system is to offer **equal educational opportunity**, which should provide all students, regardless of their backgrounds, with similar opportunities to learn and benefit from schooling. Neither educators nor policy makers agree on what constitutes equal educational opportunity. On the surface, it would seem that all students should have access to high-quality teaching, small classes, up-to-date technology, college preparatory courses, buildings that support learning, and safe environments. In reality, most equal educational opportunity programs have been designed to overcome educational deficiencies of underserved students by providing compensatory or remedial programs to reduce the educational gaps that have given advantaged students a head start.

Even when a school has the latest technology, is clean and well maintained, and is staffed by qualified professionals, equal opportunity is not automatically guaranteed. Many other factors need to be considered. What percentages of students in advanced mathematics and science classes are female or students of color? Which students make up the college preparatory and advanced placement classes? Who is assigned to or chooses a general or vocational track? Who is referred to special education classes? Who has access to the best teachers? Who participates in which extracurricular activities? Who is suspended? If the percentages of students from diverse groups in

equal educational opportunity
Access to similar education for all students regardless of their cultural background or family circumstances.

these various school settings are somewhat proportional to their representation in the school population as a whole, equal educational opportunity may be approaching the goal of its supporters.

EQUALITY OF RESULTS. Schools today are expected to provide all students with the opportunity to learn the skills outlined in national standards for mathematics, science, English, the arts, foreign languages, history, geography, civics, and economics. Policy makers not only expect U.S. students to meet minimal standards, they expect them to achieve higher scores on international tests than students in any other part of the world. If educators actually believed that all students could learn, they would ensure that all students have access to higher level knowledge. Students would not be tracked into low-ability and nonstimulating classes. They would promote critical thinking and the ability to view the world and academic subjects from multiple perspectives.

When the goal is to ensure equality of results, students who are not performing well academically or in other ways can become intellectual challenges for a team of teachers and other support personnel. The focus is on ensuring learning rather than simply moving students from one grade to another. No Child Left Behind (NCLB) recognizes that students from some groups have different experiences in schools that have resulted in white students from higher income families performing at higher levels on achievement tests. NCLB expects schools to ensure that all students achieve standards and perform at grade level in reading, mathematics, and science regardless of their race, socioeconomic status, native language, and disability. It holds schools accountable for student learning across groups and publicly identifies the schools whose students are not making adequate yearly progress (AYP) on standardized tests. Test scores for students in a school must to be disaggregated by the groups identified above to show the differential in test scores across groups. The NCLB act has had a great impact on school practices, especially in preparing students for annual achievement tests.

LOOKING AHEAD: TEACHERS AS SOCIAL ACTIVISTS

Multicultural education requires educators to be active participants in the educational process. Social justice, democracy, power, and equity are more than concepts to be discussed in class; they are guides for action in the classroom, school, and community. Educators become advocates not only for their own empowerment but also for that of students and other powerless groups.

Thinking Critically

Educators who think critically ask questions about why inequities exist in their classrooms and schools. They wonder why girls are responding differently than boys to science lessons. But they don't stop with wondering; they explore and try alternatives to engage the girls in the subject matter. They realize that teaching equitably does not mean teaching everyone the same way. Nor, however, does it mean using thirty different lesson plans each tailored to the individual learning style and cultural background of each student. Teaching equitably may mean helping students function effectively across the multiple cultural styles used by students in the classroom. Teachers who think critically figure out ways to build on the diverse cultural backgrounds and experiences of students, acknowledge the value of that diversity, and help them all learn.

Critical thinkers are able to challenge the philosophy and practices that are not supportive of equity, democracy, and social justice. They are open to alternative views; they are not limited by narrow parochialism that is based on absolutes and the notion of one right way. They question content for accuracy and biases, and they value multiple perspectives. They seek explanations for the educational meanings and consequences of race, class, and gender.

Modeling Equity in the Classroom

Caring and fairness are two qualities that students praise when describing successful teachers. Students know whether teachers view them as special or as incompetent or worthless. Teacher perceptions may be based on a student's personal characteristics; sometimes they are based on group membership. A teacher may feel that homeless children who arrive in dirty clothes, smelling badly, have little chance of success. Teachers may pity children from one-parent homes and blame their lack of academic achievement on not having two parents. Teachers may ignore English-language learners until they learn English. Are these fair practices?

A school that provides multicultural education will not tolerate such unjust practices by teachers. Both the classroom and the school will be models of democracy in which all students

Teachers must be able to transcend their own cultural backgrounds to develop learning experiences that build on the cultural backgrounds of all of their students.

are treated equitably and fairly. In such a school, teachers and instructional leaders confront their own biases and develop strategies for overcoming them in their own interactions with students and colleagues. They learn to depend on one another for assistance, both in developing a multicultural curriculum and in ensuring that students are not subject to discrimination. As a result, students learn to respect differences and to interact within and across ethnic and cultural groups as they struggle for social justice in the school and the community.

Teachers sometimes give more help to some students than to others. They might praise some students while correcting and disciplining others. Their expectations for academic success may differ depending on students' family income or ethnic group. Most teachers do not deliberately set out to discriminate against students, especially in any harmful way. The problem is that we have been raised in a racist, sexist, and classist society in which biases are so embedded that it is sometimes difficult for us to recognize anything other than the very overt signs. We often need others to point out our discriminatory practices so that we can correct them.

A good pattern to begin to develop even now, early in your teacher education program, is to reflect on your practice and the practice of teachers you observe. Among the questions that you might ask are these:

- Are students from different gender, economic, and ethnic groups treated differently? How?
- Are there fewer discipline and learning problems among the students who are from the same background as the teacher? What contributes to the differences?
- Do the least advantaged students receive the most assistance from the teacher? What are the differences in the instruction given to students from different groups?
- How well are male and female students from different ethnic and racial groups performing on state standardized tests? How well are students from other groups performing?

A key to ensuring that interactions with students are equitable is the ability to recognize our own biases and make appropriate adjustments. We must be able to admit that we sometimes make mistakes. An ability to reflect on our mistakes and why they occurred should lead to better teaching.

Making Schools Democratic

Democratic schools are ones in which students practice democracy by being active participants in their education. These schools encourage the exchange and exploration of ideas from multiple perspectives. They develop the individual and collective capacity of students to resolve problems. Teachers in democratic classrooms teach students to analyze real-world ideas, problems, and policies. Students are involved in community issues, collecting and analyzing data, and often becoming involved in changes within the community. The goal is to understand that democracy is not so much an ideal to be pursued as an idealized set of values that we must live by and that must guide our life as a society.

Democratic schools reflect democratic structures and processes and include a curriculum that provides students with democratic experiences. These schools require students, teachers, parents, and community members to be active participants in the educational process. Equity undergirds the structure of democratic schools. All students have access to all programs. Tracking, biased testing, and other practices that deny access to some students are eliminated. The emphasis on grades, status, test scores, and winning is replaced with an emphasis on cooperation and concern for the common good. Those involved in this democratic project also work toward the elimination of inequities in the broader community as well as in the school.

A democratic curriculum encourages multiple perspectives and voices in the materials used and the discussions that ensue. It respects differences in viewpoints. It does not limit information and study to the content of textbooks. It includes discussions of inequities in society and challenges students and teachers to engage actively in eliminating them.

Establishing a democratic classroom or school is not always an easy undertaking. Sometimes colleagues and parents resist it; some people believe that teachers should be all-knowing authorities who exert control over their students. Those who want schools to prepare students for social efficiency are supportive of stratified systems using grades and test scores to sort students into tracks that prepare them for future jobs. Supporters of schooling as a route to social mobility expect competition to determine which students deserve the greatest rewards, such as acceptance into gifted programs or admission to prestigious colleges. Democratic schools, on the other hand, support equity, equal access, and equal opportunity for all students.

Teaching for Social Justice

Multicultural teaching helps students struggle in class with social problems and issues that many students face daily in their lives both within and outside of school. Racism, sexism, classism, prejudice, and discrimination are felt differently by students of color than by other students. Anger, denial, guilt, and affirmation of identity are critical elements of learning about and struggling with the inequities of society. Although it is sometimes difficult to discuss these issues in classrooms, doing so can lead to a more diverse and equitable classroom.

In teaching for social justice, teachers help students understand the inequities, oppression, and power struggles that are realities in society. But this kind of teaching does not stop there. It provides hope for a world that is more equitable and socially just. Students and teachers become engaged in confronting injustice and working to remove the obstacles that prevent equality.

Students learn to apply the knowledge and skills they are learning to a local, regional, or global issue. The learning becomes authentic because it is related to the world that students care about. Students can take on community projects that examine pollution in their neighborhoods, political stances in their regional area, or the cost of food in their neighborhood versus another part of town. Students and teachers who tackle social justice as an integral part of their classroom work are providing multicultural education and reconstructionism. They are doing more than learning about the world; they are also working toward making it better for those who are least advantaged.

SUMMARY

SOCIOECONOMIC STATUS

- The way students and their families live is greatly affected by their socioeconomic status, which is determined by income, wealth, occupation, and educational attainment.
- The population is socially stratified, providing some groups more advantage and prestige than others in society and schools.
- On achievement tests students from higher income families almost always score higher than middle- and low-income peers.

RACE AND ETHNICITY

- As a result of immigration from Asia, Mexico, Central America, and the Middle East during the past forty years, the United States is becoming more racially and ethnically diverse.
- Although race is not accepted as a scientific concept for classifying people, it is a social construct that continues to be used to sort people in the United States.
- Ethnicity is determined by the national origin of one's ancestors.
- Disparities exist in the academic achievement of students from different racial and ethnic groups.

LANGUAGE

- Nearly one in five residents of the United States speaks a language other than English at home.
- A growing number of English-language learners are found in schools.
- A number of students use a dialect that is not Standard English in their home environments.
- A number of educational strategies are used in schools to help ELLs learn English.

GENDER

- Although few biological differences exist between females and males, differences in economic status, jobs, and educational attainment do exist.
- Some theorists and researchers credit biology for these differences; others have found that culture and society determine them.
- Educators can help reduce the differences in participation and achievement in academic areas and sports.

SEXUAL ORIENTATION

- More than half of LGBT students report verbal, physical, or sexual harassment by other students, and sometimes teachers, while they are in school.
- Many educators are not knowledgeable about homosexuality and do not know how to support LGBT students.

EXCEPTIONALITIES

- Today's teachers are likely to have students with disabilities in their classrooms.
- Like members of other underserved groups in society, students with disabilities are often labeled and stereotyped in ways not conducive to learning.
- Response to Intervention (RTI) is one approach to identifying students with disabilities.

RELIGION

- Religious diversity in the United States is increasing beyond Christianity and Judaism.
- Families from other religious backgrounds do not always see their traditions and values reflected in the public schools and often feel discriminated against because of their religion.

MULTICULTURAL EDUCATION

- Multicultural education is based on the principles of democracy, social justice, and equality.
- The goal is to ensure that all students participate equally in the education system.
- Educators who value the diversity of students strive to provide educational equality in which all students are provided challenging and stimulating learning experiences that help them learn at high levels.

LOOKING AHEAD: TEACHERS AS SOCIAL ACTIVISTS

- Democratic schools and classrooms involve parents, students, teachers, administrators, and community members as partners in the design and delivery of education.
- The policies and practices of democratic schools promote equity for all students, abandoning practices that sort students and give privilege to those from advantaged backgrounds.

DISCUSSION QUESTIONS

1. What are some ways in which you can integrate the racial and ethnic background of your students into the curriculum? How can you learn more about the ethnic and racial groups that may be represented in your future classroom?

2. Research shows that some students perform better academically and socially when they are segregated in single-sex classrooms. In which cases do you think such segregation is appropriate?

3. Policy makers and politicians disagree on the importance of helping English-language learners maintain their native languages. What is your position on this issue? What programs would schools provide to ELLs if your position became policy in a school district? What results would you expect if your position became policy?

4. You may be assigned to a school in which the community includes families who are Christian, Muslim, and Jewish. How will you ensure that you are respecting their perspectives on how their children should be treated in school? When will their perspectives impact school practices?

5. Most classrooms today include one or more students with disabilities. Where will you turn for assistance in providing the necessary accommodations to help those students learn at the levels they are capable of learning?

6. Diversity, social justice, and equality are concepts of multicultural education. What conditions and practices in schools suggest that these concepts are undergirding the education system as you know it? What are signs that these concepts are being addressed and implemented in schools?

SCHOOL-BASED OBSERVATIONS

1. Identify the group memberships (e.g., race, ethnicity, language, gender, socioeconomic class, religion, physical and academic ability, and geographic background) of the students in a class that you are observing at the P–12 level. How are students' memberships in these groups interacting to impact their academic achievement?

2. Examine the curriculum, textbooks, bulletin boards, and other materials used in the classroom to determine which groups studied in this chapter are included and which never appear.

3. In a school with English-language learners, interview two or more teachers about the strategies they use to ensure that students do not fall behind academically because their native language is not English.

PORTFOLIO DEVELOPMENT

1. Identify one cultural group with which you have no or limited experience and write a paper on the group's historical and current experience in the United States. What other information will be helpful to you if students from this group are in your classroom when you begin teaching? How will you work effectively with the families from this group?

2. Write a summary of what democracy means to you. How do common good and equality fit into your perception of democracy and a democratic school?

myeducationlab To begin developing your own personal portfolio, go to MyEducationLab, select *Resources*, and then *Portfolio Builder*.

PREPARING FOR CERTIFICATION

1. The PRAXIS II Principles of Learning and Teaching (PLT) test is required by many states. The test covers four broad categories: (1) students as learners, (2) instruction and assessment, (3) communication techniques, and (4) professionalism. The "students as learners" section of the test includes reference to the following: "Understanding the influence of individual experiences, talents, and prior learning, as well as language, culture, family, and community values on students' learning
   - Multicultural backgrounds
   - Age-appropriate knowledge and behavior
   - The student culture at school
   - Family backgrounds
   - Linguistic patterns and differences
   - Cognitive patterns and differences
   - Social and emotional issues"

   Reread the chapter-opening editorial by Carrie Coppernoll, from *The Oklahoman*, August 21, 2008. The changing nature of the population in Oklahoma is described. Examples of stereotypes and racism are provided. Select one category from the PLT in the list above, and one of the factors related to diversity that have an impact on students in schools. For instance, you might select family background from the list above, and religion from the factors related to diversity. Define the diffierences that may influence your interaction with students and/or their families.

2. Answer the following multiple-choice question, which is similar to items in Praxis and other state certification tests. If you are unsure of the answer, reread the "Acceptance of Diverse Groups" section in this chapter.

   Socioeconomic status is one variable to consider when you look at the diversity of the students in classrooms. This status is primarily determined by income, but other variables are also often considered. Which of the following statements about being poor is true?
   a. In the U.S., more Hispanic families are poor than White families.
   b. In the U.S., more White families are poor than Black families.
   c. In the U.S., more Black families are poor than White families.
   d. The percentage of poor facilities is fairly consistent across all races.

3. Answer the following multiple-choice question, which is similar to items in Praxis and other state certification tests. If you are unsure of the answer, reread the "Acceptance of Diverse Groups" section in this chapter.

   Seven of Ms. Bishop's third-grade students are recent immigrants, all from different countries and all speaking little English. Ms. Bishop says her goal is for all seven students to learn English language and American customs as quickly as possible so they can rapidly become part of U.S. society. Which ideology about diversity most closely corresponds to Ms. Bishop's beliefs?
   a. cultural pluralism
   b. assimilation
   c. social stratification
   d. cultural choice

4. Answer the following short-answer question, which is similar to items in Praxis and other state certification tests.

   In this chapter, the authors explain that academic achievement is not *determined* by, but *influenced* by societal factors related to race, ethnicity, language, gender, and exceptionalities. Select one of the factors listed and describe how academic achievement can be influenced by the factor.

After you've completed your written responses to the above questions, use the Praxis general scoring guide provided in Chapter 1 to see if you can revise your response to improve your score.

MYEDUCATIONLAB

myeducationlab Now go to Topic 2 *Student Diversity* in the MyEducationLab (www.myeducationlab.com) for your course, where you can:

- Find learning outcomes for *Student Diversity* along with the national standards that connect to these outcomes.
- Complete *Assignments and Activities* that can help you more deeply understand the chapter content.
- Apply and practice your understanding of the core teaching skills identified in the chapter with the *Building Teaching Skills and Dispositions* learning units.

- Check your comprehension on the content covered in the chapter by going to the *Study Plan* in the *Book Specific Resources* section for your text. Here you will be able to take a chapter quiz, receive feedback on your answers, and then access *Review, Practice, and Enrichment* activities to enhance your understanding of chapter content.

WEBSITES

www.adl.org The Anti-Defamation League fights anti-Semitism, bigotry, and extremism. Its website includes information on religious freedom, civil rights, and the Holocaust as well as resources for teachers on fighting hate.

www.edchange.org/multicultural/index.html The Multicultural Pavilion links teachers with others who are dealing with issues related to multicultural education.

www.feminist.org The website of the Feminist Majority provides information about women's issues, Title IX, and education, including links to additional resources.

www.glsen.org The website of the Gay, Lesbian, and Straight Education Network provides resources and updates for ending bias against LGBT students.

www.kineticcity.com Developed by the American Association for the Advancement of Science (AASA) for students in grades 3–5, this website is designed to interest female and students of color in science with interactive games, experiments, and other games.

www.rethinkingschools.org The Rethinking Schools website was designed by a group of teachers who wanted to improve education in their own classrooms and schools and to help shape school reform that is humane, caring, multiracial, and democratic.

www.splcenter.org The Southern Poverty Law Center combats hate, intolerance, and discrimination through education and litigation against hate groups. It publishes *Teaching Tolerance*, which is available at no cost to teachers, and numerous other teaching resources.

FURTHER READING

Corbett, C., Hill, C., and St. Rose, A. (2008). *Where the girls are: The facts about gender equity in education.* Washington, DC: American Association of University Women. This review of factors that influence student achievement finds that both boys and girls are performing better today than in the past, but too many of them are not acquiring the educational skills necessary for today's economy.

Gollnick, Donna M., and Chinn, Philip C. (2009). *Multicultural education in a pluralistic society* (8th ed.). Upper Saddle River, NJ: Pearson. A fundamental text with expanded descriptions and information about the groups outlined in this chapter. This book also discusses the pedagogical implications and applications for ethnic, racial, socioeconomic, gender, linguistic, religious, age, ability, age, and geographic groups.

Hehir, Thomas. (2002, Spring). Eliminating ableism in education, *Harvard Educational Review, 72*(1); 1–32. An excellent discussion of ableism in schools that prevents students with disabilities from fully participating in the education system, having access to high levels of academic contact, and fully participating in society. Instead of accepting different ways of seeing, moving, and thinking, schools are guilty of ableism, which results in devaluing persons with disabilities and treating them as inferior to others.

Pollock, M. (Ed.). (2009). *Everyday antiracism: Getting real about race in school.* New York: New Press. Leading experts offer concrete and realistic strategies for dealing with race in schools including how to constructively discuss race with students and teachers. The examples discussed throughout the book focus on the everyday incidents related to race in classrooms.

chapter eight

STUDENTS
AND THEIR FAMILIES

GRANT FROM TOYOTA FUNDS PROGRAM AT ELEMENTARY SCHOOLS

EDUCATION IN THE **NEWS**

By **CATHRYN STOUT**,

Memphis Commercial Appeal, April 7, 2009

Chappell's English as a second language [ESL] students are older than the other students at Egypt Elementary School. In fact, they are all parents of children enrolled in the school. As part of the Toyota Family Literacy Program, Hispanic parents take classes at Egypt, Berclair, and South Park elementary schools to improve their language, literacy and job skills.

Operating in 25 cities nationwide, the six-year-old program is coordinated by the National Center for Family Literacy in Louisville, Ky., and funded by Toyota.

The Memphis City Schools system is a new participant in the program and the three local schools that qualified for the grant have about 30 percent Hispanic enrollment.

To help bridge the cultural and achievement gaps over the next three school years, Toyota will funnel $600,000 in cash and resources into the local elementary schools.

At Egypt, the money has already paid for instructors that teach day and evening adult ESL classes. While the parents are in class, the school also pays "casual care" workers to supervise their infants. School officials said the extra staff is helping them serve a rapidly evolving population.

"We had a large influx of Hispanic students about five years ago," said Wendee Beller, the school's instructional facilitator. "We went from virtually no Hispanic students to 26 percent Spanish speaking students in three years."

Children of recent immigrants have a "steep hill to climb," said Sharon Darling, president and founder of the National Center for Family Literacy. "In order for the children to succeed, their parents need to be educated and their parents need to learn English and their parents need to have skills."

Twice a week at Egypt, about 30 participating parents attend adult education classes. Additionally, once a week they spend a couple of hours in their children's classrooms learning alongside their little ones.

On Monday, Rocio Valenzuela sat next to 8-year-old son William, helping him read the children's book "If You Give a Mouse a Cookie." As the second-grader sounded-out the word "probably," he gave his mom a big smile.

"When I'm here in the classroom, I think he feels more confident," whispered Valenzuela.

QUESTIONS FOR REFLECTION

1. What is unique about the ESL classes at Egypt Elementary School?
2. Why do Toyota and school officials think it is important to help the parents learn English?
3. What are some advantages to having the parents of these students involved in their children's education?

Source: The Commercial Appeal, Memphis, TN. Used with permission. http://www.commercialappeal.com

LEARNING OUTCOMES

After reading and studying this chapter, you should be able to:

1. Respect the different family backgrounds from which students come and understand the importance of not stereotyping student behavior or academic potential on the basis of the structure of students' families.

2. Understand that young people need caring adults to help them maneuver through the tribulations and challenges of childhood and the teenage years. (INTASC 2: Intellectual, Social, and Personal Development)

3. Identify the challenges that many students face as a result of societal factors such as poverty, over which they have little or no control. (INTASC 3: Diversity)

4. Understand the role that prejudice and discrimination play in marginalizing many students. (INTASC 3: Diversity)

5. Be aware that not all students have access to the same technology at home and school, and the impact those differences could have on future academic achievement.

TODAY'S FAMILIES

Families in the United States have changed dramatically during the past sixty years. In the 1950s, the norm was a working father and a mother at home with two or more school-aged children. To-day only 68 percent of children who are under eighteen years old live in families with two parents (U.S. Census Bureau, 2008, Table 66). Seldom does a mother remain at home until her children finish high school. Families today include mothers working while fathers stay at home with the children, single-parent families, families with two working parents, remarried parents, childless marriages, families with adopted children, gay and lesbian parents, extended families, grandparents raising grandchildren, and unmarried couples with children. As pointed out in the Professional Dilemma feature on the next page, we must learn to value and respect the diversity of the families in our schools as we work with parents and other caregivers to help students learn.

Parents are generally older than in the past, in part, because they marry later. More than 85 percent of today's young people ages eighteen to twenty-four years old have never been married (U.S. Census Bureau, 2008, Table 56). Most men and women work for a number of years before marrying. However, they do not always stay married to the same person, leading to children who are being raised by a single parent; parents who live in separate households, but have joint custody; a stepparent; other family members; or a nonrelated family. More than one-third of first-time married couples have separated or divorced after ten years. More than half of divorced women remarry within five years and 75 percent of them by ten years (Bramlett & Mosher, 2002).

At the same time, two in three children live with two parents, even though one of them may be a stepmother or stepfather. One in four children in the United States lives with his or her mother only; 5 percent live with their father only. African American children are more likely to live with a single mother than children from other groups (Planty et al., 2008). Ideally, it would be advantageous for children to have two caring and loving parents to nurture children. However, children from all types of families are academically successful in school and become well-adjusted adults. It is not the type of family that disadvantages students or makes it difficult for them to adjust appropriately and achieve well in school. The factor that is most correlated with such disadvantage is the economic well-being of families. Those in poverty, who are more likely to be living with single mothers, are more likely than their better-off peers to have problems in school.

As a teacher, you will need to monitor your interactions with students and their families to avoid labeling a child as dysfunctional because he or she lives in a family structure different than your own. Too often, teachers develop a self-fulfilling prophecy about students in nontraditional families not being able to achieve academically. Instead, we should have high expectations for the academic success of all students and do everything possible to help them learn.

Thirty percent of children under eighteen years of age live in nontraditional families that provide the love and support necessary to raise children.

PROFESSIONAL DILEMMA   Family Diversity

In the 1950s, most students came from families with both a mother and a father. But for decades now, schools have been populated with students whose families do not fit that model. In the subsequent fifty years, more and more students have been raised by single mothers and now by a growing number of single fathers. Some students do not live with either parent but stay instead with relatives or in a foster home. As society becomes more tolerant of a variety of family structures and as adults become more open about their sexual orientation, teachers will also be introduced to lesbian and gay parents who may be living with a partner or separated from a partner.

The curriculum and instructional materials seldom mirror the diversity of families, which may include parents with special needs, interracial parents, single parents, gay and lesbian parents, and foster parents. The dilemma for teachers extends beyond the curriculum. They must figure out how to value and respect the diversity of families. Otherwise, both students and parents will feel ignored, isolated, and discriminated against by educators. Teachers may also have to help other students develop an understanding of this diversity. Sometimes students respond to such differences in negative and hurtful ways.

Questions for Reflection

1. How do you characterize families headed by a mother who has never been married? How do you expect her children to behave in school?
2. How will you respond when two men meet with you to discuss the academic progress of their child?
3. How can a school develop a climate of acceptance of all students regardless of the structure and nature of the families in which they live?

Parenting

Most parents want what's best for their children, but there is no simple guidebook for steering children through the complex terrain they will have to navigate as they grow up. Often parents draw from their own experiences as children and adults. However, the world is different than when they grew up. For example, they did not have access to the technology that is an integral part of the lives of their children. The Internet was not used broadly by the population until the 1990s. Cell phones, texting, avatars, chat rooms, MySpace, Facebook, YouTube, wikis, and tweeting did not exist when most of the parents of your students were born.

Parents and caretakers are critical in setting the stage for future learning during the early years before children begin school. Reading to young children and limiting the amount of time children spend watching TV have a strong relationship to reading scores. By age four, the children of professional parents have a much larger vocabulary than do other children. Access to resources such as books, computers, and the Internet also contributes to academic success. Parental involvement in school activities and ensuring that homework is done also are correlated with good grades (Barton & Coley, 2007).

To increase students' chances of making it safely through childhood and adolescence, teachers and parents need to work together, setting high standards and helping young people meet them. Some schools are beginning to hire a school–parent coordinator to help bridge the gap between the two. They encourage parents to participate in their children's education and try to improve their communications with parents, which will be discussed later in this section.

Socioeconomic Status

Families from socioeconomic and racial backgrounds similar to those of the teachers seem to have more successful interactions with educators. Upper-middle-class families are more likely to volunteer to assist teachers and support school activities at a higher rate than other families. In turn, teachers see these parents as supportive, caring families who monitor the academic progress of their children. Family members at lower income levels may want to volunteer for work at the school, but their employers will not allow them the time off of work. Other families may feel uncomfortable because the school culture is unfamiliar or they speak little or no English. In this section, we examine how limited family incomes affect families and the schooling of their children.

HOMELESSNESS. Individuals and families with no or low incomes often lose the ability to pay their rent or maintain mortgages, ending up homeless on the streets of small and large cities. During the economic crises such as the one that occurred in 2008–2009, newly homeless people set up tents in and near cities or began living in their cars. The National Law Center on Homelessness and Poverty estimates that up to 3.5 million people in the United States are without shelter at some point during a year (National Law Center on Homelessness and Poverty [NLCHP], 2007). This figure does not

Poverty and the lack of affordable housing are the major reasons for the growing number of homeless adults, children, and families in both rural and urban areas.

include the burgeoning number of people who have become homeless as a result of the recent global recession. The homeless also includes people with disabilities, veterans, people using illegal drugs, people with mental health problems, and working people who do not earn enough to rent housing. One in four of our homeless adults had lived in foster care, a group home, or other institutional setting earlier in his or her life (National Center on Family Homelessness [NCFH], 2009). Life is very rough when living on the streets. Homeless people are physically attacked and suffer disproportionately from health and mental problems to the level that their life expectancy is twenty-one to twenty-four years less than that of the rest of the population (NLCHP, 2007).

One of the reasons for an increase in homelessness since the late 1970s is a shortage of affordable rental housing. Another is the large number of people and families in poverty. Forty-four percent of the homeless population is working (NLCHP, 2007), but employment is part time or sporadic or they are earning wages too low to purchase necessary food, clothing, and housing. A full-time minimum-wage job often does not provide enough income for a family to rent a one-bedroom unit at fair market prices.

More than 1.5 million children or 1 in 50 children in the United States are homeless at some time during the year. Every night more than 200,000 children have no home; many are staying in shelters at night or doubling up in the homes of friends or relatives (NCFH, 2008). Homeless families comprise 34 percent of the homeless population. They disproportionately are headed by women as shown in Figure 8.1. The mother of a homeless family is generally in her late twenties with two young children. Most of the mothers already have been the victims of violent incidents. They and their children suffer from chronic health problems such as asthma, anxiety, and depression (NCFH, 2009). Homelessness is devastating to families. Only 65 percent of homeless mothers live with at least one of their children; of the homeless men, only 7 percent of them live with at least one of their own children (NCFH, 2008). Most of their children are placed in foster care or left with relatives or friends.

FIGURE 8.1

Characteristics of Homeless Families

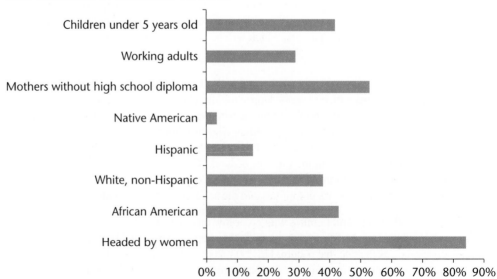

Source: National Center on Family Homelessness. (2008). *The characteristics and needs of families experiencing homelessness.* Newton, MA: Author.

Young people are also homeless because they have run away from home or been released from foster care or some other institutional setting. Nearly half of them report that family conflict and violence have been the primary reason for their homelessness. Twenty to 40 percent of them are gay, lesbian, bisexual, or transgendered (NCFH, 2008). Like the adult homeless, homeless young people live in shelters, in abandoned buildings, and on the street. One in four of them goes to school from shelters. Children who live in shelters and on the streets often suffer from inadequate health care. They may be surrounded by diseases such as whooping cough and tuberculosis. They are not always inoculated against common childhood diseases, making them more susceptible to illness than most other children. They suffer from asthma and ear infections at disproportionately high rates. Children in homeless shelters also face hypothermia, hunger, and abuse by their parents or other adults. These illnesses may prevent homeless children from attending school on a regular basis. Their lack of regular medical and dental services can cause treatable problems to interfere with their ability to concentrate in classrooms and focus effectively on academic lessons. Completing homework on the street or in a homeless shelter may be difficult if not impossible without supportive adults.

Survival alone can be all encompassing for families who are homeless as they worry about where they will sleep, what they will eat, and how to remain safe. Homeless children usually do not want their school peers or teachers to know they are homeless. The school environment may not be welcoming because these children cannot participate at the same level as other students.

Most homeless children are under fourteen years old as shown in Figure 8.2. How do those students fare in schools? Their proficiency in reading and mathematics is, on average, 16 percent below the scores of all students. They are twice as likely to repeat a grade, be expelled, or be suspended. Fewer than one in four of them graduates from high school (NCFH, 2009). Some homeless students are very resilient and able to succeed in school against all odds. Many homeless youth who are living on their own and know the value of an education are enrolled in high school. As a teacher, you may have to be creative in ensuring that these students participate equally in class work and have time to complete homework assignments. Finishing high school and college can provide these students the skills needed for a path to economic stability in the future.

Almost all homeless children move during the year. Half of them transfer from school each year; one in ten misses at least one month of school annually (Homes for the Homeless, 2006). Although the McKinney-Vento Homeless Assistance Act, which was passed in 1987, eliminated the residency requirement for students, homeless children sometimes are not allowed to attend the school that would best serve their needs. Provision of transportation back to the student's school of origin is not always deemed feasible by school systems. Homeless students are sometimes

FIGURE 8.2

Age of Homeless Children

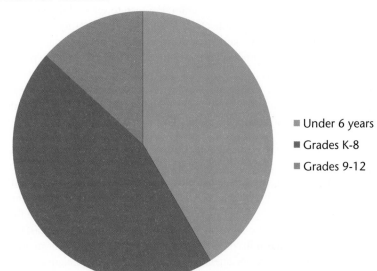

■ Under 6 years
■ Grades K-8
■ Grades 9-12

Source: National Center on Family Homelessness. (2009). *America's youngest outcasts: State report card on child homelessness.* Newton, MA: Author.

forced to wait to enroll in a school while personal records are collected. However, access to schools is less of a problem than it was in the past.

Today's advocates focus on students' classroom success. A high-quality education offers homeless children a chance for academic and economic success. To ignore them because they do not have a home or are not well groomed deprives them of the opportunity to rise above their current circumstances. They need more, not less, of our attention. Your support can be the difference in whether they continue to come to school. Your advocacy for their learning and belief that they can learn can help them through a rough economic period for their families.

SCHOOL PROGRAMS FOR STUDENTS FROM LOW-INCOME FAMILIES Federal legislation in the 1960s provided an influx of financial support to schools to support students from low-income families with the goal of making up some of the educational disadvantages with which many of them entered school. The programs are available for low-income students at all levels of the educational system. African American, Hispanic, and American Indian students are more likely to attend high-poverty schools, which would make them eligible for these federal funds, than white and Asian American students. Urban areas have twice as many high-poverty schools as suburban areas. This section summarizes some of the programs that you are likely to encounter in the schools in which you will work in the future.

Title I. Title I is the cornerstone of the programs for students from low-income families. It has been part of the Elementary and Secondary Education Act since it was first passed in 1965, most recently as part of No Child Left Behind. The assistance is provided to public schools with large numbers of students whose families meet the federal poverty level or are close to the poverty level to help these students meet state academic standards. The school district must also provide services to eligible private schools. Current Title I provisions require the involvement of parents as advisers to school leaders.

Title I serves around twenty million students. Seven in ten of them who receive these services are enrolled in preschool through grade 6. In the largest school districts, more than half of the students attend schools eligible for Title I (Stullich, Eisner, & McCrary, 2007).

No Child Left Behind requires that all teachers in Title I schools be highly qualified teachers. Highly qualified teachers must have a bachelor's degree, be fully licensed by the state, and demonstrate competence in the subjects they are teaching, usually by passing a state licensure test. Title I schools that do not meet adequate yearly progress (AYP) for two consecutive years must offer families the option to transfer their children to another school. After three years of not meeting AYP, low-income students must be offered supplemental education services, which include free tutoring to students to help them raise their academic achievement. After five years of not meeting AYP, the school district must begin planning the restructuring of the school.

Head Start. Head Start is a federally funded program designed to serve children from low-income families by addressing the needs of the whole child. In addition to educating three- to five-year-old children, teachers work with social workers, nurses, other health professionals, and directly with parents. Teachers and social workers make periodic home visits to work with the parents, providing them parenting/teaching skills to use when they work with their children. Head Start children receive breakfast and lunch daily at school. Along with working on academic skills, Head Start teachers also teach social skills, play skills, healthy habits, and table manners. Head Start was expanded in 1995 to include Early Head Start programs to service the needs of two-year-olds and their families.

Free or Reduced-Price Lunch. Many of the nation's children face food insecurity—they are not sure they will always have a meal, let alone a nutritious one. The National School Lunch Program helps to bridge this gap by providing nutritionally balanced **free or reduced-price lunches** daily in schools. Students eligible for this program live in families with an annual income of 185 percent or less of the federal poverty level, which would be $40,793 for a family of four in 2009. Most of the schools that serve free or reduced-price lunches also serve breakfast through the School Breakfast Program. These breakfasts provide more fruits and milk than most of these students would normally consume. In addition, breakfast contributes to greater attention in class, improved academic achievement, and fewer discipline problems. To continue providing food throughout the summer, the Summer Food Service Programs provide free meals at local summer education and enrichment programs in areas where half of the children are eligible for free or reduced-price school meals (NCFH, 2009).

Other aspects of No Child Left Behind are discussed in greater detail in Chapters 1, 9, and 11.

Title I A federal program, first passed by Congress in 1965, that provides financial assistance to schools with large numbers of low-income students to help students meet state standards.

Head Start A federally funded early childhood education program for three- to five-year-olds from low-income families designed to close the academic gap between them and more advantaged students before kindergarten.

free or reduced-price lunch The National School Lunch Program that provides school lunches to students who live in families with an annual income of 185 percent of the federal poverty level.

Fifteen percent of all elementary and secondary students are eligible for free or reduced-price lunches (Planty et al., 2008, Indicator 29). Nearly half of the students in the largest one hundred school districts are eligible, compared to 38 percent of suburban students (Garofano & Sable, 2008).

Children Left Alone after School

Most single parents work outside the home; both parents work in many two-parent families. Unless working parents have been lucky enough to have a job that supports a flexible schedule that allows them to be home when their children are not in school, they are not available to care for their children during the period immediately after school. The result is children of all ages being left alone or in the care of others.

Parents provide supervision after school for more than half of the students in grades K–5. Older students are more likely to care for themselves after school, as shown in Figure 8.3. Other children stay with adults other than their parents, attend center-based programs, or participate in extracurricular activities such as sports, arts, or clubs. Children in poverty are slightly more likely to stay with relatives than other children. Most parents have to pay a fee for child care, especially if it is not provided by relatives (National Center for Education Statistics, 2004). Some families cannot afford the cost of such care, leaving their children with other family members or to fend for themselves.

Children who are responsible for their own care after school experience more accidents and injuries. They also are at risk of behavior problems, lower social competence, and poorer academic performance. Adolescents left on their own are more likely to engage in risk activities such as smoking, drinking alcohol, and using drugs. Self-care is more prevalent among children over age ten than younger ones. It is also more prevalent when mothers work full time or there is a single parent. Families make choices about whether to leave children alone after school based, in part, on the safety of their neighborhoods and the health and maturity of their children (Vandivere, Tout, Zaslow, Calkins, & Capizzano, 2003).

FIGURE 8.3

Before- and After-School Care Received by U.S. Children

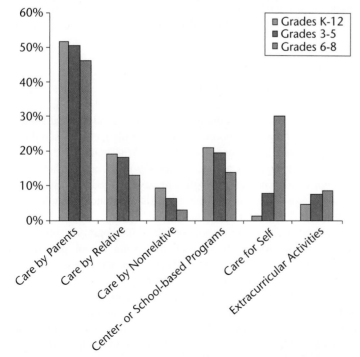

Source: U.S. Department of Education, National Center for Education Statistics. (2004). *The condition of education 2004* (NCES 2004-077, Indicator 33). Washington, DC: Author.

FIGURE 8.4

Participation in After-School Activities by Gender

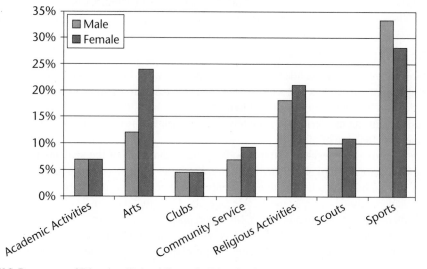

Source: U.S. Department of Education, National Center for Education Statistics. (2007). *The condition of education 2007* (NCES 2007-064, Indicator 29). Washington, DC: Author.

More than two in five children participate in after-school activities such as sports, religion, and the arts. Some students are involved in the Scouts, academic activities, community services, and clubs as shown in Figure 8.4. Students from families with higher incomes and whose parents are college graduates are more likely to participate in these activities. Girls are more involved than boys in all of these activities except sports (U.S. Department of Education, 2007).

Educators should be sensitive to the realities faced by children left alone after school. They are sometimes frightened to be at home alone, especially when they have no siblings. The process of traveling from school to home can be dangerous and scary in neighborhoods where drugs are being sold and peers are tempting one another to misbehave. Adolescents may be tempted to experiment with drugs and sex while adults are not around. Television may become the babysitter, providing children with the opportunity to learn from educational programs—or from inappropriate programs. In most cases, children are thankful for caring adults who can provide supervision and assistance.

Communicating with Families

Go to the *Assignments and Activities* section of Topic 3: *Schools and Society* in the MyEducationLab for your course and complete the activity titled *Incorporating the Home Experiences of Culturally Diverse Students*.

Regular and consistent communication with families has long been considered vital to the success of students. The focus of communications between you and your students' families should be on their children's learning. You should help them understand the academic expectations for the class and how they can help their children at home. Family members should be equal partners in conversations with teachers and other school officials. You should not do all of the talking; you should ask questions and listen to the answers. A translator can be very helpful in conversations with family members who do not speak English or have limited proficiency. Ask your faculty leader or principal for assistance in identifying a translator. Remember to tell families about the positive as well as negative behaviors of their children.

You should follow up with families after report cards and progress reports are released to them, especially if a child is not performing up to expectations. Some schools provide assistance to families as shown in the news article that opened this chapter. Teachers in some schools organize workshops with families in the evening to assist them in helping their children with homework.

In the past, teachers were dependent on mail, phone, and students to facilitate this communication. Today, Internet technologies are augmenting these standard tools in some exciting ways. Most schools have websites that can provide valuable information for families and students. Contact information and a staff directory can be very helpful. In addition, schools find that providing significant information on their website reduces the number of phone calls to school staff for frequently asked questions (FAQs). Some school districts make homework assignments available via the web and utilize the Internet to share students' grades with parents.

You might also use e-mail messages, short newsletters, and written notes to maintain regular communications with families. Internet services such as *Parent Connect* provide families password-protected access to their children's attendance records, schedules, grades, health records, and assignments. Evening activities for families provide additional opportunities for you to interact with family members in workshop settings, student performances, and athletic events.

JOURNAL FOR REFLECTION

In what ways do you envision using technology to communicate with the families of your students? How might your choices be affected by the economic level of the community in which you are teaching?

DANGERS CHILDREN FACE

The love and care of adults help children and young people pass safely through childhood and adolescence. Unfortunately, some children face danger at home, in the streets of their neighborhood, and at school that is difficult for most of us to imagine. As an educator, you should be able to recognize signs of the violence that can greatly affect children's well-being and future lives. You should know when to intervene and provide support that can make a difference in their lives as well as their academic performance at school. In this section, we examine some of the immediate dangers faced by today's students.

Child Abuse

Domestic violence is often hidden or ignored by society. Unlike other crimes, the victims of domestic violence are predominantly women and girls. Nearly one in three of the females murdered in this country are killed by someone they know intimately—a current or previous spouse or boyfriend—compared to 5 percent of murdered males being killed by someone with whom they have been intimate (Fox & Zawitz, 2007). Physical violence against women and girls is near epidemic levels in some countries. A report on domestic violence by the United Nations Children's Fund (UNICEF) indicates that up to half of the females in some countries have been abused by a family member or boyfriend. More than 60 million females in these countries have been killed by their own families either deliberately or through neglect (UNICEF, 2000). Domestic violence is one of the primary causes of homelessness for women in the United States with 22 to 57 percent of them reporting that they were fleeing domestic violence in cities around the country (NLCHP, 2008).

Most children have probably been faced with angry parents who raise their voices or even spank them on occasion. However, some family members seriously hurt children. Child abuse is investigated annually for more than 3.5 million children for the abuses identified in Figure 8.5 (U.S. Census

FIGURE 8.5

Type of Child Abuse Substantiated by Authorities

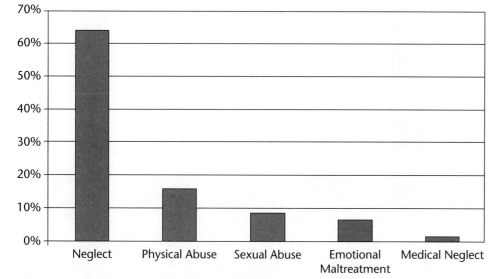

Source: U.S. Census Bureau. (2008). *Statistical abstract of the United States: 2009* (128th ed. Table 329). Washington, DC: U.S. Government Printing Office.

Bureau, 2008, Table 330). One in every one hundred children is the victim of serious abuse or **neglect**, which means the child is not being provided with his or her basic needs by parents, caretakers, or relatives, with females slightly more likely to be the victims (U.S. Census Bureau, 2008, Tables 329 and 330). Children under age five are the most vulnerable, representing more than two in five of all of the victims under eighteen years old (U.S. Census Bureau, 2008, Table 329). High school girls (11 percent) are more likely than boys (6 percent) to be sexually abused (Centers for Disease Control and Prevention [CDC], 2008a). Sensational news stories report sexual abuse of children by strangers, but the abusers usually are family members, intimate partners, friends, or acquaintances.

When old enough, some abused youths run away from home, choosing to confront possible abuse on the streets rather than the known abuse at home. For many of these children, the negative experiences and conditions of their childhood may become the foundation for mental health problems and delinquent behaviors later in life.

Children and young people who are abused or neglected may arrive at school hungry, bruised, and depressed. They may arrive early at school and seem to have little desire to leave the safety of the school. These children, like all others, need teachers who are caring, retain high expectations for them, and can provide hope for the future. School and other social service professionals may be the only adults available to support youngsters who have been abused.

Bruises, burns, broken bones, depression, withdrawal, extreme thinness, and nervousness that appear more often than one should expect may be signs of abuse. Educators should not investigate cases that they think may be abuse; they should instead report them as required by law. Not reporting could lead to fines and/or prison terms. Most school districts have procedures for reporting suspected abuse, including to whom the abuse should be reported. Even though a teacher has told his or her supervisor about possible abuse, the teacher should check to ensure that the appropriate agency was notified (Cambron-McCabe, McCarthy, & Thomas, 2004).

What might educators do to help eliminate, or at least reduce, the number of students who suffer from abuse? Parents are key to making necessary changes. Some schools and family services organizations are working with parents to help them develop better parenting skills and to be able to more effectively manage their children's behavior through time-outs and interacting positively with them (CDC, 2009a). As you interact with the parents of your students, you may be able to encourage them to participate in such sessions for improving their ability to interact effectively with their children with the goal of improving children's learning and academic achievement.

neglect The lack of providing basic needs of housing, food, clothing, education, or medical care to children.

Sexual Harassment

Harassment is not rare in schools; it is a common occurrence for many students as shown in Figure 8.6. Eighty percent of the students in a national survey indicated that they had been sex-

FIGURE 8.6

Sexual Harassment of Students in Schools

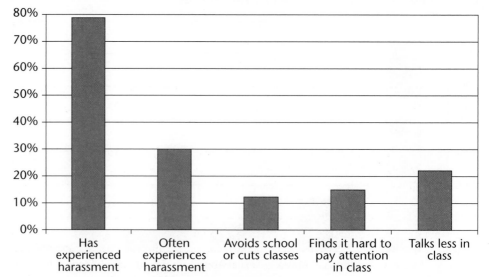

Source: American Association of University Women Educational Foundation. (2002). *Harassment-free hallways: How to stop sexual harassment in schools: A guide for students, parents, and teachers* (Section III). Washington, DC: Author.

ually harassed at school, with one in three experiencing it often (American Association of University Women [AAUW], 2002). The harassment of girls and young women in the hallways, classrooms, and cafeterias of schools ranges from name-calling to touching and, in some cases, rape. LGBT students report verbal, sexual, and physical harassment that ends in physical assault for one in five LGBT students.

The most common harassment experienced by LGBT students is in the form of verbal abuse. Almost all of them report hearing sexist and homophobic name-calling such as "that's so gay," "faggot," or "dyke" from other students. These students also indicate that faculty or school staff sometimes make homophobic remarks. In many schools, these homophobic remarks are applied to both LGBT and non-LGBT students as derogatory terms meant to call into question a student's masculinity or femininity (Greytak, Kosciw, & Diaz, 2009). Students most often make these remarks when faculty and staff are not around. However, faculty do not always intervene when they hear students making homophobic remarks; students intervene even less often. Many students do not report harassment incidents to teachers or other school authorities, in part, because they do not think it will make a difference (Kosciw, Diaz, & Greytak, 2008). How could a teacher respond when they hear students making such remarks? You could pull the students aside to let them know that their behavior is not acceptable. You might be able to use the incident as a teachable moment in which your class could talk about respect and the treatment of others in a caring way. Not confronting students about their name-calling is seen by both the victim and perpetrator as condoning the action.

How does such harassment affect students? A biennial study of school climate found that academic success is negatively affected when students feel unsafe or uncomfortable in school. LGBT students are more likely than other students to skip a class or miss a day of school because of the harassment. When they have been verbally or physically attacked, they miss school even more often (Kosciw et al., 2008). The patterns were more likely to occur for LGBT students of color (Diaz & Kosciw, 2009). Not attending classes makes it even more difficult to maintain good grades and think about attending college.

What makes schools safer and more attractive to LGBT students? Sexual harassment is reduced when clubs such as Gay-Straight Alliances exist. Supportive educators help reduce the marginalization and negative experiences for these students. An inclusive curriculum in which they see positive portrayals of the contributions of LGBT people also enhances their school experience. Finally, safe school laws and policies that include sexual orientation, gender identity, and gender expression affirm a school's commitment to providing safe schools to all students (Kosciw et al., 2008).

Sexual orientation is also discussed in Chapter 7.

Other Violence

Many adults think that young people commit a larger proportion of violent crime than they actually do. Fewer than two in one thousand juveniles are arrested for a violent crime. The most serious charges in half of juvenile arrests are larceny/theft, simple assault, disorderly conduct, drug abuse, or a liquor law violation (Snyder & Sickmond, 2006). Juvenile arrest rates for violent crimes are at the lowest level in two decades for all areas except aggravated assault in which a weapon such as a gun or knife is used. Although most crimes are committed by males, juvenile arrest rates for females are increasing. African American youth are almost four times more likely to be incarcerated than their white peers. American Indian and Hispanic youth are 2.6 and 1.8 times, respectively, as likely to be incarcerated (Snyder & Sickmond, 2006). Students with disabilities such as mental disorders, attention deficit/hyperactivity disorder (ADHD), and learning disabilities are also overrepresented in the prison population (Aron & Mears, 2003).

Automobile accidents account for 77 percent of teen deaths (Snyder & Sickmond, 2006). However, homicides are the second leading cause of teen death, but the leading cause for African American young men. A juvenile is one in every four victims of violent crime with the perpetrator most often being an adult. Although females are more often the victim of a violent crime, murder victims are much more likely to be male. African American youth are four times more at risk of being murdered than white youth (Snyder & Sickmond, 2006).

Go to the *Assignments and Activities* section of Topic 3: *Schools and Society* in the MyEducationLab for your course and complete the activity titled *Tragedy at School.*

Crime is related more directly to poverty than to the age of the criminal. At all age levels, persons in poverty are more likely than persons with high incomes to commit crimes. They are also more likely to be the victims of violent crimes. One reason for the higher crime rate for burglary and auto theft among teens is that a larger proportion of teens than adults live in poverty. Teenagers from low-income families commit crimes at about the same rate as adults who live in poverty. However, you should remember that most low-income people do not commit crimes.

FIGURE 8.7

High School Students Involved in Violence-Related Behaviors

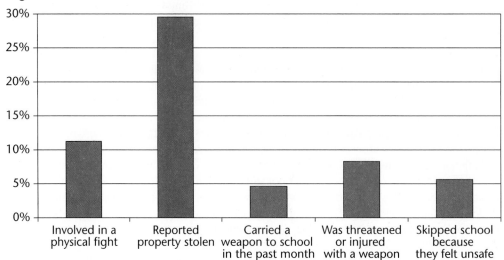

Source: Centers for Disease Control and Prevention, National Center for Injury Prevention and Control. (2008, Summer). *Youth violence: Facts at a glance.* Retrieved May 2, 2009, from http://www.cdc.gov/ViolencePrevention/pdf/YV-DataSheet-a.pdf.

Many schools are combating youth violence through conflict resolution and other programs that help students learn to respect others, stop harassment, and effectively handle interpersonal problems.

How is juvenile violence reflected in schools? One percent of all homicides in the country occur at school or as students travel to school or return home after school. Other crime does exist in schools as indicated in Figure 8.7. Two in five public schools report at least one violent incident during an academic year. Teachers are not immune from being the victims, especially of threats of bodily harm by students. Ten percent of the teachers in urban schools report receiving threats from students, compared with 6 percent in suburban schools and 5 percent in rural schools. Not all of the injuries in schools are physical. Students and teachers may suffer depression, stress, and fear because of the violence that they have witnessed or worrying that they may be the next victim (CDC, 2009b).

Some schools have initiated programs to reduce aggressive and violent behavior by students. These programs help students develop skills for conflict resolution or controlling their emotions. They may help students develop higher self-esteem and positive social skills. Other school programs assist families in improving their relations with and support of their children to reduce the chances of discipline problems arising in school. Mentoring programs that pair an adult with a student have also been helpful in redirecting the behavior and interests of students. Strategies that have been effective in controlling student aggression in classrooms include effective classroom management, cooperative learning, and reducing bullying (CDC, 2009b).

BULLYING. Another form of aggression in schools is bullying by bigger, stronger, or more aggressive students to establish dominance over their victims. For younger students, the bully may be the student who pushes them out of the cafeteria line. The bully may be the student who forces others to turn over their money or do his or her homework. The bully is usually the perpetrator of sexual harassment against female and LGBT students described in a previous section. Such behavior cannot be excused as just "boys being boys." Bullying takes the form of belittling weaker students, calling them names, and harassing or threatening them.

Sometimes the outcome of bullying is assault or murder. Bullies are 3.2 times more likely to carry weapons to school and be involved in fights in and out of school. In a survey of more than 15,000 sixth to tenth graders, nearly a third of the males and 6 percent of the females reported that they had been bullies, victims, or both in the previous thirty days. The small group of children who begin bullying classmates early in elementary school are rated by their teachers as more aggressive than their peers as they progress through school (Nansel, Overpeck, Haynie, Ruan, & Scheidt, 2003). These bullies tend to get into fights, vandalize property, skip school, and leave school early (CDC, 2008c). Psychologists report that victims of bullies experience anxiety, stress, and depression. Twenty percent of the students responsible for multiple shootings in schools were victims of bullying (CDC, 2008c).

A relatively new type of bullying occurs electronically via the Internet and cell phones. The attacks occur on social networking websites, in chat rooms, and in instant messages. The types of technology that make electronic bullying possible will probably grow as young people engage with new, easily accessible technologies. Nine to 35 percent of young people report that they have been victims of these attacks. Making rude or nasty comments is the most common electronic aggression, followed by rumor spreading and threatening or aggressive comments (Hertz & David-Ferdon, 2008). Just like regular bullying in schools, some of the young people are both the victim and the bully. However, the victim does not always know the aggressor as they would with bullying on the school grounds.

Educators cannot afford to ignore the bullying that occurs in schools. It can lead to serious future problems for the bullies and their victims (Hertz & David-Ferdon, 2008). Research shows that bullying can be prevented by working with students and parents. States and schools are developing safe school laws and policies that promote changing the behaviors of bullies. They include procedures for reporting and investigating incidences.

School should be a safe haven for children and youth. You can assist in the elimination of harassment, bullying, and other youth violence. Modeling appropriate behavior with students by avoiding sexual references, innuendos, and jokes is among the strategies recommended by the Sexual Harassment Task Force of the American Association of University Women (AAUW). Teachers should not be passive bystanders. Harassment and bullying that you witness directly or indirectly should be reported to the appropriate school official (AAUW, 2002). School districts are being sued by families when school authorities do not intervene to stop the harassment of their children.

GANGS. Gangs are attracting more students than ever. Approximately 785,000 active street gang members live in the United States (National Drug Intelligence Center, 2008). Gangs are found in all states and in most large cities; a growing number of smaller cities and rural areas are also becoming home to gangs. In 2005, gangs were reported in their schools by 24 percent of students (CDC, 2009c). City schools (13 percent) are more likely to report a gang crime in school than suburban, town, or rural schools (3 to 5 percent) (Neiman & DeVoe, 2009). Some female gangs exist, but most gangs are made up of young men. For youths of both sexes, gangs can provide a sense of place and a feeling of importance as well as a strong identity structure. Gangs often provide a discipline that has been missing from the experiences of many young people. School programs that were described earlier sometimes substitute for the need to become involved in gangs as children find a meaningful place for themselves in school.

SUICIDE. Suicide is another form of violence that affects the student population. Fifteen percent of high schoolers report seriously considering suicide in the previous year; almost 7 percent actually attempt it. Hispanic female high school students are more likely than their white peers to commit suicide. Suicide rates are higher for adolescents and young adults (fifteen to thirty-four years old) who are American Indian or Alaska Native than other groups of the same age. Adolescent and young adult males are more likely to commit suicide, but females are more likely to think about it and make nonlethal attempts (Neiman & DeVoe, 2009). Gay teens are at particular risk, being two to three times more likely to attempt suicide than their peers.

Suicide attempts are often calls for help. As a teacher, you should be alert for signs that may suggest the need for a referral to other professionals. Warning signs include changes in a person's mood, diet, or sleeping pattern (CDC, 2008d). Suicide attempts are often precipitated by interpersonal conflicts or severe stress. Being aware of these signs could help you know to alert a health professional or principal in your school. Providing support for gay students could also lead to a reduction in teen suicide rates.

CHALLENGES OF GROWING UP

Most U.S. teenagers are not the dangerous, drug-using, sexually promiscuous, nonproductive adolescents of the stereotypes in the media. Young people might not always agree with the adults with whom they interact, and sometimes they even break the rules, but most finish high school and attend postsecondary education. In many other respects, today's teens are more like their counterparts of past generations than different from them.

Nevertheless, young people face numerous challenges as they mature to adulthood. Increased pressures to grow up quickly, peer pressures, and the media provide conflicting messages that contribute to the difficulty of this period. Many students are able to draw on the support of friends, family, religion, and their own inner strength to resist being drawn into negative responses. Others find their own ways of countering circumstances over which they appear to have no control.

Teenagers are trying to figure out who they are and how they fit into the family, neighborhood, school, and larger world. They are searching for answers, but in their own ways. One of the challenges for parents, caretakers, educators, and youth workers is to encourage young people to make sound choices among the unlimited possibilities while avoiding excessive interference. You can provide the guidance they are seeking by listening to them if they decide to share their concerns and provide positive suggestions as they try to sort out their options. Believe it or not, many teenagers want adults to recognize them and help them through difficult periods and important decision-making points such as whether to go to college or participate in a project.

Adults usually regard teenagers as too young to deserve the benefits of adulthood. They expect teenagers to enjoy youth, begin dating, develop friendships, plan their future, and learn how to behave like responsible adults. Other adults see adolescents as teenage mothers, gang members, drug abusers, and troublemakers. Young people are bombarded by messages about themselves in music, movies, books, and television. Other potent influences are the circumstances in which teenagers live, which may include drugs, violence, and the lack of adult support. Young people must sort through all of these influences as well as the messages given by significant peers and adults in their lives.

Many teens, especially inner-city youths, report that the messages they receive about themselves in the media and schools are usually negative. They feel that adults and communities do not care about them. This feeling is validated by cuts in funding for the schools, parks, and community centers needed to assist youths in many communities. They have learned to feel that schools have rejected them and do not expect much of them.

Respect from adults is critical in helping youths to develop self-esteem. Teenagers don't always have appropriate adult support at home; their parents may be too tired or too busy or have too many problems themselves to care adequately for their children. For many teens, schools and neighborhood organizations are their primary sources of adult supervision and guidance. A caring adult can help teenagers develop their self-esteem by serving as a mentor, a gentle but firm critic, and a coach or advocate. Young people who believe in themselves and think they can be academically successful usually are. You can help your students develop positive self-esteem and see themselves as academically capable by giving them positive feedback and support as you push them to produce at high levels. In this section we examine some of the societal challenges that our children and youth face on the way to adulthood.

Sexuality and Pregnancy

The defining of our sexuality—our nature as sexual beings—begins in the early teens and continues throughout life. Coming to terms with our sexuality often involves turmoil both within ourselves and with parents and caretakers during the teen years. The development of a healthy sexual self is a complicated process.

Many teenagers associate sex with the freedom and sophistication of adulthood. The decision to have sex is one that causes much consternation among young people. Their uncertainty is fueled by the mixed messages they receive from parents, teenage friends, religious doctrines, the media, and older friends. At the same time that one medium glamorizes sex, other voices tell teenagers that sex is sinful and that abstinence before marriage is the only moral option.

Girls and women often connect sex with being accepted, being attractive, and being loved. Boys and men, by contrast, sometimes link sex with status, power, domination, and violence—a far cry from the loving relationship that many females have envisioned. Thus, ideal sexuality for men and women may differ.

Teenage sex is not as prevalent as some believe. The percentage of young people who have ever had sexual intercourse has decreased during the past two decades from more than 50 percent to 48 percent of high school students, with males being slightly more sexually active than females. Approximately one in three high schoolers was sexually active (that is, had had sex in the past three months), with the majority of them using contraceptives (CDC, 2008b).

One of the results of early sexual activity is teenage pregnancy. Although the number of teenage pregnancies and births has declined during the past decade, the number remains higher in the United States than in any other industrialized nation. Most (88 percent) pregnant teenage girls indicate that they had not planned or intended to become pregnant (Abma, Martinez, Mosher, & Dawson, 2004).

Poverty appears to be the most important factor in determining teenage mothers. It is a key risk factor for teen pregnancy, but its damaging impact can be buffered through strong social networks and supportive institutions (Abma et al., 2004). Most unmarried teenage mothers continue to live with their parents, but their families are disproportionately low income. Reducing family poverty may also reduce teenage pregnancy. Many teenage parents, especially mothers, are forced to take on adult responsibilities much earlier than society expects of its youth. Teenage mothers are sometimes forced to fend for themselves in impoverished conditions. Their own parents can provide little or no support, and the fathers of their children are often absent and either not contributing or unable to contribute financially.

More than 60 percent of teenage mothers are enrolled in school, have graduated, or have obtained a General Educational Development (GED) credential (Acs & Koball, 2003). Staying involved in school is important. Otherwise, statistics show, "eight to twelve years after birth, a child born to an unmarried, teenage, high school dropout is ten times as likely to be living in poverty as a child born to a mother with none of these three characteristics" (Annie E. Casey Foundation, 2003). Poverty also contributes to the births of babies with low birth weights, who are more likely than other children to experience health problems, developmental delays, abuse, neglect, and poor academic performance (Annie E. Casey Foundation, 2003).

Overall, teenagers are becoming more responsible about their sexual activity and are using contraception to reduce the risk of pregnancy and the transmission of AIDS and other sexually transmitted diseases. School programs such as sex education and health clinics are helpful, but they are not always supported by families and communities. However, the programs that have proven most effective are ones that convince teenagers that they should either practice abstinence or use contraceptives consistently and carefully (National Campaign to Prevent Teen and Unplanned Pregnancy, 2009). As many young people struggle with the development of their sexuality, they may seek guidance from teachers and other adults whom they respect. Teenagers' apprehensions and activities related to sex may affect their school behavior and their ability to perform satisfactorily in school.

Substance Abuse

Another perplexing question with which many teenagers struggle is whether to experiment with cigarettes, alcohol, or drugs. Although not as glamorized in films and advertisements as in the past, drinking and smoking are still associated with independence and adult behavior. Teens use drugs for different reasons. Sometimes biological predispositions or psychological problems trigger drug use. In other cases, social pressures, family problems, or self-hate lead young people to test drugs.

The public worries about drugs in schools. In the 2008 Phi Delta Kappa/Gallup Poll of the public's attitudes toward public schools, respondents ranked drugs as the fifth greatest problem that public schools face behind funding, discipline, overcrowding, and fighting (Bushaw & Gallup, 2008). Parents worry about drug use interfering with their child's ability to function effectively. Drug use may lead to cutting school, hanging out with the wrong crowd, being arrested, and **chemical dependency** that may require professional treatment to break.

A large percentage of teenagers do try one or more drugs, but alcohol is their favorite, being used more than twice as often as other drugs. Nearly half (47 percent) of our high school seniors have tried an illicit drug at some time, but most are not regular users. Younger students are experimenting with drugs, but the rate of illicit drug use by eighth graders has been declining since its peak in 1996. One in fifteen eighth graders is already smoking cigarettes. Although the rate of usage is higher than the public may find acceptable, current usage by all teenagers is at the lowest

chemical dependency The habitual use, for either psychological or physical needs, of a substance such as drugs, alcohol, or tobacco.

FIGURE 8.8

Students in Grades 8, 10, and 12 Using Selected Substances in the Past Month

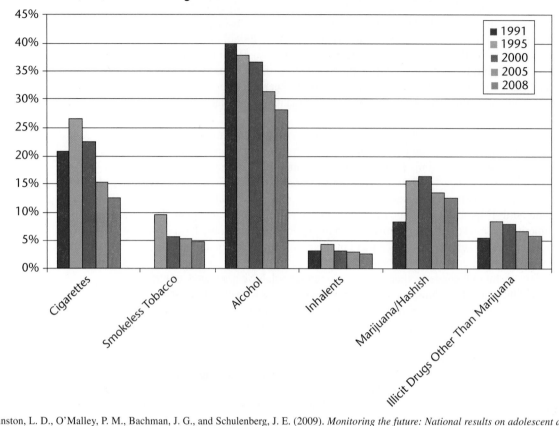

Sources: Johnston, L. D., O'Malley, P. M., Bachman, J. G., and Schulenberg, J. E. (2009). *Monitoring the future: National results on adolescent drug use: Overview of key findings, 2008* (NIH Publication No. 09-7401). Bethesda, MD: National Institute on Drug Abuse.

level in thirty-three years as shown in Figure 8.8. The bad news is the high rates of nonmedical use of prescription painkillers such as Vicodin and OxyContin as well as sedatives and barbiturates (Johnston, O'Malley, Bachman, & Schulenberg, 2006).

Drug use varies by group membership. Students who plan to attend college are less likely to use drugs. Male teenagers are more likely than females to use illicit drugs (National Center for Health Statistics, 2002). Differences in the overall use of illicit drugs in urban, suburban, and rural areas are small. They are also small across socioeconomic groups. White students are more likely to use licit and illicit drugs than Hispanic and African American students.

Economic Realities

Young people may be worried and somewhat pessimistic about their future economic conditions. However, they continue to seek out postsecondary education to improve their job and career opportunities. Sixty-six percent of high school graduates go to college immediately after high school although African American (56 percent) and Hispanic (58 percent) students enroll immediately after high school at lower rates than whites (69 percent). Fifty-one percent of low-income students go to college as compared to 81 percent of high-income students (Planty et al., 2008). Females make up 58 percent of the students enrolled in college (U.S. Census Bureau, 2008, Table 268).

Many young people begin to work while they are in high school. Students from middle- and high-income families whose parents are more likely to have finished college are more likely to work as teenagers. Nearly half of white teens work as compared to one-fourth of African American and Hispanic teens. More than 40 percent of sixteen- and seventeen-year-olds have jobs, with males more likely to work than females. There is evidence of a strong positive link between working in high school and obtaining a job after graduation. However, teens working more than twenty hours a week are more likely to have been suspended and neglect homework than their peers. At the same time, they are less likely to skip school or have serious behavioral or emotional problems (Lerman, 2000).

Many high school students work after school and in the summer.

After-school jobs are particularly beneficial to students from low-income families who do not have family or school connections to help them find employment. Unfortunately, many students who could derive long-term benefits from working while in high school—those in inner-city areas—have limited access to jobs. The lack of employment opportunities contributes to low self-esteem and to pessimism about the future and the value of school. In addition, in communities experiencing high unemployment, many young people do not have opportunities to learn how to work either through their own experiences or through the modeling of working adults.

JOURNAL FOR REFLECTION

Thinking back on your childhood and youth, which of the challenges discussed in this section did you face? How were you able to manage the challenge in positive ways? How did your family or educators provide support to you during this period?

PREJUDICE AND DISCRIMINATION

A democratic society is built on the principles of social equality and respect for individuals within society. However, many persons of color, limited English speakers, women, persons with disabilities, gays and lesbians, people with low incomes, and people affiliated with religions other than Christianity do not experience the equality to which most other members of society are entitled.

Power relationships among groups influence young people's perceptions of themselves and the members of other groups. Schools are one example of institutions in which power relationships exist. Students' work and class rules are determined by teachers. Teachers are evaluated and disciplined when necessary by principals who report to a superintendent of schools. The rules and procedures for managing schools traditionally have been established by authorities who are not directly involved with the school and who may not even live in the community served by the school. Parents, especially in economically disadvantaged areas, often feel powerless in the education of their children.

Power allows access to societal benefits such as good housing, tax deductions, the best schools, and social services. A more equitable sharing of resources for schools would guarantee that all students, regardless of family income or ethnic background, would have qualified teachers, sufficient books and other instructional resources, well-maintained buildings and playgrounds, and access to high-level academic knowledge. Unfortunately, such equality does not exist in all of our schools.

Prejudice

One of the struggles of youth is the construction of self, including identification and affiliation with one's gender and a racial or ethnic group. This process appears to be integrally tied to identifying "otherness," which involves assigning characteristics and behaviors to members of other groups to distinguish oneself from them. The construction of "others" places us either in a dominating or submissive role relative to others. Some young men identify themselves in relation to young women. They exert their masculinity as power over their female counterparts in academics, sports, and sometimes relationships. Believing that they are the ones who should wield power over others, white males in some communities build their identity in opposition to males of color.

Our perceptions of others not only affect how we see ourselves in relationship to them, but also influence how society treats members of different groups. **Prejudice** is a preconceived negative attitude toward members of specific ethnic, racial, religious, or socioeconomic groups. This prejudice sometimes extends to people with disabilities or people of a different sexual orientation or gender. Such negative attitudes are based on numerous factors, including information about members of a specific group that is stereotypical and many times not true. Prejudiced individuals may have had little or no direct social contact with members of other groups, which would present them with experiences that counteract such stereotypes.

An individual's prejudice may have a limited negative impact on members of the other group. However, these attitudes are often passed on to children through the **socialization** process. Also, prejudiced attitudes can be transformed into discriminatory behavior that prevents members of a group from being interviewed for jobs, joining social clubs, or being treated like other professionals. Prejudices are often reinforced by schools in which a disproportionate number of students in low-achieving or special education tracks are males, English-language learners, students of color, or students from low-income families. Observing that these students are not enrolled in academically challenging courses, some students form stereotypes of their low-income and foreign-born peers as academically inferior. Through this process, many students from low-income families and ethnic minority groups are prevented from gaining the skills and knowledge necessary to enter college or an apprentice trade.

You can take a number of steps to keep your prejudices from hurting students. A first step is to be conscious of your interactions with students in the classroom and hallways. If you are interacting with some students differently, analyze why. The differences may be appropriate, but you want to make sure you are not giving some students more attention and advantages than others. Also, consider asking a colleague to periodically observe your interactions with students and parents to provide a more objective review of your treatment of students from diverse groups. If you find that a group of students is not learning at the same level or is always having discipline problems, you should examine your own behaviors in the classroom to make adjustments for equality across groups.

Discrimination

Many of your students or their family members have experienced **discrimination** through practices that excluded them from equal access to housing, jobs, and educational opportunities. Discrimination is different than prejudice in that it is more than an attitude against the member of a specific group. It is a process that prevents members of a specific group from participating equally in society. Most students of color, females, low-income students, students with disabilities, and gay students have already experienced discrimination in some aspect of their lives. For example, discriminatory practices lead to African Americans receiving more severe sentences in the judicial system than members of some other groups. They lead to women not being paid at the same rate as men for the same type of work. Individuals and groups that have been discriminated against may have not acknowledged it, or they may be angry or frustrated by it.

If we do not experience discrimination in our everyday experiences, we may have a difficult time acknowledging that it exists. For example, many white students do not see themselves as advantaged or privileged in society. They do not think they receive any more benefits from society than anyone else. These students may have a difficult time fighting social injustices because they have neither experienced them nor become aware of their existence. As a result, rights based on group membership versus those of individuals are debated on college campuses, in board meetings of corporations, by politicians, and in many formal and informal neighborhood meetings. These discussions focus on programs that are perceived to favor one group over another, such as affirmative action, bilingual education, or equal funding for male and female athletes.

prejudice A preconceived negative attitude toward the members of a group.

socialization The process of learning the social norms of one's culture.

discrimination The process that prevents members of a specific group from participating equally in society. These include legislation, policies, and practices that treat persons differently in the judicial, educational, and social systems based on their group memberships.

Laws and systems that promote and support members of one group maintain the superiority and power of its members. "English only" laws that prevent official documents and communications from being printed or spoken in any language other than English represent one example of these efforts. Such practices have become so ingrained in state and federal laws, the judicial system, schools, and other societal institutions that it is difficult to recognize them unless one is directly affected by the discriminatory policies.

Legal issues on discrimination are discussed in Chapter 10.

Racism

An assumption of superiority is at the center of **racism**. It is not a topic easily discussed in most classrooms. It is intertwined with the lived experiences of many people and evokes emotions of anger, guilt, shame, and despair. Most students have learned that the United States is a just and democratic society. They find it difficult to confront the societal contradictions that support racism. Educators must acknowledge how racism has benefited some groups because it gave them advantages over others for receiving an interview for a job or access to a home in some neighborhoods. One project that is helping young people understand the importance of combating racism is described in the Global Perspectives feature below.

GLOBAL PERSPECTIVES — Coming to Justice

In 1957 the Anne Frank House was established as a museum in Amsterdam in memory of Anne Frank and members of her family who were victims of the Holocaust during World War II. The Anne Frank House is now also a nonprofit organization with the goal of combating racism in all of its forms around the globe. One of its guiding principles is the Universal Declaration of Human Rights, which is available on the Internet at www.unhchr.ch/udhr.

One of the Anne Frank House's projects is a four-day program for older teenagers to introduce them to justice and injustice in an international context. The program, *Coming to Justice,* "is confrontational, challenging youth to think critically about their own views and assumptions, dispelling many myths regarding international conflicts and justice along the way."[1] During the first day of the program, students reflect on definitions of justice and injustice and are introduced to the experiences of Anne Frank and her family. Attention changes on the second day to the early 1990s conflict in the Balkans. On the third day students attend a trial at the International War Crimes Tribunal in The Hague, The

Netherlands. On the final day students meet with people who have been eyewitnesses to these conflicts with a focus on justice and appropriate remedies for injustice. Participants report that they learn in this international context how complex the concepts of justice and injustice are as they relate them to their own local situations.

Questions for Reflection

1. What is the Universal Declaration of Human Rights and why is it important in fighting racism and discrimination around the world?
2. What does the Anne Frank House Project *Coming to Justice* have to do with racism?
3. What are the complexities of justice and injustice that students may confront during their experience at The Hague?

[1]van Driel, B. (2005, May). *Coming to Justice*: A program for youth around issues of international justice, *Intercultural Education, 16*(2), 161–169.

Families with a history of discrimination in society and schools may worry about how their children will be treated at school. They may distrust educators who are unable to acknowledge the role that racism has played in their lives. They may be very confrontational in their approaches to teachers or they may be very guarded and afraid to question a teacher. They may accuse teachers of being racist. These parents are standing up for their children and doing all they can to ensure that their children are treated equitably and have the same opportunities to be academically successful as other students. However, the behavior of these parents is usually incongruent with the school's view of positive and supportive parents. Teachers and school officials should avoid reinforcing the parents' perception of the school as racist and not caring about the success of their children. You will need to monitor your own interactions with students and families of color to ensure that you acknowledge and confront school policies and practices that appear racist. When parents believe that you care about their children and their academic and social achievement, you are beginning to develop a partnership with the students at the center.

racism The conscious or unconscious belief that racial differences make one group superior to others.

Students and adults go through stages of racial identity as they address issues of discrimination and their own racial identification. Teachers should recognize that students will be moving back and forth across the stages outlined in Table 8.1 in their struggle to know themselves. One of the first steps in this process is to begin to confront one's own racial identity. How close is one to an internalization or autonomy stage? If educators have not struggled with issues of racism, how it affects their lives, and how they may contribute to its perpetuation or elimination, it will be impossible for them to develop antiracist classrooms.

━ JOURNAL FOR REFLECTION ━

How have you personally experienced racism? What racism have you observed in your community? How could you become involved in combating racism, especially in the classroom?

Table 8.1 • Development of Racial Identity

Black Racial Identity	White Racial Identity	Latino Identity
Preencounter: African American individuals have assimilated into the mainstream culture, accepting many of the beliefs and values of the dominant society, including negative stereotypes about blacks.	*Contact:* White individuals are not aware of themselves as racial beings and are oblivious to acts of individual racism. They have a color-blind view of race and racism.	*White:* They identify themselves as white, not acknowledging their Latino culture.
Encounter: African Americans usually enter this stage when they are confronted directly by a racist act such as rejection by white peers or racial slurs or attacks. They are then forced to confront their own racial identity.	*Disintegration:* Whites usually enter this stage as a result of some experiences with race that lead to the recognition that race does matter, that racism exists, and that they are white. They may show empathy when blacks experience racial discrimination but often fail to understand their anger.	*Undifferentiated:* They accept the norms of the dominant culture without question.
Immersion–Emersion: One's identification as an African American becomes paramount. At first this identification is manifested in anger against whites, but it evolves into a growing knowledge base about African American history and culture. The result of this exploration is an emerging security in a newly defined and affirmed sense of self.	*Reintegration:* Individuals believe consciously or unconsciously that whites are superior to people of color.	*Person of color:* They identify themselves as persons of color, but lack knowledge about their Latino culture.
	Pseudoindependence: One begins the intellectual process of learning about and fighting against racism. One begins to understand that whites have responsibility for maintaining or eliminating racism.	*Latino ethnic group:* They see themselves as members of one of many groups in the United States. They also can identify both the negative and positive aspects of their group.
Internalization: Individuals begin to build coalitions with members of other nonwhite or nondominant groups and to develop relationships with whites who respect and acknowledge them.	*Immersion–Emersion:* Individuals begin to grasp the need to challenge racism. They often experience feelings of guilt and shame for the racist ideas that they believed in the past.	*Latino:* They place their Latino culture, history, and traditions at the center of their lives.
Internalization–Commitment: Individuals are able both to maintain and to move beyond their personal racial identity—to be concerned with African Americans as a group.	*Autonomy:* White individuals have abandoned cultural, institutional, and personal racism. They have a more flexible view of the world, their own whiteness, and other racial groups. They value and seek out cross-racial/cultural experiences.	*Latino-integrated:* They begin to identify themselves not just as Latino, but by their specific ethnic group (e.g., Mexican American).

Sources: "Black Racial Identity" column is based on the five stages of black racial identity developed by W. E. Cross, Jr. and described in Beverly Daniel Tatum, "Talking about Race, Learning about Racism: The Application of Racial Identity Development Theory in the Classroom," *Harvard Educational Review, 62*(1) (1992), pp. 1–24. The "White Racial Identity" column is based on the six stages of white racial identity developed by J. F. Helms and described in Robert T. Carter, "Is White a Race? Expressions of White Racial Identity," in Michelle Fine, Lois Weis, Linda C. Powell, and L. Mun Wong, Eds., *Off White: Readings on Race, Power, and Society,* New York: Routledge, 1997. The "Latino Identity" column is based on B. M. Ferdman and P. I. Gallegos, "Racial identity development and Latinos in the United States," in C. L. Wijeyesinghe and B. W. Jackson, III, Eds., *New Perspectives on Racial Identity Development: A Theoretical and Practical Anthology* (pp. 32–66). New York: New York University Press, 2001.

Sexism and Other "Isms"

Women of all racial and ethnic groups, people with disabilities, gays, lesbians, persons with low incomes, the elderly, and the young suffer from discrimination and their lack of power in society. Many individuals are members of more than one of these groups. For example, a low-income Latina may be triply harmed as a result of racism, classism, and **sexism**—the cultural attitudes and practices that devalue women.

Some persons with disabilities and their advocates argue that **ableism** greatly disadvantages people with disabilities and their ability to live a full and productive life. Ableism not only leads to viewing persons with disabilities as inferior to others but also results in treatments and accommodations designed to help them become more like persons without disabilities. These efforts are not necessarily in the best interests of individuals with disabilities. For example, activists with a hearing disability may reject the view that they should become hearing through surgery and other aids. Being deaf is their normality, even though it does not seem normal to those who hear. In other instances, teachers and aides without disabilities sometimes provide assistance or do things for persons with disabilities rather than encouraging them to learn for themselves. For educators, the strategy of overhelpfulness may be easier and less time consuming. Allowing individuals with disabilities to make the effort themselves may require a great deal of patience, but the long-term payoff for the student could be self-sufficiency.

ENGAGEMENT IN SCHOOL

Another challenge faced by some teenagers is becoming engaged in the academic work at school. Some do not see the value of finishing their education. When students in grades 5 through 12 were asked how they were feeling about school, half of them said that they were engaged, but one in five were "actively disengaged." One in three students were struggling in schools (Poll adds "youth voice" on school, 2009). Others do not see themselves as academically able students and find no reason to participate actively in their own learning.

Sometimes they are not meeting the minimal standards as determined by standardized tests, resulting in grade retention, which will prevent them from graduating with peers of the same age. They believe they can learn the lessons for survival more effectively outside school. As a result, they drop out of high school and college for different reasons, without realizing the harm it is likely to cause them in the long term. The issue of retention or social promotion is debated from two perspectives in this chapter's Teacher Perspectives.

Leaving School Early

According to federal reports, 79 percent of eighteen- to twenty-one-year-olds had completed high school in 2006, the most recent year for which figures are available. However, by age twenty-five, 86 percent of the population had completed high school (U.S. Census Bureau, 2008, Table 264). When we examine the data on how many students receive a regular standards-based diploma on time with the class with which they began high school, we find a different picture of high school graduation. The Editorial Projects in Education Research Center reports that only seven in ten students who enter ninth grade graduate with a regular diploma at the end of the twelfth grade. The problem is particularly critical in large, urban, segregated schools. American Indians, African Americans, and Hispanics have only about a fifty–fifty chance of completing high school (Swanson, 2009), placing them at great risk of not earning sustainable wages or being employed as adults. School districts with low graduation rates are more often in central cities with disproportionally high numbers of low-income and immigrant families as shown in Figure 8.9.

Graduation rates vary across gender, ethnic, and racial groups, as shown in Figure 8.10. American Indian students have the lowest graduation rate. Hispanic students also have less than a 60 percent graduation rate. The largest proportion of Hispanic dropouts were born outside the United States. They may have not attended U.S. schools nor have completed more than elementary school in their countries of birth. Although first- and later generation Hispanics graduate at higher rates than immigrants, they are still almost twice as likely to drop out of school than their white peers (National Center for Education Statistics, 2005).

sexism The conscious or unconscious belief that men are superior to women and subsequent behavior and action that maintain the superior, powerful position of males.

ableism The conscious or unconscious belief that persons with disabilities are inferior to persons without disabilities.

Is Retention Better Than Social Promotion for Students?

Today's emphasis on academic achievement may lead to students not meeting state standards as measured by standardized tests. As a result, they may not be able to graduate on time or even be pushed out of school because they fail the required tests, lowering the pass rates for a school district. What are the appropriate strategies for ensuring that students meet standards? These two educators debate the effectiveness of retention as an effective approach to help students learn at an acceptable level before being promoted to the next grade.

YES

John Mohl teaches German and social studies at Cedarbrook Middle School in Wyncote, Pennsylvania.

When I first called on "Brendan," a recent transfer to the district, to read, he refused. His homework was copied from a friend if done at all and he failed to comprehend a passage after fumbling over words when I finally got him to read aloud. Despite his third-grade reading level, Brendan was allowed into eighth grade. He was a product of social promotion.

Social promotion has three detrimental effects on the educational system. It taxes both teachers and students. Promoting a student into a higher level of English when he lacks basic reading skills, as was the case with Brendan, places undue burden on future teachers and students. Socially promoted students monopolize teacher attention, and other students' learning opportunities are limited as a result.

Second, it sends a message to students that they can move on to the next level even if they lack the required knowledge or effort. I once taught a summer school class with two particularly unruly students who were unfazed by the threat of being held back for failing. They knew they'd be eighth graders regardless of their performance. They were right, and became burdens to their new teachers (that oversight, fortunately, was later rectified).

Social promotion also distances schools from their goals of fulfilling the No Child Left Behind standards. How can anybody expect a student with elementary math skills to perform proficiently on an eighth-grade standardized math exam?

Some argue that social promotion maintains the self-esteem of low-achieving students. I agree that humanism should be an important component in our teaching. But the "real world" has neither time nor regard for making sure every person feels worthwhile. Teachers have the responsibility to introduce, to some degree, the benefits of making the mark and the consequences of not doing so. Truth be told, I'd rather see Brendan held back in eighth than held back in life.

NO

Jennifer Slifer teaches sixth-grade language arts at Thomas Edison Magnet Middle School in Meriden, Connecticut.

Each year, we all have a "Brendan" or two and we are frustrated and angry that he advances with such evident skill deficiencies. But would Brendan be helped by retention, the traditional solution for struggling students?

Social promotion by itself is not a good practice. Retention does not, however, solve the problems of low-achieving students. Research shows that retained students do not improve their academic performance compared with similar counterparts who were promoted, and retained students struggle with self-esteem.

Social promotion isn't the answer if it means we send students on to the next grade ill prepared for the workload. "Brendan" is failing, but so are we as educators if we don't provide the help he needs to keep up with his peers. So let's provide that help.

Is it time to review our centuries-old system of grouping students by age? Perhaps all students should be placed in multi-age classrooms. This arrangement would assist students who struggle to learn as quickly as their peers of the same age and would eliminate self-esteem issues caused by retention.

Another approach: Instead of retaining a student, why don't we promote struggling students with an individualized education plan (as we do for our special education students) to help them catch up to their peers? Most struggling students who are promoted do not meet the requirements for special education but they do need assistance that, unfortunately, we are not mandated to provide.

Maybe it's time to get serious about early intervention and provide funding for programs for struggling students *before* they reach middle and high school.

Our choices should not be just promoting students versus retaining them.

Passing struggling students to the next grade is a failure of the system if we don't have a plan to help them catch up. But retention isn't the answer, either.

Source: "Is Retention Better Than Social Promotion for Students?" (2005, March). *NEA Today*, p. 48. Reprinted by permission of the National Education Association.

myeducationlab To explore both sides of this issue and think about each perspective, go to the *Book Specific Resources* in the MyEducationLab for your course, select your text, and then select *Teacher Perspectives* for Chapter 8.

FIGURE 8.9

Graduation Rates by the Population of Schools

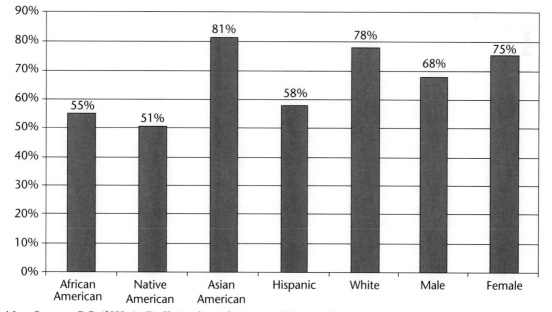

Source: Orfield, G., Losen, D., Wald, J. and Swanson, C. B. (2004). *Losing our future: How minority youth are being left behind by the graduation rate crisis.* Cambridge, MA: The Civil Rights Project at Harvard University with Contributions from Urban Institute, Advocates for Children of New York, and The Civil Society Institute.

FIGURE 8.10

High School Graduation Rates by Sex and Racial or Ethnic Group

Source: Adapted from Swanson, C. B. (2009, April). *Closing the graduation gap: Educational and economic conditions in America's largest cities.* Bethesda, MD: Editorial Projects in Education.

Students from low-income families drop out of high school at a rate six times greater than that of students from middle- and high-income families (Planty et al., 2008, Indicator 22). A greater percentage of females finish high school than males, leading to concerns about fewer young men attending and completing college. Only 57 percent of students with disabilities complete high school (U.S. Census Bureau 2008, Table 752). As one might expect, students who complete high school are more likely than dropouts to be employed. By age twenty-five, 63 percent of high school graduates without a college degree are in the labor force as compared to 47 percent of the population who did not complete high school. More education does make a difference; 78 percent of college graduates are working (U.S. Census Bureau, 2008, Table 580).

The ninth grade is a critical period in which students decide to leave school (Swanson, 2009). Middle school and the beginning of high school are key times in which we need to be engaging students in their education. The emphasis on the reform of high schools is to change these statistics by identifying effective ways of involving students in their education. While we maintain high expectations for student achievement, we must make the curriculum relevant to the real lives of students. They need to be engaged with the subject they are studying, not by listening to a lecture, but by being involved with each other in projects and problem solving to develop a deeper understanding. Urban high schools are particularly ineffective in engaging their students in learning, as shown in the Reflect on Diversity feature.

Resiliency

Many young people have the **resiliency** to overcome disastrous childhood and adolescent experiences and go on to become successful workers, professionals, and community leaders. The challenges discussed earlier in this chapter along with growing up in poverty can place children and youth at risk for developmental delays, behavior problems, and poor academic performance. The students who are most at risk live in dangerous environments that lead to health risks and threats to their safety. They may be attending schools in which students are not expected to perform at high levels and are not being pushed to do so. Their own parents may be so busy coping with several jobs and their own problems that they cannot support their children (Love, Eisman, & Popkin, 2005).

With all of these problems, some students are still able to perform well, even at high levels, in school. Their personal attributes give them strength and fortitude and help them confront overwhelming obstacles that seem designed to prevent them from reaching their potential. Children who are resilient are able to cope effectively with stress. They believe in their own **self-efficacy**, can handle change, and have good social skills.

PEARSON
myeducationlab

Go to the *Building Teaching Skills and Dispositions* section of Topic 3: *Schools and Society* in the MyEducationLab for your course and complete the activity titled *Keeping Students in School.*

resiliency The ability to overcome overwhelming obstacles to achieve and be successful in school and life.

self-efficacy The belief that one can control one's life.

REFLECT on DIVERSITY   Why Bother?

Carlos's mother just received another call from Roosevelt High School. Carlos was not in school again today. She called his cell phone, asking where he was. "In school," he responded.

"I know better Carlos. The school just called, and you have not been there for the past three days. If you miss another day, you won't be able to graduate. What is wrong with you? Get yourself back to school now."

Carlos turned back to his friends. "It was just my mom. The damn truant officer called her again. What's she want from me? I don't learn anything there anyway. I'm gonna get a job."

Carlos actually has been at school most of the past three days. He just can't find a reason to go to class. He's failing anyway, and it is much more interesting to hang with his friends in the halls. At least they talk about what is real.

Even Carlos wonders what has happened to him. He used to go to his classes. Before he got to high school, he earned As and Bs and liked school. For some reason, he no longer has any interest in doing the homework. And when he goes to class, he is usually late.

His teachers are also stumped as well. Carlos does not usually cause trouble. He is a joker and spends most of his time talking to other students rather than engaging with the content. He has had both his iPod and cell phone removed several times during class. The school counselor says that his mother is a good parent and has been pushing him to go to college. She knows that he has the ability to make it, but is at a loss about how to keep him in school.

Questions for Reflection
1. What are some of the reasons that Carlos has given up on school?
2. If you were one of his teachers, what would you do to try to engage him in your class?
3. The Obama administration is telling school administrators that high school graduation rates must improve. What responsibility does a school have to ensure that all students both learn at high levels and graduate from high school?

PEARSON
myeducationlab To respond to these questions online, go to the *Book Specific Resources* section in the MyEducationLab for your course, select your text, and then select *Reflect on Diversity* for chapter 8.

Higher family SES contributes positively to resiliency, but is not required. Other positive factors are family members who are involved with their children, provide caring environments, help their children with homework, attend to grades, and participate in school activities. Resilient students have positive relationships with teachers and have less exposure to violence or trauma. They are also helped by quality educational and recreational opportunities in school and their neighborhoods (Love et al., 2005). Regardless of the challenges they face, they are usually social, optimistic, energetic, cooperative, inquisitive, attentive, helpful, punctual, and on task.

EQUALITY OF ACCESS

Access to a high-quality education is one of the keys to improving the academic success of all students. A part of this formula is the belief that all students can learn, including those who seem to have so many environmental and social factors working against them as described earlier in this chapter. The use of technology for learning could assist us in bridging the learning gaps that now exist between groups of students. We explore some of these issues in this section.

Access to Technology

Although the number of Internet users is growing exponentially each year, most of the world's population do not have access to computers or the Internet. People in developing nations also have limited access to what most of us would consider a basic communications necessity—the telephone. In fact, the disparity across nations in telephone, cell phone, and computer access is quite great as shown in Figure 8.11. In many parts of the world, cell phones are becoming the cheaper and faster way to expand communication systems. The move to wireless connections may eliminate the need for telephone lines, but it does not remove the barrier of equipment costs.

Two in three U.S. students are using personal computers at home and 43 percent of them are connecting to the Internet. Who has these technologies depends on a number of factors. Just over half of the students in families with annual incomes of less than $20,000 are using a computer at home. Nine in ten students in families with incomes greater than $75,000 are using a computer at home. Similar disparities exist in terms of race: 80 percent of white, non-Hispanic students use a computer at home compared to 49 percent of African American and 48 percent of Hispanic students. Students are using computers at home primarily to play games, but nearly half of them use computers to complete school assignments and to connect to the Internet (U.S. Census Bureau, 2008, Table 253).

FIGURE 8.11

Telephones and Computers by Country

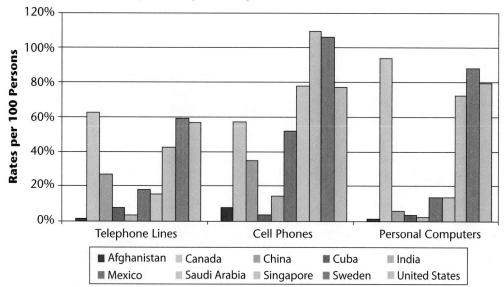

Source: U.S. Census Bureau. (2008). *Statistical abstract of the United States: 2009* (128th ed., Table 1345). Washington, DC: U.S. Government Printing Office.

FIGURE 8.12

Participation in Professional Computer and Mathematical Occupations

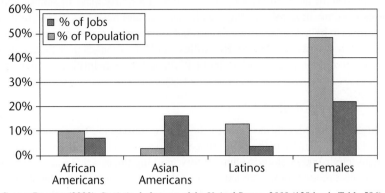

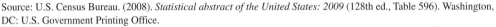

Source: U.S. Census Bureau. (2008). *Statistical abstract of the United States: 2009* (128th ed., Table 596). Washington, DC: U.S. Government Printing Office.

Another problem that exacerbates economic disparities is that African Americans, Hispanics, and women hold few of the jobs in information technology as shown in Figure 8.12. Women receive only 21 percent of the bachelor's degrees in computer and information science—a figure that has been declining during the past two decades (Planty et al., 2008, Indicator 27). The result is that women and members of the most oppressed ethnic groups are not eligible for these jobs, which offer among the highest salaries at graduation.

Do similar disparities exist in schools? Almost all schools in the country have Internet access. However, the number of classrooms with Internet connections differs by the income level of students. Using the percentage of students who are eligible for free or reduced-price lunches at a school to determine income level, we find that 95 percent of the schools with more affluent students have wired classrooms compared to 90 percent of the schools with the highest concentrations of low-income students (U.S. Census Bureau, 2008, Table 244). Figure 8.13 shows a similar disparity in the number of students per computer in schools with student populations who are students of color or from high-poverty areas. Thus, the students who are most likely to have access at home also are more likely to have access in their schools.

Classroom computers may have graphics capabilities that allow students to design interesting presentations with audio and video clips. Math teachers have graphic calculators. Students can edit their own videotapes to produce a movie instead of a traditional written paper for a class project. School districts may offer professional development courses on the use of handheld de-

FIGURE 8.13

Student Access to Computers at School

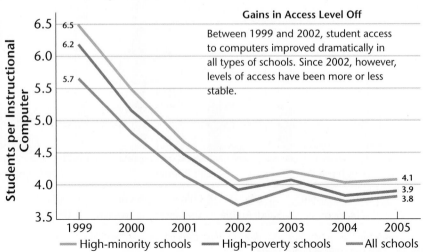

vices and podcasting for instruction. Teachers are being encouraged to communicate with parents and guardians via e-mail and postings on the school's website. Students are excited about having the opportunity to work on the computers. They like the interactivity of many of the software packages. The challenge for teachers is to figure out how best to use the technology for learning, not just for entertainment and fun.

One of the values of the Internet is to search for information about almost any subject. Search engines identify resources from many different sources and multiple perspectives. One of the skills that students should develop is how to sort through multiple sources for the information they need and how to test its accuracy. Students could use the Internet to explore topics and concepts being presented in a unit. Class time can be spent for such research activities, but it may be difficult for all students to spend the time needed, especially if a classroom has a limited number of computers. Thus, a teacher may be tempted to assign homework that requires using the Internet. A problem with assigning homework on the Internet, however, is that not all students have computers at home. Even if an assignment does not require the use of the Internet, those students who have access to it at home have an advantage in completing school projects.

LOOKING AHEAD:
GREATER ACCESS TO QUALITY EDUCATION

The past decade has seen tremendous change in terms of the technologies available to classroom teachers and students. However, the changes we have seen thus far are minimal compared to what lies ahead. Once every child has his or her own computer or cell phone, the context changes dramatically.

Today's teachers are exploring how to use new technologies in innovative ways to engage students, improve learning, and expand creativity. At the time of this writing, the use of social networking was being tested to communicate more effectively with students. It is a tricky undertaking to determine the appropriate educational uses. Some teachers have placed themselves in compromising positions by posting inappropriate pictures and writings, leading to the loss of their jobs. Other teachers are testing the use of virtual worlds such as Second Life to develop interesting learning activities. For example, in an online conference for educators and museum professionals, participants were able to virtually visit ancient Babylon, New York's Harlem in the 1920s, the White House during Lincoln's tenure, and England at the time of Henry VIII. The section on websites at the end of this chapter provides sources that you might want to explore for more innovations on using the online world in your classroom.

Go to the *Building Teaching Skills and Dispositions* section of Topic 13: *Technology in the Schools* in the MyEducationLab for your course and complete the activity titled *Distance Education*.

Some school districts are providing laptops to teachers as well as students to encourage the use of technology in their work.

Computers and the Internet can also help you better manage the administrative tasks that can detract from instruction time. Attendance records, seating charts, and parent contact information all become much easier to access as web-based information systems mature into robust tools. More importantly, teachers will be able to monitor student learning related to standards, compare performance to other students in the school district or state, and access lesson plans for addressing areas in which students are having problems. When teachers are able to commit more time to planning they are better able to develop learning activities that are more engaging and effective.

Teachers remain the critical component to providing students access to a quality education. The problem has been that many schools with the largest number of students from low-income families have been staffed by too many teachers who were not adequately prepared for their work. Many of the teachers of mathematics and science did not major in those subjects in college. Teachers in these schools were less likely to be licensed in the subjects or grade levels they were assigned. Absentee rates for teachers in these schools was much higher than schools in other communities, leading to students being taught by substitute teachers day after day. Support systems and mentoring for new teachers, who were usually the least experienced teachers in the school district, were limited. Changes to this bleak picture are underway.

No Child Left Behind required that all teachers in Title I schools be highly qualified and that teacher assistants have associate degrees. Major school districts such as New York City and Chicago have increased their expectations for teachers. Not only are they required to be highly qualified for their assignments, they are expected to show evidence that they can help their students learn. Student achievement in many of their schools is beginning to improve. Good mentoring programs are contributing to this success. Every student deserves good teachers who are competent and caring. The Obama administration appears to be willing to financially support efforts to reform schools by hiring and retaining the teachers that students need.

SUMMARY

TODAY'S FAMILIES

- Students in schools today come from diverse family structures. Although a majority of children live with their mother and father, many live with single parents, grandparents, adoptive parents, foster parents, gay or lesbian parents, or relatives.
- Students from low-income families face food insecurity and sometimes find themselves homeless when their families can no longer pay their rent or mortgage with the wages they earn.
- Achievement is helped when educators and families work together to support the academic and social growth of children.

DANGERS CHILDREN FACE

- One in one hundred children is abused by a family member or caretaker, with children under age five being the most vulnerable.
- Four in five students report being sexually harassed at some time during their school career with female and LGBT students most often being the victims of the attacks.
- Violence in the school setting is often the result of bullying in the hallways or school grounds, but it also includes electronic bullying through the Internet and cell phones.

CHALLENGES OF GROWING UP

- Adolescents struggle with economic and social realities that can affect their lives in negative ways when they make inappropriate decisions related to sexuality and the use of drugs and alcohol.
- As young people worry about what today's economic realities mean for their future, the majority are making positive decisions about postsecondary education.

PREJUDICE AND DISCRIMINATION

- Being white, high income, and English speaking provides benefits over people who are not white or speak a language other than English.
- The prejudice that young people learn at home and in school can lead to discriminatory practices that harm people who are different from themselves.

ENGAGEMENT IN SCHOOL

- Less than 60 percent of African American, Hispanic, and American Indian students complete high school in four years. In many urban areas, the percentage drops to less than 50 for these students.
- Many young people exhibit amazing resiliency, allowing them to overcome economic and social hardships to finish school and become productive adults.

EQUALITY OF ACCESS

- Developing digital equity among students who have access to computers and the Internet and those who do not is one of the challenges faced by educators in providing equity and social justice.

LOOKING AHEAD: GREATER ACCESS TO QUALITY EDUCATION

- New technologies, including social networking, are being added to teachers' toolboxes to engage students in learning and to support creativity.
- Effective teachers are critical to student learning and make a difference in the academic achievement of students.

DISCUSSION QUESTIONS

1. Families face a number of social and economic challenges that affect the well-being of their children. Which factors do you think are most damaging to children? What should teachers and schools do to help students develop resiliency and be able to achieve academically under adverse circumstances?

2. What signs might teachers see to make them wonder whether a child or adolescent is being abused? What steps should you take if you suspect abuse or other risk-taking behaviors?

3. Children and teenagers need adult support as they cope with the challenges of adolescence. Who do you think should be providing this support? What should be the role of teachers in providing the support?

4. Some researchers are suggesting that the testing requirements of No Child Left Behind (NCLB) are pushing students out of school. Some school districts have been accused of underrepresenting the number of dropouts. Why might a school system want to underreport the number of dropouts? Why would a sceptic suggest that the NCLB requirements are pushing some students out of school?

5. Based on what you learned in this chapter and know from your own experiences, how do you see technology affecting education during the next ten years? Do you think technology will lead to digital equity between population groups? Why or why not?

SCHOOL-BASED OBSERVATIONS

1. As you observe classrooms, pay attention to how teachers are interacting with students from different racial and socioeconomic groups. What, if any, differences do you observe? Are the differences appropriate? Why or why not? What adjustments in the interactions would you make if you were the teacher?

2. Technology can be used in a wide variety of ways in classrooms and within lessons. In classrooms that you are observing this semester, how is technology being used? What innovative practices have you observed? How is technology being used to promote student learning? How would you rate the use of technology to promote student learning?

PORTFOLIO DEVELOPMENT

1. Prepare a paper on the educational opportunities for homeless students in your community or another area of the state with larger numbers of homeless families. What services is the school district providing to these students? How are they being integrated into the schools they attend? What is the school district doing to ensure that homeless students will be able to keep up with their academic work? Conclude your paper by reflecting on how you will work with homeless children when you become a teacher.

2. Compare the high school graduation rates in a suburban and urban school district in your area or state. To access graduation rates for a school district, visit the website of the National Center for Education Statistics at www.nces.ed.gov and prepare graphs and a summary of the most recent data available.

PREPARING FOR CERTIFICATION

1. One of the topics covered in the Praxis II Principles of Learning and Teaching (PLT) test is "becoming familiar with relevant aspects of students' background knowledge and experiences." "Understanding the influence of individual experiences, talents, and prior learning, as well as language, culture, family, and community values on students' learning."

   Effective teachers identify methods and procedures for gathering background information about their students. What types of information will you want to have about your students and their backgrounds? What methods will you use to gather background information that will help you teach more effectively and also respect the privacy of students and their families?

2. One of the topics covered in the Praxis II Principles of Learning and Teaching (PLT) test is a section covering instruction and assessment. This section of the test includes reference to "Methods for enhancing student learning through the use of a variety of resources and materials

   *Computers, Internet resource, Web pages, e-mail

   *Audiovisual technologies such as videotapes and compact discs (CDs). . . . . . ."

   Other are also listed; however, the impact of electronic media on schools and society is changing at a rapid pace. Reflect on technology use in your school as a child and compare your experiences then to students in schools today. How might this affect you as a teacher is today's schools?

3. Answer the following multiple-choice question, which is similar to items in Praxis and other state certification tests.

   Six-year-old Heather lives with her mother, who works as a waitress. Ms. Atwater, Heather's teacher, notes that Heather often arrives at school late and is inattentive in class. Heather says she frequently stays up past midnight if other people in the house are up. Ms. Atwater has observed bruises on Heather's arms and legs, suggesting that Heather is being abused. What is the first action Ms. Atwater should take?

   a. Visit the home to investigate
   b. Arrange a conference with Heather's mother
   c. Report the suspected abuse to the principal or supervisor
   d. After reporting the abuse to the principal or supervisor, follow up to make sure the appropriate agency has been notified.

4. Answer the following short-answer question, which is similar to items in Praxis and other state certification tests.

   We know that achievement is helped when educators and families work together to support the academic and social growth of children. Identify two specific actions a teacher might take to connect school and the student's home environment for the benefit of the student. For each action, explain how that action will benefit the student's learning. Base your response on principles of fostering positive relationships with families to support student learning and well-being.

After you've completed your written responses for the above questions, use the Praxis general scoring guide provided in Chapter 1 to see if you can you revise your response to improve your score.

MYEDUCATIONLAB

myeducationlab Now go to Topic 3: *Schools and Society* in the MyEducationLab (www.myeducationlab.com) for your course, where you can:

- Find learning outcomes for *Schools and Society* along with the national standards that connect to these outcomes.
- Complete *Assignments and Activities* that can help you more deeply understand the chapter content.
- Apply and practice your understanding of the core teaching skills identified in the chapter with the *Building Teaching Skills and Dispositions* learning units.

- Check your comprehension on the content covered in the chapter by going to the *Study Plan* in the *Book Specific Resources* section for your text. Here you will be able to take a chapter quiz, receive feedback on your answers, and then access *Review, Practice, and Enrichment* activities to enhance your understanding of chapter content.

WEBSITES

www.globalkids.org After-school programs are hosted on this site as well as activities on Teen Second Life for teenagers in urban schools. The mission of Global Kids is "to educate and inspire urban youth to become successful students and global and community leaders by engaging them in socially dynamic, content-rich learning experiences."

www.iste.org The International Society for Technology in Education (ISTE) is an educator's resource for advancing the effective use of technology in PK–12 and teacher education. Check out ISTE's "Your Learning Journey" under "Educator Resources" to access its space on Facebook, LinkedIn, MySpace, Second Life, and Wikispaces.

www.nsta.org The website of the National Science Teachers Association includes online and other resources for teaching science.

www.storyofmysecondlife.com A blog of educators from around the world who are using Second Life for educational activities.

www.teachersdomain.org Developed by WGBH, a Boston public TV and radio station, the website includes multimedia resources that show science in action.

www.teachertube.com A YouTube-like site in which teachers are sharing videos of class projects.

www.TeachersHelpingTeachers.org This website for and by teachers will help you find quality curriculum materials, including virtual field trips.

FURTHER READING

Children's Defense Fund. (2008). *State of America's children 2008 report—Are our children ready to compete in the global arena?* Washington, DC: Author. Information on the status of children today, including state-by-state data on poverty, health, child welfare, youth at risk, early childhood education, nutrition, and housing. The report compares the United States' investment in and protection of its children with other industrialized countries.

Flores-Gonzalez, Nilda. (2002). *School kids/street kids.* New York: Teachers College Press. Explores why Puerto Rican students in an urban high school stay, leave, and return to school. The implications of identification as a "school kid" or "street kid" are examined.

Kozol, Jonathan. (2000). *Ordinary resurrections: Children in the years of hope.* New York: Crown. A description of living and being educated in the inner city through the experiences of inner-city children and the adults who try to assist them. The stories of individual children raise issues about recognizing the value and dignity of students as we teach.

chapter nine

ORGANIZING AND PAYING FOR EDUCATION

EDUCATION
IN THE **NEWS**

PANEL APPROVES SCHOOL FINANCE OVERHAUL

By **THE ASSOCIATED PRESS**

SANTA FE—Lawmakers are moving ahead with a proposal to overhaul how New Mexico finances public schools

The House Education Committee unanimously approved a measure Monday for a new school funding formula that supporters say will help improve the educational programs offered to New Mexico's students.

However, the school changes carry a hefty price tag: nearly $350 million a year.

Supporting the legislation is a coalition of educational groups representing teachers and other school workers, administrators and school boards.

"If not now, when?" Christine Trujillo of the American Federation of Teachers and the New Mexico Federation of Labor said in urging lawmakers to approve the funding formula overhaul despite the state's dismal budget outlook.

The proposed revision is the product of a two-year study that concluded schools need a 15 percent increase in state aid to provide necessary programs for students.

"What this bill is about is investing in our schools," said Sen. Cynthia Nava, D-Las Cruces, chairwoman of the Senate Finance Committee.

According to a legislative panel's survey of districts, schools propose using the additional state money to hire more teachers to help reduce class sizes; extend school days; hire specialists such as nurses, counselors and social workers; support teachers with instructional coaches and mentors; and expand programs for students, including music, art and vocational courses.

The Senate and House committee jointly held a hearing to consider the formula revisions. The House panel then endorsed the legislation. The next stop for the bill is the Appropriations and Finance Committee, which handles budget issues.

Currently, the state distributes more than $2 billion a year for school operations through a formula established in 1974. Although the system is supposed to treat schools equitably, critics say it shortchanges some districts, particularly those that are smaller or fast-growing.

The proposed funding formula is based on the idea of educational "sufficiency," financing districts based on what it costs to provide the programs and services to meet the educational needs of all students. Schools would get more state aid for students who are from families living in poverty, those with learning difficulties or who can't speak English.

The legislation will require a longer school year—185 instructional days starting in the 2012–13 school year, up from 180 currently.

Of the state's 89 school districts, all but three would receive more state aid under the revised funding formula. However, the legislation provides a "hold harmless" provision to make certain the three districts—Los Alamos, Pecos and Mosquero—don't lose state money for at least three years under the new funding formula.

The Greater Albuquerque Chamber of Commerce opposed the legislation. Terri Cole, the business group's president and chief executive, said there wasn't enough accountability in the measure to ensure schools spend the additional taxpayer money to achieve specific goals, such as reducing New Mexico's high dropout rate.

Separate legislation is pending that would increase the state's gross receipts and income taxes to provide additional money—about $360 million next year—to implement the funding formula overhaul.

Note: The school funding formula revision is HB331.

QUESTIONS FOR REFLECTION

1. What do you think about the idea of educational "sufficiency"? Is this principle being applied in your state?
2. The New Mexico legislation will increase the school year by five days. How does this total compare to the length of the school year in your state?
3. The Chamber of Commerce opposition to this legislation includes wanting more accountability. What would you suggest for increased accountability?

Source: Reprinted by permission of The Associated Press.

LEARNING OUTCOMES

After reading and studying this chapter, you should be able to:

1. Describe the organizational structure of schools, school districts, states, and the federal government. (INTASC 10: School and Community Involvement)

2. Describe the organizational relationship of teachers to their principal and how the responsibilities of the principal relate to those of the school district superintendent and the school board. (INTASC 10: School and Community Involvement)

3. Summarize the key sources of funding for public education and issues related to overreliance on any one

of these sources. (INTASC 10: School and Community Involvement)

4. Summarize the key issues related to equity and equality in the financing of public education. (INTASC 3: Diverse Learners)

5. Understand that politics are a characteristic part of education, schools, and teaching and that it is important for you to see how teachers can be effective in this arena. (INTASC 10: School and Community Involvement)

6. Identify themes related to expectations for school accountability. (INTASC 9: Reflective Practice)

SCHOOL DISTRICTS: ORGANIZATION AND FINANCES

All families and communities in the United States have access to a public school. The school may be located around the corner or a very long bus ride away. Unless a community is very small and remote, it will have more than one school organized as a school district. During the 2005–06 school year, 14,166 districts were operating. These districts have many common features and also some different features. For example, some districts only have elementary schools and others only secondary schools. One of the significant differences is their size. According to the National Center for Education Statistics, in 2005–06 the one hundred largest school districts had at least 47,595 students, while 72 percent of the school districts had fewer than 2,500 students (National Center for Education Statistics, 2007b). Another way to think about these statistics is that the many more smaller school districts serve fewer (17 percent) students, while the fewer in number larger districts serve the most (83 percent) students. (*Note*: All data in Chapter 9, unless otherwise noted, are from the U.S. Department of Education, National Center for Education Statistics.)

One important task of school districts is to obtain and spend the money required for schooling. The amount of money involved is significant. For example, in the 2006 fiscal (budget) year across the United States, $449.6 billion was expended. This was an average of $9,154 per pupil. All of this money has to come from somewhere (including your taxes) and must be allocated in ways that are equitable.

School District Organization

The school district is governed by a school board, and its day-to-day operations are led by a superintendent. In most districts, your official hiring as a teacher will be done by the superintendent making a recommendation to the school board. Each district has its own district office, which houses an array of administrative, instructional, financial, and clerical support staff. As the state and federal levels of government have become increasingly active in setting educational agendas, a concomitant response has occurred at the district level in the form of an ever-increasing list of tasks that must be accomplished. The typical school district **organization chart** presented in Figure 9.1 reflects the additional functions and personnel that are part of the district office.

LOCAL BOARD OF EDUCATION. Legal authority for operating local school systems is given to local boards of education through state statutes. The statutes prescribe specifically how school board members are to be chosen and what duties and responsibilities they have in office. The statutes also specify the terms of board members, procedures for selecting officers of the board, duties of the officers, and procedures for filling any vacancies. Local citizens serving as school board members, also called *trustees*, are official agents of the state.

Most school boards in the United States are elected by popular vote in special **nonpartisan** elections, in which candidates are not associated with a particular political party. In some cities the mayor will appoint board members. The percentage of appointed school boards is higher in

organization chart A graphic representation of the line and staff relationships of personnel in a school, school district, or other type of organization.

nonpartisan Candidates and elections that are not associated with a particular political party.

FIGURE 9.1

Typical School District Line and Staff Organization Chart

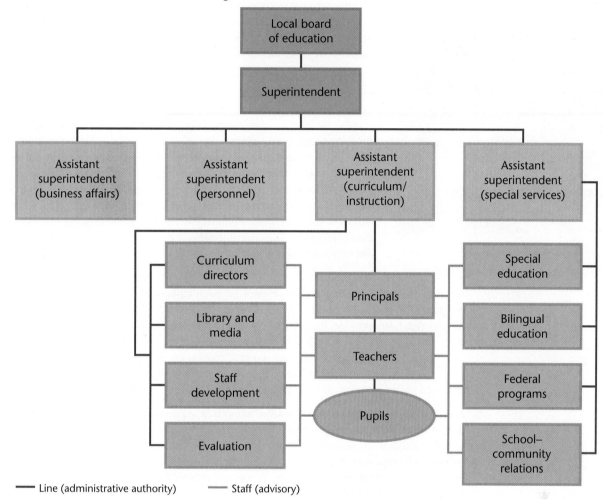

— Line (administrative authority)   — Staff (advisory)

school districts enrolling more than 25,000 pupils; yet even in three-fourths of these larger districts, the board members are elected.

Usually, teachers cannot be board members in the districts where they teach; however, they can be board members in districts where they live if they teach in different districts. The trend toward more teachers becoming board members most likely results from the goal of professional associations to secure seats on school boards.

Powers and Duties of School Boards. The powers and duties of school boards vary from state to state; the school codes of the respective states spell them out in detail. A school board's major function is the development of policy for the local school district—policy that must be in harmony with both federal and state laws. Boards have only those powers granted or implied by statute that are necessary to carry out their responsibilities. These powers usually include the power to act as follows:

- Obtain revenue.
- Maintain schools.
- Purchase sites and build buildings.
- Purchase materials and supplies.
- Organize and provide programs of study.
- Employ necessary workers and regulate their services.
- Admit and assign pupils to schools and control their conduct.

Some duties of school boards are **mandatory**, whereas others are **discretionary**. Some duties cannot be delegated. If, for example, the state has given boards the power to employ teachers, they must do this; the power cannot be delegated—even to a school superintendent. Boards can

mandatory Duties and responsibilities that must be accomplished.

discretionary Duties and responsibilities that may be done by the designated body or may be delegated to another.

More than 90 percent of school boards are elected by popular vote; the rest are appointed.

delegate much of the hiring *process* to administrators, however, and then act officially on administrative recommendations for employment. An illustration of a discretionary power left to the local board is the decision whether to participate in a nonrequired school program—for example, a program of competitive athletics. Another illustration of discretionary power is the decision to employ only teachers who exceed minimum state certification standards.

SUPERINTENDENT OF SCHOOLS. One of the primary duties of the local board is to select its chief executive officer, the superintendent. There is one notable exception to the general practice of selection of the superintendent by school boards. In a few states, especially in the Southeast, some school district superintendents are elected by the voters. In these situations, school superintendent selection is a political process just like that used for the election of mayors, county commissioners, some judges, and others. In either case, whether named by the board or elected by the people, the superintendent is responsible for the day-to-day operations of the school district, responding to school board members' interests, planning the district's budget, and defining the district's long-term aspirations. The superintendent is expected to be visible in the community and to provide overall leadership for the district.

THE CRITICAL IMPORTANCE OF LEADERSHIP. The importance of leadership by the superintendent and board members cannot be overemphasized. The quality of the educational program of a school district is influenced strongly by the leadership that the board of education and the superintendent provide. Without the communication and support of high expectations by boards and superintendents, high-quality education is not likely to be achieved. For example, offering curriculum programs that exceed state-required minimums is discretionary. For a school district to excel, the local authorities, board members, and superintendent must convince their communities that specified school programs are needed and desirable.

LINE AND STAFF RELATIONSHIPS. Another important organizational concept to keep in mind is the difference between line and staff relationships. In any organization, some people will have the job of being executives, bosses, managers, or directors. Other people will be supervised by these persons. The supervisor typically has the authority, at least to some degree, to direct, monitor, and evaluate the work of the subordinate. When one person has this type of authority over another, there is a **line relationship**.

When there is no formal supervisory authority of one person over the other, they have a **staff relationship**. This distinction becomes especially important in education because in many instances it is not clear or absolute who has the authority or responsibility to direct the work of others. For example, teachers, as professionals, can legitimately claim more independence than can employees of other organizations. But teachers are not completely free to do whatever they want. If they were, the system of education would break down, at least in the experience of the students who must move through it.

CENTRAL OFFICE STAFF. The superintendent of schools works with a staff to carry out the district's program of education. Although the size of the staff varies with the school district, some kind of formal organization is necessary. Each school district will have an organization chart similar to the one shown earlier in Figure 9.1.

In an organization chart, line officers hold the administrative power as it flows from the local board of education down to the pupils. Superintendents, assistant superintendents, and principals are line officers vested with authority over the people below them on the chart. Each person is directly responsible to the official above and must work through that person in dealing with a higher official. This arrangement is frequently referred to as the *chain of command*.

Administrative staff positions are shown in Figure 9.1 as branching out from the direct flow of authority. Staff includes librarians, curriculum coordinators, staff developers, guidance officers, transportation officers, and others. They are responsible to their respective superiors but have no line authority over teachers. They assist and advise others using their special knowledge and abilities. Teachers are generally referred to as staff even though they are in the direct flow of authority. However, their line authority in this arrangement prevails only over pupils.

line relationship An organizational arrangement in which a subordinate is directly responsible to a supervisor.

staff relationship An organizational arrangement in which one party is not under the direct control or authority of another.

You will learn more about the role of district curriculum staff when you read Chapter 12.

FIGURE 9.2

Percentage Distribution of Total Current Expenditures for Public Elementary and Secondary Schools, by Function: School Year 2005–06

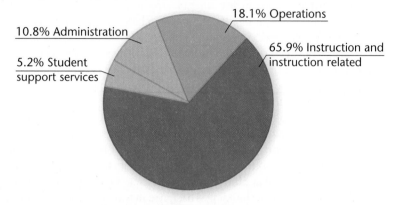

18.1% Operations

10.8% Administration

65.9% Instruction and instruction related

5.2% Student support services

Note: Percentages may not sum to 100 due to rounding. Percentage distribution of total current expenditures reported here may differ from a previously published report of such expenditures due to rounding.

Source: Data from National Center for Education Statistics, U.S. Department of Education, Common Core of Data, "National Public Education Financial Survey (NPEFS)," Fiscal Year 2006, Version 1a.

School District Expenditures

The many functions, staff, and facilities in a school district have to be paid for. The categories and percentages in Figure 9.2 are general averages for how education funds are expended. As you would expect, the largest percentage, approximately two-thirds, is spent on instruction. However, more than one-third is spent on other components. School buses must be purchased and have drivers; district staff and administrators must report to the state and federal governments about activities and how funds are spent; school buildings have to be constructed and maintained. All of the funds cannot go directly to instruction.

INTERMEDIATE UNITS. One other type of organization that you as a teacher should know about is the **intermediate unit**. These organizations function between the state department of education and the local school districts. They may be organized by county or represent a consortium of several districts. These units have different names in different states. For example, in some states, such as New York and Colorado, they are called BOCES (boards of cooperative educational services); in Texas they are called regional service centers; in California, county education offices, and in Georgia, regional education service agencies (RESAs).

A fundamental purpose of the intermediate unit is to share services that an individual district cannot efficiently or economically provide. Cooperative provisions for special education and vocational–technical education have been very successful. Other services that intermediate units can provide include audiovisual libraries, centralized purchasing, inservice training for teachers and principals as well as other school workers, health services, instructional materials, laboratories, legal services, and special consultant services. Stimulated by educational reform, the inservice dimension of the intermediate units has escalated in some states in recent years.

THE ORGANIZATION OF SCHOOLS

The basic building block of the U.S. education system is the school. To an amazing extent, schools are organized in the same way in each state. In fact, schools are organized pretty much the same in other countries too.

The all-too-typical school building consists of a set of classrooms, with corridors for the movement of students, and a central office. It has one or more large spaces for a cafeteria and gymnasium/auditorium. Schools also have staff lounges where teachers can make preparations, relax, and exchange ideas. School campuses have outside spaces for a playground, athletics, parking (staff and students), and a driveway for dropping off and picking up students. Wherever you go, you will find this basic architecture.

This typical design of schools is frequently criticized for resembling an egg crate. If you viewed a school building with the roof off, you would see that it resembled an egg carton: a series

intermediate unit An education organization located between local districts and the state that delivers support services to one or more school districts.

of cells or pockets with routes running between them. Some educational critics see this architecture as interfering with the need to introduce new educational practices. For example, the walls restrict communication between teachers and channel the flow of student traffic. Teachers have to make an effort to see what goes on in any other classrooms.

Even when a school is built with modest attempts to change the interior space, teachers and students still seem to want to preserve the egg-crate concept. For example, you may have visited an elementary school that had an open-space design. Instead of self-contained classrooms, there might be an open floor plan equivalent in size to three or four classrooms. However, if you observed the arrangement of furniture, bookshelves, and screens, you probably noted that teachers and students had constructed zones and areas that were equivalent to three or four self-contained classrooms.

This is not meant to criticize teachers for how they have adapted to new school architectures; rather, it is meant to point out how the organization of the space parallels the activities of the people who use it. There are many good reasons for organizing schools around self-contained classrooms. And in the case of the open-space concept, the noise from three or four teachers and 90 to 120 students can be so disruptive that little learning can occur. One key to the successful use of open-space plans, then, is to be sure the building is designed in ways that control and dampen noise.

The physical arrangement of a school into individual classrooms has organizational as well as instructional implications. For example, it is easy for teachers to be isolated in their classrooms. This geographic isolation contributes to their not knowing about or becoming engaged with issues that affect the whole school. Geographic isolation can affect the school as a whole too. The school staff might not be aware of community concerns or of what is going on in other schools across the district. Teachers and administrators must make deliberate efforts to learn about other parts of the education system.

The School Organization Chart

All of the people within a school have to be organized in some way. Their formal working relationships can be pictured in the organization chart shown in Figure 9.3. The principal is the single line authority for all of these adults *and* for all of the students! Interestingly, most experts on organizations advocate that no more than five to seven people should be directly supervised by one administrator. Yet in nearly all schools, the principal is responsible for a minimum of thirty adults and several hundred students. In very large schools, the principal may have two hundred people to supervise. As you can see, the simple picture of "top-down" leadership breaks apart when one considers the wide array of tasks and the sheer number of people at work in each school. A number of formal roles and structures must exist for arranging the relationships among the varied role groups and for facilitating coordination and communication.

PEARSON
myeducationlab

Go to the *Assignments and Activities* section of Topic 5: *Governance and Finance* in the MyEducationLab for your course and complete the activity titled *The Principal as Leader*.

FIGURE 9.3

A School Organization Chart

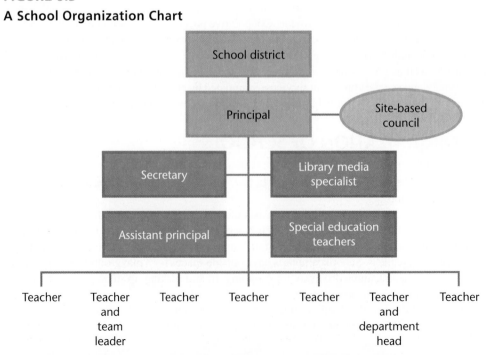

PRINCIPALS. As in school districts, schools also have line and staff relationships. At the top of the school organization chart is the principal. In law the principal is the final authority at the school. The principal's responsibilities include instructional leadership, community relationships, supervision of staff (including teachers, secretaries, and custodians), teacher selection and evaluation, students, building and grounds, provisions of contracts, administration of the attendance office, and all budgets. The principal is in a line relationship with the school district superintendent. In larger school districts, the principal may have an intermediate supervisor, such as an assistant superintendent or a director of elementary or secondary education.

The principal is responsible for the actions of all school personnel and must work closely with the superintendent and the school community.

The tasks and responsibilities of principals are expanding. For example, there has been a push to increase teacher and parent participation in making school decisions. This pressure has led to the creation of special committees of teachers and parents to work with the principal. For example, as a result of the No Child Left Behind Act, all schools must have a School Improvement Process and committee that includes teachers and parents.

═══════════ JOURNAL FOR REFLECTION ═══════════

Think about principals you knew when you were a student. How would you feel about having one of them as your principal when you are a teacher? What do you think those principals would expect from you as a teacher?

Go to the *Assignments and Activities* section of Topic 5: *Governance and Finance* in the MyEducationLab for your course and complete the activity titled *Carol Bartlett, Principal.*

ASSISTANT PRINCIPALS. Larger elementary schools and most junior high schools, middle schools, and high schools have one or more additional administrators. Normally, they are called assistant principals, although sometimes in high schools they are titled vice principals. Large high schools will have several assistant or vice principals and other administrators that have "director" or "dean" titles, such as director of athletics and dean of students. These administrators share the tasks of the principal and provide additional avenues of communication between teachers, students, staff, parents, the community, and the district office.

In elementary schools, the job differentiation between the assistant principal and the principal is less clear, and both administrators will be a part of most operations. In the high school setting, specific roles and tasks will frequently be assigned to the different administrator roles. For example, in most districts, each teacher must be observed formally. This activity takes more time than the principal has available, so the vice principal(s) observes and evaluates some teachers. Usually, the principal concentrates on observing the new teachers because he or she makes the recommendation on rehiring beginning teachers.

DEPARTMENT HEADS AND TEAM LEADERS. Elementary schools normally have another, less formal level of leadership: grade-level or team leaders. These are full-time teachers who assume a communication and coordination role for their grade level(s) or team. Junior high schools and high schools have department chairs. Normally, departments are organized around the major subject areas (mathematics, science, English, and social studies) and the cocurricula (athletics and music). Teachers are members of one of the departments, and regular meetings are held to plan curriculum and to facilitate communication. In middle schools, the leaders of interdisciplinary teams likely serve in the same way. In each case, these department heads or team leaders meet with the principal from time to time and meet regularly with their teachers. In most districts department chairs and team leaders are considered to be teachers, not administrators. One implication of this organizational arrangement is that they will not be a part of the formal teacher evaluation process.

Go to the *Assignments and Activities* section of Topic 6: *School Organization* in the MyEducationLab for your course and complete the activity titled *Grade Level Meeting.*

TEACHERS. The single largest group of adults in the school is the teachers. A typical elementary school has from fifteen to thirty-five teachers, and a large high school may have more than one hundred. Teachers are busy in their classrooms working with their students, and this is where the egg-crate architecture of schools can be a problem. Unless special mechanisms are used, such as regular department/grade-level meetings, individual teachers can easily become isolated from the school as a whole. The self-contained classroom architecture and the work of attending to twenty to forty students in the classroom at any one time means teachers have little time or opportunity to communicate with other adults. As a consequence, the principal and all of the teachers need to work hard with the other members of the school staff to facilitate communication. All must make an effort to work together to continually improve the school.

SCHOOL SUPPORT STAFF. A school has other personnel who support the administrators and teachers. One of the most important of these supporting roles is filled by the school secretary. Every teacher and principal will advise you to be sure to develop a good working relationship with the school secretary, who is at the nerve center of the running of the school. When a student has a problem, when a teacher needs some materials, when the principal wants a piece of information from the files, or when a student teacher wants to know about parking a car, the first person to contact is the school secretary.

Another useful education professional in most schools is the library media specialist. This person is a good instructional resource for teachers and certainly is key to students being able to access information and becoming skilled in using technology. A third important resource is the custodians. The cleanliness of your classroom and school depends on the efforts of the custodians, and they also can be helpful to teachers in locating supplies and moving furniture. Keep in mind that they observe and talk with students. Frequently, custodians and other support staff will know about something that is going on before the teachers do. Cafeteria workers are another group of adult workers in the school who can make a positive difference in how the school feels and functions.

Chapter 6 includes description of several innovations in school organization that increase parental involvement and choice.

Innovations in School Organization

There are several interesting and innovative approaches to school organization. Several of these, including charter schools and vouchers, were described in Chapter 6. Two others that increase school decision making are site-based decision making and empowerment.

SITE-BASED DECISION MAKING. Another approach for increasing participation is called **site-based decision making (SBDM)**, or school-based management (SBM). SBDM includes a school governance committee whereby an individual school within a district can make more of its own decisions related to the educational operations of that school—for example, budgeting, personnel selection, and curriculum design.

EMPOWERMENT. An emerging innovative variation on authority and responsibility for schools is called empowerment. In an **empowerment** school the principal and school staff are freed from many of the policies, rules, and procedures of the district and perhaps the state. Empowerment schools receive a total budget and are able to decide for themselves how the money will be spent, including the number of teachers they will employ and which programs they will purchase.

YEAR-ROUND SCHOOLS. The normal school year of nine to ten months with the full summer off is often criticized. One concern is that students will forget too much over the summer. Critics point out that the current school year was instituted back in the 1800s, when most people lived on farms and the children were counted on to perform summer chores.

One interesting solution is the **year-round school**. This is not an extended school year in that students attend school for more days. Rather, year-round schools spread the time in school across twelve months. One way a school might do this is by having multiple "tracks" of six to eight weeks. During any one cycle, one-fourth to one-third of the students will be on vacation and the others will be attending classes. In this way, students have more frequent but shorter times away from school. An additional advantage is that the school site can handle more students on an annual basis. Curiously, much of the resistance to year-round schools comes from parents who are concerned about being able to schedule family vacations; however, once the schedule is implemented, they discover that being able to schedule vacations throughout the year has advantages.

FOUR-DAY WEEK. Some rural districts that have school buses traveling long distances have implemented four-day school weeks. Each of the four days is longer, but on the fifth day there is no school. Although there has been no research on this approach, the prevailing impression is that students accomplish just as much. One of the complicating factors in this structure is scheduling athletic and cocurricula activities.

site-based decision making (SBDM) A school governance process that gives greater voice to teachers, parents, and community representatives in school policies.

empowerment The process of providing a school with the authority to allocate all, or nearly all of its budget.

year-round school School that is open all year, with only a proportion of the students attending at any one time.

ORGANIZATION OF EDUCATION AT THE STATE LEVEL

In certain countries, such as Taiwan, the national constitution specifies responsibility for education, but the U.S. Constitution does not specifically provide for public education. As will be explained in more detail in Chapter 10, the Tenth Amendment has been interpreted as granting this power to the states. As a consequence, the states are the governmental units in the United States charged with the responsibility for education. Local school districts, then, receive through state law the power to administer and operate the school system for their communities. State legislatures, within the limits expressed by the federal Constitution and by state constitutions, are the chief policy makers for education. State legislatures grant powers to state boards of education, state departments of education, chief state school officers, and local boards of education. These groups have only the powers granted to them by the legislature, implied powers from the specific grant of power, and the necessary powers to carry out the statutory purposes. The responsibilities and duties of intermediate units are also prescribed by the state legislatures. Figure 9.4 shows a typical state organization chart for education.

Stability, continuity, and leadership for education can come from the state board. However, as identified in Figure 9.4, many other individuals and groups are increasingly likely to engage in education issues. For example, many legislators have established records of heavy influence on the direction of education. Through their initiatives, new laws may affect any and all parts of the education system. There are "education governors" as well (see later section). Many state leaders have been very involved in supporting and attempting to shape education in their states. Suffice it to say, numerous participants and agencies and many kinds of influence have impacts on the shape and direction of the U.S. education system.

Chapter 10 has an analysis of how the U.S. Constitution cedes responsibility for education to the states.

State Board of Education

State boards of education are both **regulatory** and **advisory**. Regulatory functions include the establishment of standards for issuing and revoking teaching licenses, the establishment of standards for

regulatory Functions for which the state board has the authority to establish rules and regulations that limit and permit action.

advisory Functions and areas in which the state board can only offer suggestions and indicate preference for action.

FIGURE 9.4
State Organization Chart

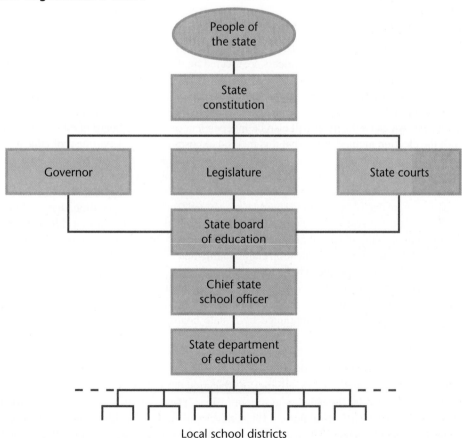

Local school districts

The states are the governmental units charged with the primary responsibility for education.

approving and accrediting schools, and the development and enforcement of a uniform system for gathering and reporting educational data. Advisory functions include considering the educational needs of the state, both long and short range, and recommending to the governor and the legislature ways of meeting these needs. State boards of education, in studying school problems and in suggesting and analyzing proposals, can be invaluable to the legislature, especially because the legislature is under pressure to decide so many issues. A state board can provide continuity over time for an educational program that annual or biannual legislative procedures do not accommodate. A state board can also coordinate, supplement, and establish study commissions. These commissions frequently include groups studying textbooks, finance, licensure, student learning standards, school building standards, and teacher education.

STATE BOARD MEMBERSHIP. Members of state boards of education get their positions in various ways. Usually, they are appointed by the governor, with confirmation by the senate. In some states they may be elected by the people, the legislature, or the local school board members in a regional convention, also with confirmation by the senate. The terms of members of state boards of education are usually staggered to avoid a complete changeover at any one time. Board members usually serve without pay but are reimbursed for expenses. The policies of nonpayment and staggered terms are considered safeguards against political patronage.

Chief State School Officer

Every state has a chief state school officer, commissioner of education, or superintendent of public instruction. Some state superintendents are elected by the people; others are appointed either by the state board or by the governor.

Arguments advanced for electing the chief state school officer hold that, as an elected official, the person will be close to the people, responsible to them, and free from obligations to other state officials. An elected person will also be independent of the state board of education. Opponents of the election method argue that this method exposes the state department of education to partisan politics, that an elected official is obligated to other members of the same political party, and that many excellent candidates prefer not to engage in political contests.

Those who advocate that the chief state school officer should be appointed by a state board of education claim that policy making should be separated from policy execution, that educational leadership should not rest on the competence of one elected official, and that this method enhances the state's ability to recruit and retain qualified career workers in education. Opponents of appointment by a state board of education claim mainly that an appointed chief school officer will not be responsible to the people. The principal objection to gubernatorial appointment is the inherent danger of the appointee's involvement in partisan politics.

Another perspective on this issue is that an elected state school officer is legally an "official" of the state, whereas an officer appointed by a state board of education is generally an "employee," not a legal official.

State Department of Education

The state government carries on its activities in education through the state department of education, which is directed by the chief state school officer. These activities have been classified in five categories: operational, regulatory, service, developmental, and public support and cooperation activities. Operational activities are those in which the state department directly administers schools and services, such as schools for the blind. Regulatory activities include making sure that teachers meet license standards, that school buses are safe, and that curricular requirements are fulfilled. Service activities include advising and consulting, disseminating research, and preparing materials (on state financial aid, for example). Developmental activities are directed at the improvement of the department itself and include planning, staffing, and research into better performance for the operational and regulatory as well as the service functions. Public support and cooperation activities involve public relations, political activities with the legislature and governor, and relations with various other governmental and nongovernmental agencies.

State Legislature

State legislatures are generally responsible for creating, operating, managing, and maintaining state school systems. The legislators are the state policy makers for education. State legislatures create state departments of education to serve as professional advisers and to execute state policy. State legislatures, though powerful, also operate under controls.

In these difficult economic times, the most important actions of state legislatures involve making decisions about the financing of schools. The sources of funds, including tax structures, and the distribution of funds for education are determined by state legislatures. Legislatures also can become involved in other education issues such as licensure standards, tenure rights of teachers, programs of study, standards of building construction for health and safety, and compulsory attendance laws.

State legislatures, in their legislative deliberations about the schools, are continually importuned by special-interest groups. These groups, realizing that the legislature is the focus of legal control of education, can exert considerable influence on individual legislators. Some of the representative influential groups are illustrated in Figure 9.5.

FIGURE 9.5
Influences on Legislative Decision Making

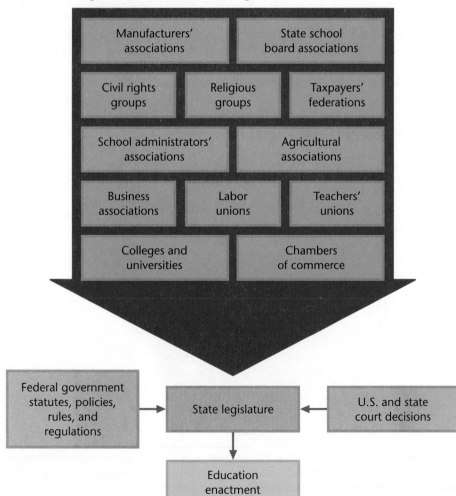

It is not uncommon for more than a thousand bills to be introduced each year in a state legislative session. Many of these bills originate with special-interest groups. In recent years, state legislatures have dealt with education bills on a wide range of topics, including accountability, finance, textbooks, adult basic education, length of the school year, legal holidays, lotteries, teacher and student testing, no pass/no play policies, and school standards of various sorts.

Governors

The top executive in each state is the governor. Many governors have emphasized the importance of education in their states. Governors can veto school legislation as they can other legislation. When there is a dispute over the interpretation of legislation, the attorney general and the state judiciary system, when called on, will rule on its constitutionality.

SOURCES OF REVENUE FOR SCHOOLS

Figure 9.6 is a diagram of the percentages of revenues that school systems nationwide receive from federal, state, and local sources. As you can see, public education is primarily funded by local and state sources of revenue. This means that each state has the major say in how well their schools will be funded and where the majority of funds will come from.

When the financing of education is considered, the first questions asked by many are "How much do I have to pay?" and "How much will my school(s) receive?" In the last thirty years, two other questions have sharpened the discussions about education finance: "Does each school across the state have the same amount of funding?" This is the **equity** question. "Is there enough funding so that students can achieve?" This is the **adequacy** or **sufficiency** question. The equity question was at the center of many school funding lawsuits in the 1980s and 1990s. In 1989 a decision of the Kentucky Supreme Court brought the adequacy question to the front. That court decision held that every child in the state had the right to an "adequate" education. The direct consequence of that decision was the state legislature passing the Kentucky Education Reform Act (KERA). The significance of KERA is that it did not deal solely with equalizing spending by each school district—that is, equity. KERA went further by specifically connecting funding with implementation of school and curriculum reforms, specifying student outcomes and development of a statewide strategy for assessing academic achievement.

Now questions related to the financing of education have to deal with all three questions: "How much?" "Is there equity in the distribution?" and, as pointed out in the *Education in the News* feature, the adequacy question, "Are the resources adequate so that all students can achieve the identified outcomes?"

equity Provision of the same amount of funding to all schools or students.

adequacy The provision of sufficient funds so that all students can achieve.

sufficiency The provision of adequate funding so that all students can achieve.

FIGURE 9.6

FIGURE 9.6

Percent Distribution of Revenues for Public Elementary and Secondary Schools, by Source: School Year 2005–06

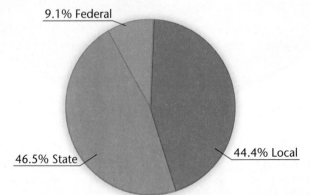

Note: Percentages may not sum to 100 due to rounding. Intermediate revenues were combined with local revenues.

Source: Data from National Center for Education Statistics, U.S. Department of Education, Common Core of Data, "National Public Education Financial Survey (NPEFS)," Fiscal Year 2006, Version 1a.

System of Taxation and Support for Schools

Money to support education comes from a variety of taxes paid to local, state, and federal governments. These governments in turn distribute tax money to local school districts to operate the schools. The three principal kinds of taxes that provide revenue for schools are property taxes, sales or use taxes, and income taxes. The property tax is generally a local tax, whereas the sales tax generally is a state and local mix, and the income tax is collected at the state and federal levels. As mentioned earlier, more than $520.6 billion in revenues were raised by local, state, and federal governments to fund public education in the 2006 fiscal year.

Each type of tax has advantages and disadvantages, yet it is unlikely that any one of these taxes used by itself for education would be sufficient. In evaluating a system of taxes, one should consider the varying ability of citizens to pay, the economic effects of the taxes on the taxpayer, the benefits that various taxpayers receive, the total yield of the tax, the economy of collection, the degree of acceptance, the convenience of paying, the problems of tax evasion, the stability of the tax, and the general adaptability of the system. Clearly, systems of taxation are complicated; each system is an intricately interdependent network.

PROPERTY TAXES AND LOCAL REVENUE. Until recently, the **property tax** was the primary source of local revenue for schools. It is based on the value of property, both real estate and personal. Real estate includes land holdings and buildings such as homes, commercial buildings, and factories. Personal property consists of automobiles, machinery, furniture, livestock, and intangibles such as stocks and bonds. The property tax has both advantages and limitations.

Property Taxes: Advantages and Limitations. The main advantage of the property tax is its stability. Although the tax tends to lag behind changes in market values, it provides a steady, regular income for the taxing agency. Another advantage of taxing property is that it is fixed; it is not easily moved to escape taxation, as income might be. Also, because the owners of property pay the tax, it is easy to identify them.

The property tax has numerous limitations, however. It can have a negative impact on the value of housing: It tends to discourage rehabilitation and upkeep because both of these tend to raise the value of the property and therefore its taxes. The tax is often a deciding factor in locating a business or industry, and it is likely not to be applied equally on all properties.

Determining the Value of Property. One problem with the property tax lies in the potential unfairness of inconsistent property assessments. In some areas, assessors are local people, usually elected, with no special training in evaluating property. Their duty involves inspecting their neighbors' properties and placing values on them. In other areas, sophisticated techniques involving expertly trained personnel are used for property appraisal. In either circumstance, assessors are likely to be subject to political and informal pressures to keep values low in order to keep tax rates low.

The assessed value of property is usually only a percentage of its market value. This percentage varies from county to county and from state to state. Attempts are made within states to equalize assessments or to make certain that the same percentage of full cash value is used in assessing property throughout the state. In recent years, attempts have been made to institute full cash value for the assessed value. For the property tax to be a fair tax, equalized assessment is a necessity.

Property Tax: Progressive or Regressive. Property tax is most generally thought of as a **progressive tax**—that is, one that taxes according to ability to pay; the more wealth one has in property, the more one pays. But because assessments can be unequal and because frequently the greatest wealth is no longer related to real estate, the property tax can be regressive. **Regressive taxes**, such as sales and use taxes, are those that affect low-income groups disproportionately. Some evidence supports the contention that people in the lowest income groups pay a much higher proportion of their income in property taxes than persons in the highest income groups.

Inequities of the Property Tax. Significant support for schools across the nation has been provided by the property tax. However, as has been described, because of schools' heavy dependence on property taxes for financing, enormous discrepancies in resources and quality have built up between schools located in rich and in poor communities.

To illustrate the school finance consequences of differences in local wealth, let's look at a simple example. A school district having assessed property valuations totaling $30 million and a responsibility for educating one thousand pupils would have $30,000 of assessed valuation per pupil.

property tax A tax based on the value of property, both real estate and personal.

progressive tax A tax that is scaled to the ability of the taxpayer to pay.

regressive tax A tax that affects low-income groups disproportionately.

Property taxes are calculated on the basis of assessed valuations, so a district with a high assessed valuation per pupil is in a better position to provide quality education than is one with a low assessed valuation per pupil. If school district A has an assessed valuation of $90 million and one thousand pupils, for example, and school district B has an assessed valuation of $30 million and one thousand pupils, a tax rate of $2 per $100 of assessed valuation would produce $1.8 million for education in district A and only $600,000 in district B. School district A could therefore spend $1,800 per pupil, compared with $600 per pupil in school district B, with the same local tax effort.

THE PERSPECTIVE OF THE COURTS ON TAXATION AND EDUCATION. Can the property tax continue to be the primary base for financing schools? This question was asked of the U.S. Supreme Court in *San Antonio (Texas) Independent School District v. Rodriguez* (1979). Keep in mind that the U.S. Constitution does not mention education, so any litigation has to be based on indirect connections. In the *Rodriguez* case, the challenge was initiated under the equal protection clause of the Fourteenth Amendment. This clause prohibits state action that would deny citizens equal protection. The U.S. Supreme Court, in a five-to-four decision, reversed the lower court decision in *Rodriguez* and thus reaffirmed the local property tax as a basis for school financing. Justice Potter Stewart, voting with the majority, admitted that "the method of financing public schools . . . can be fairly described as chaotic and unjust." He did not, though, find it unconstitutional. The majority opinion, written by Justice Lewis F. Powell, Jr., stated, "We cannot say that such disparities are the product of a system that is so irrational as to be invidiously discriminatory." Justice Thurgood Marshall, in the dissenting opinion, charged that the ruling "is a retreat from our historic commitment to equality of education opportunity." Another part of the opinion in *Rodriguez* addressed the role of the states in supporting public education:

> The consideration and initiation of fundamental reforms with respect to state taxation and education are matters reserved for legislative processes of the various States, and we do no violence to the values of federalism and separation of powers by staying our hand. We hardly need add that this Court's action today is not to be viewed as placing its judicial imprimatur on the status quo. The need is apparent for reform in tax systems which may well have relied too long and too heavily on the local property tax. And certainly innovative thinking as to public education, its methods, and its funding is necessary to assure both a higher level of quality and greater uniformity of opportunity. These matters merit the continued attention of the scholars who already have contributed much by their challenges. But the ultimate solutions must come from the lawmakers and from the democratic pressures of those who elect them.

These comments in *Rodriguez* foreshadowed the continuing string of school finance suits that have been filed in most states.

State Differences in the Funding of Education

A very useful statistic for evaluating differences in school funding is **per-pupil expenditure**. This is a standardized statistic compiled by the National Center for Education Statistics that takes into account local, state, and federal funds invested in K–12 education state by state. The most recently available data are presented in Figure 9.7.

━━━━━━━━━━━━━ **JOURNAL FOR REFLECTION** ━━━━━━━━━━━━━

Do you think the level of per-pupil expenditure for your state (see Figure 9.7) is sufficient? In comparison to other states, how well is education funded in your state? If you think a higher level of funding is needed, how would you present your opinion to parents?

State Sources of Revenue

On average in the United States, the states provide about 46.5 percent of the fiscal resources for local schools. This money is referred to as **state aid**, and within most states all or a major portion of this money is used to help achieve equality of opportunity.

The main sources of tax revenue for states have been classified by the Department of Commerce into four groups: sales and gross receipt taxes, income taxes, licenses, and miscellaneous. Sales and gross receipt taxes include taxes on general sales, motor fuels, alcohol, insurance, and amusements; income taxes include both individual and corporate; licenses include those on motor vehicles, corporations, occupations, vehicle operators, hunting, and fishing. The miscellaneous

per-pupil expenditure Average dollars spent per student.

state aid The money that states provide for the fiscal resources of local schools.

FIGURE 9.7

Current Per-Pupil Expenditures for Public Elementary and Secondary Education in the United States: School Year 2005–06

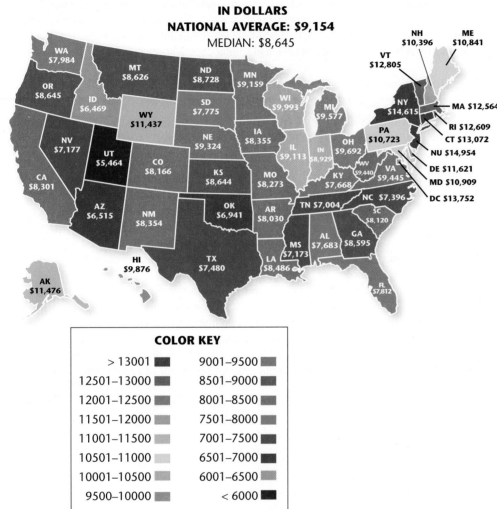

IN DOLLARS
NATIONAL AVERAGE: $9,154
MEDIAN: $8,645

COLOR KEY

> 13001	9001–9500
12501–13000	8501–9000
12001–12500	8001–8500
11501–12000	7501–8000
11001–11500	7001–7500
10501–11000	6501–7000
10001–10500	6001–6500
9500–10000	< 6000

Note: Current expenditures include salaries, employee benefits, purchased services, and supplies, but exclude capital outlay, debt service, facilities acquisition and construction, and equipment.

Source: Data from National Center for Education Statistics, U.S. Department of Education, Common Core of Data, "National Public Education Financial Survey (NPEFS)," Fiscal Year 2006, Version 1a.

classification includes property taxes, taxes on severance or extraction of minerals, and death and gift taxes. The two largest sources of state revenues are sales and income taxes.

SALES AND INCOME TAXES. Sales and income taxes are lucrative sources of state revenue, and it is relatively easy to administer both. The sales tax is collected bit by bit, in a relatively painless way, by the vendor, who is responsible for keeping records. The state income tax can be withheld from wages; hence, collection is eased. Income taxes are considered progressive taxes because they frequently are scaled to the ability of the taxpayer to pay. Sales taxes are regressive; they affect low-income groups disproportionately. All people pay the sales tax at the same rate, so people in low-income groups pay as much tax as people in high-income groups. Part of the advantage of sales taxes and income taxes is that they can be regulated by the legislature.

GAMBLING: AN INCREASING SOURCE OF REVENUE. In 1964, New Hampshire implemented a lottery. By 2009, forty-two states and the District of Columbia were operating lotteries. Legalized gambling in its many forms, from casinos and riverboats to horse racing, has become the newest source of state and local revenues. Gambling is an indirect source of revenue in the sense that it is not seen as a direct tax on citizens; instead, the revenues come through taxes on the games. Commercial casinos (not including Native American casinos) operating in twelves states paid $5.79 billion in taxes to state and local governments in 2007. Income for states from lotteries grew from $978 million in 1980 to $14 billion in 2003. In some states, part or all of the net proceeds from the lottery are allocated to education. In most states, such as California and Florida, the original intent was for these funds to be used for educational enhancements. But within three years of the California lottery's implementation, in a tight budget year, the California legislature incorporated the lottery funds into the base education budget. Other states have had similar experiences.

Recent Challenges to School Finance within the States

The number of court cases related to school finance has increased in recent years. Some states have had new suits initiated, while others are continuing to struggle to respond to earlier court decisions and directives. In all, nearly forty states have experienced or are experiencing court cases that deal with school finance.

THE STATE PERSPECTIVE ON TAXATION AND EDUCATION. Equal protection challenges have been or are currently being made at the state level. In some states, the plaintiffs have emphasized a claim of equal protection; in others the focus has been on specific language in the state's constitution. In all cases, the issue is whether the state has fulfilled its constitutional obligation to provide for education. The answer by the state supreme courts in some states has been that education is not a fundamental right, and that as long as there is provision for a minimally adequate education, the equal protection clause is met.

For example, in *Serrano v. Priest* (1971), the California Supreme Court was called on to determine whether the California public school financing system, with its substantial dependence on local property taxes, violated the Fourteenth Amendment. In its six-to-one decision, the California court held that heavy reliance on unequal local property taxes "makes the quality of a child's education a function of the wealth of his parents and neighbors." Furthermore, the court declared, "Districts with small tax bases simply cannot levy taxes at a rate sufficient to produce the revenue that more affluent districts produce with a minimum effort." Officially, the California Supreme Court ruled that the system of school financing in California was unconstitutional but did not forbid the use of property taxes as long as the system of finance was neutral in the distribution of resources. Within a year of *Serrano v. Priest,* five other courts—in Minnesota, Texas, New Jersey, Wyoming, and Arizona—ruled similarly.

STATES' RESPONSIBILITY TO GUARANTEE EQUAL EDUCATIONAL OPPORTUNITY. In 1989 and 1990, several state supreme courts made significant decisions about school finance. Since then, in a number of states, the education finance systems were knocked down by the courts, and the state legislatures were directed to remedy the wrongs.

In Montana, in *Helena Elementary School District v. State* (1989), the Montana Supreme Court ruled that the state's school finance system violated the state constitution's guarantee of equal educational opportunity. The state's constitution article mandates that the state establish an educational system that will develop the full educational potential of each person. In 1990 the court delayed the effects of its decision to allow the legislature time to enact a new finance system.

The Kentucky Supreme Court also ruled that the state's entire system of school governance and finance violated the state constitution's mandate for the provision of an efficient system of common schools throughout the state (*Rose v. The Council for Better Education Inc.,* 1989). The Kentucky Supreme Court's opinion stated:

> The system of common schools must be adequately funded to achieve its goals. The system of common schools must be substantially uniform throughout the state. Each child, *every child,* in this commonwealth must be provided with an equal opportunity to have an adequate education. Equality is the key word here. The children of the poor and the children of the rich, the children who live in poor districts and the children who live in the rich districts must be given the same opportunity and access to an adequate education. This obligation cannot be shifted to local counties and local school districts.

The court directed the state legislature to develop a new educational system, which was adopted as the Kentucky Education Reform Act (KERA) in 1990.

Throughout the 1990s, there continued to be suits, court actions, and legislative initiatives regarding how best to address funding inequities for public schools. Earlier court decisions were also revisited. For example, in a turnaround of earlier decisions, in 1994 the State Supreme Court of

Arizona ruled that the state's property tax–based school financing system was unconstitutional because it created wide disparities between rich and poor school districts. As has been true in other states, the court left it up to the legislature to rectify the problem.

Undoubtedly, changes are occurring in the state provisions for financial support for education.

Entrepreneurial Efforts to Fund Education

The combination of tight budgets, increasing enrollments, and demands for better educational services is pressuring schools, school districts, and state officials to search for new funding sources. Some sources that were highly controversial in the past, such as the lottery, have now become a regular part of the main revenue stream. Other potential new sources of funds are now being considered, debated, and utilized.

As the financing of education gets tighter, novel strategies and new sources of funds such as advertising are being sought. Some of these potential sources are the subject of intense debate.

ADVERTISING: A NEW SOURCE OF REVENUE. School districts have found that they can raise money by selling space for advertising. For example, soft drinks and fast foods are advertised on the sides of school buses. School districts are seeking corporate sponsorships to support music and sports programs. For example, the Denver public schools solicited $500,000 from four companies to sponsor education programs and ran the companies' ads on school buses and at the district's main football stadium. One school district near the Dallas–Fort Worth International Airport sold space for advertising on the rooftops of district buildings to catch the eye of travelers on incoming flights. The Teacher Perspectives feature presents two diverse opinions about the topic of advertising in schools.

MORE STUDENT FEES. Expanded use of student fees, especially for noncore subjects and extracurricular activities, is prevalent. Fees for enrollment, gym clothes, yearbooks, and lab equipment have become standard. Fees for student parking are becoming routine as well. For parents with more than one child in a secondary school, these fees can total more than $500 a year. Through various fees, a large high school can increase its revenues by $50,000 to $250,000 annually, which can add up to $1 million in four years. Participation in an athletic program means yet more fees.

MORE FUND-RAISING SCHEMES. The entrepreneurial spirit seems to have no bounds once school and school district administrators jump on the capitalist bandwagon. Bake sales and parent booster groups are routine compared to some of the more innovative approaches being tried around the United States. For example, several school districts in California sent students home with forms their parents could sign to switch their long-distance telephone carrier. The school's parent–teacher association would receive 10 percent of the long-distance payment from each family. If the students signed up friends, neighbors, and relatives, the school would gain more revenue. Projections were that through this mechanism a large school could gain as much as half a million dollars a year. One step further is being tried by the San Francisco school district with the installation of cell phone towers on school grounds. This represents another source of revenue, but also raises concerns about the possibility of the electronic waves damaging children's health.

Several years ago, Del Oro High School in Loomis, California, tested a novel way of raising money to support its sports teams. At one fall football game, three cows were turned loose on the football field for "cow-chip bingo." The field was marked off in one-yard squares and chances were sold. The owners of squares where the cows made a "deposit" were the winners.

Questions about Fund-Raising Efforts. Given the special place and role of schools in society, important questions are being raised about the appropriateness of many of these newer fund-raising efforts. Equity is one important issue. Schools in wealthy communities can raise more money than

TEACHER PERSPECTIVES

Should Schools Accept Corporate Advertising and Sponsorship?

The need for additional funds for schools, in addition to those provided by taxpayers, is resulting in a number of innovative approaches being used, including sponsored advertising. What do you think about advertisements being placed in and around schools?

YES

Kathleen McMahon teaches fourth grade at Alice Costello School in Brooklawn, New Jersey.

In an ideal world, schools would have all the money they need to fund programs and buy equipment, but we're not living in Utopia. Public and private colleges accept money from plutocrats every day. I'm not very happy that our gym is named for Shop Rite, the local supermarket, but I do think that public schools should accept well-meaning contributions from the community, and businesses are an important part of the community. I believe that we can't educate our children without the efforts of everyone.

Shop Rite has been very kind to our school. They allow our special education students to intern at the store, and they donate food for needy families when we ask them. The store never attempts to push any curriculum ideas on us; they don't require us to do business with them. The management has been enormously supportive over many years. They have also pledged $100,000 over a 20-year period. In return, we have their name and a shopping cart logo on our new gymnasium.

I have mixed feelings about this. The sign smacks of advertising and commercialism. This neighborhood store, one of a small chain, is owned by members of the Brown family, and I would prefer having their name on the gym.

Another generous local business family gave us money for library books in honor of their parents. I am quite happy to say our new library is called the Flowers Media Center.

NO

Manny Lopez teaches fourth grade at the International Community School in Oakland, California.

It is unacceptable the in the richest and most powerful country in the world, a public school should lack the resources necessary to educate its children. A free, quality public education must be one of a democracy's top priorities, and it must be immune to any market-driven force. We as a nation, must unite and rally for well-funded schools for all. Our children deserve nothing less. Allowing advertising in our schools opens a Pandora's box. We must resist selling out our schools to the highest bidder.

The idea that advertisers would take advantage of the financially beleaguered conditions of many of our public schools should come as no surprise. Advertising is a market-driven enterprise, and schools represent an untapped market potential. Upon entering our schools, the advertisers would dictate the placement of their billboards, banners, and lightboxes. The highly visible areas normally reserved for students' artwork, bulletin boards, and school/community message centers would be taken over. It would only be a matter of time before advertisers would attempt to have a hand in the curriculum, molding a school into a corporate image.

Studies show that Americans are subjected to thousands of commercial images every day. There are already more than enough forces vying for our children's attention. Schools must remain sacred spaces whose sole purpose is the education of our youth, not the manipulated development of product loyalty.

Source: "Should Schools Accept Corporate Advertising and Sponsorship?" *NEA Today,* (October, 2006), p. 43. Reprinted by permission of the National Education Association.

What is your perspective on this issue?

myeducationlab To explore both sides of this issue and think about each perspective, go to the *Book Specific Resources* in the MyEducationLab for your course, select your text, and then select *Teacher Perspectives* for Chapter 9.

---

schools located in poor communities. If an important goal is to provide equal educational opportunity for all students, then the unequal distribution of funds and equipment is once again an issue.

A second important question has to do with children being exposed to advertising in schools. A report by Consumers Union points out how the underfunding of schools has led to students being a captive audience for marketers (Consumers Union Education Services, 1996). Many educators are concerned that students are impressionable, unsophisticated consumers and are easily influenced. In the school context, many students will have difficulty distinguishing advertising from lesson messages. Because of budget pressures, however, schools and school districts will likely continue to develop their commercial bent.

State Aid

State aid for education exists largely for three reasons: The state has the primary responsibility for educating its citizens; the financial ability of local school districts to support education varies widely; and personal wealth is now less related to real property than it once was. State aid can be classified as having general or categorical use. *General aid* can be used by the recipient school district as it desires; *categorical aid* is earmarked for specific purposes. General aid is often administered through a program that funds each school district up to a foundation level of education required per pupil. Categorical aid may include, for example, money for transportation,

FIGURE 9.8

Equalization and the Foundation Principle

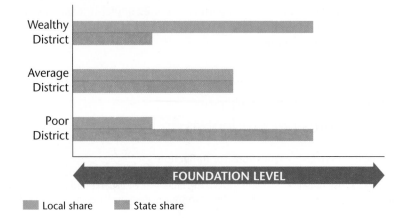

vocational education, driver education, or programs for children with disabilities. Frequently, categorical aid is given to encourage specific education programs; in some states, these aid programs are referred to as *incentive programs*. Categorical aid funds may be granted on a matching basis; thus, for each dollar of local effort, the state contributes a specific amount.

GENERAL STATE AID: EQUALITY OF OPPORTUNITY. Historically, general aid was based on the idea that each child, regardless of place of residence or the wealth of the local district, is entitled to receive a basic education. General state aid was established on the principle of equality of opportunity and is usually administered through a foundation program. Creating a *foundation program* involves determining the dollar value of the basic education opportunities desired in a state, referred to as the foundation level, and determining a minimum standard of local effort, considering local wealth. The foundation concept implies equity for taxpayers as well as equality of opportunity for students.

How State Foundation Programs Work. Figure 9.8 shows how a foundation program operates. The total length of each bar represents the foundation level of education required per pupil, expressed in dollars. Each school district must put forth the same minimum local effort to finance its schools; this effort could be, for example, a qualifying tax rate that produces the local share of the foundation level. This tax rate will produce more revenue in a wealthy district than it will in a poor district; therefore, the poor district will receive more state aid than the wealthy district. Local school districts do not receive general state aid beyond that amount established as the foundation but are permitted in most instances to exceed foundation levels at their own expense. See the Reflect on Diversity feature for more information about the potential effects of a state foundation funding program.

REFLECTonDIVERSITY   **Robin Hood Tax Laws**

One of the states' responses to lawsuits about equity and adequacy in the funding of schools is to take property tax revenues from a wealthy district and redistribute the funds to lower wealth districts. For example, Texas has well over four million students and more than one thousand school districts. One hundred and thirty-five of the more wealthy school districts must share their property tax revenue with the other 900 districts. The 900 districts educate 88 percent of the public school students. Many are calling this a "Robin Hood" system of school finance.

Questions for Reflection
1. What is your gut reaction to the idea of a Robin Hood school finance policy? What are the strengths and weaknesses of this strategy?
2. How would you feel about this if you were a property owner in one of the more wealthy districts?
3. How would you feel if you were a property owner in a less wealthy district?
4. If you were a taxpayer in a Robin Hood state, what type of accountability would you want to see?

myeducationlab To respond to these questions online, go to the *Book Specific Resources* section in the MyEducationLab for your course, select your text, and then select *Reflect on Diversity* for Chapter 9.

State Foundation Programs: Limited Effectiveness. The effectiveness of using various state foundation programs to bring about fiscal equalization has been limited. A major limitation is that the foundation established is frequently far below the actual expenditure or far below the level needed to provide adequate educational opportunity. For example, if a state established a per-pupil foundation level of $1,500 and the average actual per-pupil expenditure was $3,000, equalization would not have occurred.

GLOBAL PERSPECTIVES

International Comparisons: Expenditures per Student as an Indicator

Many indicators are used to demonstrate how the United States compares to other countries in education. Frequently the data are chosen to show that the United States is underperforming. One useful resource for international comparisons is the Organization for Economic Cooperation and Development (OECD) website at www.oecd.org. OECD is a partnership of the most developed nations, including those of Western Europe, the United States, Japan, and Australia.

One interesting set of financial data prepared for the U.S. Department of Education's NCES is expenditures per student. The data for six countries are presented in Figure 9.9.

Questions for Reflection

1. Given the intense demands for accountability, how would you explain the high level of expenditure in the United States given the perceptions that students in other countries perform better?
2. How would you explain these findings, especially for higher education? (*Hint:* "Total expenditure" means funds from all sources.)
3. How could you use these data to make a case for more or less spending for schools in the United States?

FIGURE 9.9

Annual Education Expenditure per Student, by Education Level and Country, 2005

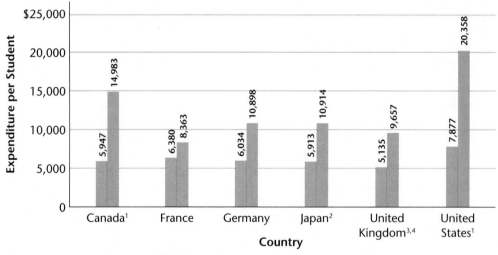

[1] Postsecondary nontertiary data included in secondary and higher education for Japan, and in secondary education for the United Kingdom.

[2] The United Kingdom includes England, Northern Ireland, Scotland, and Wales.

Note: Countries are arranged according to increasing levels of gross domestic product (GDP) per capita, as shown in parentheses. Education levels are defined according to the International Standard Classification of Education (ISCED97). Primary education refers to ISCED97 level 1. Secondary education refers to ISCED97 levels 2 and 3 (lower secondary and upper secondary, respectively). Higher education refers to ISCED97 levels 5A (academic higher education below the doctoral level), 5B (vocational higher education), and 6 (doctoral level of academic higher education), except where otherwise noted. Shown is total expenditure that corresponds to the nonrepayable current and capital expenditure of all levels of the government and private sources directly related to education; interest on debt is not included. Data are converted to U.S. dollars using 2004–05 national purchasing power parities (PPPs) exchange rate data. Includes all institutions, public and private, with the exception of Italy, which includes public institutions only.

Source: Organization for Economic Cooperation and Development (OECD), (2008). *Education at a glance: OECD Indicators 2008* (table B1.1a and table X2.1). Paris: Author; and OECD. (2008). Education Database, previously unpublished tabulation (Retrieved September 22, 2008).

A second limitation is that most general state aid programs do not provide for different expenditure levels for different pupil needs. Special education and vocational education, for example, both require more money to operate than the usual per-pupil expenditure for the typical elementary or secondary school pupil.

TAXPAYER REVOLT. In the past forty years, there have been a number of political initiatives by taxpayers to reduce their tax burden, especially the amount they pay in property taxes. This movement has been called the **taxpayer revolt**. A most dramatic instance of taxpayer revolt occurred in California in June 1978 with the passage of a citizens' ballot initiative called Proposition 13, which limited by constitutional amendment the property tax as a source of revenue. Subsequent and similar propositions have been added in other states. The trend is toward tax limitation, which reduces funds available for education. These efforts, along with a low success rate of local school bond referenda and the closing of school districts for periods of time because of insufficient operating funds, indicate problems ahead for the funding of public schools.

In many countries most of the funding for education comes from the national government. The amount of funding is quite varied as you can see from the Global Perspectives feature.

THE FEDERAL GOVERNMENT'S ROLE IN EDUCATION

As mentioned earlier, under the Tenth Amendment to the U.S. Constitution, education is a function of the states. Although the states have the primary responsibility for education and the schools are operated at the local level, during the past sixty years the federal government has assumed an ever-increasing involvement in education. In the 1960s and 1970s, the rationale for this interest and involvement was linked to national security and solving social problems. In the early 1990s, the rationale was based on economic competitiveness. In the late 1990s, the focus shifted to standards and testing, as well as concerns about funding of the infrastructure of schools.

The arrival of No Child Left Behind (NCLB) in 2002 accelerated the involvement of the federal government in education. This increasing centralization of power is called **federalism**. One consequence of federalism has been the establishment of more federal agencies, programs, and laws that address various aspects of the U.S. education system.

taxpayer revolt Political movement by citizens to freeze, or reduce, the amount of taxes paid.

federalism The process of centralizing more power over education at the federal level.

Leadership

The federal government has historically provided leadership in education in specific situations, usually in times of need or in crises that could not be fully addressed by the leadership in states or local school districts. In the 1980s, policy maker concerns over the quality of schools led to more active leadership on the part of the federal government, such as moves to establish national priorities in education and to raise major issues. For example, *A Nation at Risk,* the report prepared by the National Commission on Excellence in Education, was published in 1983.

That report was not a mandate, nor was funding recommended, but it did sound an alarm and also provided recommendations to be considered by states and local school districts. Identifying national educational issues and encouraging forums on these issues at the state and local levels, along with soliciting responses, have been appropriate federal activities. Other activities include research on significant national educational issues and dissemination of exemplary practices. During the past sixty years, the federal government has insinuated itself more and more by tying school district access to federal funds to education mandates. If states, and schools, accept federal dollars then they also accept the mandates that come with the funds.

In the past 60 years, the federal government has increased its involvement in education, taking a bigger role in determining the direction education should be heading.

The U.S. Department of Education

The first-ever agency of education in the federal government, established in 1867 through the diligent efforts of Henry Barnard, was called the Department of Education. Later, it was called the Office of Education (1869); at another time, it was the Bureau of Education within the Department of the Interior. In 1939 the Office of Education became a part of the Federal Security Agency, which in 1953 became the Department of Health, Education, and Welfare, wherein the U.S. Office of Education was assigned. In October 1979, President Jimmy Carter signed legislation creating a cabinet-level federal agency, the Department of Education. The new Department of Education took on the functions of the U.S. Office of Education. The latest version of the Department of Education, in contrast with the first in 1867, has become a powerful agency, which is seen in its authority under NCLB.

The U.S. Department of Education has some 4,500 employees and its 2008 budget was $68.6 billion. The department includes many offices and resources, including the National Center for Education Statistics, which compiles a wide range of statistics about education, the Office of Special Education and Rehabilitative Services, and the Office of Civil Rights. Information about grants, teacher resources, and statistics is available through the various Department of Education offices and programs or online at www.ed.gov.

There is no question that offering aid and awarding grants are effective ways to influence the goals of education nationally. However, debate continues about whether the offices of the federal government should have a stronger or weaker influence on education. Some people maintain that the socioeconomic forces of society are not contained within local school districts or state boundaries and therefore that direct federal intervention is needed. Others advocate dissolution of the department, insisting that education is a state responsibility. As is easy to see with the No Child Left Behind legislation, the clear trend in terms of acts of Congress and presidential leadership is toward a greater federal role in education.

Educational Programs Operated by the Federal Government

The federal government directly operates some school programs. For example, the public school system of the District of Columbia depends on Congress for funds. The Department of the Interior has the educational responsibility for children of national park employees, for Samoa (classified as an outlying possession), and for the trust territories of the Pacific, such as the Caroline and Marshall Islands. Many of the schools on Native American reservations are financed and managed through the Bureau of Indian Affairs (BIA) of the Department of the Interior. Twenty-five of these schools have become what are called contract schools, in which the tribe determines the program and staff but the BIA supports the schools financially. The Department of Defense (DOD) is responsible for the Military Academy at West Point, the Naval Academy at Annapolis, the Coast Guard Academy at New London, and the Air Force Academy at Colorado Springs. The DOD also operates a school system (DOD Dependents Schools, or DoDDS) for the children of military staff wherever members are stationed. The instruction supplied by the vocational and technical training programs of the military services has made a big contribution nationally to education as well.

The federal government also funds education research by individual university faculty and a set of ten regional education laboratories, which provide curriculum development, technical assistance, and evaluation services to school districts and states. Another important resource for teachers has been the Education Resources Information Center (ERIC). This center maintains digital archives of research reports and curriculum materials. Teachers can request specific information and literature searches from the ERIC databases.

No Child Left Behind

The widest sweeping effort by the federal government to improve student learning and schools across the nation is the 2002 reauthorization of the Elementary and Secondary Education Act (ESEA). The first ESEA was passed by Congress in 1965 as one of President Lyndon Johnson's Great Society initiatives. Since then, the ESEA has been reauthorized every four or five years. Each time the scope of the bill has expanded. Unfortunately, although a major intent of the ESEA was to increase the success of poor and minority students, the results during the past fifty years have not been dramatic. With the leadership of President George W. Bush, the 2002 ESEA reauthorization represented a major rethinking based around the theme of No Child Left Behind (NCLB). Two major purposes of NCLB were to raise student achievement across the board and to eliminate the **achievement gap** among students from different backgrounds. The nearly 2,100

myeducationlab

Go to the *Building Teaching Skills and Dispositions* section of Topic 5: *Governance and Finance* in the MyEducationLab for your course and complete the activity titled *The Impact of NCLB on School Governance and Financing*.

achievement gap The systematic difference in learning between majority and minority, or rich and poor, students.

pages of this bill contained many directives and initiatives for states and school districts. Three of these are particularly important for future teachers to understand: HQT (highly qualified teachers), AYP (adequate yearly progress), and SINOI (schools in need of improvement).

HIGHLY QUALIFIED TEACHERS (HQT). The NCLB Act requires that school districts employ only teachers who are highly qualified. The law specifies what "highly qualified" means:

- Public elementary and secondary teachers must be fully licensed or certified by the state and must not have any certification or licensure requirements waived on an emergency, temporary, or provisional basis.
- New public elementary school teachers must have at least a bachelor's degree and pass a rigorous state test demonstrating subject knowledge and teaching skills in reading, writing, mathematics, and other areas of any basic elementary school curriculum.
- New middle or secondary school teachers must have at least a bachelor's degree and demonstrate competency by passing a rigorous state test in each subject they will teach, or successfully complete a major, or graduate degree, or advanced certification in each subject they will teach.

ADEQUATE YEARLY PROGRESS (AYP). This is the basis for determining whether schools, districts, and states are in compliance with the law. The primary criterion is student performance on standardized tests. A key difference from the past is that under NCLB all students must be making progress, and there must be improvement each year so that by the school year 2013–14, all students in all schools will be "proficient." Student test scores are to be **disaggregated** by the subgroups of:

- Economically disadvantaged students
- Major racial or ethnic groups
- Students with disabilities
- English-language learners (ELL).

An additional step in the NCLB mandate is that student performance in the 2001–02 school year is to serve as the baseline. States then have twelve years to have all students meet the 2013–14 proficiency level, which means that students within each subgroup who had test scores in 2001–02 below the proficient level need to, on average, improve by one-twelfth each year. This is where the AYP concept comes from; states have to report to the federal government each year that test scores for students in all subgroups are moving toward being at least proficient.

SCHOOLS IN NEED OF IMPROVEMENT (SINOI). NCLB sets timelines and establishes consequences for states, school districts, and schools in which student performance on test scores does not meet the AYP targets. One unfortunate consequence is that these schools will be labeled as "low performing" or "failing" schools. Another consequence of the way AYP is defined is that sooner or later most schools are likely to be labeled as SINOI schools. These schools receive a label such as "N3" or "N4," which indicates the number of years during which the students in one or more subcategories did not meet AYP. These schools and districts are then subject to one of the following "corrective actions":

1. Schools that fail to meet AYP for two consecutive years must be identified as "needing improvement."
2. Schools that fail to meet the state AYP standard for three consecutive years (N3) must offer pupils from low-income families the opportunity to receive instruction from a supplemental services provider of the parents' choice.
3. Schools that fail to meet AYP for four consecutive years (N4) must take one or more of the following corrective actions: Replace school staff, implement a new curriculum, decrease management authority, appoint an outside expert to advise the school, extend the school day or year, or change the school's internal organizational structure.
4. Schools that fail to meet AYP standards for five consecutive (N5) years must be restructured, which includes reopening as a charter school, replacing all or most school staff, state takeover of school operations, or other "major restructuring" of school governance.

OTHER NCLB REQUIREMENTS. Many more elements, mandates, and expectations are part of the 2002 version of the NCLB Act, such as annual testing of students in grades 3 through 8 in math and reading/language arts, as well as testing them three times in science by grade 12. Annual state report cards are required, in which, among other things, SINOI schools must be listed. Also, school

disaggregated The process of separating test scores based on student characteristics such as gender, ethnicity, and socioeconomic status.

districts must make available to parents, on request, the following information about their child's classroom teacher:

- Whether the teacher has met state qualification and licensing criteria for the grade levels and subject areas taught
- Whether the teacher is teaching under emergency or other provisional status
- The baccalaureate degree of the teacher and any other graduate certification or degree held by the teacher and the subject area of the certification or degree
- Whether the child is provided service by paraprofessionals and, if so, the paraprofessional's qualifications.

School choice is a strategy for addressing the social challenges described in Chapters 6 and 7.

IMPACT OF NCLB. The NCLB legislation has placed heavy demands on teachers, schools, school districts, and states. There are many positive outcomes as well as many criticisms. One important outcome of the requirement to disaggregate test scores is that schools must strive to increase test scores for *all* students. No longer can expectations for achievement by minority, special needs, or ELL students be lower than for other, more "mainstream" students. Another impact is the reality that more and more schools are failing to achieve AYP in all student categories and therefore are labeled as "needing improvement."

A number of tactics are being used to increase test scores:

- "Bubble kids" are those who scored a few points below the proficient level. By targeting them it is hoped that at the next testing they will score higher.
- "Safe harbor" is the status of a school that was in need of improvement and has made progress in reducing the number of students scoring below proficient, but has not reached the AYP target.
- "District in need of improvement" is the label applied when AYP is not maintained for all schools and categories of students.
- "Corrective actions" are the steps that must be taken if a school/district fails to achieve AYP over time.
- "Supplemental services" are being provided, such as consultants to analyze data and provide training, as well as the addition of after-school programs.

Thoughtful critics and historians have offered some interesting comparisons between the original 1965 ESEA and the 2002 NCLB reauthorization. Some critics of the original ESEA say that it failed because it provided money without accountability, and the NCLB Act will succeed because it requires strict accountability. The ESEA of 1965 may have offered money without much educational accountability, but the NCLB Act demands heavy accountability without much greater federal financial and technical assistance—an approach no more likely to succeed.

In 1965, extensive federal requirements like those of NCLB would never have made it through Congress. At that time, the federal role in education was marginal, and most state education agencies had limited authority and capabilities. Local people were extremely wary that more federal aid would bring federal control. Since then the federal and state roles in education have grown, and states and school districts recognize that accepting federal requirements goes along with receiving federal funding.

In summary, the No Child Left Behind Act is a far-reaching, long-lasting federal statute intended to improve accountability, as defined in terms of student performance on standardized state testing in all states, all school districts, all schools, and all classrooms.

Federal Aid

As illustrated earlier in Figure 9.6 the federal government provides the smallest proportion (9.1%) of revenue for public education. Still, the United States has a history of federal aid to education, but it has been categorical and not general aid; it has been related to the needs of the nation at the time. Federal aid actually started before the U.S. Constitution was adopted, with the Northwest Ordinance of 1785, which provided land for public schools in "western territories." Such specialized federal aid has continued in a steady progression to the present. Almost 200 federal aid-to-education laws have been passed since the Northwest Ordinance.

local control Educational decision making by citizens at the local level rather than at the state or national level.

LOCAL CONTROL VERSUS FEDERALISM. In the past, an important and unique feature of education in the United States was **local control**, the belief that educational decisions should be made at the local level rather than at the state or national level. The rationale has been that people at the local level, including teachers and parents, know what is best for the students in their community. As has been described in this chapter, the trend during the past sixty years has been toward more federalism. The No Child Left Behind Act is the latest and heaviest centralization initiative by the federal government and includes many mandates to states, school districts, schools, and teachers.

Those who advocate for more federal and state involvement argue that education is a responsibility of all society. Some also argue that national survival requires centralized policies and programs. The underlying questions are not just about what is best for students and the nation; they are about power, authority, and who gets to decide.

Technology and School Administration

It would be very time consuming and in many ways impossible to operate today's schools and school districts without technology. One of the most obvious uses of technology is for computing and managing budgets. Another important application is in planning class schedules for students and teachers. In the "old" days school principals used entire chalk boards to sketch out, arrange, and rearrange teacher assignments and student schedules. Now there are computer programs to do this task.

A more significant use of technology and one that teachers experience weekly, if not daily, is for compiling, analyzing, and displaying student data. Many schools have a **school improvement team (SIT)** that meets once a week. The team has representatives from each grade level and/or content area. The special education resource teacher and literacy specialists are often members of the SIT. In each meeting the progress of all students who have been identified as in need of extra help is reviewed. Technology has been used to score and store the various tests and assessments for each student. During the meeting the data for each student is displayed on a screen. The student's progress is reviewed and agreement is reached on what instructional interventions should be done next. Due to the use of technology, the records of several hundred students can be compiled and retrieved as needed for these weekly reviews.

Technology is important at the district level too. Nearly all districts now have a **student information system (SIS)**, which allows all test scores to be compiled and analyzed at the district office. District administrators can review how students are performing across the district, for each school, and even for type of students. For example, the performance of students who receive free or reduced lunches can be compared to those who come from more wealthy neighborhoods. In the best SIS, teacher-friendly, up-to-the-day data displays are available for each student through the computer on the teacher's desk.

POLITICS AND ACCOUNTABILITY IN EDUCATION

So far this chapter has provided information about the formal structures of public education and revenues and expenditures at the local, state, and federal levels. Although these organizational structures illustrate the line and staff relationships, another set of relationships is important to consider and understand. Each of these levels is involved in politics—the politics of education. Reread the *Education in the News* story at the beginning of this chapter. Imagine all of the interest groups—and conflicting agendas—around the development of a new statute for the financing of education in New Mexico. Local school districts also are interested in federal educational programs and grants, so they will contact members of Congress to express their opinions. The purpose is to influence representatives' understanding of local needs and their actions on relevant legislation.

Local school districts and professional associations follow closely what is happening in their state legislature. These groups do not hesitate to let members in the legislature know their opinions or to urge action. It is not unusual for local school superintendents, board members, as well as teacher association members, to meet with their senators and representatives in person. These contacts with federal and state agencies are representative of **political action**. You as a teacher education candidate, and in the future as a teacher, cannot escape politics. So learn all you can now and begin developing your political knowledge and skills.

Besides paying for schools, the most enduring theme in politics at this time is **accountability**. The president, congress, governors, legislators, school boards, and district administrators all want schools (and teachers) to be accountable. The elements of accountability vary from school finances, to school and teacher quality, to student test scores. At all levels the politics of accountability are intense and hard fought.

school improvement team (SIT) A team representing all subject areas or grade levels that reviews student progress on a weekly basis.

student information system (SIS) A computer-based data management system that is designed to compile and analyze test scores so that district administrators can review the performance of all students and each school.

political action Becoming involved to influence decision making.

accountability A school's obligation to take responsibility for what students learn.

Special-interest groups organize to influence elections, funding of education, and how funds are expended.

Politics: Neither Positive nor Negative

Although many of the examples presented here might appear to be negative, keep in mind that politics are neither good nor bad. Instead, politics influence the way in which all organizations work. Areas of disagreement will always exist in all organizations, including schools. People have varying interests and agendas. In many cases, there are basic differences in points of view that need to be resolved for the organization to move ahead.

This is where knowledge and political skill become a special strength for teachers and school administrators. Those who are skillful in talking with all parties and negotiating areas of agreement make significant contributions. Rather than judging "politics" as bad, successful teachers learn how politics work and develop the skills to contribute to and influence the political process. Closing the classroom door guarantees that your positions and ideas will not be considered. Learn more about organizations and political processes and you will see politics as fascinating and, yes, even fun.

Politics across the Education System

There is no escaping politics as a basic force within organizations and across society. Graphic examples in recent times include the desperate attempts in each state to balance the budget while legislators and governors hear from different interest groups all wanting more money for themselves, pressing for less money for some other agency or effort, while also advocating that there be no increases in taxes. At the national level the wide-ranging, sharply stated, and often opposing views about what should be done in the reauthorization of the NCLB legislation illustrates how complex the issues and the difficulty of coming to a decision can be. Politics can be just as intense and conflicted at the local level.

SCHOOL BOARD POLITICS. Most school districts have "at-large" elections to select board members. In at-large elections every voter in a community is able to vote for a candidate for each seat on the board. The alternative is to have each board seat represent a particular region of the district. Either way there will be strong interest on the part of each voter in having a board member that will represent his or her interests. Nearly every decision a board makes has a political component. Issues such as approving the superintendent's salary, changing the boundaries of a school, raising taxes, reducing staff or extracurricular programs, busing students, and tolerating a losing athletic season bring out strong voices with often competing points of view.

SUPERINTENDENT POLITICS. As the chief executive officer, the superintendent has to listen to the opinions of all board members and strive to maintain a majority of the board's support to be retained (Hunter, 1997). The superintendent also has to work with and listen to teachers, principals, central office staff, and various members of the community. All will have suggestions for the superintendent and for what the school district should be doing.

School Politics

Schools are not devoid of politics, nor are you free from politics in your teacher education program. Principals, other teachers, parents, students, and teacher education faculty have certain things they would like to see accomplished. There also are likely to be conflicting views about how to accomplish the end. Resolving these issues requires leadership and skill.

PROFESSIONAL DILEMMA

What Is the Appropriate Role for Teachers When the Politics Get Rough?

The education accountability movement of the past decade has demanded that teachers and school administrators make serious efforts to change the way schools operate and to implement new approaches to help students learn. Policy makers, business leaders, and citizens at large have demanded that schools "reform" and "restructure." As discussed in Chapters 11 and 12, schools are now expected to implement curriculum standards and to administer newly created tests of student learning. Yet major changes in the structure and operation of schools are difficult to accomplish. It is hard for teachers to give up or change what they have been doing. It takes a great deal of time to work through the process that is necessary to develop a consensus among teachers, administrators, and parents about how a school should be restructured and what it should become. It also takes several years to work out the kinks when trying something new.

Suppose that after you had spent three years discussing and then two years implementing a major restructuring of your school and saw that it was working with students, a newly elected majority on the school board demanded that you return to the old way. As a teacher, what would you do?

This is not a hypothetical question. In one recent example, after more than three years of broad-based discussions involving teachers, administrators, students, parents, and community members, one school district's school board approved new performance-based graduation requirements for one of its high schools. The new requirements were based on student accomplishments rather than on seat-time. In fact, the high school had received national recognition for its efforts.

In November of the second year of implementation, three conservative members were elected to the five-member school board. A major theme in their election campaign was an attack on the new graduation requirements, which they promised to remove. In January the new majority on the school board proceeded to implement its campaign promise. Although students from the school, parents, and school staff members asked that the board not do this, or that the board at least allow the new graduation requirements to be optional, the board voted three to two to return to the traditional requirements. Remember that there were now students in their second year of high school who had been told that they were expected to meet the new graduation requirements.

The school board did not stop there. In the same month, January, the board terminated the superintendent, who was viewed as a very able educator by most and was well known and respected nationally. By the end of the school year, several school principals and teachers had taken positions elsewhere, and the district was running advertisements nationwide for principals and teachers who held "traditional" educational values. This might sound like an extreme case, but similar events have happened in other school districts, and similar cases will happen in one form or another during your years as an educator.

If you were a teacher in a school district where something like this occurred, what would you do? Your colleagues, the school, your students, and the innovative program have been challenged. It is clear that there is the potential for casualties, including your job. Of course, your actions will depend partly on which side of the issue you are on. Either way, what will you do?

Questions for Reflection
1. Will you speak out or wait for others to do so?
2. What will you tell your students?
3. Will you support your principal publicly or leave the principal on his or her own?
4. How do you think you would feel the next time you were asked to invest four or five years in designing and implementing a major change in your school?

TEACHERS AS POLITICIANS. Teachers often state that they do not wish to become involved in politics—as if they have a choice. Schools are not devoid of politics. Teachers lobby the principal for preferred teaching assignments, parents want particular teachers for their children, and teachers join together to advocate for a particular instructional approach. Decisions about what committees and tasks (e.g., lunch duty) each teacher will do entail some political elements. The Professional Dilemma feature asks you to consider your response to a political situation involving graduation requirements.

CLASSROOM POLITICS. Yes, there are politics in classrooms. When students approach the teacher to request clarification about an assignment or lobby to have a test rescheduled, they are engaging in politics. So are the parents who talk with the teacher about how their child is progressing. These are not bad actions; instead they are key to success in organizations and social systems.

JOURNAL FOR REFLECTION

How do you feel about the suggestion that education is political and that you should develop your political knowledge and skill? In what ways do you see this being important to you, your teaching, your students, your school? Or, do you think that you can avoid politics as a teacher?

WHEN TO TALK TO WHOM. When teachers have an idea about the school, want to try something different, or see a problem, it is important for them to talk with others to see what they think. Others may share an interest in the idea or may know about related thoughts of others. However, if you are aware of a serious problem, such as safety or a potentially illegal incident, then it is important to report this immediately to your direct supervisor. If department heads or team leaders are in place, then the first discussions should be with them. In any organization, including schools, if there is a serious problem, the normal protocol is to talk first with the person at the next level up the "chain of command." In any instance, a beginning teacher, or one who is new to the system, should seek advice from an experienced colleague before taking action. In addition to knowing the system, one must know how the system works; colleagues and principals can be helpful in this regard.

SOURCES OF POWER. Often when thinking about politics the idea of power comes to mind. Some people are seen as having more power than others. What may not be understood is that there are different sources of power. The early sections of this chapter introduced you to one important source, **position power**. For example, administrators in line positions have authority over the people under them in the organization chart.

There are other forms of power that at times can be more influential than position power. For example, **expertise** can be important. A teacher who has expert knowledge about teaching ELL students and a reputation for their excelling in his or her classroom has power. Being a member of certain **networks** or associations such as teacher unions and professional associations is another source of power.

Another important source of power is to form an **interest group** or **coalition**. Suppose several teachers are interested in using a certain computer program that the school does not have. By working together the group may be able to influence the principal, or a parent association, to purchase the program. Each teacher individually could not get the support, but by forming a coalition, together they have more power.

Accountability

With the arrival of the No Child Left Behind Act, states, school districts, and schools are being held accountable as never before. Although there are many definitions of the term *accountability*, in education it means that schools must devise a way of relating the vast expenditure made for education to the educational results, especially student performance on tests. For many years, the quality of education was measured by the number of dollars spent or the processes of education used. In other words, a school system that had a relatively high cost per pupil or used educational techniques judged to be effective was considered an excellent system. Seldom was the effectiveness of school systems judged by student outcomes—the educational achievements of students. Now those outcomes and their cost must be clearly accounted for.

Assessing student learning is a significant component of accountability, which is described in Chapter 11.

position power Power derived from holding a certain office, title, or job.

expertise Having a higher level of knowledge about a certain topic or skill than most people.

networks Personal connections gained through membership in an organization, club, or association.

interest group Group of people who have a shared agenda.

coalition Two or more interest groups that join in an effort to advance a shared agenda.

ROOTS OF ACCOUNTABILITY. Accountability has its roots in two fundamental modern problems: the continuous escalation of educational costs and, closely related, the loss of faith in educational results. The failure of the U.S. educational system, particularly in the cities and in some remote rural areas, has been accurately documented. The expectations of citizens for their children have not been met. Although U.S. public schools historically have done the best job of any nation in the world in providing education for *all of the children of all of the people,* they still have failed some of their constituents.

THE IMPORTANCE OF TEACHER ACCOUNTABILITY. Teachers play an important role in the quest for accountability. They are the primary contact with students, and they are directly responsible for instruction and student achievement. Therefore, they are expected to do their utmost to motivate students to learn and achieve. The assessment of accountability relies on data; therefore, teachers need to keep accurate records with respect to student achievement and be certain that instruction is well aligned with what is being tested.

REWARDS FOR BEING ACCOUNTABLE. The other side of the accountability coin is determining the rewards for success and the sanctions for failure. In the 1980s, many reward programs consisted of bestowing special designations and plaques on schools. In the 1990s, there was a shift to the use of money as a reward or sanction. Under NCLB, few rewards exist. Instead, different forms of threats and sanctions hang over states, school districts, and schools that "need improvement."

REWARDING TEACHERS AND PRINCIPALS. Other accountability initiatives target teachers and principals directly through focused evaluation and training programs, as well as offering financial rewards. For example, some states and school districts pay teachers more for becoming board certified.

SCHOOL AND SCHOOL DISTRICT REPORT CARDS. In the past, report cards were used only to evaluate students. A new element in the accountability movement is the use of new forms of report cards to "grade" schools, school districts, and states. Advocates of report cards argue that parents and voters need to know how well their school or school district is doing in comparison to others. They also point out that evaluating schools is complex; many factors need to be considered. A report card can incorporate many factors and present a clear picture. Opponents express concern that report cards still are overly simplistic representations. They argue that report cards increase competition, which is not supposed to be a part of public education. Proponents argue back that competition will make low-performing schools improve and/or inform parents so that they can make the choice of sending their children to another school.

LOOKING AHEAD:
THE CONTINUING CHALLENGE OF FUNDING EDUCATION

There is no doubt that as your career as a teacher unfolds the topics addressed in this chapter will continue to be with you. The organization of schools and the public education system will continue to evolve. We know that finding the necessary funds and spending them wisely will continue to be a major challenge. Taxes, spending, school efficiencies, and accountability will continue to be hot topics and will continue to be addressed through politics. Your success as a teacher and the learning successes of your students will depend heavily on the decisions that are made within the political arena of each school, district, state, and at the federal level.

Teachers truly are part of the large and complex system of education that includes all levels of government from the local, to the state, to the federal. Historically, since the U.S. Constitution does not address education directly, the primary authority and responsibility for schools has been assigned to the states. However, in the past sixty years the federal government has become directly involved. The No Child Left Behind statute is a clear example of this increasing federalism. It is likely that the role of the federal government will continue to increase.

The financial challenges affecting the nation that began in the fall of 2008 are continuing to be difficult for education. An early major response from the Congress and President Obama was the American Recovery and Reinvestment Act (ARRA) of 2009. This bill provided approximately $100 billion for education. Its intentions include saving jobs in school districts and advancing reforms

> that will create long-lasting results for our students and our nation including early learning, K–12, and post-secondary education. . . . The overall goals of the ARRA are to stimulate the economy in the short term and invest in education and other essential public services to ensure the long-term economic health of the nation. (U.S. Department of Education, 2009a)

A major challenge for all will continue to be that of obtaining sufficient funds from various sources to support schools and teachers, improve student performance, and at the same time not cause a taxpayer revolt.

Politics and accountability will continue to be linked. Teachers are not likely to receive pay increases by simply having one more year of teaching experience. Public and political pressures to have any increases in funding tied to increases in performance are not going to diminish. Student test scores, qualifications of teachers and principals, and indicators of increasing efficiency are key indicators. Also, keep in mind that within an organization a line administrator, such as a principal, represents only one of several sources of power. Another important source of power in politics is the various interest groups and coalitions. They will have a big say in determining future indicators of accountability.

SUMMARY

SCHOOL DISTRICTS: ORGANIZATION AND FINANCES

- There are more than 14,000 school districts in the United States.
- In fiscal year 2006 the average expenditure per student was $9,154.
- School boards have the authority to hire teachers and principals.
- Superintendents are the chief executive officer of the school district.
- Curriculum coordinators in the district office have staff authority.

THE ORGANIZATION OF SCHOOLS

- Principals have line authority to supervise teachers.
- Department heads and team leaders are important communication sources.
- Don't forget to work well with school secretaries, custodians, and cafeteria workers.

ORGANIZATION OF EDUCATION AT THE STATE LEVEL

- The U.S. Constitution passes authority for education to the states.
- Each state has a superintendent of public instruction also called the chief state school officer.
- The state department of education licenses teachers and administrators.

SOURCES OF REVENUE FOR SCHOOLS

- On average 46+ percent of the expenditures for education comes from the state.
- Until recently, the property tax has been the primary source of revenue for schools.
- The property tax is progressive, whereas the sales tax is regressive.
- Adequacy, equity, and equal opportunity are key themes that must be addressed in the financing of education.
- Foundation programs are one way in which states adjust funding to achieve equity.

THE FEDERAL GOVERNMENT'S ROLE IN EDUCATION

- The federal government has increased its influence by offering the carrot of extra funds along with the stick of mandates.
- No Child Left Behind was the name given to the 2001 reauthorization of ESEA.
- Adequate yearly progress (AYP) is the key to evaluating school performance.

POLITICS AND ACCOUNTABILITY IN EDUCATION

- Politics are neither positive nor negative.
- Teachers need to be political too.
- Accountability is important at all levels from states to school districts to schools to teachers.

LOOKING AHEAD: THE CONTINUING CHALLENGE OF FUNDING EDUCATION

- Funding of education will continue to be challenging.
- Taxes, spending, school efficiencies, and accountability will continue to be hot topics addressed through politics.

DISCUSSION QUESTIONS

1. Do you think the federal government should be assuming such a strong role over states, school districts, and schools? What are some likely consequences of this increasing federalism?
2. What are the advantages of using sales and income taxes to fund elementary and secondary education instead of relying on the property tax?
3. What situations have you encountered that illustrate the tension between state and local education interests? Is local control an issue in your state?
4. When is it appropriate for teachers to engage in politics? How can teachers influence what goes on in their schools? How can they influence decisions at the district and board levels?
5. What forms or types of accountability do you believe should be used to evaluate schools and teachers? What about the increasing use of test scores to judge effectiveness?
6. Many states have turned to gaming (lotteries, riverboat casinos, and slot machines) as a source of revenue for schools. What are the arguments in support of this funding mechanism? What do you see as possible downsides?

SCHOOL-BASED OBSERVATIONS

1. When you have the opportunity to visit a school or interview a teacher/principal, ask a teacher/principal to draw an organization chart and place him- or herself in it. Did the person just draw line relationships or did he or she also consider staff relationships? If the person did not consider staff relationships, ask about organization relationships with the district office (e.g., relationships with curriculum coordinators and staff developers). Does the person see these relationships as line or staff?
2. Seek an opportunity to study a school budget. Determine the different sources of revenue (e.g., local, state, federal, grants, activity fees). What are the biggest line-item expenditures? Are some monies discretionary for teachers? Note that in most schools, especially high schools, a surprising number of activities generate cash. Inquire about the implications of having cash on hand, and ask how these amounts are secured and what policies guide their uses.

PORTFOLIO DEVELOPMENT

1. Develop an organizational chart for a school you are familiar with. Use solid lines to represent line relationships and dotted lines to signify staff relationships. Draw the arrangement of personnel in regard to each of the following decisions: (a) determining a child's grade on his or her report card, (b) expelling a student (hint—don't forget that the school is part of a school district), (c) deciding on the topic for a staff development day, and (d) determining whether a particular teaching activity will be used. After considering these different decisions, explain your thoughts and feelings about the authority and accountability of teachers within the school as an organization.
2. One important component of the No Child Left Behind Act is the part mandating that each state set standards for highly qualified teachers (HQTs). Check your state's department of education website for the requirements for being an HQT in your state and then analyze your résumé. What will you need to accomplish to become an HQT?
3. School finance and spending will continue to be hot topics for school districts, state legislatures, and taxpayers. Start a file of articles from newspapers and news magazines and notes from television and radio news reports that deal with school finance and spending. Review the items in your file. Do certain topics and themes, such as concern about high taxes, emerge? When you are ready to apply for a position, having knowledge about finance and spending issues will make you better informed and prepared.

PREPARING FOR CERTIFICATION

1. The Praxis II Principles of Learning and Teaching (PLT) test includes cases and items that address the following skills that are required of beginning teachers: "Develop and utilize active partnerships among teachers, parents/guardians, and leaders in the community to support the educational process
   • Shared ownership
   • Shared decision making
   • Respectful/reciprocal communication"

   Reread this chapter's discussion of innovative organizational structures for schools. How might these alternative forms of school organization and management affect your role as a teacher? What skills will you need to function in such restructured schools?

2. Answer the following multiple-choice question, which is similar to items in Praxis and other state certification tests.

   The federal government fully funds several of today's schools. Which of the following schools does it NOT fund?
   a. Department of Defense schools
   b. The District of Columbia schools
   c. West Point
   d. Inner-city schools

3. Answer the following short-answer question, which is similar to items in Praxis and other state certification tests.

   The support of public schools comes from a variety of taxes paid to local, state, and federal government, including property taxes, sales or use taxes, and income taxes. Identify one other form of financial support as defined in the legal cases presented in the chapter that relate to the use of public funds for private education. Discuss the pros and cons of this financial support. Justify your answer within the context of providing an equal educational opportunity for all children. Describe how the selected form of support could affect equity and adequacy.

After you've completed your written responses for the above questions, use the Praxis general scoring guide provided in Chapter 1 to see if you can revise your response to improve your score.

MYEDUCATIONLAB

myeducationlab Now go to Topic 5: *Governance and Finance* and Topic 6: *School Organization* in the MyEducationLab (www.myeducationlab.com) for your course, where you can:

• Find learning outcomes for *Governance and Finance* and *School Organization* along with the national standards that connect to these outcomes.

• Complete *Assignments and Activities* that can help you more deeply understand the chapter content.

• Apply and practice your understanding of the core teaching skills identified in the chapter with the *Building Teaching Skills and Dispositions* learning units.

• Check your comprehension on the content covered in the chapter by going to the *Study Plan* in the *Book Specific Resources* section for your text. Here you will be able to take a chapter quiz, receive feedback on your answers, and then access *Review, Practice, and Enrichment* activities to enhance your understanding of chapter content.

WEBSITES

www.ed.gov The U.S. Department of Education is a very important and useful resource for teachers. Each of the department's offices are linked from this home page.

www.ed.gov/nces The National Center for Education Statistics is the main resource for statistical data about schools, ranging from school size to teacher qualifications to an interactive link that allows comparison of your school or district to others.

www.eric.uoregon.edu The University of Oregon Clearinghouse on Educational Policy and Management has many reports and publications (including ERIC) related to the organization of schools.

www.nasbe.org The National Association of State Boards of Education is a good source of information about issues and topics being addressed in each state.

www.oecd.org The Organization for Economic Cooperation and Development (OECD) is a useful resource for comparative data and policies from many developed countries.

www.edweek.org *Education Week* is the weekly newspaper that reports on all education topics including finance, organization, and legal issues. It also has a classified section for open positions.

www.ncsl.org The National Council of State Legislatures is an easy resource to find out about state legislatures and education-related policy initiatives.

www.wested.org WestEd is a major education research and development organization that produces useful reports and develops innovative approaches to curriculum and school organization.

FURTHER READING

Bolman, L. G., & Deal, T. E. (2008). *Reframing organizations: Artistry, choice and leadership* (4th ed.). San Francisco: Jossey-Bass. Many books about organization theory are complicated and provide few examples. This book is the exception. All of the theories and research about organizations and leadership are described in terms of four frames or perspectives. Each frame is described separately, along with plenty of interesting examples from all types of organizations, including schools. The focus throughout is the implications for teacher and administrator leadership.

Odden, A., & Picus, L. (2004). *School finance: A policy perspective*. New York: McGraw-Hill. This text explores school finance and expenditures beginning with a historical review. The growth of equity and adequacy issues is presented along with several chapters that address legal parameters and court cases from recent years. Throughout, the ultimate purpose of education, student achievement, is kept in mind.

chapter ten

LEGAL PERSPECTIVES
ON EDUCATION

EDUCATION IN THE **NEWS**

TEACHER FIRED FOR INAPPROPRIATE BEHAVIOR ON MYSPACE PAGE

By **JEFFREY D. NEUBURGER**,

PBS, Mediashift, October 15, 2008

It's not just students who can get into difficulty for school-related blogging.

In a recent case, a federal court rejected a challenge brought by a non-tenured teacher when the public school at which he taught decided not to renew his contract. The school had accused the teacher of overly familiar contacts with students via his My-Space page that were deemed "disruptive to school activities."

SPANIERMAN V. HUGHES

In *Spanierman v. Hughes,* 2008 U.S. Dist. LEXIS 69569 (D. Conn. Sept. 16, 2008), Jeffrey Spanierman, a teacher at Emmett O'Brien High School in Ansonia, Connecticut, created a MySpace page, ostensibly "to communicate with students about homework, to learn more about the students so he could relate to them better, and to conduct casual, non-school related discussions."

One of Spanierman's school colleagues became concerned about the page, which she said contained, among other things, pictures of naked men with "inappropriate comments" underneath them. She was also concerned about the nature of the personal conversations that the teacher was having with the students, and she convinced Spanierman to remove the page, which she considered "disruptive to students." Spanierman subsequently created a new MySpace page, however, that included similar content and similar personal communications with students. When the colleague learned of the new page, she reported it to the school administration, which placed Spanierman on administrative leave and ultimately declined to renew his teaching contract for the following year. After hearings that he attended with his union representative and later with his attorneys, he received a letter stating that he had "exercised poor judgment as a teacher."

LEGAL ISSUES

The discipline of a teacher for conduct outside the classroom raises a number of legal issues, depending upon the circumstances: Is the school public or private? Did the teacher have a contract with the school that gives the teacher rights with respect to job termination? Are there state statutes that impose standards on the teacher, or obligations on the school with respect to teacher discipline? Did the conduct involve expression that may be protected by the First Amendment? Did the conduct have a connection to the school environment?

Spanierman was employed by a public school, consequently, the school's ability to take disciplinary action was limited by both the federal and state constitutions, in particular the First Amendment and the "due process" clause of the Fourteenth Amendment. Spanierman claimed that both his "procedural" and his "substantive" due process rights were violated.

As a non-tenured teacher, Spanierman was more vulnerable to the school's evaluation of his conduct than a tenured teacher might have been.

The nature of the "procedure" to which an individual is entitled under the due process clause depends upon the nature of the right the individual is claiming. The minimum procedure to which an individual is usually entitled is notice and an opportunity to be heard. Spanierman based his procedural due process claim on the Connecticut Teacher Tenure Act, which he claimed gave him certain procedural rights, i.e., a period of notice and a hearing, and termination only for just cause. The court found that Spanierman had received notice and a hearing, but that neither the Connecticut Statute nor the teacher's union-negotiated agreement required a showing of just cause for a decision not to renew a non-tenured teacher's contract.

A claim of substantive due process focuses on the nature of the action taken by government rather than the procedure by which it is undertaken, i.e., whether the governmental action is arbitrary or without justification. The court also rejected Spanierman's substantive due process claim that the public school's action was arbitrary, egregious and outrageous, again relying on Spanierman's non-tenured status, and the fact that non-renewal of a non-tenured teacher's contract was the type of event specifically anticipated in the union-negotiated employment agreement.

NOTHING NEW?

It's possible to view the Spanierman case as a cautionary tale on using new forms of communication in the educational environment. Spanierman said he intended to use his MySpace page to better relate to his students; indeed the case demonstrates that such a page can facilitate easy communication between teachers and students. But it is that easy familiarity that, in the view of the school district, drew Spanierman over the line between acceptable discourse and inappropriate communications. The severity of the punishment may also reflect an institutional discomfort with a new means of student–teacher communication that is outside the channels customarily controlled by the school district.

And, of course, the Spanierman case could also be viewed as a simple case of inappropriate communications with students, regardless of the medium involved. Although reasonable minds may differ on whether Spanierman's communications warranted the discipline he received, the court ruled that, under the circumstances, it was the school district's call to make.

IT'S NOT THE FIRST, AND IT WON'T BE THE LAST

This is not the first case in which a teacher, or an aspiring teacher, was discharged or disciplined for conduct involving a MySpace page. In another recent case, the so-called "drunken pirate" case, a teacher in training was denied a teaching degree just prior to her graduation when officials at her teaching school found a photo on her MySpace page showing her in a pirate hat, drinking alcohol. In *Snyder v. Millersville University*, filed in federal court in Pennsylvania, there was apparently no contact with students, and it is disputed whether any students at the school ever saw the photo or the MySpace page. The school district also contended that Snyder's conduct as a student teacher was unprofessional in ways unrelated to her MySpace page.

Following a trial, the federal court judge came to a conclusion similar to that in *Spanierman*. The court rejected Snyder's challenge to the denial of her teaching degree because she failed to complete the required curriculum. The court also

concluded that her First Amendment claim should be evaluated under the standards applicable to teachers, not to students, and thus she would be protected by the First Amendment only if the material on her MySpace page involved matters of "public concern." Because Snyder admitted herself that the contents of her MySpace page were personal in nature, the court rejected her claim that her free speech rights were violated by discipline resulting from the contents of the MySpace page.

THE BOTTOM LINE

Both the *Spanierman* and *Snyder* cases are a subset of a larger category of disputes that involve posting in online forums, blogs and social networking sites. Regardless of the rights implicated, these cases remind us to be mindful of the ramifications that may flow from online personal expression that is readily accessible to students, co-workers, and employers.

QUESTIONS FOR REFLECTION

1. What do you think—was the district right or wrong to not renew Jeffrey Spanierman's contract?
2. What are the legal questions being addressed in this case?
3. Do you have any material on any of your websites that might become a problem during your student teaching or first years as a teacher?

Source: Excerpted from "Teacher Fired for Inappropriate Behavior on MySpace Page" by Jeffry D. Neuburger, October 15, 2008. Used with permission of PBS MediaShift.

LEARNING OUTCOMES

After reading and studying this chapter, you should be able to:

1. Explain the relationships between the U.S. Constitution and the role and responsibilities of the states in ensuring the availability of public schools for all children. (INTASC 7: Planning)
2. Describe critical issues about the role of public schools for which the courts are being used to resolve points of debate. (INTASC 9: Reflective Practice)
3. Identify and describe court-established guidelines related to religious activities in public schools. (INTASC 7: Planning; INTASC 9: Reflective Practice)

4. Summarize key components of the rights and responsibilities of teachers as determined by key U.S. Supreme Court decisions. (INTASC 7: Planning; INTASC 9: Reflective Practice)
5. Be clear about a teacher's responsibilities and liabilities related to negligence. (INTASC 7: Planning)
6. Reflect about the legal implications of teacher and student potential misuses of technology.
7. Distinguish between students' rights and responsibilities as citizens and their rights and responsibilities as students. (INTASC 7: Planning; INTASC 9: Reflective Practice)

LEGAL ASPECTS OF EDUCATION

The legal perspective for learning about education in the United States begins with describing the importance of the U.S. Constitution and the Bill of Rights. All else evolves from interpretations of the Constitution. Within the boundaries of U.S. law, each state is guided by its own constitution. Several additional sources of laws exist at the federal, state, and local levels, and a number of processes are in place for addressing disputes. As illustrated in Figure 10.1, in many ways the teacher is the implementer at the intersection between those who enact laws and those who interpret them.

FIGURE 10.1

Sources of Legal Control in U.S. Education as They Affect the Classroom Teacher

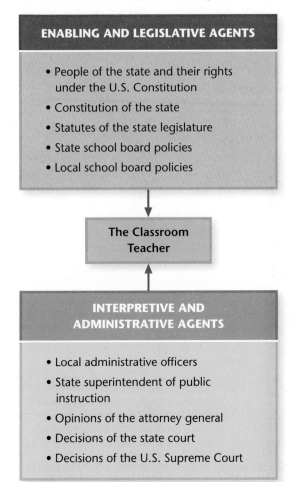

ENABLING AND LEGISLATIVE AGENTS

- People of the state and their rights under the U.S. Constitution
- Constitution of the state
- Statutes of the state legislature
- State school board policies
- Local school board policies

The Classroom Teacher

INTERPRETIVE AND ADMINISTRATIVE AGENTS

- Local administrative officers
- State superintendent of public instruction
- Opinions of the attorney general
- Decisions of the state court
- Decisions of the U.S. Supreme Court

Some laws are developed out of the legislative process. These are referred to as **enabling laws,** or those that provide opportunity or make it possible for educators to do certain things. Also, laws can impose restrictions or prohibitions. Another form of law, **administrative law,** is made up of the rules and regulations that the executive branches of government create. Once the legislative branch of government has established a new statute or policy, a government office, such as the U.S. Department of Education or a local school district, will develop rules and procedures related to implementing the new policy. These rules and procedures can have the force of law too.

Once legislation is enacted into law and the rules and procedures are in place, if a question of interpretation is raised, then the **judicial interpretive process** is engaged. The judicial process also is used when it appears that a law has been violated. The interpretations of the state and federal court system decisions form a body of **case law.** The sampling of legal topics presented in this chapter includes examples from constitutional law, state and federal statutes, and case law based on court interpretations. All apply directly to schools, teachers, and students.

Legal Provisions for Education: The U.S. Constitution

The U.S. Constitution is the fundamental law for the nation. When a state legislature makes laws that apply to education, these laws must be in accordance with both the U.S. Constitution and that state's constitution.

Three of the amendments to the U.S. Constitution are particularly significant to the governance of education, both public and private, in the United States. Interpretations of each of these amendments—the Tenth, First, and Fourteenth—by the courts have had profound impacts on the

enabling laws Laws that make it possible for educators to do certain things.

administrative law Rules and regulations that the executive branches of government create.

judicial interpretive process The judicial process of drawing conclusions about the intent of the wording in the Constitution and statutes.

case law Decisions of state and federal courts.

FIGURE 10.2

FIGURE 10.2

Key elements of the U.S. Constitution That Are Significant to the Governance of Education

> **Not Provided for:** Responsibility for education.
>
> **Tenth Amendment:** Grants responsibility for education to each state.
>
> **First Amendment:** Ensures freedom of speech, of religion, and of the press.
>
> **Fourteenth Amendment:** Ensures equal educational opportunity.

The U.S. Constitution laid the groundwork for the notion of equal access to education for all.

role and purpose of schools, the opportunities of all students to have access to an education, and the responsibilities and rights of teachers, students, and school administrators (see Figure 10.2).

TENTH AMENDMENT. *The powers not delegated to the United States by the Constitution, nor prohibited by it to the States, are reserved to the States respectively, or to the people.*

The U.S. Constitution does not specifically provide for public education; however, the Tenth Amendment has been interpreted as granting this power to the states. Therefore, education in the United States is not nationalized as it is in many other nations of the world. Each state has provided for education either in its constitution or in its basic statutory law. For example, Part 6, Section 2, of the Ohio Constitution reads:

> The General Assembly shall make such provisions, by taxation, or otherwise, as, with the income arising from the school trust fund, will secure a thorough and efficient system of common schools throughout the state; but no religious or other sect, or sects, shall ever have any exclusive right to, or control of, any part of the school funds of this state.

Through such statements, the people of the various states commit themselves to a responsibility for education. The state legislatures are obliged to fulfill this commitment.

FIRST AMENDMENT. *Congress shall make no law respecting an establishment of religion, or prohibiting the free exercise thereof; or abridging the freedom of speech, or of the press; or the right of the people peaceably to assemble, and to petition the Government for redress of grievances.*

As illustrated in the cases presented later in this chapter, two important clauses in the First Amendment have been applied repeatedly to issues confronting public education: (1) the *establishment clause*, "Congress shall make no law respecting an establishment of religion," and (2) the *free speech clause*, which has direct implications for teacher and student rights.

FOURTEENTH AMENDMENT. *No state shall make or enforce any law which shall abridge the privileges or immunities of citizens of the United States; nor shall any State deprive any person of life, liberty, or property without due process of law; nor deny to any person within its jurisdiction the equal protection of the laws.*

The application of the Fourteenth Amendment to public education as considered in this chapter deals primarily with the equal protection clause: "nor shall any State . . . deny to any person within its jurisdiction the equal protection of the laws." Equal educational opportunity is protected under the Fourteenth Amendment. In effect, the rights of citizens of the United States are ensured by the Constitution and cannot be violated by state laws or action.

JOURNAL FOR REFLECTION

Before reading this chapter, did you know that the state has the responsibility for education, or did you think it was the role of the federal government? What do you see as the ideal balance between the state, the federal government, and local control?

Church and State

Our nation has a strong religious heritage. For example, in colonial times, education was primarily a religious matter; furthermore, much of this education was conducted in private religious schools. Many private schools today are under religious sponsorship. But debate about the rightful role of religion in public education continues. Should public funds be used to support students in religious schools? Can prayer be said at high school commencement services or in classrooms? Does the teaching of creationism amount to public support for religion, or is it merely the presentation of an alternative scientific view? Agreements have not been reached through the debate process, so proponents of differing viewpoints have turned to the courts.

Court cases concerned with separation of church and state most frequently involve both the First and Fourteenth Amendments of the U.S. Constitution. The First Amendment is interpreted as being applicable to the states by the Fourteenth Amendment. For example, a state law requiring a daily prayer to be read in classrooms throughout the state could be interpreted as "depriving persons of liberty" (see the Fourteenth Amendment's due process clause) and as the state establishing a religion, or at least "prohibiting the free exercise thereof" (see the First Amendment's establishment clause). States are not permitted to make laws that abridge the privileges of citizens, and the right to the free practice of religion must be ensured.

Court cases related to the separation of church and state can be classified in three categories: (1) those dealing with the use of public funds to support religious education, (2) those dealing with the practice of religion in public schools, and (3) those dealing with the rights of parents to provide private education for their children. Key cases related to each of these categories are presented next.

PUBLIC FUNDS AND RELIGIOUS EDUCATION. The use of public funds to support religious schools has been questioned on many occasions. Typically, state constitutions deny public funds to sectarian institutions or schools. However, public funds have been used to provide transportation for students to church schools and to provide textbooks for students in parochial schools.

Approximately 85 percent of the students who attend nonpublic schools are attending church-related schools. Of this number, some 70 percent are enrolled in parochial (Catholic) schools. In states with relatively large enrollments in parochial schools, ongoing efforts have been made to obtain public financial assistance of one form or another for nonpublic school students. These attempts have often been challenged in the courts. We present a sampling of these cases and issues here to illustrate the reasoning and to assess trends in this difficult area. A summary of cases related to the use of public funds for private education is presented in Table 10.1.

Transportation for Students of Church Schools. The landmark case on the use of public funds to provide transportation for students to church schools was *Everson v. Board of Education,* ruled on by the U.S. Supreme Court in 1947. The Court held that in using tax-raised funds to reimburse parents for bus fares expended to transport their children to church schools, a New Jersey school district did not violate the establishment clause of the First Amendment. The majority of the members of the Court viewed the New Jersey statute permitting free bus transportation to parochial school children as "public welfare legislation" to help get the children to and from school safely and expeditiously. Since the *Everson* decision, the highest courts in several states, under provisions in their own constitutions, have struck down enactments authorizing expenditures of public funds to bus children attending denominational schools; others have upheld such enactments.

The *Lemon* Test: Excessive Entanglement. A useful rubric emerged from the U.S. Supreme Court decision in *Lemon v. Kurtzman* (1971). This case dealt with an attempt by the Rhode Island legislature to provide a 15 percent salary supplement to teachers who taught secular subjects in nonpublic schools and a statute in Pennsylvania that provided reimbursement for the cost of teachers' salaries and instructional materials in relation to specified secular subjects in nonpublic schools. The Court concluded that the "cumulative impact of the entire relationship arising under the statutes in each state involves excessive entanglement between government and religion." The Court pointed out another defect of the Pennsylvania statute: It provided for the aid to be given directly to the school. In the *Everson* case, the aid was provided to the students' parents, not to the church-related school. The Court posed three questions that have since become known as the *Lemon* test: (1) Does the act have a secular purpose? (2) Does the primary effect of the act either advance or inhibit religion? (3) Does the act excessively entangle government and religion? Most subsequent cases dealing with the use of public funds in nonpublic school settings have referred to this test.

Table 10.1 • Selected U.S. Supreme Court Cases Related to the Use of Public Funds for Private Education

Case	Issue	Decision
Everson v. Board of Education (1947)	Use of tax-raised funds to reimburse parents for transportation of students to church schools	Court ruled that reimbursement did not violate the First Amendment.
Lemon v. Kurtzman (1971)	Legislation to provide direct aid for secular services to nonpublic schools, including teacher salaries, textbooks, and instructional materials	Court ruled the legislation unconstitutional because of the excessive entanglement between government and religion.
Wolman v. Walter (1977)	Provision of books, standardized testing and scoring, diagnostic services, and therapeutic and remedial services to nonpublic school pupils	Court ruled that providing such materials and services to nonpublic school pupils was constitutional.
	Provision of instructional materials and field trips to nonpublic school pupils	Court ruled that providing such materials and services to nonpublic school pupils was unconstitutional.
Grand Rapids School District v. Ball (1985), and *Aguilar v. Felton* (1985)	Instruction of nonpublic school students in supplementary education by public school teachers	Court ruled that the action violated the establishment clause in that it promoted religion.
Zobrest v. Catalina Foothills School District (1993)	Provision of a school district interpreter for a deaf student attending a Catholic high school	Court ruled that government programs that neutrally provide benefits to a broad class of citizens without reference to religion are not readily subject to an establishment clause challenge.
Board of Education of Kiryas Joel Village School District v. Grumet (1994)	Creation and support of a public school district for Hasidic Jews by New York State	Court ruled that the district violated the establishment clause in that it was a form of "religious favoritism."
Agostini v. Felton (1997)	School districts' provision of Title I teachers to serve disadvantaged students in religious schools	Court overturned ban provided the district assigns teachers without regard to religious affiliation, all religious symbols are removed from classrooms, teachers have limited contact with religious personnel, and public school supervisors make monthly unannounced inspections.

PEARSON
myeducationlab

Go to the *Building Teaching Skills and Dispositions* section of Topic 4: *Ethical and Legal Issues* in the MyEducationLab for your course and complete the activity titled *Accommodations for Students with Exceptionalities.*

child benefit theory A criterion used by the U.S. Supreme Court to determine whether services provided to nonpublic school students benefit children and not a particular school or religion.

Special Situations. The U.S. Supreme Court seems to have wavered from a strict application of the *Lemon* test in two more cases: *Kiryas Joel v. Grumet* and *Zobrest v. Catalina.*

In a 1994 case, *Board of Education of Kiryas Joel Village School District v. Grumet,* the U.S. Supreme Court ruled that a New York State law that created a public school to serve children with disabilities in a village of Hasidic Jews was a form of "religious favoritism" that violated the First Amendment. Interestingly, in this case, as in some others recently, the justices ignored the *Lemon* test in making the decision. Instead, the focus was on the legislature's creation of a special school district; the justices noted the risk that "the next similarly situated group seeking a school district of its own will receive one." Another implication of this decision was the indication that the court was willing to revisit *Aguilar v. Felton* (1985) and *Grand Rapids School District v. Ball* (1985), which invalidated sending public school teachers to private religious schools to provide supplemental instruction.

Whether a public school district could provide an interpreter for a student who was deaf who attended a Catholic high school was the central question in *Zobrest v. Catalina Foothills School District* (1993). Under a federal statute, the Individuals with Disabilities Education Act (IDEA), students who are deaf are entitled to have a sign language interpreter in all regular classes. In *Zobrest v. Catalina,* the Court concluded that no establishment clause violation occurred because the provision of the interpreter was a "private decision of individual parents." In terms of the federal statute, the Court determined that this was a situation in which "government programs that neutrally provide benefits to a broad class of citizens defined without reference to religion are not readily subject to an establishment clause challenge just because sectarian institutions may also receive an attenuated benefit."

Child Benefit Theory. The use of public funds to provide secular services has led to a concept referred to as the **child benefit theory**. The child benefit theory supports the provision of benefits to children in nonpublic schools with no benefits to the schools or to a religion. More recent decisions supporting the use of public funds for transportation and textbooks for students in

In *Zobrest v. Catalina* the Supreme Court ruled that no establishment clause was violated in the case of providing an interpreter for a student who was deaf who attended a Catholic school.

private schools have generally been based on the child benefit theory; this theory emerged out of commentary about the *Everson v. Board of Education* case. The reasoning was that transportation and books provide benefits to the children and not to the school or to a religion. Those opposed to the child benefit theory argue that aid to children receiving sectarian education instruction is effectively aiding the institution providing instruction.

The child benefit theory, as supported by the U.S. Supreme Court, has penetrated federal legislation. For example, the Elementary and Secondary Education Act of 1965 (ESEA) and its subsequent amendments, including No Child Left Behind, provide assistance to both public and nonpublic school children. Title I of ESEA, which deals with assistance for the education of children from low-income families, states that children from families attending private schools must be provided services in proportion to their numbers. When a school is demonstrated to be failing, the school district is required to provide transportation and access to other schools.

Title I Teachers in Religious Schools. In a more recent decision, *Agostini v. Felton* (1997), the U.S. Supreme Court seemed to be providing increased flexibility and easing the tensions created by *Aguilar v. Felton* (1985). In *Aguilar* the court struck down the use of Title I funds to pay public school teachers who taught in programs to help low-income students in parochial schools. But in *Agostini,* the court decided that under specific safeguards Title I teachers can be sent to serve disadvantaged students in religious schools; refer to Table 10.1 (p. 272).

The issue of public aid to church-related schools is still in the process of being settled. Although it is clear that aid for certain secular services (such as transportation, textbooks, and—under prescribed circumstances—testing, diagnostic, therapeutic, and remedial services) can be provided, it is not yet absolutely clear what further aid will be approved. In fact, the whole body of law in this area continues to be somewhat confused and contradictory. Figure 10.3 summarizes statements related to public funds and religious education.

RELIGIOUS ACTIVITIES IN PUBLIC SCHOOLS. The limits and boundaries of the First Amendment in relation to public schools have been and will continue to be tested in the courts, especially in relation to religion. Several cases have dealt with the teaching of creationism and evolution, the practice of religion, and the religious use of public facilities. Each case has contributed to a gradual process of clarification of what can and what should not be done to ensure the separation of church and state. Table 10.2 summarizes U.S. Supreme Court judgments in some of these cases.

FIGURE 10.3

Summary Statements on Church and State Related to Public Funds and Religious Education

- Laws and policies that have the effect of establishing religion in the schools will not be upheld by the courts.
- Use of public tax funds to pay for secular textbooks for loan to students and transportation of religious school children has been upheld by the courts.
- Use of public tax funds to pay for salaries of teachers in religious schools has not been upheld by the courts.
- Use of public funds to pay tuition of religious school children has not been upheld; in Minnesota, a tax deduction has been upheld for parents of children in public *and* private schools.
- Special support services such as speech and hearing teachers may be provided to students in religious schools.
- Religious schools may be reimbursed for administrative costs of standardized tests, test scoring, and record keeping required by the state.
- Public tax funds may not be used in support of public school teachers offering remedial or enriched instruction in religious schools.

Table 10.2 • Selected U.S. Supreme Court Cases Related to the Practice of Religion in Public Schools

Case	Issue	Decision
Creationism		
Edwards v. Aguillard (1987)	Balanced treatment of biblical and scientific explanations of the development of life	A state cannot require that schools teach the biblical version of creation.
Practice of Religion		
Wallace v. Jaffree (1985)	Legislation authorizing prayer in public schools, led by teachers, and a period of silence for meditation or voluntary prayer	Court held that state legislation authorizing a minute of silence for prayer led by teachers was unconstitutional.
Mozert v. Hawkins County Public Schools (1987)	Request that fundamentalist children not be exposed to basal reading series in the public schools of Tennessee	Rejected by the Court of Appeals for the Sixth Court, which reasoned that the readers did not burden the students' exercise of their religious beliefs.
Board of Education of the Westside Community Schools v. Mergens (1990)	The right of a student religious club to hold meetings at a public school	Court ruled that based on the Equal Access Act (EAA) of 1984, if only one non-curriculum-related student group meets, then the school may not deny other clubs.
Lee v. Weisman (1992)	Inclusion of a religious exercise in a graduation ceremony where young graduates who object are induced to conform	Prayers as an official part of graduation exercises are unconstitutional.
Use of Facilities		
Police Department of the City of Chicago v. Mosley (1972)	Government's refusal of use of a public forum to people whose views it finds unacceptable	"There is an equality of status in the field of ideas," and "government must afford all points of view an equal opportunity to be heard."
Lamb's Chapel v. Center Moriches Union Free School District (1993)	A church's screening of a family-oriented movie on public school premises after school hours	The district property had been used by a wide variety of audiences, so there was no danger of the district's being perceived as endorsing any given religion.
Santa Fe Independent School District, Petitioner v. Jane Doe (2000)	School district policy supporting student-led prayer before football games	"The policy is invalid on its face because it establishes an improper majoritarian election on religion, and unquestionably has the purpose and creates the perception of encouraging the delivery of prayer at a series of important school events."

Prayer in School. A number of attempts have been and continue to be initiated by school districts to incorporate some form of prayer into public school classrooms and activities. One such case began when the school district for Santa Fe High School, in Texas, adopted a series of policies that permitted prayer initiated and led by a student at all home athletic games. In June 2000, the U.S. Supreme Court ruled in *Santa Fe Independent School District, Petitioner v. Jane Doe* that the clear intent of the district policies was in violation of the establishment clause. The six-to-three majority observed, "the District, nevertheless, asks us to pretend that we do not recognize what every Santa Fe High School student understands clearly—that this policy is about prayer." Later in the decision, the Court noted, "This policy likewise does not survive a facial challenge because it impermissibly imposes upon the student body a majoritarian election on the issue of prayer." In other words, the district would be imposing a particular religious activity of the majority on all, a clear violation of the establishment

A continuing topic of debate and judicial action is the place of prayer in public schools as determined by the First Amendment.

clause. "It further empowers the student body majority with the authority to subject students of minority views to constitutionally improper messages. The award of that power alone, regardless of the students' ultimate use of it, is not acceptable." In concluding, the Court stated, "the policy is invalid on its face because it establishes an improper majoritarian election on religion, and unquestionably has the purpose and creates the perception of encouraging the delivery of prayer at a series of important school events." Figure 10.4 summarizes findings related to the practice of religion in public schools.

See Chapter 6 for an informative discussion on the place of religion in the culture of families and school.

Evolution versus Intelligent Design. Education has been placed at the center of what seems to be a never-ending debate between science and certain religious perspectives. The beginning of this debate is traced to the publication of *The Origin of Species* by Charles Darwin in 1859. Following years of careful observation and documentation of the characteristics of plants and animals, Darwin theorized that today's animals and plants were the results of natural selection over thousands of years, in other words, evolution. In the approximately 150 years since that publication, the scientific base for evolution has become well established through study of the geologic record and more recently analysis of the genetic history of plants and animals.

FIGURE 10.4

Summary Statements on Church and State and the Practice of Religion in Public Schools

- To teach the Bible as a religion course in the public schools is illegal; to teach about the Bible as part of the history of literature is legal.
- To dismiss children from public schools for one hour once a week for religious instruction at religious centers is legal.
- Reading of scripture and reciting prayers as religious exercises are in violation of the establishment clause.
- Public schools can teach the scientific theory of evolution as a theory; a state cannot require that the biblical version of evolution be taught.
- If school facilities are made available to one group, then they must be made available to all other groups of the same general type.

Table 10.3 • Selected Court Cases Related to the Teaching of Evolution in Science Classes

Case	Issue	Decision
"Scopes Monkey Trial"	The teaching of evolution in science classes	The teacher was guilty. The decision was later overturned on a technicality.
Epperson v. Arkansas (1968)	Can the state ban the teaching of evolution?	The "anti-evolution" statute violated the establishment clause.
Edwards v. Aguillard (1987)	Can the state require that the teaching of creationism be given equal time with the teaching of evolution?	The Court ruled that the Arkansas legislature violated the establishment cause.
Kitzmiller v. Dover Area School District (2005)	Can a school board require its science teachers to discuss intelligent design?	The district judge ruled that "intelligent design cannot uncouple itself from its creationist, and thus religious, antecedents."

Some religious perspectives, and a large proportion of the population, view evolution as an unproven "theory." The critics have used various strategies to challenge its teaching, or to require an alternative view based on religion to be taught as well.

One of the most famous trials involving religion and a teacher occurred in Tennessee in 1925, when a science teacher, John Scopes, was found guilty of teaching evolution. Although the decision was later reversed on a technicality, the "Scopes Monkey Trial" has been kept alive in the theater and through the more recent efforts of certain religious groups advocating for the teaching in science classes of alternative views based on the Bible. In the 1970s the alternative view was to advocate for a biblical account as scientific theory; this was called *creationism*. As the courts failed to support this theory, a new one, called *intelligent design,* has been advanced. Each of these views has argued that life is too complicated to have developed without there being a higher power involved. As summarized in Table 10.3, the courts have tended to view each of these efforts as attempts to advance religion.

Regardless of past Supreme Court decisions, some topics, such as the posting of the Ten Commandments in classrooms and Bible reading in public schools, continue to be challenged by legislatures, individuals, and various groups. One of the outcomes of these ongoing challenges is an accumulating series of judicial interpretations that can serve as guidelines about what can and cannot be done. The summary statements presented earlier in Figure 6.4 outline the overall pattern of the many judicial decisions related to religion and the public schools.

Segregation and Desegregation

A troublesome problem for U.S. society has been the history of legal and social separation of people based on their race—in other words, **segregation**. Up until the middle of the twentieth century, the public school systems in many states contributed to this problem through the operation of two separate sets of schools, one for Caucasians and one for African Americans ("Negroes"). Segregated schools were supported by the court, state laws, and by the official actions of state and local government administrators. This kind of segregation, based in legal and official actions, is called *de jure* **segregation**.

Since 1954 the courts and communities have made intensive efforts to abolish the racial segregation of school students, a process that has been called **desegregation**. A major instrument the courts have used to accomplish this end has been **integration**, the busing of students to achieve a balanced number of students, in terms of race, in each school within a school district. A second instrument has been the use of magnet schools, which are schools that emphasize particular curriculum areas, disciplines, or themes. The hope is that these schools will attract a diverse set of students. These efforts to integrate the schools have had mixed success, and now there is increasing concern over the **resegregation** of schools based on where people live. Segregation—or resegregation—caused by housing patterns and other nonlegal factors is called *de facto* **segregation**.

"SEPARATE BUT EQUAL": NO LONGER EQUAL. Before 1954 many states had laws either requiring or permitting racial segregation in public schools (*de jure* segregation). Until 1954 lower courts adhered to the doctrine of "separate but equal" as announced by the Supreme Court in *Plessy v. Ferguson* (1896). In *Plessy v. Ferguson,* the Court upheld a Louisiana law that required railway companies to provide

segregation Legal and/or social separation of people on the basis of their race.

de jure **segregation** The segregation of students on the basis of law, school policy, or a practice designed to accomplish such separation.

desegregation The process of correcting illegal segregation.

integration The process of mixing students of different races in school.

resegregation A situation in which formerly integrated schools become segregated again because of changes in neighborhood population patterns.

de facto **segregation** The segregation of students resulting from circumstances such as housing patterns rather than law or school policy.

separate but equal accommodations for the black and the white races. The Court's reasoning at that time was that the Fourteenth Amendment implied political, not social, equality.

The Failure of the Separate-but-Equal Doctrine. This separate-but-equal doctrine appeared to be the rule until May 17, 1954, when the Supreme Court repudiated it in *Brown v. Board of Education of Topeka*. The Court said that in education the separate-but-equal doctrine has no place and that separate facilities are inherently unequal. In 1955 the Court rendered the second *Brown v. Board of Education of Topeka* decision, requiring that the principles of the first decision be carried out with all deliberate speed.

From 1954, the time of the *Brown* decision, to 1964, little progress was made in eliminating segregated schools. On May 25, 1964, referring to a situation in Prince Edward County, Virginia, the Supreme Court said, "There has been entirely too much deliberation and not enough speed in enforcing the constitutional rights which we held in *Brown v. Board of Education*." The Civil Rights Act of 1964 added legislative power to the 1954 judicial pronouncement. The act not only authorized the federal government to initiate court suits against school districts that were laggard in desegregating schools but also denied federal funds for programs that discriminated by race, color, or national origin.

Subsequently, many efforts have been made to meet the expectations of the Court decisions and legislation. The objective of these initiatives has been to promote integration, that is, to achieve a representative mix of students of different races in schools. In the sixty-plus years since *Brown*, there have been many efforts by school districts and communities and many additional lawsuits. Table 10.4 summarizes some key Supreme Court decisions on school desegregation and integration.

One of the positive long-term effects of desegregation can be seen in today's highly diverse schools and classrooms.

PEARSON
myeducationlab

Go to the *Assignments and Activities* section of Topic 4: *Ethical and Legal Issues* in the MyEducationLab for your course and complete the activity titled *Brown vs. Board of Education.*

Table 10.4 • Selected U.S. Supreme Court Cases Related to School Desegregation and Integration

Case	Issue	Decision
Plessy v. Ferguson (1896)	Whether a railway company should be required to provide equal accommodations for African American and white races	The Court indicated in its decision that the Fourteenth Amendment implied political, not social, equality. Thus the doctrine of "separate but equal" was established.
Brown v. Board of Education of Topeka (1954)	Legality of separate school facilities	The separate-but-equal doctrine has no place in education, and dual school systems (*de jure* segregation) are inherently unequal.
Griffin v. County School Board of Prince Edward County (1964)	Whether a county may close its schools and provide assistance to private schools for whites only	The Court instructed the local district court to require the authorities to levy taxes to reopen and operate a nondiscriminatory public school system.
Board of Education of Oklahoma City Public Schools v. Dowell (1991)	The conditions under which a school district may be relieved of court supervision	Court supervision was to continue until segregation was removed from every facet of school operations.
Freeman v. Pitts (1992)	Whether court supervision may be withdrawn incrementally, and whether a school district is responsible for segregation based on demographic changes (*de facto* segregation)	A district court is permitted to withdraw supervision in discrete categories in which the district has achieved compliance; also "the school district is under no duty to remedy imbalance that is caused by demographic factors."

Release from Court Orders. After fifty-plus years of court actions related to desegregation and school district responses, questions were raised about the conditions that must be in place for a school district to be released from federal court supervision. Three cases in the 1990s offered instances of conditions under which the courts would back away. *Board of Education of Oklahoma City Public Schools v. Dowell* (1991) is important for at least three reasons: First, the U.S. Supreme Court made it clear that "federal supervision of local school systems was intended as a temporary measure to remedy past discrimination." Second, the Court stated that in relation to desegregation, "the District Court should look not only at student assignments, but to every facet of school operations—faculty, staff, transportation, extracurricular activities and facilities." Third, for the first time the Court defined what full compliance with a desegregation order would mean.

Two other cases added additional clarity to what the Court expects in order to release a school district from supervision. In *Freeman v. Pitts* (1992), the U.S. Supreme Court ruled that districts do not have to remedy racial imbalances caused by demographic changes, but the districts still have the burden of proving that their actions do not contribute to the imbalances. The third case was a return to *Brown*. The Court had ordered the Court of Appeals for the Tenth Circuit to reexamine its 1989 finding that the Topeka district remained segregated. In 1992 the appellate court refused to declare Topeka successful. The court concluded that the district had done little to fulfill the duty to desegregate that was first imposed on it in 1954. The judges wrote that to expect the vestiges of segregation to "magically dissolve" with so little effort "is to expect too much."

These three cases in combination made it clear that it is possible for school districts to be released from court orders. The decisions also made it clear that school districts have to make concerted efforts across time to address any and all remnants of *de jure* segregation. Further, it now appears that school districts are not expected to resolve those aspects of *de facto* segregation that are clearly beyond their control.

THE SUCCESSES OF THE DESEGREGATION AGENDA. Desegregation has had some measurable benefits. For example, African Americans who graduated from integrated schools have higher incomes than those who graduated from segregated schools. They are more likely to graduate from college and to hold good jobs. In addition, the number of middle-class black families is growing. Still, there is a long way to go before the dream of full socioeconomic equality is achieved. It seems certain that schools will continue to be a primary vehicle for advancing this dream from the points of view of the courts.

ACHIEVING INTEGRATION IN TODAY'S DIVERSE SOCIETY. At present more than 500 school districts have experienced some form of federal court oversight to address segregation. At the same time, instead of schools and communities becoming fully integrated, there is a clear trend toward resegregation, especially in urban areas. As well intentioned as the efforts have been to erase *de jure* segregation, *de facto* segregation is increasing. There also is increasing diversity in the number of other racial and ethnic groups in most communities. Schools continue to be challenged to ensure that all students have equal access to a quality education. The current strategy for achieving this end is some form of **race-conscious assignment** of students. Strategies such as magnet schools, including consideration of diversity in admissions, and giving priority to siblings in school assignment are being tried. As well intentioned as these efforts may be, some perceive inequities and each is being challenged in the courts.

Equal Opportunity

The equal protection clause of the Fourteenth Amendment has been instrumental in shaping many court cases and federal statutes that are directed toward preventing discrimination in schools. A judgment of **discrimination** can be defined as a determination that an individual or a group of individuals—for example, African Americans, women, or people with disabilities—has been denied constitutional rights. In common usage, the term applies to various minorities or to individual members of a minority who lack rights typically accorded the majority. The principle that discrimination violates the equal protection clause was reinforced in Titles VI and VII of the Civil Rights Act of 1964 and in Title IX of the Education Amendments Act of 1972. Title VI of the Civil Rights Act states:

> No person in the United States shall, on the ground of race, color, or national origin, be excluded from participation in, be denied the benefits of, or be subjected to discrimination under any program or activity receiving federal financial assistance.

race-conscious assignment The strategy of taking race into account for placement of students without making it the primary or single consideration.

discrimination Denial of constitutional rights to an individual or group.

Title VII states:

> It shall be an unlawful employment practice for an employer (1) to fail or refuse to hire or to discharge any individual, or otherwise to discriminate against any individual with respect to his compensation, terms, conditions, or privileges of employment, because of such individual's race, color, religion, sex, or national origin; or (2) to limit, segregate, or classify his employees or applicants for employment in any way which would deprive or tend to deprive any individual of employment opportunities or otherwise adversely affect his status as an employee, because of such individual's race, color, religion, sex, or national origin.

Title IX of the Education Amendments Act of 1972 states:

> No person in the United States shall, on the basis of sex, be excluded from participation in, be denied the benefits of, or be subjected to discrimination under any education program or activity receiving federal financial assistance.

AFFIRMATIVE ACTION. In the years since the 1964 Civil Rights Act, numerous statutes and court cases have encouraged steps designed to ensure that underrepresented populations have equal opportunity. These **affirmative action** initiatives have included such actions as formalizing and publicizing nondiscriminatory hiring procedures and setting aside a certain number of slots in hiring or college admissions programs. Over time, concern has increased about the possibility of **reverse discrimination**—situations in which a majority or an individual member of a majority is not accorded equal rights because of different or preferential treatment provided to a minority or an individual member of a minority. This concern has resulted in a new set of court cases, each of which is attempting to redress what is perceived as a new imbalance. A summary of the events, policies, and court cases related to affirmative action are presented in Figure 10.5.

As mentioned, the legal basis for affirmative action is found in Titles VI and VII of the Civil Rights Act of 1964 and in Title IX of the Education Amendments Act of 1972. However, affirmative action procedures and methods continue to be clarified and, in some instances, questioned. For example, in 1996 the citizens of California passed Proposition 209, which bans the state and its local governments from using racial and gender preferences in hiring, contracting, and college admissions. Proposition 209 and other legal initiatives will be examined in the courts.

Opportunities for Students with Disabilities

The judicial basis for current approaches to the education of students with disabilities also is closely linked to the civil rights and equal opportunity initiatives. In addition, several specifically targeted statutes address the education of people with disabilities. Three particularly important statutes are Section 504 of the Rehabilitation Act; Public Law 94-142, the Education for All Handicapped Children Act (EAHCA); and the Individuals with Disabilities Education Act (IDEA).

affirmative action Policies and procedures designed to compensate for past discrimination against women and members of minority groups (for example, assertive recruiting and admissions practices).

reverse discrimination A situation in which a majority or an individual of a majority is denied certain rights because of preferential treatment provided to a minority or an individual of a minority.

FIGURE 10.5

Events in the History of Affirmative Action

1941	President Roosevelt issues an executive order prohibiting discrimination by government contractors.
1961	President Kennedy makes the first reference to affirmative action in an order mandating that federal contractors make employment practices free of racial bias.
1964	Congress passes the Civil Rights Act.
1965	President Johnson outlines specific steps federal contractors must take to ensure hiring equality.
1970	The Nixon administration orders federal contractors to set "goals and timetables" for hiring minorities.
1972	Congress passes Title IX of the Education Amendments Act that states that no person can be excluded from participation based on their sex.
1978	In *University of California v. Bakke,* the Supreme Court rules that colleges can consider race as one factor in admissions.
1995	The Supreme Court limits racial preferences in federal highway contracts.
2003	In *Grutter v. Bollinger* and *Gratz v. Bollinger* the Supreme Court rules that race can be considered by colleges in their efforts to have a diverse student body, but it cannot be done through a set formula or quota.

These acts encourage the education of individuals with disabilities by making grants to states and local education agencies for children ages 3 to 5, requires the federal government to be responsive to the increasing ethnic diversity of society and those with limited English proficiency, and funds programs to provide education to all children with disabilities.

SECTION 504 OF THE REHABILITATION ACT. Under this civil rights act established in 1973, recipients of federal funds are prohibited from discriminating against "otherwise qualified individuals." Note that Section 504 is a federal statute and regulations, not a court decision. Three important themes addressed in Section 504 are equal treatment, appropriate education, and people with disabilities. Equal treatment, as in other civil rights contexts, must be addressed. However, this does not necessarily mean the *same* treatment. For example, giving the same assessment procedure to students with disabilities and other students may not be equal treatment. Educational judgments in relation to students with disabilities require a "heightened standard." The measures must fit the students' circumstances, and procedural safeguards must be employed. Appropriate education means that the school system and related parties must address the individual needs of students with disabilities as adequately as do the education approaches for other students. In Section 504, a "handicapped person" is defined as follows:

> Any person who (i) has a physical or mental impairment which substantially limits one or more major life activities, (ii) has a record of such an impairment, or (iii) is regarded as having such an impairment. (34 CFR 104.3)

PUBLIC LAW 94-142 (EAHCA). First passed by Congress in 1975, Public Law 94-142 has been amended several times since. This law ensures "a free appropriate public education" to all children with disabilities between the ages of 3 and 21. Children with exceptional needs cannot be excluded from education because of their needs. The law is very specific in describing the kind and quality of education and in stating that each child with a disability is to have an individually planned education. Details of this plan must be spelled out in a written individualized education plan (IEP), formulated by general and special education teachers, and subject to the parents' approval. Originally, the law provided for substantial increases in funding; in subsequent years, however, the funding authorizations have been lower than the original commitment. Two priorities for funding were identified: (1) the child who currently receives no education and (2) the child who is not receiving all the services he or she needs to succeed. These priorities place the emphasis on need rather than on the specific disability.

THE INDIVIDUALS WITH DISABILITIES EDUCATION ACT (IDEA). Since its original inception in 1975, PL 94-142 has been amended and reauthorized several times; it is now called *IDEA*. The statute addresses how states and schools, and other public agencies, provide services to children with disabilities. The purpose of IDEA is to make available to all children with disabilities a free appropriate public education. Federal funds are made available through various grants to support services for children from birth to 26 years of age.

Increased Quality and Rigor. Significant updates and changes were made in the 2004 reauthorization of IDEA. There was a need to align IDEA with NCLB including making definitions, such as "highly qualified" teachers and "limited English proficient" consistent. Another important element was the heavy emphasis placed on "scientifically based research." Teachers and schools are expected to use classroom practices that are based on rigorous research.

Response to Intervention (RTI). As you become a teacher, *RTI* is an acronym that you will need to understand. A key IDEA theme now for teachers, schools, and school districts is to not just say "This kid needs to be in special education." Rather, there needs to be a systematic approach to assessing what the student already knows and determining identifiable needs. Secondly, documented efforts must be made to improve the students' learning by providing student need-specific (and research-based) interventions. More than likely, these interventions will be purposeful instruction, but they could be related to student behavior or other needs.

2009 Stimulus Support for IDEA. The American Recovery and Reinvestment Act of 2009 added significant funding for IDEA activities. A priority for these funds has been children ages three to five having early access to a free appropriate public education. Funding also was made available to governors to implement statewide systems of coordinated, multidisciplinary interagency programs to provide early intervention service (EIS) programs.

Look back in Chapter 6 for a discussion of early childhood education.

AIDS AS A DISABILITY. The 1990 Americans with Disabilities Act expanded the definition of disability in such a way as to include people with AIDS. Also, under IDEA the courts have found that AIDS is a disabling condition. But AIDS is an issue charged with emotion, as was desegregation. People do not always approach these difficult situations with calmness or equanimity. The courts, as well as school administrators and teachers, are constantly struggling to determine what is appropriate education for students with AIDS and what are suitable educational environments for children with AIDS-related disabilities. The Centers for Disease Control and Prevention is a useful resource for information about AIDS (phone: 800-232-5636; website: www.cdc.gov/hiv/dhap.htm).

TEACHERS' RIGHTS AND RESPONSIBILITIES

Teachers have the same rights as other citizens. The Fourteenth Amendment gives every citizen the right to **due process** of law: both *substantive due process* (protection against the deprivation of constitutional rights such as freedom of expression) and *procedural due process* (procedural protection against unjustified deprivation of substantive rights). Most court cases related to teachers evolve from either liberty or property interests. Liberty interests are created by the Constitution itself; property interests are found in forms of legal entitlement such as tenure or certification.

Teachers also have the same responsibilities as other citizens. They must abide by federal, state, and local laws and by the provisions of contracts. As professionals they must also assume the heavy responsibility of educating young people. We discuss specific court cases briefly here to illustrate some of the issues and decisions related to aspects of teacher rights and responsibilities. Note that the cases selected do not necessarily constitute the last word regarding teacher rights but rather provide an overview of some of the issues that have been decided in the courts. Table 10.5 summarizes the issues and decisions in selected cases involving teacher rights and

due process The legal procedures that must be followed to safeguard individuals from arbitrary, capricious, or unreasonable policies, practices, or actions.

Table 10.5 • Selected U.S. Supreme Court Cases Related to Teachers' Rights and Responsibilities

Case	Issue	Decision
Discrimination		
North Haven Board of Education v. Bell (1982)	Allegation by former women faculty members of sex discrimination in employment	Court ruled that school employees as well as students are protected under Title IX.
Cleveland Board of Education v. LeFleur (1974)	Rights of pregnant teachers	Court struck down the board policy forcing all pregnant teachers to take mandatory maternity leave.
Burkey v. Marshall County Board of Education (1981)	Paying female coaches half the salary of male coaches	Court ruled that the policy violated the Equal Pay Act, Title VII of the Civil Rights Act of 1964.
Contract Rights		
Board of Regents of State Colleges v. Roth (1972)	Rights of nontenured teachers	Teacher had been hired under a one-year contract. Court concluded that he did not have a property interest that would entitle him to procedural rights under the Fourteenth Amendment.
Perry v. Sindermann (1972)	Rights of nontenured teachers	Court ruled that a state employee may acquire the property interest if officially fostered customs, rules, understandings, and practices imply a contract promise to grant continuing contract status and thus establish a *de facto* tenure system.
Bargaining		
Hortonville Joint School District No. 1 v. Hortonville Education Association (1976)	Rights of boards of education to dismiss teachers who are striking illegally	Court said the law gave the board power to employ and dismiss teachers as a part of the municipal labor relations balance.
Academic Freedom		
Pickering v. Board of Education (1968)	Dismissal of an Illinois teacher for criticizing a school board and superintendent in a letter published by a local newspaper	Court upheld teacher's claim that his First and Fourteenth Amendment rights were denied.

responsibilities. This summary table is not intended to provide a complete understanding of the court decisions cited. Note also that most of the court cases were decided in the 1970s and 1980s; more recently, new federal statutes have been the defining force.

Conditions of Employment

Many conditions must be met for you to be hired as a teacher. These include your successful completion of a professional preparation program, being credentialed or licensed by the state, and receiving a contract from the hiring school district. In each of these instances, you have rights established in law and statute, as well as responsibilities.

teacher certification and licensure The process whereby each state determines the requirements for certification and for obtaining a license to teach.

tenure A system of school employment in which educators retain their positions indefinitely unless they are dismissed for legally specified reasons through clearly established procedures.

TEACHER CERTIFICATION AND LICENSURE. The primary purpose of **teacher certification and licensure** is to make sure the teachers in public schools are qualified and competent. Certification laws usually require, in addition, that the candidate show evidence of citizenship, good moral character, and good physical health. A minimum age is frequently specified. All states have established requirements for teacher certification and licensure. Carrying out the policies of certification is usually a function of a state professional standards board. The board first has to make certain that applicants meet legal requirements; it then issues the appropriate license/certificates. Certifying agencies may not arbitrarily refuse to issue a certificate to a qualified candidate. The courts have ruled that local boards of education may prescribe additional or higher qualifications beyond the state requirements, provided that such requirements are not irrelevant, unreasonable, or arbitrary. A teaching certificate or license is a privilege that enables a person to practice a profession—it is not a right. But teacher certification is a property interest that cannot be revoked without constitutional due process.

TEACHER EMPLOYMENT CONTRACTS. Usually, boards of education have the statutory authority to employ teachers. This authority includes the power to enter into contracts and to fix terms of employment and compensation. In some states, only specific members of the school board can sign teacher contracts. When statutes confer the employing authority to boards of education, the authority cannot be delegated. It is usually the responsibility of the superintendent to screen and nominate candidates to the board. The board, meeting in official session, then acts officially as a group to enter into contractual agreements. Employment procedures vary from state to state, but the process is fundamentally prescribed by the legislature and must be strictly followed by local boards. A contract usually contains the following elements: the identification of the teacher and the board of education, a statement of the legal capacity of each party to enter into the contract, a definition of the assignment specified, a statement of the salary and how it is to be paid, and a provision for signature by the teacher and by the legally authorized agents of the board. In some states, contract forms are provided by state departments of education, and these forms must be used; in others, each district establishes its own.

A big moment: Signing a contract to teach is a professional commitment by the teacher and a legal one for the school district.

Teachers are responsible for making certain that they are legally qualified to enter into contractual agreements. For example, a teacher may not enter into a legal contract without having a valid teaching certificate issued by the state. Furthermore, teachers are responsible for carrying out the terms of the contract and abiding by them. In turn, under the contract they can legally expect proper treatment from an employer.

TEACHER TENURE. Teacher tenure legislation exists in most states. In many states, tenure or fair dismissal laws are mandatory and apply to all school districts without exception. In other states, they do not. The various laws differ not only in extent of coverage but also in provision for coverage.

Tenure laws are intended to provide security for teachers in their positions and to prevent removal of capable teachers by capricious action or political motive. Tenure statutes generally include detailed specifications necessary for granting tenure and for dismissing teachers who have tenure. These statutes have been upheld when attacked on constitutional grounds. The courts reason that because state legislatures create school districts, they have the right to limit their power.

Becoming Tenured and Tenure Rights. A teacher becomes tenured by serving satisfactorily for a stated time. This period is referred to as the **probationary period** and typically is three years. The actual process of acquiring tenure after serving the probationary period depends on the applicable statute. In some states, the process is automatic at the satisfactory completion of the probationary period; in other states, official action by the school board is necessary. Teachers may be dismissed for any one of numerous reasons, including "nonperformance of duty, incompetency, insubordination, conviction of crimes involving moral turpitude, failure to comply with reasonable orders, violation of contract provisions or local rules or regulations, persistent failure or refusal to maintain orderly discipline of students, and revocation of the teaching certificate" (LaMorte, 2008).

A school board in Tennessee dismissed Jane Turk from her tenured teaching position after she was arrested for driving under the influence of alcohol (DUI) (*Turk v. Franklin,* 1982). Turk's appeal was upheld by the lower court judge because there was no evidence of an adverse effect on her capacity and fitness as a teacher. The school board appealed to the Tennessee Supreme Court, which rejected the board's appeal, finding that the school board "acted in flagrant disregard of the statutory requirement and fundamental fairness in considering matters that should have been specifically charged in writing." Tennessee law requires that before a tenured teacher can be dismissed, "the charges shall be made in writing specifically stating the offenses which are charged." Nevertheless, teacher tenure may be affected by teacher conduct outside school as well as inside. This issue, in a sense, deals with the personal freedom of teachers: freedom to behave as other citizens do, freedom to engage in political activities, and academic freedom in the classroom.

Tenure laws are frequently attacked by those who claim that the laws protect incompetent teachers. There is undoubtedly some truth in the assertion, but it must be stated clearly and unequivocally that these laws also protect the competent and most able teachers. Teachers who accept the challenge of their profession and dare to use new methods, who inspire curiosity in their students, and who discuss controversial issues in their classrooms need protection from politically motivated or capricious dismissal. Incompetent teachers, whether tenured or not, can be dismissed under the law by capable administrators and careful school boards that allow due process while evaluating teacher performance.

Rights of Nontenured Teachers. Although due process has been applicable for years to tenured teachers, nontenured teachers do not, for the most part, enjoy the same rights. As an example, reread the Education in the News feature at the beginning of this chapter. In the end, the courts ruled that the nontenured teacher should be dismissed for his actions that were judged "disruptive to school activities."

In general, tenured teachers enjoy two key rights: protection from dismissal except for cause as provided in state statutes and the right to prescribed procedures. Nontenured teachers may also have due process rights if these are spelled out in state statutes; however, in states that do not provide for due process, nontenured teachers may be nonrenewed without any reasons being given. If a nontenured teacher is dismissed (as distinguished from nonrenewed) before the expiration of the contract, the teacher is entitled to due process. Twenty-two states afford nontenured teachers the right both to know the reasons for their nonrenewal and to meet with the school board or superintendent to argue to keep their jobs. Cases in Massachusetts (Lucia v. Duggan, 1969) and Wisconsin (*Gouge v. Joint School District No. 1,* 1970) point to the necessity of following due process in dismissing nontenured teachers. In the Massachusetts case, the court said: "the particular circumstances of a dismissal of a public school teacher provide compelling reasons for application of a doctrine of procedural due process" (Freedman, 1970, p. 100). In the Wisconsin case, the court said:

> A teacher in a public elementary or secondary school is protected by the due process clause of the Fourteenth Amendment against a nonrenewal decision which is wholly without basis in fact and also against a decision which is wholly unreasoned, as well as a decision which is impermissibly based. (*Gouge,* 1970)

In 1972 the Supreme Court helped to clarify the difference between the rights of tenured and nontenured teachers. In one case (*Board of Regents v. Roth,* 1972), it held that nontenured teachers were assured of no rights that were not specified in state statutes. In this instance, the only right that probationary teachers had was the one to be notified of nonrenewal by a specified date. In a second case (*Perry v. Sindermann,* 1972), the Court ruled that a nontenured teacher in the Texas system of community colleges was entitled to due process because the language of the institution's policy manual was such that an unofficial tenure system was in effect. Guidelines in the policy manual provided that a faculty member with seven years of employment in the system acquired tenure and could be dismissed only for cause.

probationary period The required time, typically one to three years, during which a beginning teacher must demonstrate satisfactory performance as a basis for seeking tenure.

FIGURE 10.6

Summary Statements on Teachers' Rights and Responsibilities

- Prospective teachers must fulfill the requirements of laws and policies regarding certification before being employed as teachers.
- Boards of education have the authority to employ teachers, including authority to enter into contracts and to fix terms of employment and compensation.
- School districts are prohibited from use of discriminatory practices; discrimination in employment and salary of teachers on the basis of sex is in violation of Title IX of the Education Amendments Act.
- Most states have tenure laws that provide teachers with protection against arbitrary dismissal; rights of nontenured teachers are found in state laws.
- Teachers may speak out on matters of public concern, even in criticism of their school board, as long as their speech is not disruptive or a lie.
- Boards of education may remove books from library shelves under their authority to select materials for schools; however, the removal of a book merely because someone disagrees with its content was not upheld by the U.S. Supreme Court.
- Many states provide for school boards and teacher unions to bargain collectively on wages, hours, and terms and conditions of employment.
- Teacher strikes are unlawful when a statute is violated; in some states, it is legal for teachers to strike.
- Teachers are expected to exercise due care in foreseeing possible accidents and in working to prevent their occurrence; teachers may be sued for their negligence that led to pupil injury.

Whether or not a teacher is tenured, that person cannot be dismissed for exercise of a right guaranteed by the U.S. Constitution. A school board cannot dismiss a teacher, for example, for engaging in civil rights activities outside school, speaking on matters of public concern, belonging to a given church, or running for public office. These rights are guaranteed to all citizens, including teachers. However, as in the Education in the News case, if a teacher's behavior is judged to be disruptive or dishonest, a school board can dismiss the person without violating the right to freedom of speech. Figure 10.6 provides a summary of teacher rights and responsibilities. Be sure to check how well you match with these requirements.

Right to Bargain Collectively

The right of teachers to bargain collectively has been an active issue since the 1960s. In the past, teacher groups met informally with boards of education to discuss salaries and other teacher welfare provisions. Sometimes the superintendent was even the spokesperson for such teacher groups. In more recent years, however, formal collective procedures have evolved. These procedures have been labeled collective bargaining, professional negotiation, cooperative determination, and collective negotiation. Teachers' groups have defined collective bargaining as a way of winning improved goals and not the goal itself. The right of employees to bargain collectively and the obligation of the district to bargain are not constitutionally granted but are typically guaranteed by statute.

A contract arrived at by a teachers' union means that salaries, working conditions, and other matters within the scope of the collective bargaining agreement can no longer be decided unilaterally by the school administration and board of education. Instead, the contract outlines how the teachers' union and its members will participate in formulating the school policies and programs under which they work.

The first teachers' group to bargain collectively with its local board of education was the Maywood, Illinois, Proviso Council of West Suburban Teachers, Union Local 571, in 1938. In 1957 a second local, the East St. Louis, Illinois, Federation of Teachers was successful in negotiating a written contract. The breakthrough, however, came in December 1961, when the United Federation of Teachers, Local 2 of the American Federation of Teachers (AFT), won the right to bargain for New York City's teachers. Since then, collective bargaining agreements between boards of education and teacher groups have grown phenomenally. Both the AFT and the National Education Association

Legal Aspects of Education in Other Countries

The legal aspects of school systems in other countries offer some interesting differences in comparison to the U.S. system. For example, other democratic countries do not have the apparently never-ending debates about the separation of church and state. As nearby as provinces of Canada and as far away as Belgium and the Netherlands, public dollars fund nondenominational and church-based schools. In the Dutch system, there are three separate school systems: public, Catholic, and Protestant. Each is supported with public funds, yet each is governed independently.

Germany incorporates instruction in religion in all schools. In fact, often one teacher is hired specifically to teach religion in regularly scheduled classes. Students have to take instruction on religion and are given a choice of Protestant or Catholic classes. In the higher grades, this instruction shifts toward more emphasis on human values.

Also, in Germany there are no school boards, and there are no publicly elected state boards of education. The school system is run by government bureaucracies. The curriculum and exams are set by the state. However, parents are actively involved in the education of their children at the school site. For example, when there is a parent evening, *both* parents usually attend. At these evenings, much of the talk between parents is about the homework assignments their children have been doing. This level of involvement is possible because parents are expected to help their children with homework. In Germany children have three to four hours of homework

assignments *every day*. The school day ends at 1:00 P.M. Children return home and work on their homework during the afternoon.

Germany takes a different approach to consideration of children with special needs. These children either have tutors or are assigned to different schools. If a child cannot keep up with the others at a school, he or she is told, "You do not belong here." The parents and the child then either have to work harder at keeping up or move to a different school.

Another legal aspect of the education system in Germany is that teachers, as government employees, cannot be sued. One consequence is that teachers do not supervise children during non-teaching times. Also, as government employees, teachers are not evaluated after their first year of teaching. As this description of schooling in Germany illustrates, the legal aspects of education and schools can be very different from country to country. Be careful not to assume that schools are the same everywhere.

Questions for Reflection

1. Given the establishment clause, do you think it would be possible for schools in the United States to be both public and church based as in Canada, Belgium, and the Netherlands?
2. How would you feel about the stance of German schools that if your child can't keep up, she or he needs to change schools?

(NEA) have been active in promoting collective bargaining. Today, approximately 75 percent of the nation's teachers are covered by collective bargaining agreements. As you read the Global Perspectives feature, compare the rights and responsibilities of teachers in other countries with U.S. teachers.

Academic Freedom

A sensitive and vital concern to the educator is **academic freedom**—freedom to control what one will teach and to teach the truth as one discovers it without fear of penalty. Academic freedom is thus essentially a principle of pedagogical philosophy that has been applied to a variety of professional activities. A philosophical position, however, is *not necessarily* a legal right. Federal judges have generally recognized certain academic protections in the college classroom while exhibiting reluctance to recognize such rights for elementary and secondary school teachers. For example, the contract of a history teacher at the University of Arkansas–Little Rock was not renewed after he announced that he taught his classes from a Marxist point of view. The court ordered that the teacher be reinstated in light of the university's failure to advance convincing reasons related to the academic freedom issue to warrant his nonrenewal (*Cooper v. Ross*, 1979). In another case, a university instructor claimed that he was denied tenure because he refused to change a student's grade. He argued that awarding a course grade was the instructor's right of academic freedom. Because the university had given several valid reasons for the nonrenewal of the instructor's contract, however, the court did not order a reinstatement (*Hillis v. Stephen F. Austin University*, 1982).

ACADEMIC FREEDOM FOR ELEMENTARY AND SECONDARY TEACHERS. Although federal courts generally have not recognized academic freedom for elementary and secondary school teachers, the most supportive ruling was made in 1980 (*Kingsville IDS v. Cooper*, 1980). In a case that involved a high school history teacher whose contract was not renewed after she used a simulation game to introduce her students to the characteristics of rural life during the post–Civil War Reconstruction era. Although the role playing evoked controversy in the school and the community, there was no evidence that the teacher's usefulness had been impaired. Therefore, the school erred in not renewing the teacher's contract, and she was ordered reinstated.

academic freedom The opportunity for a teacher to teach without coercion, censorship, or other restrictive interference.

In *Pickering v. Board of Education* (1968), the U.S. Supreme Court dealt with academic freedom at the public school level. Marvin L. Pickering was a teacher in Illinois who, in a letter published by a local newspaper, criticized the school board and the superintendent for the way they had handled past proposals to raise and use new revenues for the schools. After a full hearing, the board of education terminated Pickering's employment, whereupon he brought suit under the First and Fourteenth Amendments. The Illinois courts rejected his claim. The U.S. Supreme Court, however, upheld Pickering's claim and, in its opinion, stated:

> To the extent that the Illinois Supreme Court's opinion may be read to suggest that teachers may constitutionally be compelled to relinquish the First Amendment rights they would otherwise enjoy as citizens to comment on matters of public interest in connection with the operation of the public schools in which they work, it proceeds on a premise that has been unequivocally rejected in numerous prior decisions of this Court. (*Pickering,* 1968)

It is difficult to define precisely the limits of academic freedom. In general, the courts strongly support it yet recognize that teachers must be professionally responsible when interacting with pupils. In most instances, teachers are not free to disregard a school board's decision about which textbook to use, but they are able to participate more when it comes to their choice of supplementary methods. Teachers have usually been supported in their rights to criticize the policies of their local school boards, wear symbols representing stated causes, participate in unpopular movements, and live unconventional lifestyles. But when the exercise of these rights can be shown to have a direct bearing on a teacher's effectiveness, respect, or discipline, these rights may have to be curtailed. For example, a teacher may have the right to wear a gothic costume to class, but if wearing the outfit leads to disruption and an inability to manage students, the teacher can be ordered to wear more conventional clothes.

In summary, academic freedom for elementary and secondary teachers is more limited than it is for higher education faculty. First Amendment protection of free speech is increasingly limited to a teacher's actions outside of the classroom and school. Before arguing for academic freedom and free speech in the classroom, a teacher must show that she or he did not defy legitimate state and local curriculum directives, followed accepted professional norms, and acted in good faith when there was no precedent or policy.

⟳ See Chapter 12 for information about how curriculum and instruction can be offered in ways that allow for teacher creativity.

BOOK BANNING AND CENSORSHIP. Ever since the United States has had public schools, some people have taken issue with what has been taught, how it has been taught, and the materials used. The number of people challenging these issues and the intensity of feelings have escalated since the mid-1970s. Well-organized and well-financed pressure groups have opposed the teaching of numerous topics, including political, economic, scientific, and religious theories; the teaching of values grounded in religion, morality, or ethnicity; and the portrayal of stereotypes based on gender, race, or ethnicity. Some complaints have involved differences of opinion over the central role of the school—whether the school's job is to transmit traditional values, indoctrinate students, or teach students to do their own thinking.

Several court cases since the 1970s have involved the legality of removing books from the school curriculum and school libraries. The courts have given some guidance but have not fully resolved the issue. In 1972 a court of appeals held that a book does not acquire tenure, so a school board was upheld in its removal of *Down These Mean Streets*. The Court of Appeals for the Seventh Circuit in 1980 upheld the removal of the book *Values Clarification,* ruling that local boards have considerable authority in selecting materials for schools. Removal of books on the basis of vulgar language has also been upheld.

The U.S. Supreme Court treated this issue in 1982 (*Board of Education, Island Trees v. Pico,* 1982). The decision disappointed people who had hoped that the justices would issue a definitive ruling on the banning of books. Instead, Justice William Brennan ruled that students may sue school boards on the grounds of denial of their rights, including the right to receive information. The Court also indicated that removal of a book because one disagrees with its content cannot be upheld. The net effect of this decision was that the school board decided to return the questionable books to the library.

The latest censorship battleground has to do with limiting access to the World Wide Web. Many school districts and schools are applying filters that restrict access to particular types of websites. New questions related to defining what is meant by "responsible use" and who decides—teachers, principals, or school districts—are now occupying school boards, legislative bodies, and the courts.

FAMILY RIGHTS AND PRIVACY ACT. In 1974, Congress passed the Family Educational Rights and Privacy Act (FERPA), which also is called the **Buckley Amendment**. This statute addresses the maintenance of confidentiality of student records. This statute does not prohibit teachers, principals, and other education professionals from making student information available for educational purposes as long as they take steps to maintain privacy of the information.

School Records. Before November 19, 1974, the effective date of the Buckley Amendment, the law regarding the privacy of student records was extremely unclear. Even today many school administrators—and most parents—do not realize that parents now have the right to view their children's educational records. Many teachers, too, are not yet aware that their written comments, which they submit as part of a student's record, must be shown at a parent's request, or at a student's request if the student is eighteen or older. Key points teachers should know about FERPA are presented in Figure 10.7.

Students Grading One Another's Papers. A common instructional practice for teachers is to have students grade one another's work. As common as the practice is, it resulted in a suit that went all the way to the U.S. Supreme Court. In *Owasso Independent School District v. Falvo*, the plaintiff alleged violations of FERPA in regard to "peer review." The suit was funded by the Rutherford Institute, a national conservative organization. The Court of Appeals for the Tenth Circuit agreed with an Oklahoma parent that students should not grade other students' work. In 2002 the Supreme Court was unanimous in overturning the circuit court and said that the privacy law was directed at records "kept in a filing cabinet in a records room or on a permanent secure database," not the grades on a classroom paper. The Court observed:

> Correcting a classmate's work can be as much a part of the assignment as taking the test itself. It is a way to teach material again in a new context, and it helps show students how to assist and respect fellow pupils. By explaining the answers to the class as the students correct the papers, the teacher not only reinforces the lesson but also discovers whether the students have understood the material and are ready to move on. We do not think FERPA prohibits these educational techniques. (*Owasso*, 2002)

Family Rights and Privacy Act (FERPA), 1994. Also refered to as the Buckley Amendment Schools and teachers must maintain confidentiality of student records, and parents must be able to review and challenge the records for their children.

FIGURE 10.7

Important Elements for Teachers to Know about the Family Education Rights and Privacy Act

Family Education Rights and Privacy Act (FERPA)

Protects the privacy of student's education records and gives parents access to education records.

Schools must:

- Allow for the inspection and review of all the student's education records
- Inform all parents of what rights they have
- Provide copies to a parent or eligible student if she/he is otherwise not able to inspect the records
- Set reasonable fees for copies
- Comply within a reasonable time but no later than 45 days after the request is made.

Parents or eligible students have rights to:

- Seek to amend information within the student's educational records that is believed to be inaccurate or misleading.
- Provide permission before others than teachers and administrators can access information from the student's educational record.

Definitions:

Education record—information directly related to a student that is maintained by the school or school district.

Eligible student—a student becomes an eligible student when he/she turns 18 years old or attends a postsecondary school.

Parent—natural parent, guardian, or person acting as a parent in the absence of a parent or guardian.

Teacher Responsibilities and Liabilities

With about fifty-four million students enrolled in elementary and secondary schools, it is almost inevitable that some will be injured in educational activities. Each year, some injuries will occasion lawsuits in which plaintiffs seek damages. Such suits are often brought against both the school districts and their employees. Legal actions seeking monetary damages for injuries are referred to as *actions in tort.* Technically, a **tort** is a legal wrong—an act (or the omission of an act) that violates the private rights of an individual. Actions in tort are generally based on alleged negligence; the basis of tort liability or legal responsibility is negligence. Understanding the concept of negligence is essential to understanding liability.

Legally, *negligence* is a failure to exercise or practice due care. It includes a factor of foreseeability of harm. Court cases on record involving negligence are numerous and varied. The negligence of teacher supervision of pupils is an important topic that includes supervision of the regular classroom, departure of the teacher from the classroom, supervision of the playground, and supervision of extracurricular activities. **Liability** is the responsibility for negligence—responsibility for the failure to use reasonable care when such failure results in injury to another.

EDUCATIONAL MALPRACTICE. Culpable neglect by a teacher in the performance of his or her duties is called **educational malpractice**. The courts of California (*Peter W. v. SFUSD,* 1976) and New York (*Donohue v. Copiague Union Free School District,* 1978) dismissed suits by former students alleging injury caused by educational malpractice. The plaintiffs claimed that they did not achieve an adequate education and that this was the fault of the school district. In the California case, the student, after graduating from high school, could barely read or write. The judge in his opinion stated:

> The science of pedagogy itself is fraught with different and conflicting theories . . . and any layman might—and commonly does—have his own emphatic viewpoints on the subject. . . . The achievement of literacy in the schools, or its failure, is influenced by a host of factors from outside the formal teaching process, and beyond the course of its ministries (*Peter W.,* 1976).

In essence, the judge stated that there was no way to assess the school's negligence. In the New York case, the judge said, "The failure to learn does not bespeak a failure to teach." In the twenty-first century, with the continuing push for accountability, there are likely to be more tests of the educational malpractice question.

Negligent Chemistry Teacher. In a California high school chemistry class, pupils were injured while experimenting with the manufacture of gunpowder (*Mastrangelo v. West Side Union High School District,* 1935). The teacher was in the room and had supplemented the laboratory manual instructions with his own directions. Nevertheless, an explosion occurred, allegedly caused by the failure of pupils to follow directions. A court held the teacher and the board of education liable. Negligence in this case meant the lack of supervision of laboratory work, a potentially dangerous activity requiring a high level of "due care."

Field Trip Negligence. In Oregon a child was injured while on a field trip (*Morris v. Douglas County School District,* 1966). Children were playing on a large log in a relatively dry area on a beach. A large wave surged up onto the beach, dislodging the log, which began to roll. One of the children fell seaward off the log, and the receding wave pulled the log over the child, injuring him. In the subsequent court action, the teacher was declared negligent for not having foreseen the possibility of such an occurrence. The court said:

> The first proposition asks this court to hold, as a matter of fact, that unusual wave action on the shore of the Pacific Ocean is a hazard so unforeseeable that there is no duty to guard against it. On the contrary, we agree with the trial judge, who observed that it is common knowledge that accidents substantially like the one that occurred in this case have occurred at beaches along the Oregon coast. Foreseeability of such harm is not so remote as to be ruled out as a matter of law. (*Morris,* 1966)

Although liability for negligence is a vague concept involving due care and foreseeability, it is defined more specifically each time a court decides such a case.

Liability Insurance. Many states authorize school districts to purchase insurance to protect teachers, school districts, administrators, and school board members against suits. It is important that school districts and their employees and board members be thus protected, either through school district

Go to the *Assignments and Activities* section of Topic 4: *Ethical and Legal Issues* in the MyEdcationLab for your course and complete the activity titled *Legal Responsibilities of Teachers.*

tort An act (or the omission of an act) that violates the private rights of an individual.

liability Responsibility for the failure to use reasonable care when such failure results in injury to another.

educational malpractice Culpable neglect by a teacher in the performance of his or her duties.

insurance or through their own personal policies. The costs of school district liability insurance have increased so dramatically in recent years that many school districts are contemplating the elimination of extracurricular activities. Consequently, state legislatures are being pressured to fix liability insurance rates for school districts; they are also being asked to pass laws to limit maximum liability amounts for school-related cases. For teachers, membership in the state affiliates of the National Education Association and membership in the American Federation of Teachers include the option of liability insurance programs sponsored by those organizations.

Figure 10.6, shown earlier, summarizes statements related to the rights and responsibilities of teachers.

JOURNAL FOR REFLECTION

Today's teachers have responsibilities never imagined in earlier times. School districts specify expectations and evaluate teachers—especially probationary teachers—clearly and closely. Teachers need to know about curriculum standards and be sure that their students have learned the material that will be on the tests. Always present is the possibility of legal action. Take a few minutes to summarize the key points you have learned from reading about teachers' rights and responsibilities. Which of these points had you not anticipated? Which will you need to be sure to learn more about?

TEACHER AND STUDENT USES OF TECHNOLOGY AND THE LAW

The ever-increasing various forms and uses of technology are sources of promising practices for teaching and learning. They also are potential sources of problems for teachers and students, and increasingly playing a part in disciplinary and legal actions.

E-Mail

One of the most ubiquitous forms of technology is e-mail. It has become the basic form of communication between administrators and teachers, and between teachers and other teachers. Teachers may use e-mail to communicate with students and parents. Problems can arise when the Send key is hit before the message is carefully composed, or by sending the e-mail to "All" instead of only replying to the original sender. These mistakes can create embarrassing moments. But other events can have more serious consequences.

EMPLOYER MONITORING OF E-MAILS. You may wonder whether it is legal for a school district to monitor the e-mails of its teachers or for the college where you are studying teacher education to read your e-mails. If you use the college or school district's e-mail system, then the answer is yes. The courts view the e-mail system and its content as owned by the district or college. Problems can arise if inappropriate content is discovered. Content that is of a personal or sexual nature or not business related can become problematic. Even the accidental discovery of inappropriate content can lead to the employee being dismissed as happened to Jeffrey Spanierman in this chapter's Education in the News case. Keep the tips in Figure 10.8 in mind so that you do not become another case.

FIGURE 10.8
Think Before You Send

- Remember: once sent, always available.
- Keep them separate: What is work related and what is personal?
- Acknowledge: What you have sent is yours.
- Be careful: Could this embarrass you at some future time?
- Does it add value? Will this improve teaching and learning?
- Reply to Sender or to All? Be sure your message is going only to whom you intend.
- Your personal website is not confidential. Nonwork systems can be found and reviewed by your employer.
- Wait! Take another minute to review these tips before hitting the Send key.

Social Networking Risks

The new uses of cell phones for social networking including Facebook and Twitter are causing concern and serious problems. The innocent acts of youth can lead to legal proceedings as teenagers in several states have discovered with "sexting." Officials are threatening to charge girls who allegedly sent nude photos of themselves with lewd exhibition and the boys who receive the photos with possession of child pornography. These are very serious charges that, if convicted, would affect each student's future for a lifetime.

Cheating with Technology

Another increasing challenge for teachers is to determine when students are using technology to cheat. Using a cell phone while taking a test to snap pictures of test items and have an outsider call in the correct answers is more common than teachers want to believe. Plagiarism on term papers is another problem. Fortunately, several websites and services are available that can be used to catch those who copy from published text.

STUDENTS' RIGHTS AND RESPONSIBILITIES

The rights of students have changed since the late 1960s. Before 1969, school authorities clearly had the final say as long as what they decided was seen as reasonable. A key U.S. Supreme Court decision in 1969 changed the balance by concluding that students do not "shed their constitutional rights to freedom of speech or expression at the schoolhouse gate." Going further on behalf of student rights, in 1975 the Court decided that the principle of due process applied to students. These decisions led to several successful student challenges of school policies and procedures. In the late 1980s, Court decisions moved back toward increasing the authority of public school officials. Along the way, student life has become more complex, not only because of such threats as the increased use of drugs and the presence of weapons and gangs, but also because a diverse multicultural and shifting political context has made it more difficult to determine what is and what is not appropriate to do and say within a school environment.

To illustrate some of the issues and decisions related to student rights and responsibilities, we present specific court cases here. Note that the cases do not necessarily constitute the last word regarding student rights, but rather provide an overview of some of the issues that have been decided by the courts. Table 10.6 is a summary of key cases; however, it is not intended to provide a complete understanding of the court decisions. You should read the following subsections and pursue references provided in the notes and bibliography to learn more about these and other student rights issues.

Students' Rights as Citizens

Through a series of court decisions, all children in the United States have been granted the opportunity for a public school education. Further, although school officials have a great deal of authority, children as students maintain many of the constitutional rights that adult citizens enjoy all the time. As obvious as each of these points might seem, each has been the subject of debate and court decisions.

STUDENTS' RIGHT TO AN EDUCATION. Children in the United States have a right to an education; this right is ensured in many state constitutions. It has been further defined by court decisions and is now interpreted to mean that each child has an equal opportunity to pursue education.

The right to an education, however, is not without certain prerequisites. Citizenship alone does not guarantee a free education. Statutes that establish public school systems also generally establish how operating costs will be met. Real estate taxes are the usual source of funds, so proof of residence is necessary for school attendance without tuition. *Residence* does not mean that the student, parent, or guardian must pay real estate taxes; it means that the student must live in the school district in which he or she wants to attend school. Residence, then, is a prerequisite to the right of a free public education within a specific school district. The Reflect on Diversity on the next page feature illustrates one teacher's dilemma in striving to involve an undocumented parent.

Table 10.6 • Selected U.S. Supreme Court Cases Related to Students' Rights and Responsibilities

Case	Issue	Decision
Plyler v. Doe (1982)	Rights to education of illegal aliens	Court struck down Texas law that denied a free public education to children of illegal aliens.
Goss v. Lopez (1975)	Suspension of high school students without a hearing	Court ruled that only in an emergency can a student be suspended without a hearing.
Wood v. Strickland (1975)	Question of whether school board members can be sued for depriving students of their constitutional rights (through suspension)	Students can seek damages from individual school board members but not from the school district.
Tinker v. Des Moines Independent Community School District (1969)	Free speech rights of students to wear black armbands to protest U.S. involvement in Vietnam	Court ruled against school district—recognized to an extent constitutional rights of pupils.
Board of Education, Island Trees Union Free District No. 26 v. Pico (1982)	School board's decision to remove books from the school library	Court issued decision that under certain circumstances, children may challenge board's decision to remove books.
Ingraham v. Wright (1977)	Power of states to authorize corporal punishment without consent of the student's parent	Court ruled that states may constitutionally authorize corporal punishment.
Bethel School District No. 403 v. Fraser (1986)	Power of school officials to restrain student speech	School officials may discipline a student for making lewd and indecent speech in a school assembly attended by other students.
Hazelwood School District v. Kuhlmeier (1988)	School district control of student expression in school newspapers, theatrical productions, and other forums	School administrators have broad authority to control student expression in the official student newspaper, which is not a public forum but is seen as part of the curriculum.
Honig v. Doe (1988)	Violation of the Education for All Handicapped Children Act (P.L. 94-142); school indefinitely suspended and attempted to expel two emotionally disturbed students	P.L. 94-142 authorizes officials to suspend dangerous children for a maximum of ten days. Justice Brennan said, "Congress very much meant to strip schools of unilateral authority to exclude disturbed students."
New Jersey v. T.L.O. (1985)	Search and seizure	School officials must have a reasonable cause when engaged in searches.

REFLECT on DIVERSITY

What If Your Student's Mother Is Undocumented?

Bill, a second year teacher of science, was in a reflective mood. He had found that following his weekend bike rides was a good time to reflect on how his classes were going this year ("A lot better than last year") and to think about how much his students were learning ("Most of them seem to be getting it"). One of the challenges was the continual arrival of new students, especially those whose first language was not English.

For example, one of the girls, Neide, had recently arrived from Brazil. It was amazing how fast she was learning English in social situations. However, her academic vocabulary most definitely needed help. One of the strategies for improving vocabulary in the content areas is to have a parent go over a vocabulary list with the student in the evenings. Bill had checked about the possibility of his meeting with Neide and her mother

to work out a vocabulary homework plan. But Neide avoided answering and seemed somehow reluctant. As he reflected further, a light bulb went on: "What if her mother is an illegal alien?" "Now, what do I do?"

Questions for Reflection
1. What is the problem(s) for Bill?
2. What should Bill do next?
3. If Neide's mother is an illegal alien, will Neide be removed from school? (*Hint:* for part of the answer take a look at Table 10.6.)
4. What would you do, or not do, in this situation?

PEARSON **myeducationlab** To respond to these questions online, go to the *Book Specific Resources* section in the MyEducationLab for your course, select your text, and then select *Reflect on Diversity* for Chapter 10.

ALIEN AND HOMELESS CHILDREN HAVE THE RIGHT TO GO TO SCHOOL. In 1982 the Supreme Court ruled that the children of illegal aliens had a right to a free public education. There are more than 500,000 homeless children in the United States. Because access to public school usually requires a residence address and a parent or guardian, as well as transportation, in the past homeless children were squeezed out of the system. Congress addressed this growing problem in 1987 with passage of the Stewart B. McKinney Homeless Assistance Act, which requires that "each State educational agency shall assure that each child of a homeless individual and each homeless youth have access to a free, appropriate public education." The law was amended in 1990 to require each school district to provide services to the homeless that are comparable to the services offered other students in the schools. These services include allowing homeless children to finish the school year in the school they were in before they lost their housing, providing transportation to school, tutoring to help catch students up, and giving homeless children the opportunity to take part in school programs offered to other children.

STUDENTS' RIGHT TO SUE. The U.S. Supreme Court has affirmed that students may sue school board members who are guilty of intentionally depriving students of their constitutional rights. In *Wood v. Strickland* (1975), the Supreme Court held that school officials who discipline students unfairly cannot defend themselves against civil rights suits by claiming ignorance of pupils' basic constitutional rights. As a result of this decision, Judge Paul Williams, a federal judge in Arkansas, ordered that certain students who had been suspended could seek damages from individual school board members—though not from the school district as a corporate body. The judge also ruled that the school records of these pupils must be cleared of the suspension incident. From these decisions, it is apparent that the U.S. Supreme Court is taking into account the rights of students.

STUDENTS' RIGHT TO DUE PROCESS. Much of the recent involvement of the courts with student rights has concerned due process of law for pupils. Due process is guaranteed by the Fourteenth Amendment. The protection clause states, "nor shall any state . . . deny to any person within its jurisdiction the equal protection of the laws." Due process of law means following those rules and principles that have been established for enforcing and protecting the rights of the accused. As explained earlier, due process falls under two headings—procedural and substantive. *Procedural due process* has to do with whether the procedures used in disciplinary cases are fair; *substantive due process* is concerned with whether the school authorities have deprived a student of basic substantive constitutional rights such as personal liberty, property, or privacy (LaMorte, 2008, pp. 6–9).

in loco parentis Meaning "in the place of a parent," this term describes the implied power and responsibilities of schools.

The application of due process to issues in schools is a recent phenomenon. Historically, schools functioned under the doctrine of ***in loco parentis*** ("in the place of a parent"). This doctrine meant that schools could exercise almost complete control over students because they were acting as parent substitutes. Under the doctrine of *in loco parentis*, the courts have usually upheld the rules and regulations of local boards of education, particularly about pupil conduct. However, the courts have not supported rules that are unconstitutionally "vague" and/or "overboard." The cases discussed next illustrate the difficult balance between protecting students' right to due process and giving schools sufficient authority to pursue their mission.

PROCEDURAL DUE PROCESS IN CASES OF SUSPENSION AND EXPULSION. Zero tolerance policies have complicated the local schools' ability to balance students' right to due process and serving students' educational needs. Procedural due

Students have procedural due process rights, including the opportunity for some kind of hearing.

process is scrutinized especially in cases of suspension and expulsion. These cases most often result from disciplinary action taken by the school, which may or may not have violated a pupil's substantive constitutional rights. For example, in *Goss v. Lopez* (1975) the U.S. Supreme Court dealt with the suspension of high school students in Columbus, Ohio. In that case, the named plaintiffs claimed that they had been suspended from public high school for up to ten days without a hearing. The action alleged deprivation of constitutional rights. Two students who were suspended for a semester brought suit charging that their due process rights were denied—because they were not present at the board meeting when the suspensions were handed out.

In ruling that students cannot be suspended without some kind of hearing, the Court said:

> The prospect of imposing elaborate hearing requirements in every suspension case is viewed with great concern, and many school authorities may well prefer the untrammeled power to act unilaterally, unhampered by rules about notice and hearing. But it would be a strange disciplinary system in an educational institution if no communication was sought by the disciplinarian with the student in an effort to inform him of his defalcation and to let him tell his side of the story in order to make sure that an injustice is not done. Fairness can rarely be obtained by secret, one-sided determination of the facts decisive of rights. . . . Secrecy is not congenial to truth-seeking and self-righteousness gives too slender an assurance of rightness. No better instrument has been devised for arriving at truth than to give a person in jeopardy of serious loss notice of the case against him and opportunity to meet it. (*Goss,* 1975)

Procedural due process cases usually involve alleged violations of the Fourteenth Amendment, which provides for the protection of specified privileges of citizens, including notice to the student, impartiality of the hearing process, and the right of representation. These cases might also involve alleged violations of state constitutions or statutory law that call for specific procedures. For example, many states have procedures for expulsion or suspension. Expulsion usually involves notifying parents or guardians in a specific way, perhaps by registered mail, and giving students the opportunity for a hearing before the board of education or a designated hearing officer. Suspension procedures are usually detailed as well, designating who has the authority to suspend and the length of time for suspension. Teachers and administrators should know due process regulations, including the specific regulations of the state where they are employed.

SUBSTANTIVE DUE PROCESS AND STUDENTS' RIGHTS TO FREE SPEECH. Substantive due process frequently addresses questions of students' constitutional rights to free speech versus the schools' authority to maintain order in support of education. The *Tinker* case (*Tinker v. Des Moines Independent Community School District,* 1969) was significant. It involved a school board's attempt to keep students from wearing black armbands in a protest against U.S. military activities in Vietnam. In 1969 the U.S. Supreme Court ruled against the Des Moines school board. The majority opinion of the Court was that

> [T]he wearing of armbands in the circumstances of this case was entirely divorced from actually or potentially disruptive conduct by those participating in it. It was closely akin to "pure speech" which, we have repeatedly held, is entitled to comprehensive protection, under the First Amendment. . . . First Amendment rights, applied in the light of the special characteristics of the school environment, are available to teachers and students. It can hardly be argued that either students or teachers shed their constitutional rights to freedom of speech or expression at the schoolhouse gate.

In the *Tinker* opinion, the Court clearly designated that the decision "does not concern aggressive, disruptive action or even group demonstrations." The decision did make it clear that whatever their age, students have constitutional rights, and the decision has had a widespread effect on the operation of schools in the United States. Schools have had to pay attention to U.S. law. Educators as well as lawyers have been guided by the principles set forth in the decision regarding the constitutional relationship between public school students and school officials.

A more recent U.S. Supreme Court decision appears to have at least narrowed the breadth of application of the *Tinker* ruling. The case involved Matthew Fraser, a high school senior in a school outside Tacoma, Washington. In the spring of 1983, Fraser was suspended from school for two days after he gave a short speech at a school assembly nominating a friend for a position in student government. School officials argued that Fraser's speech contained sexual innuendos that provoked other students to engage in disruptive behaviors unfavorable to the school setting. The U.S. District Court for the Western District of Washington held that Fraser's punishment violated his rights to free speech under the First Amendment and awarded him damages. The U.S. Court of Appeals for the Ninth Circuit affirmed the decision, holding that Fraser's speech was not disruptive under the standards of *Tinker* (Flygare, 1986). However, the Supreme Court reversed the decision. In the majority opinion in *Bethel School District No. 403 v. Fraser* (1986), Chief Justice Warren Burger wrote, "The determination of what manner of speech in the classroom or in school assembly is inappropriate properly rests with the school board."

Students' Rights and Responsibilities in School

 As is described in Chapters 4 and 5, a teacher's philosophy of education will influence what is seen as important student rights.

The right, or privilege, of children to attend school also depends on their compliance with the rules and regulations of the school. To ensure the day-to-day orderly operation of schools, boards of education have the right to establish reasonable rules and regulations controlling pupils and their conduct. Boards' actions have been challenged in numerous instances, however. Challenges have concerned questions such as dress codes, corporal punishment, the rights of married students, dress codes, abuse and neglect, student publications' freedom of expression, disabilities, and searches.

DRESS CODES AND GROOMING. Lower court cases dealing with grooming have been decided in some instances in favor of the board of education—in support of their rules and regulations—and in other instances in favor of the student. A general principle seems to be that if the dress and grooming do not incite or cause disruptive behavior or pose a health or safety problem, the court ruling is likely to support the student. Dress codes, once very much in vogue, are less evident today. Although the U.S. Supreme Court has yet to consider a so-called "long hair" case, federal courts in every circuit have issued rulings in such cases; half of them found regulations on hair length unconstitutional, and half upheld them. In all, over a two-decade period, federal and state courts decided more than 300 cases on this subject. If there is a trend, it is that students have won most of the cases that dealt with hairstyle. The courts have usually refused to uphold dress and hair length regulations for athletic teams or extracurricular groups unless the school proves that the hair or dress interfered with a student's ability to play the sport or perform the extracurricular activity (*Long v. Zopp*, 1973).

In the late 1970s and continuing through the 1980s, courts entertained fewer challenges to grooming regulations. The later decisions, however, continued to be consistent with earlier court rulings. Courts have supported school officials who attempted to regulate student appearance if the regulation could be based on concerns about disruption, health, or safety. Presumably, controversy over the length of students' hair or grooming in general is no longer critical because officials and students have a more common ground of agreement about what is acceptable. However, as the new century begins, new questions could be raised in relation to school efforts to control the clothing and other grooming symbols of gangs. The Teacher Perspectives feature on the next page presents two viewpoints about the appropriateness of student dress.

CORPORAL PUNISHMENT. In 1977 the U.S. Supreme Court ruled on and finally resolved many of the issues related to corporal punishment (*Ingraham v. Wright,* 1977). The opinion established that states may *constitutionally* authorize corporal punishment without prior hearing or notice and without consent by the student's parents, or may as a matter of policy elect to prohibit or limit the use of corporal punishment. It also held that corporal punishment is not in violation of the Eighth Amendment (which prohibits "cruel and unusual punishments").

In response to the greater sensitivity to student rights, many school districts have adopted administrative rules and regulations to restrict the occasions, nature, and manner of administering corporal punishment. Some school districts specify that corporal punishment can be administered only under the direction of the principal and in the presence of another adult.

SEX DISCRIMINATION. Until relatively recently, educational institutions could discriminate against females—whether they were students, staff, or faculty. In 1972 the Ninety-Second Congress enacted Title IX of the Education Amendments Act to remove sex discrimination against students and employees in federally assisted programs. The key provision in Title IX states, "No person in the United States shall, on the basis of sex, be excluded from participation in, be denied the benefits of, or be subjected to discrimination under any education program or activity receiving federal financial assistance." Title IX is enforced by the Department of Education's Office of Civil Rights. An individual or organization can allege that any policy or practice is discriminatory by writing a letter of complaint to the secretary of education. An administrative hearing is the next step in the process. Further steps include suing for monetary damages under Title IX, which the U.S. Supreme Court affirmed in *Franklin v. Gwinnett County Schools* (1992).

Should Students Be Suspended for Inappropriate Dress?

An important theme in this chapter has been the challenges that schools face in balancing students' rights as citizens and the schools' responsibilities to provide a safe environment that supports learning. As norms of student dress change, so do the questions about what can, and cannot, be worn at school.

YES

Pernell Collett teaches social studies and public speaking at Ledford High School in Thomasville, North Carolina, and is president of the Davidson County Association of Educators.

I am a strong supporter of the freedom of expression, and am strongly opposed to school uniforms. However, I feel that students who dress inappropriately after knowing the dress code should be suspended.

Typically, students purposely violate the dress code to elicit a response from their peers or from others in the school community. I've seen students arrive at school wearing revealing clothing; T-shirts promoting sexual behavior, alcohol, and drug use; or clothing designed to offend different social groups. A student once walked into school wearing a T-shirt emblazoned with a swastika. He was told to go home to find another shirt, and that refusing to do so would be insubordination, resulting in suspension. Does anyone really think that he wore that shirt because it was the only clean one that he had at home?

By failing to act decisively, we are sending the message that we don't care about proper behavior, which includes proper dress. It can lead to other, more serious behavior issues as well. Students need to learn self-control and personal responsibility and a dress code, including the power to suspend students for violating it, can help do that.

NO

Leticia Colin, a future parent of a teenage daughter, teaches AIMS language arts at Carl Hayden Community High School in Phoenix, Arizona.

Although teens everywhere want to wear the latest fashions and believe their dress styles should be acceptable anywhere, it is universally accepted that schools have an appropriate dress code that must be maintained. However, we need to consider carefully the manner in which we discipline students who break that code. Suspending students for dress code violations is an ineffective punishment that accomplishes nothing except disrupting student learning.

A better approach would be to seek parental or guardian involvement. If the student is allowed to leave home inappropriately dressed, why not involve the parent and have them bring appropriate clothing to school? Parents and guardians need to be held accountable for student dress code violations. Many parents leave the house before their children, but a phone call from the school asking them to bring in appropriate clothing will certainly give parents a good reason to pay attention to their child's wardrobe decisions and to talk about what is acceptable attire for school.

Suspension should be a last resort, coming only after other interventions have failed. After all, one of the major goals of any educational system is attendance. We want to keep students in school, not out.

What is your perspective on this issue?

myeducationlab To explore both sides of this issue and think about each perspective, go to the *Book Specific Resources* in the MyEducationLab for your course, select your text, and then select *Teacher Perspectives* for Chapter 10.

Source: "Should Students be Suspended for Inappropriate Dress?" NEA Today, (April 2007), p. 43. Reprinted by permission of the National Education Association.

MARRIAGE AND PREGNANCY. In the past, it was not unusual for school officials to expel students who married. Some educators reasoned that marriage brought on additional responsibilities, such as the establishment of a household, and therefore that married students could not perform well in school. They also believed that exclusion would help deter other teenagers from marrying. Courts tended to uphold school officials in these positions. Both courts and school officials acted consistently in not rigidly enforcing compulsory attendance statutes for underage students who married.

School officials today cannot prohibit a student from attending school merely because he or she is married. This position is based on the above-mentioned Title IX and on the notion that every child has a right to attend school. Public policy today encourages students to acquire as much education as they can. Not only are married students encouraged to remain in school, but they are also entitled to the same rights and privileges as unmarried students. Thus, they have the right to take any course the school offers and to participate in extracurricular activities open to other students. That is, participation in extracurricular activities cannot be denied a student solely on the basis of marital status. However, a student's attendance and participation rights can be removed if his or her behavior is deleterious to other students.

Today's schools also enroll more pregnant students than ever before. Title IX prohibits their exclusion from school or from participation in extracurricular activities. Many school systems have reorganized their school programs so that courses can be offered during after-school hours or in the evenings to accommodate married and pregnant students. This arrangement makes it easier for students to work during the day and complete their education at a time that is convenient for them. Such programs often include courses and topics aimed at the specific audience, as well as counseling programs to assist students with their adjustment to marriage and family life.

CHILD ABUSE AND NEGLECT. Government bodies in the United States have the right to exercise police power, which means that the government is entrusted with the responsibility of looking after the health, safety, and welfare of all of its citizens. In effect, each state acts as a guardian over all of its people, exercising that role specifically over individuals not able to look after themselves. This guardianship extends to care for children who have been either abused or neglected by their parents. All fifty states have statutes dealing with this issue. These statutes generally protect children under the age of eighteen, but the scope of protection and definitions of abuse and neglect vary considerably among the states. In 1974, Congress passed the Child Abuse Prevention and Treatment Act, which provides financial assistance to states that have developed and implemented programs for identifying, preventing, and treating instances of child abuse and neglect.

The severity of this problem has been highlighted by the requirement of mandatory reporting of suspected abuse and neglect. Formerly, this reporting was limited mainly to physicians, but today educators are also required to report instances of suspected abuse and neglect. Some teachers are reluctant to do so because they fear a breakdown in student–teacher–parent relationships and the possibility of lawsuits alleging invasion of privacy, assault, or slander. Their fear should be diminished, however, by statutes that grant them immunity for acting in good faith.

STUDENT PUBLICATIONS. A significant decision relative to "underground" student newspapers was made in Illinois in 1970 (*Scoville v. Board of Education,* 1970). Students were expelled for distributing a newspaper named *Grass High,* which the students produced at home and which criticized school officials and used vulgar language. The students were expelled under an Illinois statute that empowered boards of education to expel pupils guilty of gross disobedience or misconduct. A federal court in Illinois supported the board of education, but on appeal the Court of Appeals for the Seventh Circuit reversed the decision. The school board was not able to validate student disruption and interference as required by *Tinker.* The expelled students were entitled to collect damages. An implication is that the rights of students regarding newspapers they print at home are stronger than their rights of free expression in official school publications.

Early in 1988, in a landmark decision (*Hazelwood School District v. Kuhlmeier*), the U.S. Supreme Court ruled that administrators have broad authority to control student expression in official school newspapers, theatrical productions, and other forums that are part of the curriculum. In reaching that decision, the Court determined that the *Spectrum,* the school newspaper of the Hazelwood District, was not a public forum. A school policy of the Hazelwood District required that the principal review each proposed issue of the *Spectrum.* The principal objected to two articles scheduled to appear in one issue. One of the articles was about girls at the school who had become pregnant; the other discussed the effects of divorce on students. Neither article used real names. The principal deleted two pages of the *Spectrum* rather than delete only the offending articles or require that they be modified. He stated that there was no time to make any changes in the articles and that the newspaper had to be printed immediately or not at all.

Three student journalists sued, contending that their freedom of speech had been violated. The Supreme Court upheld the principal's action. Justice Byron White decided that the *Spectrum* was not a public forum, but rather a supervised learning experience for journalism students. In effect, the censorship of a student press was upheld by the Supreme Court. In Justice White's words:

> [S]chools must be able to set high standards for the student speech that is disseminated under [their] auspices—standards that may be higher than those demanded by some newspaper publishers and theatrical producers in the "real" world—and may refuse to disseminate student speech that does not meet those standards.
>
> Accordingly, we hold that the standard articulated in *Tinker* for determining when a school may punish student expression need not also be the standard for determining when a school may refuse to lend its name and resources to the dissemination of student expression.

The issue of institutional control over publications has not yet been fully resolved. In response to questions about student publications and their distribution, school boards have endeavored to write rules and regulations that will withstand judicial scrutiny. A prompt review and reasonably fast appeal procedures are vital. Students should also be advised of distribution rules and abide by them.

RIGHTS OF STUDENTS WITH DISABILITIES. Before the early 1970s, the access to education of students with disabilities was left to the discretion of different levels of government. In the early 1970s, court decisions established the position that students with disabilities were entitled to an "appropriate" education and to procedural protections against arbitrary treatment. Congress subsequently specified a broad set of substantive and procedural rights via Section 504 of the Rehabilitation Act and Public Law 94-142, the Education for All Handicapped Children Act (EAHCA). Since that time there has been a continuing series of legislative and legal refinements and extensions of the intents to see that students with special needs have appropriate educational opportunities. The problem has been to define what is meant by "appropriate." This examination and clarification process continues to unfold.

One recent case regarding student rights dealt with a violation of P.L. 94-142. That law requires public school officials to keep disruptive or violent students with disabilities in their current classrooms pending hearings on their behavior. In the decision made in *Honig v. Doe* (1988), the U.S. Supreme Court upheld lower court rulings that San Francisco school district officials violated the act in 1980 when they indefinitely suspended and then attempted to expel two students who were emotionally disturbed and dangerous as officials claimed.

The act authorizes officials to suspend dangerous children with disabilities for a maximum of ten days. Longer suspensions or expulsions are permissible only if the child's parents consent to the action taken or if the officials can convince a federal district judge that the child poses a danger to himself or herself or to others. The rules under which school officials must operate also are more limiting if the misbehavior is a manifestation of the student's disability.

It is clear that Congress meant to restrain the authority that schools had traditionally used to exclude students with disabilities, particularly students who are emotionally disturbed, from school. But P.L. 94-142 did not leave school administrators powerless to deal with dangerous students.

STUDENT AND LOCKER SEARCHES. Most courts have refused to subject public school searches to strict Fourth Amendment standards. In general, the Fourth Amendment protects individuals from search without a warrant (court order). Many lower courts, however, have decided in favor of a more lenient interpretation of the Fourth Amendment in school searches. The rationale is that school authorities are obligated to maintain discipline and a sound educational environment and that that responsibility, along with their *in loco parentis* powers, gives them the right to conduct searches and seize contraband on reasonable suspicion without a warrant. First, however, school officials may only search for evidence that a student has violated a school rule or a law. Also, there must be a valid rule or law in place.

School authorities do not need a warrant to search a student's locker or a student vehicle on campus. For searches of a student's person, however, courts apply a higher standard. Where reasonable suspicion exists, a school official's actions will likely be upheld. Reasonable suspicion exists when one has information that a student is in possession of something harmful or dangerous or when there is evidence of illegal activities such as drug dealing (money, a list of customers, or rolling papers). The second consideration is the way in which the search of a student's person is conducted. School officials are advised to have students remove contents from their clothing rather than having a teacher or administrator do it.

A further caution is not to force students to remove all their clothing or undress to their underwear. In a nearly unanimous eight-to-one decision in 2009 the Supreme Court put school districts on clear notice that strip searches are "categorically distinct" from other efforts to combat illegal drugs. In *Safford Unified School District #1 v. Redding* the court concluded that an intrusive search of a thirteen-year-old girl for suspicion of hiding ibuprofen was an overreaction. In writing for the majority, Justice Souter said that what was missing "was any indication of danger to the students from the power of the drugs or the quantity, and any reason to suppose that Savana was carrying pills in her underwear." Concern about strip searches being degrading has led a number of states and school districts to ban strip searches.

PEER SEXUAL HARASSMENT. Title IX prohibits sex discrimination, and this includes students' harassing other students. Teasing, snapping bra straps, requesting sexual favors, making lewd comments about one's appearance or body parts, telling sexual jokes, engaging in physical

Where reasonable suspicion exists, school authorities do not need a warrant to search a student's locker or a student's vehicle on campus.

FIGURE 10.9

Summary Statements on Students' Rights and Responsibilities

- State constitutions provide that a child has the right to an education; to date, students have been unsuccessful in suing school board members on the ground that they have not learned anything.
- The due process clause provides that a child is entitled to notice of charges and the opportunity for a hearing prior to being suspended from school for misbehavior.
- Students enjoy freedom of speech at school unless that speech is indecent or leads to disruption; courts are in agreement that school officials can regulate the content of student newspapers. Underground newspapers are not subject to this oversight.
- Students may be awarded damages from school board members for a violation of their constitutional rights if they can establish that they were injured by the deprivation and that the school official deliberately violated those rights.
- The use of corporal punishment is not prohibited by the U.S. Constitution, but excessive punishment may be barred by the Fourteenth Amendment.
- Students may be restricted in their dress when there are problems of disruption, health, or safety.
- Assignments of students to activities or classes in general on the basis of sex is not consistent with Title IX. These assignments may be made in such areas as sex education classes or when sports are available for both sexes.
- Restricting a student's activities on the basis of marriage or pregnancy is inconsistent with the equal protection clause and Title IX.
- Teachers are required to report to proper authorities suspected instances of child abuse and neglect.
- Parents have the right to examine their children's educational records. Students age eighteen or older have the right to examine their records.
- School officials may search students, lockers, and student property without a search warrant, but they must have reasonable grounds for believing that a student is in possession of evidence of a violation of a law or school rule.

abuse, and touching inappropriately are examples of peer sexual harassment. It is important for teachers to make it clear that sexual harassment will not be tolerated. School districts are supposed to have in place a grievance procedure for sex discrimination complaints. Students and/or their parents can file a complaint with the Office of Civil Rights also. All allegations must be investigated promptly, and schools must take immediate action in cases in which harassment behaviors have been confirmed. Keep in mind that sexual harassment is not limited to high school students; middle school and in some cases elementary school children are also sexually harassed. To summarize the topics covered in this section, Figure 10.9 lists brief statements related to the rights and responsibilities of students.

═══════════ **JOURNAL FOR REFLECTION** ═══════════

Now, it should be clear to you that students have rights and that teachers need to be aware of them. Teachers should always be sure that another teacher or administrator is present when disciplinary action is taken. When taking any such action, teachers must be sure that the principal or other administrators are informed. As a way of making the rights and responsibilities real for you, think back across your years as a student. Compare some of the things that you experienced or witnessed with what you have just read about the legal rights and responsibilities of students.

LOOKING AHEAD: THE EVOLVING LEGAL ASPECTS OF EDUCATION

During the coming decade, more issues and legal challenges related to education will arise. Teachers, students, and administrators must continually be aware of their responsibilities and the legal safeguards that protect students as well as educators. We can expect additional attempts to increase the amount of religious activities in public schools. There are likely to be new cases related to drug testing, searches, weapons, and assaults. There most certainly will be new policies, administrative directives, and court cases related to uses of technology, especially around appropriate and inappropriate social networking. Some teachers and administrators will become consumed in irresolvable disputes that will end as court cases. Be sure that you, as a teacher education candidate and in the future as a teacher, are fully cognizant of your responsibilities under the law. As the saying goes, ignorance of the law is no excuse.

SUMMARY

LEGAL ASPECTS OF EDUCATION

- The U.S. Constitution is the starting point for viewing schools from the legal perspective.
- Education is not mentioned directly in the Constitution.
- The Tenth Amendment has been interpreted as assigning responsibility to each state for education of its citizens.
- How education is addressed in each state's constitution is of paramount importance.
- Interpretations of law and the resolution of disputes, whether they are about separation of church and state, desegregation, or teachers' rights, ultimately are decided by the U.S. and state supreme courts.
- Public funds can be used to support some kinds of education services offered by church schools.

TEACHERS' RIGHTS AND RESPONSIBILITIES

- Teachers' rights as citizens and employees, including procedural and substantive due process, are protected.
- However, teachers do not have absolute academic freedom.
- FERPA protects the privacy of student records.
- Teachers must be vigilant in guarding against placing students in risky situations.
- Teachers can be sued for negligence and malpractice.

TEACHER AND STUDENT USES OF TECHNOLOGY AND THE LAW

- Teacher and student use of school district e-mail systems can be monitored.
- Teachers and teacher education candidates need to be careful in what they place on social networking websites.
- Teachers must be vigilant in monitoring the use of technology to cheat.

STUDENTS' RIGHTS AND RESPONSIBILITIES

- Students too have rights as citizens, including the right to an education.
- They have due process rights, protection from discrimination, and, within limits, freedom of expression.
- However, schools have the authority to determine when student conduct is disruptive.

LOOKING AHEAD: THE EVOLVING LEGAL ASPECTS OF EDUCATION

- The legal aspects of education will continue to evolve.
- Teachers must always be aware of their legal rights and responsibilities.

DISCUSSION QUESTIONS

1. How do you view the use of public funds to support certain activities in church schools? Do you see a trend toward "excessive entanglement"? If not, where do you see the line needing to be drawn so as not to conflict with the establishment clause?
2. How should you as a teacher accommodate the religious interest of children in your class who are of a religion other than Christianity, such as Judaism, Islam, or Buddhism?
3. In *Ingraham v. Wright* (1977), the U.S. Supreme Court ruled that states may authorize the use of corporal punishment as school policy. The U.S. military has not allowed corporal punishment for one hundred years. Why should it be disallowed in the military but be permissible in schools? Is it ever appropriate in schools?
4. Should teachers be granted tenure, or would renewable contracts be better? Why?

5. What are your thoughts about balancing student rights against school officials' need to maintain an environment conducive to learning? Should school officials have more authority? Should students have greater freedom?

6. AIDS is a legally recognized disability. If, as a teacher, you are to have an HIV-positive student in your classroom, what are that student's rights under the law? What are your responsibilities as a teacher?

SCHOOL-BASED OBSERVATIONS

1. Beginning teachers do not have the same rights as tenured teachers, but they do have rights. With a partner, compare and contrast the rights of beginning teachers in two school districts. Some of the items to check are length of the probationary period, the basis for a tenure decision, how the tenure decision-making process works, and the due process rights of probationary teachers.

2. Interview an experienced teacher about students' rights. Ask him or her to provide examples of situations in which it was important for the teacher to be aware of student rights. What were the critical points to be considered? What were the related responsibilities of the teacher? What advice would this teacher have for today's beginning teachers?

PORTFOLIO DEVELOPMENT

1. Pick a school district where you think you would like to work as a teacher. Obtain a copy of the teacher employment contract from the district human resources/personnel office and study it. What does the contract say about your rights as a district employee and as a teacher? What does it say about your responsibilities? There may be references to other legal documents such as an employee handbook and board policies; if so, become familiar with those documents too. Together, these documents set the parameters for what you can, should, and should not do as a teacher. Place these documents and your notes in a folio file folder and save them for later use.

2. From time to time, newspapers and weekly news magazines carry reports about disagreements between students and school officials. Collect these reports, paying special attention to the legal interpretations drawn by each side, and consider the implications for you. In all instances, keep in mind that both teachers and students have legal responsibilities as well as rights. These clippings and notes may be a useful resource for you someday, when as a teacher you are confronted with a question about student and teacher rights.

PREPARING FOR CERTIFICATION

1. The Praxis II Principles of Learning and Teaching (PLT) test includes cases and items that address "Major laws related to students' rights and teacher responsibilities [including]
   - Equal education
   - Appropriate education for students with special needs
   - Confidentiality and privacy
   - Appropriate treatment of students
   - Reporting in situations related to possible child abuse."

   Review the tables in this chapter that present key legal decisions affecting teachers' and students' rights. Then list the five law-related issues that you think will influence you the most in the subject area or geographic location in which you plan to teach.

2. One of the topics covered in the Praxis II Principles of Learning and Teaching (PLT) test is instruction and assessment. This section of the test includes reference to the following information: "Methods for enhancing student learning through the use of a variety of resources and materials [including]
   - Computers, Internet resources, Web pages, e-mail

   - Audiovisual technologies such as videotapes and compact discs (CDs). . . ."

   Others are also listed; however, the impact of electronic media on schools and society is changing rapidly. What collaborative Internet applications do you now use? How might your current use of social networking applications affect you as a prospective teaching candidate for a job in today's schools?

3. Answer the following multiple-choice question, which is similar to items in Praxis and other state certification tests.

   The Buckley Amendment
   a. permits corporal punishment as long as district policies and procedures are in place.
   b. allows all parents access to their children's academic records.
   c. establishes that married or pregnant students have the same rights and privileges as other students.
   d. states that all students with disabilities are entitled to an "appropriate" education.

4. Answer the following short-answer question, which is similar to items in Praxis and other state certification tests.
   What are the arguments for and against tenure for teachers? What is your position, and why?

After you've completed your written responses for the above questions, use the Praxis general scoring guide provided in Chapter 1 to see if you can you revise your response to improve your score.

MYEDUCATIONLAB

myeducationlab Now go to Topic 4: *Ethical and Legal Issues* in the MyEducationLab (www.myeducationlab.com) for your course, where you can:

- Find learning outcomes for *Ethical and Legal Issues* along with the national standards that connect to these outcomes.
- Complete *Assignments and Activities* that can help you more deeply understand the chapter content.
- Apply and practice your understanding of the core teaching skills identified in the chapter with the *Building Teaching Skills and Dispositions* learning units.

- Check your comprehension on the content covered in the chapter by going to the *Study Plan* in the *Book Specific Resources* section for your text. Here you will be able to take a chapter quiz, receive feedback on your answers, and then access *Review, Practice, and Enrichment* activities to enhance your understanding of chapter content.

WEBSITES

http://catalog.loc.gov The Library of Congress Catalog provides a quick way to access the text of government bills, including those related to education.

http://janweb.icdi.wvu.edu and **www.schoolnet.ca/sne** There are many websites with information on special education topics. The ADA (Americans with Disabilities Act) Document Center and the Special Needs Education Network are two useful sites to check first.

www.abanet.org The American Bar Association's website provides access to its journal, analyses of court decisions, and a large database of court decisions.

www.dirksencongressionalcenter.org The Dirksen Congressional Center is a very useful resource for teachers. It offers a newsletter, curriculum resources, and links for educators to aid in improving understanding of Congress. One feature describes how a bill becomes a law.

www.lawschool.cornell.edu The Cornell Law School's Legal Information Institute (LII) website is easy to use and provides access to court decisions, news related to court cases, directories, and current awareness items.

www.cnn.com/law CNN operates a number of useful websites including Law Center, which reports on state, national, and international court proceedings.

www.stateline.org The Pew Center on the States operates this very informative website that reports about policy developments in all of the states. It has a dedicated section for education policy.

www.nea.org The National Education Association website offers legal information and a number of teaching supports for beginning teachers.

FURTHER READING

Essex, N. L. (2008). *School law and the public schools: A practical guide for educational leaders* (4th ed.). Boston: Pearson A&B. This book presents issues and topics briefly, and for each it provides a table called an *administrative guide* that summarizes legal points and suggests appropriate steps to take.

LaMorte, M. W. (2008). *School law: Cases and concepts* (9th ed.). Boston: Allyn & Bacon. Each chapter presents an in-depth analysis of cases and points of law related to public education, teacher rights, and student rights.

Parker-Jenkins, M., Hartas, D., and Irving, B. A. (2005). *In good faith: Schools, religion and public funding.* Burlington, VT: Ashgate. Sometimes it is useful to read

how people in another country think about an issue. This book does that by examining issues in England, where different religious groups are advocating for their own schools with public support.

Underwood, J., & Webb, L. D. (2006). *School law for teachers: Concepts and applications.* Upper Saddle River, NJ: Pearson Merrill Prentice Hall. An easy-to-read primer for teachers that covers the important topics and includes brief descriptions of key cases.

Zirkel, P. A. Courtside. *Phi Delta Kappan.* A regular column in the *Phi Delta Kappan* that provides timely and pertinent information about legal issues.

chapter eleven

STANDARDS, ASSESSMENT, AND ACCOUNTABILITY

HIGH MARKS FOR SCHOOLS MAY BECOME HARD TO GET

EDUCATION IN THE NEWS

By **LESLIE POSTAL AND DAVE WEBER**,
Orlando Sentinel, Orlando, Florida, January 11, 2009

A tough new system to evaluate Florida's high schools could make it harder for them to earn good grades, but it may provide a more in-depth look at what is happening on their campuses.

Local educators had hoped high schools would shine if the state looked beyond scores on the Florida Comprehensive Assessment Test that is now used to calculate the A-to-F grades handed out each year. They had complained for years that the current system was too narrow and made it difficult for high schools to earn good grades. Those schools often posted more C's, D's and F's than A's and B's.

But a trial run of the proposed new system by the Florida Department of Education suggests grades for high schools would drop—not improve—at least in the first year the new plan is in place. High-flying schools such as Winter Park High and struggling ones such as Oak Ridge High in Orange County would slip a notch, the simulated calculation showed.

That has some educators upset and hoping that the state delays carrying out the new system, scheduled to post its first set of grades in 2010.

"I was certainly hoping that it was not going to be something that would make schools look worse," said Lee Baldwin, who oversees testing and accountability for Orange County schools and serves on the state panel that provided advice on the new system.

The Education Department simulation found that about 35 percent of the high schools in Florida would drop a grade, about 7 percent would improve, and about 58 percent would stay the same. The number of F-rated high schools could increase by 15 schools, totaling 44 statewide.

Baldwin says the new plan is "definitely, without a doubt, a broader look," but he fears it is also "harsh."

The new system—still under consideration and subject to revision—relies less on FCAT and more on other indicators such as graduation rates and student success in advanced courses or on college-admissions tests. Once in place, it would be the most sweeping change to the system since Florida started grading public schools in 1998.

But it would impact only high schools, with elementary and middle schools continuing to be graded only on how students do on FCAT's math, reading, science and writing exams.

Despite complaints, state education officials and lawmakers say they are unlikely to delay the new high-school-grading system, which they say is a great improvement.

"It will bring high-school accountability to reflect more what the schools are truly doing," said Education Commissioner Eric Smith, adding, "I would not be one to advocate for delay in this."

State legislators passed a law requiring the new grading system last spring, saying FCAT should count for only half of a high school's grade. They wanted a system that also graded high schools on items key to their basic mission, such as getting students to earn diplomas and prepare for college.

"The purpose of the legislation was not to improve high-school grades," said Sen. Don Gaetz, R–Niceville, who crafted the bill. "The purpose of the legislation was to provide a more well-rounded picture of high-school performance."

Some educators fear low grades.

Gaetz said many of the educators "who were among the loudest and most insistent voices calling for change" are the same ones now asking for the state to hold back on the new grading system because they fear their schools may not show well.

The state's simulated grades were based on 2007 data, and many high schools improved in 2008, meaning they may fare better under the new system than the test run suggested. The simulation also did not have all the pieces of data the state hopes to include in the final version.

"The concept is good, and I support it. But I recommend we put it off for one more year," said Bill Vogel, superintendent of Seminole County schools, which have some of the best high-school grades in the state.

Like other officials, Vogel said the system's complicated calculations still need some work. He and others do not like that students who earn GEDs will not count as graduates, for example.

Frank Casillo is principal at B-rated Lyman High, which in the test run dropped to a D. He said schools that don't have a lot of acceleration programs, such as Advanced Placement or International Baccalaureate, won't show as well. Counting how many kids take and pass those courses is unfair, especially when the state is cutting back funding to offer the courses, he said.

"I don't like it. But we will do what we have to do," Casillo added.

The *Orlando Sentinel* in March created an online database to evaluate Central Florida high schools on up to 20 criteria, from reading scores to dropout rates to college readiness. The analysis showed that looking beyond FCAT created a broader and much more detailed picture of high-school successes and struggles. For example, some schools that received C's from the state actually outperformed some A-rated schools when more criteria were added.

Gaetz and others cited the analysis as an indication that Florida's old high-school-grading system came up short and that a new one was needed.

First, public hearings must occur.

The state's Education Department, which must come up with the new grading formula, plans to finalize its proposal and then hold public hearings before it is presented to the State Board of Education for final approval this spring.

Local educators plan to continue lobbying for a delay or tweaks to the system.

Rick Fleming, principal of West Shore Junior/Senior High in Melbourne, said many high-school principals are worried,

mostly because "everyone's going to have to re-adapt to a new set of rules."

But principals are also pleased the state will be taking a broader look at high schools.

"People got tired of everything being graded solely on FCAT," Fleming added.

QUESTIONS FOR REFLECTION

1. Why are some educators in Florida worried about the state application of criteria for grading high schools that use more factors than the state's achievement test, the Florida Comprehensive Assessment Test (FCAT)?
2. Why are other educators supportive of the use of more than just the FCAT to grade high schools?
3. What is the purpose of grading schools in a state? What difference will these changes make in student learning in Florida's high schools?

Source: Used with permission of the *Orlando Sentinel*, copyright 2009.

LEARNING OUTCOMES

After reading and studying this chapter, you should be able to:

1. Identify the importance of standards in our educational system.
2. Discuss the changing role of the federal government in setting standards for P–12 student learning.
3. Understand the role of performance assessments in determining what students know and are able to do. (INTASC 8: Assessment)
4. Define accountability for student learning and describe how the No Child Left Behind Act is holding schools, school districts, and states accountable for student achievement. (INTASC 8: Assessment)
5. Discuss international comparisons of student achievement and how students from the United States are performing. (INTASC 8: Assessment)

standards A statement of a desired outcome, which in education is usually a description of student learning.

assessments The use of multiple methods, including tests, to evaluate the current level of student learning; used in planning future steps in instruction.

standards-based education The use of explicit outcomes of what students should know and be able to do, which are outlined in standards, to develop instruction and assessments.

performance Demonstration of learning through doing.

high-stakes tests Tests that have major consequences or implications.

EDUCATION STANDARDS

Education **standards** affect the entire teaching and learning process, including the curriculum, instruction, **assessments**, and professional development. Standards are a popular topic in both the business and education worlds. State and federal policy makers expect students to meet standards, which have been developed by national organizations, state boards of education, and local groups. Educators must figure out how they will ensure that students meet the standards. As an instructional approach, **standards-based education** places student learning at the center. Achievement of the standards is paramount and is increasingly linked to a student being promoted or receiving a diploma. Student **performance** against standards is often measured by achievement on standardized tests, sometimes determining whether teachers and principals retain their jobs.

Standards have different meanings to different users. Some people view them as synonymous with rigor and the setting of high expectations for schools, teachers, and students. Others focus on learner outcomes or what students or teachers should know when they finish a grade or college. Still others equate standards with **high-stakes tests** such as annual state tests, or teacher licensure tests, which must be passed to receive a license to teach.

At their simplest, standards are statements that describe what we should know and be able to do. They are developed for school construction, school accreditation, and licensure as well as student learning at each grade level. They also can range in scope from being extremely global and ambitious to very narrow and specific. Today, the focus of most standards for P–12 students is on what students have learned. Even accreditation standards for your teacher education program expect that you know the student standards and have developed the knowledge, skills, and professional dispositions for helping all students learn. In this section we explore the types of standards you will be expected to implement when you begin working in a school.

Conceptions of Standards

Diverse conceptions of standards stem from differing expectations. Business leaders tend to want high school graduates who are ready for work. They should be able to read, write, and compute as well as have the dispositions that will make them desirable workers. Business executives expect schools to prepare for them a supply of future workers. They are willing to provide specific job training, but they do not want to teach what they consider the basic skills that all students should have before entering the world of work.

Students must meet high standards before they can graduate from high school. Many states are requiring students to pass a test before they receive a diploma.

Policy makers think about the larger, long-term needs of society. They are concerned about graduates having the knowledge and skills that will help the United States maintain its competitive edge in the global economy. Therefore, they promote rigorous academic standards that will ensure that students perform at high levels on international comparisons. They want students to know more science, history, mathematics, literature, and geography than students in other countries.

Parents choose standards based on their own personal goals and family histories. Some parents want their children to go to prestigious colleges. Others want their children to obtain a job immediately after high school. Still others want their offspring to prepare for a professional career such as a medical doctor, lawyer, or engineer. These expectations influence the type of standards that parents support.

Developing and adapting a clearly articulated, coordinated set of standards is not easy. Not all members of a community agree on what standards are appropriate. Despite these difficulties, the development of clear standards enables different constituencies within the school community to clarify their needs and aspirations. The process of selecting and adapting standards also provides a forum for conducting dialogues and negotiating what schools should do and for what schools, teachers, and students should be held accountable.

WORLD-CLASS STANDARDS. One of the nation's goals is that the United States retains its competitiveness and prosperity in the global economy. Countries around the world have learned that education plays a major role in this effort. Not only does completion of college help individuals develop higher level skills, it translates into a higher income over their lifetime. The development of high skill levels also contributes to a country's competitiveness worldwide. The National Governors Association, the Council of Chief State School Officers, and Achieve, Inc., reported in 2008 that "If the United States raised students' math and science skills to globally competitive levels over the next two decades, its GDP [i.e., gross domestic product] would be an additional 36 percent higher 75 years from now." To check how we are doing, the performance of our students is annually benchmarked against that of students from countries that score the highest on international comparisons, such as Germany, South Korea, Japan, and Singapore.

World-class standards against which students' knowledge and skills are measured are visionary statements of aspiration and accomplishment at high levels. Unlike many nations, the United States does not have a common set of standards that guide curriculum development; each state has developed its own set of standards. Proponents of world-class standards are calling for the development of national standards, as discussed later in this chapter. Traditionally, states and educators have resisted the development of national standards, leaving the decisions about what to teach in our schools to the state or local district. The current focus on competitiveness has taken precedence over those arguments.

REAL-WORLD STANDARDS. Another segment of the public believes that standards should be real-world goals. This conception of standards places primary emphasis on the necessary knowledge and skills that will make students employable and enable them to live independent lives. Assessments of reading, writing, and computing skills show that too many high school graduates lack these skills. Major U.S. firms report that 34 percent of tested job applicants lack the basic skills necessary for the job (American Management Association, 2001). In contrast to world-class standards, real-world standards are seen as being achievable in schools. Real-world standards set the expectation that students learn the basic skills of reading, writing, and computing that allow them to balance checkbooks, prepare for job interviews, manage their daily lives, and maintain employment.

OPPORTUNITY-TO-LEARN STANDARDS. At the beginning of the standards movement in the late 1980s, standards were generally input standards that indicated resources and other areas of a school's organization that should be in place for quality educational programs. They required specific topics to be addressed in the curricula. They also sometimes required a maximum student-to-teacher ratio in the classroom, faculty with bachelor's degrees who were certified to teach the courses they were teaching, adequate budgets, number of library books, and adequate technology.

At the end of the 1990s, student and teacher standards moved from input to output or performance standards with the emphasis on what students and teachers should know and be able to do. These standards were sometimes accompanied by a set of **opportunity-to-learn standards** that addressed the need for adequate and appropriate instructional resources, assessments, and system structures to create the proper conditions for students to achieve the standards. The intent was to ensure that all students had an equal chance to meet the standards. Examples include guaranteeing that students have sufficient opportunities to relearn when a standard is not achieved, ensuring that sufficient time is offered to students so that they can achieve various standards at their own pace, offering alternative ways to achieve a standard based on individual needs, specifying the types of technology to be available in schools and classrooms, and regularly providing staff professional development that helps teachers fine-tune instructional techniques that lead to student achievement of standards. With the goal of fairness, students with disabilities and English-language learners had to be provided appropriate accommodations to support their learning of the proficiencies outlined in standards.

opportunity-to-learn standards Standards that identify the instructional resources, assessments, and system structures required to create the proper conditions for students to achieve content and performance standards.

content standards Standards that specify learning outcomes in a subject or discipline (for example, mathematics or social studies).

Opportunity-to-learn standards identify the resources and support needed to ensure that all students can meet content and performance standards.

Content Standards

Content standards today are performance based. They describe what teachers and students should know and be able to do in various subject areas such as science, mathematics, language arts, history, geography, social studies, physical education, and the arts. They are often accompanied by standards for what teachers should know about the content or subject to teach at the preschool, elementary, middle, or secondary level.

Content standards establish the knowledge and skills that should be learned in various subject areas. They are often linked to big ideas, themes, or conceptual strands that should be nurtured throughout a student's education. For example, in the national science standards, the big ideas of evolution and equilibrium, form and function, systems, and the nature of science are explicitly described, along with specific grade-level expectations (National Committee on Science Education Standards and Assessment, 1996). The same is true in the standards for social studies; ten themes such as culture, civic ideals and practices, and people, places, and environments provide a framework for the social studies curriculum in early grades, middle grades, and high schools. The standards of the National Council for the Social Studies (NCSS, 2009) also include learning expectations and snapshots of classroom practice for each theme. The National Council of Teachers of Mathematics (NCTM) standards, furthermore, state that students should be able to understand and use numbers and operations; specifically, they should

- *Understand numbers,* ways of representing numbers, relationships among numbers, and number systems;
- *Understand meanings* of operations and how they relate one to another;
- *Compute fluently* and make reasonable estimates (NCTM, 2000).

In addition to knowledge acquisition statements, content standards often specify what thinking and process skills and strategies students and/or teachers should acquire. These skills and strategies might include developing a plan and hypothesis; interpreting, extrapolating, and drawing conclusions; and communicating results. Standards may also include statements about the habits or dispositions that should be nurtured in students. These habits or dispositions include curiosity, perseverance, tenacity, caring, and open-mindedness.

Today, all states have their own content standards or have adapted the national standards to their own state contexts. For the first time, the governors and chief state school officers in almost every state agreed to create common standards in mathematics and English language arts. The development of these standards was on a fast track. Three national groups (Achieve, the College Board, and ACT, the group that develops college entrance tests) were charged with developing the standards for high school graduates and each grade before the end of 2009. The state officials agreed to use the common core of these national standards for at least 85 percent of their state standards; the other 15 percent could be unique to the state. Forty-six states, the District of Columbia, Puerto Rico, and the U.S. Virgin Islands committed to adapting the common core by 2012 (McNeil, 2009).

The standards are to identify what students should know by the time they finish each grade to make them ready for college and a career. The standards will bring consistency to what is to be learned across the country. A common set of academic targets will be identified and benchmarked against international standards. Such benchmarking should greatly reduce the patchwork of different proficiency levels that now exists across states that allow large numbers of students in one state with low-proficiency expectations to pass the test while the numbers are much smaller in another state with high-proficiency expectations.

21st Century Knowledge and Skills Framework

Since standardized tests became an integral part of the educational landscape following the passage of the No Child Left Behind Act, educators have been concerned that important areas such as critical thinking and problem solving have been ignored. A number of business leaders and policy makers agree. They are now calling for attention to be paid to twenty-first-century skills that are needed in a global economy and rapidly changing world.

Although a number of organizations are writing about standards for twenty-first-century knowledge and skills, the Partnership for 21st Century Skills has taken the lead. The partnership includes more than thirty member organizations that represent technology companies such as Adobe Systems, Dell, Apple, and Microsoft; companies that produce educational technology such as Blackboard, LeapFrog SchoolHouse, and Discovery Education; tests and publishing companies such as Educational Testing Service (ETS) and Pearson Education; communications companies such as AT&T, Corporation for Public Broadcasting, and Verizon; and foundations. Two associations are involved: the National Education Association, which is one of the teachers unions, and the American Association of School Librarians. The partnership has developed a framework for teaching and learning that stretches from preschool through graduate school. It has identified the knowledge, skills, and expertise that students should master to be successful in this century. The four broad outcomes and support systems required to support the development of these outcomes are shown in Figure 11.1.

FIGURE 11.1

21st Century Student Outcomes and Support Systems

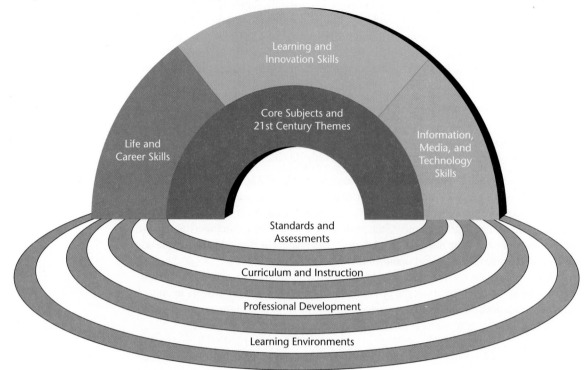

Source: Partnership for 21st Century Skills. (2009, May 27). *Framework for 21st century learning.* Tucson, AZ: Author. Retrieved June 30, 2009, from http://www.21stcenturyskills.org/index.php?Itemid=120&id=254&option=com_content&task=view.

The core subjects are the ones addressed in the content standards of what students should know and be able to do, which were described earlier in the chapter. Some of the four twenty-first-century themes can be found in specific content standards such as social studies, but they have not been integrated across the content standards. They are meant to be interdisciplinary and promote higher level understanding. The first is global awareness, which includes "learning from and working collaboratively with individuals representing diverse cultures, religions and lifestyles in a spirit of mutual respect and open dialogue in personal, work and community contexts" as well as "understanding other nations and cultures, including the use of non-English languages" (Partnership for 21st Century Skills, 2009). The other themes are financial, economic, business, and entrepreneurial literacy; civic literacy; and health literacy.

The other four outcomes demonstrate an even more dramatic change from the current standards-based curriculum. The Learning and Innovation Skills prepare students for the increasingly complex life and work environments they will face in the future. They include creativity and innovation, critical thinking and problem solving, and communication and collaboration. Having skills related to information, media, and technology will be important in a world where the Internet and other technologies provide access to an abundance of information, technology tools are rapidly changing, and technology makes it possible to collaborate with people around the globe. The Information, Media, and Technology Skills that the partnership has identified include information literacy; media literacy; and information, communications, and technology literacy. The fourth set of outcomes is Life and Career Skills for working and living in a "globally competitive information age." They include flexibility and adaptability, initiative and self-direction, and social and cross-cultural skills.

These twenty-first-century skills are growing in popularity among states. Iowa, Kansas, Maine, Massachusetts, New Jersey, North Carolina, South Dakota, West Virginia, and Wisconsin were the first states to begin to incorporate them into their own standards and curriculum as well as initiate professional development for educators on how to use them. As the states work collaboratively to develop national student standards, the inclusion of these twenty-first-century skills is likely to be a part of the vision. They are also being incorporated into the INTASC principles for the licensure of new teachers that are being revised in 2009–2010. You may have to show evidence in the future that you have developed these skills to be eligible for a state license to teach.

================ JOURNAL FOR REFLECTION ================

What skills do you think you and your students will need to develop that your parents and grandparents never needed? What is so different about the world today than when they grew up that requires different skills? What impact is technology having on the skills needed to live and work today?

Federal Role in Standards

At a meeting of governors in 1989, President George Bush called for the development of content standards to ensure that the nation's students would be first in international academic competitions. The first set of student standards was released in 1989 by the National Council of Teachers of Mathematics (NCTM). With federal support, standards for P–12 students were developed in subsequent years by professional associations and other groups such as the National Research Council. The standards developed by these associations sometimes had great support from Congress, but not always. For example, the standards for social studies, which promoted the multicultural contributions to the nation, were defeated in 1995 by Congress with a 99-to-1 vote (Symcox, 2002).

President Bill Clinton followed up by signing the Goals 2000: Educate America Act in 1994, which established a framework for moving students to world-class standards by the year 2000. The lofty goals called for the following results before the beginning of the twenty-first century:

1. All children in America will start school ready to learn.
2. The high school graduation rate will increase to at least 90 percent.
3. All students will leave grades 4, 8, and 12 having demonstrated competency over challenging subject matter including English, mathematics, science, foreign languages, civics and government, economics, the arts, history, and geography, and every school in America will ensure that all students learn to use their minds well, so they may be prepared for responsible citizenship, further learning, and productive employment in our nation's modern economy.
4. United States students will be first in the world in mathematics and science achievement (United States Congress, 1994).

Recognizing that the nation had not moved student performance to world-class standards, President George W. Bush gained bipartisan support for the new reauthorization of the Elementary and Secondary Education Act, or No Child Left Behind (NCLB), in 2001. NCLB called for a major testing program to measure student performance on state tests that were aligned with state student standards for each subject at each grade level. The testing of student achievement against content standards began with mathematics and English language arts.

No Child Left Behind required all states to set standards for what a child should know and learn for all grades in mathematics, reading, and science. In addition, the states were required to set a level of proficiency for determining whether the standards were being met by students. Schools are expected to make adequate yearly progress (AYP) as shown by their students achieving at the state's proficiency level at grade level or above on the state test. Federal expectations are that low-income students, students with disabilities, English-language learners, and students from different racial and ethnic backgrounds also will meet state proficiencies for their grade level. If AYP is not achieved by one or more of these groups for more than two years, the school will be identified as "needing improvement." By 2013 all students are expected to be at the proficiency level for their grade level.

The federal legislation requires schools to annually test all students in grades 3 through 8 on their achievement of standards in math, reading, and science. Secondary students must be tested at least once. One of the purposes is to provide feedback on student learning to students, parents, and teachers. Data are publicly reported in district and state report cards that show how students in local schools perform in comparison to students in other schools. The legislation allows parents to remove their children from a Title I school that has been found in need of improvement for two consecutive years and send them to a school at which students are achieving at a higher level.

No Child Left Behind is discussed in greater detail in Chapters 1 and 10.

The Future of Standards-Based Education

There is no escaping standards in schools today. They are not abstract statements of ideals that teachers can simply ignore. They are now driving what teachers teach and, in many districts, how schools—and in some cases teachers—are evaluated. Standards-based education is a complex and sophisticated approach to teaching and learning. It is a professional challenge for beginning teachers, as well as experienced teachers, to learn to teach this way. The teacher's role shifts from conveyor of knowledge and dispenser of grades to coach and facilitator of students as they engage in learning. The expectations and checkpoints are stated and known by the teacher and students before instruction begins. Students not only know beforehand what is to be learned, but they also know what the assessment tasks will be like—that is, the types of performances described in the expectations.

Many questions influence the future of standards. How will school organization, use of time, graduation requirements, and power relationships change because of the standards movement? How can the plethora of standards be managed by teachers and still be integrated with the move toward thematic and interdisciplinary instruction? If the standards movement is to be worth the upheaval it has generated, such questions must be answered by thoughtful, knowledgeable participants who are engaged in the process of changing what students learn and how they learn. One important step is the compilation of data about student learning related to standards. Therefore, one of the early efforts in the standards movement has been to significantly increase the attention being paid to methods for assessing student learning.

PEARSON
myeducationlab

Go to the *Assignments and Activities* section of Topic 9: *Assessment, Standards, and Accountability* in the MyEducationLab for your course and complete the activity titled *Assessment Methods.*

rubric Scoring guides that describe what learners should know and be able to do at different levels of competence, such as developing, proficient, and advanced.

ASSESSMENT

Standards are not an end unto themselves. Simply listing standards in a school brochure will make little difference in the way students learn and achieve. If standards are to have any real effect on schools and on student achievement, they need to be supported by other elements in a school's structure: an articulated curriculum, professional development sessions focused on improving student achievement, and a well-thought-out array of assessments that align with the standards.

When assessments are linked to standards, changes must occur in the types of measures used, the kinds of data collected, and the ways the results are used to enhance student achievement. These changes in the assessment process can be quite dramatic, since assessment in the past has often meant little more than teachers producing grades or students doing well on paper-and-pencil achievement tests. When assessments are interwoven into standards-based frameworks, they become much more varied and meaningful to teachers and students alike. In this section, we examine the assessments of student learning and the ways in which they can enhance the teaching and learning process.

What Is Assessment?

Assessment in education implies many things: evaluation, grades, tests, performances, criteria, **rubrics**, and more. To encompass adequately its many dimensions, we will examine assessment in a broader sense by analyzing its root meanings. The term *assessment* is derived from the Latin word *assessio,* which means "to sit beside." This image provides an excellent metaphor. Ultimately, assessment can be thought of as the act of sitting beside ourselves and analyzing what we observe. In a sense, all assessment is based on this image: the examination of ourselves through the perception of an examiner who sits beside us and provides feedback. Some theorists contend that all true assessment is ultimately self-assessment. Assessors can provide information, but in the end it is the person being assessed who accepts the information or rejects it, using the information to further his or her development or setting aside the information as unimportant.

The image of an assessor sitting beside a learner also implies the use of tools or measuring devices that enable the assessor to gather different types of information. Paper-and-pencil tests, performance assessments, portfolios, journals, and observation checklists are examples of different assessment measures. Often these tools are labeled assessments, but in fact they are merely measures that assessors use to provide feedback. Keep in mind that assessment is really the larger process of gathering information, interpreting the information, providing feedback, and ultimately using or rejecting the feedback.

Purposes of Assessment

The ultimate reason for assessment in the classroom is to help students learn. However, assessments of students and teachers today are being used for a num-

Paper-and-pencil tests remain the major type of standardized assessments used to measure student achievement.

ber of other purposes as well. It is important to clarify these different purposes before attempting to interpret assessment results. Put simply, for teachers and students, assessing in classrooms is done for two purposes. The first is a **formative assessment** to determine what students have learned and provide feedback to them so that both you and the students can understand where to next focus their energies. The second is a **summative assessment** to make a final judgment about whether a certain level of accomplishment has been attained, such as passing a course. Most assessments for these purposes have been developed by teachers for use in their own classrooms. In standards-based education, teachers are checking throughout the year for evidence that students are meeting the standards through tests and a variety of other sources. These two assessment purposes can be translated into either the assessment *of* learning or the assessment *for* learning.

ASSESSMENT OF LEARNING. State achievement tests are designed as summative assessments that tell school officials, parents, and the public whether students are meeting required benchmarks. They are assessments of learning. Educators could use them to learn what students know so that instructional strategies could be developed to ensure they meet the standards. However, assessments of learning often create high-stakes situations for students, teachers, and their schools. They help principals know which teachers are more successful at improving test scores, not necessarily learning. They help school districts and the state and federal governments know which schools are meeting AYP. They are not usually used to look at the achievement of individual students and figure out what needs to occur to improve academic achievement.

These assessments are often used as gatekeepers to determine who moves to the next grade or who is admitted to a profession. For example, college admissions offices have a long history of using students' performance on standardized tests such as the ACT and SAT to determine who can be admitted. Professions such as law, medicine, nursing, physical therapy, certified public accountancy, and architecture require persons to pass a standardized test before they are admitted to the profession and allowed to work in a specific state. Most state departments of education require new teachers to pass a standardized test to be eligible for a license to teach. The use of standards for gatekeeping purposes is also becoming a way of life at the P–12 level. One of the first steps for children entering some of the prestigious preschools in a number of metropolitan areas is passing a test. A growing number of states require students to pass a test before a diploma of graduation is granted. Some school districts expect students to meet grade proficiencies on a test to move to the next grade.

ASSESSMENT FOR LEARNING. Student essays, projects, and portfolios are valuable resources for knowing how deeply students understand the content of a subject. Observing students as they conduct experiments, demonstrate how to solve a mathematics problem, or interact with other students on a group project provides additional information about student learning. More and more teachers are recording their observations of student learning throughout the school year in journals that can show growth over time. These formative assessments help teachers determine which students know the content at the expected level and which students need additional assistance.

When used for the purpose of helping students learn at higher levels, performance assessments can help you identify student understanding of the concept or skill you are trying to teach. The analysis of the data on student learning can help you clarify what comes next in the students' learning to move them to the next level. Assessments that are conducted formally and informally on a regular basis can help you find out which students are struggling with specific lessons. When teachers collaborate on assessment activities, they are not only helping students, but also informing and improving their own instructional practice (Stiggins & DuFour, 2009).

Students of any age can be involved in the assessments of their learning. Research finds that academic achievement improves when teachers and students become partners in the assessment process (Stiggins, 2009). Students are more engaged in academic work when they are confident that they can succeed. Students can be involved in assessing themselves and their peers if the assessments are being used for learning, not a grade or other summative assessment. They can develop their own portfolios that show how they have improved their achievement over time. They can learn to do their own self-assessments to

formative assessment Collection of data to show what a student has learned in order to determine the instruction required next.

summative assessment Data about student performance that are used to make a judgment about a grade, promotion to the next grade, graduation, college entrance, etc.

Assessment is an ongoing process in which teachers collect data on student progress toward meeting standards as they interact with, listen to, and observe students on a regular basis.

know where they need help and when they are ready to move to the next level. Stiggins (2009) suggests the following steps for involving students in the assessment process:

- Let students know the learning target for instruction in student-friendly language.
- Provide samples of student work that show success along a continuum.
- Give students descriptive feedback that will help them improve their performance.
- Teach students how to conduct their own self-assessments of their progress.
- Help students improve pieces of their work as they pull it together for a final product.
- Help students learn to reflect on their work as they become more academically competent and confident.[1]

Diagnostic assessments are used to determine at what level a student is functioning compared to the level at which he or she should be able to function developmentally. The feedback from these sources should help teachers design new or different instructional strategies that will assist students who are having difficulty. For example, the teacher in the Reflect on Diversity feature is using performance assessments to help determine what a new student knows and whether he might need special services.

These types of assessments provide an array of questions and tasks for a student to perform in a specific area such as reading, writing, mathematics, or motor skills. In such assessments, the questions and tasks might be organized by difficulty. As the student performs each task successfully, she or he is given another, more difficult question.

Diagnostic assessments are also used to determine the need for special services or accommodations and are usually conducted by a special education teacher, school psychologist, speech/language pathologist, occupational therapist, or regular teacher trained to administer a specific test. Most students who take these tests have been referred by teachers or parents for special education or gifted and talented services. The RTI, which was discussed in Chapter 7, is an example of an assessment process for determining whether students need special services.

Types of Assessments

Go to the *Building Teaching Skills and Dispositions* section of Topic 9: *Assessment, Standards, and Accountability* in the MyEducationLab for your course and complete the activity titled *Assessing Student Learning*.

Educators use different types of assessments depending on the purpose of the assessments. The types described next are among the most common. Many are manifested in paper-and-pencil formats; others take the form of the demonstration of skills. Educators and parents should know the type of assessments being administered to their students and children. Are the assessments designed to compare students across the state or nation or to determine if students have developed the core knowledge and skills expected in standards? The first is usually summative in nature; the second is formative. Let's take a look at three types of assessments.

NORM-REFERENCED ASSESSMENTS. Norm-referenced assessments are used to demonstrate who is best in some area. In a norm-referenced assessment, the individual's performance is compared with that of a norm group of similar individuals. After these types of assessments are developed, they are carefully revised on a regular basis to ensure that the tests yield varied test scores from low to high. These types of assessments do not reveal all that an individual child knows or is able to do. They are not the appropriate assessment to use to determine whether students meet proficiencies outlined in standards. In some ways, norm-referenced assessments are like a contest, and it is expected that some students will excel and others fail.

Norm-referenced assessments are misused more often than most other assessments. Teachers must be cautious in concluding that individual students who score low are not doing well. Norm-referenced tests typically sample only a portion of what students in a particular class are expected to know and do. Therefore, the student may not be performing well in those areas assessed by the tests but be doing better in other areas that were not tested.

Sometimes state authorities penalize a school district or school whose students as a group perform below a specific level on a norm-referenced test. This is a flawed practice because norm-referenced tests are designed such that 50 percent will score below the fiftieth percentile. In fact, when schools begin to score regularly above this percentile, the test is made more difficult. A related problem is that the nature of the test prevents the inclusion of questions on some of the core,

---

[1]Excerpt from Stiggins, R. (2009, February). Assessment FOR learning in upper elementary grades. *Phi Delta Kappan, 90*(6): 419–421. Reprinted by permission of Richard J. Stiggins.

REFLECTonDIVERSITY   Using Assessments for Learning

When Jason arrived in Ms. Ehrenberg's multicultural third-grade class for the first time about halfway through the school year, he took an open seat next to the wall, saying nothing after he was introduced to the class. He looked out the window most of the first week, making no attempt to participate in class activities. Ms. Ehrenberg soon learned from the principal that he had already been expelled from one school because he threw a chair at the teacher.

During his second week in the classroom, Jason moped around and never appeared on task. He began snapping back at his classmates when they tried to involve him in conversations or at play during recesses. He certainly seemed unhappy at school and was becoming Ms. Ehrenberg's greatest challenge. Based on Jason's address, she guessed that his single mother was struggling financially. She was puzzled about how to engage him in the schoolwork. She knew that if she did not get him engaged this year, he was likely to become more disenchanted with school year by year, leading him to drop out or be a low-performing participant for the rest of his school career. She had to take some action.

Ms. Ehrenberg wondered if she could conduct some assessments that would help her determine what Jason already knew (that is, his prior experience) and what interested him. Maybe he had special needs that had not been detected before. She had already noticed that Jason was more disruptive when students were involved in English language arts. She decided to systematically record when the disruptions occurred. Were they at a specific time of the day or when a specific subject was being taught? She also could look for signs that would suggest she should recommend him for special testing by the school psychologist.

After a few weeks of observation and note taking, Ms. Ehrenberg found that Jason was much more engaged when he was working on a project that required him to be actively involved in problem solving or figuring out an answer. He was not comfortable talking in front of the class and never responded when asked a direct question in a whole-group lesson. He appeared to like to draw and had signs of some creative talent. He would much rather be doodling than reading a story that she had assigned.

Questions for Reflection

1. How is Ms. Ehrenberg using her knowledge of performance assessment to learn more about Jason to figure out instructional strategies that will encourage him to become more involved in his schoolwork?
2. Now that Ms. Ehrenberg has some sense of Jason's interests and areas in which he might excel, what should she do?
3. What tactic would you take if Jason arrived in your class?

myeducationlab To respond to these questions online, go to the *Book Specific Resources* section in the MyEducationLab for your course, select your text, and then select *Reflect on Diversity* for Chapter 11.

---

most important concepts in content standards. Too many students select the correct answer because their teachers focused on this key concept in their teaching to ensure that students learned it. If a large number of students select the correct answer, the test question is revised. As a result, many of the items on the test address peripheral areas of the standards, avoiding the important knowledge and skills at the heart of the standards. The goal is not to determine if most students meet standards but to make sure there is an appropriate distribution of scores.

CRITERION-REFERENCED ASSESSMENTS. Instead of comparing a student's performance with that of a group of students, criterion-referenced assessments compare a student's performance with a specific type of accomplishment or criterion. For instance, you can assess whether students can add two-digit numbers without regrouping. To measure this skill, a student could be asked to answer ten different questions. If a child successfully answers all ten, or nine or even eight of the ten questions, a teacher can state with some degree of confidence that the child knows how to add two-digit numbers without regrouping.

Most classroom tests should measure students' knowledge in a criterion-referenced manner; that is, a student should be asked to answer questions a number of times that measure the same learning. Then, instead of scoring the test by using some sort of A through F range, the teacher sets an acceptable score that determines that the student really understands a concept at an acceptable level.

CAPSTONE/SUMMATIVE ASSESSMENTS. Capstone or summative assessments can be developed to celebrate a milestone accomplishment or to demonstrate how well a person has mastered something. These types of assessments are used near the end of some major accomplishment such as recitals or graduation. For instance, after completing courses in education, a teacher candidate student teaches to show that he or she can help students learn the subject matter. Hence, student teaching is a capstone assessment. This capstone assessment is evaluated by a master teacher who notes all of the accomplishments that are shown by the student teacher throughout the performance. In such an assessment, deficiencies can also be identified, but the major focus is to uncover what a teacher candidate has mastered throughout a program of study.

At the school level, a capstone assessment can be used at the end of a school year. Students can be asked to apply all they have learned in science by completing a science project or in language by writing a short story or a research paper. Some schools require a comprehensive test, presentation of student work in a portfolio, or essay as the capstone experience for graduation.

Performance Assessments

The notion of assessment has changed during the past decade. For years, educators have called for better standardized testing, but the response was the proliferation of a number of different kinds of tests with different emphases. Tests of achievement, basic skills tests, criterion-referenced tests related to specific objectives, tests of cognitive ability, tests of flexibility, and tests of critical thinking were developed. Despite these worthy attempts, these tests provide a limited view of what students know. Many educators viewed these paper-and-pencil instruments as an intrusion and not directly related to what was really happening in the classroom and real world.

Instead, educators want assessments that allow students to demonstrate in a number of ways that they met standards in real-world or **authentic** settings—in other words, performance. The best performance assessments are designed to promote student understanding, learning, and engagement rather than simply the recall of facts. The development of performance assessments is discussed in the Professional Dilemma feature.

Performance assessments can be used to demonstrate a specific proficiency. For example, if students have been taught a specific method for using a piece of science equipment, such as a gram balance, a performance assessment would include having the student weigh several objects on a balance. The teacher would typically observe the student to see whether all the specific techniques in accurately weighing a sample were used. Assessments of specific proficiencies in schools include many teacher-made assessments that focus on the specific things a student has studied. An example of a competency-based assessment outside the classroom is the road test employed in most states as a prerequisite to receiving a driver's license. The critical characteristic of such an assessment is that the assessment is closely related to something the student must be able to do. Hence, in the road test, a person drives a car in situations that the driver will typically experience: turning left or right, backing up, parking, and so forth. The person is usually scored through an observation checklist that the assessor uses.

AUTHENTIC ASSESSMENTS. Performance assessments are examples of another important characteristic of good assessing when the tasks that students are asked to perform are authentic. The tasks are realistic in terms of being as close as possible to how the learning would be applied in a real-world setting. Too often, test items and activities are remote from what a learner would need to do in life. When assessments are authentic, the tasks are based on problems and contexts,

Go to the *Assignments and Activities* section of Topic 9: *Assessment, Standards, and Accountability* in the MyEducationLab for your course and complete the activity titled *Performance Assessment.*

authentic Assessment tasks that are grounded in real-world settings and applications of what has been learned.

PROFESSIONAL DILEMMA

Developing Performance Assessments

"Common assessments—those created collaboratively by teams of teachers who teach the same course or grade level—also represent a powerful tool in effective assessment in professional learning communities," reported Stiggins and DuFour (2009), who work with school districts and teachers on the development of formative assessments.

Your principal, Mr. Jennings, wants to try this approach. He has asked the middle school teachers to work together to identify key performance assessments that all of you would use at critical junctures of the program. The principal has made it clear that these assessments cannot be multiple-choice tests and that student performance on them must be analyzed and used by the teachers to help students develop more in-depth understanding of the key concepts and skills for the subject they are learning. He has said that improvement in state test scores would be a wonderful result, but not his bottom line. He wants students to be learning to think

critically about important issues in the subject. They should be able to problem solve about real issues in their community.

Mr. Jennings asked you to cochair this project with another teacher. He wants an initial report on your plans within a month and wants you to begin testing the new assessments next semester.

Questions for Reflection
1. Where do you begin? What will be some of the issues on the agenda for your first meeting?
2. Why does Mr. Jennings appear not to be concerned about students' performance on the state tests this year?
3. How will you and your colleagues go about developing assessments that do not include tests? What assessments might you develop?
4. How could this collaborative effort lead to gains in student learning?

Table 11.1 • Types of Performance Assessment Tasks

Type	What It Is	Uses	Tips for the Teacher for Effective Use
Learning logs and journals	Notes, drawings, data, charts, artwork, and other notes written by the student	• Encourages reflection as one is learning • Provides a record of questions and thoughts	• Generate questions for students to ponder and respond to • Make the questions as varied as possible
Folios and portfolios	Folio is the storage bin, box, or file. Portfolio is the organization and presentation of selected folio artifacts for a particular purpose.	• Documents learning and growth over time • Encourages self-assessment • Shows student's best work	• Ask students to explain why they have included the various items • Require entries to be tied to standards • Provide feedback • Discuss the portfolio with students and their parents
Interviews	Peers and/or the teacher asking a set of questions	• Helps determine what has been learned	• Use a variety of question types to obtain a range of responses
Observation with anecdotal record	Observing and note taking during day-to-day activities	• Provides documentation of performance and learning over time	• Conduct observations on a regular basis • Write notes clearly and include specific descriptions of what was observed • Review notes • Distinguish carefully between facts and interpretations
Student products and projects	Specific products such as lab reports, presentations, and digital productions	• Provides cumulative evidence about the extent of learning	• Display student work

that are clearly seen as relevant and real. Some possibilities for authentic performance tasks are presented in Table 11.1.

There are three major areas to consider in developing authentic assessments for standards. First, a rich context needs to be designed, one that permits inquiry to occur. Second, it is important to fill the context with a wide variety of questions so that different types of thinking can occur. Finally, the critical indicators for learning need to be identified.

Developing a performance assessment task begins by considering the learning standards, **benchmarks**, and objectives that are the intended outcomes of instruction. It is critical that students be assessed on the intended outcomes as described in the district/state standards and benchmarks.

An important step in developing authentic assessments is to structure the tasks so that they are complex enough to permit students to show important learning, motivating enough to encourage students to think, rich enough to offer multiple opportunities to show how and what students have shaped into an understanding, and relevant enough that students can use their own experience. Some writers call the structure of the task the **context**, by which they mean the various activities, hands-on experiences, and questions that encourage learners to think and show how they can apply what they know.

Once a context has been selected, it needs to be structured and filled with opportunities to show how and what students have learned. Asking students to display their cognitive abilities in as many ways as possible enhances the teacher's understanding of students' unique ways of knowing. This is where assessment tools are helpful. Observing students in action and recording these observations in a variety of ways are critical.

Too often teachers assess one way but teach another. For example, assessing by using paper-and-pencil tests or using single-answer questions when instruction has been emphasizing inquiry is inappropriate. The reverse is also true. Assessing students in a hands-on inquiry mode when all instruction was lecture and reading/writing is equally incorrect.

Teachers have long been aware that questioning is an important way to cue students to display their understanding. Research indicates that the types of questions students are asked determine the

benchmarks A level of performance at which a standard is met. Examples of levels include "proficient" and "correct response on 80 percent of questions or performances."

context The various elements of the experience, questions asked, and setting.

Table 11.2 • Examples of the Types of Questions That Encourage Students to Show Different Ways of Knowing

Type of Question	Examples
Analysis questions	What are the key parts? Which parts are essential and why?
Comparison questions	How are these alike? What specific characteristics are similar? How are these different? In what way(s) are they different?
Classification questions	Into what groups could you organize these things? What are the rules for membership in each group? What are the defining characteristics of each group?
Connections clarification questions	What does this remind you of in another context? To what is this connected?
Constructing support questions	What data can you cite that support this conclusion? What is an argument that would support this claim?
Deduction questions	On the basis of this rule, what would you deduce? What are the conditions that make this inevitable?
Inferring and concluding questions	On the basis of these data, what would you conclude? How likely is it that this will occur?
Abstracting questions	What pattern underlies all of these situations? What are the essential characteristics of this thing?
Error analysis	How is this conclusion misleading? What does not match?

academic culture of a classroom. Questions that focus on a single aspect of knowing (knowledge or skills) limit the opportunities for showing understanding (the interactions of knowledge, skills, and habits of mind). Having a clearer picture of the multidimensionality of understanding (ways of knowing) directs teachers to ask a wide variety of questions. This is especially true during an assessment experience. Students should be asked many different types of questions within a rich, hands-on context. Table 11.2 presents examples of the variety of question types that allow students multiple opportunities to show their various ways of knowing.

Once students are engaged in a motivating inquiry, they will be better able to exhibit learning development. It is important that teachers focus on all aspects of learning when they examine student performance and not simply focus on those aspects that are easy to assess. If a context is truly authentic, students will have ample opportunities to display what they know and can do across a variety of different standards:

- Knowledge and comprehension of concepts, application of concepts, and connection of concepts to real-world contexts
- Ability to solve problems and exercise thinking skills
- Ability to perform and apply process skills
- Ability to structure thinking
- Collaboration and other dispositions
- Communication and ability to modify ideas on the basis of new evidence.

A rich assessment context allows students to display many of these components of understanding and skill. The art of assessing well includes identifying indicators—things that can be observed that relate to different aspects of some important standard. Identifying indicators in a performance task is much like acting as an X-ray: You need to notice what behaviors count and what successful ways of doing and knowing look like. To do this, teachers need to step back from the performance, much like a physician, and identify those actions that are meaningful and, more important, the learning that those actions indicate. Once teachers develop lists of indicators, they can easily assess what a child knows and does not know. These lists can form the basis for assigning grades, discussing student progress, and making decisions about student needs.

Authentic assessment is both an art and a science. As an art, assessment is like the world of a play. Placing students in the proper context is like situating characters to play a particular role; once in this context, students cannot help but display the knowledge, thinking, and habits of mind they have developed. On the other hand, authentic assessment is also like a science in that the educator needs to meticulously identify and examine the questions and other types of learning indicators that are important to the task.

FIGURE 11.2

Examples of Rubric Levels

Absolutely	Kind of	Not Sure	No Way
4	3	2	1

Advanced	Proficient	Developing	Beginning
4	3	2	1

Target	Acceptable	Unacceptable
3	2	1

As can be seen, authentic assessment is an attempt to make testing both in and out of the classroom more closely grounded in the context of student learning and less narrowly focused on a few aspects of what has been learned. Its very name implies trying to better determine what children have really learned.

RUBRICS. In its simplest and most basic sense, a rubric is a scoring guide. It is a way of describing different levels of accomplishment or degrees of being proficient. A rubric is not the measurement itself; it is a way of interpreting, scoring, and summarizing how well a student has performed. Figure 11.2 represents three different ways of thinking about labels for the levels of a rubric. Rubrics are a tool for focusing on the important elements in an assessment and combining these elements into a single score. They also provide guidance to ensure that different assessors rate students in the same manner and that students know what is expected for each level.

Rubrics can be analytic or holistic measures. *Analytic* refers to looking at each dimension of the performance and scoring each. *Holistic* refers to considering all criteria simultaneously and making one overall evaluation. You might sum all the analytic scores for a total score, or you might have one holistic dimension within an analytic rubric to provide an overall impression score. By doing this, assessors can access the benefits of both analytic and holistic scoring procedures. Analytic scoring, of course, provides the most specific data for use as a diagnostic assessment; it also limits flexibility because the dimensions are prescribed ahead of time. Holistic scoring does not require specific dimensions to be assessed; as such, it provides more flexibility and allows an assessor to give credit for unexpected dimensions that may contribute to the overall success of a performance. However, holistic scoring provides less direction for students than analytic scoring does. Tables 11.3 and 11.4 provide examples of analytic and holistic scoring rubrics, respectively.

BASING ASSESSMENTS IN THE WORK OF A DISCIPLINE. You will need to consider how the learning goals and standards relate to the lives and actions of scientists, writers, historians, and mathematicians. Consider what professionals do and how they use their different ways of knowing. Together, these considerations will often suggest ideas for the performance context.

To illustrate this way of determining a context, consider a curriculum that is filled with learning experiences focused on food chains, prey and predator relationships, and the balance of nature. How does this translate into a real-world context? Having students dissect owl pellets and analyze findings in light of the previous concepts provides one such context that is closely tied to the real world and to environmental issues. Like practicing scientists, students could be asked to investigate a set of owl pellets that have been collected from a specific area of the country. Students can apply what they know and use skills and thinking processes throughout the investigation. The assessment should provide students with opportunities to take measurements and make and record observations about the owl pellets. Students can be asked to create data tables that summarize the types of prey that were consumed, make inferences and draw conclusions about food availability, and finally even answer direct questions about food chains.

Professional Aspects of Good Assessments

Thus far, we have examined the purposes and described a variety of the methods being applied to performance assessment. However, assessing student learning has more to it than the mechanics

Table 11.3 • Analytic Trait Rubrics for Fifth-Grade Science Experiments

The rubric below uses a scale of one to four. Level 1 is a beginning or low level of performance; level 4 is a high level of performance.

Experiment Design	Scientific Results
4 Design shows student has analyzed the problem and has independently designed and conducted a thoughtful experiment.	4 Pamphlet explained with convincing clarity the solution to the problem. Information from other sources or other experiments was used in explaining.
3 Design shows student grasps the basic idea of the scientific process by conducting experiment that controlled obvious variables.	3 Pamphlet showed that student understands the results and knows how to explain them.
2 Design shows student grasps the basic idea of scientific process but needs some help in controlling obvious variables.	2 Pamphlet showed results of the experiment. Conclusions reached were incomplete or were explained only after questioning.
1 Design shows student can conduct an experiment when given considerable help by the teacher.	1 Pamphlet showed results of the experiment. Conclusions drawn were lacking, incomplete, or confused.

Data Collection	Verbal Expression
4 Data were collected and recorded in an orderly manner that accurately reflects the results of the experiment.	4 Speech presented a clearly defined point of view that can be supported by research. Audience interest was considered, as were gestures, voice, and eye contact.
3 Data were recorded in a manner that probably represents the results of the experiment.	3 Speech was prepared with some adult help but uses experiment's result. Speech was logical and used gestures, voice, and eye contact to clarify meaning.
2 Data were recorded in a disorganized manner or only with teacher assistance.	2 Speech was given after active instruction from an adult. Some consideration was given to gestures, voice, and eye contact.
1 Data were recorded in an incomplete, haphazard manner or only after considerable teacher assistance.	1 Speech was given only after active instruction from an adult.

Source: G. Wiggins, *Educative Assessment.* San Francisco: Jossey-Bass, 1998, p. 167. Copyright © 1998 Jossey-Bass. Reprinted by permission of John Wiley & Sons, Inc.

Table 11.4 • Holistic Oral Presentation Rubric

5—Excellent	The student clearly describes the question studied and provides strong reasons for its importance. Specific information is given to support the conclusions that are drawn and described. The delivery is engaging and sentence structure is consistently correct. Eye contact is made and sustained throughout the presentation. There is strong evidence of preparation, organization, and enthusiasm for the topic. The visual aid is used to make the presentation more effective. Questions from the audience are clearly answered with specific and appropriate information.
4—Very Good	The student describes the question studied and provides reasons for its importance. An adequate amount of information is given to support the conclusions that are drawn and described. The delivery and sentence structure are generally correct. There is evidence of preparation, organization, and enthusiasm for the topic. The visual aid is mentioned and used. Questions from the audience are answered clearly.
3—Good	The student describes the question studied and conclusions are stated, but supporting information is not as strong as a 4 or 5. The delivery and sentence structure are generally correct. There is some indication of preparation and organization. The visual aid is mentioned. Questions from the audience are answered.
2—Limited	The student states the question studied but fails to describe it fully. No conclusions are given to answer the question. The delivery and sentence structure are understandable, but with some errors. Evidence of preparation and organization is lacking. The visual aid may or may not be mentioned. Questions from the audience are answered with only the most basic response.
1—Poor	The student makes a presentation without stating the question or its importance. The topic is unclear, and no adequate conclusions are stated. The delivery is difficult to follow. There is no indication of preparation or organization. Questions from the audience receive only the most basic or no response.
0	No oral presentation is attempted.

Source: G. Wiggins, *Educative Assessment.* San Francisco: Jossey-Bass, 1998, p. 166. Copyright © 1998 Jossey-Bass. This material is used by permission of John Wiley & Sons, Inc.

of constructing authentic tasks. Assessing student learning is an activity that influences and affects many people. Therefore, the professional and ethical aspects of assessment must be considered. A number of very technical issues are also related to whether each assessment task is fair and truly assesses what was intended.

PRINCIPLES FOR HIGH-QUALITY ASSESSMENTS. Like other professionals who have knowledge that their clients do not have and whose actions and judgments affect their clients, classroom teachers are responsible for conducting themselves in an ethical manner. This responsibility is particularly important in education because, unlike other professions, students have no choice about whether they will or will not attend school. The following principles are keys to developing and using powerful and responsible assessments:

- Base assessments on standards for learning.
- Represent performances of understanding in authentic ways.
- Embed assessments in curriculum and instruction.
- Provide multiple forms of evidence about student learning.
- Evaluate standards without unnecessary standardization.
- Involve local educators in designing and scoring assessments (Darling-Hammond & Falk, 1997).

ACCOMMODATIONS. Issues of assessment become even more glaring for students who are English-language learners and those with special needs and learning disabilities. State and national assessments usually allow appropriate accommodations for these groups as outlined in Table 11.5. The purpose of an accommodation is to allow these students access to the test content without changing the construct of the test so that results are comparable to students who did not need accommodations. Determining the accommodation depends on a number of factors including the student's disability, age, the nature of the assessment, and the skill or subject being assessed. An inappropriate accommodation could compromise the validity of the scores, leading to inaccurate information about students' academic achievement. Often, simply changing the way in which learning is assessed can provide significant new opportunities for these students to demonstrate their knowledge and skills against a set of standards.

FAIRNESS. Some of the attractions of state tests are that they are standardized, perceived as objective, and inexpensive in comparison to performance assessments. One of the problems is that they ignore the lived experiences of many test takers, resulting in biases that give students from one group an advantage over another. Analyses of test items show that many of them are biased against students from low-income families. Basing assessments on a set of standards provides appropriate standardization. Performance assessments, unlike standardized tests, can take into account the variations in students' learning contexts while still holding to the levels of achievement expected to meet standards (Darling-Hammond & Falk, 1997).

Table 11.5 • Testing Accommodations for English-Language Learners and Students with Disabilities

English-Language Learners	Students with Disabilities
• Use of a dictionary or glossary that defines words specific to the content areas • Use of plain or simplified English on the test • Use of a bilingual dictionary that provides equivalent meanings of terms • Dual-language or side-by-side presentation of test items • Native-language versions of the test • Small-group administrations • Allowing extra testing time	• Reading questions aloud for reading comprehension and math problem-solving tests • Use of dictation services or software programs for writing portions • Allowing extra time to complete the test • Small-group administration of the test • Individual administration of the test Source: Jablonski, G., Potts, E., & Wiley, A. (n.d.). *Providing access to assessment: How should IEP teams make decisions about accommodations?* Arlington, VA: Council for Exceptional Children.

Source: Educational Testing Service. (2008, Summer). Addressing achievement gaps: The language acquisition and educational achievement of English-language learners. *Policy Notes, 16*(2), 10.

RELIABILITY AND VALIDITY. Two critical aspects of any effort to assess student learning, whether the assessment items have been developed by an individual teacher or a national testing company, are reliability and validity. Each of these terms is regularly used in professional discussions; however, their meaning and implications might not be appreciated. The only way in which any assessment of student learning can be counted on to be fair is if each and every item is both valid and reliable.

Validity refers to whether the assessment items measure what they are intended to measure. All too frequently, test items do not measure what the test maker had in mind. For example, a history teacher could have a learning objective related to students being able to describe key social, economic, and political causes of the Civil War. If the teacher then uses a test item that asks students to describe the results of key battles during the Civil War, the test item would not be valid. It did not ask students to demonstrate what they had learned in relation to the stated learning objective. This is a simple and obvious example of an assessment item that is not valid. Problems related to validity are many and can be extremely complex. Still, it is essential that teachers make every effort in the construction of assessment items to make sure that what students are being asked to do is closely aligned with the statement of standards and learning objectives.

JOURNAL FOR REFLECTION

Consider the types of assessments that have been used throughout your college studies. Select one assessment experience that you have found to be especially helpful in displaying what you believe you really know and can do. Describe the assessment, and then list what characteristics of the assessment enabled you to express your understanding.

Reliability is an equally important technical aspect of high-quality assessments. Reliability has to do with the consistency of information about student learning that results from repeated use of each assessment item or task. If two students who have learned the same amount complete the same assessment, do they receive identical scores? If they do, then the item has high reliability. If two students with the same level of learning receive discrepant scores, then the item is not consistent or reliable. Test makers often check the reliability of their items by using an approach called test–retest. In this approach to checking reliability, the same student responds to the same test item after a carefully selected time interval, typically a week or two. Here too the reliability question is "How consistent are the results from both administrations of the assessment?" If both assessments yield similar results, then the assessment is considered to be reliable.

ACCOUNTABILITY

As illustrated in the news story at the beginning of the chapter, parents and policy makers in many areas of the country are holding their schools accountable for student learning as measured by various criteria. Student assessments can provide important information on whether school programs are effective at helping students learn. One way of assessing the success of a school program is through norm-referenced assessments, but these assessments are quite limited. They measure only how well a group of students does in comparison to other groups of students across the country on a standardized paper-and-pencil task, which is often taken on a computer nowadays. To determine how well a program is doing, it is important to use **multiple assessments**. For example, one additional way to assess a school program would be to regularly gather information about how graduates are performing in the real world. Information about how many students successfully graduate without being retained could be another useful indicator. Having a broad array of assessment data can enable school districts to take stock and redirect efforts such as changing the types of instruction being used and the types of learning being emphasized.

A growing concern of some people is that the practice of many states using the same test is just one step away from a national exam, which will lead shortly thereafter to a national curriculum. Others believe that a national curriculum already exists and that national requirements

validity An indication of whether assessment items measure what they are intended to measure.

reliability An indication that the information about student learning is consistent across repeated use of each assessment item or task.

multiple assessments Using more than one measure and type of measure in making a judgment.

are appropriate. One example of a national test is the National Assessment of Educational Progress (NAEP), which is administered each year to fourth, eighth, and twelfth graders in a sample of schools in each state. The NAEP assesses student proficiencies in mathematics, reading, science, writing, the arts, civics, economics, geography, and U.S. history. One of its purposes is to make it possible for policy makers and educators to view nationally the achievement of students. Comparisons are made with student achievement in other countries, and most assuredly comparisons are also made from state to state in this country. The NAEP is designed to make inferences about student achievement within states. It is not designed to make judgments about individual students or schools. Unfortunately, although the NAEP has existed for several decades and its findings are very useful, school districts and schools are increasingly unwilling to participate in this testing program because of the mounting pressure and time demands of the many other required tests.

Using Technology to Track Student Learning

Technology is supporting the tracking of student assessment at all levels. A critical and often missing component of an effective lesson is addressing the individual needs of students. Inevitably, teachers are faced with a very diverse class of students in terms of their understanding of any particular concept. Many schools now have database systems that collect and report student assessment results in a format that is easy to access. For example, teachers can view reports of their students that list how each student performed on assessment items specific to a standard or topic on recent district or state assessments. This information can then be used to guide decisions such as where the lesson should begin and what sort of student groupings might be most appropriate.

Many schools and school districts are purchasing database services to help them manage and retrieve all of the data stored in file cabinets and unique databases first created by teachers or school administrators. They are purchasing assessment systems from companies such as Northwest Evaluation Association (NWEA), Plato Learning, and Tungsten Learning that allow teachers to regularly assess students against state and district standards. Some schools test their students monthly, using systems that make performance data available immediately to teachers. Sophisticated systems are able to track student growth from year to year (Borja, 2006). These assessments and their instantaneous feedback are allowing teachers to intervene in the learning process to assist students in improving their academic performance. These assessments can also be designed to test other knowledge and skills such as critical thinking and problem solving that may not be assessed on the state tests. Different models, which are described in the following sections, are used to determine student, teacher, and school performance at improving student learning.

VALUE-ADDED MODEL. The **value-added model** measures student growth over a period of time by comparing student performance on the last examination with performance on the current examination. These technically sophisticated models are able to account for student characteristics such as poverty that can affect test scores. They are able to isolate student performance so that it can be matched with a specific teacher or school. When the students of a teacher or school score at a higher level than predicted, they are classified as high-performing teachers or schools. Some states are using these data to determine which teachers deserve a bonus or higher pay raise than other teachers. At some point in the future, state data systems may allow the achievement scores of your students to be used as evidence of the effectiveness of your teacher education program.

GROWTH MODEL. The **growth model** is similar to the value-added model in that it measures students' academic achievement over time at the school level. Growth models depend on data from multiple measures of performance, rather than pass rates, which are the only measure used for state reports under No Child Left Behind. The question answered by data in this model is "By how much, on average, did math scores of the students attending this school improve over the course of a year?" (Jennings & Corcoran, 2009). These data help school districts and states know more about the academic growth of students in their schools, which should lead to more appropriate interventions to improve learning than sometimes occurs by labeling a school as low performing.

value-added model A statistical model that measures student growth over a period of time by comparing student performance on the previous examination with performance on the current examination.

growth model A statistical model that measures students' academic achievement over time at the school level.

International Comparisons

When newspapers release the latest results on students' performance on international exams, educators and policy makers hold their breath. At best, U.S. students are usually around average, not in the top tier where we think we belong. Policy makers declare that our poor performance indicates that schools and teachers are not doing their job well. Educators wonder why students aren't performing at a competitive level. They want to know how other countries are doing so much better, deploying academicians to study their curricula, instructional strategies, and teachers with the goal of improving student performance in the next round of tests. Secretary of Education Arne Duncan has indicated that states should benchmark their test scores against international standards, which is one of the steps in the national standards project that most states have adopted.

Critics of testing and the use of test scores caution us against simplistic interpretations of the international test results. Some of them also worry that the average performance on test scores has become an excuse for companies moving jobs to other countries. This perspective was reflected in a commentary in *Education Week*. Iris C. Rotberg asks: "Is there a shortage of U.S. scientists, as some firms have reported, or is there a shortage at the wages the firms would prefer to pay? Are companies outsourcing jobs to China and India because Americans are not qualified for them, or because the firms can pay much lower wages to workers in these countries? . . . Is the underrepresentation of native-born U.S. students in some science, mathematics, and engineering Ph.D. programs the result of a failure of our education system, or of personal decisions made by students to select other fields—perhaps more lucrative fields like investment banking, law, or business?" (Rotberg, 2008).

Not all U.S. students score at the average level. A sizable number are among the top tier of test performers in this international competition. In all countries there is an achievement gap based on the family's socioeconomic status, but it is especially severe in the United States. The problem is that vast numbers of U.S. students are performing at low levels (Cavanagh & Manzo, 2009). The president of Educational Testing Service, which is the producer of assessment tests for elementary and secondary students as well as professional licensure tests, stated at a recent meeting that "Policymakers and reformers on both the right and left agree that achievement gaps based on race, ethnicity and class must close if the United States is to maintain its economic pre-eminence and live up to its founding principles" (Educational Testing Service, 2009).

In the next section, we review the most common international tests that are tracked by policy makers and education officials. They are often the subject of discussions in social settings as well as among your education colleagues. As you will see, performance of U.S. students varies by the test being used.

TRENDS IN INTERNATIONAL MATHEMATICS AND SCIENCE STUDY (TIMSS). TIMSS tests the math and science skills of students at the fourth and eighth grades. It is designed to measure students' knowledge of the math and science curriculum that they should be learning in school. Both developing countries with fewer economic resources and industrialized countries such as the United States participate in this program.

U.S. students do fairly well on TIMSS, scoring above the 2007 average at both grade levels. Our fourth graders scored higher, on the average, than students in twenty-three countries and lower than those in eight countries on the mathematics exam and higher, on the average, than students in twenty-five countries and lower than those in four countries on the science exams. A similar pattern existed at the eighth-grade level as shown in Figure 11.3. The top performing countries at both grade levels are in Asia: Singapore, Chinese Taipei, Japan, Hong Kong, and Korea.

PROGRAMS IN INTERNATIONAL STUDENT ASSESSMENT (PISA). Every three years, the PISA tests math, science, or reading skills that students learn in and out of schools with more of a focus on the application of what they have learned to real-life situations. The test is taken by students who are fifteen years old in industrialized countries and other jurisdictions. The program is administered by the Organisation for Economic Co-operation and Development (OECD, n.d.), which facilitates discussions and projects of the "governments of countries committed to democracy and the market economy from around the world."

FIGURE 11.3

2007 TIMSS: Average Science Scale Scores of Eighth-Grade Students by Country

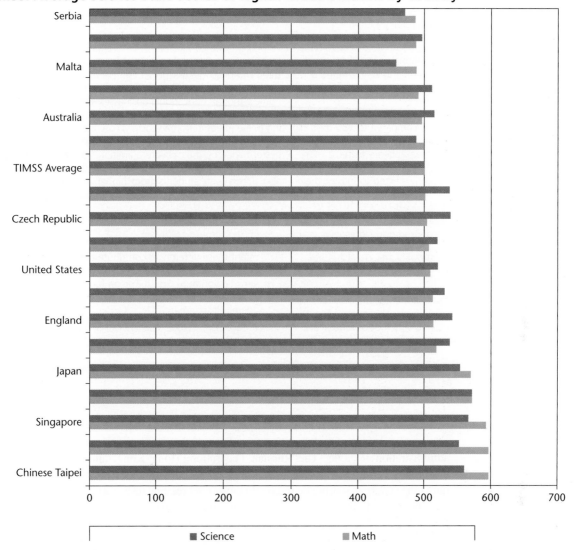

Source: Planty, M., Hussar, W., Snyder, T., Kena, G., KewalRamani, A., Kemp, J., et al. (2009). *The condition of education 2009* (NCES 2009-081, Indicators 15 and 16). Washington, DC: National Center for Education Statistics, Institute of Education Sciences, U.S. Department of Education.

The analysis of PISA data indicates that gender, origin, language, and socioeconomic status are related to top performance on the test. However, some countries have a much lower percentage of students performing at low levels regardless of the students' gender, origin, language, or socioeconomic status, which suggests that all students can achieve at high levels. Across countries, girls outperform boys in reading; boys perform somewhat better than girls in mathematics; and both genders perform about the same in science (OECD, 2009). U.S. students do not perform well on the PISA, being below the average of students in the thirty-two industrialized countries that participated. On the science assessment, U.S. students were ranked twenty-one of thirty-two participating countries. Students from Finland, Canada, and Japan were the top performers in science. In mathematics U.S. students ranked twenty-six of thirty-two countries with students from Finland, Korea, and the Netherlands scoring the highest (OECD, 2008). The Global Perspectives feature identifies characteristics of education in the United States and South Korea that may lead to some of these differences in the academic achievement of their students.

GLOBAL PERSPECTIVES — The Success of South Korea

With a population of less than 50 million, South Korea consistently ranks among the top countries on international tests. What is its secret? South Korea has a national curriculum and very talented and motivated teachers. Students attend six years of elementary school, three years of middle school, and three years of high school. However, they spend more days in school than U.S. students. Eighth graders are in school 205 days per year, compared to 180 days in the United States.

The math curriculum in South Korea appears to have more depth than in many U.S. classrooms where the goal is to teach many topics. South Korean students are expected to master their lessons before beginning a new one. Textbooks are "less bloated and redundant than U.S. brands."

South Koreans value teaching. Although potential teachers go through a rigorous screening process of exams and interviews, applicants for teaching positions outnumber the jobs available, particularly at the secondary level. The payoff for meeting high standards is a higher salary for both beginning and veteran teachers than is earned in the United States.

The curriculum and talented teachers are not the only reason South Korean students achieve at high levels. The country has an "enormous network of private tutoring and out-of-school academic services, which are in heavy demand." Families may spend 10 percent of their incomes to ensure their children are enrolled in these services. More than half of South Korean students are tutored by nonschool teachers, compared to one-fourth of U.S. students. Many of these tutoring businesses are operated out of a home although educational businesses also provide services.

The need for academic support outside of school may be leading to inequities in Korean society. Low-income families cannot always afford the outside services, often resulting in lower academic performance by their children, limiting their access to additional education and higher prestige jobs. The quality of these services also differs with students from higher income families because they usually have greater access to high-quality support systems.

Questions for Reflection

1. How would you characterize the major differences between the education of South Korean and U.S. students? How might these differences contribute to higher performance on international tests?
2. Why do you think South Korean families are willing to spend so much of their income to ensure that their children are academically competitive?

Source: Cavanagh, S. (2009, April 22). Out-of-school classes provide edge. *Education Week, 28*(29), 26.

PROGRESS IN INTERNATIONAL READING STUDY (PIRLS). The PIRLS tests the literary and informational skills of fourth graders on a five-year cycle. Forty countries participated in the last administration in 2006. The Russian Federation, Hong Kong, and Singapore were the top performing countries, but U.S. fourth graders scored well above the international average with only nine countries scoring better. As on most other reading tests, girls scored significantly higher than boys in all but two countries. Other findings included the confirmation of a positive relationship between reading achievement and parents engaging their children in early literacy activities before they started to school, including reading books, telling stories, and singing songs. Other contributors to higher scores were the presence of children's books in the home, parents who were frequent readers, and parents who had a favorable attitude toward reading. Across countries, 40 percent of the students reported reading for fun on a daily basis; another 28 percent read for fun at least weekly (Mullis, Martin, Kennedy, & Foy, 2007).

Testing Challenges

The nationwide movement toward standards, performance, and a variety of assessment strategies is a good one, especially for teachers and their students. The goals of teaching and learning are made clear, which then makes it easier for teachers to know what to teach and how. Having standards certainly aids students in understanding what is most important to learn. And having standards helps teachers, schools, school districts, and states in determining the learning outcomes that should be assessed. Still, as with any education initiative, the standards movement has had a number of unintended consequences that have provided challenges for schools and teachers. You are likely to find some of these challenges when you begin to teach.

HIGH-STAKES TESTING. As the focus on student performance has intensified, the federal government has mandated that students be tested annually. At a minimum, the student test results are compiled by schools and reported to the public. Schools are named and ranked in the newspaper, and sharp questions are asked about those schools that are not meeting adequate yearly progress.

Testing becomes high stakes when the assignment of rewards and sanctions is determined by a test score. In a few states, high-performing schools receive additional funds. In some districts,

FIGURE 11.4

Criteria for High-Stakes Testing Practices

The American Education Research Association's (AERA) *Public Policy Statement on High-Stakes Testing in PreK–12 Education,* adopted in July 2000, provides twelve criteria, based on solid research, that state education leaders, local school leaders, parent, and others can used to assess the assessments. AERA states that every high-stakes testing program should ensure:

- Protection against high-stakes decisions based on a single test
- Adequate resources and opportunity to learn
- Validation for each separate intended use
- Full disclosure of likely negative consequences of high-stakes testing programs
- Alignment between the test and the curriculum
- Validity of passing scores and achievement levels
- Opportunities for meaningful remediation for examinees who fail high-stakes tests
- Appropriate attention to language differences among examinees
- Appropriate attention to students with disabilities
- Careful adherence to explicit rules for determining which students are to be tested
- Sufficient reliability for each intended use
- Ongoing evaluation of intended and unintended effects of high-stakes testing.

For more information, visit AERA's website at www.aera.net.

teachers and/or principals receive salary bonuses if test scores improve. Some states provide rewards to high-performing schools, but much more likely is some sort of sanctioning of the low-performing schools. On the positive side, some states provide assistance to schools that are "in need of improvement" by assigning an experienced master teacher or principal to work with the schools. In other cases, principals are reassigned and entire school staffs replaced. In some states an entire school district that is designated low performing can be taken over by the state. Criteria for high-stakes testing are listed in Figure 11.4. Tests can be high stakes for students and their future as well. For example, many states now use standardized exams to determine graduation from high school, and most colleges used standardized tests to help determine admission.

Effective schools are also discussed in Chapter 6.

═══ JOURNAL FOR REFLECTION ═══

Have you ever taken a performance assessment that had high-stakes implications for your future? What kind of assessment was it? What would have been the impact on your life if you had not passed it? Why do you think parents worry about the testing programs in schools today?

PRESSURES TO CHEAT. In high-stakes conditions, teachers and principals invest concerted effort in helping their students do well on the tests. In nearly every school and classroom, teachers stop their regular instruction for a week or more to help students prepare for the test. These preparations can be as practical as practicing answering multiple-choice questions and reviewing what has been taught during the year. The problem arises when teachers—and in some cases principals—help their students cheat. Cheating ranges from telling students how to answer specific test items to teachers, principals, and school district administrators actually changing students' responses on individual tests. In other instances, schools have encouraged some students, such as those with learning disabilities, to stay at home on the day of testing.

TEACHING TO THE TEST. Any single test is bound to sample a very limited part of what students learn. Also, state tests might have little overlap with the various sets of content standards and the emphasis in district curriculum materials. Time spent on preparing for high-stakes tests reduces the time available to teach related material and other subjects, such as the performing arts, that are not being tested or for which the stakes are not as high. Teaching to the test also often means that the development of critical thinking and higher order thinking skills is neglected. If the entire district

High-stakes conditions have led to an increase in student pressure to cheat.

curriculum is aligned with state standards, then those students whose instruction covers more of the standards should perform better on the tests.

A related issue has to do with balancing the time teachers spend on topics that are likely to be on the test versus instructional time spent on the rest of the curriculum. About two-thirds of teachers indicate that their instruction is too focused on content that will be tested, to the detriment of covering other material. Almost 80 percent of teachers report that they teach test-taking skills to students (Olson, 2001), reducing the amount of time to teach the content itself. Two experienced teachers provide their views about teaching to the test in the Teacher Perspectives feature.

Other data refute the claim that teachers spend less time teaching content than in the past, at least at the elementary school level. Lorin W. Anderson at the University of South Carolina reviewed this claim by teachers by comparing their concerns with conditions in the 1970s and 1980s before testing became so prevalent. He found that elementary school teachers have always spent much more time teaching English language arts than any other subject. The amount of time teaching mathematics has remained constant; attention to science and social studies has always been limited (Anderson, 2009).

ONE-SIZE-FITS-ALL. Another critical issue related to the heavy focus on testing is the assumption that the same test is appropriate for all students, schools, and states. Historically, heavy emphasis has been placed on the importance of addressing individual differences and emphasizing that all students do not develop at the same rate. Now policy makers are mandating that one test be given to all students at a certain grade level at a specified time—in other words, "one-size-fits-all." No matter how unique individuals might be, all are to take the same relatively narrow test, and major decisions about individual students and/or schools are based on the test results. Students who are economically advantaged in suburban schools take the same test that low-income urban students take. This practice undermines the credibility of the test and its results clearly disadvantage some students and schools.

INCREASED TEACHER BURDEN. As exciting and important as the new approaches to assessment are, one of the downsides is the increased work for teachers. Developing more authentic tasks takes more time than does constructing multiple-choice and true/false test items. Deriving scoring devices for authentic tasks is added work too. Holistic scoring entails first developing a scoring rubric and then examining each student's response in sufficient detail to determine a total score. The load on teachers becomes even heavier in secondary schools because each teacher has contact with more students. One of the important solutions to the risk of an increased burden is for teachers within a school or school district to collaborate in the development of assessment tasks. There also is national sharing of assessment items through discipline-based professional associations and various chat rooms on the web. A related key for individual teachers is to keep in mind that many of the traditional activities that teachers have been doing to assess student learning, such as noting their performance in laboratories and in the field, have become more legitimate with the move to authentic assessment.

Equity within Accountability

No Child Left Behind expects schools to help all students meet standards at defined proficiency levels regardless of their socioeconomic status, ethnicity, race, first language, disability, migrant status,

Does Prepping for High-Stakes Tests Interfere with Teaching?

More and more states require students to pass tests in order to graduate or to receive a diploma. Some states offer different types of diplomas based on how well a student performs on a test. This type of testing is called high-stakes testing and it poses several philosophical questions. What do high-stakes tests say about the nature of knowledge? What does it mean to be educated in a high-stakes testing environment? What behaviors do high-stakes testing encourage? How do high-stakes tests influence teaching? The following debate raises these types of questions.

YES

Nancy Buell teaches fourth grade at the Lincoln School in Brookline, Massachusetts. She has taught for thirty-two years and serves on the state Board of Education's Advisory Council for Mathematics and Science.

As I watch my students debate how much taller fourth graders are than first graders, I am struck by their intuitive use of significant features of the data. As in:

Lee: Fourth graders are 10 inches taller because the tallest fourth grader is 64 inches and the tallest first grader is 54 inches.

Tamara: A first grader is about 5 inches shorter. I found the middle height for each and just subtracted. The middle for the fourth graders is 57 inches and the middle for the first graders is between 51 inches and 52 inches.

Dana: 5 inches or 4 inches, because the most common height for first graders is 53 inches and the most common height for fourth graders is 58 inches or 57 inches.

These students are exploring ideas involving maximum, median, and mode. They are considering what features to use to tell what is typical of the two groups so they can be compared. Students support their ideas with information in the data itself. They are developing ways to think about data that will lead to a deep understanding of more formal statistics.

The rich mathematical discussions in my class are an outgrowth of my participation in professional development that focused on inquiry-based teaching and the big ideas we should be teaching.

But since high-stakes testing arrived, professional development meetings often focus on how to improve test scores, not on how to improve learning.

Teaching that concentrates on improving test scores is very limited—by the nature of both testing and teaching. Testing involves sampling student knowledge. It is fragmented and only examines learning outcomes. It seldom looks at how well a student understands complex ideas.

A typical test item might give students a set of data and ask for the median. Students would not be asked to select the appropriate statistic to address a question and justify their choice. Yet knowing how to find the median, without knowing when to use it, is useless, except on tests.

If we teach facts and procedures likely to be on the test, without the deeper understanding behind them, we shortchange our students. We must not limit what we teach to what will be tested.

Many teachers feel pressured to choose teaching techniques that help with testing more than learning. They're urged to spend more time on information that mimics test items.

Students should, of course, know how to answer multiple choice, short answer, and open response questions, but teaching these test-taking skills should not be confused with teaching a subject. Some teachers spend a day a week using test-like items, not to sample what children know, but to try to teach the content.

Teaching should build on what students already know and help them develop a rich web of interconnected ideas. Real learning involves inquiry, hypothesis testing, exploration, and reflection.

Teaching to the test will not help my students think about how to use features of data sets to answer real questions. Teaching to the test is not teaching.

NO

Charlotte Crawford teaches fourth grade at Coteau-Bayou Blue School in Houma, Louisiana. A twenty-seven-year teaching veteran, she helped set the cut scores for her state's high-stakes fourth-grade test and now serves on a state panel for staff development.

Preparing students to take high-stakes tests does not interfere with teaching. It enhances teaching. When used properly, high-stakes tests can focus attention on weaknesses in the curriculum and in the teaching of it, as well as furnish an assessment of student progress. Once identified, student weak areas can be strengthened.

When the new high-stakes tests and revised curriculum were introduced in Louisiana, along with new accountability standards, many teachers were bewildered at the prospect of being held accountable for teaching a new curriculum without being told how to teach it.

Yet many of these teachers were also open to the new ideas and began working to find ways to implement them. They were aided by funding from the state for additional reading materials and in-service training.

Teachers often feel overwhelmed by the changes involved in our state's rigorous new standards, but many Louisiana educators are beginning to take ownership of their new curriculum. They're growing confident when making scope and sequence decisions. They're consistently reevaluating what they have taught, and how they have taught it, so they can do better next time.

These educators are revamping their classroom activities and their teacher-made tests to match them more closely to the format and tone of the state-mandated tests.

Helping students become familiar with the state-mandated test formats, by using them in the classroom, prevents having to spend valuable class time to "practice" for the high-stakes tests.

Learners, meanwhile, are reaping the benefits of having teachers who are determined that their students will be as prepared as possible to relate the skills they learn in school to real-life situations. They're becoming lifelong learners, besides performing well on standardized tests.

(continued)

TEACHER PERSPECTIVES

Some educators complain that they must "teach to the test."

But others consider this to be a weak objection since the state tests focus on information and skills students are expected to know at certain points in their schooling.

These educators say the curriculum objectives covered by the state tests should be taught before the tests are given, with the remaining objectives covered afterwards. This is a very workable arrangement when high-stakes tests are given early in the spring.

To be sure, some Louisiana educators are still resisting the changes that come with the state tests.

But most realize this is an idea whose time has come.

In 1998, my school helped pilot the fourth-grade language arts test. I was nervous about how my students would fare. When they finished, I asked for reactions.

Much to my surprise, students calmly informed me that the state test was "kind of hard, kind of easy, kind of fun."

That day, my students unwittingly reassured me that learners who are prepared for high-stakes tests need not fear them.

Source: "Does Prepping for High-Stakes Tests Interfere with Teaching?" *NEA Today* (January 2001), p. 11. Reprinted by permission of the National Education Association.

What is your perspective on this issue?

myeducationlab To explore both sides of this issue and think about each perspective, go to the *Book Specific Resources* in the MyEducationLab for your course, select your text, and then select *Teacher Perspectives* for Chapter 11.

or gender. In fact, performance by students from each of these groups must be reported on the school's and district's annual report card. Thus, teachers are held responsible for helping all students learn as reflected on a single assessment—the state content test. Meeting this goal is more difficult in some settings than others, especially when resources are limited or nonexistent for providing students with the facilities and support necessary to promote learning at a high level and providing teachers the necessary professional development. Nevertheless, it is a goal worth achieving.

A continuing point of criticism about these traditional tests is that they do not address or accommodate the diversity of students in today's classrooms. Each student brings a unique set of background experiences, prior knowledge, and cultural perspectives to learning. Asking all students to show what they know on a narrow standardized test is a very real problem.

The gap between the test scores of white students and most students of color remains wide as does the gap between students from low-income and higher income families. NAEP data on achievement levels for mathematics show an achievement gap between white and African American, Hispanic, and American Indian students of more than 21 percentage points at the fourth grade and more than 27 percentage points by the eighth grade (see Figure 11.5). The gap grows even wider by the twelfth grade. Ironically, many researchers have found that state tests are much better determiners of the family's socioeconomic level or parents' education than of academic ability. Students who perform at low levels on these tests are disproportionately from low-income families.

Supporters of NCLB argue that African American and Hispanic students will perform at a more equal level over time because schools will be able to raise their test scores by hiring only **highly qualified teachers**, teaching reading more effectively, basing instruction on what is known to work from "scientifically based research," and allowing parents to remove their children from low-performing schools and place them in higher performing schools. Critics also believe that all students can learn and that highly qualified teachers are essential. They also question the ability of schools, especially in high-poverty areas, to raise test scores without intensive professional development of teachers, reduction of student-to-teacher ratios, greater involvement of parents, and more stimulating curriculum and instruction—all areas that require financial resources that are not usually available in communities with the greatest need.

Researchers are finding that multiple assessments demonstrate that students from different cultural groups perform at higher levels on different assessments. Some students who do poorly on standardized tests effectively demonstrate their knowledge and skills on other assessments based on their interests or real-life settings. The teacher's assessment of prior knowledge and development of instruction with those data in mind are particularly helpful in improving the academic achievement of low-income students and students of color (Shepard et al., 2007).

LOOKING AHEAD:
LEARNING TO ASSESS FOR STUDENT LEARNING

You should have a good sense by now that you will need to know the standards that your students will be expected to achieve when you begin to teach. In fact, it would probably be very helpful to know the standards before you are interviewed for a teaching job to show the interviewer that you

highly qualified teachers Teachers who are licensed without a provision and have passed a standardized content test in the subject they teach or for the grades they teach.

FIGURE 11.5

Performance on NAEP Mathematics Tests by Race and Ethnicity

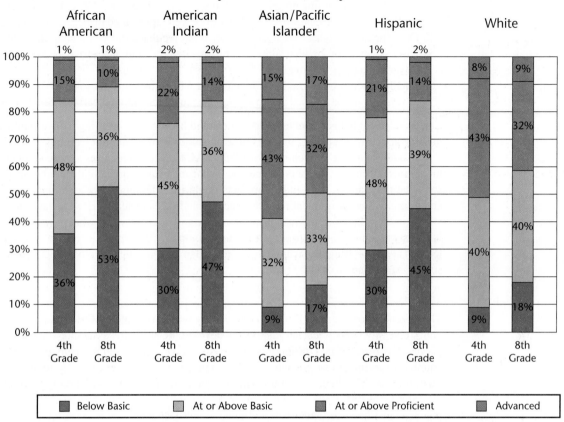

know the importance of standards. Of course, you will be held accountable for the academic performance of your students against these standards. How are you going to learn to develop appropriate assessments for student learning that will help you know what students are learning and the instructional strategies that will help ensure that they all are learning? In this section, we discuss two approaches that a growing number of teacher education programs are using to help candidates develop their assessment skills. You should begin now to practice developing performance assessments that you can use when you begin to teach.

Performance Assessment for California Teachers (PACT)

The PACT project is a consortium of more than twenty colleges and universities in California that are using this particular performance assessment with teacher candidates to determine if they are ready to teach. Institutions in a number of other states will be testing PACT over the next few years. You may be required to use this assessment or the Teacher Work Sample, which is described in the next section.

The assessment package includes a "Teaching Event," which is modeled after the portfolio that experienced teachers complete for national board certification, which was discussed in Chapter 1. Teacher candidates complete the assessment near the end of their teacher education program. During student teaching, they "plan and teach a unit of instruction, including development of an assessment plan, and to analyze their students' learning in relation to their teaching" (Shepard et al., 2007). They identify two students in their class with different instructional challenges; one of them must be an English-language learner. As part of the assessment, they include three samples of each student's work to show their learning. With the samples of student work, they respond to the following issues and questions:

1. Describe the student as a person and learner. What are the students' strengths and approaches to learning, levels of knowledge and skills, academic needs, individual learning goals, and other relevant characteristics?

2. Discuss what each work sample illustrates about the student's developing skills and understandings. What was the student able to do? In what areas did the student have difficulty?
3. Describe what learning progress you can see across the samples. Are there aspects of the student's learning you have observed that are not well represented in these particular assessments?
4. Describe how you assess each response. What feedback did you give to the student?
5. Discuss what you believe supported or impeded the student's progress. Were there particular modifications you made to support the student's success?
6. Finally, discuss what you have done or you will do as a teacher to build on what the student has already accomplished and to support the student's ongoing learning (Shepard et al., 2007).

This assessment helps future teachers understand how student learning evolves and pushes them to think about their teaching in terms of what students are or are not learning.

In addition to the "Teaching Event," the PACT portfolio requires a more summative assignment in which student teachers present the data from an assessment of the whole class around lessons that they taught. The student artifacts might include homework assignments, papers, tests, and journals. The assignment requires teacher candidates to summarize the data for the full class and provide samples of the responses from three students to show what they understood and in what areas they were still struggling. In an accompanying commentary, they describe what they learned about the students' achievements related to the learning objectives and what their next instructional choices will be.

Teacher Work Sample

The Teacher Work Sample (TWS) methodology was developed by Del Shalock at Western Oregon University to help teacher candidates develop the skills for assessing student learning. The process has been refined during the past twenty years and is used by many programs across the country. Even though your teacher education program may not require you to use the TWS, you may find it another helpful tool for thinking about what students are learning as you teach.

Similar to PACT, the TWS requires teacher candidates to demonstrate their ability to assess, plan, and instruct in a standards-based educational system and impact positively on student learning. The standards that candidates must show they can meet through the TWS at Western Oregon University require them to do the following:

1. Analyze contextual information to determine relevant factors that influence curriculum instruction, learning goals, and management decisions.
2. Set developmentally appropriate, challenging, varied learning goals and objectives that are derived from the district, state, or national content standards and/or common curriculum goals.
3. Demonstrate the ability to plan a unit that connects learning goals and objectives, methods of teaching and assessment, and the knowledge of students and their prior knowledge.
4. Develop lessons for a unit that includes activities using a variety of instruction and assessment strategies that help students meet learning outcomes.
5. Demonstrate the ability to design valid assessments and analyze assessment data to determine student learning relative to expected outcomes.
6. Reflect thoughtfully about the relationship between their own teaching and student learning.

For the TWS, student teachers identify the context of their classroom, including the characteristics of students such as English-language learners and students with disabilities. They test students' knowledge of the unit to be taught. They plan the lessons and discuss why they chose certain instructional strategies instead of others. After the unit is taught, they assess what students learned, compile the data, and analyze them to determine what additional teaching is needed. Their reflections on their teaching and the data of student learning help the teacher candidates determine if their teaching made a difference. They also consider what worked well and what they would do differently the next time.

In both PACT and the Teacher Work Sample, you would learn how to develop good assessments, collect data on what students are learning, and analyze the assessment data to promote student learning. Both systems include reflection in which you think about whether your teaching has actually helped students learn and the next steps needed to ensure that students are learning, which should be the goal of all teaching.

SUMMARY

EDUCATION STANDARDS

- The focus of standards today is on what students know and are able to do.
- Expectations for learning are being described in the form of standards, which have been developed for all subject areas and grade levels.

ASSESSMENT

- Once the standards of learning have been set, teachers, as well as curriculum developers and policy makers, want to know how well students are doing.
- Assessing is more than testing. It entails developing and using good measures along with making interpretations and judgments about what has been accomplished and what needs to be done next.
- Assessment of student learning has become very important and increasingly technical.
- Using multiple measures to make judgments about the amount of student learning is very important for teachers when making high-stakes decisions.

ACCOUNTABILITY

- The pressures on states, school districts, schools, and teachers have never been higher. Everyone wants to see higher levels of student learning.
- Two tools are being used to hold educators accountable: standards and testing.
- The stakes of testing can be high for states, school districts, schools, teachers, and students.
- Every effort must be taken to ensure that the tests are of high quality and that high-stakes decisions are based on multiple sources of evidence.

LOOKING AHEAD: LEARNING TO ASSESS FOR STUDENT LEARNING

- The Performance Assessment for California Teachers (PACT) and Teacher Work Sample (TWS) are performance assessments that allow teacher candidates to demonstrate their ability to develop effective assessments, plan lessons and units, analyze data on what their students are learning, make appropriate decisions about instruction, and reflect on the effectiveness of their teaching with the goal of helping students learn.

DISCUSSION QUESTIONS

1. Standards-based education is now the paradigm that teachers are expected to use. Thinking about your own education at the high school and college level, how would you describe the integration of standards in the curriculum and instruction? How were you made aware of the standards that you were supposed to be meeting? Did the standards support higher order thinking or were they more factual in nature?

2. Assessing has been described as being more than testing. What does this mean for you as a teacher? How will you know if you are assessing, rather than simply testing?

3. Standards-based education calls for the use of performance assessments in determining whether students meet standards. How could student portfolios be used to show what students have learned? What problems might such assessments cause?

4. How fair is it to demand that all students, regardless of their ability or socioeconomic status, master a common set of learning standards before obtaining a diploma? In what cases, if any, do you think students should be exempt from testing requirements for graduation?

5. What do you see as your role as a teacher in a standards-based education classroom? What professional development will you need as a new teacher in order to implement standards-based curriculum and performance assessments in your classroom?

SCHOOL-BASED OBSERVATIONS

1. Talk with teachers in the schools that you are observing and review the school district's website to identify the standards that teachers are supposed to use. During your observations, record the evidence that convinces you that standards are (or are not) integrated into classroom instruction. What evidence indicates that the school is (or is not) supporting teachers in preparing students to meet the standards?

2. Interview several teachers who are required to administer state assessments that reflect standards. Ask the teachers to identify what they do to help students prepare for these tests. Record the results of your interviews and then write your own perspective on the value of statewide and high-stakes assessment.

3. One of the distinguishing characteristics of standards-based education is that students, regardless of grade level, are supposed to be able to describe the expectations for learning (standards and benchmarks). Interview some students and see how they describe what they are doing in a particular lesson. Do they tend to describe the instructional activity ("We are studying the Civil War"), or do they describe what they are supposed to be learning ("We are learning about the economic factors that led to the Civil War"). Can they describe how much they have learned?

PORTFOLIO DEVELOPMENT

1. Authentic assessments attempt to provide students with opportunities to show what they know and can do within a real-world setting. Go to the website of the organization that has developed standards for the subject that you plan to teach or the students that you plan to teach (e.g., special education or early childhood education) to locate the student standards for your field. Select one of the standards and develop an authentic assessment that would enable students to demonstrate what they have learned in relation to that national standard.

2. Rubrics are used to assess performance in many classrooms. To gain practice in developing and using a rubric, design one that could be used to assess the level at which you have learned and are able to demonstrate the information presented in this chapter. After you have completed the rubric, use it to rate your performance.

PREPARING FOR CERTIFICATION

1. Two topics in the Praxis II Principles of Learning and Teaching (PLT) test relate to this chapter: "addressing curriculum goals, selecting content topics, incorporating learning theory, subject matter, curriculum development and student development and interests" and "techniques for creating effective bridges between curriculum goals and students' experiences." With regard to assessment, two topics emerge in the Praxis PLT: (1) "Understanding of measurement theory and assessment-related issues," and (2) "Interpreting and communicating results of assessments."

   In this chapter, you learned about the importance of the standards movement in establishing curriculum goals and assessing student learning. Learn more about the national student standards for the subjects and grade levels you plan to teach. What goals for learning are contained? What are some ways you might assess those goals?

2. Answer the following question, which is similar to items in Praxis and other state certification tests. Mr. Harding has been asked to construct objectives for the lessons he is teaching in his second grade class. He is having trouble determining which of these are standard statements, benchmark statements, and statements that are objectives for the lesson. Which of the following is an objective:
   a. The students use numerical and computational concepts and procedures in a variety of situations.
   b. Students will be able to add numbers 0–100 using base 10 blocks.
   c. The students demonstrate number sense for whole numbers.
   d. The students demonstrate number sense for whole numbers, money, and time on their final exam.

3. Answer the following short-answer question, which is similar to items in Praxis and other state certification tests.

   As a teacher, your students' performance will be compared to how the students of other teachers and students in your school, in other school districts, and in other states are doing. Take a position for or against these comparisons and provide your reasons.

After you've completed your written responses for the above questions, use the Praxis general scoring guide provided in Chapter 1 to see if you can revise your response to improve your score.

MYEDUCATIONLAB

myeducationlab Now go to Topic 9: *Assessment, Standards, and Accountability* in the MyEducationLab (www.myeducationlab .com) for your course, where you can:

- Find learning outcomes for *Assessment, Standards, and Accountability* along with the national standards that connect to these outcomes.
- Complete *Assignments and Activities* that can help you more deeply understand the chapter content.
- Apply and practice your understanding of the core teaching skills identified in the chapter with the *Building Teaching Skills and Dispositions* learning units.

- Check your comprehension on the content covered in the chapter by going to the *Study Plan* in the *Book Specific Resources* section for your text. Here you will be able to take a chapter quiz, receive feedback on your answers, and then access *Review, Practice, and Enrichment* activities to enhance your understanding of chapter content.

WEBSITES

www2.edtrust.org/edtrust Education Trust's site provides data, policies, and recommendations related to academic achievement with an emphasis on students who have not been served well in the educational system.

www.nces.ed.gov/nationsreportcard The National Assessment of Educational Progress website provides information about the national testing programs and national report card.

www.relearning.org This site for Relearning by Design provides information on standards and authentic assessment and is hosted by the Coalition for Curriculum and Assessment (CCA).

www.nctm.org Information about the National Council of Teachers of Mathematics and its standards can be found at this website.

www.ccsso.org The website of the Council of Chief State School Officers, which is the professional association for state superintendents of education, provides links to each state where it is possible to explore that state's standards and information about test results.

FURTHER READING

Chappuis, J. (2009). *The seven strategies of assessment FOR learning*. Portland, OR: ETS Assessment Training Institute. This practical guide identifies the key strategies for using assessments in the classroom to help all students learn.

Popham, W. J. (2001). *The truth about testing: An educator's call to action*. Alexandria, VA: Association for Supervision and Curriculum Development. This critique of the tests being used by states for high-stakes testing programs helps the reader understand the biases that exist in tests. Guidelines are included to help teachers use tests for instructional benefits.

Stiggins, R. J., Arter, J., Chappuis, J., & Chappuis, S. (2006). *Classroom assessment FOR student learning: Doing it right—Using it well*. Portland, OR: ETS Assessment

Training Institute. These authors recommend changing the focus of classroom assessment from summative to formative assessments with the goal of using assessment information to know what students are learning and identifying strategies to ensure that they have developed understanding before moving to the next level.

Symcox, L. (2002). *Whose history? The struggle for national standards in American classrooms*. New York: Teachers College Press. This firsthand account describes the drafting of the history standards, the controversy, and their subsequent rejection by Congress. The analysis provides valuable insights into how decisions are made about the history to be taught in schools and about developing national content standards.

chapter twelve

DESIGNING PROGRAMS FOR LEARNERS: CURRICULUM AND INSTRUCTION

EDUCATION IN THE NEWS

"DEPTH" MATTERS IN HIGH SCHOOL SCIENCE STUDIES

By **SEAN CAVANAGH**,
Education Week, March 11, 2009

The scientific world is vast. One key to students' developing a strong understanding of it could be having them focus on relatively few topics, in great depth. That is the main conclusion of a recent study that examines one of the most enduring debates in science instruction—whether "depth" or "breadth" of knowledge is most important. Its authors come down on the side of depth.

High school students who focus more intensely on core topics within their biology, chemistry, and physics classes fared better in beginning college science than those who delved a little bit into a larger list of topics, the study found. Observers say those findings could offer direction to developers of science curricula, tests, and textbooks.

A central finding is that "breadth-based learning, as commonly applied in high school classrooms, does not appear to offer students any advantage when they enroll in introductory college science courses," the authors conclude, "although it may contribute to scores on standardized tests."

Arguments over depth vs. breadth are common across subjects. In science, however, that debate is especially vexing. Numerous scientific organizations and researchers have called for teaching and tests that are more focused on mastery of big topics. In their view, that position is backed up by the opinions of scientific experts and research on cognition and how humans build knowledge.

Yet paring down scientific topics, and determining which ones merit the most attention, is not easy. Many textbooks are written to meet the academic standards of multiple states, and as a result, are crammed with information, or "encyclopedic," as the study notes. Teachers also face pressure to prepare students for the questions they will encounter on state-mandated science tests, which are in turn based on the content found in state academic standards.

A study, published online in December 2008 by the journal *Science Education,* suggests that approach is misguided. It was written by Marc S. Schwartz, a professor of mind, brain, and education of the University of Texas at Arlington; Philip M. Sadler, the director of the science education department at the Harvard-Smithsonian Center for Astrophysics, in Cambridge, Mass.; Gerhard Sonnert, a research associate, also at the Harvard center; and Robert H. Tai, an associate professor of science education at the University of Virginia, in Charlottesville.

The authors build their research on a national survey of 8,310 undergraduates enrolled in their first college science course. Students were asked how much time they spent in high school biology, chemistry, and physics classes on various subtopics. In each subject, the researchers said students had been exposed to a topic in depth if they reported spending at least one month on it—for instance, mechanics or electromagnetism in physics or evolution in biology. They controlled for other factors, such as students' socioeconomic background and math proficiency.

The results show that students who had spent at least one month on one particular topic earned higher grades in college science courses than students who had not. By contrast, those who had been exposed to a relatively long list of topics, but not in depth, did not have any advantage in college chemistry or physics and were at a disadvantage in biology.

In-depth teaching can have a major impact, the authors maintain. Students who experience deeper coverage of physics in high school perform in college as if they had received two-thirds of a year more preparation than those who had the opposite mix of depth and breadth. In chemistry, students appeared to gain the equivalent of one-quarter of a year's worth of study from in-depth lessons, the authors found. In biology, students taught under an approach emphasizing breadth performed as if they had received a half-year less preparation in high school in that subject.

The researchers acknowledge that the study does not address important questions, such as how much depth is the right amount. The study also points to high-stakes science tests as a factor promoting overly scattered science teaching. Francis Eberle, the executive director of the National Science Teachers Association, in Arlington, Va., said the study does not address an important issue: the disconnect between high school and college science courses. Too many postsecondary courses emphasize "straight, rote learning" through lectures, and suggest to undergraduates that their goal is to "prepare the best" among them, a departure from the more nurturing approach many students encounter in high school, Mr. Eberle argued.

Even so, the study will likely challenge a common assumption in the scientific community that schools need to focus on breadth to produce professional-level scientists, who know all aspects of the subject, he said. Changing teaching and testing methods is difficult, Mr. Eberle added. "Our traditions are so strong. Our system is designed for breadth," he said. There are other factors, too. "Any time you change the system" for teaching science, Mr. Eberle said, "parents will say, 'That's not the way I had it.'"

QUESTIONS FOR REFLECTION

1. A school curriculum specifies what students will learn across different grade levels. Even though there are now national and state standards that guide decisions about what students should know and be able to do, these standards can be interpreted very differently. How would you tend to interpret these standards: Would you want students to master a wide variety of information or know a smaller number of concepts well? Provide reasons for your answer.

2. Think about your own school experiences in science. Did your teachers focus on a few key concepts and use a variety of experiences to help you learn these concepts or did your teachers focus on a wide variety of information and help you master the information? Describe how this curricular approach did or did not help you to meet the demands of college and life.

3. Education is often criticized for being slow to change. What reasons do you think parents, school administrators, and other teachers would cite if they were asked to change the curriculum of their schools to one that has depth versus breadth?

Source: Copyright Editorial Projects in Education, Inc. March 11, 2009. Reprinted with permission.

LEARNING OUTCOMES

After reading and studying this chapter, you should be able to:

1. Describe and compare different curriculum designs. (INTASC 1: Subject Matter; INTASC 4: Teaching Methods; INTASC 7: Planning; INTASC 8: Assessment)

2. Analyze the effects of different influences on the selection and design of curricula in your state. (INTASC 10: Collaboration)

3. Identify different curriculum evaluation approaches and studies across multiple levels including classrooms, schools, districts, nations, and globally.

4. Identify and apply different types and forms of learning objectives to instruction. (INTASC 4: Teaching Methods; INTASC 7: Planning)

5. Describe and analyze characteristics of direct and indirect teaching strategies. (INTASC 4: Teaching Methods)

6. Compare the learning needs of different types of learners and the relative effectiveness of different teaching strategies. (INTASC 2: Development & Learning; INTASC 4: Teaching Methods)

WHAT IS CURRICULUM?

Curriculum relates to anything and everything that supports learning. As such, it is a general term that is used in many different ways depending on the circumstances in which it is used. For example, in textbook selection committees, curriculum implies the scope of learning content and the grade-level sequence in which that content will be taught. In a school improvement meeting, curriculum might imply the types of competencies that students should be able to master at a certain grade level. At a daily teacher planning session, curriculum can mean that type of teaching that teachers use to help students learn. Curriculum also includes the informal and less obvious parts of the school day such as mottos or slogans on school walls, the types of student work displayed in classrooms, and even the way desks are arranged in classrooms. Ultimately, **curriculum** is the environment that is created by the interaction of all of the elements that support learning: the content taught, the materials selected, the teaching strategies used, the learning activities in which children engage, and the way a school is organized.

You might be wondering how this curriculum environment developed. Clearly, the curriculum of a school comes together over time and results from many different decisions made by state officials, administrators, teachers, and the community.

For more information about school curriculum throughout history, see Chapters 2 and 3.

curriculum An environment created by the interaction of all of the elements that support learning: the content taught, the materials selected, the teaching strategies used, the learning activities in which children engage, and the way a school is organized.

Developing Curriculum

As described in the philosophy and sociology chapters, those who are engaged in developing curriculum bring their own views and beliefs to the effort. For example, people who believe that students can be trusted will press for activities that allow for student initiative and open-ended explorations, whereas curriculum developers who believe that students will make a mess and break manipulative materials will develop activities that rely more on the teacher and are more structured for the students.

Beliefs about student learning and effective teaching come into play as well. Some theorists believe that what is to be learned should be broken down into subparts and each of these taught separately and sequentially, whereas others advocate for presenting the whole and letting the students "figure it out." Consider how different perspectives can influence the teaching of addition. Should students be taught a single way to do addition and be expected to always do it that way, or should they be encouraged to do addition in different ways, as long as they can explain how they obtained the correct answer? There is not a single correct answer to any of these questions; the best answer is a matter of perspective. Depending on the perspectives of the developers, curricula they produce can be quite different. Three key questions must be addressed for each curriculum development initiative:

1. What should be taught?
2. Who should decide?
3. How will it be taught?

Think about each of these questions. Determining what will be taught has serious implications for the learner, the teacher, and society. Should the content prepare students for the world of work? Should it contribute to the development of "good" citizens? To what extent should the selected content prepare the student to learn advanced content?

Who should make these decisions—teachers, experts, politicians, or citizens? Should we ask community members for their input? Should we bring in experts from different disciplines to help decide the content? Should we include principals and teachers? The more people involved in the decision, the more differences that will arise and this leads to another difficulty— getting agreement.

Question 3 brings up another new set of challenges: How will the curriculum be taught? Each teacher will have her or his own views about which way is best. What is to be done when the curriculum developers and teachers have different views? Answering each of these three overriding questions begins with philosophical assumptions and beliefs about what is important for society and individuals, as well as understanding the discipline. What should happen during instruction also requires careful deliberation.

STEPS IN THE CURRICULUM DEVELOPMENT PROCESS. A good place to start understanding how the curriculum of a school develops is to consider some general steps in which the design of a curriculum is made explicit in the form of outcomes, learning objectives, teaching activities, and assessment. Over the next several pages, we describe these steps in the curriculum development process along with implications for classrooms, teachers, and their students.

Curriculum theorists of the past identified a logical sequence of steps when developing new curriculum, as shown in Table 12.1 (Taba, 1962; Tyler, 1950). The steps may seem overly simple, logical, and sequential; however, they continue to be as essential as they were in the past. The development of any curriculum should incorporate each of these steps. When one or more of these steps is neglected, teachers and their students struggle to fill in the missing pieces.

The seven steps to curriculum development outlined in Table 12.1 make the work look easy. However, the reality is that developing curriculum is hard work and involves answering a number of very important value-laden questions that will be addressed either explicitly or implicitly. As each step is completed, theses value-laden questions must be reasked and reanswered:

1. To what extent should the learning outcomes support preserving a democratic society?
2. Which outcomes are important for the individual learner's self-worth?
3. Is the curriculum biased in some way against certain individuals or groups?
4. Will the curriculum be available to all? Or is it too expensive, too hard to teach, or does it have components that are inaccessible to some?
5. Is it built around the essential center of the discipline or is it composed of peripheral and isolated elements?

You will likely be asked to participate in one or more steps in the curriculum process. When you do, keep in mind these challenging, value-laden questions and carefully determine your personal point of view. This will help you, as a curriculum committee member, recognize how the ideas of other committee members resemble or contradict your own. This clarity will assist you and

Table 12.1 • Basic Steps of the Curriculum Development Process

Step	Purpose	Example Activity
1	Determine what needs to be learned and why.	Survey parents or business leaders about what future citizens/workers will need to know; or identify the big ideas in a discipline.
2	Describe the desired learning outcome(s).	Write standards, benchmarks, and objectives for each grade level.
3	Select the specific content.	Relate what is expected in the standards with the important topics in the discipline.
4	Organize the content.	Design a topic and objectives sequence so that what is learned first builds toward what will be learned later.
5	Select the learning activities.	Identify the specific lesson activities, tasks, and materials that will engage the learner and be congruent with the core ideas of the discipline.
6	Sequence the learning activities into a whole.	Sequence the learning from the early grades through high school and organize the topics within each year so that they are coherent and rigorous, with objectives that can be learned.
7	Evaluate the effectiveness of the materials, instruction, and student learning.	Collect evidence from teachers about instruction and from students about learning outcomes.

Go to the *Building Teaching Skills and Dispositions* section of Topic 11: *Curriculum* in the MyEducationLab for your course and complete the activity titled *Identifying Curriculum Types*.

For more information about subject-centered curriculum in the past, see Chapter 2.

big ideas The organization of content around major themes and principles.

others in the process of coming to a consensus. For, as challenging as these questions are, coming to a consensus about their answers is critical and at the core of the curriculum development process.

Curriculum Designs

Over time, a number of curriculum designs have been identified by comparing the way curricula are structured. Each curriculum design has particular strengths and weaknesses, and each has different implications for teachers. Some designs are typically found in U.S. schools, whereas others are more apt to be seen in schools in other countries. Each design is based on assumptions about what is important for students to learn as well as particular philosophies about teaching and how students learn best. Summaries of common designs are presented in Table 12.2.

TYPES OF CURRICULUM. The earliest curriculum design in American schools was the *subject-centered curriculum*, which focused on content disciplines. There were only three subjects or disciplines: religion, Latin, and Greek. The only teaching style was lecture. Students were expected to learn—in other words, memorize—the content. Surprisingly, the subject-centered curriculum is still the most common curriculum design in the United States, albeit the subject areas have changed as has the number of subject areas taught. Schools now include mathematics, reading, literature, social studies, science, physical education, and so forth.

Because of the explosion in the number of subject areas taught, there has been a move toward integrating subjects into themes or big ideas. *Themed curriculum* design focuses on teaching generalizations or big ideas that underlie various subjects. **Big ideas** such as change, cause and effect, symmetry, and interaction are studied through the perspectives of different disciplines. So, students might study change as it looks in chemistry and change as it looks in social science. Students might study symmetry through the lens of mathematics and through the lens of biology. A *spiral curriculum* is closely related to a themed curriculum in that it also focuses on big ideas. The main difference is that in a spiral curriculum the big ideas or cross-disciplinary concepts are taught over and over again across grade levels. Over time, the ideas are taught in an increasingly more abstract manner and students' understandings about these big ideas deepen.

Another curriculum design that has developed in response to the explosion of subjects that need to be taught is the core curriculum. A *core curriculum* focuses on key concepts and skills that are extremely important to learning and further understanding. So, key ideas and concepts are selected that must be mastered by all students. Once students show mastery of the core, they are permitted to investigate other related ideas and deepen their understanding. A *mastery curriculum* is closely related to the core curriculum design, but a mastery curriculum focuses more on very specific content and skills that must be mastered a certain way. For example, students in

Table 12.2 • Varied Curriculum Designs and Implications for Teachers and Students

Curriculum Design Name	Design	Role of the Teacher	Role of the Student
Subject centered	Selected subjects are identified. Organization is tight and narrow, and the sequence is specified.	Primary strategy is lecture. Teachers are expected to teach to the prescribed sequence and use the prescribed materials.	Students learn the content. The narrow focus allows students to learn more content in less time.
Theme or big idea centered	A number of subjects are integrated and theme generalizations from each subject become the big ideas.	Teachers may lecture. Focus is on the broad generalizations instead of depth in a particular content.	Students are expected to develop a broad understanding across a number of content areas. Students may not understand the broad themes and may instead simply memorize them.
Spiral	The curriculum is viewed across the P–12 continuum, the assumption being that key content will be taught more than once. In an early grade, a particular topic will be introduced in a general way. Several years later, the subject will be taught a second time with more depth. Then in the high school years, the topic will be taught again with even greater depth.	Teachers will use a variety of teaching strategies. The key is that teachers must have sufficient depth of knowledge to offer more content depth with each cycle in the spiral. Teachers also must make a concerted effort to add depth to student understanding with each subsequent pass.	Students are expected to learn the content at the depth taught each time. The risk is that they will not retain the knowledge and understanding developed in the previous cycle.
Core	Includes some contents all students should know. Depending on the philosophical perspective, a set of subjects is selected to be the center of the curriculum.	Rather than discrete content courses, integrated blocks may be offered. The content is taught in relation to problems or topics. Each problem uses each of the content areas. Typically, teachers teach as interdisciplinary teams.	Students learn through the study of interdisciplinary problems. Accompanying this learning is learning in related subjects.
Mastery	Levels of learning that all students are to reach are identified. Students are given as much time as they need and a variety of activities to aid their reaching mastery.	Teachers must be able to provide a variety of activities and ways for students to reach mastery. Teachers also must be skilled at assessing what students do and do not know.	Once students have met the criterion for a particular learning objective, they move on to addressing the next learning target.
Problem based	Students work in groups and are presented with a problem. Solving the problem requires that they learn new content.	The teacher is a guide and coach rather than a dispenser of content. Only when the need arises does the teacher present content.	Students are expected to be able to work cooperatively as members of problem-solving teams. They must be self-starters and motivated to study the problem.
Standards based	The standards of learning become the content.	Student learning is placed at the center rather than the topic being taught. Teachers use a wide variety of lessons and assessment strategies, all of which are aimed at assisting students in constructing their own understanding.	Students know the standards and specific benchmarks they are studying. They self-assess in relation to these.

a mastery curriculum setting would be required to answer very specific mathematics questions (like adding two-digit numbers with no regrouping) on a test.

A second change is that curriculum designs take into account the importance of motivating students and making them more interested in their learning. Instead of focusing only on abstract content, newer curriculum designs focus on current problems and issues. The decreasing popularity of teacher lecture and the increased use of learning activities are also examples of a way to increase student motivation. The problem-based curriculum design emphasizes the importance of students' motivation. A *problem-based curriculum* focuses more on authentic, contemporary problems, rather than abstract ideas or skills, that are under investigation in the world of work. Students are invited to tackle a problem with the intent of helping society find a solution. Ideas and skills are learned as students investigate the problem.

Although all of today's curricula are in some way standards based, some school districts have adopted a total *standards-based curriculum* design. By total standards based, we mean that the standards themselves are the key components of the design. The standards statements are used directly with no intervening organizational overlay. In some ways this makes the standards more prominent but it also can chop up curricular content in artificial ways. Examine the Global Perspectives feature concerning curriculum in Germany.

GLOBAL PERSPECTIVES   German Education

Studying curricula in other countries can broaden our perspective about the U.S. curricula. For example, German curricula focus on the three Rs, special education, and socialization. Extracurricular activities, from music to sports, are the responsibility of the communities, churches, and amateur athletic associations. Vocational education is the primary responsibility of business and industry. Health and safety are the responsibility of health maintenance organizations, government, churches, private institutions, and the home. In contrast, U.S. schools, in addition to the major charges of teaching the three Rs, must provide social education, including understanding and appreciating differences in ethnicities, races, creeds, and cultures; recreation; avocational education; vocational education; art, music, and theater—and the list goes on.

After the sixth grade, German students elect, by choice and examination, their main school: *Hauptschule* (about a third of the students), the *Realschule* (about one-fourth of the students), or the *Gymnasium* (about one-third of the students). Whereas the *Hauptschule* and *Realschule* prepare students for vocational education and apprenticeship programs, the *Gymnasium* is the academic school for the development of the mind and preparation for college attendance for professional careers. Special education students, about 10 percent of the student body, attend well-supported special schools called *Sonderschule*. Although a comprehensive-type high school, *Gesamtschule*, which is patterned after the American comprehensive high school, has been started, fewer than 10 percent of German students attend it.

There is little or no heterogeneous grouping in German schools, and teachers are firmly supportive of ability grouping. In the college preparatory schools, students can shift programs on the basis of interest and societal need, but the longer they wait to do so, the longer it takes them to complete their education because they must make up deficient prerequisites. Classes are spread over twelve months of the year and meet six days a week. However, with time allowed for vacations and holidays, German schools are open about 180 days a year, much like those in the United States. College-bound high school students experience a program that is closer to that of the U.S. college than of the U.S. high school.

Questions for Reflection
1. Do you think that American schools should be organized into the three types of German schools: *Hauptschule, Realschule,* and *Gymnasium*? Why or why not?
2. In German schools students are ability grouped. Is this a good idea? If so, why?

For more information about school funding see Chapter 9.

cocurriculum/extra-curriculum
School activities and programs, before, during, and after regular school class hours, that enrich the curriculum and provide extended opportunities for student participation.

hidden curriculum The implicit values and expectations that teachers and schools convey about what is important for students to learn.

COCURRICULUM AND EXTRA-CURRICULUM. When most teachers, parents, and the public think about curriculum, they think about the core academic subjects of language arts, science, mathematics, and social studies. However, school includes other subjects, such as world languages, physical education, and, especially in secondary schools, athletics, band, drama, choir, and many clubs. These other subjects, after-school activities, and clubs make up the **cocurriculum**, which sometimes is called the **extra-curriculum**. In many ways, it can be argued that the cocurriculum is of equal importance to the basic subject areas. The cocurriculum is especially important in high schools. Unfortunately, during times of budget cuts, various pieces of the cocurriculum are targeted. For example, driver education used to be a free component of the cocurriculum in most public high schools. Now, if it is offered through the school at all, a fee is required. This is unfortunate because for many students participation in the cocurriculum is a prime reason for staying in school. Cocurriculum teachers are excited about their programs and spend long hours after school, at night, and on weekends working with students to publish the student newspaper or yearbook or to prepare the team or band for the next competition. These highly dedicated teachers and their programs provide students with experiences and skills they will carry with them throughout their adult lives.

THE HIDDEN CURRICULUM. As the name implies, the **hidden curriculum** is not readily seen. In fact, it is invisible! At the same time it is a very critical and significant component of teaching and schools.

The hidden curriculum is experienced through the messages that are sent to students about expectations and about what is important to succeeding with each teacher and across the school. The hidden curriculum can be detected through examining the meaning behind the rules of the classroom and school, noting what is celebrated, what is deemed to be important, and what is rewarded, punished, and ignored. For example, are academic accomplishments celebrated as well as athletic? Are students with special needs included or isolated? Do all students have equal access to algebra and advanced placement classes or just certain groups of students?

When a teacher emphasizes neatness or speaking one at a time or is open to divergent student talk, messages are made clear about what is important for students to do and not do. Social behavior, dress codes, and rules about how to behave in the corridors become important ways that students learn about expectations. Whatever teachers value about learning, the subject matter, and the uniqueness of their students become elements of the hidden curriculum. Students learn what is important or not important through this invisible curriculum.

Student participation in the cocurriculum and extra-curriculum such as involvement with school plays, as shown here, can provide important opportunities for learning, as well as encouragement for staying in school.

Curriculum Resources

The curriculum delivered in each classroom has a rich and complex foundation. The tangible items for the teacher and the students include curriculum guides, textbooks, student workbooks, available technologies, and manipulative materials and lab supplies. However, the curriculum is more than printed documents. It also encompasses schoolwide resources and special-purpose facilities such as the media/resource center, playground and athletic facilities, cafeteria, auditorium, band practice hall, and arts and crafts classroom. As stated previously, the curriculum also includes the expectations for student learning. Each of these curriculum resources is important for teachers to understand, carefully examine, and use wisely.

STANDARDS. Of all the resources available to teachers the most important are the standards. As has been described earlier, for most subject areas there will be at least three sources of standards: (1) those published by the professional associations such as the National Council of Teachers of English (www.ncte.org) or the National Council of Teachers of Mathematics (www.nctm.org), (2) the statement of standards developed within each state and available through each state's department of education website, and (3) a school district's own list of standards, often called **power standards**, which are a reduced or more focused set of the state and national standards. These standards will clearly identify the subject matter and content that should be taught in a specific school district. The standards will not describe how to teach to the standard; teachers will need to turn to the many other curriculum materials and resources to plan instruction.

ASSESSMENTS. As a student, how often have you thought about asking or heard someone else ask the teacher, "Will this be on the test?" An important indicator of which elements of the curriculum are seen as most important is what is actually tested. With the continuing emphasis on high-stakes testing, teachers and their students must be knowledgeable about what is tested. A core assumption in some school districts and states, such as Texas or Florida, that have no pass/no play rules is that students will work harder to learn the material if they are tested and experience the direct consequences of the results.

For you as a teacher, understanding what is on the test is important for at least two reasons: (1) Your students will be highly motivated to learn what will be on the test and (2) you will quickly discover that for your grade level or subject, some critical topics are not covered on the high-stakes test. Both of these reasons illustrate an important aspect of the curriculum: The curriculum is not just what is in the textbook, nor just what is in the classroom lessons; it also is embedded in the expectations for learning and related assessments.

power standards A reduced set of standards that focuses on the most critical learning outcomes that must be taught and learned within each school year.

TEXTBOOKS. For teachers, one of the primary sources of information about the curriculum is the commercially published textbook. Textbook publishers employ expert author teams and invest large sums of money to provide students and teachers with up-to-date and well-designed materials. In U.S. schools, for most subjects textbook packages provide the bulk of the content, lesson objectives, and audiovisual resources, as well as student assignments. Most textbooks have an accompanying instructor's guide that provides the teacher with additional background subject information, lesson plans, suggestions for extensions and special assignments, and test items. A number of additional resources exist for teachers who use textbooks in the major subject areas such as science, mathematics, and English. These additional resources include training workshops, access to supporting websites, and perhaps videos of classroom lessons in which the textbook is used.

CURRICULUM GUIDES AND COURSE SYLLABI. Another important curriculum resource consists of the support materials for the teacher prepared by the school district and state. These include syllabi and curriculum guides for each subject area and grade level. Syllabi and curriculum guides draw the connections between what is to be taught at each grade level and the expectations for student learning in state and district standards. These guides also provide a vertical view of how the subject is to be covered from grade level to grade level. This is important because students experience school one year at a time, but their learning needs to be cumulative across the years. Teachers need to see how what they are teaching this year relates to what students learned last year and what they will be expected to learn next year. District and state curriculum guides are very useful for teachers as they plan daily lessons, especially when information is provided about the specific benchmarks for student learning that must be addressed and assessed at each grade level and for each subject. In some cases, such as in California, instead of having curriculum guides the state curriculum is organized around the big ideas for each subject area and published as *curriculum frameworks*. For example, in describing the nature of science, three broad assumptions are stated:

> The scientific method is a process for predicting, on the basis of a handful of scientific principles, what will happen next in a natural sequence of events. Because of its success, this invention of the human mind is used in many fields of study. The scientific method is a flexible, highly creative process built on the broad assumptions:
>
> • Change occurs in observable patterns that can be extended by logic to predict what will happen next.
> • Anyone can observe something and apply logic.
> • Scientific discoveries are replicable (California Department of Education, 2003).

CURRICULUM LIBRARIES AND THE WEB. Today's teachers have many easy-to-access supplementary resources to help them understand the curriculum and to obtain ideas for teaching to the standards. One invaluable resource now is the web. For any subject matter or topic, a large number of websites exist. Professional associations, regional education laboratories, intermediate agencies, and individual teachers and professors make available tips and full lesson plans. The school resource center and the curriculum resources in the district office and at any nearby colleges also have much useful information to offer. In addition, the textbooks and activities you used during your teacher preparation program are valuable resources.

THE MANY INFLUENCES ON CURRICULUM

At the beginning of this chapter, we observed that in today's schools teachers play a limited role in selecting the curriculum. In the past, teachers could teach their favorite lessons without worrying that there would be dire consequences for them or their students as a result of not following the guide or syllabus. Teachers today do not have this flexibility; they are responsible for helping all students achieve in terms of the published standards and benchmarks. So then, who does select the curriculum?

As befits our democracy, many people and groups have a say in selecting the curriculum for public schools. Figure 12.1 illustrates the many different actors and forces involved in determining the curriculum. Around the outer circle is the array of forces and interest groups that represent the

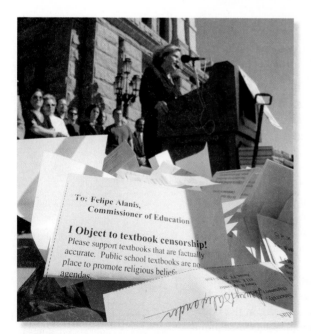

Special interest groups are a powerful influence on the selection of curriculum.

FIGURE 12.1

The Many Influences on Curriculum

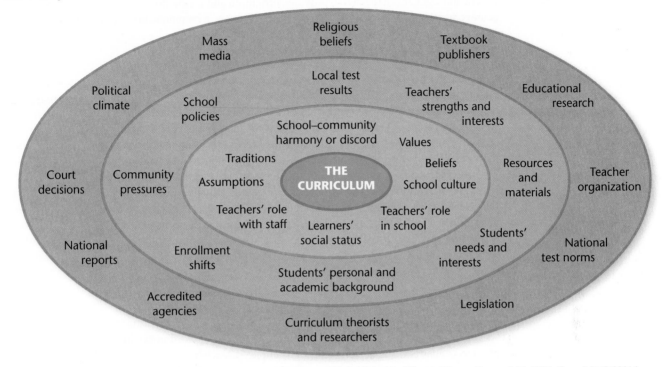

Source: F. W. Parkey and B. H. Stanford, *Becoming a Teacher*, 5th edition, p. 378. Published by Allyn and Bacon, Boston, MA, 2001. Copyright © 2001 by Pearson Education. Reprinted by permission of the publisher.

macro view. The middle ring summarizes many of the local factors and conditions that influence curriculum decisions. The inner ring shows the school context and influences. The product of this array of forces and interests is the curriculum that is selected and implemented in each classroom.

Large-Scale Influences on Curriculum

The primary effect of the various elements that form the outer ring in Figure 12.1 is to influence what will be common for curriculum in all states and school districts. Court cases, state and federal legislation, national reports, and educational research, as well as textbook publishers, determine much of what will be taught and learned in all schools and classrooms. In fact, this set of influences works against local control of schools. Instead of local control, there is a growing movement toward the establishment of a statewide and even national curriculum.

Another macro-level influence on the curriculum is the various interest groups, such as teacher and administrator organizations, political parties, and religious advocacy groups. **Interest groups** are informal and formal organizations of individuals who hold a common interest and shared agenda in regard to a particular topic or policy. These groups pay close attention to the work of committees charged with developing standards, curriculum guides, and test items. Each group is likely to have its own unique perspective and agenda. For example, teacher associations tend to resist any accountability moves that would link student performance on tests with the identity of the teachers who taught them. Many religious groups advocate that their positions, such as intelligent design, be included and that contrary positions, such as evolution, receive less emphasis. A different perspective might be represented by groups of administrators, who are concerned more about costs.

The various accrediting bodies, such as the Southern Association of Colleges and Schools (SACS) and the New England Association of Schools and Colleges (NEASC), influence the curriculum through the standards they apply to all schools they accredit. These standards in some ways set a common curriculum for all schools. For example, school accrediting bodies require each school to have a **school improvement process (SIP)**. A SIP usually is written by a school committee and the principal during the spring of the year. The plans include analyses of data about student learning, reports about the year's efforts to improve the school, and specific plans for the next year. Key expectations for these plans include analyses of student success on state tests such

For more information about school improvement, see Chapter 9.

interest groups Informal and formal organizations of individuals who hold a common interest and shared agenda in regard to a particular topic or policy.

school improvement process (SIP) A plan for future action that results from a school leadership team review of current successes and needs.

as those in mathematics, literacy, and, in some states, writing. The accrediting body expects improved student performance on state tests; a direct consequence of this expectation is that each school and teacher is expected to provide curriculum and instruction designed to enhance student achievement on the prescribed test. In ways such as this, a common curriculum is defined and implemented for all accredited schools.

Community Influences on Curriculum

At the local school district level, many additional factors influence the curriculum. Clearly, community interests and priorities are an influence. If the community values high school football and marching band, these two program areas will be an integral part of the cocurriculum. The personal background of students also influences the curriculum. For example, in many school districts a significant proportion of the students are English-language learners. **English-language learners (ELLs)** are students whose first language is not English and who therefore are learning English at the same time they are learning the content specified in the curriculum standards.

The curriculum influences of this ELL population are many. This population creates demand for teachers who speak their native languages. ELL students also need more assistance in learning academic subjects because they are learning English at the same time. One likely consequence is that ELL students do less well on high-stakes tests, especially if they are expected to read and respond in English. The overall result is that the curriculum in the classroom needs to be adjusted in response to these influences.

School Site Influences on Curriculum

The inner circle of Figure 12.1 summarizes some of the school's influences on the curriculum. Assumptions about learning, for example, make a significant difference in which subjects are emphasized, what is taught, and how. For example, if teachers in a particular school truly believe that all students can learn, then the curriculum is organized and delivered in ways that support all students learning: Students are grouped according to their needs; regular classrooms include students with special needs; and most group activities are organized to take advantage of the diverse talents and interests of students rather than having like students grouped together. In comparison, if teachers in a particular school believe that some of the children cannot learn, then "those" children are given less opportunity and more limited access to the curriculum. The result confirms the teacher's beliefs: Those students do less well.

In spite of the many influences on curriculum selection, its development, and its implementation, it is clear that in the end the curriculum is delivered in classrooms. This has two important implications. The first is that the role of the teacher in implementing today's curriculum is enormous. Although teachers have relatively little say in curriculum selection, they have the primary responsibility for helping students learn and achieve the desired outcomes. The second implication is that teachers have a plethora of curriculum resources to work with: curriculum guides, teacher-training sessions, and textbooks, as well as standards and benchmarks. All of these curriculum resources assist teachers in understanding what they should be teaching, and help them see what came before and what will happen next year with the students they teach this year.

══════ JOURNAL FOR REFLECTION ══════

Use Table 12.2 to think about a subject area that you plan to teach. Which curriculum design(s) did you experience when you were in school learning this subject? What do you see as the strengths and weaknesses of that design(s)?

SELECTION AND MANAGEMENT OF CURRICULUM

Clearly, many levels of interest and many perspectives directly influence the selection of a curriculum. This large and diverse set of influences also affects the processes for designing curricula. Without some sort of control mechanisms or an organized authority, it would be impossible for each teacher to choose what to teach and how to teach it in ways that satisfy a majority of the influences. Without some sort of overall authority, there would be no continuity in the curriculum from teacher to teacher, grade level to grade level, or school to school.

For more information about English-language learners see Chapters 7 and 8.

English-language learners (ELLs) Students whose first language is other than English and who therefore are learning English at the same time they are learning the content specified in the curriculum standards.

In the United States, the legal responsibility for schools and, therefore, for the curriculum, lies with each state. In large part, state legislatures and state boards of education determine the curriculum. Additional structures exist to set and support the curriculum at the school district level. In addition, even with the centralizing roles of the state and district, schools and teachers retain a number of important roles and responsibilities.

The State's Role in Managing Curriculum

Because each state has the primary responsibility for setting the curriculum for schools within that state, teachers need to know how this is done and what they can do to contribute to the process. The states have assumed two major areas of responsibility for curricula. The first is establishing what students are expected to learn, and the second is determining the instructional materials that can be used.

THE STATE SETS STANDARDS. The statements of expectation for student learning are determined at the state level. The typical process is to establish a statewide committee comprising teachers, school administrators, higher education faculty, and state policy makers, such as a representative state board of education member or a legislator, such as chair of the House Education Committee. Standards committees with similar composition are established for each content area. Each committee reviews the national curriculum standards for its content area. These committees hold public hearings around their state so that the various interest groups (remember the different circles in Figure 12.1) can present their positions. When each of these committees completes its work, members recommend a set of state standards to the state board of education. Once the state board approves them, all districts, schools, and classrooms in the state are required to teach to those standards.

THE STATE MAY CHOOSE CURRICULUM MATERIALS. There is some variation from state to state in the extent of state-level involvement in selecting curriculum materials. The main area of involvement is in selecting textbooks. States have either open adoption or state adoption policies. An **open adoption policy** permits local school districts to select curriculum materials and textbooks based on their own specific needs. A **state adoption policy** requires school districts to purchase curriculum materials and textbooks based on a list approved by the state. Most southeastern states as well as Texas and California have formal state-level processes for adopting textbooks; these are state adoptions. In these states, a committee is charged with reviewing the various available textbooks and establishing an adoption list. School districts and schools then select the textbooks they will use from this list of approved materials. If schools wish to select curriculum materials from the adoption list, they receive state funding to support the purchase. If a district or school decides to select materials not on the state's adoption list, it will have to pay the full cost of those materials. In open states, the adoption of textbooks is a matter of local choice; that is, the state leaves responsibility for the selection of curriculum materials to each school district, even when there is state funding for their purchase.

The District's Role in Managing Curriculum

Regardless of whether a school district is subject to a state adoption or open adoption policy, major curriculum-related tasks and responsibilities are assumed by each school district. These often include textbook selection or review of a list of state-adopted texts as well as provision of curriculum specialists.

DISTRICT TEXTBOOK SELECTION. One obvious district task is to select the textbooks and related curriculum materials to be purchased and used within the district. A curriculum committee is established that includes teachers, principals, parents, and perhaps higher education faculty. The committee reviews the current status of the subject area, including how well students are doing on tests. The committee examines available text and materials options, and then recommends to the district superintendent and school board which materials should be purchased. Teacher participation on these committees is important since they are the ones required to use these textbooks and other curriculum materials.

DISTRICT OFFICE CURRICULUM SPECIALISTS. School districts also employ a number of professional specialists whose responsibility it is to see that each curriculum area is supported and that teachers are prepared to teach the chosen curriculum. One important role is that of curriculum

open adoption policy A state text adoption policy that allows each school district the autonomy to review and select whichever textbooks it chooses.

state adoption policy A state textbook adoption policy that limits financial support and selections to those that are included on a state-approved list.

coordinator/liaison/specialist. Typically, earlier in their careers these individuals were master teachers. Now their role is to guide, support, and champion their subject areas. In smaller districts, an individual might have responsibility for a number of content areas, such as language arts and social studies. Larger school districts have curriculum specialists assigned for at least each of the "big four" areas: reading, mathematics, science, and social studies. There are also specialists for special education, bilingual/ELL education, compensatory education, and other need areas.

In addition to the subject-specific specialists, most school district office staffs include **generalists**. Instead of being experts in a particular content area, these individuals are experts in helping teachers learn and apply different teaching strategies, assessment procedures, and use of technology. District office generalists include:

- Experts in general teaching strategies, such as cooperative grouping and assessment methods, that can be used in most content areas
- Induction specialists, who are responsible for offering workshops, mentoring, and other support for beginning teachers
- Staff developers, who coordinate and present teacher inservice workshops, including those offered district-wide at the beginning of each school year
- **Teachers on special assignment (TOSAs)** are expert teachers who leave the classroom for one to three years to participate in a curriculum review, including selection of new materials, and to support teachers during the implementation phase.

Local Schools' Role in Managing the Curriculum

Even with all of the activities done at the national, state, and district levels, each school has major tasks and responsibilities for managing the curriculum. It still is up to each school and teacher to bring the curriculum alive in each and every classroom. Each teacher must do his or her part by being informed about the state standards and the benchmarks for his or her students' grade level. Teachers must also use the materials and strategies that will help all students learn. In secondary schools, an important curriculum management structure is the department. When teachers for one subject are organized as a department, they can easily seek ideas from colleagues who know the content, and they can coordinate across grade levels to determine what is taught in each course. The same ends are obtained in elementary schools by having grade-level teams and in larger schools by establishing content-specific curriculum committees.

EVALUATING CURRICULA

How do we know if the selected and implemented curriculum is making any difference? The obvious answer is that without systematic and well-organized evaluation studies, we cannot know. Evaluation of the curriculum has to be done carefully and at all levels, from teachers in classrooms, to school- and district-level evaluation, to statewide evaluation. In addition, national and international curriculum evaluation studies are conducted.

Curriculum evaluation is primarily based on what occurs in the classroom. Until the curriculum is implemented and student learning is assessed, direct evidence of effectiveness cannot be obtained. The first evaluation step is done by each teacher who implements the curriculum. Teachers' informal assessments of how easy it is to teach, the effectiveness of textbooks and materials, and the amount of student interest and motivation are early indicators of how effective any curriculum will be. Another early indicator is teacher assessments of the extent of student learning. Through informal teacher assessments and the formal testing done in the classroom, teachers and curriculum specialists can obtain early evidence of how well a curriculum is working.

Researchers and curriculum evaluators also focus on classrooms to determine curriculum effectiveness. Whereas the teacher examines only his or her classroom, researchers systematically document use of the curriculum and related student learning in a large number of classrooms. For example, in a study of teaching and learning mathematics with a curriculum designed around the NCTM standards, researchers documented classroom processes and student learning in more than one hundred classrooms. The results of their study included the following findings: (1) Classrooms where the teaching most closely approximated the best practices as outlined in the NCTM standards had the highest levels of student performance, the corollary being that in classrooms with less use of the new curriculum, students achieved less; and (2) students in classrooms with

generalists Professional educators housed in the district office who provide classroom support across a number of content areas.

teachers on special assignment (TOSAs) Teachers who are assigned to the district office for a limited time in order to accomplish a specified curriculum support task.

teachers who were collaborating with other teachers in teaching the new curriculum had higher levels of achievement (George, Hall, & Uchiyama, 2000).

District and State Curriculum Evaluation Practices

In today's high-stakes testing environment, school districts and states are focusing on student performance on standardized tests. Unfortunately, there is little examination of what goes on in classrooms. Instead, schools and school districts are often judged and labeled based on overall test score results. The No Child Left Behind (NCLB) Act mandates that the test scores for each school be published in the local newspaper. In extreme situations, when test scores are at the bottom year in and year out, (such as in Hartford, Connecticut; Compton, California; and Trenton, New Jersey), the state may "take over" operation of the school district. The results of these state takeovers are mixed, at best. In some districts, such as Hartford Public Schools, student test scores have gone up. In other districts, they have remained low.

National Curriculum Evaluation Studies

Two important national approaches to curriculum evaluation are the National Assessment of Educational Progress (NAEP) and the testing at most grade levels mandated in NCLB. These approaches reflect two very different philosophies about curriculum evaluation. In NAEP a random sample of students is selected from across each state. The sample is drawn from all students in the state, but does not include all of the students in one school or from one classroom. Therefore, the findings from NAEP indicate how well students are doing in reading, science, or mathematics by state. NAEP cannot make judgments about the effectiveness of particular schools or school districts.

In NCLB, Congress has mandated that all public school students be tested each year in grades 3 through 8 and in one year of high school. Each state can select the test, but the major content areas must be tested. These data will allow the labeling of schools and districts, even ranking each in terms of student performance on the selected tests.

International Curriculum Evaluation Studies

During the last twenty years, concern has been escalating about how well U.S. students do in comparison with students from other countries. Here again, student performance on standardized tests is the benchmark. The most widely reported study is the Trends in International Mathematics and Science Study (TIMSS; http://nces.ed.gov/timss). In this major study, the performance of students in grade 4 and/or 8 in the different countries is compared. The study was first done in 1995 and has been repeated in 1999, 2003, and 2007. In the 2007 study, 58 countries and educational jurisdictions participated in TIMSS at the fourth- or eighth-grade level, or both. The focus of this TIMSS report (Gonzales, 2008) is on the performance of U.S. students relative to their peers in other countries in 2007 and on changes in mathematics and science achievement since 1995. The report also describes additional details about the achievement within the United States such as trends in the achievement of students by sex, race/ethnicity, and enrollment in schools with different levels of poverty.

Each country is required to draw a random sample of students and schools. All students take the same test and scores are compared across countries. For example, in 2003, U.S. fourth-grade students scored 518, on average, in mathematics while the international average was 495. U.S. fourth-grade students outperformed students in Australia, Italy, and Norway, but did less well than students in Belgium-Flemish, England, Hungary, Japan, and the Netherlands. Eighth-grade U.S. students performed above the international average in mathematics but were outperformed by students in nine countries including Japan, Korea, Singapore, Belgium-Flemish, Hungary, and the Netherlands.

The average science scores for both U.S. fourth- and eighth-grade students in 2007 were similar to those in 1995. The U.S. fourth-grade average science score was 539 in 1995 and 542 in 2007. The U.S. eighth-grade average science scores were 520 in 2007 and 513 in 2005. In 2007, 15 percent of U.S. fourth graders and 10 percent of U.S. eighth graders were at or above the advanced science international benchmarks. Singapore and Chinese Taipei had higher percentages of fourth-grade students at or above the advanced international science benchmarks than the United States. At grade 8, six countries had higher percentages of students at or above the advanced international science benchmarks: Singapore, Chinese Taipei, Japan, England, Korea, and Hungary. These six countries also had higher average science scores than the United States.

INSTRUCTION: THE TEACHING SIDE OF CURRICULUM

Once the influences and committees have converged and a curriculum has been designed, teachers have the responsibility to bring it to life in classrooms. This is extremely important work. If teachers fail in the delivery of the curriculum, students cannot learn material required in the stated benchmarks and standards. One dire consequence of students not learning is failure—failure for the students and the teacher as well as for the school and community that have supported development of the curriculum.

Just like curriculum development, instruction begins with what students need to learn. Teachers need to think about student learning in relation to the outcomes for each lesson and how these lessons will unfold across days and weeks. Based on the expectations for learning and the characteristics and interests of the students, particular teaching strategies are selected. Another important influence on instruction is the schoolwide effort to improve learning that includes components that are expected to be implemented in all classrooms. For example, all elementary teachers in a school or school district may be expected to use the same instructional approach when teaching reading.

Instructional Objectives for Student Learning

Standards and benchmarks are descriptions of expected student learning that represent relatively long-term steps. Teachers and their students need more focused and short-term statements in order to focus on individual lessons. The instructional tools for creating this focus are called **objectives**; these are the statements of expected student learning for each lesson. The difference between objectives and standards is the size and scope of learning described. Standards represent the broad learning outcomes that students are expected to achieve across several years. Benchmarks address parts of standards, but they still are quite broad and can describe learning accomplishments that can take months. Instructional objectives address the daily learning expectations for students; they help both teachers and students identify the focus for the day's learning. Daily

objectives Statements of learning outcomes for a lesson or several weeks of lessons.

lessons, classroom activities, and quizzes need to be clearly tied to the important expectations for learning stated in the standards and benchmarks. Contrary to what some teachers practice, objectives for instruction should be known and understood by both the teacher and the students.

One of the important elements of writing objectives is understanding their purpose. Frequently, when teacher education candidates first write objectives they write them as input statements, which describe what the teacher will do and what will happen in the lesson. The following objective is one example: "The students will be assigned to groups and they will read the chapter in the text." Such an input objective is no longer acceptable because it fails to clarify what students need to learn.

Objectives should be written as output statements, which describe what students are to learn as a result of experiencing the lesson or lessons. For example, "As a result of this lesson, students will be able to compare the reasoning behind the economic and political arguments for and against sending troops into Afghanistan."

The difference between thinking in terms of inputs and outputs is crucial to becoming a successful teacher (see Figure 12.2). The natural tendency of teachers and professors is to think in terms of "what I am teaching." They may even say things such as "I teach English." In the past, this way of thinking about instruction was acceptable; however, in today's schools teachers need to be thinking and talking in terms of what their students are learning. "My students have been learning about the Civil War and the terrible cost of life that occurred." Fortunately, the use of instructional objectives can help teachers make this important shift in thinking.

Types of Instructional Objectives

As an additional support for teachers, scholars have identified different ways of writing learning outcomes. The development and refinement of these typologies has occurred during the last thirty to forty years. Each type of instructional objective addresses a different kind of learning, and assessing student learning

Analysis of the various skills that students are to learn is an important early step in planning instruction.

FIGURE 12.2

Two Emphases to Teacher Thinking: Which Should Be First?

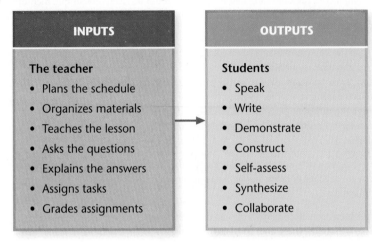

requires different methods, depending on the type of objective. For most lessons, teachers will likely have at least two kinds of learning objectives, which also means that careful thought has to be given to how the learning outcomes will be assessed.

BEHAVIORAL OBJECTIVES. As the name implies, **behavioral objectives** focus on an observable performance or task. In fact, the proponents of behavioral objectives advocate that if the learning cannot be described in terms of observable behaviors, then there is no way to tell if learning took place. From this point of view, student learning is to be described in terms of behaviors. This means that in behavioral objectives, the verb, or *action word*, is key. The objective needs to focus on a behavior that can be perceived, such as to *observe, classify, name, list,* or *interpret,* and not on words, such as *appreciate* and *understand.*

Behavioral objectives are a useful instructional tool for teachers in planning, teaching, and assessing student learning. A useful approach to identifying student behaviors is to perform a **task analysis**, which is the systematic identification of the key skills that someone needs to be able to do to complete a task or satisfy a benchmark. The typical steps for a task analysis include the following:

- Examine the related standards and benchmarks in order to identify the observable skills that students must demonstrate.
- Identify the small learning steps that in combination would result in students being able to do the whole task.
- Describe each step in terms of behaviors that can be observed.
- Determine the sequence in which students will need to learn the behaviors.
- Write behavioral objectives for the most central and important of these behaviors.
- Be attentive as the lesson unfolds to facilitating students' acquisition of those behaviors.
- Create an end-of-lesson, or unit, test that focuses on whether the students can exhibit the behaviors described in the behavioral objectives.

This approach to thinking about learning and teaching has been criticized as too linear and rational. Still, it is a useful way for teachers and students to maintain a focus on the key elements of a lesson. The real risk with behavioral objectives is having too many objectives and/or objectives that are so specific and narrow that they are trivial. It is one thing to write a behavioral objective that describes what both hands are doing when a person is touch typing, but it's another thing—and on a much more micro level of task analysis—to have an individual objective for the placement of each finger on the keyboard.

LEARNING OBJECTIVES FOR THE COGNITIVE DOMAIN. In 1956 a significant book was published titled *Taxonomy of Educational Objectives: The Classification of Educational Goals Handbook 1: Cognitive Domain.* The lead author of this book was a scholar named Benjamin Bloom (1956). He and his coauthors had developed a typology of different types of learning objectives in the area of knowledge. The basic premise was that educational objectives should be classified

Go to the *Assignments and Activities* section of Topic 12: *Instruction* in the MyEducationLab for your course and complete the activity titled *Cognitive Development 3.*

---

behavioral objectives Expectations for student learning that are stated in terms of observable behaviors.

task analysis The process of systematically identifying and sequencing the small learnings that must be accomplished in order for students to demonstrate mastery of a particular task or benchmark.

Table 12.3 • The Six Levels of Bloom's Revised Taxonomy of the Cognitive Domain

1.00 Remember	Knowledge and behaviors that emphasize remembering and recall. This could be relatively simple memorization such as facts, word spelling, and the multiplication tables. This domain also includes knowledge of criteria, rules, principles, methods, and theories.
2.00 Understand	Students are able to communicate the key components of an idea and can use the idea. The communication may be oral, written, or an equation or some other symbolic form. Three types of comprehension are translation, interpretation, and extrapolation. Translation entails the ability to understand an idea presented in one form, such as a graph, and be able to describe its meaning in another form, such as a written paragraph. Interpretation moves beyond translation to being able to weigh the different parts of a communication and to identify and understand the major ideas as well as the interrelationships. Extrapolation is extending beyond the presented communication by predicting consequences or likely next steps.
3.00 Apply	The student is able to apply learning to a new situation. Furthermore, the student is able to select the correct application without coaching by the teacher or other students. Using a principle to predict what will happen when a certain factor is changed is application.
4.00 Analyze	Analysis addresses the ability to break something down into its parts or pieces. Analysis also deals with detection of the relationships between the parts and how the whole is organized. Analysis begins with identifying the elements and then the relationships and interactions between the elements. Analysis goes beyond the stated and also includes recognition of the implicit.
5.00 Evaluate	Evaluation is about making judgments about the value or worth of ideas, products, or problem solutions. Although evaluation is presented as the last level, Bloom emphasizes that some effort at evaluation is a component of most of the other levels as well. At this level, evaluation is seen as a considered process based on criteria. It is not a simplistic rush to opinion. Instead, there is a reasoned analysis of all facts and weighing of alternatives and the consequences of each.
6.00 Create	To create is the process of putting together the parts to make a whole. Bloom points out that this is the level of the taxonomy that addresses creative behavior. This does not mean completely free creative effort, because there are likely lesson and problem contexts that set outside limits. At this level, the learner is working with a given situation. The product of this type of thinking might be an original idea.

according to the type of knowledge the learner was acquiring. This book and the classification system it introduced have become cornerstones of curriculum and instruction; the classification system is known as **Bloom's taxonomy**. Rather than treating all knowledge that is learned as being the same, Bloom and his colleagues identified six different levels of learning and therefore educational objectives. Over time, Bloom's colleagues revised his original list slightly. The revised version of Bloom's taxonomy includes six levels of learning and is summarized in Table 12.3 (Anderson & Krathwohl, 2001).

In Bloom's taxonomy, each of the six levels of the cognitive domain represents different amounts of complexity of knowledge and different extents of knowledge use. Teachers require different types of learning of students, depending on which level of the taxonomy is being addressed. In addition, teachers must keep in mind that this taxonomy is also a learning hierarchy. Students cannot perform at the higher levels unless they have already learned the necessary knowledge at the lower levels. The level of learning must be reflected in the way the learning objective is written. Simple memory and recall is a very different level of learning than is application or analysis.

LEARNING OBJECTIVES FOR THE AFFECTIVE DOMAIN. The **affective domain** of student learning also is important for teachers to consider as they plan instruction, teach lessons, and assess student learning. The affective domain addresses human reactions and responses to the content and subject matter. Student attitudes, feelings, and dispositions are a key component of instruction. Shortly after the development of the cognitive domain taxonomy, a parallel effort was under way to develop a taxonomy of educational objectives in the affective domain. The leader of this team was David Krathwohl (Krathwohl, Bloom, & Masia, 1964).

An unavoidable part of instruction is consideration of students' attitudes and beliefs because these affective elements are related to classroom behaviors. Krathwohl's affective domain taxonomy provides an analytical tool for planning instruction and an aid for teachers to think about different levels of student learning in terms of values and beliefs (see Table 12.4). In planning instruction and during teaching, the affective domain can be used to assess the openness to and

Bloom's taxonomy A system for classifying knowledge learning outcomes in terms of the complexity of mental activity required.

affective domain A system for classifying learning outcomes in the area of human reactions and responses.

Table 12.4 • The Five Levels of Krathwohl's Taxonomy of Affective Domain

1.0 Receiving (Attending)	The learner is sensitized to the condition, phenomenon, or stimulus that is the aim of the lesson or topic of study. At the most basic level, the learner is *aware* of the object or phenomenon. For example, in music students are aware of differences in mood or rhythm. Another component of this level is the *willingness to receive* or to attend to the topic of study. If there is not openness to learning more, then higher levels of the affective domain cannot be reached.
2.0 Responding	At this level, the learner is motivated beyond simply attending and is actively attending. At the lowest level of responding, there is *acquiescence in responding;* in other words, the learner is willing to go along. Slightly higher is the *willingness to respond,* in which the student looks for additional information or experience. A higher level of responding is indicated when the student shows *satisfaction in response.*
3.0 Valuing	At this level, the student is behaving in ways that reflect a sense of belief or attitude. Within this level, there is the range of behavior from *testing for acceptance of a value* to *commitment.* Actions of reaching out to learn more about a new topic, such as asking questions or searching out the topic on the web, are indicative of acceptance. With commitment there is a conviction and loyalty to the topic, position, or group.
4.0 Organization	As more than one value becomes relevant, there is a need to develop an internal system of organization of values. Organization begins with *conceptualization* of particular values and beliefs. This does not necessarily require verbal expression, but the learner is able to compare one value or belief to another. This process leads to *organization of a value system,* which brings together a number of values and their relationships.
5.0 Characterization by a Value or Value Complex	At this level, the learner has a set of values in place, the values are organized into some kind of internal system, and behaviors are consistent over time in relation to these values. The values represent a *generalized set,* and there is a *characterization* of the person in terms of the internal consistency of thought and an external consistency of action that is characteristic of the person.

interest of students in learning about a particular topic. If certain students are at level 1.0, Receiving (Attending), the lesson will need to be aimed at having students become more engaged with the topic and opening a willingness to move toward level 2.0, Responding, and level 3.0, Valuing. If students are already at level 4.0, Organization, then the learning objectives can ask students to weigh, compare, and form judgments. Values and beliefs, as well as motivation and interests, are a core component of learning. Students of teachers who continually attend to the affective domain will have greater learning success in the cognitive domain. When students are interested in learning and see the value of learning certain content, they will more intensely engage with the curriculum, which makes instruction more interesting and successful.

LEARNING OBJECTIVES FOR THE PSYCHOMOTOR DOMAIN. Another domain for learning objectives relates to learning physical skills, which require the mind and body to work together. Music, art, drama, industrial arts, and other vocational courses require students to perform tasks physically. The corresponding taxonomy, the **psychomotor domain**, has received attention from curriculum theorists and was developed by E. J. Simpson (1972). The first two levels are Perception and Set, which address the learner becoming aware of a particular stimulus and becoming ready to act. For example, the band director raises the baton and all members prepare to play the first note. Levels 3 and 4 of Simpson's psychomotor domain taxonomy address Guided Response and Mechanisms. When trying something for the first time, it helps to have suggestions and directions as a guide. With time the steps become automatic. At Level 5, Complex Overt Response, the learner can accomplish more complex tasks and movements. At the still higher level, Adaptation, the learner is able to adjust his or her behavior and accommodate its application in different settings or under different conditions. At the highest level, Origination, creativity is demonstrated. For example, the trumpet student moves beyond playing the written music to improvisation.

TEACHING STRATEGIES

Once the curriculum has been established and instructional objectives have been written, it is time to plan for and teach lessons that will help students learn the knowledge, dispositions, and skills identified in the objectives, benchmarks, and standards. Two hundred years ago, there was only

psychomotor domain A system for classifying learning outcomes that require physical activity and performance.

FIGURE 12.3

Key Characteristics of Effective Direct Instruction

1. Direct instruction works best when the learning objectives are clear and narrow in scope.
2. Information and/or tasks should be presented in sequence and one step at a time.
3. The teacher should check carefully for student understanding as the presentation unfolds.
4. Build in student practice with corrective feedback.
5. Avoid negative criticism.
6. Include review at key points.
7. Tasks and assignments should be clearly structured.

Go to the *Building Teaching Skills and Dispositions* section of Topic 12: *Instruction* in the MyEducationLab for your course and complete the activity titled *Effective Teaching Methods.*

Go to the *Assignments and Activities* section of Topic 12: *Instruction* in the MyEducationLab for your course and complete the activity titled *The Direct Instruction Model.*

direct instruction A teaching approach in which the teacher clearly and succinctly provides clear, precise information about a specific topic, concept, or skill.

active learning time (ALT) The proportion of time within a lesson that students are actively engaged with the task of learning the objectives.

indirect instruction A set of teaching approaches in which students have greater responsibility for structuring and managing their own learning.

Guided Discovery Carefully designed learning activities that require students to investigate a specific question.

inquiry An instructional approach that begins with a problem or puzzle posed by either the teacher or students.

one teaching strategy—lecture; the teacher talked and the students memorized. Today this "stand and deliver" strategy is but one of many teaching methods. Students are not willing to sit through continuous lectures and a variety of teaching strategies have been demonstrated to be significantly more effective in engaging students and having students achieve at higher levels.

Direct Instruction

Although the lecture method continues to receive criticism, there is an appropriate time for teachers to impart information directly. **Direct instruction** is a teaching approach in which the teacher clearly and succinctly provides precise information about a specific topic, concept, or skill. During the last thirty years, extensive research has been done on the behaviors of the teacher and the effectiveness of direct instruction (Rosenshine & Stevens, 1986). When direct instruction is done well and with appropriate learning objectives, students learn. Two basic, underlying assumptions of this teaching strategy are that the teacher knows the content and that the easiest way for students to learn it is for the teacher to directly communicate it to them.

Although with direct instruction information is passed from teacher to students, additional ways to communicate information exist besides teacher lecture. Reading the textbook, asking questions that require answers, and using different technologies such as videos, television programs, and information searches on the web are ways to impart information and to make direct instruction more interesting and motivating for students.

To be most effective in using direct instruction, the teacher must manage a number of important steps (see Figure 12.3). With direct instruction, the teacher is at the center and maintains full control of the lesson. The teacher must control the flow and keep all talk focused. Sidebars and off-topic discussion are discouraged. A primary purpose of direct instruction is to maintain a high amount of on-task learning time, or **active learning time (ALT)**. Higher proportions of class time in which students are engaged will yield higher levels of student learning.

Indirect Instruction

The opposite approach to direct instruction is **indirect instruction**, which covers a large number of teaching strategies in which students have greater responsibility for structuring tasks and managing their own learning. The teacher still has overall responsibility, but students have to initiate more, to organize more of the tasks and their thinking, and in the end be able to construct their own product or way of demonstrating what they have learned. Key characteristics of indirect instruction are presented in Figure 12.4.

GUIDED DISCOVERY. Guided Discovery lessons are carefully designed learning activities that require students to investigate a specific question. The procedures for the investigation are carefully designed by the teacher so that students eventually arrive at an understanding that is the desired learning outcome. Students are allowed to work through the investigation at their own pace but the instructions designed by the teacher guide them in a preferred direction. Gradually students discover the learning concept. Students are sometimes critical of this teaching methodology because they are led to believe that they are discovering something on their own when, in fact, the activities lead them to a specific concept.

INQUIRY AND PROBLEM-BASED LEARNING. Inquiry lessons begin with a problem or puzzle being posed by either the teacher or students. Then, the students initiate investigations or problem-

FIGURE 12.4

Key Characteristics of Effective Indirect Instruction

1. The teacher or students pose a problem or puzzle.
2. The problem or puzzle is one that stimulates student interest and inquisitiveness.
3. The teacher does not provide the answer or problem solution.
4. Students initiate activities and investigations to analyze the problem or puzzle.
5. The teacher serves as a guide or coach only when students are stymied.
6. All possible solutions/answers are given open consideration.
7. Students articulate orally, in writing, and/or through presenting the reasoning behind their answer/solution.

solving strategies in an effort to construct an answer. *Problem solving* is another name for this general approach. Students assume major responsibility for their learning with this approach.

In an inquiry lesson, the first phase is to define the problem. The teacher might pose a dilemma, or in a science lesson do a demonstration, for which the answer is not obvious. The students then have to define the specific question or problem. The second major phase in inquiry lessons is discovery of the solution. The discovery phase might include conducting an experiment, seeking out information from reading or on the web, or, in a mathematics lesson, using manipulative materials. In the end, the students will have constructed new understanding and have learned new concepts and principles.

One innovative adaptation of the inquiry approach, which was first used in medical education, is **problem-based learning (PBL)**. In this approach, a real or simulated problem

When using an inquiry approach to instruction, the teacher acts more like a coach than a lecturer.

is posed, and students work in groups to develop a solution. The problem does not have a quick or obvious answer, nor is it one about which the students will already have sufficient knowledge. The purpose of PBL is to engage a team of four to six students in systematic inquiry, decision making, and problem solving. The result is deeper understanding of the subject as well as the development of skills in inquiry and collaborative work. In medical education, the students will need to seek out information in journals, attend lectures by professors, meet in their group to analyze the problem, and pool their developing understanding. Many medical schools have small seminar rooms reserved for PBL teams to study the problem and concentrate their efforts for weeks. The evaluations of the use of PBL in medical education have demonstrated that future doctors do just as well on the standardized licensure exams and they are better at information retrieval and problem solving.

MODEL-CENTERED INSTRUCTION. Models are an important device for organizing and explaining knowledge, and they are used widely in science. In the **model-centered learning** approach, a twelve- to fourteen-week curriculum allows the students to explore and evaluate models and to create their own models for explaining and predicting phenomena (such as force and motion in astronomy). Research on this approach shows improvements in student content knowledge (Schwarz, 2002).

Increased Emphasis on Science and Technology

With the passage of No Child Left Behind, which requires annual testing in reading and mathematics, there is now an increased emphasis on teaching reading and mathematics. One unexpected

myeducationlab

Go to the *Assignments and Activities* section of Topic 12: *Instruction* in the MyEducationLab for your course and complete the activity titled *Model Inquiry Unit.*

problem-based learning An inquiry learning approach in which an authentic, contemporary, or simulated problem is posed and students work in groups to develop a solution.

model-centered learning An instructional approach that allows the students to explore and evaluate models and to create their own models for explaining and predicting phenomena (such as force and motion in astronomy).

outcome from this emphasis is that other subjects (such as social studies and science) have been somewhat neglected. For example, teachers have begun to emphasize reading skills rather than science and social studies concepts. Science classrooms, which at one time had students investigating various science phenomena, now have students reading from textbooks while using some new reading strategy.

President Barack Obama believes that there is an urgent need to strengthen not just reading and mathematics but science education as well. In a major position paper, both President Obama and Vice President Biden (2009) have announced that they will work to increase the number of science and engineering graduates, encourage undergraduates studying math and science to pursue graduate studies, and work to increase the representation of minorities and women in the science and technology pipeline.

Obama and Biden will also recruit math and science degree graduates to the teaching profession and will support efforts to help these teachers learn from professionals in the field. They will also work to ensure that all children have access to a strong science curriculum at all grade levels.

In addition to this increased emphasis on science education, Obama and Biden intend to build on existing federal education technology programs. This education technology fund will encourage school and community leaders to:

- Integrate learning technologies such as simulations, interactive games, and intelligent tutoring systems into their teaching and learning programs.
- Use technology to provide assessments that allow teachers and parents to build on students' individual needs and talents.
- Create new technology-based curricula that help students develop high-demand twenty-first-century skills and work on authentic projects.
- Use technology-supported social networks that enable collaboration among peers across the country.

Clearly, these bold initiatives have the potential to change the current curriculum and instruction landscape.

Organizing Students to Maximize Learning

One important component of all teaching strategies has to do with how students are grouped. Should students be taught as a whole class? When should students be divided into groups? What should be the size of the groups? Should the groups be kept the same? What should be done about the different ability levels and skills of students? All of these questions must be answered to determine the best organizational model for learning.

myeducationlab

Go to the *Assignments and Activities* section of Topic 12: *Instruction* in the MyEducationLab for your course and complete the activity titled *Cooperative Learning*.

---

homogeneous grouping Grouping students who are alike in terms of their ability to learn or interests.

heterogeneous grouping Grouping students who are diverse in their interests and ability to learn.

cooperative learning A strategy for grouping that provides specific roles and responsibilities for each member.

HOMOGENEOUS OR HETEROGENEOUS GROUPING. Grouping together students who have similar levels of achievement and abilities is called **homogeneous grouping**. Grouping together students with different levels of achievement and different abilities is called **heterogeneous grouping**. The best way to group depends to some extent on the task. Deciding on which way to group students is philosophical too. Proponents of heterogeneous grouping point out that high-achieving students help the lower achieving ones and that everyone learns. On the other hand, the proponents of homogeneous grouping believe that mixed-ability grouping slows down the fast learners. Note that the unstated assumption in this debate is that the only learning that counts is that of each student individually; but the accomplishment of the group also should be considered. The Professional Dilemma feature presents a scenario to help you determine which type of grouping you might prefer.

COOPERATIVE LEARNING. A widely used approach to grouping is **cooperative learning**, in which students are expected to work together to accomplish tasks and are held accountable for both individual and group achievement. In this approach, the general plan is to have a mix of students, so that each group will include students with high, middle, and lower abilities. An alternative is to have students grouped according to interest and assign them activities according to those interests. Typically, cooperative learning groups work together for several weeks or longer. Each group member has an assigned role, including group leader, monitor, resource manager, recorder, and reporter. In this way, leadership and task responsibilities are shared. Extensive research has been done on this approach to grouping. Some of the outcomes are improvement in understanding of content, development, and support of using acceptable social skills; opportunities for student decision making; and encouragement of student responsibility (Johnson & Johnson, 1999).

PROFESSIONAL DILEMMA

Should I Use Homogeneous or Heterogeneous Ability Grouping?

The issue of how to group students for instruction can be very controversial. Some propose homogeneous grouping and others argue for heterogeneous grouping. Homogeneous ability grouping is a practice that seems to have merit. Permitting students who require the same level of instruction to be clustered in a single setting makes planning and resource allocation much easier. Such grouping patterns permit students to receive instruction that is tied to their specific needs, because they are with others who need the same information or skill development.

Those who oppose homogeneous ability grouping contend that labeling students and placing them in similar ability groups based on their academic skill sets up structures that often inhibit future growth and development. Both teachers and parents begin to view students according to these labels; once tracked by ability, students seldom break out of the initial labels assigned at an early age. These critics call for multiability or heterogeneous grouping. They believe that having students from a variety of backgrounds and ability levels work together is more in keeping with a democratic society. Furthermore, such multiability grouping permits students to help one another, fostering cooperativeness and caring among those from different backgrounds. Indeed, opponents of tracking programs have pointed to the disproportionate number of minority and low-income students who seem to make up the lower level groups.

Questions for Reflection

1. List other pros and cons of homogeneous ability grouping. List other pros and cons of heterogeneous ability grouping. Using these pro and con lists, what educational philosophies are compatible with homogeneous grouping and what educational philosophies are compatible with heterogeneous ability grouping?
2. Should one type of grouping be used in all instructional settings or circumstances, or should the types of grouping be varied according to task and context?
3. What type of grouping would you choose to use most of the time and why?

To answer these questions online, go to MyEducationLab, select the *Assignments and Activities* section, and click on this chapter's *Professional Dilemma.*

Criticisms of cooperative learning include the arguments against homogeneous grouping cited previously. Other critics, including many parents, object to grading students based on group accomplishments. Examine the Reflect on Diversity feature, which examines issues that arise when using cooperative learning approaches.

DIFFERENTIATED INSTRUCTION. It is critical to employ different types of instructional grouping approaches based on the unique needs of students. **Differentiated instruction** is the regular practice of employing a variety of instructional methods and learning activities to match the different ways

REFLECT on DIVERSITY

This Is Science Class, Not Language Arts

Joanna Wilenski has taught sixth-grade science in the same middle school for more than ten years. Over time, Joanna noticed a gradual but significant change in the composition of the student body. The number of Spanish- and Vietnamese-speaking children had increased to such a degree that her school had adopted and now implemented a language immersion program. She, along with other experienced teachers, attended a variety of language immersion workshops. Thanks to this effort, Joanna was certain that more of her language diverse students would succeed.

As she has always done, Joanna started the new school year with an introduction to cooperative learning in science. She knew, from experience, that it is important to teach students how to cooperate in a learning environment. Joanna explained that in science it is helpful to investigate the world together and learn from different perspectives.

After several class sessions practicing different cooperative learning techniques, Joanna created small science groups to work on a science investigation. Students were asked to determine how many drops of water would fit on a penny before spilling over. She asked students to assume different roles as they investigated this question together including materials handler, recorder, and observer. Students seemed eager and ready to explore this question about surface tension.

After several minutes, however, Joanna noticed that some groups were not working well. She walked over to one of the groups and noticed that only two of the four students were working and the other two were sitting quietly and uninvolved. Concerned, she asked the students if they needed help. Immediately, one of the participating students said: "Yes, tell Juanita and Chou to learn English or go to another group. We don't have time to teach them ourselves."

Questions for Reflection

1. Why do you think that the student felt it was a burden to have students who were not versed in English in the group?
2. What could Joanna say to the student that might help her work with language diverse students in the classroom?
3. Would it have been better to group students according to their different languages? Why or why not?

myeducationlab To respond to these questions online, go to the *Book Specific Resources* section in the MyEducationLab for your course, select your text, and then select *Reflect on Diversity* for Chapter 12.

differentiated instruction The regular practice of employing a variety of instructional methods and learning activities to match the different ways that students learn and to accommodate the different levels of learning that students require.

that students learn and to accommodate the different levels of learning that students require. Regardless of the type of instruction approach used, students will respond differently to the intended learning outcomes. Some students may immediately show mastery of the outcome, others may exhibit misconceptions, while other students may end up confused. This type of outcome is typical when students are taught in a classroom setting. The key to success is to immediately design follow-up learning activities based on the different needs of students. The group of students who showed immediate mastery could be provided with an inquiry lesson in an effort to allow them to deepen their understanding. The group of students with specific misconceptions could receive direct instruction focused on the misconceptions. The group of students who are confused might benefit from exposure to a totally different instructional method to reteach the content. This process is ongoing and is at the heart of differentiated instruction.

One debate that continues to concern both parents and teachers is the role of homework. Given what we know about the differences in students' home lives, assigning homework can pose problems. The Teacher Perspectives feature explores this issue.

Research on the Use of Technology to Enhance Instruction

Research has supported the value of technology in classrooms. When technology is used to actively engage students in learning, applying, and analyzing important concepts, achievement gains result. For example, researchers have found that in classrooms in which computer simulations are used to support higher level cognitive tasks, subsequent achievement gains can result (Wenglinsky, 2005).

TEACHER PERSPECTIVES

Should We Abolish Homework?

The value of homework remains a controversial topic. Although some research confirms the value of homework, other studies question the wisdom of assigning homework to students who have limited resources at home.

YES

Mike Burman *teaches high school English and journalism at Horace Mann High School in North Fond du Lac, Wisconsin.*

If students are in school seven hours a day, what right do I have to interfere with their family time? One of my fellow teachers had a son in middle school who would come home from basketball practice, then go to the basement to do, on average, three hours of homework a night. Does this sound healthy?

At the younger grades, it is almost criminal to assign homework. I spoke to a mother of a first-grader who was getting 30 minutes a night. She is very frustrated that instead of quality time with her son, she has to go through homework that at times is frustrating for him.

In my own classroom, I have actually noticed an increase in achievement, thanks to my reduction in homework. I used to assign a big project at the end of a novel or unit, and then give students a week or so to do it on their own. Later, I tried giving students time in class to work on these projects. Two positive things happened as a result: a higher percentage of students turned in a project and there was an increase in the quality of the projects.

Educators have about seven hours a day to create meaningful learning experiences. If they cannot then they are not using time efficiently. Children are not machines. They need "downtime" just like any adult.

NO

Henry Adeoye *is a special education teacher at Moorhead Junior High School in Conroe, Texas.*

Abolishing homework will negatively impact students' learning in no small measure. First, it would be detrimental to continuity. Homework allows students to practice the skills they learned earlier in the day, so that when they return to school the next day, those skills aren't lost. I don't know of many students who willingly study the next chapter without being asked. There are exceptions, but most students do not study on their own. They need direction; homework is just one tool to keep them on track.

Also, when students have assignments that are to be completed at home, it often encourages parents to become more involved with their children's education. When reviewing homework assignments, parents are able to see firsthand what their children are learning in school, which fosters communication between teachers and parents. This has been an invaluable tool in my classroom to foster the home/school relationship.

Teachers should not relent in using homework to enhance students' performance, but it should not be assigned to the extent that students become inundated or overwhelmed, and it should never be assigned as punishment.

Although homework is an essential ingredient to a quality education, breaks from homework can certainly be given from time to time—students sometimes need breaks just as we need breaks from our work.

Source: "Should We Abolish Homework?" *NEA Today* (March 2007), p. 51. Reprinted by permission of the National Education Association.

What is your perspective on this issue?

myeducationlab To explore both sides of this issue and think about each perspective, go to the *Book Specific Resources* in the MyEducationLab for your course, select your text, and then select *Teacher Perspectives* for Chapter 12.

Another major study (called a meta-analysis) focused on the effective use of technology in education by examining more than 122 studies involving 11,317 learners (Yiping, 2001). The study found that when using technology, the following instructional features make a positive difference: (a) Students who worked in small groups learned more than those who worked alone; (b) students achieved across a variety of learning outcomes including cognitive, process or skill, and affective growth; (c) students needed to have prior experience in working in groups, (d) students needed instruction in specific cooperative learning strategies, and (e) the content needed to include tutorials, practice software, an opportunity to learn computer skills, and an interdisciplinary subject matter such as social science.

The potential for technology to support learning is substantial and is a large reason why so many educators are excited about its use. The key to using any technology effectively is to always keep the instructional goal in mind rather than simply focusing on the technology. This may seem obvious but can you can easily get lost in many new and exciting technologies that emerge. Keep this important focus in mind (the instructional goal comes first) as you review the many technology tools available to you.

Go to the *Assignments and Activities* section of Topic 13: *Technology in Schools* in the MyEducationLab for your course and complete the activity titled *Technology Improves Teaching Skills.*

TEACHING STRATEGIES FOR DIVERSE STUDENTS

A central consideration in designing instructional strategies is how well they match up with the learning needs of diverse students. In many ways, each student in a classroom is unique. Effective teachers use strategies that take advantage of each student's strengths and that accommodate areas of need. Students will vary in their ability to read and calculate. They will vary in their ability to use English and in how well they can communicate orally and through writing. Some will be exceptionally fast at learning, and others will be slow.

One important component of instruction that teachers must examine and understand is how best to address the array of students with special needs and those who are English-language learners. For example, students with learning disabilities are apt to have difficulty with direct instruction strategies, especially lecture. However, they benefit from having clear and concrete teacher directions and activities that are well structured and sequenced. ELL students can be very successful with strategies that facilitate their interaction with other students and that provide ample time for processing what is happening. ELLs also benefit from indirect instruction strategies, because their learning is less dependent on understanding everything the teacher says. ELL students in secondary school classes in particular do not benefit from direct instruction. Fortunately, a number of well-developed approaches exist for accommodating the needs of diverse learners.

Teaching Students with Language Diversity

A seemingly never-ending debate deals with selecting the best instructional approach for ELL students. Some advocate **immersion** programs, or English as a second language (ESL), in which students are taught primarily in English, and their native language is limited and used only on a case-by-case basis to clarify instructions. Other experts advocate that ELL students be placed in **transitional** programs, also called **bilingual** education, in which their native language is used along with English to ensure content understanding, but only until the student can make the full transition to all-English instruction. The Institute for Education Sciences (IES) of the U.S. Department of Education is currently funding a major research study related to this debate. Table 12.5 was developed by IES as a summary of distinctions between these two program models.

Resources for Teaching ELL Students

Among the many resources for teachers who work with ELL students are several federally funded centers. One of these is the National Clearinghouse for English Language Acquisition (www.ncela.gwu.edu). The NCELA is a repository for best practices, research, and related information for teachers who work with ELL, dual language, and migrant education. Subjects on the NCELA website include assessment and accountability, curriculum and instruction, and parent and community involvement. The website also includes links to legislation and regulations related to the No Child Left Behind Act, searchable databases, and strategies and activities for ELL teachers.

In practice, teachers of ELL students should include two kinds of objectives: language and content. Content objectives are established for all students. For the ELL students, adding a language objective helps with their language development. For example, a language objective could be that the ELL students will be able to identify and say vocabulary words when shown a picture.

immersion A program approach in which ELL students are taught primarily in English, with use of their native language only on a case-by-case basis.

transitional/bilingual A program approach in which ELL students are taught in their native language along with English.

Table 12.5 • Comparison of English Immersion and Transition Programs

	Structured English Immersion	Transition
Content Instruction	Instruction is in English with adjustments to proficiency level so that subject matter is comprehensible. Instruction is supplemented by visual aids and gestures.	Literacy and academic content areas begin in student's primary language and continue to grade-level mastery of academic content. As proficiency in oral English develops, the language gradually shifts to English. The transition usually begins with math computation, followed by reading and writing, then science, and finally social studies. Students transition to mainstream classes in which all academic instruction is in English once they acquire sufficient English proficiency.
Language Arts Instruction	English is taught through content areas. Subject matter knowledge and English are taught together by teaching content through learner-appropriate English. A strong language development component is included in each content lesson.	Begins in student's primary language with instruction in English oral language development. The goal is to achieve both basic oral English proficiency and content knowledge, mainstreaming to an all-English program by the end of grade 3.
Language Goals	English acquisition and content knowledge by grade 3.	English acquisition and content knowledge by grade 3.
How Primary Language Is Used	Primary language is limited to use on a case-by-case basis, primarily to clarify English instruction.	Primary language is used to ensure grade-level mastery of academic content but only until the student can make a full transition to all-English instruction.
How English Is Used	To teach content instruction, adjusted to proficiency level.	Shifts from student's primary language to English as proficiency in oral English develops. English is frequently used in nonacademic subjects such as art, music, and physical education.

Source: U.S. Department of Education, Institute of Education Sciences.

During an elementary school lesson, the teacher could speak the key words while pointing to them in a *Big Book* or writing them on the whiteboard. In a secondary classroom, the teacher could use a worksheet that has sentences with blanks where the key vocabulary words should go. This task will help the ELL student focus on the key words and concepts. Another useful technique in both elementary and secondary classrooms is to have one or two of the students model the task before the whole class begins individual or group work. ELLs, as well as all the other students, are able to see what is expected of them. Figure 12.5 presents another useful set of tips for assisting ELL students.

Accommodating Students with Exceptionalities

There is a wide range of variability in student needs and the resources that teachers have to address them. In the past, most students with special needs were isolated and placed in "special education" classrooms. This self-contained model came under heavy criticism for a number of reasons, including the absence of contact with general education student role models and special education students losing out on many school activities and events. One conse-

Often, determining students' dispositions is as easy as looking at each student individually.

FIGURE 12.5

Entrees to English: Tips for Assisting Language Learners

- **Engage cooperative groups of English language learners (ELLs) and English speakers in common tasks.** This gives students a meaningful context for using English.
- **Develop content around a theme.** The repetition of vocabulary and concepts reinforces language and ideas and gives ELLs better access to content.
- **Allow student nonverbal ways to demonstrate knowledge and comprehension.** For example, one teacher has early primary students hold up cardboard "lollipops" (green or red side forward) to indicate "Yes" or "No" to questions.
- **Don't constantly correct students' departure from standard English.** It's better to get students talking; they acquire accepted forms through regular use and practice. A teacher can always paraphrase a student's answer to model standard English.
- **Consider using visual aids and hands-on activities to deliver content.** Information is better retained when a variety of senses are called upon.
- **Use routines as way to reinforce language.** This practice increases the comfort level of second language learners; they then know what to expect and associate the routine with language.

Source: "Entrees to English: Tips for Assisting Language Learners," by Terrey Quindlen, *Curriculum Update*, Fall 2002, p. 2. © 2002 by ASCD. Reprinted by permission. Learn more about ASCD at www.ascd.org.

quence of P.L. 94-142 was establishment of the resource room and a major change in philosophy. Now there is an expectation that students with special needs are members of the general education classroom and go to the resource room only for special instruction—in other words, inclusion.

The first step in addressing teaching and learning for students with special needs is to help them develop appropriate attitudes. There is a strong tendency on the part of all students to look for differences and to prefer to interact with peers who are like themselves. Rather than accepting and valuing diversity (here is a hint of the need for affective learning objectives), students may have a predisposition to reject and isolate peers who are different in gender, race, socioeconomic class, or ability to learn. The expectations that students in any classroom hold and act on in regard to students with special needs begins with the attitudes and behaviors of the teacher. There is no escaping the fact that how well students in a classroom value and respect diversity is in large part related to the values and behaviors of the teacher. This is true for each school as a whole. In schools where the principal and teachers share the belief that all students can learn and there is a shared responsibility for helping all students learn, all students do learn more. This is a matter of disposition and begins with the adults in the school. **Dispositions** are habits of mind or ways of acting that develop overtime (e.g., respect for others, openmindedness, perseverance). A useful set of questions for assessing how well students are doing to promote a sense of community and social acceptance is presented in Figure 12.6.

dispositions Habits of mind or ways of acting that develop over time (e.g., respect for others, perseverance, open-mindedness).

FIGURE 12.6

Questions for Determining the Extent to Which a School/Classroom Is Promoting a Sense of Community and Social Acceptance

- Are students with disabilities disproportionately teased by other students?
- Do students with disabilities seem to enjoy being in the general education classroom?
- Do students without disabilities voluntarily include students with disabilities in various activities?
- Do students without disabilities seem to value the ideas and opinions of students with disabilities? Do students with disabilities seem to value the ideas and opinions of students without disabilities?
- Do students with disabilities consider the general education classroom to be their "real class"? Do they consider the general education teacher to be one of their "real teachers"? (p. 25).

Source: D. Voltz, N. Brazil, and A. Ford, "What Matters Most in Inclusive Education: A Practical Guide for Moving Forward," *Intervention in School and Clinic, 37* (2001), pp. 23–30.

━━━━ **JOURNAL FOR REFLECTION** ━━━━

An important part of teacher success is related to how well teachers implement the learning standards of the school district. Select one standard from your state standards and develop one behavioral learning objective that would relate to the standard on a specific grade level.

LOOKING AHEAD: MODELS FOR SCHOOL CURRICULUM REFORM

During the past three decades, there has been continuing and ever-increasing frustration with U.S. schools. National, state, and local policy makers frequently use criticism of schools in their campaigns for political office. Education researchers and leading educators also regularly express concern about the quality of schools and the readiness of high school graduates to enter the workforce. In response, educators have developed a number of school reform models. **School reform** models are comprehensive schoolwide efforts to change curriculum and instruction with the expressed intent of increasing student test scores. School reforms are systematic, multiyear, involve all school staff and all subject areas, and are organized to focus all efforts on curriculum and instruction in order to increase student learning.

Each of these reform models is led by a university scholar, and the participating schools will often belong to a regional or national network of schools engaged in the same approach. Teachers receive special training and are expected to use certain instructional approaches. Each approach involves a number of schoolwide elements including acceptance of certain beliefs about students and learning, use of specified curriculum and teaching strategies, and a special vocabulary that draws attention to the core philosophy and principles of the reform model. A sampling of these reform models is described briefly in the next few paragraphs.

School Improvement

school reform The use of comprehensive programs that are intended to bring about schoolwide changes in curriculum and instruction and thereby increase learning outcomes for all students.

The most widespread approach for gradual improvement of schools is generally the school improvement process (SIP), discussed earlier. An example of an organizing framework for school improvement is presented in Figure 12.7. Note what is placed at the center of this framework, as well as how arrows are used to indicate the importance of drawing connections between goals, data about past performance, and action plans for next steps. The typical SIP requires a number of steps,

FIGURE 12.7

Hartford (Connecticut) Public Schools' Organizing Framework for School Improvement

Source: Italia Negroni, Hartford Public Schools, and Jonathan Costa, Performance Innovations. Reprinted with permission.

including principal leadership, and the establishment of a school SIP team composed of teachers, department chairs or grade-level team leaders, and parents. School improvement processes have an annual rhythm to them. During spring the SIP team will hold meetings and examine test scores and other data about how well students are performing. The SIP team produces a school improvement plan that identifies specific targets that everyone in the school will work on during the next year. The intention behind the selection of the targets is to identify specific areas, such as writing, algebraic reasoning, or SAT vocabulary, in which a schoolwide effort should be able to lead to increases in student learning. The SIP plan will be reviewed and approved by district office staff. As schools open in August, the school staff may receive related professional development, and during the entire school year the specific objectives stated in the SIP plan will be monitored. The following spring the SIP team will meet and start the school improvement process cycle all over again. Ideally, there will be data documenting gains in the target areas, and for the next year a different set of specific targets will become the focus of improvement efforts.

Accelerated Schools

SIP is a widespread generalized approach to improving schools. Most other reform models are more customized. Each reform model is based on a particular philosophy of teaching and learning. Each reform model is also based on a particular line of research, which was directed by the lead proponent of the reform model. For example, Henry Levin, formerly of Stanford University and more recently Teachers College of Columbia University, is the founder and conceptual leader for the Accelerated Schools approach to school reform. Professor Levin proposed that rather than slowing down instruction for low-achieving students, teachers should accelerate their expectations for students as well as the way they teach. For more information and print materials related to Accelerated Schools, see the website www.creativelearningpress.com.

Success for All

The leading scholar for the Success for All (SFA) school reform model is Robert Slavin (1996) of Johns Hopkins University. The foundations for SFA demonstrate another important feature of school reform models—they are based on findings from classroom research. In the case of SFA, much of the research was done in inner-city schools with children who were truly at risk of failure and in schools with track records of failure. As a result, SFA was developed around the core assumption that every child can read. Implementation of SFA begins with a structured approach to the curriculum and support for children as they learn to read. For example, the first step is the use of strategies designed to get children ready for school, including strong preschool and kindergarten reading readiness programs. Curriculum instruction and classroom management are addressed through training for all teachers.

The approach includes specific reading books, the use of reading tutors, and eight-week reading assessments. All reading teachers employ a prescribed strategy. For example, reading time begins by having the teacher read children's literature to the students and engage them in a discussion of the story. Another component is Story Telling and Retelling (STaR), which engages the students in listening, retelling, and dramatizing literature. Each of these components has been derived from earlier research studies, and SFA is regularly evaluated to assess how well it is working in terms of increasing student achievement.

Institute for Learning

The Institute for Learning (IFL), which is housed at the University of Pittsburgh, is directed by Lauren Resnik. As with SFA, the IFL approach is based on decades of research in classrooms. The IFL model is grounded in a set of principles of learning, which have been derived from the many research studies. In the IFL model, there are clear and high expectations for student work. Curriculum and instruction are tied to standards, as are evaluations. There is an expectation of academic rigor and a thinking curriculum. The curriculum focuses on a knowledge core that is to "progressively deepen" understanding of core concepts. This approach also expects students to self-manage their learning.

JOURNAL FOR REFLECTION

Think about the curriculum forms that were presented. Which of these would you personally endorse and why?

SUMMARY

WHAT IS CURRICULUM?

- Curriculum is the environment that is created by the interaction of all of the elements that support learning.
- Establishing the curriculum is a complex and dynamic process that takes place well before teachers plan for instruction.
- The various curriculum designs include subject-centered, themed, spiral, core, mastery, and problem- or standards-based approaches.
- Two other significant components of the curriculum are the cocurriculum and the hidden curriculum. For many students these are their reasons for staying in or dropping out of school.

THE MANY INFLUENCES ON CURRICULUM

- As befits our democracy, many people and groups have a say in selecting the curriculum for public schools. The most important beginning step in developing a curriculum is gaining consensus about desired learning outcomes.
- Large-scale influences on curriculum include court cases, state and federal legislation, national reports, and educational research, as well as textbook publishers. Another macro-level influence on the curriculum is the various interest groups, such as teacher and administrator organizations, political parties, and religious advocacy groups.
- The local community's unique population and characteristics also influence the design of a curriculum. Ultimately, curriculum is delivered in classrooms and the role of the teacher in implementing today's curriculum is critical.

SELECTION AND MANAGEMENT OF CURRICULUM

- In the United States, the legal responsibility for schools and for the curriculum lies with each state. In general, states establish what students are expected to learn and what instructional materials can be used.
- School districts assist in the management of curriculum by setting up textbook selection committees and hiring professional specialists whose responsibility it is to see that each curriculum area is supported and that teachers are prepared.
- On the local level, teachers must do their part by keeping informed about the state standards and the benchmarks for their students' grade-level teaching with the materials and strategies that help all students learn.

EVALUATING CURRICULA

- Curriculum evaluation is primarily based on what occurs in the classroom. Until the curriculum is implemented and student learning is assessed, direct evidence of effectiveness cannot be obtained.
- In today's high-stakes testing environment, school districts and states are focused on student performance on standardized tests as an evaluation of the curriculum.
- Two important national approaches to curriculum evaluation are the National Assessment of Educational Progress and the testing at most grade levels mandated in the No Child Left Behind Act.
- Recently, international studies in science and mathematics have been implemented.

INSTRUCTION: THE TEACHING SIDE OF CURRICULUM

- Teachers have primary responsibility for translating the standards for learning and the curriculum into minute-to-minute and day-to-day learning experiences for students—in other words, instruction.
- Following analysis of the standards and benchmarks, teachers must develop instructional objectives for each lesson and employ teaching strategies that will engage the students.
- Teaching involves the development of cognition, skills, and dispositions.

TEACHING STRATEGIES

- Historically, direct instruction was the only recognized teaching strategy. Indirect instruction strategies are those that cover a large number of teaching strategies in which students have greater responsibility for structuring tasks and managing their own learning.

- Indirect instruction strategies include guided discovery, inquiry, problem-based, and model-centered approaches.
- In addition to an increased emphasis on science education, President Obama and Vice President Biden intend to build on and extend federal education technology programs.
- Grouping students is an important component of instruction. Three common types of grouping are homogeneous, heterogeneous, and cooperative.

TEACHING STRATEGIES FOR DIVERSE STUDENTS

- Competing programs are available to students with language diversity: immersion programs, in which students are taught primarily in English and use of their native language is limited, and transitional programs, in which students' native language is used and English is gradually introduced.
- Teachers must make sure that all students, including ELLs and students with special needs, are able to participate and develop understanding.

LOOKING AHEAD: MODELS FOR SCHOOL CURRICULUM REFORM

- Many schools are implementing one of the reform models that provide teachers with additional curriculum resources and instructional strategies.
- School improvement programs are the most general type of school reform in that they propose setting target achievement levels and making changes to the curriculum based on annual evaluations.
- Another reform focuses on accelerating expectations rather than slowing down expectations for students.
- Success for All reform implements a structured approach to the curriculum and support for inner-city children to read. Curriculum instruction and classroom management are addressed through training for all teachers. The approach includes specific reading books, the use of reading tutors, and eight-week reading assessments. All reading teachers employ a prescribed strategy.
- The Institute for Learning model is grounded in a set of principles of learning, including clear and high expectations for student work, the tying of curriculum and instruction to standards, an expectation of academic rigor focused on a knowledge core that is progressively deepened, and a thinking curriculum that leads students to self-manage their own learning.

DISCUSSION QUESTIONS

1. Revisit the news story presented at the beginning of this chapter. Identify the different interest groups that spoke to the state board of education. What aspects of their views differed, and in what ways were they the same? Where do each of the views fit in Figure 12.1?

2. The curriculum comprises not only the formal statement of standards, materials, and teacher guides, but also the cocurriculum and the hidden curriculum. For a particular subject such as literacy, mathematics, or science, how have you seen these three types of curriculum affect you and other students? What roles did your teachers play with each type of curriculum?

3. Today's teachers have the major responsibility for instruction. For the most part the curriculum is set. What do you see as being keys to teachers being effective in instruction? What can you do to be sure that the instructional objectives you set for a given lesson engage all your students?

SCHOOL-BASED OBSERVATIONS

1. During practicum and other classroom observation experiences, be sure to examine the curriculum materials provided for the teacher. Which elements of the curriculum designs can you trace back to the various sources and influences on curriculum development?

2. Examine a teacher's lesson plans in order to see the connections to state and district standards, to yearly benchmarks, and to the learning objectives for the lesson(s) you are observing. What are the clear themes in terms of expectations for student learning? In what ways does the lesson facilitate students learning the stated objectives?

3. When observing classrooms, look for the students who have limited English language skills. What special

steps does the teacher take to facilitate these students' learning? What are these students doing to learn the content of the lesson as well as the English language?

4. Technology can be used in a wide variety of ways in classrooms and within lessons. In classrooms where you are observing, how is technology used? Which types of technology are supports for the teacher? Which types are used directly by the students? What types of integrated technology are used?

PORTFOLIO DEVELOPMENT

1. Find a copy of a curriculum guide for a subject that you plan to teach. As you study the guide, make notes about the topics you already know well enough. Also identify those topics where you will need to learn more before you can be an effective teacher. Make a table for these two lists that has a "Comments" column so that in the future you can make notes about what you have learned as you continue with your teacher education program.

2. At the library or when visiting a school curriculum resource room, examine the curriculum materials for a subject that you plan to teach. For one lesson, use Bloom's taxonomy as a guide and write a set of learning objectives. This task will provide you with experience and a sample product that you can use as you are planning lessons in the future.

myeducationlab For additional information about portfolios, go to the MyEducationLab for your course, select *Resources* and then *Preparing a Portfolio*.

PREPARING FOR CERTIFICATION

1. A topic in the Praxis II Principles of Learning and Teaching (PLT) test related to curriculum and instruction is "addressing curriculum goals, selecting content topics, incorporating learning theory, subject matter, curriculum development and student development and interests" and "techniques for creating effective bridges between curriculum goals and students' experiences."

In this chapter, the authors emphasized the importance of developing valued dispositions both in their students and themselves. *Dispositions are habits of mind or ways of acting that develop over time (e.g., respect for others, open-mindedness, perseverance, etc).* In most cases, teacher education programs have a set of dispositions for their teacher candidates. What are the dispositions required of you in your program? Identify the disposition that best fits your having the appropriate disposition for working with students with special needs. Explain how your demonstration of that disposition will affect your teaching.

2. Answer the following multiple-choice question, which is similar to items in Praxis and other state certification tests.

Ms. Sanchez, a second-grade teacher, after assessing the reading levels of students in her classroom, brought a group of five low-achieving students to work with her on the \ea\ sounds. She asked students to brainstorm words that contained \ea\ and recorded students' responses on the board. She then asked, "Does the \ea\ in all of these words have the same sound? How many sounds do you think \ea\ makes in English? Today you will find out how many different sounds \ea\ can make." After working with students on the concept, she showed a series of flashcards with words containing \ea\ and asked students to read the words. She recorded the number of correct responses each child made on an informal assessment sheet. This instruction is an example of

a. homogeneous grouping and direct instruction
b. heterogeneous grouping and direct instruction
c. homogeneous grouping and indirect instruction
d. heterogeneous grouping and indirect instruction

3. Answer the following short-answer question, which is similar to items in Praxis and other state certification tests.

Some states have passed legislation requiring that all schools use immersion programs rather than bilingual programs for English as a second language (ESL) students. Define the immersion and bilingual approaches to teaching students who are not proficient speakers of English. What are the arguments for and against each approach? Which position do you support, given your current level of knowledge?

After you've completed your written responses for the questions above, use the Praxis general scoring guide provided in Chapter 1 to see if you can revise your response to improve your score.

MYEDUCATIONLAB

PEARSON **myeducationlab** Now go to Topic 11: *Curriculum* and Topic 12: *Instruction* in the MyEducationLab (www.myeducationlab. com) for your course, where you can:

- Find learning outcomes for *Curriculum* and *Instruction* along with the national standards that connect to these outcomes.
- Complete *Assignments and Activities* that can help you more deeply understand the chapter content.
- Apply and practice your understanding of the core teaching skills identified in the chapter with the *Building Teaching Skills and Dispositions* learning units.

- Check your comprehension on the content covered in the chapter by going to the *Study Plan* in the *Book Specific Resources* section for your text. Here you will be able to take a chapter quiz, receive feedback on your answers, and then access *Review, Practice, and Enrichment* activities to enhance your understanding of chapter content.

WEBSITES

www.csrclearinghouse.org A one-stop site to learn about many of the school reform models, including an "ask-the-expert" link.

www.ascd.org Founded in 1943, the Association for Supervision and Curriculum Development is dedicated to advancing best practices and policies for the success of each learner. The professional organization of more than 175,000 members in 119 countries includes professional educators from all levels and subject areas: superintendents, supervisors, principals, teachers,

professors of education, and school board members. The site has a wealth of resources about curriculum improvement.

www.ncela.gwu.edu The website of the National Clearinghouse for English Language Acquisition, sponsored by the U.S. Department of Education, is a great resource for information about teaching ELLs.

www.acceleratedschools.org An informative site for learning about Accelerated Schools that includes descriptions of schools and a Q&A link.

FURTHER READING

Educational Leadership, the journal of the Association for Supervision and Curriculum Development. This periodical is designed for teachers who are interested in learning about the latest curriculum and instruction ideas, approaches, and issues.

Joyce, B., Weil, M., & Calhoun, E. (2003). *Models of teaching* (7th ed.). Boston: Allyn & Bacon. An entire book devoted to the description and analysis of different teaching strategies and how to use them in instruction.

Kelly, A. V. (2004). *The curriculum: Theory and practice* (5th ed.). Thousand Oaks, CA: Sage Publications. An informative text that addresses what is entailed in developing curriculum and the central role that teachers play. There also is an examination of the meaning of knowledge.

Smith, T. E., Polloway, E., Patton, J. R., & Dowdy, C. A. (2004). *Teaching students with special needs in inclusive settings* (4th ed.). Boston: Allyn & Bacon. This text is a useful resource for teaching students with special needs. There are chapters devoted to suggestions for each type of disability as well as chapters on teaching in elementary and secondary school classrooms.

Tanner, D., & Tanner, L. (2006). *Curriculum development: Theory into practice* (4th ed.). Upper Saddle River, NJ: Prentice Hall. Information about the historical roots of current curriculum, connections to today's reforms, along with descriptions of applications in the classroom.

chapter thirteen

BECOMING A HIGH-QUALITY TEACHER IN A CHANGING WORLD

EDUCATION
IN THE NEWS

NEWMARKET TEACHER EARNS "ED"IE AWARD

By **JOSHUA CLARK**,

Seacoastonline.com (online newsletter)

In her five years as a teacher at the Newmarket Junior/Senior High School, Venera Gattonini has endeavored to inspire and instill within her students the same passion and understanding for the industrial arts that she has.

On Saturday, she was rewarded for her work with a 2009 New Hampshire Excellence in Education Award for Program Excellence in Technology Education. In a ceremony held at the Radisson Hotel in Manchester, the 16th Annual "ED"ies, hosted by the New Hampshire Excellence in Education Award Program organization, gave out 40 awards to outstanding public schools, programs and educators.

Gattonini said she was both excited and encouraged to be honored with the award.

"It makes me feel encouraged to keep moving forward and continue to get students excited about what I feel passionately about," she said.

Chris Andriski, principal of the Newmarket Junior/Senior High School, said the school is truly excited to see one of its teachers recognized for her hard work in such a manner.

"An award like this is long overdue for the amount of time and work she puts in both inside and outside the classroom creating high-quality work that makes us all proud," Andriski said.

Through her work Gattonini teaches students in grades 6 to 12. She instructs them to understand and properly use each of the tools in the wood shop. She also introduces them to each of the disciplines within the industrial arts program, including manufacturing, construction, architecture and design.

"I want them to understand and experience each of the different facets [of industrial arts]," she said.

Gattonini has made it a point to make it clear to her students that "they have a voice they can imbue within whatever they make." This point was evidenced by her work with grades 6 to 8 students that showcased each of their aesthetic sensibilities.

Students are asked to infuse personal experiences and tastes into their work whether it be a fork, spoon, cutting board, clock or coat rack.

The goal is to design and ultimately create what Gattonini hopes will be "something completely different from what they're used to seeing."

"I want the students to know they have the ability to accomplish anything they set out to do," she said.

One of the most important aspects of the program, said Gattonini, is providing students with practical, hands-on experience that enables them to leave school with viable tools and skills that can be utilized in a number of areas.

Providing them with real-world skills aside, Gattonini said the greatest part of working with the students comes from being able to see them "light up at seeing what they've created," after confronting any fears they may have had about using the tools.

"Hopefully, the skills they learn here can be something they carry with them throughout life, whether in their career, as a hobby or being able to fix something around the house," she said.

"It truly delights me to see the reactions in students when they become confident in their abilities," she said.

QUESTIONS FOR REFLECTION

1. What are some of the qualities of Ms. Gattonini that make her a high-quality teacher?
2. Ms. Gattonini teaches industrial arts. To what extent are you aware of the dramatic changes in this program area in recent years?
3. What are some ways in which this program area can help all students succeed?
4. If you were a teacher in this school, how would you collaborate with Ms. Gattonini so that the students you share benefit?

Source: From Seacoastline.com (online newsletter), June 16, 2009.

LEARNING OUTCOMES

After reading and studying this chapter, you should be able to:

1. Describe how the information provided in the preceding chapters of this text come together to provide you with a solid foundation and understanding of the expectations for today's schools and teachers. (INTASC Standard 9: Reflective Practice: Professional Development)
2. Present an overview of the continuing national pressures to reform schools.
3. Describe key characteristics of high-quality schools. (INTASC Standard 9: Reflective Practice: Professional Development)

4. Clarify your philosophy of what high-quality teaching and high-quality schools are like. (INTASC Standard 1: Content Pedagogy, INTASC Standard 4: Multiple Instructional Strategies)
5. Present the case for why and how high-quality teachers use evidence. (INTASC Standard 8: Assessment)
6. Summarize key sources of support that you will have access to as a first-year teacher. (INTASC Standard 9: Reflective Practice: Professional Development)

DIFFERENT PERSPECTIVES FOR VIEWING EDUCATION AND TEACHING

This text has been organized around a major theme: perspectives on education in a changing world. Two very important components of this theme are (1) the differing viewpoints about education and (2) the rapidly changing environment of education. There are many different viewpoints (or perspectives) regarding education. Some viewpoints are similar and others are diametrically opposed such as idealism versus realism or local control versus direction from central governments. The world has been, is, and will continue to change rapidly. For example, as society becomes more diverse, so do schools. Different philosophical perspectives lead to different expectations for the curriculum and for the teacher's role.

This is an exciting and very important time during which to become a teacher. The United States has a three hundred plus year history of development of education policies, sixty plus years of findings from systematic research, and continuing development of innovative practices that offer a rich foundation for teachers to use in making a difference. From here forward, the most critical factor for you to keep in mind is that high-quality teachers are continually focused on doing those things that make a positive difference in student learning. Every effort is first and foremost aimed at improving the learning of all students.

Recent Trends in Attempts to Improve Education

> Chapters 2 and 3 provide rich descriptions of the historical background, events, and actions that have led to the shape of education today.

As we have seen in the past several years, as economic conditions have declined schools have suffered the consequence of lower funding. As is highlighted in Table 13.1, a number of other trends have emerged that have significant implications for schools, teachers, and students. Each of these trends has an additional implication for you and your teaching career. There will be change! Much of what teachers did well in the past will not work in the future. Much of what you see as high-quality teaching today will not be what excellent teachers will be doing a decade from now.

CONTINUING PRESSURES TO REFORM SCHOOLS

school reform Major schoolwide initiatives to change curriculum, instruction, and/or within-school organizational arrangements.

In many ways, the concerns about and expectations for education and for teachers have always been based on the contemporary problems and concerns of American society. For example, when you read Chapters 2 and 3 you would have seen how societal issues of different times led to different expectations for schools. Quite often when there has been a problem in society, business, or world politics, policy makers, business leaders, and key educators have turned to the schools as a source of the problem and/or as a resource for solving the problem. This pattern of moving from crisis to **school reform** has happened repeatedly as discussed next.

Table 13.1 • Key Trends with Implications for Schools, Teachers, and Students

Trends	Implications for Schools, Teachers, and Students
Economic recession, mortgage defaults, bankruptcies, and increased unemployment	• Reduced taxes lead to reductions in school budgets • Loss of extra-curriculum activities • Increases in class size • Fewer teachers being hired
Increased expectations for accountability	• Annual testing as required by NCLB • Increased criteria for teacher licensure • School reform • School improvement plans • Evaluation of schools based on student performance • Teacher pay based on student and school performance
Availability of research and evaluation findings	• Required use of evidence-based curriculum • Expectation that schools will use data in planning improvement efforts • Expectations that teachers will use data in planning instruction
Increasing student diversity	• Use of multicultural curriculum • Teaching limited-English-proficient students • Reducing the achievement gap • Enssuring appropriate assessment, placement, and instruction for students with special needs
Rapid technology developments	• More tools and resources to support classroom instruction • More tools for administration of budgets, schedules, and communication • Social networking

Sixty Years of Increasing Federal Pressure to Change Schools

Figure 13.1 summarizes efforts during the past sixty plus years to change schools. The combination of world events, political leadership, economic conditions, and international competition have led policy makers at the federal level to respond with priority initiatives that are intended to improve/reform/change schools. For example, following the launch of Sputnik in 1957, national concerns arose over being competitive with the Soviet Union and that the school curriculum was out of date and in some instances inaccurate. This led to a major national push in the 1960s to develop new curriculum, especially in the sciences and mathematics. In 1982 a national report stated that the "nation was at risk" due to the poor quality of education. This led to another round of initiatives to "reform" schools. In 1989 President G. H. W. Bush held the first meeting ever between the president and all state governors to examine the problems with education. This led to President Clinton's *Goals 2000* report, which set targets such as all students being ready for school by the age of five by the year 2000. Subsequently, in 2001 President G. W. Bush signed into law the No Child Left Behind Act, which mandates that all students will be performing at grade level by the 2013–14 school year.

As you can see, an important theme that has emerged during the last half century is one of increasing federal involvement in education. A name for this theme is **federalism**. As explained in Chapter 10, although the U.S. Constitution is interpreted as leaving responsibility for education to the states, in the past sixty years the federal government has used the combination of legislation and money as an incentive to move from stimulating implementation of various programs to mandating particular uniform practices that all states and schools must follow. This trend is well illustrated in Figure 13.1. For example, the original 1965 version of the Elementary and Secondary Education Act (ESEA) offered

federalism Increasing role of the national government in directing education practices and procedures at the state and/or local level.

FIGURE 13.1

Timeline of Efforts to Change Schools

	1953–61	1961–69	1969–74	1974–77	1977–81	1981–89	1989–93	1993–2001	2000s	2008–
Presidents	Eisenhower	Kennedy, Johnson	Nixon	Ford	Carter	Reagan	G. H. W. Bush	Clinton	G. W. Bush	Obama
Crisis	*Sputnik*	Civil rights	Viet Nam			Ending the Cold War			Two wars and declining economy	Stimulating economic recovery
Federal Office for Education	U.S. Office of Education	U.S. Office of Education	U.S. Office of Education, National Institute of Education	U.S. Office of Education	U.S. Department of Education	U.S. Department of Education	U.S. Department of Education	U.S. Department of Education	U.S. Department of Education	U.S. Department of Education
Policies	Build state and local capacity to educate people with disabilities	Elementary and Secondary Education Act (ESEA)	Reauthorization of ESEA linking federal aid to student achievement	Education for All Handicapped Children Act (P.L. 94-142)	Reauthorization of ESEA with federal aid dependent on rising test scores	Education summit; first meeting of president and governors	Reauthorization of ESEA, with high-stakes testing	Reauthorization of ESEA; now called No Child Left Behind (NCLB), response to intervention (RTI)	Public posting of test scores for all public schools	American Recovery and Reinvestment Act
Related Reports and Publications						*A Nation at Risk*		*Goals 2000*		
Change initiatives Based on Research		Major curriculum development projects: science and math	Effective teachers: direct instruction and classroom management			Effective schools: whole school and principals		School reform programs, school improvement, and value added	Standards, data-driven decision making, professional learning communities (PLCs)	Early childhood reform and investment in K–12, restore leadership in higher education

During the last 50 years, federal involvement in educational policy has continued to increase.

grants that states and school districts could apply for to support implementation of innovative practices and programs, rather than mandating reforms.

Reauthorization of ESEA as No Child Left Behind

The 2001 reauthorization of ESEA, called the No Child Left Behind Act (NCLB), did not simply offer grant programs that schools could apply for, but mandated various education practices that all states and public schools must do. As described in Chapter 9, NCLB prescribed that all states implement a number of actions including:

- Annual testing at most grade levels and for most subjects,
- Specifying teacher minimum qualifications
- Setting sanctions for schools and school districts that fail to reach the prescribed annual increases in the proportion of students with passing test scores.

Chapters 6, 9, and 10 provide more details about NCLB and its legal context.

REFLECTING ON THE OVERALL PATTERN OF FEDERAL REFORM STRATEGIES. One of the challenges for you as a teacher education candidate, and in your future as a teacher, is to be able to see overall patterns and themes. It is all too easy to become fully occupied with details of the moment. Each day, each class period, and each week will be filled with tasks and demands. Be sure to regularly take time to pull back and view the big picture of what is happening. Otherwise, you run the risk of not seeing professional growth in yourself and each student's growth in learning. This is an important reason for taking time to reflect, instead of act. The metaphor of not only seeing the details of a tree but also being able to see the forest is appropriate. High-quality teachers do both. They see the details of how each of their students is doing within each lesson, and they also can see patterns of student growth across lessons, days, weeks, and months.

DIFFERENT LEVERS FOR "FIXING" SCHOOLS. Two scholars have done this type of reflection in relation to the trend toward increased federalism in education. Sashkin and Egermeier (1993) developed a forest view of how federal education policy has changed over the decades. They offered three perspectives for understanding a thirty plus year history of education change. Their analysis suggests that four different levers have been used with the intention of reforming education:

- *Fix the parts:* This perspective is reflective of the massive curriculum development projects of the 1960s. (Reread parts of Chapters 11 and 12.)
- *Fix the people:* Some see teacher training and professional development as the key to improving education. (Reread parts of Chapters 6, 7, and 8.)

- *Fix the school:* Implementing one of the various whole school reform models and reorganizing schools are seen as ways to change whole schools. (Reread parts of Chapters 9 and 10.)
- *Fix the system:* We now are in a time when the whole system of education is seen as needing change. (This requires consideration of all perspectives covered in the six parts of this text.)

As a teacher you will be part of many efforts to change and improve education. To help you in being reflective, you can use these four "fixes" as a way of considering the intent of future change approaches.

A New President, A New Agenda for Education

The arrival of President Barack Obama has spurred new initiatives to improve education. Education was seen as a key lever for addressing the economic crisis. The policy response was for Congress to pass the American Recovery and Reinvestment Act in 2009. The act included heavy investments in education. For example, $5 billion was provided for early learning programs, $77 billion for reforms to strengthen K–12 education, and $8.5 billion was to be used to encourage states to make improvements in teacher effectiveness, make progress toward college and career-ready standards, and improve achievement in low-performing schools. A key rationale was to link improving the nation's economic competitiveness with every child receiving an education "that will enable them to succeed in a global economy that is predicated on knowledge and innovation" (*Issues: Education*, 2009).

Findings from Education Research and Development: Another Pressure for Changes in Teaching and Schools

Beginning with President Johnson's Great Society initiatives, education research, like education itself, also came under the direction of the federal government. Both the 1965 and 1966 ESEA statutes included major multiyear funding for education R&D. This was unprecedented for education. Results from these efforts include many studies of what teachers do, identification of school characteristics that are correlated with student test scores, the role of principals, and the importance of teacher training and professional development. In all cases the criterion for quality and effectiveness is whether there are improvements in student learning.

EFFECTIVE TEACHING AND CLASSROOM MANAGEMENT. In the 1970s researchers funded through ESEA grants identified strong correlations between student test scores and teacher behaviors. Across school years some teachers' students always scored higher, whereas the students of other teachers always scored lower (Brophy & Good, 1974). This research has resulted in the formulation of a model called the effective teaching model. The first principle in this model is for teachers to create a classroom climate that is supportive and where students feel comfortable making mistakes.

Other researchers at that time identified important characteristics of classroom management (Emmer, Evertson, & Anderson, 1980). For example, effective teachers have a middle range number of classroom rules. Fewer than five rules means the rules are too broad, and more than ten means they are too specific.

EFFECTIVE SCHOOLS. In the 1980s researchers examined the characteristics of whole schools where students had higher test scores. This research led to the formulation of an effective schools model. Characteristics of these schools included a shared vision and goals, concern about teaching and learning, purposeful teaching, high expectations, and home–school partnerships. One concern to keep in mind about both the effective teaching and effective schools models is that the criterion for effectiveness is student academic achievement. Much less is known about social and affective outcomes.

"VALUE ADDED" FOR SMALL CLASS SIZE. In the 1990s, another approach to identification of the relationships between teachers and student learning emerged out of Tennessee. In this project, the Student/Teacher Achievement Ratio (STAR) study, students entering kindergarten were assigned at random to "small classes" (thirteen to seventeen students), a "regular class" (twenty-two to twenty-six students), or a "regular class with a full-time teacher aide" within each participating school. A total of 329 classrooms in seventy-nine schools in forty-six districts participated. The study followed the students throughout the 1990s. Findings include the following: (1) Students in small classes had superior academic performance. (2) No differences were found between teacher-aide classes and regular classes. (3) Small classes were advantageous for boys and girls, there were greater benefits for minority students and students attending inner-city schools, the small-class advantages were found for all subjects, and students in small classes had higher engagement behaviors (Finn & Achilles, 1999).

In the 1990s these types of benefits became known as **value-added** benefits. In other words, making an investment in a particular change, such as small class size, resulted in gains above what would normally be observed. Through research, an improvement in outcomes from making a particular change or an additional investment was documented.

Today's corollary of value-added benefits is **evidence-based practice**. The first question that is likely to be asked whenever a new practice, an innovative approach, or change in instruction is proposed is "What evidence is there that this makes a positive difference in student outcomes?" If the initiator of the change cannot provide data related to this question, there is not much likelihood that it will be adopted.

━━━ JOURNAL FOR REFLECTION ━━━

As you can see, across the last sixty years, having evidence that documents the effectiveness of classroom practices has become increasingly important. As you become a teacher, what types of evidence will you want to be able to provide about the quality of your teaching?

EMERGING PRESSURES AND INDICATORS OF ACCOUNTABILITY REQUIRE CHANGE IN SCHOOLS

As you well know, all of the problems of society and of schools have not been solved. Also, when a particular problem has been fixed, attention quickly moves to another problem that needs attention. A key part of the solution process will be establishing specific measures of accountability. The following are examples of emerging issues, problems, and pressures that are having direct implications for change in what schools and teachers are expected to do.

Expectations for Accountability Are Increasing

Accountability is the theme that cuts across teachers, schools, and school districts. As explained in Chapters 9 and 10, much of this movement toward increased accountability began with the 1991 Kentucky Education Reform Act (KERA). The Kentucky Supreme Court had declared the state's public education system unconstitutional. The court's decision was based on the extreme disparities across the state in funding and in student performance. This was the first of now more than thirty-five states that have experienced law suits related to unequal funding of schools. The Kentucky legislature then had to come up with a constitutionally defendable state system of public education. KERA was the result.

As you know, the 2001 No Child Left Behind legislation raised the level of accountability for all levels of the education system. Since then the number of priority indicators for accountability has increased.

TEST-BASED ACCOUNTABILITY. At this time the primary accountability indicator for public education is test scores. However, instead of simply looking at the average score for the school, the focus is on disaggregation of scores by subgroups such as IEP, LEP, and free and reduced lunch. The near-term consequence is that states, districts, schools, and school staffs are consumed with analyzing standards, test prep, increasing student attendance, and making sure that all categories of students perform well on the annual state-mandated tests. It is not uncommon for two plus months of the school year to be invested in preparing students for these tests. One consequence is that all of this time on test prep becomes lost time for instruction in additional subject matter or subjects and activities that are "not on the test." Another consequence is media preoccupation with finding what is wrong with a school based on these single test scores.

RANKING OF SCHOOLS, DISTRICTS, AND STATES. One use of the test scores is to rank schools and school districts. In every state the test scores for each school are published by the state education department. If you go to the website for any state you can find this information. Most states have sophisticated statistical models that compare each school to all the schools within the state. In some states, such as California and Connecticut, the comparisons go further: Schools are compared to other schools with similar social and economic demographics. These data are now

value-added A product or process for which there is evidence of greater gain than if the approach were not used.

evidence-based practice A curriculum or instructional approach for which there is research and/or evaluation studies of its effectiveness.

being used in national rankings too. For example, *U.S. News & World Report* uses test scores and other indicators to publish "America's Best High Schools," a ranking of the top one hundred public schools and what makes them great. Another consequence of this intense focus on accountability is that all schools are now in competition with all other schools to increase their place in the rankings.

GRADUATION RATES. Test scores are not the only indicator, especially for high schools. A high school's **graduation rate** is increasingly being used to evaluate school, district, and state performance. It is alarming to see high school graduation rates of less than 50 percent, but this is the case for many schools. A related indicator that is receiving increased attention is the proportion of high school graduates that move on to some form of postsecondary education. In some districts attention is given to how many students attend which prestigious four-year colleges.

Although you might think calculating this indicator would be easy, it has turned out not to be that simple. For example, should the graduation rate be a simple count of how many students receive a diploma? If so, which diplomas should be counted? Do **certificates of attendance** count? Should the rate be a percentage of all students who entered ninth grade or just the percentage of seniors who "walk"? This statistic is problematic because many students disappear between the spring of eighth grade and the beginning of ninth grade. Maybe graduation rate should be calculated beginning with all sixth graders, but what if they move out of the district before the end of high school?

DROPOUTS. The number of **dropouts** is receiving increased attention. However, this is another indicator that is difficult to determine. The first problem is defining who is a dropout. Is it young adults who are old enough that they "should" have graduated? What about the youth who drops out before age sixteen? The U.S. Census Bureau determines a dropout to be individuals between sixteen and twenty-four years of age who are not enrolled in and have not completed high school. Within this definition 84 percent of students graduate from high school. Of the approximately 20 percent who do not complete high school on time, 63 percent return to get their diploma or earn a **general education diploma (GED)**.

Although some may think that the dropout rate is getting worse, it actually has been declining. It declined between 1972 and 2005 from 15 percent to 9 percent. However, the dropout rate is more of a factor for certain schools and students. Black (11 percent) and Hispanic (23 percent) youth drop out at higher rates than whites (6 percent). Also, less than half of first-generation immigrants graduate. The good news is that second-generation immigrants graduate at a rate of more than 80 percent (Child Trends DataBank, 2008).

Those of you who plan to teach in middle/junior high school or elementary school may think that you will be free from the accountability pressures related to graduation rates—but that is not so. If the school district or state is aware of the related research, then teachers at all levels will be held accountable for addressing the problem. Researchers have identified **risk factors** that are early indicators of the potential for certain students to become future dropouts. Elementary teachers, as well as middle school and junior high school teachers, should know and be ready to respond to these factors.

In an earlier study, Roderick (1993) followed a cohort of students in a small district in Massachusetts. She discovered two subgroups of dropouts: the "early dropouts" and the "later dropouts." The early dropouts could be predicted by low grades beginning in elementary school. But the later dropouts could not be predicted in terms of having low grades until they entered middle or high school. Roderick also identified that "transition years" were critical turning points. The transition from elementary school to middle school and the transition to high school were critical years.

In more recent research, Neild and Balfanz (2006) have identified specific risk factors that predict 50 percent of future dropouts as early as sixth grade:

* Sixth graders with poor attendance (less than 80 percent), a failing mark for classroom behavior, a failing grade in math, or a failing grade in English had only a 10 percent chance of graduating within four years of entering high school.
* Eighth graders with poor attendance or a failing grade in math or English had less than a 25 percent chance of graduating high school within eight years.
* Ninth graders who had not exhibited eighth-grade risk factors but had poor ninth-grade attendance (less than 70 percent), who earned fewer than two credits, or did not earn promotion to tenth grade had only a one in four chance of graduating within eight years.

graduation rate A calculation of the proportion of high school students who fail to graduate.

certificates of attendance Provided to students who failed to pass tests and/or other requirements necessary for receiving a diploma.

dropouts Students who have left school without completing graduation requirements.

general education diploma (GED) An alternative equivalent to receiving a high school diploma.

risk factors Characteristics that are predictive of students not succeeding.

Table 13.2 • Early Intervention Strategies That Make a Difference

- Highly personalized supports and services
- Strong relationships with adult counselors who pay a great deal of attention to students
- Systematic strategies to monitor and address "alterable" risk factors
- Formal coaching in specific problem-solving strategies
- Substantial communication with and support for parents
- Connections between schools, families, and community services, while managing to keep the primary focus on educational progress

Source: As summarized in Jerald, C. (2007). *Keeping kids in school: What research says about preventing dropouts.* Alexandria. VA: The Center for Public Education.

The findings from these studies make it clear that all teachers, elementary and secondary, have a major responsibility for identifying students who are at risk of not graduating high school and for doing something about it.

WHAT TEACHERS CAN DO TO PREVENT DROPOUTS. In the past many teachers did not feel that they had any responsibility for, or could make any difference in, the potential of students to drop out sometime in the future. This view is no longer acceptable. If academic difficulties and disengagement are predictors of the probability for students to drop out, then these should be key target areas for **early interventions**. Table 13.2 summarizes steps that can be taken to help prevent students from dropping out. Devising instructional strategies that are designed to help students catch up can help. Intensive counseling with support for parents also has been found to be important. Creating smaller schools within large schools can help students feel that they belong. These strategies cannot be accomplished by a single teacher in isolation. Still, a key responsibility for you as a teacher is to create lessons and to teach in ways that are interesting, engaging, and challenging to all of your current students.

HOW TO RECOGNIZE A HIGH-QUALITY SCHOOL

One important outcome of the accountability movement and the pressures to reform schools is that many indicators are now available that can be used to judge the quality of schools. High-quality schools are different in a number of identifiable ways. The characteristics presented next have been selected because knowing about them is important to your success as a teacher education candidate. Chances are good that the schools where you have clinical experiences and do your student teaching will be attending to each of these indicators. When the time comes for you to seek a teaching position, these indicators will be good predictors of what being a teacher in the school would be like.

Data-Driven Decision Making

High-quality schools use data continually, especially in relation to student achievement. Data are used to make instructional decisions, as well as budgetary ones. These schools do not rely heavily on the annual federal- and state-mandated testing because they do not delay making decisions until these results are made available. Instead, they continually study, refer to, and use three levels or *tiers* of data:

- *Tier 1:* standardized tests typically administered once a year by the state and/or the district.
- *Tier 2:* interim assessments that may have been developed for district-wide use or developed specifically by a school. These assessments are administered one to four times a year. They are both diagnostic and predictive. They are designed to measure the same learning outcomes as the Tier 1 tests and are scored quickly. The results are used as an early predictor of how well students will do on the Tier 1 tests. The scores from Tier 2 assessments are also diagnostic. Areas where students do not do as well can then be targeted for further instruction.
- *Tier 3:* teacher-developed measures, teacher judgment, and examples of student work. This information is used by the teacher to plan instruction daily and weekly. It also can be of use to other teachers who work with a particular student and for grade-level and department meetings.

In combination, these three tiers of evidence provide each teacher, each grade level or department, and the whole school with information to guide the next steps in instruction. Obviously, these data

early interventions Actions that are taken early to reduce the possibility of students dropping out of school or not graduating on time.

School personnel, including the principal and teachers, meet regularly to review how well all students are succeeding, using teacher-developed data, teacher judgment, and examples of student work.

also provide indicators of how well the school is doing in terms of having all students succeed. Another indicator of the quality of a school is how it uses data in the development and implementation of its school improvement plan and process.

School Improvement Process

An important annual effort for all schools is a **school improvement process (SIP)**. The process begins with the school reviewing data and developing a set of **action steps** that address areas of student learning that are deficient. The data, the action steps, and a timeline for implementation are placed in a major document, the **school improvement plan**. In some schools principals write the plan and teachers may not even see it. In high-quality schools a committee of teachers and administrators will lead the SIP work and at times all staff will be engaged with studying data and proposing action steps. In high-quality schools the plan will not be left on a shelf; it will be a guide for what happens across the school year, including staff development and how school resources will be allocated.

Two other important indicators of a high-quality school are the relationships and interactions among the adults, as discussed next.

Professional Learning Communities

High-quality schools have a special organizational culture that is known as a **professional learning community (PLC)**. When you visit a PLC school you will see teachers working collaboratively. They visit each other's classrooms and openly share plans, resources, and ideas. They also have a shared vision for the school and what teaching and learning should be like. There is mutual respect, high levels of trust, and regular introduction of innovative solutions to problems. An additional critical feature is that of **collegial learning**. In a PLC school there is an expectation that the adults are continually learning along with the students (Hord, 2004). A caution to note with this indicator of a high-quality school is that a PLC is not something that happens at a scheduled time: "We have PLC every Friday at 9:30." Rather, a true PLC is an indicator of the organizational culture of the school: "This is how things are done around here."

Parent and Community Involvement

Unfortunately, some schools seem to structure rules and activities in ways that limit parent involvement. Visits to classrooms are restricted, parent conferences are scheduled at times when most parents are still at work, and school office staff are not welcoming. In contrast to this, high-quality school staff members understand the importance of parent involvement.

High-quality schools use many strategies to involve parents in addition to the traditional PTA and parent volunteer programs. Strategies include sending frequent newsletters, using voice mail calling to homes to inform parents about student homework assignments, and holding early morning activities such as "Donuts with Dads" and "Muffins with Moms." They hold parent meetings on different nights for different languages and sponsor school fairs and student performances specifically designed to draw in parents and community members.

Parent involvement is particularly important and challenging to achieve with immigrant families, minorities, and families with cultural differences. Parent and community involvement is also challenging in communities with a high percentage of poor families and where many of the adults have limited or no English. To address these factors, many schools employ a parent/community liaison to visit parents and facilitate communications.

Some communities have organizers who help develop parent advocacy groups. For example, in Los Angeles, a grassroots parent advocacy group called Parent U-Turn conducts surveys of parents and youth and then develops proposals for urban school reforms. As described in this

PEARSON
myeducationlab

Go to the *Assignments and Activities* section of Topic 14: *Professional Development* in the MyEducationLab for your course and complete the activity titled *Peer Observation and Feedback*.

school improvement process (SIP) The annual activities that school staff members engage in to identify and resolve shortcomings in student learning.

action steps The procedures such as teacher training and use of new assessments that are implemented to address the deficiencies identified in the school improvement plan.

school improvement plan The document produced each year that summarizes the data analyses and specifies the actions steps that will be taken.

professional learning community (PLC) A school organization culture that emphasizes collaboration and all members continuing to learn.

collegial learning Teachers learning from other teachers.

In addition to the traditional PTA and parent volunteer programs, high-quality schools use many strategies to involve parents in school life.

chapter's Reflect on Diversity feature, finding better ways to involve parents in schooling is not just the school administrators' jobs, it is a teacher responsibility too.

High-Quality Schools Have Leaders That Make a Difference for Teachers and Students

Another important characteristic of high-quality schools is leadership. Regardless of whether the students come from poor families or middle class families, and whatever the mix of ethnic groups, how the principal and teachers lead the school makes a difference. In this section some of the important characteristics of leadership in high-quality schools are described.

PEARSON
myeducationlab

Go to the the *Assignments and Activities* section of Topic 14: *Professional Development* in the MyEducationLab for your course and complete the activity titled *Working with Parents and the Community*.

REFLECTonDIVERSITY   Parent–Teacher Conference

As the holiday season approaches, it is time for Bill to schedule his second round of parent–teacher conferences. The Red Rock school district mandates that teachers schedule a conference at the end of each report marking term. Bill's students are diverse with the majority being Latino, and the parents are recent immigrants many of whom cannot speak English. Before the first round of conferences, he had asked other teachers how they conducted parent–teacher conferences with parents who did not speak English. Most teachers had used their students who were proficient in English to serve as translators.

Bill had done this and found that the parents were not very talkative. This was discouraging since he believed that developing parent support for education was a key to preventing so many of these kids from dropping out. His first thought was that both he and the parents had selfconcerns (see Table 13.7). He sure knew that he was uncertain about how the conferences would go. It also made sense that parents would have self concerns about meeting with this teacher and hearing evaluations of their child. Also, in checking his class notes from his Foundations of Education class he remembered reading that for Latino parents placing children in a position of equal status can upset the traditional family

relationships. So this time Bill decided to form small-group parent conferences for Latino parents who could not speak English. He scheduled parents based on their children's academic progress and hoped that this way there would be more parent talk and dialogue. He planned to start each conference by having the students walk their parents around the classroom and show their individual work.

Questions for Reflection
1. Do you think having small-group parent conferences will work?
2. In what ways is this approach culturally sensitive?
3. How well do you think the idea of Self concerns, which was described in this chapter, fits this situation for Bill? For the parents?
4. What problems/challenges would you anticipate in having several sets of parents and students meeting at the same time?
5. What do you think Bill should do about issues of student confidentiality?

PEARSON
myeducationlab   To respond to these questions online, go to the *Book Specific Resources* section, select your text in the MyEducationLab for your course and then select *Reflect on Diversity* for Chapter 13.

Table 13.3 • Three Principal Facilitator Styles

INITIATORS: Have clear and strongly held images for what the school should be like. They focus on what will be best for students, have a passion for the school, and support their teachers. They use data, expect teachers to be involved beyond their classrooms, and champion the school to parents, the community, and the district.
MANAGERS: Are very knowledgeable about policies, rules, and procedures. They also are skilled at obtaining and managing resources including dollars and materials. They expect teachers to follow the procedures, get lesson plans and reports in on time, and maintain a focus on instruction.
RESPONDERS: Respect their teachers and assume that they know what needs to be done. They trust teachers and others to take the lead and don't believe principals need to monitor each classroom closely. They are friendly and always ready to chat about what is happening with teachers beyond their classrooms.

Note: For more information about principals, leadership, and school change, see Hall & Hord, 2011.

myeducationlab

Go to the *Assignments and Activities* section of Topic 1: *The Teaching Profession* in the My EducationLab for your course and complete the activity titled *Teachers as Professionals: Two Principals' Views.*

VISIONARY AND SUPPORTIVE PRINCIPAL LEADERSHIP. Effective schools have principals that have a vision for what the school should be like and what will make a difference in student success. They also have high expectations for their teachers. However, not all principals are like this. Recent research can be used to illustrate some of the differences in principals and their leadership. For example, one set of researchers has identified three different leadership styles of principals. They are called *initiators, managers,* and *responders* (Hall & Hord, 2011). See Table 13.3 for a brief description of each style. If you were to interview for a teaching position with each of these types of principals, they would ask you some very different questions. Study the descriptions in Table 13.3 and then think about how you would respond to their interview questions.

Initiator-Style Principal Interview Question: What evidence do you have that you can make a difference in student learning?

You should be ready to pull from your portfolio examples of lessons you have taught and the assessments you used with the lessons. You should also be ready to explain what went well, what you would do next for any students who did not do well, and how you would do the lesson differently next time.

Manager-Style Principal Interview Question: Tell me about how you would organize your classroom and schedule for a typical day.

Be ready to draw from your portfolio—which should be well organized with tabs and nothing falling out—examples of schedules you have used in your field experiences. If you have a PDA or other form of technology be ready to show how you have used this as an organizer. Be ready to show a well-organized and clearly written plan.

Responder-Style Principal Interview Question: We have a wonderful school. I want everyone to enjoy working here. Now tell me, how would you fit in?

Yes, you will have to take more of a lead in this interview. Be ready to describe how you are prepared to teach and that you can manage your classroom well. Do not count on a lot of direct supervision or support; you will be more on your own. You also will want to indicate that you are social and friendly in your contact with colleagues.

JOURNAL FOR REFLECTION

How do the descriptions of three principal styles compare with your experience? When you were a student and now in your field experiences which style of principal have you found to be most effective? What did the more effective principals do, that the less effective did not do?

PRINCIPAL LEADERSHIP IS CORRELATED WITH TEACHER SUCCESS IN CHANGE AND STUDENT TEST SCORES. In addition to identifying these different principal styles, researchers also have found that teachers have more success with change when their principal leads with the initiator or manager

Table 13.4 • Checklist of Characteristics of a High-Quality School

High-Quality Characteristics	Indicators of High-Quality School Characteristics	Question to Think About or Observation to Make
Data-Driven Decision Making	• Data about student learning are readily available. • Data are used by teachers, the principal, and other leaders. • Instructional decisions are data based. • Professional development strategies are data based.	• What types of data (Tier 1, 2, or 3) do teachers talk about? • What data are analyzed within the school improvement plan? • How easy is it for teachers to access evidence of student learning? • How often does the principal refer to data?
Visionary Leadership	• The principal has a strongly held vision for the school. • The learning needs of students come first. • The principal supports teachers. • The principal is visible in classrooms.	• What's most important to the principal? • What leadership style does the principal use? • What leadership styles do the assistant principal(s), team leaders, and department chairs use? • Do the teachers talk with the principal about instruction?
Professional Learning Community	• Teachers are collegial. • Teachers share ideas about teaching. • Teachers own all of the students in the school (not just those in their classroom). • Adults are also expected to be learners.	• What do teachers talk about in the staff lounge? • Are opportunities to attend workshops valued? • Do teachers observe in other teachers' classrooms? • Do teachers discuss what they see in other teachers' classrooms?
Parent and Community Involvement	• Parents are participating members of the school community. • One or more businesses support the school.	• Are parents regularly in classrooms? • Are parents involved in a variety of activities? • Does the school have one or more business partners?
Continuous Refinement and Testing of New Approaches	• Evidenced-based curricula are used. • Emerging new approaches are tested.	• Are there changes in curriculum and instruction approaches each year? • Are staff informed about current research and best practices?

style. Also, students have higher test scores in schools with principals who have a vision for what teaching and learning should be like (initiators) and those who are well organized (managers). A complicating factor for teachers is that initiator-style principals press teachers, students, and parents to do more and to work together, whereas responder-style principals leave teachers alone to do the teaching in their classrooms (Hall, Negroni, & George, 2008). You will discover that each principal you work with will make a major difference in the quality of the school and your quality as a teacher.

Checking a School for Indicators of High Quality

Any given school is likely to have some of the characteristics of a high-quality school, but probably not all. Table 13.4 is a sample checklist that could be used to assess the extent to which some of these characteristics are found in a school. This checklist is not intended to be used to evaluate a school. Instead the checklist is provided as one way to summarize some of the characteristics of a high-quality school.

HIGH-QUALITY TEACHERS PROVIDE EVIDENCE OF STUDENT LEARNING

In the end, the goals of having all students learning and graduating and having schools of high quality require that you become a high-quality teacher. As described in this chapter's Education in the News feature about Venera Gattonini, high-quality teachers like to teach and they do everything possible to have all their students learn and succeed. These factors will increasingly be the basis for judging your quality as a teacher.

Table 13.5 • Emerson Elliott's Six Steps to Student Learning–Centered Teaching

- *Judges prior learning:* Undertakes an assessment to understand the prior P–12 student learning in the area he or she will teach.
- *Plans instruction:* Plans an appropriate sequence of instruction to advance P–12 student learning, based on the prior assessment.
- *Teaches:* Teaches P–12 students to acquire and use content knowledge in meaningful ways, engaging those who bring differing background knowledge and learning needs, and providing students with opportunities to demonstrate the use of critical and creative thinking skills.
- *Assesses:* Conducts a concluding objective test or alternative assessment(s).
- *Analyzes:* Analyzes the results of the concluding assessment(s), documenting the student learning that occurred at individual and group levels, including explanations of results from students who learned more or less than expected, and results from each subgroup of students.
- *Reflects:* Reflects on changes in teaching that could improve results.

Source: Elliott, E. (2005). *Student learning in NCATE accreditation.* Washington, DC: National Council for the Accreditation of Teacher Education.

What Evidence Will You Have to Show You Are a High-Quality Teacher?

As your career unfolds a key term for documenting accountability will be *evidence-based practice.* Your teaching and the quality of your school will be judged based on data about student performance. In the past schools were most likely to be judged in terms of the quality of facilities and the quantity of resources such as the number of books and computers. Now schools and teachers are evaluated in terms of test scores and other indicators of student success such as graduation rates. This is what evidence-based practice is about: collecting and compiling data and providing documentation related to how well students are performing. Schools as a whole must do this, and so must individual teachers. Be sure to collect evidence of how well students have performed and what they have learned as a part of every lesson you teach.

High-Quality Teachers Use Student Learning–Centered Instruction

High-quality teachers plan their lessons, manage instruction, and assess student progress. A useful general model for instruction is presented in Table 13.5. This model can be applied when you are asked to develop a lesson plan, to teach a small group, or to teach a whole class. Each of the components is well established as an important part of best practice.

High-Quality Teachers Are Reflective and Have a Stated Educational Philosophy about Teaching and Learning

Throughout this text one of the emphases has been on your becoming reflective. Reflection is an important characteristic of high-quality teachers. They reflect *before* teaching on what each student now knows, what they need to learn next, and what can be done in terms of instruction. High-quality teachers also are reflective *during* the act of teaching. They are thinking about how the lesson is going, continually checking for student understanding, and refining what they will do next. Of course, teachers are also reflective *after* instruction. They examine assessments for each student and

High-quality teachers plan their lessons, manage instruction, and assess student progress.

Table 13.6 • Refining Your Philosophy of Education Statement

From time to time it is important for teachers to take a half hour or so to revisit their personal framework or philosophy of education. One useful way to approach this activity is to use the parts and chapters of this textbook as a guide. Each chapter has offered a different perspective, or lens, for viewing education. Depending on your personal assumptions and beliefs, you will have a preference for some of these perspectives. If there is a perspective that you do not like, or feel less comfortable with, rather than rejecting it you probably should consider it to be a clue about a topic(s) for which you need to do more study and reflection.

As you engage in reflecting on and refining your philosophy of education statement, consider the following questions:

1. What elements of schools and teaching from the past do you see as being important to continue using today? (Review Part II, Historical Foundations of Education.)

2. Which philosophy do you think best matches your approach to teaching? (Review Part III, Philosophical Foundations of Education.)

3. What role do you think schools should have in a diverse society? (Review Part IV, Sociological Foundations of Education.)

4. Don't forget that there are legal, financial, and organizational aspects of schools. How do these perspectives play out in your philosophy? (Review Part V, Governance, Organization, and Legal Foundations of Education.)

5. What are your views of the standards movement, curriculum, and the current focus on student learning? (Review Part VI, Curricular Foundations of Education.)

6. Given your views, what does it mean for you to be an ethical teacher?

think through how the lesson unfolded, what they should do next, and what they will do the next time they teach that lesson.

All of this reflection is based on a personal framework or philosophy of education. As your study of the foundations of education comes to a close, you should take a half hour to update your philosophy statement. Revisit Chapter 5 and reflect on how far you have come in your thinking about what high-quality teaching entails. This is important to do for several reasons. For instance, you will be asked about what's important to you as a teacher when you interview for that first teaching position. Key topics and questions for you to think about in refining your statement are provided in Table 13.6.

Chapter 5 provides guidance for developing an educational philosophy and rich examples of elements to be considered.

Ethics Is an Important Component of a High-Quality Teacher's Philosophy

Not only should you continue to reflect on which philosophies will ground your point of view as a teacher, you also should be considering what is ethical. Much of what teachers should, can, and cannot do is specified by law. Statutes, case law, policies, and procedure manuals all specify what teachers can and cannot do. Ethics, however, is a more principled view of what it means to be a high-quality teacher. As you continue to reflect on your philosophy, be sure to consider the ethical component. One statement of a code of ethics for education professionals that has stood the test of time is that of the National Education Association (see Figure 13.2). In studying this statement, you will see several core principles that truly are indicative that teaching is a profession. Note, for example, that "Commitment to the Student" comes first.

Review Chapter 10 as a reminder of how the law affects the ethics of teachers.

High-Quality Teachers Have Three Types of Knowledge

Teacher education researchers have identified three domains of professional knowledge and skill that expert teachers possess: *content knowledge, pedagogical knowledge,* and *pedagogical content knowledge* (Berliner, 2001). Each is important and each is essential. You might want to think about your current level of understanding within each of these domains. Becoming a high-quality teacher requires continuing to develop knowledge and skill within each of these domains.

CONTENT KNOWLEDGE: HOW WELL DO YOU KNOW THE SUBJECT(S) YOU WILL TEACH? Needing to have knowledge about and an understanding of the subject one teaches is obvious, but difficult to achieve. This is especially challenging for elementary school teachers who may have to teach

FIGURE 13.2

NEA Code of Ethics

Preamble

The educator, believing in the worth and dignity of each human being, recognizes the supreme importance of the pursuit of truth, devotion to excellence, and the nurture of the democratic principles. Essential to these goals is the protection of freedom to learn and to teach and the guarantee of equal educational opportunity for all. The educator accepts the responsibility to adhere to the highest ethical standards.

The educator recognizes the magnitude of the responsibility inherent in the teaching process. The desire for the respect and confidence of one's colleagues, of students, of parents, and of the members of the community provides the incentive to attain and maintain the highest possible degree of ethical conduct. The Code of Ethics of the Education Profession indicates the aspiration of all educators and provides standards by which to judge conduct.

The remedies specified by the NEA and/or its affiliates for the violation of any provision of this Code shall be exclusive and no such provision shall be enforceable in any form other than the one specifically designated by the NEA or its affiliates.

PRINCIPLE I

Commitment to the Student

The educator strives to help each student realize his or her potential as a worthy and effective member of society. The educator therefore works to stimulate the spirit of inquiry, the acquisition of knowledge and understanding, and the thoughtful formulation of worthy goals.

In fulfillment of the obligation to the student, the educator—

1. Shall not unreasonably restrain the student from independent action in the pursuit of learning.
2. Shall not unreasonably deny the student's access to varying points of view.
3. Shall not deliberately suppress or distort subject matter relevant to the student's progress.
4. Shall make reasonable effort to protect the student from conditions harmful to learning or to health and safety.
5. Shall not intentionally expose the student to embarrassment or disparagement.
6. Shall not on the basis of race, color, creed, sex, national origin, marital status, political or religious beliefs, family, social or cultural background, or sexual orientation, unfairly—
   a. Exclude any student from participation in any program
   b. Deny benefits to any student
   c. Grant any advantage to any student
7. Shall not use professional relationships with students for private advantage.
8. Shall not disclose information about students obtained in the course of professional service unless disclosure serves a compelling professional purpose or is required by law.

PRINCIPLE II

Commitment to the Profession

The education profession is vested by the public with a trust and responsibility requiring the highest ideals of professional service.

In the belief that the quality of the services of the education profession directly influences the nation and its citizens, the educator shall exert every effort to raise professional standards, to promote a climate that encourages the exercise of professional judgment, to achieve conditions that attract persons worthy of the trust to careers in education, and to assist in preventing the practice of the profession by unqualified persons.

In fulfillment of the obligation to the profession, the educator—

1. Shall not in an application for a professional position deliberately make a false statement or fail to disclose a material fact related to competency and qualifications.
2. Shall not misrepresent his/her professional qualifications.
3. Shall not assist any entry into the profession of a person known to be unqualified in respect to character, education, or other relevant attribute.
4. Shall not knowingly make a false statement concerning the qualifications of a candidate for a professional position.
5. Shall not assist a noneducator in the unauthorized practice of teaching.
6. Shall not disclose information about colleagues obtained in the course of professional service unless disclosure serves a compelling professional purpose or is required by law.
7. Shall not knowingly make false or malicious statements about a colleague.
8. Shall not accept any gratuity, gift, or favor that might impair or appear to influence professional decisions or action.

Adopted by the NEA 1975 Representative Assembly

Source: *NEA Code of Ethics.* (1975). Retrieved July 29, 2009 from www.nea.org/home/30442.htm.

as many as six different subjects. Having sufficient content knowledge also is a challenge for secondary school teachers because they need depth of understanding. At the secondary school level, if teachers do not have in-depth knowledge about a subject, they might teach inaccuracies and misconceptions.

PEDAGOGICAL KNOWLEDGE: HOW MUCH DO YOU KNOW ABOUT HOW STUDENTS LEARN AND DIFFERENT TEACHING STRATEGIES? Knowing about curriculum, instruction, and multiple ways to assess learning and understanding how students learn are other domains that expert teachers have mastered. Nearly all of the opportunities to learn in these areas will be found in the professional education courses that are part of your teacher education program. Also important within this domain is developing the actual skill of teaching, which is why clinical, field, and student teaching experiences are so important. How often have you heard a student say, "He really knows his subject, but he can't teach it so that I can understand it"?

PEDAGOGICAL CONTENT KNOWLEDGE: ARE YOU ABLE TO CONNECT WHAT YOU ARE TEACHING WITH THE EXPERIENCES AND BACKGROUND THAT YOUR STUDENTS BRING TO EACH LESSON? This domain of professional knowledge has a curious name, which also can be confusing. However, this domain is probably the most important for you to develop. This is where the teacher's content knowledge and pedagogical knowledge intersect with real students. This set of knowledge relationships is pictured in Figure 13.3. Students bring their personal level of understanding of the subject to the lesson. They also arrive in your classroom with a rich array of past experiences, cultural and social backgrounds, and attitudes toward learning.

Teachers with pedagogical content knowledge understand the knowledge that their students bring to the lesson and know how to build on that uniqueness. High-quality teachers also can anticipate the misconceptions that their students are likely to have when learning something new. These teachers are able to choose examples and metaphors that their students will understand. For example, using snow as an example with students who have always lived in the desert may not make the most sense. This is why the authors of this text have placed so much emphasis on the importance of your developing an understanding of the cultural and social, as well as academic, backgrounds of your students. With this knowledge, you can be much more successful in helping them to learn.

FIGURE 13.3

Intersection of Three Domains of Expert Teacher Knowledge

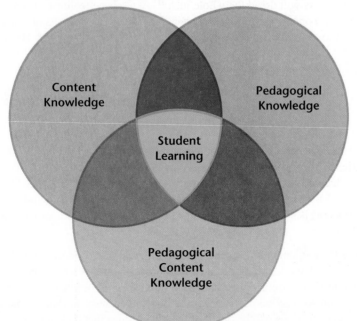

Teachers must work together to implement the changes that will always be a part of their careers.

BECOMING A HIGH-QUALITY TEACHER REQUIRES CHANGE

Given all of the pressures, expectations, and needs and the many innovations that teachers are expected to implement means that change will be a regular part of your career. Frequently, teachers have just become comfortable with an approach when they are asked to start doing something differently. There is no escaping the fact that we are living in a time of change. As ready as you may be to accept the new, each innovation brings with it challenges and uncertainties. Will the new way really work better? Will you be able to make the change successfully? These and other questions face teachers every time something new is proposed.

Teachers Have Different Kinds of Concerns about Change

As you have read through this chapter you can see that teachers are being asked to make many changes. Some of these will make sense to you and reinforce things you already are doing. Some will seem foreign and will cause you concern. Some will likely be very challenging to understand and to use in your classroom. And, for many you will have no alternative but to implement the new way. You will have mixed feelings and perceptions about each of these change efforts.

Think some more about Venera Gattonini, the teacher in this chapter's Education in the News feature. Clearly, Ms. Gattonini loves teaching. She is doing all that she can think of to provide her students with "practical, hands-on experiences." She wants her students to leave school with skills they can use for the rest of their lives. She is delighted when her students gain confidence. She also is pressing them to do "something completely different." It appears that Ms. Gattonini is excited about change and thinking mainly about what will benefit her students.

There is a personal side to change that is reflected in the different perceptions and feelings people have. Teachers, their students, principals—in fact, everyone—has mixed feelings about their experiences with change. There are perceptions about what the change will mean. Some will be excited, while others will dread the whole idea. Having these feelings, attitudes, and perceptions is a natural component of the change process. In fact, forty plus years of research have been conducted related to understanding people's **concerns** about change (Hall & Hord, 2011).

What Are Your Concerns about Becoming a Teacher?

To illustrate what researchers have learned, let's think about your concerns right now. Before reading any further, write a paragraph in Figure 13.4 about your concerns.

Use the following subsections and Table 13.7 to assess what you have written.

DIFFERENT CONCERNS AS A CHANGE PROCESS UNFOLDS. People's concerns about change vary as they experience the process. Researchers have identified four phases or groupings of concerns: Unconcerned, Self, Task, and Impact concerns (Hall & Hord, 2011). The basic description for each of these concerns is presented in Table 13.7. Keep in mind that each of these categories of concerns is not good or bad. Instead they are characteristic of what all of us feel as we experience change.

Concerns before the Beginning of a Change Process. In addition to identifying the four types of concerns, researchers have found that as a change process unfolds some concerns will be most intense at different times. Before the change initiative begins, teachers are most likely to be *Unconcerned*. "I am so busy with _____ that I don't even want to think about it right now." Thoughts and preoccupations will be on all of the other things that they are doing already.

concerns The composite of mental thoughts, attitudes, worries, and enthusiasms about teaching or an innovation.

FIGURE 13.4

What Are Your Concerns About Becoming a Teacher?

> **Open-Ended Concerns Statement about Becoming a teacher?**
>
> When you think about becoming a teacher, what are your concerns? Do not think about the concerns of others, but about what concerns you have right now. Please be frank and write your response using complete sentences (not a list of topics).

Concerns at the Beginning of a Change Process. As the time to actually learn about and begin using the innovation gets closer, *Self* concerns become most intense. Questions about one's ability to be successful with the new approach will be raised: "I don't know if I can do this." Concerns may also arise about whether there will be support from supervisors to do things the new way. "What if my principal doesn't agree?" This is a time of high uncertainty during the change process.

Concerns as Implementation of the Change Gets Under Way. When implementation of the innovation begins, *Task* concerns become very intense. "It is taking me hours to prepare for the next day, and still everything doesn't go smoothly." Concerns about time, logistics, and organizing materials can go on for months or even several years if the change is big and complex.

Concerns When Use of the Innovation Is Mastered. Ultimately, if the change process unfolds successfully and principal support for it is strong, then teachers' Self and Task concerns will be resolved, and *Impact* concerns will become the most intense. "By collaborating and working together we are seeing big improvements in what our students are learning." Impact concerns are the ideal end for a change process. However, to successfully complete a change process and experience all four areas of concern normally takes three to five years.

REFLECTING ON YOUR CONCERNS. Now, let's check back on what you wrote in response to the question in Figure 13.4. Read what you wrote and compare it to each of the four categories of concerns using Table 13.7 as a scoring guide. Which phase(s) of concern is most intense for you at this time? Are you Unconcerned about becoming a teacher and more concerned about something else? ("I have to get a different roommate.") Do you have more intense Self concerns? ("When I am student teaching, I hope I will know enough and can control the students.") What about Task concerns? ("I have so much to do just to finish this course/semester.")

What about Impact concerns? Did you write down anything related to student success? ("I want each of my students to learn all they can.") Or, did you write anything about what you want to do to improve your effectiveness as a teacher? ("I think I will take that other methods course because it will help me work with ELL students.")

Table 13.7 • Four Types of Concerns That Teachers Can Have as They Experience Change

IMPACT: The most intense focus is on how use of the change/innovation is affecting student learning. Thoughts are on how to be sure all students are "getting it," what can be done to further improve student learning, and possibly collaborating with one or more colleagues so that together the outcomes are even better.

TASK: Time, scheduling, organizing tasks and materials, fitting everything into the available time are of utmost concern. Attention related to implementing the innovation/change is heavily focused on time, logistics, and coordination of tasks.

SELF: Uncertainty about what is being demanded, whether you can do it well, and whether you will be supported are key concerns. There is a need to have more information about the change, what it entails, and how it will work.

UNCONCERNED: The teacher is concerned about things other than the current innovation. This does not mean that the teacher is opposed to the change. However, for some reason, other efforts, some other initiative, or perhaps something outside of school is of more concern.

Note: For more information about people's concerns regarding change, see Hall & Hord, 2011.

myeducationlab

Go to the *Assignments and Activities* section of Topic 1: *The Teaching Profession* in the MyEducationLab for your course and complete the activity titled *The Multiple Roles of Teachers*.

It is likely that your Impact concerns are much lower in intensity at this time. It would not be unusual for you, at this point in your teacher education program, to not have written anything related to student learning. Impact concerns do not normally become intense until the end of student teaching and after several years of teaching full time. So, don't be worried about not having intense Impact concerns at this time. You are very early in the change process of becoming a teacher. Keep in mind that having intense Impact concerns is a positive indicator that you are becoming a high-quality teacher. High-quality teachers are first and foremost concerned about their students learning rather than themselves or the tasks of teaching.

GLOBAL PERSPECTIVES

Teacher Induction Programs Have a Long History in Australia

Concern about providing formal programs of support for beginning teachers has a long history in Australia. In fact the term *induction* was used in the United Kingdom and Australia long before it became a common term in the United States. There also is a history of research on teacher induction in Australia. In the 1970s Professor Richard Tisher led a research team that conducted the first major study of the experiences of beginning teachers. The researchers found that 50 percent of beginning teachers received no help with their teaching in the first week (Tisher, Fyfield, & Taylor, 1978). The researchers expressed contempt for the "cavalier treatment of new teachers." Today there are comprehensive induction programs for all teachers in all parts of Australia. If you would like to know more about their programs, as well as find useful information for beginning teachers, check out this website: www.aussieeducator.org .au/teacher_beginning.html.

Questions for Reflection
1. Do you think it would be possible to discover some useful ideas for you as a beginning teacher based on what is done in Australia? Why or why not?
2. As you think ahead to your first week of teaching, what kind of help would you like to have from a mentor or colleague?
3. What kind of support would you like to have from your principal?

myeducationlab

Go to the *Assignments and Activities* section of Topic 14: *Professional Development* in the MyEducationLab for your course and complete the activity titled *Teaching at Different Grade Levels*.

SUPPORTIVE RESOURCES FOR YOUR FIRST YEAR

You are now near the end of a semester in which you have probably taken your first professional education course(s). Becoming a high-quality teacher is up to you. It will take time, study, and practice to transition from novice to expert. Still, as you know from your own experiences in schools, high-quality teachers do exist. They know more and teach in different ways than do those who are less effective. Fortunately, many resources and supports are available to help you succeed. A sampling of these resources is given next. (The Global Perspectives feature describes what has been done in Australia to better support beginning teachers.)

Induction of New Teachers

During the past twenty years, the thinking about and approaches to **induction** of beginning teachers have changed dramatically. In earlier times little or no accommodations were made for new teachers. They were assigned to a classroom, given a key, and expected to be up and functioning just as well as the veteran teachers. Now, most school districts offer a number of programs and resources to support novice teachers.

In the past, little accommodation was made for new teachers. Today, most school districts offer a number of programs and resources to support novice teachers.

NEW EMPLOYEE WORKSHOPS. In early August, after you have signed your contract, you and the other newly hired teachers will be invited to a new employee workshop. These sessions are usually conducted by the district's Human Resource Department. Typically these sessions will not address your concerns about teaching students or organizing your classroom. Instead, likely topics will include your rights and responsibilities as an employee of the district, how to sign up for health insurance, sick leave policies, how you get paid, and reminders about legal protections and responsibilities.

NEW TEACHER ORIENTATIONS. Larger school districts usually offer one or more meetings for all new teachers that will address many of your teaching-related questions. In smaller districts the new teacher orientation may be more informal and school based. These sessions often review classroom management techniques, the school year calendar, report cards, and the schedule for testing. If you will be teaching in a district that has teacher-friendly computer systems for scoring tests and monitoring student progress, these topics will be introduced as well.

ASSIGNED TEACHER MENTORS. A very important resource for new teachers is mentors. Mentors are experienced teachers from whom the novice teacher can seek advice. They are not evaluators; that is the job of the principal. In many states and most larger districts, someone will be assigned to be your mentor for at least the first year. Mentors are master teachers who can help you with the design of lessons. They can sit in your classroom when you are teaching and follow up with suggestions to help you reflect.

COLLEAGUE TEACHER MENTORS. Frequently beginning teachers will discover an experienced teacher who can serve as an informal mentor. This person might be another teacher at your grade level or within your department. As the school year unfolds, you will likely find yourself turning to one of these colleagues more and more often.

SCHOOL-BASED SPECIALISTS AS NEW TEACHER RESOURCES. Another source of support will be the various specialist teachers within the school. The special education resource teacher can be of great help to you in teaching the students with special needs in your classroom. Other specialists that might be in your school include a technology coordinator, library/media coordinator, literacy specialist, mathematics specialist, ELL coordinator, and possibly a home–school community liaison person.

The Future of Technology for Teaching and Student Learning

Each of the preceding chapters in this text addressed one or more forms of technology and explored connections to teaching and student learning. These descriptions have been based on what is available today. The one certainty for the future is that new forms of technology will be created and innovative applications of current forms will be developed. Any of these might be used in classrooms and schools.

The Teacher Perspectives feature outlines the dilemma for teachers. How much of and which applications should teachers be using? There is no doubt that as a teacher you will be confronted with opportunities and questions about whether or not to use various new technologies in your classroom. The following paragraphs use a sampling of some emerging technologies and applications to illustrate the dilemma. Each technology has potential benefits for teaching and learning, and each also has potential risks.

induction The entry phase of teaching: normally covers the first three years.

Should Technology Be Used in Every Classroom?

TEACHER PERSPECTIVES

The various forms and possible uses of technology in schools seem to be never ending. Whiteboards, the web, personal computing, cell phones, and more recently various social networking applications can be made available for use by teachers and/or students in classrooms. But should they be made available? How much technology and which types do you want to use in your classroom? Two teachers offer opposing views below.

YES

Keith Parker is a history education student at Austin Peay State University in Clarksville, Tennessee.

When I begin teaching history and social studies in the fall of 2007, I'll require students to use as much technology as I have the resources for. They'll learn how important technology is for conducting research and how best to leverage it for that purpose. However, the students who aren't as interested in history will still learn skills that will help them when they enter the workforce. In almost every field of work, some type of technology is used. Students must be prepared.

If we complement and reinforce our lessons with technology—from Microsoft PowerPoint to streaming media, and computer spreadsheets to podcasts—we'll help students to be more receptive of the material and to become more familiar with the sorts of technology that have become a part of everyday life at home and in the workplace.

Finally, while students might not be familiar with workplace technologies and software, they are whizzes when it comes to Internet and telecommunications technology. By using more technology in the classroom, we're speaking their language and teaching them in a way that they might learn. Ignacio "Nacho" Estrada once said, "If a child can't learn the way we teach, maybe we should teach the way they learn."

NO

Timothy Kubinak teaches algebra and geography at King's Fork Middle School in Suffolk, Virginia.

Overuse of technology has inadvertently provided students with a deck of "get out of work free" cards. As a math teacher, I've seen that the use of technology, such as graphing calculators, has some positive effects—students can check their work, create graphs, and work together to solve problems. But too often I see students using technology to perform basic operations that should have been mastered in elementary school.

Some of my colleagues in the English department attribute their students' writing skills, or lack thereof, to the heavy use of instant messaging and spell check. These technologies, though useful when used as directed, can lead to a decrease in proficiency. The need for core skills development must be the first priority of the student and teacher.

Our generation learned how to read, write, and do arithmetic by learning from our teacher's example—with pencils, paper, and our minds. True, educators have learned that our students' needs are unique from past generations, but we remember what is truly important in our children's education. The need to learn how to organize, apply, analyze—in essence, we're teaching them how to learn. Yes, technology is an integral part of this process, but that does not mean it is a required component of every classroom setting.

Source: "Should Technology Be Used in Every Classroom?" *NEA Today* (September 2006), p. 43. Reprinted by permission of the National Education Association.

What is your perspective on this issue?

myeducationlab To explore both sides of this issue and think about each perspective, go to the *Book Specific Resources* in the MyEducationLab for your course, select your text, and then select *Teacher Perspectives* for Chapter 13.

RAPID DEVELOPMENT OF NEW FORMS OF TECHNOLOGY. Older adults will reminisce about the "days before we had the web and e-mail," while today's students have no memory of life without cell phones. In terms of history both of these forms of technology are recent developments. They also are indicators of how fast new forms of technology are created. An additional unique characteristic of technology is that, once created, never-ending adaptations and refinements follow. For example, when watching a movie that was made ten years ago, note what cell phones were like then compared to now. They were larger and were capable only of making phone calls. Now they are multifunction devices. As another indicator of rapidly changing technology, you merely have to chart the annual evolution and increasing capacity of iPods.

This rapid creation of new forms and applications of technology has important implications for teachers:

1. Tech-savvy teachers will see interesting and useful ways to incorporate some of the new forms, yet will be uncertain about the usefulness of others.
2. Students will be early to adopt and creative in using the new forms and applications.
3. The establishment of school and district policies related to appropriate and inappropriate uses of new forms of technology will lag behind the technologies' introduction in the classroom.

These three implications pose a dilemma for teachers in the future. Which forms and applications will you encourage, and what are your guiding principles for what will not be allowed? This is the underlying theme of the Teacher Perspectives feature. It is likely that you will be confronted with the need to make decisions about uses in your classroom before your school or district has a rule or policy in place. You will need to be thoughtful about your reasoning and understand the legal, ethical, and instructional elements related to your decision.

SOCIAL NETWORKING TECHNOLOGY. The unbelievably rapid growth of websites such as FaceBook, digital photos, text messaging, and unique applications such as Twitter illustrate the dilemma for teachers and school officials. Each of these applications can be used in ways that enhance teaching and student learning, yet they also can be used to cheat. Some districts have decided to suspend students who bring cell phones or iPods to school. Others have decided that students may carry them as long as they are turned off. These policies, however, still mean that teachers must monitor the availability and uses of each.

Unfortunately, teachers also must be continually attentive to the possibility of students using technology to cheat. One indicator of the extent of the problem is found in a survey of nearly 30,000 high school students conducted by the Josephson Institute for Ethics (2008) in Los Angeles: 64 percent reported cheating on a test with 38 percent indicating they did so two or more times. As sad as it may be, teachers need to view each new form and application of technology as possibly providing a new way for students to cheat.

PROMISING NEW APPLICATIONS. Often forms and applications of technology that have been around for some time are merged into new systems of classroom support. This will most certainly happen in the future. A current example that is just now showing up in classrooms is based on integrating several technologies that have been around for a long time.

Microphones, speakers, and amplifiers have been around for more than one hundred years. In the early days each microphone had to have its own wire and if two were turned on at the same time, a very loud screeching noise would be heard. Now, with the addition of computer software and advances in technology, many wireless microphones can be on at the same time. What do you suppose could be done in classrooms by combining these "old" technologies?

Several vendors have created **classroom audio technology** systems. One of the stresses for teachers and students is having to talk loud enough to be heard. This effort is tiring for teachers and usually means that some students will not have heard everything. For relatively little investment, technology systems are now available that can fix this problem. In these classrooms speakers are located strategically so that all can hear. The teacher has a wireless microphone and others are available for students. Everybody can talk in normal voices and all can hear what is being said.

INCREASING INTEGRATION OF TECHNOLOGY USES. Teachers in the future will have even more forms and applications of technology to learn about and use. Two keys to taking advantage of this future are flexibility and imagination. Teachers need to be flexible and open to consider whether some new technology really is better. They also can be creative in thinking up new ways to use technology. A third key, and one that will be increasingly important, is to devise strategies to integrate the uses of technology.

As just described with classroom audio technology, each technology and application can be used by itself, but the high-quality classroom will integrate these uses. For example, technology makes possible differentiation according to student needs. A variety of ways should be available for each student to achieve each objective. Students in the same classroom with different needs should be able to use books on tape, writing templates, charts, and instruction in different languages to learn the same material. Connecting to the Internet to retrieve content or to communicate with students in another state or country can be another integrated practice. Teachers in the future need to think about how all of the individual technology resources can be integrated to form a whole system that supports teaching and learning.

School-Based Administrators Can Be Important Supports for New Teachers

As described in Chapter 9, teachers have a line relationship with the principal. This is an especially important relationship because one of the principal's responsibilities is to evaluate first-year teachers. However, do not permit the evaluation role to block out any possibility of the principal being a resource. Nearly all principals have been teachers earlier in their careers. They also know what is available around the school that can be of help.

Assistant principals also can be a resource, and in schools that have deans and department chairs they too can be important resources. An important theme cutting across all of these people

Chapter 10 addresses the legal aspects and implications of the uses—and misuses—of social networking and other forms of technology.

Go to the *Assignments and Activities* section of Topic 14: *Professional Development* in the MyEducationLab for your course and complete the activity titled *Succeeding in your First Year of Teaching.*

classroom audio technology The use of wireless microphones and speakers in classrooms.

Review Chapter 9 if you are not clear about teacher organizational relationships with the principal.

resources is that beginning teachers should not become isolated in their classroom. When you need help, or just an opportunity to ask someone else what they think, get out of your classroom and seek out one or more of these resources. They will be pleased that you asked.

PARTICIPATING IN THE PROFESSION

One of the rewarding aspects of becoming a teacher is the opportunity to work with other well-educated and highly dedicated professionals. There are many types of professional organizations and associations that teachers can join. In most school districts, teachers are represented by a teachers' organization or union that is responsible for negotiating contracts and setting working conditions. These organizations and associations have had a major influence on the development of national education policy; on the determination of state policies, laws, rules, and regulations related to schooling; and (at the local level) on curriculum decisions and labor contract negotiations. At all of these levels, teachers are actively involved and are responsible participants who will eventually work with the resultant policy decisions and curriculum products.

Teachers have opportunities to become involved in professional or specialty associations as well. These associations deal directly with issues such as the development of student and teacher standards, the design of curriculum, innovations in teaching, and improving instructional processes. They provide teachers with the opportunity to collaborate with other teachers who have like concerns and interests; they also enable teachers to participate in various professional leadership activities. Some specialty associations focus on teaching specific subjects, such as science, math, literature, and reading, or specific grade levels, such as middle school and early childhood education. These associations usually have national, state, and local chapters. Clearly, teachers can profit from membership and participation in both professional organizations and professional or specialty associations.

Teacher Unions

Teacher unions were organized to improve working conditions. The National Education Association (NEA) and the American Federation of Teachers (AFT) are the two major unions for teachers in the United States. Some teachers have chosen to join other state or local organizations that are not affiliated with the NEA or the AFT but operate similarly to a union. The unions provide a number of services for their members, leadership on a number of professional issues, and a political presence at the local, state, and national levels.

National Education Association

The National Education Association is by far the largest teachers' organization, with 2.5 million members, including teachers, administrators, clerical and custodial employees, higher education faculty, and other school personnel. Teacher education candidates can join the NEA's Student Program. More than a million teacher education candidates have joined the student group since it was formed in 1937. You might wish to explore the advantages of joining this organization on your campus.

The NEA is committed to advancing public education. The organization was founded in 1857 as the National Teachers' Association (NTA). In 1870 the NTA united with the National Association of School Superintendents, organized in 1865, and the American Normal School Association, organized in 1858, to form the National Education Association. The organization was incorporated in 1886 in the District of Columbia as the National Education Association and was chartered in 1906 by an act of Congress. The charter was officially adopted at the association's annual meeting of 1907, with the name National Education Association of the United States.

The Representative Assembly (RA) is the primary legislative and policy-making body of the NEA. NEA members of state and local affiliates elect the 9,000 RA delegates who meet annually in early July to debate issues and set policies. The president, vice president, and secretary-treasurer are elected at the annual RA. The top decision-making bodies are the board of directors and the executive committee. An executive director has the primary responsibility for implementing the policies of the association, and standing committees and ad hoc committees carry out much of the work.

Given its long history of advocacy of teaching as a profession, it should not be surprising to learn that the NEA sponsors many professional initiatives designed to disseminate best practices, facilitate teacher leadership, and empower teachers to reform schools. The NEA has organized to provide professional help in student assessment and accountability; professional preparation, state licensure, and national certification; and governance and member activities. The NEA also initiated in 1954, along with four other associations, the accrediting body for teacher education, NCATE, and continues today to provide leadership through appointments to NCATE's governance board and board of examiners. The examiners are practitioners who visit college campuses to apply the standards. These and other program areas offer an array of activities and initiatives to further advance teacher professionalism.

Members of the NEA receive its newsletter, *NEA Today,* and have access to numerous other publications and products, including publications that are available online through its professional library. Recent reports from the association address diversity, portfolios, student assessment, school safety, cooperative learning, discipline, gender, inclusion, reading and writing, and parent involvement. Handbooks published by the NEA and written by experienced teachers are helpful resources for new teachers.

American Federation of Teachers

The second largest teachers' union is the American Federation of Teachers, with national headquarters in Washington, D.C. It was organized in 1916 by teachers in Winnetka, Illinois, to establish an organization to meet their needs and to create a strong union affiliation. The Chicago Teachers' Federation preceded the AFT, having been established in 1897 and affiliating with the American Federation of Labor (AFL) in 1902. Since 1916, AFT membership has grown steadily. The late Albert Shanker, who was AFT president from 1974 until his death in 1997, is given much of the credit for the growth and success of the AFT, including its national involvement in political discussions related to education. In 1965, membership was at 110,500; by 2000, membership exceeded one million. The organization of the AFT includes a president, numerous vice presidents, a secretary-treasurer, and administrative staff. The membership serves on standing committees and council committees.

Since its inception, the AFT has boasted of its affiliation with the AFL, and later the AFL-CIO. AFT has stressed that organized labor was an important force in establishing our system of free public schools and that it has actively supported school improvement programs. Affiliation with organized labor gives the AFT the support of the more than fifteen million members of the AFL-CIO. Support from local labor unions has often worked to the advantage of local AFT unions in their efforts to gain better salaries and improved benefits from local boards of education.

The AFT has diverse resources available to its members. Its lobbying and political action activities support a number of professional issues, in addition to bargaining issues at the local, state, and national levels. Its publications include the journal *American Educator.* Jointly with the NEA, the AFT conducts the annual QUEST conference to convene the leadership of both organizations to discuss professional issues. The Educational Research and Dissemination Program helps make selected findings from recent research on classroom management and effective teaching available to teachers.

POLITICAL ACTION. Both the NEA and AFT have political action committees and government relations departments. Political action committees are engaged in actions to elect political candidates who are sympathetic to education and teachers' issues. They monitor elected officials' voting records on education bills and analyze the platforms of new candidates. They actively participate in the election campaigns of the president, governors, and key legislators. The state and national political action committees of the NEA and AFT have a common aim: to promote education by encouraging teachers to participate in the political life of their local, state, and national communities. These committees throughout the states are responsible for recommending political endorsements to their respective boards of directors.

Professional Associations

Teachers can join, participate in, and provide leadership for many professional associations that focus on their chosen professional interests. These associations are organized around academic disciplines and specific job assignments, such as science teaching, mathematics teaching, special education, school psychology, reading, cooperative learning, and multicultural education.

PHI DELTA KAPPA INTERNATIONAL. The professional association Phi Delta Kappa International (PDK) is one of the largest and most highly regarded organizations for educators in the world. Today it is open to all educators, although in its earlier years women were not allowed to join. It publishes excellent professional material, including the journal *Phi Delta Kappan,* a newsletter, *Fastback* booklets on timely educational topics, research reports, books, and various instructional materials. The organization also sponsors many surveys, research projects, grants, awards, conferences, training programs, and trips. Local PDK chapters bring together teacher candidates,

PEARSON
myeducationlab

To see a list of professional educational associations with website addresses, go to the MyEducationLab for your course, select *Resources, Preparing for and Beginning Your Career,* and then *Professional Education Associations.*

higher education faculty, and local teachers and administrators. You might want to consider a student membership and become involved in your local chapter.

SPECIALTY PROFESSIONAL ASSOCIATIONS. There are more than five hundred specialty associations in education based on different academic disciplines, different types of students, and different instructional approaches. Over time, you will find those specialties that apply to your unique role in education. Participation in these associations will enable you to network with others who have similar interests and focus.

Of the specialty associations that could be described, the Association for Supervision and Curriculum Development (ASCD) is profiled here because it provides an international forum focused on all aspects of effective teaching and learning. Founded in 1943, ASCD is a nonprofit, nonpartisan organization representing 175,000 educators from more than 135 countries and more than sixty affiliates. Members span the entire profession of education—superintendents, supervisors, principals, teachers, professors of education, and school board members. ASCD offers broad, multiple perspectives in reporting key policies and practices. The association focuses on professional practice within the context of public and private schools and cites as its primary goal the building of an engaged diverse community to improve learning and teaching for each student.

LOOKING AHEAD: BE THE BEST YOU CAN BE

Now that you have studied the different perspectives that comprise the foundation of education, you should be ready to reflect on implications for your career as a teacher. As you have seen, our profession is rich in history and expertise and diverse in thoughts and perspectives. No matter which perspective is selected, which chapter(s) you found most interesting, or the contexts you considered, one theme stands out: Education and the profession of teaching will continue to change. The pressures to continuously find better ways to teach and to improve student learning will not cease.

The theme of continuous efforts to improve and change will be with you throughout the remainder of your teacher education program and throughout your career as a teacher. You have the responsibility of trying new approaches and providing evidence about the difference each makes in your teaching, your students, and your school.

The authors of this text represent very different perspectives and personal histories. Interestingly, regardless of their academic discipline and teaching experiences, the authors frequently observe that this is an exciting time to become a teacher. In your developing career you will continue to learn and all along you will have opportunities to make a difference in student learning and in the learning of your colleagues. We hope you, your students, and your colleagues benefit as much from the American education system as we have.

═══════════════ **JOURNAL FOR REFLECTION** ═══════════════

The authors of this text believe that this is an exciting time to become a teacher. Do you agree? What excites you about becoming a teacher?

We, the authors, wish you the very best in your developing career. We need many more high-quality teachers. As you now know from reading this text, there is a long and rich legacy of efforts, people, and ideas to help you grow. You will likely have moments of doubt (those Self concerns again), and you most certainly will have days where you have too much to do (Task concerns). We hope, though, that you will also move on to truly experiencing the excitement and wonderment that comes from having your students "get it." As you know firsthand, high-quality teachers make a lasting difference in the lives of their students. High-quality teachers will have Self and Task concerns too, but what really drives them is their Impact concerns. As reported in the Education in the News feature about Venera Gattonini at the beginning of this chapter, high-quality teachers are always striving to be the best they can be and to do everything they can think of to help all of their students learn.

SUMMARY

DIFFERENT PERSPECTIVES FOR VIEWING EDUCATION AND TEACHING

- Different perspectives can be applied to our understanding of education and teaching: sociological, historical, philosophical, organizational, economic, legal, and multicultural.
- The United States has a three-hundred year history of trying to improve its educational system.

CONTINUING PRESSURES TO REFORM SCHOOLS

- In recent decades the federal government has been increasingly pressuring schools to change.
- Crises in society are a catalyst for school change.
- Findings from research can lead to change.
- Evidence about student learning unveils areas of needed change.

EMERGING PRESSURES AND INDICATORS OF ACCOUNTABILITY REQUIRE CHANGE IN SCHOOLS

- Expectations for accountability are increasing.
- Test scores are being used to rank school districts as well as individual schools.
- Graduation rates are becoming an important indicator of school quality.
- Dropout rates also are becoming an important indicator of school quality.
- All teachers have an important role in reducing dropouts and increasing graduation rates.

HOW TO RECOGNIZE A HIGH-QUALITY SCHOOL

- Today's expectations for students and for teachers are higher than in the past.
- Data are used to make instructional and budgetary decisions.
- School improvement is a process, not just a plan.
- High-quality schools have a special organizational culture called a professional learning community.
- Many strategies are employed to involve parents and community members in student learning.
- The principal has a vision for the school and provides supportive leadership.
- Accountability is centered on student learning.

HIGH-QUALITY TEACHERS PROVIDE EVIDENCE OF STUDENT LEARNING

- High-quality teachers use evidence to determine if they are making a difference in student learning.
- High-quality teachers are reflective and have a stated philosophy.
- Ethics is an important component of a high-quality teacher's philosophy.
- High-quality teachers have depth in three types of knowledge: content, pedagogical, and pedagogical content knowledge.

BECOMING A HIGH-QUALITY TEACHER REQUIRES CHANGE

- Four categories of concerns are Unconcerned, Self, Task, and Impact concerns.
- Teacher concerns change as the teacher becomes more expert.
- Beginning teachers will have more Self concerns than other types of concerns.
- High-quality teachers have more Impact concerns than other types.
- Reflecting on your concerns can be helpful.

SUPPORTIVE RESOURCES FOR YOUR FIRST YEAR

- Induction is the first one to three years of teaching.
- Beginning teachers have many resources available to them: workshops and orientations, mentors, and professional associations.

PARTICIPATING IN THE PROFESSION

- Associations provide opportunities for teachers to work together.
- The NEA and AFT advocate for teachers' rights.
- Professional associations provide opportunities for teachers to specialize in activities related to a particular professional interest or curriculum subject.

- High-quality teachers strive to have all of their students learn.
- High-quality teachers are always looking for ways to improve their teaching and increase student learning.

DISCUSSION QUESTIONS

1. What changes have you seen in your lifetime that have affected what today's schools are like?
2. Which indicators of accountability for schools do you think are most important?
3. Do you think that the trend toward increased federal direction of public education has gone too far, or should the federal government take even more control?
4. What characteristics of high-quality schools do you agree with? Are there other characteristics that you think should be added or deleted?
5. How have your concerns about becoming a teacher changed since this academic term started? In what ways have they stayed the same?
6. For which domain of high-quality, or expert, teacher knowledge do you have the most to learn?

SCHOOL-BASED OBSERVATIONS

1. Ask a teacher about the various changes that she or he has made during their teaching career. Which of the changes turned out to be most beneficial? Which were the biggest challenge?
2. Obtain a copy of a school's school improvement plan and see which tiers of data were used. Did the school rely solely on Tier 1 data (standardized test scores) or were other tiers also considered? (If you don't have access to a school's plan, check the district and state website. The school's plan should be there.)

PORTFOLIO DEVELOPMENT

1. Keep a copy of the open-ended concerns statement that you wrote while reading this chapter. (If you didn't do it then, go back to Figure 13.4 and do the task now.) Every six weeks or so as you move on in becoming a teacher take time to write out your concerns. You can score them using the general definitions provided in Table 13.7. As you continue to do this you should see a developing pattern and several trends in relation to your becoming a teacher.
2. Now would be a good time for you to use the student learning–centered teaching model (Table 13.5) to sketch out a lesson plan for a topic you would like to teach. Be sure to think about what your students might know already and what you would do to incorporate their background and past experiences into the lesson. This is what pedagogical content knowledge is about.

myeducationlab For additional information about portfolios, go to the MyEducationLab for your course, select *Resources* and then *Preparing a Portfolio.*

PREPARING FOR CERTIFICATION

1. A topic in the Praxis II Principles of Learning and Teaching (PLT) test related to the teacher's role and school effectiveness is "ongoing personal reflection on teaching and learning practices as a basis for making professional decisions [including]
   - code of Ethics
   - advocacy for learners."

   The authors cite information about the four different levers used with the intention of reforming education: (1) *fix the parts,* (2) *fix the people,* (3) *fix the school,* and (4) *fix the system.* Thinking about today's schools, describe something you feel needs to be fixed. Identify which of the above levers you think might be the most successful, and describe why.
2. Answer the following multiple-choice question, which is similar to items in Praxis and other state certification tests.

   Many students drop out of school for one reason or another. Several risk factors have been identified and occur at various grade levels. Which of the following

are **not** listed as risk factors for students in sixth, eighth, or ninth grades.
 a. poor attendance
 b. poor grades in the sciences
 c. poor behavior
 d. earned fewer than two credits in ninth grade

3. Answer the following short-answer question, which is similar to items in Praxis and other state certification tests.

 The authors define many ways that partnerships exist in schools. Some include shared ownership,

some require shared decision making, and some include respectful/reciprocal communication. Identify two of these partnerships from your reading. Compare and contrast them. Identify the one you think would be the most successful in your community and explain why.

After you've completed your written responses for the above questions, use the Praxis general scoring guide provided in Chapter 1 to see if you can revise your response to improve your score.

MYEDUCATIONLAB

PEARSON myeducationlab) Now go to Topic 14: *Professional Development* in the MyEducationLab (www.myeducationlab.com) for your course, where you can:

- Find learning outcomes for *Professional Development* along with the national standards that connect to these outcomes.
- Complete *Assignments and Activities* that can help you more deeply understand the chapter content.
- Apply and practice your understanding of the core teaching skills identified in the chapter with the *Building Teaching Skills and Dispositions* learning units.

- Check your comprehension on the content covered in the chapter by going to the *Study Plan* in the *Book Specific Resources* section for your text. Here you will be able to take a chapter quiz, receive feedback on your answers, and then access *Review, Practice, and Enrichment* activities to enhance your understanding of chapter content.

WEBSITES

www.howtogetyourged.org This is a site for you and students to learn about what is entailed in earning a GED.

www.ed.gov/policy/elsec/leg/esea02/index.html This is the official U.S. Department of Education website for P. L.

107–110, which is better known as the No Child Left Behind Act of 2001. The site describes the various parts of the statute and provides links to related government documents and departments.

FURTHER READING

Dymoke, S., & Harrison, J. (Eds.). (2008). *Reflective teaching and learning: A guide to professional issues for beginning secondary teachers (Developing as a reflective secondary teacher)*. Thousand Oaks, CA: Sage. This book focuses on the special tasks and steps beginning secondary teachers should take. Topics include classroom management, inclusion, assessing student learning, and being sure to integrate national curriculum standards.

Good, T., & Brophy, J. (2007). *Looking in classrooms* (10th ed.). Boston: Allyn and Bacon. This book is a useful resource for looking at instruction. The practices described in this volume are evidence based. The authors are the lead researchers who developed the Effective Teaching model.

Kottler, E. I., & Gallavan, N. P. (2007). *Secrets to success for beginning elementary school teachers*. Thousand Oaks, CA: Corwin Press. The authors take a practical approach to being

a first-year teacher. There are many useful tips for organizing your classroom, valuing cultural diversity, and using technology. There also is a chapter advising the beginning teacher about "learning your way around the school."

Schell, L. M. (2008). *Countdown to the first day of school: A K–12 get-ready checklist for beginning teachers, teacher transfers, student/preservice teachers, mentors and more!* Washington, DC: NEA. Here is a useful guide for all teachers as they prepare for that first day and for the first months of teaching.

Trumbull, E., Rothstein-Fisch, C., Greenfield, P. M., & Quiroz, B. (2001). *Bridging cultures between home and school: A guide for teachers*. Mahway, NJ: Lawrence Erlbaum. Here is a rich resource of practical approaches for teachers and school leaders who are serious about increasing parent involvement.

REFERENCES

Abma, J. C., Martinez, G. M., Mosher, W. D., & Dawson, B. S. (2004). Teenagers in the United States: Sexual activity, contraceptive use, and childbearing, 2002. National Center for Health Statistics. *Vital Health Stat 23*(24). Retrieved on May 4, 2009, from http://www.cdc.gov/nchs/data/series/sr_23/sr23_024.pdf.

Acs, G., & Koball, H. (2003). TANF and the status of teen mothers under age 18. *New federalism: Issues and options for states,* Series A, No. A-62. Washington, DC: Urban Institute.

Aguilar v. Felton, 473 U.S. 402 (1985).

Alexander, H. G. (1987). *The language and logic of philosophy.* Lanham, MD: University Press of America.

American Association of University Women. (2002). *Harassment-free hallways: How to stop sexual harassment in school.* Washington, DC: Author.

American Management Association. (2001). *AMA survey on workplace testing: Basic skills, job skills, psychological measurement.* New York: Author.

Anderson, L. W. (2009). Upper elementary grades bear the brunt of accountability. *Phi Delta Kappan, 90*(6), 413–418.

Anderson, L. W., & Krathwohl, D. R. (Eds.) (2001). *A taxonomy for learning, teaching and assessing: A revision of Bloom's taxonomy of educational objectives.* New York: Longman.

Anderson, P. M., & Summerfield, J. P. (2007). Why is urban education different from suburban and rural education? In S. R. Steinberg and J. L. Kincheloe (Eds.), *19 urban questions: Teaching in the city* (pp. 29–39). New York: Peter Lang.

Anderson, S., Cavanagh, J., Collins, C., Pizzigati, S., & Laphan, M. (2008). *Executive excess 2008: How average taxpayers subsidize runaway pay: 15th annual CEO compensation survey.* Washington, DC: Institute for Policy Studies and United for a Fair Economy.

Annie E. Casey Foundation. (2003). *Kids count data book 2003.* Baltimore, MD: Author.

Armytage, W. H. G. (1951). William Byngham: A medieval protagonist of the training of teachers. *History of Education Journal, 2,* 108.

Arnot, M. (2004). Male working-class identities and social justice: A reconsideration of Paul Willis's *Learning to labor* in light of contemporary research. In N. Dolby, G. Dimitriadis, and P. Willis (Eds.), *Learning to labor in new times* (pp. 17–40). New York: Routledge Falmer.

Aron, L. Y., & Mears, D. P. (2003). *Addressing the needs of youth with disabilities in the juvenile system: The current status of evidence-based research (a research report).* Washington, DC: National Council on Disability.

Barton, P. E., & Coley, R. J. (2007). *The family: America's smallest school.* Princeton, NJ: Educational Testing Service.

Barton, P. E., & Coley, R. J. (2008). *Windows on achievement and inequality.* Princeton, NJ: Educational Testing Service.

Barton, P. E., & Coley, R. J. (2009). *Parsing the achievement gap II.* Princeton, NJ: Education Testing Service.

Beane, J. A. (2001). Introduction: Reform and reinvention. In T. S. Dickinson (Ed.), *Reinventing the middle school.* New York: Routledge Falmer.

Bellah, R. N., Madsen, R., Sullivan, W. M., Swidler, A., & Tipton, S. M. (2008). *Habits of the heart: Individualism and commitment in American life.* Berkeley: University of California Press.

Berliner, D. C. (2001). Learning about and learning from expert teachers. *International Journal of Educational Research, 35*(5), 463–483.

Bethel School District No. 403 et al. v. Fraser, a Minor, et al., 478 U.S. 675 (1986).

Bloom, B. S. (Ed.) (1956). *Taxonomy of educational objectives: The classification of educational goals handbook 1: Cognitive domain.* New York: David McKay.

Board of Education, Island Trees Union Free District No. 26 v. Pico, 457 U.S. 853 (1982).

Board of Education of Kiryas Joel Village School District v. Grumet, 512 U.S. 687 (1949).

Board of Education of Oklahoma City Public Schools v. Dowell, 498 U.S. 237 (1991).

Board of Education of the Westside Community Schools v. Mergens by and Through Mergens (No. 88–1597), 496 U.S. 226 (1990).

Board of Regents of State Colleges v. Roth, 408 U.S. 564 (1972).

Bob Mozert et al., Plaintiffs-Appellants, v. Hawkins County Public Schools, et al., Defendants-Appellees. U.S. Court of Appeals for the Sixth Circuit 765 F.2d 1058 (1987).

Borja, R. R. (2006). Risk and reward. *Technology Counts 2006: The information edge: Using data to accelerate achievement [Education Week, 25*(35)]. Bethesda, MD: Editorial Projects in Education.

Bowles, S., & Gintis, H. (1975). *Schooling in capitalistic America.* New York: Basic Books.

Bowles, S., Gintis, H., Boyd, R., & Fehr, E. (Eds.) (2006). *Moral sentiments and material interests: The foundations of cooperation in economic life.* New York: Basic Books.

Bramlett, M. D., & Mosher, W. D. (2002). Cohabitation, marriage, divorce, and remarriage in the United States. National Center for Health Statistics. *Vital Health Stat, 23*(22).

Bransford, J. D., Brown, A., & Cocking, R. R. (Eds.) (2000). *How people learn: Brain, mind, experience and school* (expanded ed.). Washington, DC: National Academies Press.

Bransford, J., Darling-Hammond, L., & LePage, P. (2005). Introduction. In L. Darling-Hammond and J. Bransford (Eds.), *Preparing teachers for a changing world: What teachers should learn and be able to do* (pp. 1–39). San Francisco: Jossey-Bass.

Brantmeier, C., Schueller, J., & Wilde, J. (2007). Gender equity in foreign and second language learning. In S. S. Klein, B. Richardson, D. A. Grayson, L. H. Fox, C. Kramarae, D. S. Pollard, and C. A. Dwyer (Eds.), *Handbook for achieving gender equity through education* (2nd ed., pp. 305–334). Mahwah, NJ: Lawrence Erlbaum.

Brophy, J. E., & Good, T. L. (1974). *Teacher-student relationships: Causes and consequences.* Retrieved from http://www.eric.ed.gov (ERIC Document Reproduction Service No. ED091495).

Broughman, S. P., Swaim, N. L., & Keaton, P. W. (2008). *Characteristics of private schools in the United States: Results from the 2005–2006 private school universe survey* (NCES 2008-315). Washington, DC: National Center for Education Statistics, Institute of Education Sciences, U.S. Department of Education.

Brown v. Board of Education of Topeka, 347 U.S. 483 (1954).

Buber, M. (1958). *I and thou* (Ronald G. Smith, Trans.). New York: Charles Scribner.

Buckley, J., & Schneider, M. (2007). *Charter schools: Hope or hype?* Princeton, NJ: Princeton University Press.

Burger, C., Abbott, G., Tobias, S., Koch, J., Vogt, C., Bienvenue, L., Carlito, D., Sosa, T., & Strawn, C. (2007). Gender equity in science, engineering, and technology. In S. S. Klein, B. Richardson, D. A. Grayson, L. H. Fox, C. Kramarae, D. S. Pollard, and C. A. Dwyer (Eds.), *Handbook for achieving gender equity through education* (2nd ed., pp. 255–280). Mahwah, NJ: Lawrence Erlbaum.

Burkey v. Marshall County Board of Education et al., 513 F. Supp. 1084; Northern District of West Virginia, Wheeling Division (1981).

Bushaw, W. J., & Gallup, A. M. (2008). Americans speak out—Are educators and policy makers listening? The 40th annual Phi Delta Kappa/Gallup poll of the public's attitudes toward the public schools. *Phi Delta Kappan, 90*(1), 9–20.

California Department of Education. (2003). *The nature of science and technology.* Sacramento, CA: Author.

Cambron-McCabe, N. H., McCarthy, M. M., & Thomas, S. B. (2004). *Public school law: Teachers' and students' rights* (5th ed.). Boston: Pearson.

Cavanagh, S., & Manzo, K. K. (2009). International exams yield less-than-clear lessons. *Education Week, 28*(29), 1, 16–17.

Center for Education Reform. (n.d.). *Charter school profile.* Washington, DC: Author.

Center for Education Reform. (2006). *Charter schools by the numbers.* Washington, DC: Author.

Center for Education Reform. (2007). *Charter school facts.* Washington, DC: Author.

Centers for Disease Control and Prevention. (2008a). *Sexual violence: Facts at a glance.* Retrieved on May 2, 2009, from http://www.cdc.gov/ncipc/dvp/SV/SVDataSheet.pdf.

Centers for Disease Control and Prevention. (2008b). Youth risk behavior surveillance—United States 2007. *Morbidity and Mortality Weekly Report, 57*(SS04), 1–131. Retrieved on May 3, 2009, from http://www.cdc.gov/mmwr/preview/mmwrhtml/ss5704a1.htm.

Centers for Disease Control and Prevention. (2008c). *Understanding school violence.* Atlanta: Centers for Disease Control. Retrieved on May 2, 2009, from http://www.cdc.gov/ViolencePrevention/pdf/SchoolViolence_FactSheet-a.pdf.

Centers for Disease Control and Prevention. (2008d). *Understanding suicide: Fact sheet 2008.* Retrieved on May 2, 2009, from http://www.cdc.gov/ViolencePrevention/pdf/Suicide-FactSheet-a.pdf.

Centers for Disease Control and Prevention. (2009a). *Parent training programs: Insight for practitioners.* Atlanta: Centers for Disease Control. Retrieved on May 2, 2009, from http://www.cdc.gov/ViolencePrevention/pdf/Parent_Training_Brief-a.pdf.

Centers for Disease Control and Prevention. (2009b). *Understanding youth violence: Fact sheet 2009.* Retrieved on May 2, 2009, from http://www.cdc.gov/ViolencePrevention/pdf/YV-FactSheet-a.pdf.

Centers for Disease Control and Prevention. (2009c). *Youth violence: Facts at a glance, Summer 2008.* Retrieved on May 2, 2009, from http://www.cdc.gov/ViolencePrevention/pdf/YV-DataSheet-a.pdf.

Child Trends DataBank. (2008, Summer). *High school dropout rates.* Retrieved August 25, 2009, from http://www.childtrendsdatabank.org/indicators/1HighSchoolDropout.cfm.

Christensen, C. M., Horn, M. G., & Johnson, C. W. (2008). *Disrupting class: How disruptive innovation will change the way the world learns.* New York: McGraw-Hill.

Civil Rights Project, Harvard University. (2002). *What works for the children? What we know and don't know about bilingual education.* Cambridge, MA: Author.

Cleveland Board of Education v. LeFleur, 414 U.S. 632 (1974).

Compayre, G. (1888). *History of pedagogy* (W. H. Payne, Trans.). Boston: Heath.

Conchas, G. Q., & Rodríguez, L. F. (2008). *Small schools and urban youth.* Thousand Oaks, CA: Corwin Press.

Consumers Union Education Services. (1996). *Captive kids: Commercial pressures on kids at school.* Yonkers, NY: Consumers Union.

Cooper v. Ross, 472 F. Supp. 802 (E.D. Ark. 1979).

Corbett, C., Hill, C., & St. Rose, A. (2008). *Where the girls are: The facts about gender equity in education.* Washington, DC: American Association of University Women.

Cove, E., Eiseman, M., & Popkin, S. J. (2005). *Resilient children: Literature review and evidence from the HOPE VI panel study.* Washington, DC: Urban Institute.

Dalton, B., Sable, J., & Hoffman, L. (2006). *Characteristics of the 100 largest public elementary and secondary school districts in the United States: 2003–2004* (NCES 2006-329). Washington, DC: National Center for Education Statistics.

Darling-Hammond, L. (2000). Teaching for America's future: National commissions and vested interests in an almost profession. *Educational Policy, 14*(1), 162–183.

Darling-Hammond, L., & Falk, B. (1997). Supporting teaching and learning for all students: Policies for authentic assessment systems. In A. L. Goodwin (Ed.), *Assessment for equity and inclusion: Embracing all our children.* New York: Routledge.

Davis, M. R. (2009). Breaking away from tradition: E-learning opens new doors to raise achievement. *Technology Counts 2009* [*Education Week, 28*(21)]. Bethesda, MD: Editorial Projects in Education.

Day, J. C. (n.d.). *National population projections.* Washington, DC: U.S. Census Bureau. Retrieved on May 11, 2009, from http://www.census.gov/prod/1/pop/profile/95/2_ps.pdf.

Deal, T. E., & Peterson, K. D. (1999). *Shaping school culture: The heart of leadership.* San Francisco: Jossey-Bass.

DeHass, D. M. (2009). *1981–82 – 2007–08 NCAA sports sponsorship and participation rates report.* Indianapolis, IN: National Collegiate Athletic Association.

Dewey, J. (1897). My pedagogic creed. *The School Journal, 54*(3), pp. 77–80.

Dewey, J. (1916). *Democracy and education.* New York: Macmillan.

Dewey, J. (1937). Education and social change. *The School Frontier 3*(26), 235–238.

Diaz, E. M., & Kosciw, J. G. (2009). *Shared differences: The experiences of lesbian, gay, bisexual, and transgender students of color in our nation's schools.* New York: Gay, Lesbian and Straight Education Network.

Donohue v. Copiague Union Free School District, 407 NYS 2d 874 (NY 1978).

Donovan, M. S., & Bransford, J. D. (Eds.) (2005). *How students learn: History, mathematics, and science in the classroom.* Washington, DC: National Academies Press.

Duck, L. (1981). *Instructor's manual for teaching with charisma.* Boston: Allyn & Bacon.

Education Trust. (2006). *Yes we can: Telling truths and dispelling myths about race and education in America.* Washington, DC: Author.

Educational Testing Service. (2009). Addressing achievement gaps. *Policy Notes, 17*(1), 1.

Educational Policies Commission. (1938). *The purposes of education in American democracy.* Washington, DC: National Education Association.

Educational Policies Commission. (1944). *Education for all American youth.* Washington, DC: National Education Association.

Educational Policies Commission. (1952). *Imperative needs of youth.* Washington, DC: National Education Association.

Educational Testing Service. (2008, Summer). Addressing achievement gaps: The language acquisition and educational achievement of English-language learners. *Policy Notes, 16*(2).

Edwards v. Aguillard, 482 U.S. 578 (1987).

Emmer, E. T., Evertson, C. M., & Anderson, L. M. (1980). Effective classroom management at the beginning of the school year. *The Elementary School Journal 80*(5), 219–231.

Epperson v. Arkansas, 393 U.S. 97 (1968).

Everson v. Board of Education, 330 U.S. 1 (1947).

Family income and educational attainment: 1970 to 2007. (2008, November). *Postsecondary Educational Opportunity*, No. 197.

Finn, J. D., & Achilles, C. M. (1999). Tennessee's class size study: Findings, implications, misconceptions. *Educational Evaluation and Policy Analysis 21*(2), 97–109.

Flygare, T. J. (1986). De jure. *Phi Delta Kappan, 68*, 165–166.

Foss, S. (2009). *Measuring poverty in the United States.* New York City: National Center for Children in Poverty. Retrieved on May 8, 2009, from http://nccp.org/publications/pub_876.html.

Foss, S., & Couthen, N. K. (2008). *Who are America's poor children?* New York: National Center for Children in Poverty. Retrieved on May 8, 2009, from http://nccp.org/publications/pub_843.html.

Fox, J. A., & Zawitz, M. W. (2007). *Homicide trends in the United States.* Washington, DC: U.S. Department of Justice, Bureau of Justice Statistics. Retrieved on May 2, 2009, from http://www.ojp.usdoj.gov/bjs/pub/pdf/htius.pdf.

Franklin v. Gwinnett County Public Schools, 503 U.S. 60 (1992).

Freedman, H. C. (1970). The legal rights of untenured teachers. *Nolpe School Law Journal, 1*, 100.

Freeman v. Pitts, 503 U.S. 467 (1992).

Garofano, A., & Sable, J. (2008). *Characteristics of the 100 largest public elementary and secondary school districts in the United States: 2004–05.* Washington, DC: National Center for Education Statistics.

Genesee, F. (Ed.). (1999). *Program alternatives for linguistically diverse students.* Washington, DC: Center for Research on Education, Diversity & Excellence.

George, A. A., Hall, G. E., & Uchiyama, K. (2000). Extent of implementation of a standards-based approach to teaching mathematics and student outcomes. *Journal of Classroom Interaction, 35*(1), 8–25.

Giroux, H. A. (1981). *Ideology, culture and the process of schooling.* Philadelphia: Temple University Press.

Giroux, H. A. (1985). Teachers as transformative intellectuals. *Social Education 4*, 376–379.

Giroux, H. A. (2001). *Theory and resistance in education: Towards a pedagogy for the opposition.* Westpoint, CT: Bergin and Garvey.

Glasser, W. (1986). *Control theory in the classroom.* New York: Harper & Row.

Glasser, W. (2000). *Counseling with choice theory: The new reality therapy.* New York: Harper Collins.

Glickman, C. D., & Wolfgang, C. H. (1978). Conflict in the classroom: An eclectic model of teacher–child interaction. *Elementary School Guidance and Counseling, 13,* 82–87.

Gonzales, P. (2008). *Highlights for TIMSS 2007: Mathematics and science achievement of U.S. fourth- and eighth-grade students in an international context.* Washington, DC: National Center for Education Statistics.

Goodlad, J. (1984). *A place called school: Prospects for the future.* New York: McGraw-Hill.

Goodlad, J. (2004). *A place called school, twentieth anniversary edition.* New York: McGraw-Hill.

Goss v. Lopez, 419 U.S. 565 (1975).

Gouge v. Joint School District No. 1, 310 F.Supp. 984 (W.D.Wis.1970).

Grand Rapids School District v. Ball, 473 U.S. 373 (1985).

Greene, M. (1975). Curriculum and consciousness. In William Pinar (Ed.), *Curriculum theorizing: The reconceptualists* (p. 12). Berkeley, CA: McCutchan.

Greene, M. (1988). *The dialectic of freedom.* New York, NJ: Teachers College Press.

Greene, M. (2000). *Releasing the imagination: Essays on education, the arts, and social change.* New York: Jossey Bass.

Greytak, E. A., Kosciw, J. G., & Diaz, E. M. (2009). *Harsh realities: The experiences of transgender youth in our nation's schools.* New York: Gay, Lesbian and Straight Education Network.

Griffin v. County School Board of Prince Edward County, 377 U.S. 218 (1964).

Hall, G. E., & Hord, S. M. (2011). *Implementing change: Patterns, principles and potholes* (2nd ed.). Upper Saddle River, NJ: Pearson.

Hall, G. E., Negroni, I. A., & George, A. A. (2008). *Examining relationships between urban principal leadership and student learning.* Paper presented at the annual meeting of the American Education Research Association, New York.

Handwerk, P., Tognatta, N., Coley, R. J., & Gitomer, D. H. (2008). *Access to success: Patterns of advanced placement participation in U.S. high schools.* Princeton, NJ: Educational Testing Service.

Hazelwood School District et al. v. Kuhlmeier et al., 484 U.S. 260 (1988).

Heath, S. B. (1983). *Ways with words: Language, life, and work in communities and classrooms.* New York: Cambridge University Press.

Heidegger, M. (1993). The question concerning technology. In D. Krell (Ed.), *Basic writings* (p. 21). New York: HarperCollins Publishers. (Originally published in 1954).

Helena Elementary School District No. 1 v. State, 236 Mont. 44, 769 P.2d 684 (1989).

Hertz, M. F., & David-Ferdon, C. (2008). *Electronic media and youth violence: A CDC issue brief for educators and caregivers.* Atlanta: Centers for Disease Control. Retrieved on May 2, 2009, from http://www.cdc.gov/ViolencePrevention/pdf/EA-brief-a.pdf.

Hillis v. Stephen F. Austin University, 665 F.2d 547 (5th Cir.), cert. denied, 457 U.S. 1106 (1982).

Homes for the Homeless. (2006). *Facts.* Retrieved on May 7, 2006, from http://www.homesforthehomeless.com/index.asp?CID=3&PID=20.

Honig, California Superintendent of Public Instruction v. Doe, No. 86-728, 484 U.S. 305 (1988).

Hord, S. M. (Ed.) (2004). *Learning together, leading together: Changing schools through professional learning communities.* New York: Teachers College Press.

Hortonville Joint School District No. 1 v. Hortonville Education Association, 423 U.S. 1301 (1976).

Howell, W. G., & Peterson, P. E. (2002). *The education gap: Vouchers and urban schools.* Washington, DC: Brookings Institution.

Hunter, R. C. (1997). The mayor versus the school superintendent. *Education and Urban Society, 29*(2), 217–232.

Hussar, W. J., & Bailey, T. M. (2008). *Projections of Education Statistics to 2017.* Washington, DC: National Center for Education Statistics, U.S. Department of Education.

Ingraham v. Wright, 430 U.S. 651 (1977).

Issues Education. (2009). Retrieved from http://www.whitehouse.gov/issues/education/.

Jennings, J. L., & Corcoran, S. P. (2009). "Beware of geeks bearing formulas": Reflections on growth models for school accountability. *Phi Delta Kappan, 90*(9), 635–639.

Jerald, C. (2007). *Keeping kids in school: What research says about preventing dropouts.* Alexandria, VA: The Center for Public Education.

Johnson, D. W., & Johnson, R. (1999). *Learning together and alone: Cooperative, competitive and individualistic learning* (5th ed.). Boston, MA: Allyn & Bacon.

Johnson, S. M. (1990). *Teachers at work: Achieving success in our schools.* New York: Basic Books.

Johnston, L. D., O'Malley, P. M., Bachman, J. G., & Schulenberg, J. E. (2006). *Monitoring the future—National results on adolescent drug use: Overview of key findings, 2005.* Bethesda, MD: National Institute on Drug Abuse.

Josephson Institute for Ethics. (2008). *The ethics of American youth—2008 summary.* Los Angeles, CA: Author.

Kandel, I. L. (1938). *Conflicting theories of education.* New York: Macmillan.

Kelley, M. (2000). Indian affairs head makes apology. *The Free Press.* (September 8, 2000).

Kentucky Education Reform Act of 1990 (KERA, House Bill 940). *Kentucky Acts of 1990* (pp. 1209 ff.). Frankfort, KY.

Kingsville Independent School District v. Cooper, 611 F.2d 1109, 1114 (5th Cir. 1980).

Kor, A.-L., Self, J., & Tait, K. (2001). *Pictorial Socratic dialogue and conceptual change.* Paper presented at 2001 International Conference on Computers in Education (ICCE 2001), Seoul, Korea, November 2001.

Kosciw, J. G., Diaz, E. M., & Greytak, E. A. (2008). *2007 national school climate survey: The experiences of lesbian, gay, bisexual and transgender youth in our nation's schools.* New York: Gay, Lesbian and Straight Education Network (GLSEN).

Kozol, J. (2000). *Ordinary resurrections: Children in the years of hope.* New York: Crown.

Krathwohl, D. R., Bloom, B. S., & Masia, B. B. (1964). *Taxonomy of educational objectives: The classification of educational goals handbook II: Affective domain.* New York: David McKay.

Labaree, D. F. (1997). Public goods, private goods: The American struggle over educational goals. *American Educational Research Journal, 34*(1), 39–81.

Lacampagne, C., Campbell, P. B., Damarin, S., Herzig, A., & Vogt, C. (2007). Gender equity in mathematics. In S. S. Klein, B. Richardson, D. A. Grayson, L. H. Fox, C. Kramarae, D. S. Pollard, and C. A. Dwyer (Eds.), *Handbook for achieving gender equity through education* (2nd ed., pp. 235–254). Mahwah, NJ: Lawrence Erlbaum.

Lamb's Chapel v. Center Moriches Union Free School District, 508 U.S. 384 (1993).

LaMorte, M. (2008). *School law: Cases and concepts* (9th ed.). Boston: Allyn & Bacon.

Langdon, C. A., & Vesper, N. (2008). The sixth Phi Delta Kappa poll of teachers' attitudes toward the public schools. *Phi Delta Kappan, 81*(8), 607–611.

Lee v. Weisman, 505 U.S. 577 (1992).

Leithwood, K., & Jantzi, D. (2009). A review of empirical evidence about school size effects: A policy perspective. *Review of Educational Research, 79*(1), 464–490.

Lemon v. Kurtzman, 403 U.S. 602 (1971).

Lerman, R. I. (2000). *Are teens in low-income and welfare families working too much?* Washington, DC: Urban Institute. Retrieved on May 22, 2006, from www.urban.org/publications/309708.html.

Lerner, P. K. (2007). Gender equity in physical education and athletics. In S. S. Klein, B. Richardson, D. A. Grayson, L. H. Fox, C. Kramarae, D. S. Pollard, and C. A. Dwyer (Eds.), *Handbook for achieving gender equity through education* (2nd ed, pp. 381–410). Mahwah, NJ: Lawrence Erlbaum.

Lipsky, D. K., & Gartner, A. (1996). Inclusion, school restructuring, and the remaking of American society. *Harvard Educational Review 66*(4), 762–796.

Locke, J. (1812). Some thoughts concerning education. In *The works of John Locke,* Volume X. London: Printed for W. Otridge [and others].

Long v. Zopp, 476 F.2d 180 (4th Cir. 1973).

Lucia v. Duggan, 303 F. Supp. 112 (D.Mass.1969).

Mander, J., & Tauli-Corpuz, B. (2006). *Paradigm wars: Indigenous peoples' resistance to globalization.* San Francisco: Sierra Club Books.

Martin, J. R. (1985). *Reclaiming a conversation: The ideal of the educated woman.* New Haven, CT: Yale University Press.

Mastrangelo v. West Side Union High School District, 2 Cal 2d, 540 (1935).

McEwin, C. K., Dickinson, T. S., & Jenkins, D. M. (2003). *America's middle schools in the new century: Status and progress.* Westerville, OH: National Middle School Association.

McNeil, M. (2009). 46 states commit to common-standards push. *Education Week, 28*(33), 16.

Mondimore, F. M. (1996). *A natural history of homosexuality.* Baltimore: Johns Hopkins University Press.

Monroe, P. (1905). *History of education.* New York: Macmillan.

Morris v. Douglas County School District, 403 P.2d 775, 776 (Or.1965).

Mullis, I. V. S., Martin, M. O., Kennedy, A. M., & Foy, P. (2007). *PIRLS 2006 international report: IEA's progress in international reading literacy study in primary schools in 40 countries.* Chestnut Hill, MA: TIMSS & PIRLS International Study Center, Boston College.

Nansel, T. R., Overpeck, M. D., Haynie, D. L., Ruan, J., & Scheidt, P. C. (2003). Relationships between bullying and violence among US youth. *Archives of Pediatrics and Adolescent Medicine, 157*(4), 348–357.

National Campaign to Prevent Teen and Unplanned Pregnancy. (2009). *What works: Curriculum-based programs that prevent teen pregnancy.* Washington, DC: Author.

National Center for Children in Poverty. (2008). *Basic facts about low-income children: Birth to age 18.* New York: Author. Retrieved on January 27, 2009, from http://www.nccp.org/publications/pub_845.html.

National Center for Education Statistics, U.S. Department of Education. (2004). *The condition of education 2004* (NCES 2004-077), Indicator 34. Washington, DC: Author.

National Center for Education Statistics, U.S. Department of Education. (2005). *The condition of education 2005.* Washington, DC: Author.

National Center for Education Statistics, U.S. Department of Education. (2006). *Navigating resources for rural schools.* Washington, DC: Author. Retrieved on January 27, 2009, from http://nces.ed.gov/pubs2007/ruraled/hl_demographics.asp#top.

National Center for Education Statistics, U.S. Department of Education. (2007a). *The condition of education 2007* (NCES 2007-064). Washington, DC: Author.

National Center for Education Statistics, U.S. Department of Education. (2007b). *Revenues and expenditures for public elementary and secondary education school year 2005–06 (fiscal year 2006).* Washington, DC: Author.

National Center for Education Statistics, U.S. Department of Education. (2008). *Projections of education statistics to 2017.* Washington, DC: Author. Available at http://www.nces.ed.gov/programs/projections/projections2017/.

National Center for Education Statistics, U.S. Department of Education. (2009). *NAEP 2008 trends in academic progress.* Washington, DC: Author.

National Center for Health Statistics. (2002). *Health, United States, 2002 with chartbook on trends in the health of Americans,* Table 65. Hyattsville, MD: Author.

National Center on Family Homelessness. (2008). *The characteristics and needs of families experiencing homelessness.* Newton Centre, MA: Author.

National Center on Family Homelessness. (2009). *America's youngest outcasts: State report card on child homelessness.* Newton Centre, MA: Author.

National Commission on Excellence in Education. (1983, April). *A nation at risk: The imperative for educational reform.* Washington, DC: U.S. Government Printing Office.

National Committee on Science Education Standards and Assessment, National Research Council. (1996). *National science education standards.* Washington, DC: National Academies Press.

National Conference on Citizenship. (2006). *American civic health index: Broken engagement.* Washington, DC: Author.

National Council for the Social Studies. (2009). *Expectations of excellence: Curriculum standards for social* studies. Silver Spring, MD: Author.

National Council of Teachers of Mathematics. (2000). *Principles and standards for school mathematics.* Reston, VA: Author.

National Drug Intelligence Center. (2008). *National drug threat assessment 2009.* Retrieved on May 3, 2009, from http://www.usdoj.gov/ndic/pubs31/31379/index.htm.

National Federation of State High School Associations. *NFHS participation figures for 2006–07.* Retrieved on May 17, 2009, from http://www.nfhs.org/custom/participation_figures/default.aspx.

National Governors Association, Council of Chief State School Officers, and Achieve, Inc. (2008). *Benchmarking for success: Ensuring U.S. students receive a world-class education.* Washington, DC: National Governors Association.

National Law Center on Homelessness and Poverty. (2007). *2007 annual report: National Law Center on Homelessness & Poverty.* Washington, DC: Author.

National Law Center on Homelessness and Poverty. (2008). *Some facts on homelessness, housing, and violence against women.* Washington, DC: Author.

National Research Council. (2000). *How people learn: Brain, mind, experience and school, expanded edition.* Committee on Developments in the Science of Learning and Committee on Learning Research and Educational Practice. J. D. Bransford, A. Brown, and R. R. Cocking (Eds.), Commission on Behavioral and Social Sciences and Education. Washington DC: National Academies Press.

National Research Council. (2005). *How students learn: History, mathematics, and science in the classroom.* Committee on How People Learn: A Targeted Report for Teachers. In M. S. Donovan and J. D. Bransford (Eds.), Commission on Behavioral and Social Sciences and Education. Washington DC: National Academies Press.

Neild, R. C., & Balfanz, R. (2006). *Unfulfilled promise: The dimensions and characteristics of Philadelphia's dropout crisis, 2000–2005.* Philadelphia, PA: Project U-Turn.

Neiman, S., & DeVoe, J. F. (2009). *Crime, violence, discipline, and safety in U.S. public schools: Findings from the school survey on crime and safety: 2007–08* (NCES 2009-326). Washington, DC: National Center for Education Statistics.

Nelson-Barber, S., & Estrin, E. T. (1995). Bringing Native American perspectives to mathematics and science teaching. *Theory into Practice, 34*(3), 174–185.

New Jersey v. T.L.O., 469 U.S. 325 (1985).

Newport, F. (2009). *Despite recession, no uptick in Americans' religiosity.* Princeton, NJ: Gallup Organization, March 23, 2009. Retrieved on May 14, 2009, from http://www.gallup.com/poll/117040/Despite-Recession-No-Uptick-Americans-Religiosity.aspx.

Nietzsche, F. (1986). The wanderer and his shadow. In R. J. Hollingdale (Trans.), *Human, all too human* (p. 6). Cambridge: Cambridge University Press. (Originally published in 1880)

Noddings, N. (1993). *The challenge to care in schools.* New York, NY: Teachers College Press.

Noddings, N. (2005). *The challenge to care in schools: An alternative approach to education* (2nd ed.). New York: Teachers College Press.

North Haven Board of Education v. Bell, 456 U.S. 512 (1982).

Obama, B., & Biden, J. (2009). *Investing in America's future: Barack Obama and Joe Biden's plan for science and innovation.* Retrieved from http://www.barackobama.com/pdf/issues/FactSheetScience.pdf.

OECD. (2008). *Growing unequal-income distribution and poverty in OECD countries* (C08: Child poverty). Paris: Author. Retrieved on May 11, 2009, from http://www.oecd.org/dataoecd/52/43/41929552.pdf.

Olson, L. (2000). The common good. In *Lessons of a century: A nation's schools come of age.* Bethesda, MD: Editorial Projects in Education.

Olson, L. (2001). Overboard on testing? *Quality Counts 2001: A better balance* [*Education Week, 20*(7)]. Bethesda, MD: Editorial Projects in Education.

O'Mara, M. P. (2006). Uncovering the city in the suburb: Cold war politics, scientific elites, and high-tech spaces. In K. M. Kruse and T. J. Sugrue (Eds.), *The new suburban history* (pp. 57–79). Chicago: The University of Chicago Press.

Organisation for Economic Co-operation and Development. (n.d.) *About OECD.* Paris: Author. Retrieved on June 9, 2009, from http://www.oecd.org/pages/0,3417,en_36734052_36734103_1_1_1_1_1,00.html.

Organisation for Economic Co-operation and Development. (2008). *OECD factbook 2008.* Paris: Author.

Organisation for Economic Co-operation and Development. (2009). *Equally prepared for life? How 15-year-old boys and girls perform in school.* Paris: Author.

Ost, J., & Gates, G. J. (2004). *The gay & lesbian atlas.* Washington, DC: Urban Institute.

Owasso Independent School District No. 1 v. Falvo, 534 U.S. 426 (2002).

Ozman, H. A., & Craver, S. M. (2008). *Philosophical foundations of education.* Columbus, OH: Merrill.

Partnership for 21st Century Skills. (2007). *Framework for 21st century learning.* Tucson, AZ: Author. Available at http://www.21stcenturyskills.org/index.php?Itemid=120&id=254&option=com_content&task=view.

Partnership for 21st Century Skills. (2009). *P21 framework definitions document.* Tucson, AZ: Author. Retrieved on June 8, 2009, from http://www.21stcenturyskills.org/documents/p21_framework_definitions_052909.pdf.

Peirce, C. S. (1955). The fixation of belief. In Justus Buchler (Ed.), *Philosophical writings of Peirce* (pp. 5–22). New York: Dover. (Originally published in 1877)

Perrone, V. (Ed.) (1991). *Expanded student assessment for supervision and curriculum development*. Alexandria, VA: Association for Supervision and Curriculum Development.

Perry v. Sindermann, 408 U.S. 593 (1972).

Peter W. v. San Francisco Unified School District, 131 Cal. Rptr. 854 (Cal. Ct. App. 1976).

Pickering v. Board of Education, 391 U.S. 563 (1968).

Planty, M., Hussar, W., Snyder, T., Provasnik, S., Kena, G., Dinkes, R., KewalRamani, A., & Kemp, J. (2008). *The condition of education 2008* (NCES 2008-031). Washington, DC: National Center for Education Statistics, U.S. Department of Education.

Plessy v. Ferguson, 163 U.S. 537 (1896).

Plyler v. Doe, 457 U.S. 202 (1982).

Police Department of the City of Chicago v. Mosley, 408 U.S. 92 (1972).

Poll adds "youth voice" on schools. (2009, May 13). *Education Week, 28*(31), 4.

Quaid, L. (2008). Girls are equal to boys on state math tests, study finds. *Education Week, 27*(44), 12.

Quintilian. (1905). *The institutes of oratory* (W. Guthrie., Trans.). London: Dewick and Clark.

Ravitch, D. (1985). *The schools we deserve: Reflections on the educational crisis of our times*. New York: Basic Books.

Ravitch, D. (2001). *A century of battles over school reform*. New York: Simon and Schuster.

Recruiting New Teachers, Inc. (1998). *The essential profession: A national survey of public attitudes toward teaching, educational opportunity and school reform*. Belmont, MA: Author.

Roderick, M. (1993). *The path to dropping out: Evidence for intervention*. Westport, CT: Auburn House.

Rose v. Council for Better Education, 790 S.W.2d 186, 60 Ed. Law Rep. 1289. (Supreme Court of Kentucky 1989).

Rose, S. J. (2000). *Social stratification in the United States: The new American profile poster*. New York: New Press.

Rosenshine, B., & Stevens, R. (1986). Teaching functions. In M. C. Wittrock (Ed.), *Handbook of research on teaching* (3rd ed., pp. 376–391). New York: Macmillan.

Rotberg, I. C. (2008). Quick fixes, test scores, and the global economy: Myths that continue to confound us. *Education Week, 27*(41), 27, 32.

Rousseau, J-J. (1979). *Émile* (Alan Bloom, Trans.). New York: Basic Books. (Originally published in 1782)

Sabo, D., & Veliz, P. (2008). *Go out and play: Youth sports in America*. East Meadow, NY: Women's Sports Foundation.

San Antonio (Texas) Independent School District v. Rodriguez, 411 U.S. 1 (1973).

Sanders, W. L., & Rivers, J. C. (1996). *Cumulative and residual effects of teachers on future academic achievement*. Knoxville: University of Tennessee Value-Added Research and Assessment Center.

Santa Fe Independent School District, Petitioner v. Jane Doe, 530 U.S. 290 (2000).

Sashkin, M., & Egermeier, J. (1993). *School change models and processes: A review and synthesis of research and practice*. Washington, DC: U.S. Department of Education.

Schmuck, R., & Schmuck, P. A. (1983). *Group processes in the classrooms*. Dubuque, IA: Wm. C. Brown.

Schwarz, C. V. (2002, April). *Using model-centered science instruction to foster students' epistemologies in learning with models*. Paper presented at the annual meeting of the American Educational Research Association, New Orleans, LA.

Scoville v. Board of Education of Joliet Township High School District 204, 425 F.2d 10 (7th Cir. 1970).

Serrano v. Priest, 5 Cal.3d 584 (1971).

Sheive, L. T., & Schoenheit, M. B. (1987). Vision and the worklife of educational leaders. In L. T. Sheive and M. B. Schoenheit (Eds.), *Leadership: Examining the elusive* (p. 99). Alexandria, VA: Association for Supervision and Curriculum Development.

Shepard, L., Hammerness, K., Darling-Hammond, L., Rust, F., Snowden, J. B., Gordon, E., Gutierrez, C., & Pacheco, A. (2007). Assessment. In L. Darling-Hammond and J. Bransford (Eds.), *Preparing teachers for a changing world: What teachers should learn and be able to do* (pp. 275–326). San Francisco: Jossey-Bass.

Simpson, E. J. (1972). *The classification of educational objectives in the psychomotor domain: The psychomotor domain*, Vol. 3. Washington, DC: Gryphon House.

Sizer, T. (2004). *The red pencil: Convictions from experience in education*. New Haven, CT: Yale University Press.

Slavin, R. (1996). *Education for all*. Exton, PA: Swets & Zeitlinger.

Smith, L. G., & Smith, J. K. (1984). *Lives in education*. Ames, IA: Educational Studies Press.

Snyder, H. N., & Sickmund, M. (2006). *Juvenile offenders and victims: 2006 national report*. Washington, DC: U.S. Department of Justice, Office of Justice Programs, Office of Juvenile Justice and Delinquency Prevention.

Spanierman v. Hughes, 2008 U.S. Dist. LEXIS 69569 (D. Conn. Sept. 16, 2008).

Spring, J. (2001). *The American school: 1642–2004* (5th ed.) Boston: McGraw-Hill.

State v. Scopes, 152 Tenn. 424, 278 S.W. 57 (Tenn. 1926).

Staurowsky, E. J., Hogshead-Makar, N., Kane, M. J., Wughalter, E., Yiamouyiannis, A., & Lerner, P. K. (2007). Gender equity in physical education and athletics. In S. S. Klein, B. Richardson, D. A. Grayson, L. H. Fox, C. Kramarae, D. S. Pollard, & C. A. Dwyer (Eds.), *Handbook for achieving gender equity through education* (2nd ed., pp. 381–410). Mahwah, NJ: Lawrence Erlbaum.

Stiggins, R. (2009). Assessment FOR learning in upper elementary grades. *Phi Delta Kappan, 90*(6), 419–421.

Stiggins, R., & DuFour, R. (2009). Maximizing the power of formative assessments. *Phi Delta Kappan, 90*(9), 640–644.

Stullich, S., Eisner, E., & McCrary, J. (2007). *National assessment of Title I, volume I: Implementation* (NCEE2008-4012). Washington, DC: Institute of Education Sciences, U.S. Department of Education.

Swanson, C. B. (2009). *Cities in crisis 2009: Closing the graduation gap*. Bethesda, MD: Editorial Projects in Education.

Symcox, L. (2002). *Whose history? The struggle for national standards in American classrooms*. New York: Teachers College Press.

Taba, H. (1962). *Curriculum development theory and practice*. New York: Harcourt, Brace & World.

Tammy Kitzmiller, et al. v. Dover Area School District et al., 400 F. Supp. 2d 707 (M.D. Pa.) U.S. District Court for the Middle District of Pennsylvania (2005).

Thorne, B. (2002). Do girls and boys have different cultures? In S. M. Bailey (Ed.), *The Jossey-Bass reader on gender in education* (pp. 125–150). San Francisco: Jossey-Bass.

Tinker v. Des Moines Independent Community School District, 393 U.S. 503 (1969).

Tisher, R. P., Fyfield, J. A., & Taylor, S. M. (1978). *Beginning to teach, Vol. 1. The induction of teachers: A bibliography and description of activities in Australia and the U.K.* Canberra: Australian Government Publishing Service.

Toch, T., Jerald, C. D., & Dillon, E. (2007). Surprise—High school reform is working. *Phi Delta Kappan, 88*(6), 433–437.

Trotter, A. (2008). McCain and Obama share basic views on ed. tech. *Education Week, 28*(8), 8–9.

Turk v. Franklin Special School District, 640 S.W.2d 218, 220 (Tenn. 1982).

Two lenses: Academic achievement, Quality counts. (2009, January 8). *Education Week, 28*(17), 39.

Tyler, R. W. (1950). *Basic principles of curriculum development*. Chicago, IL: University of Chicago Press.

UNICEF. (2000). *Domestic violence: An epidemic*. New York: Author.

United States Congress. (1994). *Goals 2000: Educate America Act*. Retrieved on June 8, 2009, from http://www.ed.gov/legislation/GOALS2000/TheAct/index.html.

U.S. Census Bureau. (n.d.). *Table 8: Poverty of people, by residence: 1959 to 2004*. Retrieved on May 7, 2006, from www.census.gov/hhes/www/poverty/histpov/hstpov8.html.

U.S. Census Bureau. (2008). *Statistical abstract of the United States: 2009* (128th ed.). Washington, DC: U.S. Government Printing Office.

U.S. Census Bureau, American FactFinder. (2008a). *Disability characteristics*. (2005–2007 American Community Survey 3-Year Estimates). Retrieved on May 13, 2009, from http://factfinder.census.gov/servlet/STTable?_bm=y&geo_id=01000US&-qr_name=ACS_2007_3YR_G00_S1801&-ds_name=ACS_2007_3YR_G00_&-_lang=en&-_caller=geoselect&-state=st&-format=.

U.S. Census Bureau, American FactFinder. (2008b). *Language spoken at home by ability to speak English for the population 5 years and over.* (2005–2007 American Community Survey 3-Year Estimates). Retrieved May 11, 2009, from http://factfinder.census.gov/servlet/DTTable?_bm=y&-geo_id=01000US&-ds_name=ACS_2007_3YR_G00_&-SubjectID=15261972&-_lang=en&-mt_name=ACS_2007_3YR_G2000_B16001&-mt_name=ACS_2007_3YR_G2000_C16001&-format=&-CONTEXT=dt_.

U.S. Census Bureau, American FactFinder. (2008c). *People reporting ancestry, BO4006.* (2005–2007 American Community Survey 3-Year Estimates). Retrieved May 11, 2009, from http://factfinder.census.gov/servlet/ DTTable?_bm=y&-state=dt&-ds_name=ACS_2007_3YR_G00_&-mt_name=ACS_2007_3YR_G2000_B04006&-redoLog=false&-_caller=geoselect&-geo_id=01000US&-geo_id=NBSP&-format=&-_lang=en.

U.S. Department of Commerce, Bureau of the Census. (1982). *Digest of education statistics 1982.* Washington, DC: U.S. Government Printing Office.

U.S. Department of Education. (2009a, March 7). American Recovery and Reinvestment Act of 2009: Saving and creating jobs and reforming education. Retrieved on August 17, 2009, from http://www.ed.gov/policy/gen/leg/recovery/implementation.html.

U.S. Department of Education. (2009b). *The Blue Ribbon Schools Program: Recognizing excellent American schools.* Washington, DC: Author. Retrieved on June 1, 2009, from http://www.ed.gov/programs/nclbbrs/about-brs.pdf.

U.S. Department of Education, Institute of Education Statistics. (2005). *America's charter schools: Results from the NAEP 2003 pilot study* (NCES 2005-456). Washington, DC: Author, 2005.

U.S. Department of Education, Institute of Education Statistics. (2008). *1.5 million homeschooled students in the United States in 2007. Issue brief.* Washington, DC: National Center for Education Statistics.

U.S. Department of Education, National Center for Educational Statistics. (2003). *The condition of education 2003* (NCES 2003-067). Washington, DC: Author.

U.S. Department of Education, National Center for Educational Statistics. (2005). *The condition of education 2005* (NCES 2005-094). Washington, DC: Author.

Vandivere, S., Tout, K., Zaslow, M., Calkins, J., & Capizzano, J. (2003). *Unsupervised time: Family and child factors associated with self-care (Occasional Paper Number 71).* Washington, DC: The Urban Institute.

van Driel, B. (2005). Coming to justice: A program for youth around issues of international justice. *Intercultural Education, 16*(2), 161–169.

Wallace v. Jaffree, 472 U.S. 38 (1985).

Wenglinsky, H. (2005). *Using technology wisely: The keys to success in schools.* New York: Teachers College Press.

West, C. (1993). *Prophetic thought in postmodern times.* Monroe, ME: Common Courage Press.

Whitehead, A. F. (1929). *The aims of education.* New York, NY: Free Press.

Willard, E. (1893). A plan for improving female education. In A. C. Brackett (Ed.), *Women and the higher education* (pp. 12–14). New York: Harper & Brothers.

Wilson, T. P. (1994a). *Navajo: Walking in beauty.* San Francisco, CA: Chronicle Books.

Wilson, T. P. (1994b). *Lakota: Seeking the great spirit.* San Francisco, CA: Chronicle Books.

Wilson, T. P. (1994c). *Hopi: Following the path of peace.* San Francisco, CA: Chronicle Books.

Wolman v. Walter, 433 U.S. 229 (1977).

Wood v. Strickland, 420 U.S. 308 (1975).

Yiping, L., Abrami, P. C., and Apollonia, S. (2001). Small group and individual learning with technology: A meta-analysis. *Review of Educational Research 71*(3), pp. 449–521.

Zobrest v. Catalina School District, 509 U.S. 1 (1993).

Abbott, G., 182
Abma, J. C., 215
Abrami, P. C., 357
Achieve, Inc., 305
Achilles, C. M., 373
Acs, G., 215
Adeoy, H., 356
Alexander, H. G., 82
American Association of University Women, 211, 213
American Association of University Women Educational Foundation, 210
American Federation of Teachers, 21
American Management Association, 306
Anderson, L. M., 372
Anderson, L. W., 326, 350
Anderson, P. M., 159
Anderson, S., 169
Annie E. Casey Foundation, 215
Apollonia, S., 357
Armytage, W. H. G., 67
Arnott, M., 181
Aron, L. Y., 211

Bachman, J. G., 216
Bailey, T. M., 11
Balfanz, R., 374
Barton, P. E., 171, 175, 203
Beane, J. A., 154
Bellah, R. N., 144, 145
Berliner, D. C., 381
Biden, J., 354
Bienvenue, L., 182
Bloom, B. S., 349, 350
Borja, R. R., 321
Bowles, S., 130
Bradley, E., 36
Bramlett, M. D., 202
Bransford, J. D., 99, 160
Brantmeier, C., 182
Brazil, N., 359
Brophy, J. E., 372
Brougham, S. P., 150, 151
Brown, A., 99
Buber, M., 116
Buckley, J., 148, 150
Buell, N., 327
Burger, C., 182
Burman, M., 356
Bushaw, W. J., 6, 7, 215

California Department of Education, 342
Calkins, J., 207
Cambron-McCabe, N. H., 210
Campbell, P. B., 182
Capizzano, J., 207
Carlito, D., 182
Carter, R. T., 220
Cartier, M., 146
Cavanagh, J., 169
Cavanagh, S., 322, 324, 335
Center for Education Reform, 149, 150
Centers for Disease Control and Prevention, 210, 212, 213, 215
Child Trends DataBank, 374
Choy, S., 187
Christensen, C. M., 152
Civil Rights Project, Harvard University, 178
Clark, J., 367
Cocking, R. R., 99

Coley, R. J., 171, 175, 182, 203
Colin, L., 295
Collett, P., 295
Collins, C., 169
Conchas, G. Q., 155
Consumers Union Education Services, 250
Coppernoll, C., 167
Corbett, C., 181
Corcoran, S. P., 321
Council for American Private Education, 151
Council of Chief State School Officers, 142, 305
Coutnen, N. K., 169, 170
Cowgill, C., 60
Craver, S. M., 97
Crawford, C., 327
Cross, W. E., Jr., 220

Dalton, B., 156, 159
Damarin, S., 182
Darling-Hammond, L., 17, 160, 319, 328, 329, 330
David-Ferdon, C., 213
Davis, M. R., 152
Dawson, B. S., 215
Day, J. C., 173
Deal, T. E., 147, 160
DeHas, 183
Dejaeghere, J. G., 141
DeVoe, J. F., 213
Dewey, J., 93, 114, 129
Diaz, E. M., 211
Dickinson, T. S., 154
Dillon, E., 155
Dinkes, R., 148, 154, 158, 175, 177, 184, 186, 202, 216, 224, 226, 323
Donovan, M. S., 99
Duck, L., 109, 111
DuFour, R., 311, 314

Educational Policies Commission, 59
Educational Testing Service, 177, 319, 322
Education Trust, 160
Egermeier, J., 371
Eisner, E., 206
Elliott, E., 380
Elrod, E., 96
Emery, S., 146, 180
Emmer, E. T., 372
EPE Research Center, 178
Estrin, E. T., 176
Evertson, C. M., 372

Faulk, B., 319
Ferdman, B. M., 220
Fine, M., 220
Finn, C. E., Jr., 29
Finn, J. D., 373
Flygare, T. J., 294
Ford, A., 359
Foss, S., 169, 170
Fox, J. A., 209
Foy, P., 324
Freedman, S. W., 189
Fyfield, J. A., 386

Gallegos, P. I., 220
Gallup, A. M., 6, 7, 215
Garofano, A., 207
Gartner, A., 186
Gates, G. J., 183, 184

Gathercoal, P., 102
Genesee, F., 178, 179
George, A. A., 347, 379
Gintis, H., 130
Giroux, H. A., 115, 127
Gitomer, D. H., 182
Glasser, W., 124
Gonzalez, P., 347
Good, T. L., 372
Goodlad, J., 126
Gordon, E, 328, 329, 330
Greene, M., 95, 128
Greytak, E. A., 211
Gutierrez, C., 328, 329, 330

Hall, G. E., 347, 378, 379, 384, 386
Hammerness, K., 328, 329, 330
Hampden-Thompson, G., 187
Handwerk, R., 182
Haynie, D. L., 213
Heath, S. B., 144
Heidegger, M., 85
Helms, J. F., 220
Hertz, M. F., 213
Herzig, A., 182
Hill, C., 181
Hoffman, L., 156, 159
Hogshead-Makar, N., 183
Hollinbeck, K., 60
Homes for the Homeless, 205
Hoover, V., 22
Hord, S. M., 376, 378, 384, 386
Horn, M. G., 152
Howell, W. G., 150
Hunter, R. C., 258
Hussar, W. J., 11, 148, 154, 158, 175, 177, 184, 186, 187, 202, 216, 224, 226, 323

Jablonski, G., 319
Jackson, B. W., III, 220
Jacobson, L., 153
Janzi, D., 159
Jenkins, D. M., 154
Jennings, J. L., 321
Jerald, C. D., 155, 375
Johnson, C. W., 152
Johnson, D. W., 354
Johnson, R., 354
Johnson, S. M., 127
Johnston, L. D., 216
Josephson Institute for Ethics, 389

Kandel, I. L. 1938, 129
Kane, M. J., 183
Kaplan, B., 22
Karayan, S., 102
Keaton, P. W., 150, 151
Kelley, M., 174
Kemp, J., 148, 154, 158, 175, 177, 184, 186, 202, 216, 224, 226, 323
Kena, G., 148, 154, 158, 175, 177, 184, 186, 202, 216, 224, 226, 323
Kennedy, A. M., 324
KewalRamani, A., 148, 154, 158, 175, 177, 184, 186, 202, 216, 224, 226, 323
Koball, H., 215
Koch, J., 182
Kor, A. L., 89
Kosciw, J. G., 211
Kozol, J., 159

Krathwohl, D. R., 350
Kubinak, T., 388

Labaree, D. F., 140
Lacampagne, C., 182
LaMorte, M., 283, 292
Langdon, C. A., 5
Laphan, M., 169
Leithwood, K., 159
LePage, P., 160
Lerman, R. I., 216
Lerner, P. K., 183
Lippman, C., 123
Lipsky, D. K., 186
Locke, J., 91
Longman, T., 189
Lopez, M., 250
Losen, D., 223

Madsen, R., 144, 145
Mander, J., 144
Manzo, K. K., 322
Martin, J. R., 89
Martin, M. O., 324
Martinez, G. M., 215
Masia, B. B., 350
McCarthy, M. M., 210
McCrary, J., 206
McEwin, C. K., 154
McMahon, K., 250
McNeil, M., 307
Mears, D. P., 211
Mohl, J., 222
Mondimore, F. M., 183
Monroe, P., 44
Morris, V. C., 107
Mosher, W. D., 202, 215
Mullis, I. V. S., 324
Murphy, K., 189
Musial, D., 108

Nansel, T. R., 213
National Campaign to Prevent Teen and Unplanned Pregnancy, 215
National Center for Children in Poverty, 157, 170
National Center for Education Statistics. *See* U.S. Department of Education, National Center for Education Statistics
National Center for Health Statistics, 216
National Center on Family Homelessness, 204, 205, 206
National Committee on Science Education Standards and Assessment, National Research Council, 307
National Council for the Social Studies, 307
National Council of Teachers of Mathematics, 307
National Drug Intelligence Center, 213
National Education Association, 222, 356, 382
National Federation of State High School Associations, 183
National Governors Association, 142, 305
National Law Center on Homelessness and Poverty, 203, 204, 208
Negroni, I. A., 360, 379
Neild, R. C., 374
Neiman, S., 213
Nelson-Barber, S., 176
Neuberger, J. D., 267
Newport, F., 185
Nietzsche, F., 95
Noddings, N., 85, 117

Obama, B., 354
Olson, L., 155, 326
O'Malley, P. M., 216
O'Mara, M. P., 157

Orfield, G., 223
Organisation for Economic Co-operation and Development, 170, 252, 322, 323
Ost, J., 183, 184
Overpeck, M. D., 213
Ozman, H. A., 97

Pacheco, A., 328, 329, 330
Pai, Y., 107
Parker, K., 388
Parker, L. O., 159
Parker, R., 139
Parkey, F. W., 343
Partnership for 21st Century Skills, 142, 308
Peirce, C. S., 128
Perrone, V., 127
Peterson, K. D., 147, 160
Peterson, P. E., 150
Pitts, L., 131
Pizzigati, S., 169
Planty, M., 148, 154, 158, 175, 177, 184, 186, 202, 216, 224, 226, 323
Postal, L., 303
Potts, E., 319
Powell, L. C., 220
Provasnik, S., 148, 154, 158, 175, 177, 184, 186, 187, 202, 216, 224, 226, 323

Quaid, L., 181
Quindler, J., 359
Quintilian, 32

Ravitch, D., 127
Recruiting New Teachers, Inc., 4, 5, 11, 20
Rice, R., 131
Rivers, J. C., 160
Roderick, M., 374
Rodríguez, L. F., 155
Rooney, P., 187
Rose, S. J., 169
Rosenshine, B., 352
Rotberg, I. C., 322
Rousseau, J. J., 115
Ruan, J., 213
Rust, F., 328, 329, 330

Sable, J., 156, 159, 207
Sabo, D., 183
Sanders, W. L., 160
Sashkin, M., 371
Scheidt, P. C., 213
Schmuck, P. A., 123
Schmuck, R., 123
Schneider, M., 148, 150
Schoenheit, M. B., 132
Schueller, J., 182
Schulenberg, J. E., 216
Schwartz, C. V., 353
Self, J., 89
Sheive, L. T., 132
Shepard, L., 328, 329, 330
Sickmond, M., 211
Simpson, E. J., 351
Sizer, T., 110
Skinner, B. F., 110
Slavin, R., 361
Slifer, J., 222
Smith, J. K., 34
Smith, L. G., 34
Snowden, J. B., 328, 329, 330
Snyder, H. N., 211
Snyder, T., 148, 154, 158, 175, 177, 184, 186, 202, 216, 224, 226, 323
Sosa, T., 182
Spring, J., 148
St. Rose, A., 181
Stanford, B. H., 343
Starnes, B. A., 176

Staurowsky, E. J., 183
Stevens, R., 352
Stiggins, R., 311, 312, 314
Stout, C., 201
Strawn, C., 182
Stullich, S., 206
Sullivan, W. M., 144, 145
Summerfield, J. P., 159
Swaim, N. L., 150, 151
Swanson, C. B., 155, 221, 223, 224
Swidler, A., 144, 145
Symcox, L., 309

Taba, H., 337
Tait, K., 89
Taturn, B. D., 220
Tauli-Corpuz, B., 144
Taylor, S. M., 386
Thomas, S. B., 210
Thorne, B., 181
Tipton, S. M., 144, 145
Tisher, R. P., 386
Tobias, S., 182
Toch, T., 155
Tognatta, N., 182
Toledo, E., 36
Tout, K., 207
Trotter, A., 152
Tyler, R. W., 337

Uchiyama, K., 347
UNICEF, 209
U.S. Census Bureau, 59, 142, 155, 156, 157, 158, 168, 169, 170, 173, 174, 176, 181, 183, 184, 188, 202, 209–210, 216, 221, 224, 225, 226
U.S. Congress, 309
U.S. Department of Education, 7, 57, 159, 160, 208, 261
U.S. Department of Education, Institute of Education Sciences, 148
U.S. Department of Education, National Center for Education Statistics, 10, 149, 150, 152, 157, 158, 171, 184, 185, 186, 207, 208, 221, 234, 237, 244, 247, 323

Vandivere, S., 207
Van Driel, B., 219
Veliz, P., 183
Vesper, N., 5
Viadero, D., 105
Vogt, C., 182
Voltz, D., 359

Wald, J., 223
Ward, D., 180
Waters, R., 96
Weaver, R., 3
Weber, D., 303
Weinstein, H. M., 189
Weis, L., 220
West, C., 83, 85
Whitehead, A. F., 91
Wiggins, G., 318
Wijeyesinghe, C. L., 220
Wilde, J., 182
Wiley, A., 319
Willard, E., 49
Wilson, T. P., 99
Wirt, J., 187
Wolfgang, C., 123
Wong, L. M., 220
Wughalter, E., 183

Yiamouyiannis, A., 183
Yiping, L., 357
Young, E., 24

Zaslow, M., 207
Zawitz, M. W., 209

SUBJECT INDEX

Ableism, 219
Abstinence-only sex education, 36
Abstracting questions, 316
Abstraction, 82, 84
Academic achievement
  of English-language learners, 178
  poverty and, 171
  racial and ethnic disparities in, 175, 328, 329
  schools' role in, 143
Academic freedom, 285–286
Academies, 68
Accelerated Schools, 361
Accommodations, testing, 62, 319
Accountability, 320–328
  defined, 257
  district report cards, 261
  equity within, 326, 328
  Florida high schools, 303–304
  funding without, 256
  growth model, 321
  importance of, 260
  increasing expectations for, 373–375
  international comparisons, 322–324
  politics and, 257–258
  principals, 261
  ranking of schools, districts, and states, 373–374
  rewards for, 260–261
  roots of, 260
  school report cards, 261
  teachers, 260, 261
  test-based, 373
  testing challenges, 324–326
  using technology to track student learning, 321
  value-added model, 321
Accreditation programs, 14–15, 343–344
Achievement gap, 255, 328, 329
Achievement tests, 181
Actions in tort, 288
Actions steps, 376
Active learning time (ALT), 352
Adaptation, 129
Adequacy, 244
Adequate yearly progress (AYP), 142, 143, 206, 255, 309
Administrative law, 269
Adult education, 63–64
Advanced certification, 16–17
Advertising, as revenue source, 249, 250
Advisory functions of state boards of education, 241, 242
AERA (American Education Research Association), 325
Aesthetic development, 107
Affective domain, 350–351
Affirmative action, 279
African Americans
  academic achievement, 175, 328, 329
  access to technology, 225, 226
  college enrollment, 216
  crime, 211
  desegregation benefits, 278
  disproportionate placements, 186
  dropout rate, 374
  educational history, 45–47
  graduation rate, 221
  high-poverty schools, 206
  jobs during high school, 216
  as racial and ethnic group, 173, 174
  racial identity development, 220

AFT (American Federation of Teachers), 284–285, 390, 391
Age groups, and poverty, 170–171
Age of Pericles, 31
Age of Reason, 35
Age of the revival of learning, 33
Aging of population, 155
Agostini v. Felton (1997), 272, 273
Aguilar, Ayeh, 167
Aguilar v. Felton (1985), 272, 273
AIDS as disability, 281
Alcuin, 33
Aliens, illegal, 291–292
Allen, Dwight, 71
ALT (active learning time), 352
American Academy, 40
American Education Research Association (AERA), 325
American Federation of Teachers (AFT), 284–285, 390, 391
American Indians
  academic achievement, 328, 329
  crime, 211
  disproportionate placements, 186
  early educational history, 30
  graduation rate, 221
  high-poverty schools, 206
  knowledge and learning strategies, 98–100, 175–176
  racial and ethnic groups, 173, 174
  suicide, 213
  teaching about, 176
American Psychological Association (APA), 117
American Recovery and Reinvestment Act (2009), 261, 280, 370, 372
American Sign Language (ASL), 177
Americans with Disabilities Act (1990), 281
America's Civic Health Index, 141
Amish, 188
Analysis
  in Bloom's taxonomy, 350
  of teaching, 70–71
Analysis questions, 316
Analytic rubrics, 317, 318
Analytic thinking, 82–83, 84
Anderson, Gabrielle, 167
Andriski, Chris, 367
Anecdotal records, 315
Angelis, Angelo, 79
Anne Frank House, 219
Anytown, Okla. (diversity camp), 167
APA (American Psychological Association), 117
Application, in Bloom's taxonomy, 350
Apprenticeships, teaching, 68
Appropriate education, 280, 297
Aquinas, Thomas, 33
Architecture, school, 238, 240
Aristotle, 31–32, 33, 91
Arizona Connections Academy, 139
Arizona Supreme Court, 248–249
Arizona virtual schools, 139
ASCD (Association for Supervision and Curriculum Development), 392
Asian Americans
  academic achievement, 175, 329
  access to technology, 226
  educational history, 47–48
  as racial and ethnic group, 173, 174
ASL (American Sign Language), 177

Assertive discipline, 125
Assessment, 310–320
  authentic, 12, 314–317
  basing in work of the discipline, 317
  capstone, 313–314
  criterion-referenced, 313
  curriculum and, 341
  defined, 304
  described, 310
  diagnostic, 312, 313
  educational philosophy and, 121–122
  fairness, 319
  formative, 311–312, 313, 328–330
  for learning, 311–312, 313, 328–330
  of learning, 311
  multiple, 320
  norm-referenced, 312–313
  performance, 17, 314–317, 318
  performance-based, 160
  principles, 319
  professional aspects, 317, 319–320
  purposes, 310–312
  reliability and validity, 320
  rubrics, 310, 317, 318
  summative, 311, 313–314
  testing accommodations, 319
  types, 312–314
Assistant principals, 239, 389
Association for Supervision and Curriculum Development (ASCD), 392
Association for the Study of Negro Life and History, 190
Associations, professional, 391–392
Athens, early educational history of, 31
Attendance, certificates of, 374
Attending, in Krathwohl's taxonomy of affective domain, 351
Attestations, 20
Attire, business, for teachers, 96
Audio technology, classroom, 389
Australia
  citizenship education, 141
  teacher induction programs, 386
Authentic assessment, 12, 314–317
Authentic public space, 128
Autonomy stage of racial identity development, 220
Axiology, 81, 90
AYP (adequate yearly progress), 142, 143, 206, 255, 309

Baldwin, Lee, 303
Banks, James, 73
Barnard, Henry, 40
Battledores, 41
Behavioral objectives, 349
Behavioral theory, 72
Behaviorism, 110–111. *See also* Realism
Beller, Wendee, 201
Belonging, sense of, 141
Benchmarks, 315
Benefits, fringe, 20–21
Bethel School District No. 403 v. Fraser (1986), 291, 293–294
Bethune, Mary McLeod, 49
Biden, Joe, 354
Big ideas, 338, 339
Bilingual education, 178–179, 357, 358
Bilingualism, 179, 180
Bilingual teachers, 11

Bill and Melinda Gates Foundation, 155, 159
Blacks. *See* African Americans
Bloom, Benjamin, 72, 349–350
Bloom's taxonomy, 349–350
Blue-Backed Speller (Webster), 43, 44
Blue Ribbon schools, 160
*Board of Education, Island Trees Union Free
      District No. 26 v. Pico* (1982), 286, 291
*Board of Education of Kiryas Joel Village School
      District v. Grumet* (1994), 272
*Board of Education of Oklahoma City Public
      Schools v. Dowell* (1991), 277, 278
*Board of Education of the Westside Community
      Schools v. Mergens* (1990), 274
Board of Regents of State Colleges v. Roth
      (1972), 281, 283
Boards, school, 234–236, 258
Boards of cooperative educational services, 237
Boards of education, state, 241–242
Book banning, 286
Boston, early African American educational
      history of, 46
Bowles, Samuel, 130
Brennan, William, 286
Brodinsky, Ben, 73
Brown v. Board of Education of Topeka (1954),
      277, 278
Bruner, Jerome, 72
Bubble kids, 256
Buber, Martin, 116, 117
Buckley Amendment, 287
Buddhism, 188
Building a High-Quality Education Workforce
      (National Governors Association), 142
Bullying, 13, 212–213
Burger, Warren, 294
Burkey v. Marshall County Board of Education
      (1981), 281
Bush, George H. W., 309, 369, 370
Bush, George W., 309, 369, 370
Business attire for teachers, 96
Busing, 59
Byngham, William, 67

Cafeteria workers, 240
California
      affirmative action, 279
      curriculum frameworks, 342
      educational malpractice, 288
      intermediate units, 237
      Performance Assessment for California
            Teachers, 329–330
      ranking of schools, 373
      school finance, 248, 249, 253
      state adoption policy, 345
California Supreme Court, 248
Canter, Lee, 125
Capstone assessments, 313–314
Cardinal Principles of Secondary Education
      (Commission on Reorganization of
      Secondary Education), 65
Caring, environment of, 117
Carter, Jimmy, 370
Case law, 269
Casillo, Frank, 303
Catechetical schools, 33
Catechumenal schools, 33
Categorical federal aid, 61–62
Categorical state aid, 250–251
Cathedral/monastic schools, 33
Celebrationist historians, 30
Censorship, 286, 296
Central office staff, 236–237
Certificates of attendance, 374
Certification, 16–17, 282
Chain of command, 236

Change, 129–130, 384–386
Change agents, 129–130
Character development, 107
Characterization by value/value complex, in
      Krathwohl's taxonomy of affective
      domain, 351
Charlemagne, 32–33
Charter schools, 133, 148, 149–150
Chautauqua movement, 64
Chavis, John, 46–47
Cheating, 79, 290, 325, 389
Chemical dependency, 215
Chief state school officers, 242
Child abuse, 209–210, 296
Child Abuse Prevention and Treatment Act
      (1974), 296
Child benefit theory, 272–273
Children left alone after school, 207–208
Chinese language instruction, 11
Chinese thought, 97
Choices, school, 148–152
Choice theory, 124–125
Church and state, 271–276
Citizenship education, 140–142
Civil Rights Act (1964), 277, 278–279
Classification questions, 316
Classroom audio technology, 389
Classroom climate, 126–128
Classroom management, 123–126, 372
Classroom organization, 120–122
Classroom politics, 259
Class size, 372–373
Class structure, social, 168–169
Cleveland Board of Education v. LeFleur
      (1974), 281
Climate, classroom, 126–128
Clinton, Bill, 309, 369, 370
Coalition of Essential Schools, 110
Coalitions, 260
Cocurriculum/extra-curriculum, 340
Code of ethics, National Education Association,
      381, 382
Cognitive development, 72
Cognitive domain, 349–350
Cole, Sydney, 167
Cole, Terri, 233
Collective bargaining rights, 284–285
Colleges and universities. *See also specific
      institutions*
      academic freedom, 285
      early African American, 47
      early American, 39
      medieval, 33
      state teachers' colleges, 69
      teacher preparation in, 69
Collegial learning, 376
Colonial education, 37–39, 66–68
Comenius, Johann Amos, 35
Coming to Justice program, 219
Commissioners of education, 242
Commission on Reorganization of Secondary
      Education, 65
Committee of Ten, 65. *See also* National
      Education Association (NEA)
Common culture, 142, 144–145
Common elementary schools, 40
Common School Journal, The, 40
Communicating with families, 208–209
Community
      influences on curriculum, 344
      of inquiry, 128
      involvement in education, 376–377, 379
      partnering with, 147–148
Comparison questions, 316
Compulsory education, 40
Computers, 225, 226–228. *See also* Technology

Comte, Auguste, 111
Conant, James, 64
Concerns, about change, 384–386
Concrete operations stage, 72
Conditions of employment, 282–284
Conferences, parent-teacher, 377
Confidentiality of student records, 287
Conflict resolution, 125–126
Confucianism, 97
Connecticut Teacher Tenure Act, 267
Connection, in prophetic thinking, 83, 85, 86
Connections clarification questions, 316
Consequences, 125
Constructing support questions, 316
Constructivism, 117–118. *See also* Existentialism
Contact stage of racial identity development, 220
Content knowledge, 381, 383
Content standards, 306–307
Context, 315
Continuing professional development, 24
Control continuum, teacher-student, 123
Control theory, 124–125
Controversial topics in the classroom, 131
Convergent thinking, 109, 111
Cooperative learning, 142, 354–355
Cooperative Research Program, 61
Cooper v. Ross (1979), 285
Core curriculum, 338, 339
Corporal punishment, 294
Corporate advertising and sponsorship, 249, 250
Corrective actions, under NCLB, 256
County education offices, 237
Course syllabi, 342
Courts, 246, 248–249. *See also specific courts*
Crandall, Prudence, 47
Creating, in Bloom's taxonomy, 350
Creationism, 39, 274, 275–276
Crichton, Michael, 118
Criterion-referenced assessments, 313
Critical thinking, 193
Critics, educational, 72
Cultural capital, 158
Cultural values, 145–147
Culture
      common, 142, 144–145
      defined, 142
      school, 147, 160
      in schools, 144–148
      schools' role in transmitting, 143
Cultures of families, 145
Curriculum, 336–347
      behaviorist, 111
      constructivist, 118
      core, 338, 339
      defined, 336
      designs, 338–341
      developing, 336–338
      Eastern ways of knowing and, 97
      essentialist, 109–110
      evaluating, 346–347
      existentialist, 107
      hidden, 142, 340–341
      history curriculum in Rwanda, 189
      humanistic, 116–117
      idealist, 107
      influences on, 342–344
      mastery, 338–339
      mathematics, 346–347
      No Child Left Behind Act and, 347, 353–354
      positivist, 113
      pragmatist, 107
      problem-based, 339, 340
      realist, 107
      resources, 341–342
      selection and management of, 344–346
      spiral, 338, 339

standards-based, 160, 339, 340
subject-centered, 338, 339
themed, 338, 339
trends, 59–60
types, 338–340
Curriculum frameworks, 342
Curriculum guides, 342
Curriculum libraries, 342
Curriculum specialists, 345–346
Custodians, 240

Da Feltre, Vittorino, 34
Dame schools, 39
Dark Ages, 32–33
Darling, Sharon, 201
Dartmouth College, 50–51
Darwin, Charles, 275
Decision making, 240, 375–376, 379
Deduction, 83, 316
De facto segregation, 276, 278
De jure segregation, 276, 278
Del Oro High School (Loomis, Calif.), 249
Democracy, 114
Democratic schools, 194–195
Department heads, 239
Departments of education, state, 242–243
Depth, in high school science studies, 335–336
Descartes, René, 35
Desegregation, 276–278
Development, professional, 24
Developmental bilingual education, 179
Dewey, John, 87, 93, 114, 117, 129
Diagnostic assessments, 312, 313
Dialectic, change as, 130
Dialectical diversity, 177
Dialogues, Plato's, 88, 89
Differentiated instruction, 355–356
Digital media, 105. *See also* Technology
Direct instruction, 352
Disabilities
  defined, 184, 280
  diversity and, 184–187
  learning, 62
  legal aspects, 279–281, 297
  teaching strategies for, 358–359
  testing accommodations for, 319
Disaggregation, 255
Discernment, 83, 86
Discipline, 40, 124–126
Discretionary school board duties, 235, 236
Discrimination, 218–219, 278–279, 294, 297
Disintegration stage of racial identity
  development, 220
Dispositions, 12, 359
Disproportionate placements, 186, 187
District in need of improvement, 256
District of Columbia, vouchers in, 150
Districts. *See* School districts
Divergent thinking
  constructivism and, 118
  defined, 109
  humanism and, 116
  positivism and, 113
  progressivism and, 114, 115
Diversity, 167–195. *See also* Reflect on Diversity
  feature
  exceptionalities, 184–187
  family, 202–203
  gender, 179, 181–183
  language, 176–179, 180
  multicultural education, 73, 189–193
  race and ethnicity, 172–176
  religion, 187–189
  sexual orientation, 183–184
  socioeconomic status, 168–171
  teachers as social activists, 193–195

teachers from diverse backgrounds, 11
teaching strategies for, 357–359
in urban communities, 158
Diversity training for teachers, 146
Domestic violence, 209
Donohue v. Copiague Union Free School District
  (1978), 288
Douglass, Frederick, 46
Dress codes, 294, 295
Dropouts, 221, 223–224, 374–375
"Drunken pirate" case, 268
Du Bois, W. E. B., 190
Due process, 267, 281, 292–294
Duncan, Arne, 322

Early childhood education, 152–154
Early dropouts, 374
Early interventions, 375
Eastern ways of knowing, 95–98
Eberle, Francis, 335–336
Economic Opportunity Act (1964), 64
Economic realities, 216–217
Edgewood Independent School District (San
  Antonio, Tex.), 150
Editorial Projects in Education Research
  Center, 221
Edmonds, Ron, 160
Educational critics, 72
Educational history. *See* History of education
Educational malpractice, 288
Educational management organizations
  (EMOs), 150
Educational philosophy, 106–133. *See also*
  Philosophy
  beyond the classroom, 129–133
  classroom climate and, 126–128
  classroom management/discipline and,
    123–126
  classroom organization and, 120–122
  described, 107
  developing, 118–129, 381
  educational implications of philosophy,
    106–107
  motivation and, 122–123
  personal learning focus and, 128
  sample, 108
  student-centered educational philosophies,
    113–118, 119
  teacher-centered educational philosophies,
    109–113, 119
  technology and, 128–129
Educational research, 12, 45, 50, 61, 372
Educational technology, 71
Educational Testing Service (ETS), 16, 64
Education Amendments Act (1972), 279
"Education for All American Youth"
  (Educational Policies Commission), 66
Education for All Handicapped Children Act, 60,
  280, 297
Education in the News feature
  cheating, 79
  digital media and ethics, 105
  diversity, 167
  federal role in education, 57
  Florida high school accountability, 303–304
  heroes in education, 3
  high school science studies, 335–336
  New Hampshire Excellence in Education
    Award Program, 367
  school finance overhaul in New Mexico, 233
  teacher's MySpace behavior, 267–268
  teaching patriotism, 29
  Toyota Family Literacy Program, 201
  virtual schools, 139
Education Resources Information Center
  (ERIC), 254

Education Trust, 160, 161
Edwards v. Aguillard (1987), 274, 276
Effective schools, 159–161, 372
Effective teaching, 71, 160, 372
Egg-crate school architecture, 238, 240
Egypt Elementary School (Memphis, Tenn.), 201
Eight-Year Study, 65
Eisenhower, Dwight D., 370
Elections, nonpartisan, 234
Elementary and Secondary Education Act
  (1965). *See also* No Child Left Behind Act
    (NCLB)
  education research and development, 372
  federal role in education, 57
  funding without accountability, 256
  grants, 369, 371
  reauthorization of, 254
  Title 1, 273
Elementary education, 39–40
Elementary schools, 40, 154
Elementary teachers, 285–286
ELLs. *See* English-language learners (ELLs)
E-mail, 289
Emergence of Common Man, 36–37
Émile (Rousseau), 36, 115
Emmett O'Brien High School (Ansonia, Conn.),
  267–268
EMOs (educational management
  organizations), 150
Employment, conditions of, 282–284
Employment contracts, teacher, 282
Empowerment, 132–133, 240
Enabling laws, 269
Encounter stage of racial identity development, 220
Enculturation, 144
Enframing, 85
England, teacher training in, 67
English, Standard, 177
English as a second language (ESL), 179, 357, 358
English-language learners (ELLs)
  cooperative learning, 355,
  curriculum, 344
  defined, 344
  disproportionate placements, 186
  diversity, 177–179
  family literacy programs, 201
  resources for teaching, 357–358
  teaching strategies, 357–358, 359
  testing accommodations, 319
English-only movement, 177
Enrollment growth, 58
Entanglement, excessive, 271, 272
Entrepreneurial efforts to fund education, 249–250
Environment of caring, 117
Epistemology, 81
Epperson v. Arkansas (1968), 276
Equal educational opportunity, 62, 192–193
Equality, 192–193, 217, and
Equal opportunity, 278–279
Equal protection clause of the Fourteenth
  Amendment, 246, 278, 292
Equal treatment, 280
Equity, 182, 193–194, 244, 326, 328
Erasmus, 34
ERIC (Education Resources Information
  Center), 254
Error analysis, 316
ESL (English as a second language), 179, 357, 358
Essentialism, 109–110. *See also* Idealism;
  Realism
Essential Schools movement, 110
Establishment clause, 272
Estrada, Ignacio "Nacho," 388
Ethics, 105, 381, 382
Ethnic groups, defined, 168. *See also* Race and
  ethnicity

Ethnicity, 145, 172–175. *See also* Race and ethnicity
ETS (Educational Testing Service), 16, 64
European Americans. *See* Whites
Evaluation, in Bloom's taxonomy, 350
Everson v. Board of Education (1947), 271, 272, 273
Evidence-based practice, 373, 380
Evolution *versus* intelligent design, 39, 274, 275–276
Exceptionalities. *See* Disabilities
Existentialism, 93–95, 107. *See also* Constructivism; Humanism
Expenditures
    per-pupil, 246, 247, 252
    school districts, 237
Expertise, 260
Expulsion, 292–293
Extra-curriculum, 340

Facilitator styles, 378
Fairness, in assessment, 319
Families, 201–209
    children left alone after school, 207–208
    communicating with, 208–209
    cultures of, 145
    diversity of, 202–203
    literacy programs for, 201
    parenting, 203
    socioeconomic status, 171, 186, 203–207
Family Educational Rights and Privacy Act (1974), 287
Far Eastern Indian thought, 97
FCAT (Florida Comprehensive Assessment Test), 303, 304
Federal aid, 61–62, 256–257
Federalism, 253, 369–371
Federal role in education. *See also specific laws and cases*
    educational programs, 254
    federal aid, 61–62, 256–257
    history of, 57, 61–62, 369–372
    leadership, 253–254
    standards, 309
    U.S. Department of Education, 57, 160, 254
Fees, student, 249
Finance, school. *See* Revenue sources
Financial challenges, 261
First Amendment
    academic freedom, 286
    church and state, 271, 273
    students' right to free speech, 293–294
    teacher use of MySpace, 267, 268
    text of, 270
Flanders, Ned, 70–71
Fleming, Rick, 304
Florida
    high school accountability, 303–304
    school finance, 248
    vouchers, 150
Florida Comprehensive Assessment Test (FCAT), 303, 304
Florida Department of Education, 303, 304
Folios, 19–20, 315
Ford, Gerald, 370
Formal operations stage, 72
Formative assessment, 311–312, 313, 328–330
Foundation programs, 251–253
Four-day school weeks, 240
Fourteenth Amendment
    church and state, 271
    due process, 267, 293
    equal protection clause, 246, 278, 292
    separate-but-equal doctrine, 277
    taxation and education, 248
    text of, 270

Fourth Amendment, 297
Framework for 21st Century Learning (Partnership for 21st Century Skills), 142–143
Franklin, Benjamin, 40, 68
Franklin v. Gwinnett County Schools (1992), 294
Fraser, Matthew, 293–294
Frederick the Great, 35
Freeman v. Pitts (1992), 277, 278
Free/reduced-priced lunch, 206–207
Free speech, 293–294
Friedenberg, Edgar, 72
Froebel, Friedrich, 37
Funding, school. *See* Revenue sources
Fund-raising schemes, 249–250

Gaetz, Don, 303, 304
Gambling, as revenue source, 247–248
Gangs, 213
Gardner, Howard, 105
Gates, Bill, 155
Gattonini, Venera, 367, 379, 384
Gays, 183–184, 211
GED (general education diploma), 374
Gender diversity, 179, 181–183
Gender-sensitive education, 182
General education diploma (GED), 374
Generalists, 346
Generalization, 83, 84
General state aid, 250, 251
George-Barden Act (1946), 57
Germany
    education practices, 340
    legal aspects of education, 285
GI Bill (1944), 57, 61
GI Bill (1966), 61
Gibson, Kayla, 139
Gifted education programs, 186
Gintis, Herbert, 130
Giroux, Henry, 115, 127
Glasser, William, 124
Global Perspectives feature
    Anne Frank House, 219
    Chinese language instruction, 11
    citizenship education in Australia, 141
    Eastern ways of knowing, 98
    educational ideas borrowed from around the world, 41
    English beginnings of teacher training, 67
    German education, 340
    history curriculum in Rwanda, 189
    legal aspects of education, 285
    Montessori, Maria, 49
    per-pupil expenditures, 252
    Piaget, Jean, 72
    South Korean education, 324
    teacher induction programs in Australia, 386
    world as classroom, 133
Goals 2000, 369, 370
Goals 2000: Educate America Act (1994), 309
Goodlad, John, 126, 127
GoodPlay Project, 105
Goss v. Lopez (1975), 291, 293
Gouge v. Joint School District No. 1 (1970), 283
Governors, 244
Graduation rates, 221, 223–224, 374–375
Grand Rapids School District v. Ball (1985), 272
Gratz v. Bollinger (2003), 279
Greene, Maxine, 95, 128
Griffin v. County School Board of Prince Edward County (1964), 277
Grooming regulations, 294
Grouping, heterogeneous *versus* homogeneous, 354, 355
Growth model, 321
Grutter v. Bollinger (2003), 279

Guest speakers, 147–148
Guided Discovery, 352

Hall, G. Stanley, 152, 154
Hall, Primus, 46
Hall, Samuel, 68
Hartford Public Schools (Conn.), 347
Harvard College, 39
Havighurst, Robert, 71
Hazelwood School District v. Kuhlmeier (1988), 291, 296
Head Start, 206
Helena Elementary School District v. State (1989), 248
Herbart, Johann Friedrich, 37
Herbartian teaching method, 37
Heroes in education, 3
Heterogeneous grouping, 354, 355
Hidden curriculum, 142, 340–341
Higher education. *See* Colleges and universities
Higher Education Act (1965), 57
Highly qualified teachers, 14, 206, 228, 255, 328
High-quality schools, 375–379
High-quality teachers, 367, 379–383
High schools, 41, 155, 303–304, 335–336
High Scope model, 153
High-stakes testing, 304, 324–325, 327–328
Hillis v. Stephen F. Austin University (1982), 285
Hinduism, 188
Hispanics
    academic achievement, 175, 328, 329
    access to technology, 225, 226
    college enrollment, 216
    crime, 211
    disproportionate placements, 186
    dropout rate, 374
    educational history, 48
    as ethnic group, 173, 174, 175
    family literacy programs, 201
    graduation rate, 221
    high-poverty schools, 206
    jobs during high school, 216
    parent-teacher conferences, 377
    racial identity development, 220
Historian types, 30
History curriculum in Rwanda, 189
History of education, 30–52, 57–74
    African Americans, 45–47
    Age of Reason, 35
    Asian Americans, 47–48
    beginnings of education, 30–32
    changing aims of education, 65–66
    colonial education, 37–39
    development of teaching profession, 61–64
    elementary education, 39–40
    Emergence of Common Man, 36–37
    federal role in education, 57, 61–62, 369–372
    Hispanic Americans, 48
    Middle Ages, 32–33
    private education, 50–51
    Reformation, 34–35
    Renaissance, 33, 34
    secondary schools, 40–41
    teacher preparation, 66–70
    teaching materials, 41–45
    trends, 58–61, 70–74
    women, 48–50
Holistic rubrics, 317, 318
Homelessness, 203–206, 292
Home schooling, 63, 152
Homework, 356
Homogeneous grouping, 354, 355
Honig v. Doe (1988), 291, 297
Hope, 85, 86
Hopi thought, 99
Hornbooks, 41, 42

Hortonville Joint School District No. 1 v. Hortonville Education Association (1976), 281
Humanism, 33, 34, 115–117. *See also* Existentialism
Hutterites, 188
Hypocrisy, tracking, 85, 86

I and Thou (Buber), 116
IDEA (Individuals with Disabilities Education Act), 186, 280, 281
Idealism, 87–89, 90, 92, 107. *See also* Essentialism
IEP (individualized education plan), 185
Ignatius of Loyola, 34–35
I-It relationships, 116
Illich, Ivan, 72
Illinois
   academic freedom, 286
   student publications, 296
Illinois Supreme Court, 286
Imagination, 82–83, 84
Immersion, 179, 357
Immersion-emersion stage of racial identity development, 220
Immigrants, 174, 374
Impact Aid laws (1950), 57
Impact concerns, 385, 386
"Imperative Needs of Youth" (Educational Policies Commission), 66
Incentive programs, 251
Inclusion, 185–186
Income taxes, 245, 246, 247
Indentured servants, teachers as, 67–68
Indian thought, 97
Indirect instruction, 352–353
Individualized education plan (IEP), 185
Individuals with Disabilities Education Act (IDEA), 186, 280, 281
Induction, 8, 15, 386, 387
Inductive logic, 83
Inequity, 217, 245–246
Inferring and concluding questions, 316
Information age, 5
Ingraham v. Wright (1977), 291, 294
Initiators (facilitator type), 378
In loco parentis, 292
Input objectives, 348, 349
Inquiry, 128, 352–353
Institute for Learning, 361
Institutes of Oratory, The (Quintilian), 32
Instruction, 348–359. *See also* Teaching
   Chinese language, 11
   differentiated, 355–356
   direct, 352
   English-language learners, 357–358, 359
   indirect, 352–353
   objectives, 348–351
   organizing students to maximize learning, 354–356
   science and technology emphasis, 353–354
   sheltered, 178
   student learning-centered, 380
   students with exceptionalities, 358–359
   teaching strategies, 351–359
   using technology to enhance, 356–357
Insurance, liability, 288–289
INTASC (Interstate New Teacher Assessment and Support Consortium), 15, 16
Integration, 276
Intelligent design, 39, 274, 275–276
Interactionists, 123
Intercultural Service Bureau, 190
Interest groups, 243–244, 260, 343
Intermediate units, 237
Internalization-commitment stage of racial identity development, 220

Internalization stage of racial identity development, 220
International comparisons of accountability, 322–324. *See also* Global Perspectives feature
Internet
   bullying and, 213
   for communicating with families, 208–209
   as curriculum resource, 342
   equality of access to, 225, 227
   limiting access to, 286
   multicultural education and, 191
   researching educational history on, 45
   researching educational information on, 61
   use by teachers, 227–228
Internet-based schools, 139, 152
Interstate New Teacher Assessment and Support Consortium (INTASC), 15, 16
Interventionists, 123
Interviews, for performance assessment, 315
Islam, 188
I-Thou relationships, 116
Ito, Mimi, 105

James, William, 114
Japanese thought, 97–98
Jefferson, Thomas, 29
Jesuits, 34–35
Job hunting for teachers, 23
Jobs, after-school, 216–217
Johnson, Hannibal, 167
Johnson, Lyndon, 370, 372
Josephson, Michael, 79
Journaling, reflective, 19
Judicial interpretive process, 269
Junior high schools, 41, 154
Jurassic Park (Crichton), 118

Kandel, Isaac L., 129
Kant, Immanuel, 88
Kennedy, John F., 370
Kentucky Education Reform Act (1990), 244, 248, 373
Kentucky Supreme Court, 244, 248, 373
Kingsville IDS v. Cooper (1980), 285
Kitzmiller v. Dover Area School District (2005), 276
Knowledge
   American Indian, 98–100, 175–176
   content, 381, 383
   Eastern ways of knowing, 95–98
   pedagogical, 383
   pedagogical content, 383
   professional, 12–13
   twenty-first-century, 307–308
Kohlberg, Lawrence, 82
Kozol, Jonathan, 72
Krathwohl, David, 350–351
Krathwohl's taxonomy of affective domain, 350–351

Lakota thought, 99
Lamb's Chapel v. Center Moriches Union Free School District (1993), 274
Language diversity, 176–179, 180
Lanham Act (1941), 57, 61
Later dropouts, 374
Latin grammar schools, 32, 39
Latinos. *See* Hispanics
Law. *See* Legal perspectives on education
Leadership, 130–133, 236, 253–254, 377–379
Learner-centered power style, 132
Learning
   active learning time, 352
   age of the revival of, 33
   assessment for, 311–312, 313, 328–330

assessment of, 311
assumptions about, 344
cooperative, 142, 354–355
curriculum and, 344
model-centered, 353
objectives for, 349–351
organizing students to maximize, 354–356
personal learning focus, 128
problem-based, 117–118, 353
professional learning community, 376, 379
service, 148
student learning-centered instruction, 380
study of process, 71–72
using technology to track, 321
Learning disabilities, 62
Learning focus, and educational philosophy, 128
Learning logs/journals, 315
Leaving school early, 221, 223–224, 374–375
Lee v. Weisman (1992), 274
Legal perspectives on education, 267–299. *See also specific laws and cases*
   academic freedom, 285–286
   church and state, 271–276
   collective bargaining rights, 284–285
   colonial school laws, 38
   conditions of employment, 282–284
   equal opportunity, 278–279
   evolving legal aspects of education, 298–299
   history of education laws, 57
   segregation and desegregation, 276–278
   student records, 287
   students' rights and responsibilities, 290–298
   students with disabilities, 279–281, 297
   teachers' rights and responsibilities, 281–289
   technology, 267–268, 289–290
   U.S. Constitution, 269–270
Legislatures, state, 243–244
Lemon v. Kurtzman (1971), 271, 272
Lesbian, gay, bisexual, or transgender (LGBT), 183–184, 211
Lesson planning, 121
Leven, Henry, 361
LGBT (lesbian, gay, bisexual, or transgender), 183–184, 211
Liability, 288
Liability insurance, 288–289
Liberal arts, 33
Liberal historians, 30
Liberty interests, 281
Library media specialists, 240
Licensure, 15–16, 23, 24, 282
Line relationship, 236
Literacy programs for families, 201
Local control, 257
Locations, school, 155–159
Locke, John, 35, 91
Locker searches, 297
Logic, 83, 84
Logical positivism, 112
Long v. Zopp (1973), 294
Lotteries, 247, 248
Low-income families, 171, 186, 206–207. *See also* Poverty
Lucia v. Duggan (1969), 283
Lunch, free/reduced-priced, 206–207
Luther, Martin, 34
Lutheran parochial schools, 51

Magnet schools, 133, 148, 149, 159
Malpractice, educational, 288
Managers (facilitator type), 378
Mandatory school board duties, 235–236
Mann, Horace, 40, 69
Manners, teaching of, 60
Married students, 295–296
Marshall, Thurgood, 246

Martin, Jane Roland, 89
Massachusetts
  early elementary education, 40
  early school laws, 38
  nontenured teacher rights, 283
Mastery curriculum, 338–339
Materials, teaching, 41–45
Mathematics curricula, 346–347
Mathematics teachers, 11
McCullough, David, 29
McGuffey, William Holmes, 45
McKinney-Vento Homeless Assistance Act
    (1987), 205
McNayr, Seth, 167
Medieval universities, 33
Memphis City Schools, 201
Meno (Plato), 88
Mentoring, 8, 24
Metaphysical era, 111
Metaphysics, 80–81
*Metaphysics of Morals and the Critique of
    Practical Reason* (Kant), 88
Mexican Americans, 174. *See also* Hispanics
Microphones, wireless, 389
Middle Ages, 32–33
Middle class, 169
Middle Colonies, 37, 38
Middle level education, 154–155
Middle schools, 41, 154–155
Migration of population, 155
Miller, Edward, 153
Milwaukee, Wisc., 148, 150
Miner, Myrtilla, 46
Missouri Synod Lutheran Church, 51
Mobility, social, 140, 168
Model-centered learning, 353
Modeling, 132
Monastic schools, 33
Monitorial schools, 39–40
Montana Supreme Court, 248
Montessori, Maria, 49, 153
Montessori schools, 153
Morals, 82
Mormons, 188
Morris v. Douglas County School District
    (1966), 288
Motivation, 122–123
Mozert v. Hawkins County Public Schools
    (1987), 274
Multicultural education, 73, 189–193
Multiple assessments, 320
MySpace, 267–268

National Assessment of Educational Progress
    (NAEP)
  curriculum evaluation and, 347
  English-language learners and, 178
  family income and, 171
  as national test, 321
  performance by race and ethnicity, 175, 328, 329
National Association for the Education of Young
    Children, 153
National Board for Professional Teaching
    Standards (NBPTS), 8, 16–17
National Center for Family Literacy, 201
National Clearinghouse for English Language
    Acquisition, 357
National Commission on Excellence in
    Education, 253
National Council for Accreditation of Teacher
    Education, 15
National Council for Social Studies, 142
National Defense Education Act (1958), 57, 59–60
National Education Association (NEA)
  code of ethics, 381, 382
  collective bargaining, 284–285

Educational Policies Commission, 65–66
  as teacher union, 390–391
National Governors Association, 159
National School Lunch Program, 206
National Science Foundation, 61
Nation at Risk, A (National Commission on
    Excellence in Education), 253, 369, 370
Native Americans. *See* American Indians
Native North American ways of knowing,
    98–100
Naturalism, 36
Nava, Cynthia, 233
Navajo thought, 99
NBPTS (National Board for Professional
    Teaching Standards), 8, 16–17
NCLB. *See* No Child Left Behind Act (NCLB)
NEA. *See* National Education Association (NEA)
Neau, Elias, 46
Neglect, 210, 296
Negligence, 288
Networks, 260
Newcomer programs, 178–179
New England Primer, 42–43
New Hampshire Excellence in Education Award
    Program, 367
New Jersey v. T.L.O. (1985), 291
Newmarket Junior/Senior High School (N.H.), 367
New Mexico school finance overhaul, 233
New teachers, 8–9, 22, 387, 389–390
New York City
  adult education, 63
  expectations for teachers, 228
New York State
  church and state, 272
  educational malpractice, 288
  intermediate units, 237
Nietzsche, Friedrich, 94–95
Nineteenth Amendment, 50
Nixon, Richard, 370
No Child Left Behind Act (NCLB)
  accountability, 260, 261, 373
  adequate yearly progress, 142, 143, 206, 255, 309
  charter schools, 149
  curriculum, 347, 353–354
  defined, 11
  educational management organizations, 150
  effective schools, 160
  English-language learners, 178
  equality, 193
  equity within accountability, 326, 328
  federal government's role in education, 62,
      254–256
  highly qualified teachers, 14, 206, 228, 255, 328
  impact of, 256
  local control, 257, 261
  out-of-field teacher assignments, 11
  overview, 18
  requirements, 371
  school choice, 148
  school improvement process, 239
  schools in need of improvement, 255
  standards, 309
  test data for groups, 161
  testing accommodations, 62
  Title I schools, 206
Noninterventionists, 123
Nonpartisan elections, 234
Nontenured teachers, 267, 283
Non-Western education, early history of, 31
Normal schools, 68–69
Norm-referenced assessments, 312–313
Northern Colonies, 37–38
North Haven Board of Education v. Bell
    (1982), 281
Northwest Ordinance (1785), 256
Note-taking, 18–19

Obama, Barack H., 148, 150, 354, 370, 372
Objectives, 348–351
Observations, 18, 315
Oklahoma, diversity in, 167
Old Deluder Satan Act, 38
Online schools, 139, 152
Open adoption policy, 345
Open-space school architecture, 238
Opportunity-to-learn standards, 306
Organization
  classroom, 120–122
  of education at state level, 241–244
  in Krathwohl's taxonomy of affective
      domain, 351
  school, 237–240
  school district, 234–237
  of students to maximize learning, 354–356
Organization charts
  defined, 234
  school, 238–240
  school district, 235
  state, 241
Out-of-field teacher assignments, 11
Output objectives, 348, 349
Owasso Independent School District v. Falvo
    (2002), 287

PACT (Performance Assessment for California
    Teachers), 329–330
Panethnic membership, 172
Parenting, 203
Parent involvement, 376–377, 379
Parent-teacher conferences, 377
Parent-U-Turn, 376
Parochial schools, 51, 63, 148, 151
Partnering with the community, 147–148
Partnership for 21st Century Skills, 307–308
Patriotism, teaching, 29
Pedagogical content knowledge, 383
Pedagogical knowledge, 383
Peer mediation programs, 125–126
Peer review, 287
Peer sexual harassment, 297–298
Peirce, Charles Sanders, 93, 114, 128
Pennsylvania
  church and state, 271
  parochial schools, 51
Performance, 304
Performance Assessment for California Teachers
    (PACT), 329–330
Performance assessments, 17, 314–317, 318
Performance-based assessment, 160
Performance-based licensing, 15
Pericles, Age of, 31
Per-pupil expenditures, 246, 247, 252
Perrone, Vito, 127
Perry v. Sindermann (1972), 281, 283
Pestalozzi, Johann Heinrich, 37, 40
Peter W. v. SFUSD (1976), 288
Phi Delta Kappa International, 391–392
Philosophy, 80–100. *See also* Educational
    philosophy
  analytic thinking, 82–83, 84
  branches, 80–81
  defined, 80
  Eastern ways of knowing, 95–98
  educational implications of, 106–107
  existentialism, 93–95
  idealism, 87–89, 90, 92
  Native North American ways of knowing,
      98–100
  pragmatism, 91–93
  prophetic thinking, 83, 85, 86
  realism, 89–91
  technology and, 85, 87
Piaget, Jean, 71–72, 153

Pickering v. Board of Education (1968), 281, 286
PISA (Programs in International Student Assessment), 322–323
Plagiarism, 290
Plato, 31, 87, 88, 89
Play, 153
Plessy v. Ferguson (1896), 276–277
Plutarch, 31
Plyser v. Doe (1982), 291
Police Department of the City of Chicago v. Mosley (1972), 274
Political action, 257, 391
Politics in education, 257–260
Portfolios, 15, 20, 315
Position power, 260
Positive recognition, 125
Positivism, 111–113
Postmodernist historians, 30
Poverty
    academic achievement and, 171
    crime and, 211
    rural communities, 156–157
    socioeconomic status, 169–171
    suburban communities, 157
    teen pregnancy and, 215
Powell, Lewis F., Jr., 246
Power relationships, 217
Power sources, 122–123, 260
Power standards, 341
Power styles, 132
Pragmatism, 91–93, 107, 114. *See also* Progressivism
PRAXIS Series, 16
Prayer in school, 275
Preencounter stage of racial identity development, 220
Pregnant students, 215, 295–296
Prejudice, 218
Preoperational stage, 72
Primavera Online High School (Ariz.), 139
Principals
    accountability, 261
    assistant/vice, 239, 389
    leadership, 378–379
    new teacher support, 389
    responsibilities, 239
Private education, 50–51
Private schools, 63, 150–152
Probationary period, 282, 283
Problem-based curriculum, 339, 340
Problem-based learning, 117–118, 353
Problem solving, 352–353
Procedural due process, 267, 281, 292–293
Professional associations, 391–392
Professional development, 24
Professional Dilemma feature
    adjusting attitude of students, 112
    developing performance assessments, 314
    family diversity, 203
    homogeneous *versus* heterogeneous ability grouping, 355
    inclusion of students with disabilities, 185
    keeping up with research, 50
    multicultural education, 73
    play, 153
    standardized tests, 18
    teachers and politics, 259
    teaching morals and values in public schools, 82
Professionalization of teaching, 62–63
Professional knowledge, 12–13
Professional learning community, 376, 379
Professionals (social class), 169
Programs in International Student Assessment (PISA), 322–323
Progress in International Reading Study, 324
Progressive Education Association, 65, 70

Progressive taxes, 245
Progressivism, 114–115. *See also* Pragmatism
Promotion, social, 222
Property interests, 281
Property taxes, 245–246
Prophetic thinking, 82, 83, 85, 86
Prophetic Thought in Postmodern Times (West), 83
Proposition 13 (California), 253
Proposition 209 (California), 279
Protestant Reformation, 34–35
Protestants, 187
Pseudoindependence stage of racial identity development, 220
Psychomotor domain, 351
Publications, student, 296
Public funds and religious education, 271–273, 274
Public Law 94-142 (Education for All Handicapped Children Act), 60, 280, 297
Public schools
    religious activities in, 273–275
    school choices, 148–150
    teaching morals and values in, 82
Public view
    of education, 73
    of schools, 6–7
    of teachers, 5–6
Punishment, corporal, 294
Pupil/teacher ratio, 10
"Purposes of Education in American Democracy" (Educational Policies Commission), 65

Quadrivium, 33
Quality assurance, 14–18
Questioning, 315–316
Quintilian, 32

Race and ethnicity. *See also specific racial and ethnic groups*
    disparities in education and, 175
    dropout rates and, 374
    ethnicity, 172–175
    performance on National Assessment of Educational Progress, 175, 328, 329
    poverty and, 169, 170
    race, 172
    teaching from cultural context, 175–176
Race-conscious assignment, 278
Racial identity development, 220
Racism, 219–220
Ranking of schools, districts, and states, 373–374
Rationalists, 35
Rational process, change as, 129–130
Reader (McGuffey), 45
Reagan, Ronald, 370
Realism, 89–91, 107. *See also* Behaviorism; Essentialism
Real-world standards, 306
Reason, Age of, 35
Receiving, in Krathwohl's taxonomy of affective domain, 351
Recognition, positive, 125
Recruitment incentives, 21–22
Reduced-priced lunch, 206–207
Reflection, 18–20, 380–381
Reflect on Diversity feature. *See also* Diversity
    American Indians, 176
    assessments for learning, 313
    classroom management, 126
    curriculum and Eastern ways of knowing, 97
    English-language learners, 355
    illegal aliens, 291
    leaving school early, 224
    parent-teacher conferences, 377
    religious beliefs in the classroom, 39

"Robin Hood" school finance, 251
    student bullying, 13
    testing accommodations, 62
    urban schools, 159
Reform, school, 360–361, 368–373
Reformation, Protestant, 34–35
Reggio Amelia approach, 153–154
Regional accreditation, 14–15
Regional education service agencies, 237
Regional service centers, 237
Regressive taxes, 245
Rehabilitation Act, Section 504, 280, 297
Reinforcement, 111
Reintegration stage of racial identity development, 220
Reliability, 320
Religion-affiliated schools, 50, 271, 272, 273
Religious activities in public schools, 273–275
Religious beliefs in the classroom, 39
Religious diversity, 187–189
Religious education, 271–273, 274
Remembering, in Bloom's taxonomy, 350
Renaissance, 33, 34
Report cards, school and school district, 261
Republic (Plato), 31
Research, educational, 12, 45, 50, 61, 372
Resegregation, 276
Residence, 290, 291
Resiliency, 224–225
Resnik, Lauren, 361
Respect, 214
Responders (facilitator type), 378
Responding, in Krathwohl's taxonomy of affective domain, 351
Response to Intervention (RTI), 186–187, 280
Retention *versus* social promotion, 222
Retirement benefits, 21
Returning teachers, 9
Revenue sources, 244–253
    entrepreneurial efforts to fund education, 249–250
    financial challenges, 261
    New Mexico overhaul, 233
    school budget trends, 59
    school finance challenges within states, 248–249
    state aid, 246, 250–253
    state differences in education funding, 246, 247
    state revenue sources, 246–248
    taxation and support for schools, 245–246, 247
Reverse discrimination, 279
Revisionist historians, 30
Revival of learning, age of the, 33
Rewards for accountability, 260–261
Risk factors, 374
"Robin Hood" school finance, 251
Roman Catholic Church, 34
Roman Catholic parochial schools, 51, 63, 148, 151
Roman schools, 32
Rorty, Richard, 93
Rose v. The Council for Better Education Inc. (1989), 248
Rousseau, Jean-Jacques, 36–37, 115
RTI (Response to Intervention), 186–187, 280
Rubrics, 310, 317, 318
Rules, 125
Runaways, 210
Rural schools, 156–157
Rutherford Institute, 287
Rwanda, history curriculum in, 189

Sadler, Philip M., 335
Safe harbor, 256
Safford Unified School District #1 v. Redding (2009), 297

Salary schedule, 20
Sales taxes, 245, 246, 247
San Antonio (Texas) Independent School District v. Rodriguez (1979), 246
San Francisco school district, 249, 297
Santa Fe Independent School District, Petitioner v. Jane Doe (2000), 274, 275
Sartre, Jean-Paul, 94
SBDM (site-based decision making), 240
SBM (school-based management), 240
Scholastic Aptitude Test (SAT), 64
Scholasticism, 33
School architecture, 238, 240
School-based management (SBM), 240
School boards, 234–236, 258
School Breakfast Program, 206
School choices, 148–152
School culture, 147, 160
School districts
  accountability, 261
  consolidation of, 59
  curriculum evaluation practices, 347
  expenditures, 237
  organization, 234–237
  ranking of, 373–374
  report cards, 261
  role in managing curriculum, 345–346
  statistics, 234
School finance. *See* Revenue sources
School funding. *See* Revenue sources
School improvement plan, 376
School improvement process (SIP), 343, 360–361, 376
School improvement team (SIT), 257
School levels, 152–155
School locations, 155–159
School politics, 258–260
School reform, 360–361, 368–373
Schools. *See also* Public schools
  accountability, 261
  Blue Ribbon, 160
  catechetical, 33
  catechumenal, 33
  cathedral/monastic, 33
  charter, 133, 148, 149–150
  common elementary, 40
  culture in, 144–148
  curriculum management, 346
  dame, 39
  democratic, 194–195
  effective, 159–161, 372
  elementary, 40, 154
  high, 41, 155, 303–304, 335–336
  high-quality, 375–379
  Internet-based, 139, 152
  junior high, 41, 154
  Latin grammar, 32, 39
  Lutheran parochial, 51
  magnet, 133, 148, 149, 159
  middle, 41, 154–155
  monitorial, 39–40
  Montessori, 153
  need for additional, 58
  in need of improvement, 255
  normal, 68–69
  online, 139, 152
  organization charts, 238–240
  parochial, 51, 63, 148, 151
  private, 63, 150–152
  public view of, 6–7
  ranking of, 373–374
  religion-affiliated, 50, 271, 272, 273
  report cards, 261
  roles, 140–143
  Roman, 32
  Roman Catholic parochial, 51, 63, 148, 151

  rural, 156–157
  secondary, 40–41
  single-sex, 181–182
  site influences on curriculum, 344
  size of, 156
  suburban, 157–158
  urban, 158–159
  virtual, 139, 152
School secretaries, 240
School support staff, 240
Schools We Deserve, The (Ravitch), 127
School violence, 212, 213
Schwartz, Marc S., 335
Science, 335–336, 353–354
Science teachers, 11
"Scopes Monkey Trial," 276
Scoville v. Board of Education (1970), 296
Secondary schools, 40–41
Secondary teachers, 285–286
Second Morrill Act (1890), 57
Secretaries, school, 240
Section 504 of the Rehabilitation Act, 280, 297
Segregation, 276–278
Self concerns, 385, 386
Self-efficacy, 224
Self-esteem, 214
Sensorimotor stage, 72
Separate-but-equal doctrine, 276–278
September 11, 2001 terrorist attacks, 29
Serrano v. Priest (1971), 248
Service learning, 148
SES (socioeconomic status), 168–171, 186, 203–207
Seven Cardinal Principles, 65
Seven liberal arts, 33
Sex, 214–215
Sex discrimination, 294, 297
Sex education, 36
Sexism, 219
Sexual harassment, 210–211, 297–298
Sexual orientation, 183–184, 211
Shalock, Del, 330
Shanker, Albert, 391
Sheltered instruction, 178
Shinto, 97–98
Shortages, teacher, 9, 11, 58–59
Signing bonuses to new teachers, 22
Silberman, Charles, 72
Simon, Syd, 82
Single-sex education, 151–152
Single-sex schools, 181–182
SIP (school improvement process), 343, 360–361, 376
SIS (student information system), 257
Site-based decision making (SBDM), 240
SIT (school improvement team), 257
Size
  class, 372–373
  school, 156
Sizer, Theodore, 110
Skills, twenty-first-century, 307–308
Skinner, B. F., 72, 110
Slates, 44
Smith, Eric, 303
Smith-Hughes Act (1917), 57
Snyder v. Millersville University, 268
Social activists, teachers as, 193–195
Social development, 143
Socialization, 218
Social justice, 191–192, 195
Social mobility, 140, 168
Social networking, 227, 267–268, 290, 389
Social promotion, 222
Social stratification, 168
Society, importance of teachers to, 4–5, 6

Society for the Propagation of the Gospel in Foreign Parts, 38, 46
Society of Jesus, 34–35
Socioeconomic status (SES), 168–171, 186, 203–207
Socrates, 31, 88
Socratic method, 31, 88, 89
Sonnert, Gerhard, 335
Souter, David, 297
Southern Colonies, 37, 38
South Korea, educational achievement in, 324
Space, and classroom climate, 128
Spanierman, Jeffrey, 267–268
Spanierman v. Hughes (2008), 267–268
Sparta, early educational history of, 31
Special education programs, 60–61, 186
Special education teachers, 11
Spielberg, Steven, 118
Spiral curriculum, 338, 339
Sports, 183
Staff relationship, 236
Standard English, 177
Standardized tests, 18
Standards, 304–310
  about, 17–18
  conceptions of, 305–306
  content, 306–307
  curriculum and, 341
  defined, 304
  federal role in, 309
  future of standards-based education, 309–310
  opportunity-to-learn, 306
  power, 341
  real-world, 306
  state's role in, 345
  twenty-first-century knowledge and skills framework, 307–308
  world-class, 305–306
Standards-based curriculum, 160, 339, 340
Standards-based education, 304
State adoption policy, 345
State aid, 246, 250–253
State boards of education, 241–242
State departments of education, 242–243
State foundation programs, 251–253
State legislatures, 243–244
States
  curriculum evaluation practices, 347
  curriculum management, 345
  education funding differences, 246, 247
  organization of education, 241–244
  ranking of, 373–374
  revenue sources, 246–248
  school finance challenges, 248–249
State teachers' colleges, 69
Stewart, Potter, 246
Stewart B. McKinney Homeless Assistance Act, 292
Stratification, social, 168
Strip searches, 297
Student-centered educational philosophies, 113–118, 119
Student fees, 249
Student information system (SIS), 257
Student learning-centered instruction, 380
Student products and projects, 315
Student publications, 296
Student records, 287
Students
  adjusting attitude of, 112
  citizen rights, 290–294
  due process rights, 292–294
  education rights, 290–292
  free speech rights, 293–294
  grading one another's papers, 287
  married, 295–296

organizing to maximize learning, 354–356
pregnant, 215, 295–296
rights and responsibilities, 290–298
rights to sue, 292
school rights and responsibilities, 294–298
searches of, 297
Student-to-teacher ratios, 10
Subject-centered curriculum, 338, 339
Substance abuse, 215–216
Substantive due process, 267, 281, 292, 293–294
Suburban schools, 157–158
Success for All, 361
Sue, students' rights to, 292
Sufficiency, 244
Suicide, 213
Summative assessment, 311, 313–314
Summer Food Service Programs, 206
Superintendents, 236, 242, 258
Supplemental services, under NCLB, 256
Support staff, school, 240
Suspension, 292–293, 295
Swartz, Shawntae, 139
Syllabi, course, 342

Tabula rasa, 91
Tai, Robert H., 335
Taoism, 97
Task analysis, 349
Task concerns, 385, 386
Taxation, 245–246, 247
Taxpayer revolt, 253
Teacher-centered educational philosophies,
109–113, 119
Teacher-centered power style, 132
Teacher Education Accreditation Council, 15
Teacher Perspectives feature
abstinence-only sex education, 36
bilingualism, 180
business attire for teachers, 96
controversial topics in class, 131
corporate advertising/sponsorship in schools, 250
diversity training requirements for teachers, 146
dress codes, 295
high-stakes tests, 327–328
homework, 356
retention *versus* social promotion, 222
signing bonuses to new teachers, 22
teaching manners, 60
technology in classrooms, 388
Teacher preparation, history of, 66–70
Teachers
academic freedom, 285–286
accountability, 260, 261
bilingual, 11
business attire for, 96
certification, 16–17, 282
as change agents, 129–130
collective bargaining rights, 284–285
conditions of employment, 282–284
continuing professional development, 24
demand for, 8, 9–11
demographic profile, 7–8
from diverse backgrounds, 11
diversity training for, 146
effective, 71, 160, 372
elementary, 285–286
employment contracts, 282
expressing views on controversial topics in
class, 131
highly qualified, 14, 206, 228, 255, 328
high-quality, 367, 379–383
importance to society, 4–5, 6
as indentured servants, 67–68
induction, 8, 15, 386, 387
job hunting, 23
job hunting for, 23

as leaders, 130–133
licensure, 15–16, 23, 24, 282
mathematics, 11
new, 8–9, 22, 387, 389–390
nontenured, 267, 283
out-of-field assignments, 11
pay, 20–22
politics and, 259–260
professional knowledge, 12–13
professional responsibilities, 12
professional skills, 13–14
public view of, 5–6
qualities of great teachers, 24
reasons for leaving teaching, 7–8
responsibilities, 239–240, 288–289
returning, 9
rights, 281–287
as school board members, 235
science, 11
secondary, 285–286
shortages of, 9, 11, 58–59
as social activists, 193–195
on special assignment, 346
special education, 11
student records and, 287
supply of, 8–9
unconcerned, 384, 385
use of computers and Internet, 227–228
working conditions, 22–23
Teachers' colleges, state, 69
Teachers on special assignment (TOSAs), 346
Teacher-student control continuum, 123
Teacher unions, 390–391
Teacher Work Sample (TWS), 330
Teaching. *See also* Instruction
analysis of, 70–71
effective, 71, 160, 372
as framing ways of knowing, 108
Herbartian method, 37
as profession, 12–14
professionalization of, 62–63
quality assurance for, 14–18
to the test, 325–326
Teaching apprenticeships, 68
Teaching materials, 41–45
Teaching strategies, 351–359
direct instruction, 352
for diverse students, 357–359
for English-language learners, 357–358, 359
increased emphasis on science and technology,
353–354
indirect instruction, 352–353
organizing students to maximize learning,
354–356
for students with exceptionalities,
358–359
using technology to enhance instruction,
356–357
Teaching units, 121
Team leaders, 239
Technology
access to, 225–227
cheating with, 290, 389
educational, 71
educational philosophy and, 128–129
ethics and, 105
future of, 387–389
increased emphasis on, 353–354
law and, 267–268, 289–290
philosophy and, 85, 87
school administration and, 257
using to enhance instruction, 356–357
using to track student learning, 321
Technology Assisted Project-Based
Instruction, 139
Teenagers, 214–217

Tennessee
church and state, 276
teachers' rights and responsibilities, 283
Tenth Amendment, 241, 253, 270
Tenure, 282–284, 287
Terrorism, war on, 29
Test-based accountability, 373
Testing
accommodations for, 62, 319
accountability and, 324–326
achievement tests, 181
evolution of, 64
high-stakes, 304, 324–325, 327–328
standardized, 18
teaching to the test, 325–326
Texas
intermediate units, 237
school finance, 251
state adoption policy, 345
Textbooks, 342, 345
Themed curriculum, 338, 339
Theological era, 111
Thinking. *See also* Divergent thinking
analytic, 82–83, 84
convergent, 109, 111
critical, 193
prophetic, 82, 83, 85, 86
TIMSS (Trends in International Mathematics and
Science Study), 322, 323, 347
*Tinker v. Des Moines Independent Community
School District* (1969), 291, 293–294, 296
Title I, 206, 228, 273
Title IX, 182–183, 279, 294, 295, 297
Torts, 288
TOSAs (teachers on special assignment), 346
Toyota Family Literacy Program, 201
Tracking hypocrisy, 85, 86
Transitional/bilingual education, 179, 357, 358
Translators, 208
Transportation for students of religion-affiliated
schools, 271, 272
Trends in education, 58–61, 70–74, 368, 369
Trends in International Mathematics and Science
Study (TIMSS), 322, 323, 347
Trivium, 33
Trujillo, Christine, 233
Trustees, 234. *See also* School boards
Turk v. Franklin (1982), 283
Tuskegee Institute, 47
Twenty-first-century knowledge and skills
framework, 307–308
Two-way immersion, 179
TWS (Teacher Work Sample), 330

Unconcerned teachers, 384, 385
Understanding, in Bloom's taxonomy, 350
Undifferentiated stage of racial identity
development, 220
Unions, teacher, 390–391
Units, teaching, 121
Universal Declaration of Human Rights, 219
Universities. *See* Colleges and universities
University of Arkansas-Little Rock, 285
University of California v. Bakke (1978), 279
Unschooling, 63
Upper class, 169
Urban schools, 158–159
U.S. Bureau of Indian Affairs, 254
U.S. Centers for Disease Control and
Prevention, 281
U.S. Constitution, 269–270
U.S. Department of Defense, 254
U.S. Department of Education, 57, 160, 254
U.S. Supreme Court. *See also specific cases*
academic freedom, 286
church and state, 271–272, 273, 274, 275, 276

U.S. Supreme Court. *continued*
  confidentiality of student records, 287
  private schools, 50–51
  segregation and desegregation,
    276–277, 278
  students' rights and responsibilities, 290, 292,
    293, 294, 296, 297
  taxation and education, 246
  teachers' rights and responsibilities, 281, 283

Valenzuela, Rocio, 201
Valenzuela, William, 201
Validity, 320
Value-added model, 321, 372–373
Values, 82, 145–147, 351
Values Clarification (Simon), 82
Valuing, in Krathwohl's taxonomy of affective
    domain, 351
Van Deinse, Dane, 139
Vice principals, 239, 389
Violence, 209, 211–212, 213
Virtual schools, 139, 152
Vision, 131–132
Vocational Education for National Defense
    Act, 61

Vogel, Bill, 303
Voice, 127–128, 191
Voltaire, 35
Vouchers, 148, 150
Vygotsky, Lev, 71

Wall, Geoffrey, 139
Wallace v. Jaffree (1985), 274
War on terrorism, 29
Washington, Booker T., 47
Web. *See* Internet
Webster, Noah, 43, 44
Wesley, Charles C., 190
West, Cornel, 83, 85
Western education, early history of, 31–32
Western Oregon University, 330
White, Byron, 296
Whitehead, Alfred North, 91
Whites
  academic achievement, 175, 328, 329
  access to technology, 225
  college enrollment, 216
  dropout rate, 374
  as racial and ethnic group, 173
  racial identity development, 220

Willard, Emma, 48–49
Williams, Paul, 292
Wisconsin
  rights of nontenured teachers, 283
  vouchers, 148, 150
Wolman v. Walter (1977), 272
Women, educational history of, 46, 47, 48–50
Woodson, Carter G., 190
Wood v. Strickland (1975), 291, 292
Workforce readiness, 142–143
Working class, 168–169
Working conditions, 22–23
World as a classroom, 133
World-class standards, 305–306
World languages immersion, 179
World Wide Web. *See* Internet

Year-round school, 240
Young, Ella Flagg, 49

Zobrest v. Catalina Foothills School District
    (1993), 272

PHOTO CREDITS